Records of the
Moravians in North Carolina

Volume XII

1856-1866

C. Daniel Crews
Lisa D. Bailey

Editors

Raleigh
Division of Archives and History
North Carolina Department of Cultural Resources
2000

North Carolina Department of Cultural Resources
Betty Ray McCain
Secretary
Elizabeth F. Buford
Deputy Secretary

Division of Archives and History
Jeffrey J. Crow
Director
David J. Olson
Deputy Director

"If it is ever possible to fill the gap between that series [*Records of the Moravians in North Carolina*] and Bishop Rondthaler's volume [*Memorabilia of Fifty Years*] we will have given to the world an historical contribution which I think cannot be surpassed anywhere.

Truly we have a great inheritance. . . ."

Adelaide L. Fries
Moravian Customs, Our Inheritance (1936), p. 58

Contents

Map and Illustrations

Foreword

The publication of Volume XII of the *Records of the Moravians in North Carolina, 1856-1866*, is the culmination of many years of intensive work in transcribing the meticulous records of the Moravian brethren. The decade of records presented in this volume represents the inclusion of significant texts not recorded in the earlier volume in the series that covers these dates. The work also provides additional documentation about life in the Moravian communities as well as information on political and social history of the period. The exact and complete nature of the records of the Moravians is well known: the initial eleven volumes in this series have provided several generations of researchers with a wealth of documentary material and have supplemented original records from other sources. This volume covers a turbulent period in the state's history; the records included here will provide another insight into the life and work of the Moravians as well as the world in which they lived.

The work of editors C. Daniel Crews, archivist of the Moravian Church in America, Southern Province, and Lisa D. Bailey of the Division of Archives and History, along with the dedicated labor of other staff at the Moravian Archives is a testimony to and a continuation of the commitment of Dr. Adelaide Fries, archivist of the Southern Province from 1911 to 1949 and editor of Volume I of the *Records of the Moravians in North Carolina, 1752-1771*, published in 1922 as well as six additional volumes. Douglas L. Rights, Minnie J. Smith, and Bishop Kenneth G. Hamilton worked to complete her ambitious project with the publication of volumes VIII-XI. This volume fulfills the 1936 wish of Miss Fries to add to the previously published Moravian records for this period. It is the "great inheritance" that she noted in *Moravian Customs, Our Inheritance*, and it is the legacy of the Moravians who were committed to documenting their community and the world around them that provides us these documents. We are indebted to them and richer for their work.

Catherine J. Morris, *State Archivist*
North Carolina Division of Archives and History
September 2000

Preface

Beginning in 1920 and continuing through 1968, first the North Carolina Historical Commission and then the Department of Archives and History published eleven volumes of *Records of the Moravians*. Now the Moravian Archives welcomes the opportunity of once again being in partnership with the Division of Archives and History in the publication of volume 12 of *Records of the Moravians in North Carolina*.

The intention of this volume is to help fill the gap that Adelaide Fries, translator and editor of the first seven volumes, discerned in 1936. That gap, from about 1857 through 1876, spans some of the most momentous years in the history of North Carolina and the nation—the Civil War and Reconstruction. This volume will cover the period 1856-1866. It will be followed by volume 13, which will deal with the years 1867-1876.

As they had done for more than a century previously, Moravian ministers meticulously recorded in the diaries of the churches they were serving the events that affected them and their congregations, frequently mirroring the events of the nation as a whole. The weather interested them, and church services, but also battles and troop movements, going off to and returning from the war, diseases and death in the congregations, hard times and the utter poverty of a defeated land, the new freedom of a formerly enslaved people and what the future may hold for them, recovery from war and the coming of prosperity and the railroad, the impinging of other churches in an area that once was almost exclusively Moravian. These are among the themes that appear in volumes 12 and 13 of *Records of the Moravians*.

A number of people have made volume 12 possible. Certainly Jeffrey J. Crow, director of the Division of Archives and History, and Joe A. Mobley, administrator of the Historical

Publications Section, are to be thanked for graciously accepting the task of shepherding yet two more volumes of *Records of
the Moravians* into print. Lisa D. Bailey of the Division of
Archives and History had the onerous and difficult task of final
proofreading and catching all those mistakes that escaped
everyone else. At the Moravian Archives assistant archivist
Richard W. Starbuck oversaw editing, copy checking with the
originals, page layout, and indexing. The most difficult task of
all was deciphering the handwriting of the Moravian ministers
of the nineteenth century. Sometimes for days Grace S.
Robinson would wrestle with a particularly difficult scrawl of,
say, George Frederic Bahnson, but thanks to her tenacity and
her peculiar insight she brought it all to computer-entered
clarity—and with remarkable accuracy. Without Grace and her
five years of labor on the task, volume 12 would still be only a
dream.

C. Daniel Crews, *Archivist*
Moravian Church in America, Southern Province
September 2000

Editorial Method

Earlier volumes of *Records of the Moravians* were translations of church records—diaries, minutes, correspondence—from the ancient German script into modern English. Unlike those earlier *Records*, volume 12 consists of transcriptions, not translations, since the original documents are in the English language. The nineteenth-century Moravian ministers whose church diaries are transcribed here were a remarkably literate and for the most part highly educated group of writers. Their words and turns of phrases stand the test of time; however, frequently they strayed from or completely ignored any standard usage of punctuation or capitalization. Christian Lewis Right, for example, rarely punctuated the end of a sentence or capitalized the first letter of the next, leaving streams of run-on sentences for the modern-day editor to sort out. To assist the reader without altering the sense of the original, a gentle application has been made of modern rules of capitalization and punctuation.

Since the Moravian ministers were students of Scripture, the style of the King James Version of the Bible infused their diary writing. Some of the more antiquated usages have been revised. "To day" and "to morrow," for example, have been made one word, and where applicable the colon has been made a semicolon.

A few other standardizations were applied. The days and dates that begin each meeting or diary entry were made uniform and italicized. Bible books, chapters, and verses were also standardized. Isolated misspelled words were corrected, though a few consistent variations were retained, Jacob Siewers's "feaver," for example. However, the spellings of names and places have been retained as the ministers recorded them. The ministers frequently abbreviated to the point of making the diaries almost a shorthand. So as not to burden the reader, the great majority of abbreviations—recd., mtg., com., A. of S. of M., Lit., v., w., for example—were spelled out. Brackets are employed only to insert material from a separate source (e.g., [Bethania Report:]) or to indicate the rare addition or explanatory remark by the editor.

The ministers who recorded these records often identified enslaved African Americans by writing the masters' names in parentheses. That expedient is retained and is also employed in the index of this volume.

The material here is about one-third of what the ministers wrote. Every effort has been made to include material of broad historical value and to omit repetition of regular church services. Earlier volumes of *Records of the Moravians* attempted to convey genealogical information through diary entries only, but diary entries rarely give complete data. The solution was to publish abstracts or summaries of church register material of births and baptisms, marriages, and deaths and burials. These should prove especially useful to genealogical researchers. Though they are published separately as appendixes in the back of this volume, they should not be ignored by the general reader, for much of the loss and sorrow of the Civil War is recorded in the death and burial entries and sometimes in the baptism entries.

The original diaries, minutes, and reports from which these transcriptions are taken are housed at the Moravian Archives in Winston-Salem, the repository of the records of the Moravian Church, Southern Province.

RECORDS OF THE

MORAVIANS IN NORTH CAROLINA

1856

[British intervention caused the withdrawal of Persia from Afghanistan and the recognition of Afghan independence.
In the Kansas territory fighting continued between pro- and anti-slavery factions.
In January the state-owned and -financed North Carolina Railroad was completed between Charlotte and Goldsboro.]

Memorabilia of Salem Congregation, 1856
[Extracts transcribed; handwriting is that of George Frederic Bahnson.]

Another subject which had claimed our attention as members of the congregation at Salem was the so called lease system by which persons not members of the Moravian Church are prevented from owning property and carrying on business in their own name. Pleasing as the picture may present itself to the mind's eye of a place inhabited altogether by individuals that do not only worship their God in exactly the same form and according to the same theological system, but worship him in spirit and in truth and are in reality living members of that body whose head the Lord himself is, it is nevertheless an undeniable truth that such a spot cannot well be found, and much less be retained in the church militant, composed as it is of members who carry with them to their final resting place more or less of imperfections and sinfulness. Hence it did become more and more apparent that we had for some time contented ourselves with the shadow after the substance had virtually been withdrawn.

All legal impediments for the abolishment of that system having been removed, the matter was presented to the Congregation Council first on Feb. 14 and 15 and then on Nov. 17, and at the latter meeting it was resolved by an overwhelming majority of the members present that the lease system should be abolished and that property might be held in the town of Salem in fee simple and business be carried on by persons entirely irrespective of their connexion with the Moravian Church. In consequence of further measures adopted, an act of incorporation was granted for our town, and very shortly the officers called for by this act will be elected and enter upon their respective duties. In view of these great and momentous changes we can only supplicate the Lord our Savior, that his tabernacle may still be in Salem and his dwelling may abide in our beloved Zion.

Salem Congregation Council, 1856
[Extracts transcribed.]

Mon., Feb. 11, 1856. Present 72 members.

The Chairman opened the meeting by a few remarks, stating that we had assembled for the purpose of deliberating upon a subject of very great importance, and one that would require our undivided and deliberate attention, viz.: to take into consideration the question whether that part of our rules having reference to the holding of property in the town of Salem should be further retained or abolished; and that it would be very desirable that the proceedings of this body be conducted in a friendly and brotherly spirit.

The minutes of last meeting having been read and adopted, the Chairman communicated the following preamble and resolutions passed by the Town Committee on Jany. 31st and adopted by the Elders' Conference on Febr. 6th, containing their views on the subject now to be discussed by the Congregation Council.

[The preamble and resolutions are published in *Records of the Moravians in North Carolina*, v. 11, p. 5981-5982.]

Br. E. A. Schweinitz, the present Proprietor, by request of the Town Committee then gave an historical account of the Trust under which the Wachovia lands have been held, and of the transmission of the title from the beginning to the present time, and then passed over from the lands of the Unity in general to that portion of it which is known as the *Land of the Salem Diacony*. This parcel of land prior to May 1st, 1826, was held by the Diacony under a lease for an annual rent of $177; but on the above named day was bought by the Salem Diacony at 1.12_{1/2}$ per acre under certain conditions, one of which was that, as had thus far been the case already, no lots in Salem were to be sold, but should merely be held under lease; upon application, however, the Synod of 1848 gave its sanction that lots in Salem might be sold in fee, provided it was to [be] decided upon by a constitutional majority of the voting members of the Congregation at Salem, and provided no legal difficulties to such a step existed. In April 1854 a petition signed by 36 individuals, consisting partly of owners of houses or of such to whom lots had been granted in Salem, was handed to him, containing the request that the sale of lots in Salem might be taken into consideration by the proper authorities; but that owing to various circumstances no immediate action was taken thereon. Whereupon in the fall of last year his attention had again been drawn to said petition by some of the subscribers. Not being fully convinced in his own mind of the legality of the sale of these lots, he had with the consent of the Town Committee and Conference applied for a legal opinion on the subject to Bartholomew F. Moore, one of the best lawyers in the state, who after mature deliberation, in a document of great length, gave it as his opinion that no obstructions existed in the trust to the sale of lots in the town of Salem, and that any deed executed by him [the Proprietor, E. A. de Schweinitz] for such lots would be good and valid in law. In this opinion also Judge Badger, to whom it had been communicated, fully coincided. A few weeks after the receipt of this document the Town Committee and Conference entered into the consideration of the above named petition, being led into it in part also by transactions that had taken place in the town in regard to certain properties; and after mature and deliberate investigation of the subject, the Preamble and Resolutions now communicated had been passed and adopted in both bodies by a unanimous vote, with the exception of Resolution the second against which *one* vote had been given in the Town Committee; and that the opinions expressed in the Preamble and Resolutions were now before the Congregation Council either for concurrence or rejection.

After the above remarks had been made by Br. Schweinitz, the Preamble and Resolutions were read again and more or less discussed sentence by sentence, such explanations being given as would more fully convey the idea of the Town Committee and Conference.

Whereupon Congregation Council adjourned to next Thursday evening at 7 o'clock.

Thurs., Feb. 14, 1856. 76 members present.

The minutes of last meeting were first read and after a slight alteration adopted by the meeting.

1. A resolution was made, seconded, and adopted that the minutes of this body in future be written in the English language, and that those of last meeting be translated into that language.

2. The Preamble and Resolutions of the Town Committee and Elders Conference submitted to this body at its last session were again taken up and the first Resolution contained in said writing shaped in such a manner as to bring it for discussion before the Congregation Council, viz.: "Be it resolved that the Rules and Regulations contained in Chapter V, §§ 8, 9, 10, 13, and 14, of the Rules and Regulations of the Congregation of the United Brethren at Salem be stricken out," which Resolution, after being seconded, gave rise to a long and animated debate, which, however, for the present led to no final results; and Council eventually adjourned to meet again tomorrow evening at 7 o'clock.

Fri., Feb. 15, 1856. Present 73 members.

1. The English translation of the minutes of Monday 11th and of the transactions of yesterday's meeting having been read and adopted, several members rose to make personal explanations in regard to statements made by them.

2. A motion having been made, seconded, and adopted by a majority of votes present to lay the resolution proposed last time and now before this body on the table for the present, a motion was made and seconded "To appoint a Committee of 7 members from this body to assess the lots and then report to the Congregation Council." This motion led to the discussion of the question "whether this body was constitutionally empowered to carry out the views contemplated by the motion," which question, however, was finally decided by a sentence in § 79 of the English translation of the Synodal results of 1848 which says, "Each congregation or choir diacony is managed by the congregation or choir warden assisted by the Committee," from which it is apparent that the lots or land in question being the property of the Congregation Diacony can neither be sold nor their price assessed by the Congregation Council, but are constitutionally under the management and control spoken of in the above extract of the Synodal Results. Such being the case the following amendment of the last motion was made and seconded, viz.: "Resolved that the Town Committee and Conference report to the Congregation Council the price set upon

the lots if sold in fee simple," which resolution was adopted, yeas 72, nays 1.

Whereupon Council adjourned till the above named bodies are ready to report.

Mon., Sept. 29, 1856. 43 members present.

2. A number of females, at present lodging at the hotels in town, having on yesterday intruded themselves into the love-feast kept for the Children of the Congregation and greatly misbehaved on that occasion, Council almost unanimously resolved that in future all lovefeasts be strictly considered as private meetings to which none but members of the Congregation are to be admitted, and that the minister, whenever he announces them, state publicly that they are only intended for members of the Congregation.

Mon., Nov. 17, 1856. 76 members present.

The minutes of last meeting were read and adopted.

1. Congregation Council met for the purpose of hearing the report of Town Committee in reference to the prices to be asked for lots in the town of Salem (see minutes of Febr. 15, 1856), and again to enter into deliberation concerning the alteration of the Rules and Regulations of the Congregation in regard to the holding of property in our town. In order fully to call to mind the action already had on the subject, all the minutes of Congn. Council having reference thereto were read, viz., the minutes of Feb. 11th, 14th, and 15th, 1856, as also the following Resolutions of Town Committee adopted Febr. 7th and which were communicated to Congregn. Council on Febr. 11th but had not been inserted in the minutes of that day, viz.:

[The Resolutions of the Town Committee are published in *Records of the Moravians in North Carolina*, v. 11, p. 5983.]

The above preliminaries having been gone thro', it was next reported on the part of the Town Committee, that upon entering upon the consideration of the prices to be charged for town lots, they had first agreed upon and established the following points, viz.:

[The points the Town Committee established in pricing lots are published in *Records of the Moravians in North Carolina*, v. 11, p. 5984-4985.]

. . . Congregation Council again took up the Resolution laid over from minutes Febr. 14, viz.:

"Be it resolved that the Rules and Regulations contained in Chapter V §§ 8, 9, 10, 13, and 14 of the Rules and Regulations of the Congregation of the United Brethren at Salem be stricken out," which motion after some debate was carried by a vote of 57 yeas, nays none.

No. 2 of the Resolutions of the Town Committee (see minutes Febr. 11th), "That in future lots in the town of Salem may be held in fee simple," was then taken up and an amendment offered to the following effect: "That this sale of lots do not go into effect until a charter incorporating the town of Salem be received from the legislature of the State," which amendment, however, after being seconded was lost by a decided vote; whereupon the original Resolution was carried by 54 yeas, 8 nays.

No. 3 of the Resolutions of Town Committee (see minutes Febr. 11) "Recommending that the Rules and Regulations of the Congregation at Salem be so amended and altered as to conform to the new state of things" was then seconded and adopted by a unanimous vote.

2. The Resolution making lovefeasts strictly private meetings, contained in §2 of minutes of last meeting, was again taken up and amended so as to admit by ticket upon personal application to the minister such individuals as are communicant members of other Christian denominations.

Friedland Diary, 1856
[Extracts transcribed; handwriting is that of John Chapman Cooke.]

Thurs., June 5. On Thursday, June 5, we removed to Friedland as a resting place for the purpose of recovering my health, which had been ruined in the service of the Church during fourteen years service in the Danish and English W. India [Indies] missions, and which permission I had from the U.E.C.

Sun., June 8. Very feeble and suffering from fever. Preached from 2 Cor. 13:14 to a small company of persons to whom I introduced myself, and they became somewhat acquainted, if acquaintance it may be called, for none of them interested themselves enough to call upon me during the week following, and from which I inferred that it was quite a matter of indifference with them whether I lived or died.

Sun., June 22. Preached from Luke 14:18 to a full meeting. Gave them notice that I wished to form a Sunday School, and requested them to send their children on Sunday next.

Sun., June 29. Sunday School, 10 children came. Organized the School and formed classes 1 and 2.

Sun., July 6. Sunday School, 9 children. The children [are] very ignorant and generally very dull. Preached from John 1:29. The novelty of the new preacher seems to have given place to some other novelty. The meeting was a small attendance. I have since learned that at this season of the year the Methodists have their camp meetings, and when these occur or the Baptists practice immersion there is a general gathering to these places from curiosity, religious motives, and wickedness.

Sun., Aug. 3. Meeting to take into consideration the propriety of organizing the congregation. Agreed to do so on the following Sunday.

Sun., Aug. 10. (Memorial of 13th.) No Sunday School. First meeting at 10 o'clock, quite a number present. Afternoon: lovefeast, full attendance, after which an election for 3 Committee members. The following were chosen: Philip Kerner, John Kerner, Alexander Sneider. Holy Communion, 21 present. I afterwards learnt that the greater part of these were but nominal members; many of them had not been in the church for some years previous, and as curiosity was the moving principle, perhaps it would be some years again before they would make their appearance.

Sun., Aug. 24. I do not know what to make of these people. They seem to be half Christian, half heathen, without seeming to understand anything of the responsibilities of church members, and so very independent as to be incapable of subjection to the "Brotherly Agreement," and so far as the 4th article[1] of that code is concerned, even the "Committee" agree that it is altogether a dead letter as applied to Friedland, and it seems to me from this that the "Committee" itself is a dead letter, as they do not think it of use to interest themselves in any way in the matter of carrying out the intentions of the "Brotherly Agreement."

---

[1]The fourth article of the Brotherly Agreement, as printed in Salem in 1837, addresses the duties of a congregation's Committee, especially that the minister "may receive the means of a decent maintenance for himself and family."

Sun., Sept. 7. [S]mall attendance. By small attendance I mean from 5 to 15 adults; by good attendance I mean from 30 to 40 adults, exclusive of children.

Sun., Nov. 30. Conversed with the people before preaching; could not elicit much from them. They seem to be very reserved upon religious subjects, and it is labor to get them at all interested in the matter. So as to draw anything from them, preached from Job 11:7, as I could not gain much by conversation. I preached a long sermon, pointedly and plainly. The "Committee" proves to be a dead letter, as they do not act in any case, and I cannot get them even to haul wood. I have, however, informed them that unless they do furnish wood for the use of the church, that I shall not be able to continue the service this winter, as I am not able to preach during the winter unless the church is warmed.

Sun., Dec. 7. Got wood hauled by Sides and Gibbons, neither of them "Committee." Jonathan Lowder gave one day's labor chopping, and so I got wood for the church. For our own use I helped myself by sawing, chopping, etc., although very unable. Up to this time I have had fever occasionally, constantly, but the cold weather setting in has checked it, and I am recovering as the cold increases.

1857

[The year saw the beginning of persecution of Christians in Korea and the execution of missionaries. Britain began taking over governance of India from the British East India Company after the exile of the last Mogul emperor. In China, Britain and France started the Second Opium War to legalize opium and force the opening of more ports for European traders.

In March James Buchanan was inaugurated as the fifteenth president of the United States. With the *Dred Scott* decision, the Supreme Court dealt a blow to anti-slavery forces.]

Memorabilia of Salem Congregation, 1857
[Extracts transcribed; handwriting is that of George Frederic Bahnson.]

In accordance with a practice not less proper and becoming than time honored, which is observed in our church, we meet on this evening, the last of another fleeting year of our probationary state of existence here upon earth, for the purpose of unitedly casting a retrospective glance upon the weeks and months that constituted the year 1857, which will soon be numbered with the things that were.

During the forepart of the year, a severe season and other causes brought on great scarcity and exceedingly high prices of the necessaries of life, so that here and there the cry of absolute want and of all but starvation was heard in our generally highly favored country. And even after a very abundant harvest had filled almost to overflowing from one end of the land to the other the barns and storehouses, like a fatal flash of lightning shooting forth from an entirely unclouded sky, a fearful panic spread from North to South reaching from the uttermost East to the very extremes of the far distant West, by which hundreds and thousands were brought from affluence and luxury to poverty and absolute want, so that the cry for bread wherewith to feed their families (for women and children) emanated from the lips of multitudes of once free and independent, strong and hearty citizens of our glorious republic.

And moreover at this very moment the western sky is overcast with ominous clouds, and well-grounded fears intrude themselves involuntarily that they will not scatter before brother shall have lifted up sword against brother and fellow citizens shall have engaged in a fierce and bloody civil strife.

[A] General Synod was held whose results will exercise a powerful influence, and we humbly and confidently trust, for lasting good upon the 3 Provinces constituting our Brethren's Unity. Although the delegates of the two other Provinces and especially those from the continent constituted an over-whelming majority, still all the requests and propositions brought before the General Synod by our American delegates were granted, so that in regard to local matters every Province is perfectly independent and at liberty to arrange its own Provincial affairs in accordance with its peculiar wants and circumstances, provided that no measures proposed or intro-duced come into conflict with the general principles derived from the word of God and forming the basis on which alone our Unitas Fratrum or Brethren's Unity can rest and be con-tinued. [T]he results attended to are of such a nature as fully to satisfy the wishes expressed on our part at our last Provin-cial Synod, so that instead of disunion then dreaded by some, the ties of brotherly love and affection binding together the two transatlantic Provinces with ours are drawn closer and have, we confidently anticipate, become more lasting.

Among the festivals we celebrated during the course of [the year] probably several might be deserving of a particular no-tice. There is one to which special allusion must be made in as much as it was highly interesting in itself and will not return in a similar manner during the natural lifetime of any of us. It was the 1st of March, on which was celebrated the 4th centen-ary jubilee of the Moravian Church.

In consequence of the total abolition of the so called lease system by which at least nominally all who were not members of the church were prohibited from owning houses or carrying on business in town, in their own names, several alterations were called into existence. The poor fund which had existed for the benefit of the members in town (the Single Srs. excepted, who have a fund of their own) will hereafter be used for all the members (with the above mentioned exception), whether they live in town or out of it. It would be very desirable, therefore, that the fund might awaken more interest in the minds of members, so that meetings of the society may be more numer-ously attended than has been the case heretofore.

A collection was also made for the benefit of poor people not connected with our church, and we doubt not that thus the heart of many a one was gladdened.

Our town having been incorporated according to the laws of our state, it became necessary to elect the officers prescribed by the act of incorporation, and consequently on the first Monday of the year, the 5th of January, this (charter) election took place for the first time and resulted in the appointment or choice of the following individuals: for Mayor, Bro. Charles Brietz, and for commissioners, 8 [7] others, 7 [6] of whom are members of our church: Messrs. Patterson, Adam Butner, Rud. Crist, Francis Fries, Theodor Keehln, Edward Belo, and Solomon Mickey. The time for which they were elected having almost transpired and a new election being on hand, it may not be improper to return to them on this occasion deserved thanks for the manner in which they have discharged their duties and more especially to their presiding officer, on the performance of whose obligations much of the comfort and quietness to be enjoyed by the citizens of our place will depend. It is devoutly to be hoped that persons will continually be elected determined to do their whole duty without fear, favor, or affection, and that the better portion of the community, which we doubt not will always constitute the (legal) majority, may sustain the officers of their choice whenever and wherever they shall require it in the fulfillment of official duty—so that cursing and swearing, drunkenness and rowdyism of every kind and description, but too rife in many localities throughout our happy land, may be duly checked and speedily banished from the houses and streets of a town whose founders intended the same to be a place of which it could truly be said: In Salem also is the Lord's tabernacle [Ps. 76:2].

During the course of the year new streets were laid out and names were given to all, tho as yet they have not come into much use. On Friday, Feb. 27, upwards of 20 new building lots were sold; on none of which, however, thus far any houses have been erected.

The year which we are about to close was also signalized by an unusual amount of sickness and mortality, so that in all probability there have never yet been as many deaths in our town and congregation as occurred this year. [T]owards the close of April when the weather was yet anything but genial the measles and kindred diseases attacked many children and young persons both in town and more especially in our female boarding school. Several children of members of our congregation were on this occasion taken away from their parents by him who has said: Suffer little children to come unto me and forbid them not, for of such is the kingdom of heaven [Luke 18:16]. In more than one instant, though, this dispensation of our Lord was felt the more keenly by the parents, because by it was removed from their guardianship an only son or an only daughter. Later in the year great sickliness prevailed in the country, so that several of our members there had to part with their little ones, and one of our sisters had to give up to him who has the best claim upon them three of her children in very quick succession. Adults, though, were also called to their eternal home during the year, so that alongside of one another are reposing on our "God's acre" the mortal remains of three young mothers who were called away from their husbands and families.

The measles and kindred complaints attacked in an unusual manner our large and flourishing female boarding school. All the new buildings had been finished, and on the 11th of February the large and commodious dining hall had been used for the first time, about 250 persons sitting down to a substantial and well prepared meal, but the neat and well finished chapel of the institution in which that meat which endureth unto life everlasting is to be offered to young immortals could not be set apart for its sacred purpose until on Ascension day, the 21st of May, for a season of affliction had been permitted to befall that institution especially through the measles. At one time not less than 150 pupils were on the sick list, five of whom departed this life, a circumstance which had not occurred during the more than fifty years of the existence of our school and will, we humbly pray, never be allowed to take place again. Death came upon them in such quick succession that we had to accompany at one time the mortal remains of two of these young pilgrims to their last resting places.

The same diseases had, however, proved much more fatal in other localities, so that neither the belief in the healthfulness of our town nor in the care taken of pupils entrusted to our institution was at all shaken in the minds of the parents, and the boarding school filled up in a shorter time this year after vacation than ever before and has been full ever since, and good health has been universally enjoyed.

It may be observed here that the number of new scholars who entered during the year 1857 was 149. The highest number of boarders at one time during the year was 240, and the number of boarders at the close of the scholastic year is 235.

Our school for boys has likewise been in uninterrupted activity during the year, and the pupils, about 40 in number, have generally made commendable progress in their studies.

During the year a number of new houses were built by different individuals: In Main Street one by Bro. A. Welfare, another by Bro. Jul. Mickey, a third by Bro. Chas. Houser; in other streets several by Bro. F. Fries, one by Bro. Edw. Ackerman, another by Bro. Francis Mickey, a third by Bro. Chitty, a fourth near the sisters house by Bro. E. A. Vogler, a fifth by Bro. John Siewers by the side of his shop. An addition was made to the Inspector's house. Bro. Heissler renovated his house as also did Br. Wm. Peterson and Phil. Reich. Br. Wm. Lineback also built an additional house on his lot. Besides these, several sheds and stables were erected and one large shop is being fitted up to serve as a store. A lockup was also provided for evil doers and by its not infrequently being occupied, that class appears by far more numerous than it ought to be.

Among the ministers at Salem the following changes have taken place: Bro. Max Eug. Grunert was called to Salem from Bethany as co-pastor and assistant inspector and arrived with his family on the 18th of May. Bro. Reichel, having been elected a member of the Mission Department in the U.E.C., left Salem with his family on the 28th of October.

Salem Diary, 1857
[Extracts transcribed; handwriting is that of George Frederic Bahnson.]

Thurs., Jan. 1. With thanksgiving and praise we entered in the usual and solemn manner into this important year. Important it is when we look into the past and remember that we close the 4th century and enter upon the 5th of the existence of the Brethren's Unity or church, and important it must be when we call to mind that the General Synod will assemble and discuss questions of the greatest importance to us as a Unity. Business men in general have no time to come to church on this day. In the evening there was liturgy.

Mon., Jan. 5. Today the charter election took place and the following officers were elected: Mayor Charles Brietz (94 votes). Commissioners: Patterson (101), Ad. Butner (88), Rud. Crist (79), F. Fries (74), Theod. Keehln (61), Ed. Belo (61), and Solm. Mickey (47). In all 128 votes were polled. There was no unpleasant excitement.

Sun., Jan. 18. Unexpectedly the wind shifted during the night and brought on a very severe fall of snow. It snowed and drifted in a manner almost unparalleled in our latitude. It was almost impossible to get along both on account of the depth of the snow and the drifting of it. It continued to snow all day long and was very cold. Bro. Bahnson preached at the usual time to an audience composed principally of the pupils of our boarding school and a few hardy and bold churchgoers. The passage leading from the Female Academy to the church proved very useful today.

Wed., Jan. 21. Since last Saturday no mail has come to town—the railroad is impassable and even the plank road was tried in vain by a stage yesterday.

Bells are jingling merrily. The accounts from other parts of the country are truly pitiful—men and animals having perished in the snow.

Sun., Jan. 25. At 1 P.M. the so called poor society held their annual meeting. 16 persons were present. After they had transacted their business, the committee appointed by the citizens for the purpose of collecting funds for the benefit of our poor neighbors rendered an account of their stewardship. Nearly $30 had been collected and applied for the benefit of the needy around Salem.

Tues., Jan. 27. First mail since Friday last, but only as far north as Washington.

Fri., Feb. 6. The Musical Society gave a concert in the hall. Did them credit.

Wed., Feb. 11. Today there was a social solemnity connected with the opening [of] the new dining hall in the Academy. Members of Conference and others partook with teachers and scholars of a substantial and well prepared dinner. About 250 persons sat down with great ease and comfort at 10 tables. It is the largest dining hall in any of our Moravian institutions, either this side the Atlantic or on the other. It is 77 feet by 44, the ceiling resting on graceful iron pillars.

Sun., Mar. 1. Fourth centennial jubilee of the Unitas Fratrum. At 9 A.M. Bro. Reichel kept a morning blessing—singing and prayer. At 10 Bro. Bahnson preached on John 15:16. At 2 P.M. Bro Reichel kept the lovefeast with an address on the four centenaries. After this meeting Bro. Bahnson administered the holy communion in the German language and at 7 in English.

Fri., Mar. 13. Severe snowstorm, continuing all day and all night—rather strange a snow storm so late in the season, but this has been another remarkably cold and inclement winter.

Sun., Mar. 15. [M]eeting of the so called poor society, at which it was resolved to do away with the distinction between members of Salem Congregation living in or out of town. All shall have the same claims upon the funds of the society, a measure rendered necessary by the abolition of the old lease system. There is, however, but very little interest manifested in the affairs of this society. It is scarcely possible to get together a dozen or so to transact business.

Tues., Mar. 31. Bro. Bahnson lectured in the evening on the catechism, attendance quite good. Several times during the week was public sale at the store formerly kept by Boner and Clinard, which interfered somewhat with the lectures.

Tues., Apr. 7. Only 27°, on some thermometers only 20°. Fruit much injured, if not entirely, peaches particularly. Superior court was in session but broke today, having no business to transact. The jail at Winston is empty. God grant that it may be so always.

Thurs., Apr. 9. Maundy Thursday. At 2 1/2 and 4 P.M. Bro. Bahnson kept the usual meetings. There were not many men in, as sweet anticipation had led one to expect. It seems to be very hard to give up a business day. Many send their young men, stay away themselves. Well, if both the old and the young cannot come, perhaps the young are more benefited by coming.

Sat., Apr. 11. Great Sabbath. At 2 P.M. Bro. Bahnson kept the lovefeast which was well attended as all lovefeasts are, but there was no rush of strangers. At 7 1/2 P.M. Bro. Reichel kept the evening blessing, there being no sufficient reason for having it in the afternoon as was the case heretofore on account of numerous strangers camping all around Salem. The meeting in the evening was very well attended. The organ was not played, but the singing went on guided by stringed

instruments—something new and therefore of course not un-
attractive.

Sun., Apr. 12. Easter Sunday. At 5¼ in the morning we
met before the church to hail our risen Redeemer and then
proceeded as usual to the graveyard to pray our beautiful
Easter litany. Quite a number of strangers had congregated.
Good order was maintained without much difficulty. Our own
people do sometimes not set the best example and must be
reminded of their obligations.

Mon., Apr. 13. The annual meeting of Salem Bible Association was but poorly attended. Still it was resolved to supply our
county and if possible that of Stokes also.

Thurs., Apr 23. The ministers of the Province had a sociable
lovefeast for the purpose of taking leave for the present of our
Synodal delegates. Most of the wives of those Brethren and
other sisters in the service of the church were present.

Sun., Apr. 26. The attendance at church is somewhat
diminished in consequence of the prevailing sickness, in town
and in the Academy. It is said that there is sickness in 32
families, principally measles, some cases of whooping cough,
and single instances of scarlatina.

Mon., Apr. 27. Bro. Reichel left this morning on his way to
attend as one of the delegates of this Province the approaching
General Synod of our church.

Mon., May 4. The Brn. E. Schweinitz and Thom. Pfohl left
this morning in order to begin their journey to Herrnhut for the
purpose of attending the General Synod of our church to be
convened on the 8th prox. [*proximo* (*mense*), next month].

Tues., May 5. During the day two pupils of our female
boarding school, Eugenia Stow and Elisabeth Metts, departed
this life.

Thurs., May 7. At 9 A.M. Bro. Bahnson kept the funeral of
the two pupils who died on Tuesday last, and spoke on the
occasion on Jeremiah 3:4. They have sad times in our Academy. During this season of affliction 170 beds have contained
sick pupils. Another pupil, Lirry Lynch, had departed this life
in the morning, so that there were three corpses in the buildings connected with our boarding school.

Wed., May 13. Two more pupils of our Academy departed
this life today, Susan Edmonds and V. L. Joyner. The body of
the latter was taken to Tarborough by her friends.

Mon., May 18. Today Bro. Grunert came with his family to Salem and took up his abode in the house formerly occupied by Bro. Benjn. Warner.

The scarcity of provisions is very great. Far and wide the demand for grain is greater than the supply. Corn sold above Bethany at a public sale at $2.05 per bushel.

Thurs., May 21. Ascension day. At 3 P.M. the new chapel in the Female Academy was consecrated. Bro. Bahnson opened with prayer and preached on Ps. 76:2: In Salem is his tabernacle. In the evening a liturgy in German was sung, Bro. Bahnson occupying the chair. The attendance was very poor and the singing no better. Liturgies in the German language have seen their day here at Salem and ought to be abolished altogether.

Sun., May 31. Whitsunday. At 9 A.M. Bro. Grunert kept the first meeting in the English language; it was encouragingly attended. Hitherto the first meeting was always in German and a hymn was sung to a perfectly or at least almost generally unknown tune. The change of language seemed to meet with approbation.

Mon., June 1. The 44th semi annual meeting of our home mission society was held at the usual time and place. Bro. Siewers, now stationed at Bethany, was present, as were also all the other ministers from the country. Bro. Siewers gave a detailed verbal report concerning our mission at Mount Bethel.

Thurs., June 4. This morning another pupil of our institution died. She had been taken out of school by her parents and was at Butner hotel. May she only have been prepared for this all important change. Her name was Mary Alsebrook, the only daughter of her parents. Lord bless the parents and comfort them in their bereavement. In some few instances like this, whooping cough had been added to the measles, and the constitution of the patients being too weak for both diseases, death ensued. This being the last day of the session, and the public houses tolerably full of strangers, it is a matter of regret that there must be a corpse at one of them.

Wed., June 17. Today was the annual examination of our town boys' school. They did very well and the attendance was very encouraging indeed. Even the last session at candlelight was well attended. It would be very desirable indeed if some more interest could be awakened in this school of ours.

Sat., July 4. The national birthday. Firing of cannon, ringing of bells, etc., as usual. At 7 o'clock a numerous congregation assembled before which Bro. Rob. Schweinitz made some appropriate remarks and offered up a fervent prayer. At 9 o'clock there was another assemblage in the square. Alex Brietz read the national Declaration of Independence and Bro. Bahnson followed with an address. In the evening at 8 o'clock the square was beautifully and tastily illuminated. Alex Brietz read the Mecklenburg Declaration and Mr. Rufus Wharton followed with an address. Order and decorum prevailed to an unusual degree, and the manner in which this national day was celebrated gave satisfaction to all sensible and reflecting persons. Even the nuisance of a show, whose performers the older of our tavernkeepers had taken in, because the love of money is very great and powerful, did not interfere with the festivities of the day, but was rather a kind of safety valve through which superfluous steam escaped. May this nation be filled with true and practical gratitude towards that great Jehovah who has blessed us in such a signal and unmerited manner, and may all the privileges now enjoyed be handed down to our latest posterity and only end when time shall be no more.

Sat., July 11. The first weekly report from Synod arrived but in German.

Sun., July 12. Some persons living in town purposing having a dancing school for their children, some allusion was made to the impropriety of such a proceeding and that it was a striking proof that the parents had not yet drawn sufficient water from the wells of salvation in as much as the love of God shed abroad into the heart would remove altogether all taste and love for such poor vanities of the world. Wheat and chaff are separating more visibly, since there are no outward benefits connected with church membership.

Sat., July 18. At 8 P.M. Bro. Bahnson kept a meeting for our Great Boys. Not all were present. Of course they deserve less censure than their parents. The boys themselves dislike these meetings. I believe, and the question might be a timely one, whether all these Choir festivals ought not be abolished, with the exception, if any, of the Married People and Children's festivals.

Fri., July 31. This week the exercises in the female boarding school commenced. The prospects are very flattering, rather too much so, for want of accommodation in spite of the new and extensive building.

Sun., Aug. 2. A little before midnight the ringing of the bells and the cry of fire awakened us. In our Bro. Staub's room an explosion had taken place resembling, according to the testimony of some, the noise of a cannon. The front of the house (Butner's hotel) near his chamber was very much injured and he himself was so severely burnt that he breathed his last in a few hours.

Mon., Aug. 3. The sudden and mysterious death of our Bro. Staub was the universal theme of conversation. A Coroner's jury was called and all the requisitions of the law were complied with. In the evening at 7 o'clock was the funeral. Our church has scarcely ever been so full on a funeral occasion; it was crowded to overflowing and many colored people were without.

Sun., Aug. 9. At the usual hour Bro. Bahnson conducted divine worship preaching on Luke 15:17, the madness of sin. Quite a good audience, among the rest some of leading spirits of the dancing school which has been kept in our Bro. Zevely's hotel. [This sentence is in German:] O build up such swine through our mission hour. Private information was received that the great question about equal representation at future General Synods had been decided favorably. Hereafter every Province will send 9 delegates. In our country the Provincial Synods will elect them, 2 at the South, the balance at the North. In England and on the Continent the congregations will appoint them. How that can be done on the Continent I cannot well understand since the number has been so much reduced. But that is their own look out, and none of our concerns. Thus far I think the proceedings of the Synod will prove satisfactory except that they consume a long period of time in being brought to light. [This sentence is in German:] Good things take a while.

Mon., Aug. 10. This evening a complimentary party was given to a female of doubtful character who had instructed some of our would-be wise greenhorns in the art of dancing. Some of our young people, females, were persuaded not to expose themselves; others, and among them an elderly married sister and her daughter, would have it their own way. It was very pleasing, though, to notice that a loud voice was heard against this measure. O that all would heed it.

Sat., Aug. 29. An episcopal minister by the name of Houghton, who preached once in our church, applied for permission
to do so tomorrow. It so happens that the Rev. Jacob Doll, a
Presbyterian minister, has permission to preach tomorrow.
Hence Mr. H. could not have access to the pulpit in the
morning. The request being made in the name of our neighbor,
Mrs. Sheppard, that he might preach in the afternoon, Bro.
Bahnson informed her son, who was conducting the nego-
tiating, that we would have a lovefeast in the afternoon, etc.,
but that he could preach at 4 P.M. provided his coming here
somewhat regularly on the 5th Sunday of the month was not a
preconceived plan to attempt to establish an episcopalian
congregation in our midst. If the latter should be the plan we
should of course be unable to prevent the attempt, but should
necessarily feel just as unwilling to help in furthering a plan by
which we could not but be losers as far as membership is
concerned. Young Mr. Sheppard will inform Mr. Houghton
accordingly, and upon the plan pursued by the latter will his
preaching in our church depend. There are scores of neighborhoods that are very destitute of gospel means and privileges
where Mr. Houghton would find sufficient employment before
he comes into our parts.

Sun., Aug. 30. The single Brethren celebrated their annual
festival. How long this custom will continue time will show, but
it would almost appear as though the proper spirit did no
longer prevail as much as would be desirable. At 10 A.M. Br.
Bahnson prayed the litany and Rev. James Doll, a clergyman
of the Presbyterian church, delivered a very good evangelical
and practical sermon on the duty of training our hearts to the
service of God. It was very well attended. Some of the upper-
tenders [social climbers] were present, having been notified
probably that Mr. Houghton would preach. At the lovefeast of
the Single Brn., kept by Bro. Bahnson, 40 were present. A
great many of our people went out to hear Mr. Houghton
preach in the Methodist church at Winston.

Sun., Sept. 6. A camp meeting held at Maple Springs had
drawn many from our church, so that its influence would be
seen in the number who attended preaching this morning. In
the evening the whole town was roused by the cry of fire. A dry
kiln belonging to Bro. Wm. Shulz and filled with lumber had
caught fire and presented a grand spectacle. From different
parts of town it looked precisely as though houses in that

neighborhood were in full flames so that not a few were very much frightened. Thanks to the mercy of our God no further damage was done besides the destruction of the dry kiln and its contents. The fire company and many others exerted themselves faithfully.

Sun., Sept. 20. Bro. Bahnson conducted divine service, preaching on Heb. 11:26. Quite well attended, altho the quarterly Methodist meeting at Winston may have carried off some of the baser sort. The negroes had great times at Winston; some notorious ones took it out in shouting.

Wed., Sept. 23. After two cloudy and rainy days we had again a beautiful kind of weather. The heat is gone, and a cool and bracing air has come upon us. People, though, will take colds unless they are careful.

Mon., Sept. 28. At 7$1/2$ A.M. Br. Bahnson married the Single Bro. Julius Mickey and the Single Sr. Lavinia Vogler. The ceremony took place in the church. Since it is no longer obligatory to be married in church everybody likes it.

Thurs., Oct. 1. Today the Brethren L. T. Reichel and S. T. Pfohl, who had been absent for months as delegates to the General Synod, returned into our midst, and were heartily welcomed.

Sun., Oct. 11. A camp meeting at Mount Tabor about 6 miles from here exercised its usual effect. Many of our people could not but go there. Why and wherefore.

Tues., Oct. 13. Br. Emil Schweinitz arrived today, having returned from attending the General Synod.

Sun., Oct. 18. During the course of this week a kind of influenza spread rapidly throughout the whole town, In every family almost, one or more members were more or less severely attacked by it, some pretty severely.

Wed., Oct. 28. This morning Brother Reichel and his family left for the North. May the Lord our Savior watch over them and carry them safely to the place of their destination.

Sun., Nov. 1. During the latter part of the week the weather became so warm that fire had to be dispensed with, and people sat with open doors and windows, yea enjoyed themselves in front of their houses like in summer.

Fri., Nov. 13. Br. B. was called out to see Jefferson Fisher's family in which 3 children are afflicted with the same disease of the throat. Sr. Fisher, just readmitted to our church, is a sister of Bro. Ed. Blum and of Rud. Blum. The wife of the latter is dangerously ill with the same disease.

Tues., Nov. 17. There is a great deal of sickness among some of our country members. At Sr. Fisher's she herself and 6 of her children are down with what the doctor calls scarlet fever. This sickness seems to spread through the neighborhood.

Thurs., Nov. 26. Thanksgiving day according to the recommendation of the Governor. More than 20 sister states united in this pleasing and becoming duty. It was a very fine day, and generally observed here in our community, altho I believe nowhere else in this county except in our congregations.

Sun., Nov. 29. Entering upon the happy season of Advent. . . . In the evening at 7 P.M. Bro. Bahnson delivered an address, followed by the singing of Hosannah and by prayer.

Thurs., Dec. 10. At 1 P.M. was the funeral of Amanda Fisher, the 3d child removed by the Savior from the same family.

Fri., Dec. 11. In the evening some of our sisters prepared a public entertainment in the concert hall, the proceeds to be appropriated to church purposes. They succeeded very well indeed.

Tues., Dec. 15. There is a great deal of sickness throughout the country to which different physicians give various names.

Thurs., Dec. 24. Christmas Eve. At 4 1/2 P.M. Bro. Grunert kept the usual meeting for our children; it was pretty noisy. At 7 P.M. was lovefeast, etc., kept by Bro. Bahnson. It was of course rather crowded, but some had sneaked in that would have done better to stay away. One brother had to leave because his neighbors on both sides spread such a whiskey stench that he could not bear up against it. These two persons have just been excluded from the holy communion, Augustus Butner and Henry Shore, but alas they appear to pursue the downward career. May mercy arrest them. Later in the evening, these two persons with many others made themselves guilty of heathenish and abominable conduct on the streets, defying the lawful authority of our town. It is a burning shame and disgrace to the peace loving citizens. May measures be adopted to prevent a repetition.

Thurs., Dec. 31. At 10 A.M. the Elders Conference had its closing meeting. At 4 1/2 P.M. Bro. Bahnson kept a meeting for the children. At 8 o'clock Bro. Bahnson communicated the

Memorabilia of the year 1857, that were listened to attentively. At 10 o'clock the same Brother kept singing meeting, pretty well attended, and at 11 1/2 he addressed a large audience on the solemnity of the close of a year until the trombones announced the fact that 1857 belongs to the things that were.

Female Missionary Society of Salem, 1857
[Extracts of minutes transcribed.]

Sun., Jan. 25. Br. Friebele's report was read. The state of his small Negro Congregation, he writes, is upon the whole encouraging. The fifth of October [1856] had been a day of great rejoicing; for then the new melodeon which had been presented by this society was used for the first time; in the name of his congregation he returned thanks for the same.

Diary of the African Church in Salem, 1857
[Extracts transcribed; handwriting is that of John Adam Friebele.]

Sun., Mar. 15. Adaline Adams wishes to become a member of our church.

Fri., Apr. 10. Meeting; a good many people came, and after the meeting cleaned the graveyard, etc.

Sun., Apr. 12. Easter. Br. Byhan read the Litany. After which was preaching.

Sun., Apr. 19. Meeting and Bible instruction. Commenced giving instruction to Adaline Adams.

[Handwriting is now that of George Frederic Bahnson.]

Sun., May 17. Bro. Friebele having accepted a call as home missionary at Mount Bethel, the Brethren residing at Salem as ministers of that congregation will temporarily attend to the Negro church also. Today Bro. Bahnson preached on the Syrophenician woman [Mark 7:26]. The attendance was tolerable; some took it as a plea that they had not been aware that there would be preaching. There is certainly a large number of colored people in our midst, more or less perfectly careless of the one thing needful. May the spirit of God arouse them from their lethargy.

Sun., May 31. Whitsunday. By some misunderstanding a notice had been erroneously given that there would be no preaching, but after 4 o'clock Bro. Bahnson found occasion to address a few words of admonition to quite a respectable number of colored persons who had assembled at the funeral of Emma the daughter of Lewis (Geo. Folz) and Mary (Wm. Fries) and property of the latter.

[Handwriting is now that of Maximilian E. Grunert.]

Sun., June 21. At 1 o'clock the communicant members assembled for a lovefeast. Br. Grunert addressed them preparatory to the Holy Communion, which was held soon after. Fifteen members partook of it, and a few were present as spectators.

Sun., July 5. [Br. Bahnson's handwriting.] Bro. Grunert preached on Matt. 5:4. There were not many Negroes present, and even they appeared to be unusually much under the influence of drowsiness. The prospect is rather disheartening.

Sun., July 12. [Br. Bahnson's handwriting.] Owing to other engagements no brother was at leisure to preach to the Negroes. Hence there was no meeting for them.

Sun., Oct. 11. Br. Bahnson preached to a large audience, among which were many white people, on Mark 16:16. After which the youth [Church Register: Nancy Adelia] (Starbuck) was baptized, and the free woman Sophia Laws confirmed. Then followed a lovefeast for the members, and finally the Lord's supper was administered to 21 persons, several of them being Methodists.

Sun., Nov. 22. ([Colored Church Report; handwriting is that of George Frederic Bahnson:] After preaching, Bro. Bahnson called upon such as desired to give themselves up to the Savior to come forward, and give him their right hand. Several came forward, and promised to be Christ's. Bro. Bahnson gave them instruction on Thursday, the 26th; a dozen negroes attended, some of them members of another church. It is the intention to continue this instruction, and the hope is entertained that some of them will be willing and ready for confirmation. Very much cannot be expected, though, in the opinion of several ministering Brethren who have given the matter any consideration as long as the negroes are separated from the white congregation, which is dictated by necessity in as much as the church edifice of the white congregation does not possess sufficient room to admit the colored people. A wish, however, naturally intrudes itself to be able to procure a church edifice which would afford accommodations to both white and colored people. Their admission into the white people's church is in our opinion one of the causes that induce them to frequent the house of God in our neighbor town of Winston.)

Sun., Dec. 20. Br. Bahnson preached on Luke 2:1-12. Afterwards cakes and candles were distributed among the children present. Their number was of course considerably larger than usual; the attendance of adults was also good.

Aufseher Collegium (or Town & Church Committee or
Congregation Committee), 1857
[Extracts of minutes transcribed.]

Mon., Jan. 12.

Congregation Council having on the 8th inst. elected the following Brethren as members of the Committee, viz.: Wm. Petersen, Fr. Fries, C. Cooper, E. A. Vogler, Nathl. Vogler, Henry Leinbach, and Theod. Kühln, Elders Conference assembled with them in the office of the Warden on the evening of Jan. 12th, when after religious exercises Committee organized by electing Br. E. A. Schweinitz, President, and Br. S. Thos. Pfohl, Secretary.

1. The members of Conference not having a seat in the Committee having withdrawn, the minutes of last meeting (Dec. 15, 1856) were read and adopted.

4. Committee give their consent that a second story be erected on the Museum building on the Boys Schoolhouse lot, for the purpose of obtaining a separate and private room for exercises in music, provided the musicians are able to collect the requisite funds.

5. The Trustee of Boner and Clinard having advertised the public sale of the improvement on an outlot held by them, and stating at the same time that the conditions under which the improvements would be sold, were to be made known at the sale, Committee think it advisable that this opportunity be embraced to make known that the rents on such lots will have

to be increased, in as much as the assessors of taxes have valued the Diacony land at $20 per acre instead of $5 formerly, and we now pay taxes according to the new valuation, and that consequently the individual taking the above lot would do it with the understanding that a higher rent will be demanded in future.

Mon., Jan. 26. All present.

1. The minutes of last meeting having been read, Committee resolved in reference to §5 that the following notice be publicly read by the trustee of the firm before the sale of the improvement on the outlot takes place, in order to obviate all misunderstanding, viz.: "The purchaser buys no right or title to the land, and can claim only such improvement as he may remove, should the field be required by the landlord for any purposes whatsoever. It must be expressly understood that the rent will be raised, and should the land be required for building purposes or otherwise, the purchaser can claim no indemnification."

5. Whereas by the incorporation of Salem an entire separation between municipal and church expenses is effected, whereby it becomes necessary for the Congregation Diacony to defray certain expenses pertaining to the Church, which heretofore had been charged to the account of the town, and by means of which alteration an additional expense of say $150 per annum will in future devolve upon the Diacony; it becomes a case of necessity that the annual contributions of the members of the Congregation towards the support of the Church be somewhat increased; or as the case in reality presents itself, that part of the contributions heretofore paid towards municipal expenses, and which hereafter will no longer be paid to the Warden but to the Commissioners of the Town, be now added to the Congregation account. A plan how the above named sum might be raised was communicated, and a committee consisting of the Brrn. Pfohl, E. A. Vogler and H. Leinbach appointed to investigate the subject more fully and to report to this body at its next meeting.

7. As it may become desirable to be prepared for the sale of town lots, a committee consisting of the Brrn. E. A. Vogler, Nathl. Vogler and Wm. Petersen was appointed to propose a plan and to lay it before this body, with power to add some more members to their number.

Mon., Feb. 9. Not present Br. W. Petersen.

1. As the town lot of Br. Thos. Boner is to be sold tomorrow, Committee think that altho' thus far the sanction of the Unities Elders Conference to the sale of such lots has not been received, the Proprietor should nevertheless suffer the sale to take place; not being able to comprehend how that body could reasonably withhold their sanction, when permission has already been granted in 1848 by the General Synod of the Church.

2. A revised list of the contributions of members to the expenses of the Church prepared by the committee appointed for the purpose was next communicated and discussed. But in as much as this list was based upon the former regulations when a distinction was made between members residing in town and those that live in the country, it was not clear to Committee in how far such distinction should be retained since the whole system has been abolished, whereby we are in matters of this kind strictly confined to expenses pertaining to the Church, in which members living without the bounds of the town have the same interest as those living nearer the Church. It was finally resolved to lay the matter over for further advisement, and meanwhile to urge the framing of the new rules and regulations of the Congregation with the least possible delay.

3. It was resolved that the committee appointed last time for laying out of streets notify the occupants of such fields or lots thro' which the streets will pass that their term of rent will cease with the 30th of April next.

5. It was resolved that all sums to be received hereafter for the sale of town lots be entered on a separate account to be opened in the books of the Diacony, and that the amount to be received for such sales be, if possible, invested in public securities (coupon bonds issued by the State of North Carolina), such stocks being exempt from taxation.

6. Committee find it necessary for various reasons altogether to discontinue the sale of wood from the lands of the Diacony. The privilege granted heretofore to citizens of the town to cut decayed timber for firewood, or live trees for building or other purposes is consequently revoked.

Mon., Feb. 16. Not present Br. H. Leinbach (indisposed).

2. In reference to the new Rules and Regulations of the Congregation (see §2 of minutes of Feb. 9, 1857) the suggestion was made on the part of the Elders Conference, that in as far as the Brethren's Church is at this time in a state of transition, a number of very material alterations affecting its constitution and government having been proposed by the Northern and Southern Provincial Synods of America for discussion and decision at the approaching General Synod of the Church, it would appear to Conference as if the proper time for framing a new code of Rules had not yet arrived, and that in as much as all rules not stricken out by resolution of the Congregation Council of Nov. 17, 1856, are still in force, it might be most advisable to postpone the framing of the New Rules till points in our general Constitution now unsettled shall have been fully established and ratified.

Committee concur in these views.

3. With regard to the contribution of members to Church expenses, it was upon further consideration resolved, that from January 1st, 1857, members residing in town be charged at the following rates, viz.:

a married couple $4.25

widowers and single brethren $2.25 and

widows and single sisters $1.10 per year

to be placed to the credit of Congregation account, and the account heretofore carried on under the appellation of Salem Congregation, or Church and Town Expenses, to be discontinued after the close of the books at the end of April, [and] members of the Congregation not residing in town, till April 30 next, to be charged the former rates and after that time, in regard to Church expenses, to come under the same regulations as members living in town.

5. The plot of the town lots as proposed to be laid out by the sub-committee nominated Jan. 26, §7, on the fields west of the town and south of the Old Shallowford road was presented, and together with an amendment proposed by said sub-committee and relating to a slight alteration of a street thro' the premises of the Mill Co., [was] adopted by the Committee. The former sub-committee was requested now to lay out and stake off the streets and lots accordingly, leaving it discretionary with them to make slight alterations wherever deemed necessary.

Mon., Feb. 23. All present.

2. A certain piece of meadow ground joining the lot of Br. Adam Butner on the west is not to come into market until he had secured his last crop of hay this year, but may be rented by him as heretofore for that length of time.

4. In reference to the sale of town lots now contemplated the following conditions were resolved upon, viz.:

1. Application for town lots will be received by the Warden from tomorrow morning till Thursday evening (26th) at 6 o'clock.

2. Applicants will appear at the Town Hall on next Friday (Feb. 27) at 1 o'clock P.M. when the result of the applications will be made known.

3. If there is only one applicant for a lot he takes the lot at the stipulated price.

4. When there are several applicants for the same lot, it is to be bid for on Friday at 1 o'clock at the Town Hall. The bidding, however, is confined to such persons only as have made previous application for said lot within the stipulated time.

5. All purchasers to pay the cash within ten days from next Friday (say by 6 o'clock P.M. of Monday, March 9th, 1857).

6. Timber standing on a lot to be paid for separately according to valuation, and payment to be made at the same time that the lot is paid for.

5. In order to define the position of the town lots more fully on the deeds to be made out hereafter, Committee find it necessary to name the different streets in town, and resolved that those running north and south be called, respectively, Church Street, Main Street, Salt Street, Elm Street (formerly called Factory Row), Marshall Street (from Old Shallowford street to the mill lane) and Poplar Street, and those running east and west (beginning at the north corporation line) Belews Creek Street, New Shallowford Street, Bank Street, Old Shallowford Street, West Street, and Walnut Street (passing N. Vogler's and Tr. Chitty's).

Thurs., Feb. 26. All present.

3. After tomorrow's sale lots already laid out and priced will be sold by the Warden at private sale for cash, a lot not to be considered as secured to the person desiring it until paid for.

Mon., Mar. 9. Not present Brrn. F. Fries and C. Cooper.

8. Br. S. Thos. Pfohl, having been chosen by the Southern Provincial Synod as one of the Deputies to the General Synod to convene at Herrnhut June 8th of the present year, communicated to Committee his idea how his place as Warden might be filled during his absence, viz.: Br. James Leinbach to attend to the paying of salaries, taxes, interest, etc. Br. Fr. Fries to take charge of the notes of the Diacony, with power to act in case of necessity. Br. Charles Cooper to have an eye upon repairs of houses, fences, etc., and also upon the supply of firewood to those houses and persons furnished by the Warden. And Br. E. A. Vogler to superintend the affairs of the Single Sisters Diacony. This arrangement was approved by the Committee, and it had also previously already received the sanction of the Provincial Helpers' Conference.

Fri., Apr. 3. Not present Br. Theod. F. Keehln.

4. The application of Dr. Britton of Winston for permission to bury his child on our graveyard was not granted.

5. This application lead to a discussion of the necessity of laying out another graveyard in the vicinity of Salem for the interment of such persons as may reside in town but are not members of our Society, thereby enabling us to keep our burying ground as the place of interment for such persons only as belong to our congregation. A charter having been granted by the legislature for a Cemetery Association, extending such privileges as were thought necessary for the proper regulation of such a burying place, a sub-committee consisting of the Brrn. Nathl. Vogler and Chs. Cooper was appointed, who are to meet the members of said association and then report to this body.

6. The Warden was instructed to charge the Commissioners of the town with the burning fluid used since Jan. 1st and also with the tin stand, can, and lamps recently procured for the use of it, and also with the new lantern put up at the Post Office. The salary of the Watchman and Lamplighter he will pay only to the 31st of Dec. 1856.

7. The Salem Band, having contributed $100 towards the erection of the old Concert and Town Hall, would wish to receive back that amount from the Diacony in order to apply it towards the erection of a new Music Hall now in contemplation on the Museum building. Committee postponed the decision.

9. The Brrn. E. A. Schweinitz and S. Thos. Pfohl, the President and Secretary of the Committee, being about to leave shortly in order to attend the General Synod, Committee appointed Br. E. A. Vogler as President and Br. James Leinbach as Secretary during the absence of the above named brethren.

Mon., Apr. 13. Not present Brrn. H. Leinbach and Wm. Peterson.

1. The sub-committee appointed according to §5 has viewed the locality to the eastward of our graveyard, and report that in their opinion a space of ground of 100 ft. from the eastern enclosure of our graveyard should be retained for its future enlargement, from which place a line should be drawn parallel with the graveyard alley till it strike the street or alley running along the south side of Br. Edw. Leinbach's lot, which would in their opinion leave ample room for the enlargement of our graveyard, and that a piece of ground eastward of that line as far as the Company should desire it, say about 800 feet, and extending from the street south of E. Leinbach's lot to a line drawn eastwardly from the southern side of the middle walk in our graveyard, be sold to the Cemetery Company. Committee approves of this plan and resolved that in consideration of the very hilly nature of the ground and especially in consideration that the improvements contemplated by the Company may in time prove an ornament to the town and a place of resort and recreation to its inhabitants, we are willing to sell the desired spot for $50 to the Company.

2. In reference to §7 the following resolution was passed: Whereas the musicians in town contributed $100 towards the old Concert Hall and imagine that they have some claim on said Hall, they now apply for a contribution to the same amount from the Diacony towards the new music hall. This right this Committee can not understand, but to extinguish it if just, but more particularly in consideration of the gratuitous services rendered by the musicians of the town in Church music, and for the encouragement of our brethren and sisters to perfect themselves in the science and art of music, so as to

be able to serve the Congregation efficiently and acceptably in the performance of Church music, therefore resolved that the Diacony grant them one hundred dollars towards the erection of the contemplated music saloon.

4. Application having been made for Widow Beckel to move into the house formerly occupied by Martha Elis. Baumgarten in the Sisters House garden, Committee are unanimously of opinion that the application should not be granted, as they think that the Sisters House premises should be strictly retained for the purposes for which they were originally intended, viz. for the accommodation and use of our single sisters.

Fri., June 26. Br. Charles Cooper not present.

1. Br. E. A. Vogler mentioned that application had been made by Mr. Henry Hughes through Br. Lewis Belo for permission to bury his child in our graveyard. After some discussion, Committee agreed to grant that permission to Mr. Hughes, with the understanding that he obligate himself to pay $5 for keeping in repair the grave of his child and that he also procure a tombstone for the same.

4. Mention having been made that the rent, etc., due to the Diacony from Widow Holland's estate had been settled by note of William Snider, some discussion in reference to the debtors of the Diacony arose, and Committee agreed that Br. Fries, in whose hands the notes of the Diacony had been placed, should see to it that all remiss debtors be required to settle up.

Fri., July 24. The Brethren Fr. Fries, Wm. Petersen and N. Vogler absent.

President mentioned that at request of Br. Bahnson, this meeting had been called to entertain the request of Mrs. J. Reid from Mt. Airy, formerly of this place, for permission to bury her child in our graveyard. The fact that Mrs. Reid's relations living here were all members of our church and that she herself had been such until her marriage induced the Committee to consent to the burial of the child in our graveyard.

Mon., Aug. 24. Br. Wm. Peterson not present.

The minutes of last meeting were not read, as the Secretary had not brought them with him.

5. Br. Levi Blum, wishing to pay for his lot [67], requested to have the line between himself and A. Butner established.

Committee determined that the bounding lines, decided upon some time ago, should be adhered to.

6. It was further determined that Br. Butner must make purchase of his lot *before* giving possession of the same to Mr. Chaffin, with whom he had made contracts of sale.

Mon., Oct. 19. Br. F. Fries not present.

1. The Brrn. E. A. Schweinitz and S. Thos. Pfohl, having returned from Europe, again occupied their respective places, the former as President and the latter as Secretary of this body.

4. Br. Theod. Keehln as executor of the late Br. Augustus Staub asks the question whether the 8 acres of land which the deceased held under lease on the south side of the creek and which have been cultivated by him as a vineyard, orchard, nursery of trees, etc., should be sold in fee, or whether the *improvement* on the land should be merely disposed of as being held under rent or lease? As the decision of this question involves the whole policy hereafter to be pursued with all the land of the Diacony situated outside of the limits of the corporation, Committee laid the subject over for further consideration at its next session.

7. The town lots on Marshall Street between Walnut Street and the Mill lane are now to be laid out, as application has been made for some in that part of the town.

Mon., Nov. 2. Not present Brrn. Theod. Keehln and Wm. Petersen.

2. With reference to the land or lot heretofore rented to the late Augustus Staub, Committee came to the following decision, viz.: The Staub tract (containing 8 ac. 106 ps.) may be sold on these terms: The buyer (whoever he be) shall hold it as other outlots are held, paying yearly rents at the rates paid by Staub until an alteration be made in the general system of holding outlots. Say, if rents on outlots are raised, the new renter must be bound to pay whatever rent be put on that lot, at the same ratio that other rents are raised. If the authorities determine to sell outlots, the purchaser of Staub's interest must buy at such price as is determined on for lots in the same section of the Diacony land.

4. As it appears that the town lots on the west side of Main Street and between the Old and New Shallowford streets are by

measurement 200 ft. in depth, altho' only put down at 198 ft. in the town plot, Committee resolved that the true measurement be put down on the plot and the calculations of the contents be made accordingly whenever one of these lots is disposed of.

Mon., Dec. 7. All present.

2. Br. Adam Butner, having disposed of his Hotel to Mr. Nathan Chaffin, wishes also to transfer some of the fields that he held in rent to him. Committee gives its consent.

6. The yearly accounts of Salem Diacony and of the Single Sisters Diacony for the year closing with April 30, 1857, were then laid before Committee. From the former it appears that owing to increased expenses of different kinds, a loss of $795.04 has arisen, but that on the other hand $3,362.15 have been received for the sale of town lots, which amount has been reserved as a fund and invested in North Carolina state bonds at 6 percent interest.

The accounts of the Single Sisters Diacony close with a loss of $1,111.01 bro't about by the unprecedented high prices of provisions and especially of groceries, the price charged for boarding having remained the same as heretofore when provisions were at least 50 percent lower.

Mon., Dec. 14. Not present Brrn. C. Cooper and Theod. Keehln.

1. After some conversation in reference to the lot granted to Edwin Clemmons, and also regarding the price put upon the lot of Br. John Siewers—which, however, led to no results— Committee entered into the further consideration of the yearly accounts of the Diacony, and endeavoured to find ways and means to improve its condition.

As its disbursements on account of the higher taxes and salaries have been increased by about $500 per year, it has become very desirable, yea, absolutely necessary to increase its receipts also in as far as it can be done. In order to accomplish this, the following propositions were made and discussed, without, however, being finally disposed of in the present session.

     1. With regard to notes due by sundry individuals and which in part are of long standing, it was proposed to collect them as speedily as possible.

2. As the rents for rooms are in a great measure collected from widows and persons that have not abundant means at command, it was not considered expedient to increase them, but an attempt is to be made to induce the Directors of Salem Poor Fund to pay those of the sisters Cathar. Schaffner, Mahela Butner, and Anna Schaub, amounting to $35 per annum.

3. Rents for outlots have heretofore averaged at 50 cents per acre [per month] and were established at a time when the Diacony land was assessed in the tax list at $5 per acre or even at less. By the last assessment, however, the land in the vicinity of Salem has been rated at $20 per acre, for which we have to pay taxes at a much higher percentage than formerly. (In 1847 our taxes amounted to $35, this year to $247). In order to meet in some measure at least the increased expenses on land, it was proposed that hereafter the rents for land be regulated in the following manner, viz.: The minimum rent to be $1.00 per acre, but if 50 percent added to present rate brings it above $1.00, then that percent is to be added to rents now paid.

The above propositions, after having been discussed, were laid over for further consideration, and Committee resolved to meet again tomorrow evening.

Tues., Dec. 15. Not present the Brrn. H. Leinbach, C. Cooper, and Theod. Keehln.

The minutes of yesterday's meeting having been read, Committee continued the investigation of the accounts of the Congregation Diacony and added the following propositions to those already made, viz.:

1. It is proposed that hereafter firewood be not furnished to the minister and Warden but that instead thereof $40 yearly be added to the salary of each.

2. Wood for superannuated Salem ministers or their widows not to be furnished any more by the Diacony.

3. Newspapers and periodicals not published by the Church of the United Brethren not to be kept by the Diacony.

4. As the occasions for the use of a horse by the Diacony have become less frequent since the incorpora-

tion of Salem, the horse, wagon, and also the old carriage might be dispensed with and sold.

Bethania Diary, with Bethabara, 1857
[Excerpts transcribed; handwriting is that of Maximilian E. Grunert.]

Thurs., Jan. 8. Began a new catalogue of the Bethabara congregation; it was a very necessary but rather difficult task.

Sun., Jan. 18. An awful snowstorm prevailed all day. There were no meetings. Had an appointment at Spanish Grove, which thus had to be dropped.

Mon., Jan 19. Very cold. The wind blew the snow about and produced large drifts. People are mostly confined to their houses. They say that since 1800 nothing like it has been experienced in these parts.

Sat., Feb. 14. About 1 A.M. a little daughter was born to us. In the afternoon the Committee met, principally on account of the celebration of the first of March.

Sat., Feb. 28. Celebration of the first of March at Bethabara, its being the fourth centenary jubilee of the organization of the Brethren's Church. The attendance was not large. The morning meeting from 3/4 11-1/2 1. Afterwards lovefeast and the Holy Communion with 20 communicants. The Lord was nigh! It was to be regretted that the organ could not be used.

Sun., Mar. 1. This memorial day of the beginning of the Brethren's Church 400 years ago was observed here as the anniversaries of the congregation generally are, and most of the members, as well as a considerable number of others, attended. At 10 o'clock there was a short morning blessing in the German language, followed by a sermon on the doctrinal text, 1 Cor. 3:11, for the most part historical, and listened to with much attention. The church was full for once. The lovefeast, of which a number of invited guests partook with us, was enlivened by several anthems performed by the choir, and kept up by relating and reading some particulars of the ancient Br.'s Church, and also an address. Then followed the Lord's Supper, pretty well attended.

Thurs., Mar. 5. Drizzling rain all day. Our merchants, however, set out for the north.

Wed., Mar. 11. Was called to Winter's. Found their daughter Louisa perfectly deranged, and could not do anything with her; promised to call again. What wretched poverty!

Thurs., Mar. 12. Spent a long time at Winter's. The girl was reasonable and said that great things had been done for her, that she would live some years yet, and her mission was to warn people, and especially the rich, of their danger. In fact, I found that she had pitched upon me, as in her opinion a wealthy man, to help them. Found myself in rather a difficult position and often at a loss what to say. In the opinion of the whole neighborhood they are a lazy set, who will not work as they might, and claim support as a right. They say that they do as much as their circumstances will allow them.

Sat., Mar. 14. News came that E. C. Lehman lay very sick in Baltimore.

Thurs., Mar. 19. Towards evening Lewis Belo brought news of E. C. Lehman's death at Baltimore on Monday. About 10 P.M. the corpse arrived. Awful scene.

Sat., Mar. 21. At 12 was the funeral. Br. Bahnson had come. We sang a couple of verses at the house, and proceeded to the church, where a very large congregation had assembled. Br. Josh. Boner presided at the organ; the departed having served as organist for very many years, it seemed but right that his place was occupied on this occasion. The Salem brass band had also come, and performed at the outdoors exercises. The church loses with him a very valuable member whose place is hard to fill.

Tues., Apr. 14. Began in the evening to keep Ben. Chitty's melodeon instruction with a view of his learning to play the organ.

Tues., Apr. 21. Br. Bahnson came from Mount Bethel; a meeting of the Committee (town members) was called, and he notified them that br. Grunert had received and accepted a call to Salem, and that br. and sr. Siewers from Mt. Bethel had been called to take charge of this congregation.

Wed., Apr. 29. The day appointed for church scouring. The hands assembling after 2 ringings appearing too few, they were dismissed by the authority of the first sextoness, and the church left as it was. Was in Salem.

Thurs., May 7. Church scouring. Today a good many came.

Mon., May 11. Was in Salem. The new horns arrived today.

[The handwriting is now that of Jacob F. Siewers.]

Jacob F. and Matilda A. Siewers, having received and accepted a call to take charge of the Congregation at and around Bethania, left the Blue Ridge on the 19th of May with their daughter Margaret in company of Augustus Fogle. We were kindly invited to dine at Robert Gilmer's in Mt. Airy, and afterwards proceeded on our journey, the weather being very unpleasant, cold and rainy, and at night quartered quite comfortably at Mr. Pace's.

Wed., May 20. Continued our journey and arrived about noon in Bethania. The parsonage undergoing the cleaning process, we were kindly invited to dinner at Br. Grabs's sen. opposite the parsonage, and afterwards were kindly greeted by a number of the Brn. and Srs. In the evening we lodged at Br. Joseph Transou's, the steward of the congregation.

Sun., May 24. This morning Br. Bahnson arrived from Salem and at 10 A.M. in the first meeting introduced us to the congregation as their future laborers in this part of the Lord's vineyard and commended us to the Lord in prayer. Committee met, and determined not to have a general lovefeast on the Congregation Festival but only for communicants. We had the pleasure of having our children here, Caroline, Elisabeth, and Jacob, as also of seeing a number of persons whose faces had been familiar to us in past years.

Wed., June 3. Received of Thomas Lash by black boy 40 pounds of flour. I worked in the garden hoeing my cabbage and potatoes on the other side of the street.

Fri., June 5. Wrote my diary and inserted the baptisms in the Church Book.

Sun., June 14. Br. Pratt . . . gave me a short history of his life, his providential escape with his life after a serious fracture of his scull occasioned by a limb falling on him after felling a tree. Also his conviction and conversion and joining the Church, under the instrumentality of Br. Hagen. I pressed on him the duty of family worship letting his light shine around him.

Tues., June 16. The Franklin rod at the church having been disconnected, by the help of several brethren we procured a ladder and fixed it. Br. Elias Schaup [Schaub] paid me his half yearly payment: $3.

Thurs., June 18. Dropt a line to Br. Bahnson upon learning that the sacramental bread had to be procured from Salem.

Fri., June 26. Went down with Jacob and Nathaniel Siewers to Bethabara in Schaup's wagon and bro't up a table and 4 chairs from the parsonage.

Mon., June 29. After dinner Br. Transou kindly loaning us his horse, we—Sr. Siewers and myself—visited Allen Flint's, Br. Henry and Thomas Schultz's and Edwin Shultz. At the house of the latter, I found an old couple, Krauses, George who formerly belonged to the Lutheran Church under G. Shober's charge but thru' Br. Hagen attached to the Bethania Congregation. Sr. Krause in her old days has recovered her sight and can see to sew, etc.

Sat., July 4. In the morning in company with Elias Shaup went to see Br. Lash's reaping machine in operation. Caroline and Margaret also came out in company with Mrs. Livingston and M. Miller. We were all well pleased with the novelty.

Sun., July 5. By invitation I vespered with Br. Pratt. There I met with his daughter Caroline, who is deaf and dumb, having returned from the N. C. Institute where she completed her education, having been there 7 years. I conversed with her for some time by means of a slate. This evening I attempted for the first time to address an audience in the German language.

Wed., July 8. Answered the kind letter of Mr. P. A. Cregar, corresponding secretary pro tem. of the Ministers Aid Society of Philadelphia, thru' whom I received $10 as a present.

Sat., July 11. Read Spurgeon's sermons, kindly loaned to me by Miss Maria Peterson.

Thurs., July 16. I worked in my garden, the rain having put the ground in good plight. Br. Bahnson and wife stopped before our house a little before dinner, bound for Br. Thomas Lash's, who has his 50th birthday.

Fri., July 17. Last night I spoke with Br. Herman Butner in relation of the difference between Sol. Transou and himself, a very trifling but unfortunate difference.

Thurs., July 23. After going to bed I was awakened by a knocking at the front door and upon inquiry found one of the Spiece's and Steirs' desiring me to go with them. I rode on a horse to Edwin Spiece's, whose child was very low of the flux and not expected to live, and the object of my being sent for was to baptize the child. There being another infant in the family unbaptized, I was requested to baptize it also.

Sun., July 26. In the afternoon, according to appointment, I preached to the negroes under the shade of a large oak at their church. The state of the weather prevented a number from coming, still I judged some 60 persons were present. I preached on Luke 15:11-24. I thought we would be driven into the house by the rain, but we escaped being disturbed. The negroes sing very well.

Sun., Aug. 2. Without praying the Litany preached at 10 A.M. on Matthew 9:2-8 to a good audience. Took a hasty dinner and by the kindness of Br. E. Shaup was enabled to take Sr. S. along to Br. John Grabs where I preached on same text at 3 P.M. at the school house to about 250 persons. The house was thronged and some outside. It was very warm, but a more attentive congregation I have never addressed nor with more freedom.

Sun., Aug. 16. After preaching requested the members of the Committee to wait a few moments: 1. Bro't forward a desire to have the kitchen chimney taken down and rebuilt outside. 2. The fence around the lot requiring repair. The brethren agreed to the above, and Brn. Jos. Transou and Levin S. Grabs were appointed to see it done.

Fri., Sept. 4. Br. Rights, Sr. S., and myself started this morning for the Blue Ridge, stopped at Mr. Armstrong's, on Tom's Creek, where we met Br. Bahnson, who had left the day previous with his son Charles. After having our horse fed we continued our route to Mount Airy, where we arrived at night, putting up at Elisha Banner's. Br. R. complained of pain in his chest.

Sat., Sept. 5. This morning Br. R. informed us that he had spent a sleepless night with much suffering, but was well enough to proceed. We took the Ward's Gap road in company with Br. Bahnson (who with his son had staid at Rev. Mr. Reed's) and arrived at Mount Bethel, our former home. We found Br. and Sr. Friebele well and waiting for us. The arrangement for a three days meeting having been made, we immediately went up to the church. Br. Bahnson preached at 11 A.M., and I followed in a short exhortation; the assembly was small.

Mon., Sept. 7. Br. Scott appearing in the church for the first time since last fall, and I being the cause at least in part, it having been a subject of notoriety, I felt it a duty in proposing publicly a reconciliation, whereupon we stept forward before the congregation, declaring our willingness to bury all past differences and mutually to forgive one another, we confirmed this compact with a kiss. Afterwards we all partook of the Lord's Supper, several of the neighbors of other denominations in good standing after being invited joined with us in commemorating the Lord's death. Br. Rights, Sr. S., and myself spent the night at Bro. John Scott's.

Tues., Sept. 8. We all left for home, Br. B. and son taking a route along the top of the mountain, and Br. R. and we thru' Mount Airy homewards.

Fri., Sept. 11. This morning I received a note from Br. Solomon Transou requesting me to erase his name from the Church book, as he was no longer a member of the Moravian Church. After an hour or two I went to see him, and spoke to him about his differences with Br. Butner, and prevailed with him not to proceed to law, but to drop the matter. He promised to do so, but insisted that his name should be stricken from the church records, stating that he had been badly treated by Br. Bahnson, he having shown an unwarrantable partiality in H. Butner's favor, amounting to personal insult, and that he could not remain in a church where such distinctions were permitted.

Wed., Sept. 16. Sr. S. and myself started to visit Charles Rank, going down the plank road, but we altered our course in consequence of a heavy rain overtaking us, wetting us to the skin. We continued the plank road to near the Maple Springs, and then turned off for Henry Fogle's, where we arrived about noon and remained all night.

Mon., Sept. 21. Sr. S. and myself visited the old mother Butner, who is in her 88th year and with the exception of her failing sight seems to enjoy tolerable health.

Wed., Sept. 30. Sr. S. and myself went to see Benj. Hauser, found him very low and evidently weaker. As there was no male person about the house but his son, I remained till near night; he had to be lifted in and out of bed very often.

Sun., Oct. 11. Children's Festival. Afternoon Br. Reichel held the lovefeast and told the children that he had been present at a similar occasion in one of our congregations in Europe, where there were about 150 present. Here he judged there were about 50 present.

Wed., Oct. 21. Engaged br. J. Conrad's services for building our outside chimney, and the brick br. Timothy Conrad engaged to deliver.

Sun., Oct. 25. Brothers Festival. Afternoon at 2 held the lovefeast; several missed it, not having heard the bell ring. But one communicant Brother present, Wesley Karney. The sacrament of course left out.

Mon., Oct. 26. Sr. S. and myself went to Salem to be present at a vesper given as a welcome to the returned brethren from the Synod and a farewell to Br. Reichel, who having been elected to the U.E.C. is about to return to Europe.

Fri., Sat., Oct. 30, 31. Took down the kitchen chimney and cleaned the brick to get them ready for rebuilding.

Tues.-Thurs., Nov. 3-5. Occupied on the chimney, tending and helping until finished.

Sun., Nov. 8. After dinner I loaned [borrowed] Shaub's mule and buggie and started to Spanish Grove by Pfafftown, and after passing the Chittys' old fields, took the left hand road and drove about until 3 P.M., and being unable to find the road, returned by Pfafftown. I afterwards heard that a very large congregation had waited for me till near 4 P.M. It is admitted that I must have been within a 1/4th of a mile of the School house. The leaves, having fallen, made the road too indistinct for me to recognize it.

Sat., Nov. 14. Sr. Siewers went with Julious Shaub to Salem to procure sacramental bread.

[The Bethania Diary interrupts. The following excerpts are transcribed from Br. Siewers's Reports to Ministers Conference.]

Thurs., Nov. 26. Preached the Thanksgiving sermon; could scarcely get along for coughing. In consequence gave up going to Bethabara.

Mon., Dec. 7. Rode out to Shoretown, visited the widow Langly, who with a son and daughter are sick. Conversed and prayed with them; they are very poor. Farther on visited Winter's; several more sick. Visited E. Transou's. Called at Tom Conrad's, found his mother a little better. On my return called at Phillip Transou's to see the widow Wolf, she was better. Called at Sol. Pfaff's, and at Peter [Pfaff's]. A negro man named Elijah, in the last stages of dropsy with whom I conversed and prayed, assured me that he had made his peace with God in the days of health.

Wed., Dec. 9. More rain. The roads are in desperate condition; the sick in town are not much better.

([Ministers Conference minutes:] *Thurs., Dec. 17.* Br. Siewers mentioned that the membership of Nazareth Lutheran church (commonly called Dutch Meeting House) having nearly died out, the Protestant Methodists had made efforts to get possession of this church and the land adjoining. The minister at Bethania is now generally called upon to perform the services there, and it seemed but fair that this property should, if changing owners, fall to the Brethren. Br. S. will make further inquiries about this matter.)

Friedberg Diary, with Hope, Muddy Creek, Macedonia, 1857
[Extracts transcribed; handwriting is that of Christian Lewis Rights.]

Sat., Jan. 3. [F]ound our little daughter very sick; returned to Salem for medical aid. Dr. Shelton had been here in the morning.

Sun., Jan. 4. Did not go to Hope. Dr. Keehln was here.

Mon., Jan. 5. Little Mabel died 20 minutes after 8 o'clock P.M. The last struggle was painful to witness. How hard to give her up, but "thy will be done, O Lord."

Wed., Jan. 7. Buried our infant. Brothers Bahnson and Reichel were here. Brother Bahnson spoke from 2 Kings 4:26: Is it well with the child.

Sun., Jan. 18. This morning the ground was covered with snow. It continued snowing all day, and the wind drove at a furious rate. The snow drifted in the lanes as high as the fences. It was about 18 inches deep on an average. No meeting.

Tues., Jan. 20. Today I was engaged in removing the snow from the garret. It took me the whole day.

Fri., Jan. 30. Snow fell to about the depth of four inches.

Sun., Feb. 8. During the past week the weather moderated, and for several days we had had no fire in the bedroom. The snow is gone, but the roads are desperately muddy. [T]here was a meeting of the heads of families to consult in what way to celebrate the anniversary of the organization of the ancient church of the Brethren on the 1st of March 1457, 400 years ago. It was finally determined to have a Lovefeast for the whole congregation (free), and afterwards celebrate the Communion, and that the Hope Congregation be requested to celebrate with us, and also that a collection be taken up on that day to aid in defraying the expenses of the Delegates going to the Synod.

Wed., Feb. 11. Prayer meeting in the Church this evening in accordance with a wish expressed in *The Moravian* that united prayer might be offered up for a general blessing on the church, and especially that the labors of the approaching Synod might be convened with the best of consequences.

Sun., Mar. 1. Centennial Jubilee of the Moravian Church, it being 400 years since it first organized. At 11 o'clock preaching from 1 Sam. 7:12: Hitherto hath the Lord helped us. Rev. Samuel Farrabee of the Methodist E. Church closed with prayer. 2nd: Lovefeast for the whole congregation. 3d: the Communion. There were a great many persons here. Seats had to be made in the porch and front room; the kitchen was full of women. In the evening there was prayer meeting at Flat Rock school house. A collection was taken up to aid in defraying the expenses of the members elected to the General Synod, amounting $10.25.

Fri., Mar. 13. About 2 o'clock it began to snow and continued till sometime in the night. The wind blew very violently, and it is piercing cold. I was on a visit at Bro. Joseph Rothrock's. In consequence of the storm, I left my carriage and family behind, and rode home without a saddle.

Sat., Apr. 11. Went to Hope to accept the lumber furnished by brother Christian Seides to repair the graveyard. The lumber furnished amounted to $11.65, and brother Schweinitz is requested to pay it.

Thurs., Apr. 23. [Ministers] Conference in the morning and a lovefeast in the afternoon. Brother Reichel is going to start north on next Monday preparatory to sailing for Europe. The weather is still very cold, ice every morning. In the west they have snow, and here cold winds. It looks like the beginning of March, and only a few persons have begun to plant corn. The trees around the house are still as bare as in winter, and food of every kind is enormously high and scarce. In Salem they are paying 50 cents per cwt. for hay and hauling it out of the meadows. In fact the hay is all gone.

Sun., Apr. 26. Mr. Jonathan Cross, an agent of the American Tract Society, delivered a very interesting lecture at Friedberg. At the close a collection was taken up amounting to $16. Beard, Thornton, and Knauss were present. In the afternoon he went to Salem.

Tues., May 12. Friedberg anniversary. 1st, Committee meeting. Bro. Jesse Mock and Chr. Earnest agreed to cover the bake-oven, Bro. Shore to get some nails. 2nd, introductory address. 3d, lovefeast and a closing meeting. . . .

Fri., May 15. The Brethren Chr. Spach, Chr. Earnest, and Jesse Mock covered the bake-oven.

Thurs., June 18. Preaching at Muddy Creek meeting house. ([Friedberg Report:] This meeting had been appointed in order to hold a consultation in regard to building a house with a view [of] a minister here. At the close of the exercises I explained to them the difficulties connected with such an enterprise, viz., men and means, and all seemed satisfied.)

Sun., July 19. Preaching at Friedberg in the morning, and at Hope in the afternoon to the negroes. The house was well filled, and all seemed very attentive. ([Friedberg Report:] After the service a negro woman came to me and asked me to put the text on a slip of paper, so that her master could read it for her when she came home.)

Sun., Sept. 13. Commenced a protracted meeting at Friedberg.

Mon., Sept. 14. Protracted meeting continued. Six mourners, three professed. A window curtain caught on fire in our bedroom and created a considerable excitement, Sr. Rights burnt her hand trying to get it down. Nothing was burnt except the curtains.

Sat., Dec. 19. Bro. John Kanauss showed me a letter from the Tract House commending him for his faithfulness in the discharge of his duties as colporteur for the last nine months. I rejoiced with him, because through my recommendation he received the appointment.

Friedland Diary, 1857
[Extracts transcribed; handwriting is that of John Chapman Cooke.]

Remarks in general up to this time [Mar. 1]

During my ministration at Friedland, I have from time to time been enabled to arrive at certain conclusions in reference to its congregation, and its ability and willingness to support a stationary minister, and these conclusions have finally resolved into the opinion that there is neither ability nor disposition among them to carry out such a purpose. When I first went there I endeavored to collect the fragments of the congregation, and by personal intercourse and social conversation create a sympathetic feeling in favor of the Church, and this was responded to so far as to secure their attendance at church. This point gained, I next endeavored to ascertain what amount of means they could furnish towards the support of a resident minister, but nothing definite could be elicited from any of them on this subject. Nor was there any willingness on their part to subscribe any sum individually towards this object. So long as I continued to serve them free, it is all very well, and attendance at church appears to be considered as a compensation for the ministration of the Word, and this appears to be the prevailing sentiment among them. The vital principles of our Church have here degenerated into indifference, carelessness, and coldness, although I have served them constantly in the word and ordinances from the time I went there to reside. Yet I have not received a copper from them, and if I am in want of a peck of corn I have to pay for it. And if the case were brought to issue whether to remain among them and maintain a regular service (or otherwise and discontinue it), my opinion is that not even $50 per annum could be realized for a resident minister. And with such a prospect, it is very evident that the incumbent of Friedland must receive his maintenance from another source except the people, or that Friedland must become what it was before—an "outpost." The returns of the congregation for the last years have been fictitious; the numbers were counted from the book as they had then stood year after year without being revised. And thus while names and numbers appeared on the book and in the returns, the persons were not visible, having either died or removed or gone to other congregations or left the church altogether.

Sun., Mar. 8. The people in general are very indifferent toward the Church of the Brethren, and the majority in favor of Methodists and Baptists.

Sun., Mar. 15. It is very discouraging to a minister to waste his lungs upon empty benches.

Sun., July 5. It would be some satisfaction for me to have something interesting to relate, but nothing of the kind has occurred. And my labors in general seem to be without any particular results.

Sun., July 26. The Methodist camp meetings being more in vogue, the people gather to them from all quarters, and it seems as if the most consistent have the itching fancy to desert their own church and mingle with the rabble.

Sun., Aug. 2. Sunday School, 10 children. Preached from Prov. 4:23. Four grown persons present besides the children and some young people.

As I have previously stated the condition of Friedland, it appears to me to be unnecessary to add anything further upon the subject, as it would only be a reiteration of what I have before expressed. It does not improve, and the idea of building up a congregation here has proved so fallacious that I think I may dismiss the subject upon the ground that it is quite impracticable.

Sun., Sept. 27. Up to this time I have nothing particular to communicate in addition to my last. I have been to the extremity of what was once the limits of this congregation, and find in general so much apathy amongst the few survivors that [it] is a question with me whether they wish to have a regular ministry maintained at Friedland. Nearly every family which was once "Moravian" has now an admixture of Baptist or Methodist among some of its members, and this influence neutralizes the interests of our Church to such an extent that parents (Moravians) and children (Methodists or Baptists) troop off together to camp meetings or dippings, and the natural consequence of all this is a dying out of our interest in this section amongst the fragments of what was once Friedland Congregation. To enter into details would fill several pages, and after all tend to the same conclusion.

Sun., Oct. 18. I am tired of noting Small Attendance, and therefore shall discontinue it and remark only a change for the better, which is not to be expected during the camp meeting and dipping season.

Sun., Nov. 8. Our Sunday School has been steadily maintained, and although the children do not come regularly, yet we have an average attendance of 18 whilst the list numbers 29.

Sun., Dec. 27. Within the past year nearly all the neighbors of Friedland have changed places by sale of their property and removals, and others have taken their places who have no sympathy with our Church. The last of these was the sale of Elizth. Sides place, which was bought by Alexr. Martin (Oldside Baptist), and upon which he is this week to put a family named Weir, known as the Most Vagabond Set in this part of the county. It is a large family, 14 in number, and are in Martin's employ, and as he some time since bought the adjoining farm (Phillips) he has now placed them on this last purchase in order to secure the working of both places. I have it on good authority that there is 4 bastard children by one of the daughters in this family at present, and altogether they are, male and female, profligates. This family now will be one of Friedland's nearest neighbors.

Taking into consideration all the circumstances connected with Friedland at present, I cannot but consider it a very undesirable situation, holding forth no encouragement and without any proper organization, for even in the congregation (if congregation it may be called) there is Not One that will take the trouble to sweep out the church once in a week (for Sunday). All this myself and wife does besides chopping wood, cleaning ashes from the stove, making fire, etc., etc.

I do not mention this for any other purpose than merely to show what I have before stated, that there is no sympathy with the interests of the Church, and therefore [it is] questionable whether they desire a continuance of the ministry. Even the Committee, which was elected last year by advice of J. G. Sides, take no interest in the Church, no more than if they were not members of it, and neither of them have done anything, nor will they do anything towards getting in wood for the winter, and I have been obliged to help myself otherwise, and have myself got in wood for the winter for both house and church. Enough.

[New] Philadelphia Reports, 1857
[Extracts transcribed; handwriting is that of George Frederic
Bahnson.]

Sun., May 31. The Methodist local preacher, Bro. Thomas
Frye, preached at the usual time, engagements at Salem preventing the Brethren residing there from going to this church.

Sun., June 14. Bro. Bahnson preached at the usual time,
with a view of giving this congregation a sermon on every
alternate Sunday, but although the attendance is quite encouraging, especially on the part of the young people, it will be
out of the question for the present to preach regularly on every
alternate Lord's day.

Sun., June 28. A Sunday school has been commenced there
which is pretty well attended; they have also contributed
money and obtained quite a nice collection of the books published by the American Tract Society.

[Handwriting is now that of Maximilian E. Grunert.]

Sat., Oct. 31. Anniversary of the church. Bro. Grunert attended, most of the members were present. At 2 o'clock the
meetings were opened with singing and prayer, upon which an
address was delivered, based on the doctrinal text. Without
dispersing, the lovefeast immediately followed. The communicants met afterwards for the celebration of the Lord's supper.
This latter meeting was, upon request, held in the German
language. Several appeared to be much affected.

Some time ago the thought of having occasional prayer
meetings at the church was broached, and one such meeting
held, Th. Frey taking the lead; since then all has been still
again. The absence of Frey's family on the 31st was generally
remarked upon. Sunday School continues to be attended to.

[Handwriting is now that of George Frederic Bahnson.]

Sun., Nov. 29. Bro. Bahnson preached at the usual time on
John 1:11-12. The attendance was as it generally is, very encouraging, but hitherto no fruit could be perceived emanating
from the preaching of the word except that the conduct of the
young people was improving. At the close of the services Bro.
Bahnson reminded them of the many services they had lis-

tened to without any apparent practical results for the better, and invited the young especially either to come forward and give him a pledge of future faithfulness to the Savior by tendering their right hand or by speaking to him in the minister's room or by informing any of the full members of their intention. Only one young sister came to him in the minister's room. A small beginning, but we will thank God and take courage.

1858

[European expansion in Asia continued in 1858 as France seized Cochin China (southern Vietnam). In August the first transatlantic telegraph cable was completed, and Queen Victoria and President Buchanan exchanged greetings.

Minnesota was admitted as the thirty-second state on May 11. From August to October the Lincoln-Douglas debates enlivened the Illinois Senate race. Lincoln lost the election but became a national figure.

North Carolina Democrats were divided on election issues.]

Memorabilia of Salem Congregation, 1858
[Extracts transcribed; handwriting is that of Francis Raymond Holland.]

Notwithstanding the extensive and unprecedented inundations in the North and West, which occurred in the beginning of summer, and the severe drought which prevailed at a later period throughout nearly the whole of the South, the earth has yielded "seed for the sower, and bread for the eater," so that on the day appointed by the proclamation of the governor, we could assemble to give thanks unto our Father in heaven, who "opened his hand, and satisfied the desires of every living thing."

But what has most strikingly distinguished the year as a year of blessings has been the remarkable and widespread revival of religion throughout the various churches of our land. Nor has this revival of religion been confined to our own country. From across the great deep also the tidings come that in various parts of Great Britain especially the influences of the Spirit of God have been manifested in an unusual degree. From the best and most reliable information to be obtained, it appears that near 500,000 persons have made a profession of religion in our own country during this year. Who can estimate the results of this precious revival for time and eternity! Already are hundreds of young men preparing for the Christian ministry, and greatly increased efforts put forth to reach the destitute and perishing in our own and other lands.

The same pleasing and hopeful state of things can with truth be said to exist in some degree in our own Province, several of our churches having during the year experienced seasons of refreshing from on high, and considerable accessions having been made to their numbers.

Among the evidence of increasing spiritual life in our midst, we note the fact that social prayer meetings have occasionally been held in private houses, and that a public weekly prayer meeting was commenced at the request of members, and has been regularly continued on Monday evenings with an encouraging attendance to the present time.

A lively interest has also been manifested in the Sunday School, which is attended by about 200 scholars under the instruction of 30 teachers, who together with the officers of the schools, have attended to their duties with exemplary punctuality and faithfulness. A collection taken in town for the purchase of papers and library books amounted to $48.40.

During the year our institutions for education have continued in the even tenor of their way, enjoying the gracious blessing and protection of the Lord.

On Feb. 22 a Provincial Synod of the Southern Province met at this place, and after disposing of all the business before it, adjourned on Feb. 24th. At this Synod, which was the first held under the new or amended constitution of the Church, two members of the P.E.C. were chosen by a majority of votes, viz., the Brn. Geo. F. Bahnson and Robt. de Schweinitz. The former of whom was chosen president of the P.E.C. The Administrator, Br. Emil de Schweinitz, is ex officio the 3d member of P.E.C. This Synod manifested its fraternal interest and regard for the Northern Province by appointing a delegate to the Northern Provincial Synod. Br. Robt. de Schweinitz, the brother elected, accordingly attended the sessions of that Synod, which met at Bethlehem on June 2d.

On June 11th a meeting of colporteurs, principally such as were engaged in the western part of our state, was convened here by the agent of the American Tract Society for North Carolina. The meetings were continued for several days, and proved highly interesting and edifying.

In the month of July the congregation was gratified by a visit from Br. H. R. Wullschlaegel, a bishop of our Church and member of the U.E.C., who had been deputed especially to attend the Provincial Synod of the Northern Province. Br. Wullschlaegel arrived here on July 8 and left on July 19th.

A commendable degree of activity was manifested in the cause of Home Missions. The Salem Home Mission Society having contracted a considerable debt, special efforts were made for its liquidation, in which the Sisters especially took an active part. These efforts were crowned with a good degree of success.

The baptism or confirmation of a number of colored persons on March 21st also proved an occasion of special interest, and of pleasing hope for the welfare of these people for whose spiritual instruction and nurture we are made in an especial degree responsible.

The former pastor of this congregation, Br. Bahnson, having been as already stated elected to another office claiming his entire attention, the present pastor received and accepted the appointment as Br. Bahnson's successor and entered upon his duties on Sept. 5th.

Salem Diary, 1858
[Extracts transcribed; handwriting is that of George Frederic Bahnson.]

Fri., Jan. 1. A beautiful morning as we came from the meeting begun in 1857. Some rowdies had made every preparation to have a good time of it, but our commissioners had made such complete arrangements that no disturbance was made of any kind or disruption, and for years and years there has not been such a quiet, orderly, and decent New Year's morning as this year.

Sun., Jan. 3. A new Methodist minister begins his activity at Winston, which proves an irresistible temptation to many.

Mon., Jan. 4. Election of Mayor and commissioners result as follows: Mayor: Chs. Briez with 95 votes. Commissioners: Lewis Belo 72 (new), F. Fries 66, R. Patterson 65, Theod. Keehln 59, Sol. Mickey 59, Nath. Blum 53 (new) and Adam Butner 49. Not re-elected Rud. Crist and Ed. Belo (ein unähnliches Paar) [an unlikely pair].

Fri., Jan. 8. Sad news that the md. bro. Ernest Vierling had been brought home from Winston in a wagon, he being so drunk that he could not walk. What an infatuation did possess the vast majority of the members of the Congregation Council years ago to consent to the location of the county town so near to Salem. Lord God, all merciful, have pity on thy Salem, and let us not go entirely by the board.

Wed., Jan. 20. Since the 11th of November 7 persons [who] have departed this life are of the family connection of the Blums living in and near Liberty.

Wed., Jan 27. Received the affecting intelligence that Br. C. W. Jahn, bishop of the Brethren's Church, had departed at Berthelsdorf on the 1st inst. Bro. Reichel communicated this sad news in his first official letter, having arrived with his family at Herrnhut on Dec. 30th.

Mon., Feb. 1. Today the synodal results of the last General Synod came to hand. Large bodies move slowly.

Sun., Feb. 7. The audience was quite good, altho' the Methodists had quarterly meeting with 4 ministers, if not more, come on purpose to make a stir. I thanked God and took courage.

Tues., Feb. 9. Bro. Sam. Warner arrived from the Cherokee mission.

Mon., Feb. 22. Friday at 10 A.M. the Wachovia Provincial Synod met in the chapel and was held with open doors. Still the number of guests was never very large. Synod met also in the afternoon and in the evening.

Wed., Feb. 24. The Financial Committee having presented a report that was accepted by Synod, the sessions were brought to a close after all the business devolving upon Synod had been disposed of. In the afternoon the election of two members of Wachovia PEC took place. One of them was elected as chairman, the other as the 2d member. Bro. Bahnson was elected President of PEC and also nominated for a bishop. Bro. Rob. Schweinitz was elected the 2d member. Thanks to the Lord, great unanimity prevailed in the votes. Of 27 votes cast Bro. Bahnson received 21 and Bro. Rob. Schweinitz 20. The Brn. E. A. Vogler, F. Fries, and S. T. Pfohl were then elected to form, with the P.E.C. of which Bro. E. A. Schweinitz will be the 3d member by virtue of his office, the Financial Board, under whose control will be the finances of the Province.

Sat., Feb. 27. The Sisters had prepared an entertainment in the concert hall, the proceeds to be given to the home mission fund. They realized quite a nice little sum.

Fri., Mar. 12. Sr. Annie Lineback, for many years teacher of the town girls school, being about to leave for the North, Elders' Conference resolved upon appointing Sr. Theresa Peterson to fill the vacancy.

Tues., Mar. 16. In the evening Bro. Bahnson kept lecture on catechism, and at 8 o'clock, as he has done for some time, instruction for the colored people. Both well attended.

Fri., Mar. 19. Bro. Bahnson held the usual lecture on the catechism. It was the last this season for the colored people, who came after the whites had left. Ten colored persons offered either for baptism or confirmation. Thank God.

Sun., Mar. 21. At 2 P.M. Bro. Bahnson kept a meeting in which 3 colored persons were baptized, viz.: Anna, Rhoda, and Betty, and 7 were confirmed, viz.: Nicotie, Amie, Lucy, Edward, George, Louis, and Harry. According to request it was held in our church. The attendance was very good both of whites and blacks, and the form and every[thing] connected with the meeting were exactly as though the candidates had been white people. Communion lovefeast and holy communion followed, both attended by a number of guests, members principally or perhaps altogether of the Methodist Church. The Lord's presence was sensibly felt. Thanks to his never failing mercy.

Sun., Apr. 4. Easter. A glorious morning. Nature herself seemed to sympathize with the heart-cheering event we commemorate. At 5 1/2 o'clock a large number of persons had assembled before the church and after the singing of a verse, etc., a procession was formed as usual to the graveyard, where our sublime Easter litany was prayed by Bro. Bahnson, after which all returned similarly to our moving up to that hallowed spot. In general good order prevailed.

Mon., Apr. 5. For several reasons the board of managers postponed the anniversary meeting of Salem Bible Association. It will probably be held sometime in June.

Fri., Apr. 9. A negro by the name of Frank was found guilty of the murder of another negro whose name had been Eli. A free negro woman, Lucy, Eli's wife, is also implicated, but has moved her trial to Rockingham County.

Mon., Apr. 12. In the evening we had a very severe thunder gush with excessively vivid and long continued lightning. The season is rather wet but very fertile. Most glorious prospect for every kind and species of fruit.

Sun., Apr. 25. Quite a cool day. Winter clothing felt very comfortable. The Dunkers' annual meeting about 6 or more miles from here had attracted some of our youngsters. Yesterday evening these Dunkers had washing of feet, etc., which attracted a crowd. At 7½ P.M. Bro. Grunert delivered an address in English on the doctrinal text, behold I make all things new, referring among the rest to the blessed and wide spreading religious awakening of which every public print speaks.

Sun., May 2. Early this morning an infant son was born in Bro. Bahnson's family, but not only did he draw but a few breaths, but it pleased the Lord in his unsearchable wisdom to take to himself with the little infant the faithful wife and mother, and make his servant for the second time a lonely widower. O Lord, help to bear the cross which thou hast prepared for thy servant and his afflicted and bereaved family.

Fri., May 21. Today was the public examination of the infant school. The little ones acquitted themselves very well indeed, and Sr. Pfohl deserves much credit for the degree of patience and perseverance she constantly manifests. But few could do what she performs.

Thurs., May 27. Examination of the pupils of our Female Academy. A large number of friends and patrons of the school were here. In the evening a musical performance, "The Coronation of the Rose," gave universal satisfaction.

Tues., June 1. Bro. Rob. Schweinitz left this morning to attend the northern Provincial Synod as a delegate of Wachovia Synod. His family went with him.

Fri., June 4. Examination of our Boys' School. There was a larger audience than had assembled for years. The boys acquitted themselves very creditably, so that it is presumed the examination gave general satisfaction to parents and friends. Fine shower in the evening, much needed.

Sun., June 6. At 8½ A.M. Bro. Bahnson kept the usual meeting for the Great Girls. . . . At 2 P.M. Bro. Bahnson kept the lovefeast. The number of Great Girls is very considerable, and with their hoops they occupy a very considerable space.

Fri., June 11. A meeting of colporteurs principally engaged in the western part of our state having been called here by Wil. W. Crowder, the agent of the Amer. Tract Society for N.C., Bro. Bahnson preached at 7½ P.M. to an encouraging audience on Mark 16:15. Whereupon Bro. Crowder addressed the audience.

Sun., July 4. At 7½ P.M. Bro. Bahnson kept monthly prayer meeting. He referred, of course, to this day and its events in 1776, the glorious Declaration of Independence, and exhorted all to show their gratitude for our great religious liberty, the grander when compared with what occurred on July 6, 1415. He also announced formally Bro. Holland's accepting of the call to become minister, etc., of Salem congregation, and commended said brother to their brotherly kindness and intercession before the throne of grace.

Thurs., July 8. Bro. Rob. Schweinitz returned from the North, where he had attended the Provincial Synod held at Bethlehem as the delegate of the Wachovia Synod. In his company was Bro. Henry Rudolph Wullschlägel, one of the members of the U.E.C. in the mission department, who had been sent to be present at the Northern Provincial Synod and now came on a friendly visit to Wachovia.

Sun., July 18. At 4 o'clock P.M. the Female Missionary Society held its semi-annual meeting. Bro. Wullschlägel addressed them in German, giving them a very interesting account of our mission in Surinam of which he was superintendent for a number of years. In the evening at 8 o'clock Bro. Bahnson delivered an address in English, at the close of which he called the attention of the congregation to Bro. Wullschlägel's intended departure on tomorrow, and this brother was thereupon commended to our Lord's protection by the singing of suitable verses.

Sun., July 25. In the evening Bro. Clauder, at present on a visit here with his children and friends, but the stationed pastor at Canal Dover, Ohio, preached to an overflowing audience. His text was Rom. 5:1.

Tues., July 27. Sr. Maria Schweinitz with her children returned from the north, also Sr. Caroline Siewers, who had been north on a long visit. The weather is very hot and rain is sadly needed.

Sun., Aug. 8. During the course of the week we had a few showers cooling off the air and refreshing vegetation, though many things are so completely scorched that the most plentiful rains will not revive them. In many fields the corn looks pitifully indeed, and poor land will yield scarcely anything to reward the poor labor which poor people have poorly bestowed on it.

Thurs., Aug. 19. For future reference the census taken during the month, within the lines of incorporation, be inserted here:

white males under 5 years:	27	white females:	45
white males over 5, under 21:	107	white females:	174
white males over 21, under 45:	105	white females:	174
white males over 45, under 75:	45	white females:	90
white males over 75, under 90:	5	white females:	5
		over 90:	2
		(Academy:	215)
	289		705
Colored people: males:	100	females:	61
		Sum total	1,155

Sun., Aug. 22. Children's festival. At 2 P.M. Bro. Bahnson kept the lovefeast for the children. The number of strangers boarding temporarily at our hotels in town was rather annoying. They had made their appearance in company of children and colored servants without either asking or receiving anything in the shape of an invitation or permission to be present.

Sun., Aug. 29. At 10 Bro. Bahnson prayed the litany and preached on the Good Samaritan before a large audience. At the close Bro. Bahnson attended to the circumstance that he was standing in the midst of this congregation for the last time as their regular pastor, and besought them to give evidence of the vitality of their religion, etc., by remembering liberally the deeply afflicted and sorely visited Brethren at Lebanon, Penn.

A pleasing evidence of increasing spiritual life in our midst may be found in the fact that smaller circles for praying in private houses alternately here and there have been formed. May the spirit of prayer be poured upon us in the most abundant, universal manner.

[The handwriting is now that of Francis Raymond Holland.]

Sun., Sept. 5. In the public service at 10 A.M. Br. and Sr. Holland were introduced to the congregation as their future laborers, by Br. Bahnson.

Sun., Sept. 19. At 1 P.M. the S. School, after an intermission of some weeks, was recommenced; 74 girls and about 40 boys were present, 3 male teachers and 14 female present. At 7 P.M. address, etc., by Br. Holland. Br. Bahnson, who intends (D.V. [God willing]) to set out this week on an official visitation

to the Cherokee mission, was commended to the Lord by singing a hymn and prayer.

Thurs., Sept. 23. Br. Bahnson set out on his journey,
accompanied no doubt by the best wishes and prayers of the
congregation.

Sun., Oct. 3. In the evening the monthly missionary prayer
meeting was held, in which—the daily word for the 1st Monday
of the month being Jer. 31:17—special reference was made to
the ancient covenant people of God, and they were remembered
in prayer. The situation of our dear Br. Friebele and his family
at Mt. Bethel, Va., also called for our remembrance at the
mercy seat, inasmuch as certain evil-minded persons—lewd
fellows of the baser sort—have on several occasions of late
sought to do them grievous injury. On one occasion recently a
fire was kindled in the buggy of Br. Bahnson, who was there
on a visitation, said buggy standing in the barn at the time.
Providentially the fire was discovered at 3 o'clock A.M. before it
had communicated to the barn. Since then threats have been
made, and they have been kept in a state of constant anxiety.
The enmity does not appear to be so much a personal one as to
be directed against the mission itself. May the Lord bring to
naught the wickedness of unreasonable and malicious men,
and overrule all to the furtherance of His cause.

Mon., Oct. 11. At 7 P.M. a prayer meeting was held in the
church in accordance with a resolution of the Salem Elders'
Conference that in future a prayer meeting shall be held every
Monday evening. Yesterday afternoon it commenced raining
and continued all night. Today the rain still continued steadily
but moderately to descend. This is the first rain of any consequence that has fallen since the latter part of July, and is joyfully welcomed, inasmuch as the dust had become excessive
along the roads, the vegetation parched, and the farmers unable to prepare their ground for sowing wheat.

Wed., Oct. 13. A request was sent thro' Br. Francis Fries by
Br. Thos. A. Siddall to have his name stricken from the list of
members. Br. Fries stated that the circumstances were such as
would require Siddall's exclusion at any rate, and that he (Siddall) had left home, probably never to return!

Sun., Oct. 17. The S.S. at 1 P.M. was well attended. Br.
E. A. Vogler entered upon his duties as one of the superintendents. The brn. Francis Hauser, James Lineback, and Barrow
entered as teachers. At 3 P.M. Br. Grunert preached in the

German language. The German preachings had been "dropped" for some time, owing to other afternoon meetings or the unavoidable engagements of one or the other of the ministers. At 7 P.M. "Gemeinstund" in English.

Sun., Oct. 24. Litany and preaching at 10 A.M. by Br. Holland. There being a confirmation at Friedberg this day—it is reported that about 40 persons were to be (some baptized and some confirmed)—a goodly number of people from Salem and vicinity went down. Nevertheless the attendance at preaching was very good.

Thurs., Nov. 12. Finished our first round of visits to the families in connection with the church.

Fri., Nov. 26. The day appointed for the execution of the negro Frank, convicted of the murder of another negro named Eli. The Governor, however, granted a respite of three weeks in order to gain time for a thorough examination of the petition sent in for a pardon of the prisoner. About dusk a shocking murder was perpetrated in Winston by P. T. Shultz (the wicked and worthless son of parents belonging to this congregation) on the person of one Costin Holder. Shultz has been engaged in the nefarious business of keeping a tippling house, and himself as well as his victim were under the effects of liquor. A great crowd of people, mostly of a decidedly degraded appearance, had collected to witness the execution of Frank—the news of his respite not having become generally known—and probably great quantities of whiskey were drunk in Winston. "Woe unto him that putteth the bottle to his neighbor's lips!" "The way of the transgressor is hard."

Sun., Dec. 5. Br. Bahnson, who had returned on Tuesday last from his visitation to the Cherokee mission, conducted the public service at 10 A.M., preaching from Acts 16:30-31.

Fri., Dec. 17. The negro Frank, convicted of murder, was executed. He having made a profession of faith in Christ and testified that he had obtained peace with God thro' faith in our Lord Jesus Christ, Br. Holland baptized him in the jail at Winston. Br. Holland also attended him to the gallows and preached there. Subject: the penitent thief.

Mon., Dec. 20. Examination of Boys School before the Board of Directors. Scholars acquitted themselves creditably. School closed for the holidays.

Fri., Dec. 24. The lovefeast for the children at 4½ P.M. was kept by Br. Holland, as was also the lovefeast at 7 P.M. The church was well filled and good order prevailed. A number of tickets had been issued, granting admittance to persons not members of the church.

Sat., Dec. 25. At 2 P.M. the scholars and teachers of the S. School gave an entertainment to their parents and friends. The exercises consisted of singing and recitations. It is believed that considerable interest has been hereby excited in favor of the S.S.

Female Missionary Society of Salem, 1858
[Extracts of minutes transcribed.]

Sun, Jan. 17. Br. Bahnson next communicated to the Society, the Report of the Coloured Congregation. . . . In reference to the various obstacles they had to cope with, it was deplored that one great cause of the coldness to Religion of the Coloured people, must be attributed to the apparent carelessness of their Owners in regard to the spiritual welfare of those, who were for the time committed to their care: therefore the members of the Society were entreated and urged upon, to use their influence to produce a better state of things.

Diary of the African Church in Salem, 1858
[Extracts transcribed; handwriting is that of Maximilian E. Grunert.]

Sun., Jan. 3. Bro. Bahnson preached on Matt. 11:28. Attendance only tolerable; a new preacher in Winston formed the center of attraction.

During the course of the month [of January] a number of colored people attended religious instruction, kept for them by br. Bahnson on Wednesday evening. Their regularity deserves commendation.

Sun., Mar. 21. Leave having been obtained, the Negroes met at 2 o'clock in our large church to a very considerable number. They occupied the benches in the centre, white people being seated behind and aside them. Br. Bahnson baptized: Ann Rosetta (E. A. Vogler), Rhoda Laurette and Betty Martin (F. Fries); and then confirmed the following 7 persons: Lucy (Dav. Blum), Amy (Rights), Nicotie (Waugh), Harry (Nath. Vogler),

Lewis (G. Foltz), George (F. Fries), and Edward (Chs. Brietz). The candidates appeared to be deeply affected.

After this meeting br. B. kept communion lovefeast, and then administered the Lord's Supper to about 50 persons, some of whom were members of other churches. The Lord was sensibly in our midst, and not a few of the participants were deeply moved, as their countenances and freely flowing tears indicated.

Sun., Apr. 4. Easter. A procession having been formed at 9 A.M., headed by the white people present, we proceeded to the graveyard, where the Easter morning Litany was prayed; whereupon the exercises were continued in the church, which was crowded. Good order prevailed, and the congregation appeared interested.

Sun., July 4. No meeting was held, this being communion day in Salem church.

Sun., July 11. Br. Bahnson preached on Rev. 2:4. The audience was quite good. The congregation having been dismissed, br. B. addressed the communicants in reference to the approaching celebration of the Lord's Supper.

Sun., July 18. Br. B. administered the holy communion; it was to all appearances a blessed time to the participants. Br. Wullschlägel was also present, addressed the meeting, and communed with us. Amy (Rights) had to be excluded.

Sun., Aug. 8. Preached on Mark 15:34. Not a great many, and those went to Winston afterwards, attracted by the present excitement there.

Sun., Sept. 26. Preached on Luke 7:11ff. The practice of coming late is again alarmingly on the increase. But few are generally present in the beginning, and nearly during the whole of the meeting they drop in, tho' towards the end the audience is generally good.

Sun., Oct. 31. Preached on Rom. 4:5. The audience, which was good, paid marked attention. The little boys begin to come on account of the approaching Christmas.

Sun., Dec. 12. Sophia, the daughter of br. William (Spach), was confirmed. She has been instructed by br. Rights, and also by her father, and appears to be determined to take Christ for her portion. After confirmation followed the communion lovefeast, whereupon the holy Communion was administered. A good deal of feeling and emotion was manifested by the members.

Sun., Dec. 19. The celebration of Christmas was anticipated. The same took place in the usual manner. Sr. Denke had provided cakes, etc., for the children, which they received in high glee.

Aeltesten Conferenz/ Elders Conference of Salem Congregation,
1858
[Extracts of minutes transcribed.]

Wed., Sept. 8.

Br. Holland, having reached Salem with his family during last week, and having entered upon his various duties as minister, inspector of the boys school, etc. was present for the first time, and cordially welcomed in our midst.

It was ordered that the proceedings of this body in future be held in the English language.

In consequence of the constitutional changes in this Province and more especially the president's filling no longer an office in the Salem congregation, it is understood, that in future, when the new rules of the Salem congregation will have been adopted, the president of the P.E.C. and the Administrator will not be members of this "Salem's Elders' Conference" any longer. Until then they were both requested to continue their attendance. This adoption of the new rules will necessarily be deferred till after br. Bahnson's return from the Cherokee mission, where he intends going shortly on an official visit.

3. Br. Bahnson reported, that the single br. Wesley Spaugh had been married by the Rev. Mr. Turner in Waughtown to Susan Ferrar, without having given notice. Conf. did not doubt that this was done in ignorance of our rules, and since they intended going West, his connection with this church will cease at all events. Should he apply for a certificate of membership, it shall not be refused.

Wed., Oct. 6. Br. Bahnson absent.

3. The rules of Salem Congregation were spoken of again. In view of the fact that in January next a new Committee is to be elected to stand for 2 years, it appears highly desirable that this be done under the new rules, which accordingly should go into operation before that time. Conference resolved to meet in committee on Tuesday evening next to begin the revision.

4. A communication, signed "many members," was received by br. Holland, in which a desire is expressed for more meetings for prayer. A prayer meeting, to be held every Monday evening, was proposed and sanctioned. The Monthly Concert for prayer, which of late has given place to a Sunday evening prayer meeting on the first Sunday of the month, will then be again observed at the proper time. A long debate followed in reference to the manner of conducting this meeting. Conf. thought that at this time promiscuous prayer meetings could not be commenced, in as much as few brethren would probably be willing to offer prayers in public; and to give variety to these meetings, addresses or the reading of portions of the Bible, or extracts from periodicals were approved of. Conf. regretted the want of a lecture room of larger dimensions than the present chapel, in which such meeting would be kept.

Wed., Oct. 20. br. R. Schweinitz absent.

4. Br. Holland stated that br. Fries some time since informed him of br. Ths. Siddall's request that his name be taken from the list of church members. It has now become known that this individual has deserted his family, and that it would have been necessary to exclude him from the church. It will be necessary to make a provision in the new rules to meet similar cases.

5. The single br. Eugene F. Clewell has run away from his creditors. It appears inexpedient to do anything in this case for the present.

Wed., Dec. 1. br. E. Schweinitz absent.

2. The usual semiannual collections for foreign missions have been discontinued for some time (Feb. '57), principally because no one was inclined to go round and call at the different houses. This method of obtaining contributions being therefore no longer available, it was proposed to take up from time to time collections at the church doors for this object after an appropriate sermon. For the present Conf. considered it expedient to do so in Jan. and Aug., those being the times when the house collections used to be taken up.

Aufseher Collegium (or Town & Church Committee or
Congregation Committee), 1858
[Extracts of minutes transcribed.]

Mon., Jan. 11. Not present Br. Chs. Cooper.

4. A plan for the removal of the Odd Fellows Hall from the Square and the erection of a third story on the contemplated Museum building on the corner of the Boys School lot for the use of that society being in agitation, the question has been asked whether Diacony would contribute anything towards said purpose. Committee think that under the present condition of the Diacony we cannot grant anything towards the removal of that building.

5. Committee next turned its attention again to the propositions made in the two last meetings in reference to the Congregation Diacony, and after a reconsideration passed them without amendment. Persons holding outlots or land in rent are to be notified of the change contemplated before the end of the present month, the new rates to go into operation with the beginning of our fiscal year May 1st. The President and Secretary are to examine the leases held by the Mill Company, Augustus Fockel, Henry Blum, etc., and to report what steps can be taken to increase their rent also. The alterations with regard to firewood for Salem labourers and superannuated persons also go into operation on May 1st next.

Mon., Jan. 25. Br. F. Fries not present.

1. With regard to lands held in lease it was resolved to determine that part of the lease having reference to rents and then to raise the rents correspondingly with outlots. Holders of such leases are to be notified of this alteration.

Mon., Feb. 8. Br. H. Leinbach not present.

2. A number of applications having come in for lots in the northern part of the town, principally above the Old Factory, the idea was suggested [that] during the summer to lay out a regular plan of streets and lots within the corporate limits of Salem, and in the meantime to have the occupants of outlots in that section at liberty to raise another crop on their lots. As it is desirable to act in this matter in perfect understanding with the Town Commissioners, it was resolved to notify them of our intentions and to hear their views of the matter.

3. Br. Charles Cooper applies for a building lot on Cemetery Street between the graveyard alley and the Cemetery, the front of the lot to be along said street and *not* on the alley. As Committee is of opinion that a lot embracing the whole distance between the Alley and the Cemetery would forever prevent further encroachments upon the Alley, it was resolved that 200 feet be retained for the further enlargement of our graveyard, and that the other part, being about 100 ft. along the alley by about 225 ft. along Cemetery Street, be sold to Br. Cooper . . . with the proviso, however, that it be expressly laid down as a condition in the deed for this lot [#135] that under no conditions an entrance from the lot into the alley (other than a small gate for foot passengers) be ever permitted.

4. As considerable trespass is committed upon our timber, especially near Winston, it would be very desirable to employ one or more efficient foresters, and Committee will endeavour to find some suitable persons.

Fri., Mar. 5. All present.

1. Committee is of opinion that we should endeavour to get Br. Ad. Butner to act as forester.

2. The newly elected Financial Board, entrusted with the management of the Wachovia Sustentation, being under the necessity of furnishing a dwelling for the President of the Provincial Elders' Conference of the Southern Province, ask the question whether the Church Committee would assist them in procuring a house for said purpose. Committee upon deliberation by an almost unanimous vote (1 dissenting vote) decided in favour of *selling* and not of renting to said Financial Board for the use of Wachovia Sustentation either of the two houses belonging to Salem Diacony and situated north of the church, the brick house [the "Bishop's House," lot #10] at $3,000 and the white house [lot #11] at $1,800. (The price of the latter house passed by a unanimous vote; the former, by 5 yeas.)

Tues., Mar. 9. Not present Br. F. Fries.

1. The Financial Board (see §2 of last meeting) have agreed to purchase the brick house at the stipulated price.

2. The Brrn. appointed to speak with Br. Chs. Brietz . . . report that he declares himself utterly unable at this time to make any promises with regard to enlarged payments towards his debt for the future, and that the prospects held out by him

last October . . . of being able from the beginning of this year to pay $100 per month had disappeared again, and that in fact he saw no possibility of eventually paying the debt, unless he could find the means of increasing the capital invested in the trade, which according to his opinion is too small to work successfully with such a burden of interest resting on it.

3. The lots in the lower part of town on Main and Marshall streets have now all been laid out—on the east of Main Street to the race and on the west side of Main and on Marshall Street to the Mill lane—which lots are now to be put up at public sale on next Friday.

Fri., Mar. 12. All present.

2. The butchers that formerly supplied the Sisters House with beef having discontinued, it is found necessary to buy up cattle for consumption for the school and Sisters House and to attend to the slaughtering. For this purpose it is desirable to erect a slaughter house at some convenient place for their exclusive use. Committee think that the place proposed for its location at the north end of the upper meadow is a suitable one, provided there is no objection raised on the part of the Town Commissioners.

3. . . . . Committee upon further consideration and in view of what was stated at their last meeting saw no other prospect before them than that the debt of Br. Brietz would increase from year to year, whilst the property deeded would diminish in value, whereby the loss that Diacony would eventually have to sustain would only become the greater. The motion was therefore made, seconded, and unanimously adopted, "That Br. Charles Brietz's affairs be wound up," and Committee therefore empowered the trustee of the Diacony to consult with Br. Chs. Brietz and the other trustees, and to wind up the tanyard affairs as speedily as is found practicable.

Wed., Mar. 24. Not present Brrn. H. Leinbach and F. Fries.

3. The Town Commissioners have sanctioned the erection of a slaughter house on the Sisters House premises, as stated in last minutes §2.

4. The Odd Fellows Hall having been disposed of by that society and being about to be removed from the Square to the lot of a private individual, the Town Commissioners are desirous of procuring a place for the fire apparatus. They would

prefer to have a lot in fee, or if that could not be found, to have the privilege of adapting the basement of the building about to be erected by the Young Men's Missionary Society and the Musical Society as was stated "for Commissioners purposes, for fire apparatus and other materials." After some discussion on the subject it was laid over for further action to a future meeting of the Committee.

Mon., Apr. 19. Not present Brrn. N. Vogler, and Theod. F. Keehln.

1. In reference to §4 it was stated that since our last meeting the Town Commissioners have purchased a locality [lot #69, west part] for the fire apparatus, thereby obviating the necessity of further deliberation on that subject.

3. The Inspector of the Female Academy at this place is desirous of now making use of the privilege granted to him of laying out a pleasure ground on the hill immediately east of the lots above the church. . . . Committee grant the required extension of the pleasure grounds. The lot held by the Inspector in the lower part of the town and heretofore used as a pleasure ground by the school, Committee think might soon be returned to Diacony and sold.

Mon., May 3. Not present Brrn. C. Cooper and W. Peterson.

2. There being a considerable quantity of firewood on hand at this time, it was resolved that the new arrangement to be entered into on May 1st with regard to the wood furnished to the minister and warden be postponed for some time longer (see minutes Dec. 15, 1857, §1).

3. The annual contributions heretofore paid by the Single Sisters Diacony and Female Academy to Salem Congregation account are hereafter to be entered to the credit of the Congregation account.

5. Complaint being made that the church steeple has latterly become too much of a place of resort to a number of boys, Br. Saml. Shultz is to be instructed not to lend the Church keys to them.

Mon., June 14. Not present Br. W. Peterson.

2. A bit of the furniture belonging to the Diacony and in use in the Sustentation House ["Bishop's House"] was communicated, and Committee is disposed to sell to the Financial

Board as much of it as can be spared if they should desire to purchase it, the different articles to be valued by competent persons. Bookcases, tables, and chairs belonging to the archives or conference room, however, are not to be sold.

3. The attention of Committee was next directed to the Waterworks established at this place and kept up by an annual contribution or tax paid almost exclusively by members of our Church residing in the town, and thus far managed and directed by the Committee. The duties of this body having since the incorporation of the town become exclusively confined to Church matters, it is evident that some other arrangement must be made to furnish the town with water. It was therefore resolved to refer this matter for further consideration to the Town Commissioners. The Warden will furnish them with such information about the cost, etc., of the present waterworks as he may possess.

Mon., Sept. 13. Not present Brrn. C. Cooper, F. Fries, and W. Peterson.

4. The trustees of Charles Brietz have advertised the sale of the tanyard and of his effects for the 30th of this month.

Mon., Sept. 27. Not present Br. E. A. Vogler (on a journey).

3. Town Commissioners have on their part chosen the Brrn. Theod. Keehln, Adam Butner, and Sol. Micke a committee who in conjunction with this body are to determine upon the new streets to be laid out in town.

Mon., Oct. 4. All present.

2. The Brn. Nathl. Vogler and Wm. Peterson were appointed to assist in the laying out of new streets and lots, as contemplated last spring.

3. The yearly accounts and statements of the Single Sisters Diacony and of Salem Diacony from May 1, 1857, to Apr. 30, 1858, were next laid before the Committee. From the former it appears that $1,061.56 more were received than expended.

The accounts of Salem Diacony close with a deficit of $891.65 after adding $3,708.72 to the Fund arising from the sale of lots and after deducting $3,526.30 from House account.

Committee resolved upon the following distribution of the gain of Single Sisters Diacony, viz.:

Donation to Salem Diacony	
towards covering its loss	$500.00
For Church Music	10.00
For Sisters House Library	10.00
For reserved fund of Single	
Sisters Diacony, the balance	541.56
	$1,1061.56

Mon., Oct. 18. Not present Brrn. F. Fries, C. Cooper, and W. Peterson.

1. The plan of the lots and streets as proposed to be laid out by the sub-committee appointed at the last meeting was submitted and approved by the Committee, who thereupon proceeded to name the different streets now contemplated, the whole, however, to be subject to the approval of the Town Commissioners.

Committee will endeavor to procure the services of Br. James Leinbach to make a new survey and plot of the whole town and the fields and outlots on the Salem Town Land.

It was further resolved that in case a member of the Committee should, as is not unfrequently the case, devote a considerable portion of time to the benefit of the Diacony, e.g. in laying out of lots, etc., he be compensated for his labour.

4. The family of Br. John Vogler, contemplating to bring the remains of his daughter and her infant (Sister Louisa Senseman) from New Salem, Illinois, for interment on our graveyard, would wish to bury both in one grave, and in order not to mar the uniform appearance of the square, to dig the grave at the beginning of a row in such a manner that the extra width of the grave be thrown outside of the regular square (the mound over the grave, however, not to be made wider than usual). Altho' a new row of graves has but just been commenced, Committee see no objections that for such a particular object and in so peculiar a case said grave should be dug in the next row.

Mon., Nov. 1. Not present the Brrn. E. A. Schweinitz, N. Vogler, and Wm. Peterson.

1. The streets as proposed (according to §1 of last minutes) having been sanctioned also by the Town Commissioners, the lots have since been laid off, and Committee resolved that they

be offered at public sale on Friday 19th inst., and that the sale be advertised in the *Press* and *Sentinel.*

The names given to the different streets now laid out are the following, viz.: the first street running east and west to the north of New Shallowford Street, to be called High Street, and the next (being the continuation of the street between Salem and Winston) to be called North Street throughout its whole course. The streets running north and south westwardly of Elm Street to be designated respectively as Cherry, Pine, and Spruce Streets.

Difficulties having presented themselves regarding the re-survey of the town lots and fields, the subject was postponed indefinitely.

3. It was resolved hereafter to hold the regular meetings of the Committee on Tuesday evenings, in order to give the members an opportunity of attending the prayer meetings on Monday evening.

Sat., Dec. 11. Extra meeting. Not present the Brrn. F. Fries and E. A. Vogler.

The inhabitants of the neighboring town of Winston being about to petition the Legislature for an act of incorporation for said town, extending the corporate limits 1/4 mile east and west from the middle of the Winston tract (thereby taking in part of the land belonging to Salem Diacony), stating at the same time that the corporation should be precluded from laying a tax on said land so long as it remains the property of the Diacony, the case was laid before the Committee for consideration.

As the Winston tract of land is but small, their object in asking for an act of incorporation, viz., to maintain and enforce order in the town, would be almost totally defeated if the limits of the corporation were to be confined to the land sold to the County in 1849; and as Committee does not desire to throw any obstacles in their way, members present gave their unanimous consent that the Winston corporation extend to 1/4 mile east and west of the middle of the Winston tract, with the understanding that the above clause exempting that part of the land embraced within the limits of the corporation belonging to the Salem Diacony from taxation by the Winston commis-sioners, so long as it remains the property of the Diacony, be inserted in the charter as a promise made by the leading inhabitants of Winston. Br. F. Fries, who is a member of the present legislature, is to be informed of this resolution of the Committee.

Tues., Dec. 14. Not present the Brrn. F. Fries, C. Cooper, and E. A. Vogler.

1. Br. Charles Clauder requests an increased compensation for his services as tender of the organ bellows. Committee is willing to allow him $1.00 per month.

2. Committee resolved that the horse and carriage belonging to the Diacony be retained for the present, and not sold as contemplated some time since (see minutes Dec. 15, 1857), as besides the Diacony the Pastor of the Church has use for them when visiting Church members residing at a distance from town.

3. Br. Robt. Schweinitz as Inspector of the Female Academy would prefer to buy the piece of land granted to said institution for a pleasure ground, with the understanding that in case it be no longer required by the Academy for the specified purpose, it then be given back to the Diacony. Committee have no objections to such an arrangement and fix the price of said grounds at $50 (see minutes Apr. 19, 1858, §3).

Provincial Financial Board, 1858
[Extracts of minutes transcribed.]

Wed., Mar. 3. First meeting of the Financial Board.

On this evening, Wednesday March 3, 1858, the Brn. G. F. Bahnson, E. A. de Schweinitz, and Robert de Schweinitz, at present constituting the Provincial Elders Conference of this Province, together with the Brn. Francis Fries, E. A. Vogler and S. Thos. Pfohl, the members elected by the Provincial Synod of last month, met for the purpose of organizing the Financial Board, newly instituted by the Provincial Synod. The organization was effected by the election of G. F. Bahnson as Chairman, Saml. Thos. Pfohl as Treasurer, and E. A. de Schweinitz as Secretary.

Br. E. A. de Schweinitz next submitted to the Board the propositions which he had been instructed to make by the Unity's Warden College concerning the manner of paying over to this Province the amount to which by the recent liberal action of the General Synod it was now entitled, of which propositions the following were the principal features: That he would make the settlement at once, provided the Board were willing to receive in payment the greater part thereof in good and well secured notes, and the remainder in cash. If this proposition would not be acceptable to the Board, he would give his obligation therefor, at the rate of four percent per annum, until full settlement was made. In order to give some idea to the Board as to the solvency of parties upon whom he held notes which he proposed to transfer, Br. Schweinitz read a list of them. The Board agreed not to go further into this matter tonight, but to postpone that business to the next meeting which should be held in Br. Schweinitz's office where all the papers would be convenient.

Br. Bahnson asked the Board what should be the course of procedure relative to his obtaining and occupying the House [the "Bishop's House" on lot #10] hitherto occupied by the President of the P.E.C. After some interchange of opinion upon the subject, it was agreed that as the house in question belonged exclusively to Salem Diacony and was built for the Salem minister, application must be made to the Church Committee (Aufs. Coll.), and the motion made and carried was so worded that the application should not be in direct words for that house, but that as this Board had to provide a house for the President of P.E.C., who now stood in a different relation toward our own congregation than any of his predecessors, that we ask Committee whether it would assist us in procuring a dwelling.

Mon., Mar. 8. All the members present.

1. The first subject taken up by the Board was the providing of a dwelling for the President of P.E.C. The Treasurer reported that the Church Committee (Aufs. Colleg.) had responded to the proposition submitted to it by this Board by offering to dispose of either the brick or white house to Sustent. Diacy., the former at $3,000, the latter at $1,800. The Board was anxious, before agreeing to a purchase, to know what sum would be required to put the necessary outbuildings on the lot of the brick house. After considerable debate the Board agreed that the brick house valued at $3,000 be purchased, with the express understanding that more than $150 shall not be expended by Sustentation Diacy. on the lot for outbuildings.

2. Board next proceeded to examine the notes which Br. E. A. de Schweinitz desired to transfer to the Treasurer of Wa. Sustent. Diacy. in part payment of the distributive share of this Province, which share amounts to $32,926.83. The following notes with the accrued interest were received by the Board, viz.:

	principal	interest	[total]
A. W. Cooper	$1,500	$47.50	$1,547.50
T. D. Cooper	160	9.07	169.07
Benton C. Douthit	278.46	2.08	280.54
Stephen Douthit	376.17	40.12	416.29
J. W. Eccles	2,000.	48.33	2,048.33
Wm. Huser (River)	200.	4.60	204.60
W. R. Holt	2,531.75	130.80	2,662.55
Pleasant A. Hoover	275.	15.13	290.13
Valentine Hoover	500.	23.33	523.33
Will. A. Lash	300.	4.	304
I. G. and T. B. Lash	4,000.	55.55	4,055.55
J. M. Leach	600.	35.25	635.25
John M. Morehead	1,750.	90.42	1,840.42
Will Oakely	600.	18.75	618.75
Will. Poindexter	1,100.	47.66	1,147.66
Jonathan Perry	500.	23.75	523.75
F. M. Phillips	200.	6.	206.00
			$17,473.72

Furthermore Board agreed to receive a balance
  due from Salem Congn. Diacy. to
Wa. Unity's Admin. amounting to   1,534.31
and likewise an order on Salem Female Acad. for   2,400.
and 5 N.C. State Bonds at par, ex July coupons   5,000.
                                    $26,408.03

the balance Br. Schweinitz will pay
    to the Treasurer in cash   6,518.80
                                    $32,926.83

3. On motion it was resolved that a new set of books be opened by the Treasurer.

4. After a conversation about the arrangements to be made for feeding the horses of the country ministers when they visit Salem officially, it was resolved that as Br. L. Rights is at present the only country minister who has no proper place for feeding his horse, that he be requested to procure one most convenient for himself.

5. The first Thursday of every month was, on motion, fixed upon for the stated meetings of the Board.

6. On motion, the Treasurer was directed to deposit for the present all moneys in his hands in the Salem Savings Institute.

Thurs., Mar. 18. E. A. Vogler absent.

1. Since last meeting, the whole sum of $32,926.83, being the distributive share of this Province in full, has been paid over to the Treasurer of Wa. Sustent. Diacy. by Br. E. A. de Schweinitz. The members of Board therefore proceeded, according to the resolution of the Provincial Synod empowering them so to do, to sign a receipt in full for the whole amount.

2. The chief object of this meeting being to lay down general principles for the investment of moneys in the hands of the Treasurer, Board now took up this subject, and after considerable discussion, it was on motion resolved: "That the general principle by which this Board be governed shall be, that the outstanding notes be collected and the funds thus obtained invested in public securities."

4. On motion, Treasurer was directed to buy from the funds in hand three additional $1,000 N.C. State Bonds, and to invest the balance in $1,000 certificates of Salem Savings Institute at 6 percent.

5. The application of Br. Lewis Rights for $126, the amount required by him in order to enable him to pay his debts contracted to the end of 1857, was taken up. The Chairman stated that Br. Rights had received from Friedberg Congregation for the year 1857 no more than $200 all told. The minimum sum fixed upon by the Provincial Synod of '56 for the salary of country ministers being $300 per annum and the year 1857 having been an unusually hard one, the propriety of granting Br. Rights' application was urged. On motion, Board agreed to grant $126, the amount required.

6. Treasurer informed the Board that a writing desk was required for the President of P.E.C., as the one now in use belongs to Salem Congregation Diacy.

Mon., June 7. Robert de Schweinitz absent in Pa.

1. Treasurer reported that according to §4 of last meeting, $6,000 had been deposited in Salem Savings Institute at 6% and three $1,000 N.C. State Bonds had been purchased at 9.5.

3. Br. E. A. de Schweinitz submitted the account current of Sustent. Diacy. with Unity Administration from June 1, 1857, to March 1, 1858, showing a balance of $1,200.58 due Sust. Diacy. on March 1, 1858. This balance has been paid over to the Treasurer. On motion, the 31st day of May of each year was fixed upon as the end of the fiscal year. The next annual statement of the accounts was postponed to May 31, 1859, and will therefore embrace a period of 15 months.

5. The propriety of purchasing a horse for Sustentation Diacy. was urged by Br. Bahnson. Br. Bahnson offered his own at the price which he paid for it, viz., $136, and Board agreed to buy it at that price for Sustent. Diacy.

6. In answer to a question of the Treasurer, whether it was to be considered his duty to attend to the repairs of the Sustentation House, and to the mending of furniture, etc., in the same, Board resolved that it is not the duty of the Treasurer to attend to these matters, and that Br. Charles Cooper be requested to attend to all smaller repairs, etc., on the express condition that his bills be passed on by the Board before they are presented for payment to the Treasurer.

Tues., Aug. 31. Francis Fries absent.

1. This was a special meeting of the Board, called by the Treasurer in order to submit the offer of John M. Morehead to settle his note by Craven County Bonds. Board unanimously rejected this proposition.

2. Br. Bahnson's request that a cooking stove be furnished for his kitchen was granted.

3. As Br. Charles Cooper declines accepting the appointment referred to in §6 of minutes of June 7, 1858, Board resolved that Br. Bahnson order such repairs himself, subject to the provisions and condition laid down in said §.

Bethania Diary, with Bethabara, 1858
[Extracts transcribed; handwriting is that of Jacob F. Siewers.]

Sat., Jan. 2. Theodore Hine called and informed me that his father departed on the night of the 1st instant between 11 and 12 o'clock. Afternoon rode down to John Hine's. Sr. Hine is in the last stages of consumption, and this bereavement is particularly distressing to her, as she had hoped to have preceded her husband to their eternal home.

Fri., Jan. 8. Brn. E. Shaub and Julius, Sam'l. Stauber, and Wesley Kearny came in the yard with a machine of Shaub's and sawed my wood for me, Br. W. Lehman hauling several loads as also Sam. Stauber, cutting up some 8 or 9 cords of wood for me. Thanks to these kind friends.

Sun., Jan. 10. Preached at Bethania at 10 A.M. on Matt. 3. After meeting gave public notice that the Lord permitting I would preach here every Lord's day at 10 A.M. On the 1st and 3d Lord's day in every month in the afternoon in addition at Bethabara at 2 P.M. and on the 2d at Pleasant Valley at 2 P.M. and on 4th at Spanish Grove at 2 P.M. On every 5th Lord's day, the afternoon service would be held at John Grabs' at Crooked Run at 2 P.M. After meeting it commenced drizzling. I went to Pleasant Valley, but no one attending returned home in the rain. No persons from the country being in the last Lord's day preaching, the arrangements were not known.

Thurs., Jan. 28. Snow and rain, the roads at places nearly impassable. J. G. [John Grabs] gave me $5 towards his church expenses and presented us with a fine ham.

Fri., Jan. 29. Helped to make a writing desk in the School house.

Fri., Feb. 12. Commenced snowing before day and continued . . .

Sat., Feb. 13. . . . . during the whole of today and the following night attaining to the depth of about eleven inches.

Sat. Feb. 20. Rode down to Bethabara, found all the heads of families present, except H. Fogle was from home. Preached to 9 persons in the stove room of the parsonage. A disagreeable difference of considerable time existing between William Pratt and John Shore, being both present, they were prevailed upon to drop all the past, and extend to one another the hand of reconciliation, which happy issue may the Lord bless by permanency.

Sun., Feb. 28. Preached at Bethania at 10 A.M. to a small audience on Luke 23:24. After dinner went to Spanish Grove and preached on the same to a full house at 2 P.M. At the close of the meeting gave notice that I should deliver a course of confirmation lectures of evenings at the school house, the meetings to be public and unpledged.

Matilda Amalia Winkler Siewers, wife of the Reverend Jacob F. Siewers, pastor at Bethania, 1857-1865. After the death of her husband at West Salem, Illinois, in 1867, Sr. Siewers returned to Salem, North Carolina, where she died in 1900. She is buried in the Salem Moravian Graveyard.

Mon., Mar. 29. This morning the body of Lash's Eli was found in Abr. Conrad's pond. When taken out it was plain he had been murdered. In the course of the day Lucy Hine and Lash's Frank were arrested, and committed to the county Jail. ([Bethania Report:] Lucy Hine, Eli's wife, a free woman of color, and Frank, T. Lash's servant, were arrested and committed to jail.)

Tues., Mar. 30. At noon Eli's funeral took place. Text the 6th Commandment, many negroes present.

Sun., Apr. 4. Easter. The congregation met in the church before sunrise and sang a hymn in remembrance of our Saviour's Resurrection, accompanied by the brass band; then we proceeded to the Graveyard and prayed the Easter morning Litany. Preached to a good audience at 10 A.M. Fair weather. After dinner Sr. S. and myself went to Bethabara. At 2 P.M. we prayed the Easter morning Litany and preached on the subject of the Resurrection.

Thurs., Apr. 15. Br. Bahnson called here and obtained the old Trombones belonging to the Church for which he will be responsible.

Fri., Apr. 16. [V]isited at David Shouse's and found them all well except mother Mickey, who continues to suffer in one of her eyes, which had been operated on by Doc. Williams some 5 weeks ago; conversed and prayed with the family, and went home. Towards evening rode down to Mickey's Schoolhouse, and delivered the closing lecture on confirmation course, and requested serious consideration on the subject spoken of, and stated that I should call round in a few days to ascertain who if any desired to be confirmed.

Sat., May 1. Sr. S. and myself went this morning to visit the widowed Sr. Mary Krieger some 7 miles distant going by the Dutch meeting house. We stopped awhile at Kiser's, from here it's about 2 miles. We found her well but weak, having been sick a good portion of the winter; took dinner there, and then called at the widow Jesse Styers. She was not at home, but we were prevailed on to stop to vesper, after which we returned home by night.

Sun., May 2. This morning the sad intelligence reached us of the death of Sr. Bahnson. We have repeatedly received various kindnesses at her hands. The Lord reward her abundantly, and may he also by his kind spirit comfort our dear Brother in this heavy affliction and be as he has promised, a Father to the motherless children.

Fri., May 14. Before day I was called to go to Thomas Conrad's, he having his spells again. After breakfast I rode out, found him wandering in mind, but he declared himself perfectly well, and not sensible of any distress of mind or body.

Sun., May 16. This morning I had been solicited to visit Thomas Conrad's, who it was said was perfectly deranged and had to be chained, but it being rather late I did not go.

Mon, May 17. Rode out to T. Conrad's, found him better, and they having released him of his chain, he seemed much easier, tho' not in his proper mind. I conversed with him and at his desire prayed with him. He seems desirous of attaining peace with God.

Thurs., June 24. This evening we had a hard rain and considerable storm; the rain ran through the house from the back door to the front.

Fri., June 25. By invitation, on our return from Bethabara we called and dined at William Flint's (sheriff).

Fri., July 2. My daughter Margaret had an examination of her pupils in the church.

Wed., July 14. We had a fine rain last night again. Writing out my diary, report, and duplicate of church registry.

Thurs., July 15. Sr. S. and myself went to Salem to conference, met with br. Wullschlegel, member of the U.A.C. Br. Bahnson introduced him to country ministers. Afternoon had a special vesper in conference hall. Had my carriage repaired.

Tues., July 20. Tax giving in day and candidates speaking in Town.

Sat., Aug. 7. Went out to the Dutch meeting house and preached at the funeral of Henry Shouse (deceased August 23, 1857, aged 57 y., 9 m.) to a good audience. I gave out a monthly appointment at this place, namely every 1st Saturday in each month at 3 P.M. Took supper at Sandy Kearney and returned home.

Fri., Aug. 20. Visited at Mr. Harding's, a Campbellite Baptist.

Tues., Aug. 24. The breth. Emil and Robert Schweinitz and Bahnson called. Margaret is wanted in the S.A. [Salem Female Academy]. She is to go down by Saturday, Elisabeth to come up.

Wed., Sept. 1. This morning Margaret and Jane Miller and Benj. Chitty left here for Hope, Indiana, on a visit to their parents. This afternoon we had a good rain, the first since the 18th of July.

Sun., Sept. 12. Married People's Festival. After dinner the heads of families met to elect a Committee member in place of br. Edward Butner, removed towards the Pilot. Br. Daniel Butner was elected by 13 votes, there being 16 Brethren present. It was then stated that br. Joseph Transou declined serving any longer as Steward of this congregation, having served 14 years in that capacity. It was moved and seconded to proceed to an election of a br. in his place, resulted in the election of br. Rinehold Oehman, who refused to serve. The next vote taken, br. William Lehman was elected; he also refused to serve. Br. Levin Grabs then agreed to discharge the duties for a short time, until a person could be elected to fill that office.

Tues., Sept. 21. Sr. S. and myself visited at Thomas Conrad's, who is still afflicted with fits.

Sat., Sept. 25. At 3 A.M. was awakened and requested to go to Jacob Wolf's, who it was believed was near his end and desired to see me. I found him wondering in mind; he has been drinking too much and suffering from delirium tremens.

Sat., Oct. 2. Remained at home, forgetting my appointment at the Dutch meeting house, did not attend.

Sun., Oct. 10. Sr. S. and myself went to Mickey's School house, where we were to have a union protracted meeting. A large audience having assembled and no other minister appearing on the stand, I was about to open the meeting when I observed the Rev. Mr. Baldwin (br. Sol. Transou's son-in-law) seated among the audience; introduced myself to him, and requested him to take part in our meetings, but he declined. I then opened the meeting at 10 A.M. by singing and prayer, and then preached on John 5:39-40. Before closing the service Br. Craft and John Alspach arrived on the stand. After the morning service, notice was given that the next service would commence at 2 P.M. The ministers were invited to take dinner in the school house, prepared by Br. Henry Shultz. Afternoon it being cool, we concluded to open the meeting earlier, and to drop the night meeting. Br. Craft then opened the meeting and preached on Hebrews 7:25, and after a suitable interval Br. J. Alspach preached on Malachi 3:16, after which the meeting was closed and adjourned to next morning 10 A.M. It was quite cool all day.

Tues., Oct. 12. In consequence of its raining nearly all day I did not go to Mickey's school house.

Thurs., Oct. 14. [D]rove out to Pfafftown, and preached a funeral service at Evan Transou's on Matt. 19:14. Afterwards buried his little daughter at the infant graveyard about 1/4 of a mile from town, where I was told there were *eleven* infants buried under two years of age, the only occupants of this real God's Acre.

Sun., Nov. 7. Afternoon . . . preached at the negro church on 2 Kings 5 to a small audience. Cause assigned: negro funeral in the neighborhood.

Fri., Nov. 19. I visited Frank in the Jail, conversed and prayed with him. He wept very freely.

Sat., Nov. 20. In the morning I again visited Frank, conversed and prayed with him. He seems truly penitent but has not obtained peace. "The way of transgression is hard."

Wed., Nov. 24. Evening prayer meeting in church, 1 person besides my family attended (in all four).

Fri., Nov. 26. This day Frank was to have been executed. The Governor, however, granted him a respite for 3 weeks, so that the multitude were disappointed, and this manifested itself in a strong feeling.

Sat., Nov. 27. This morning the report of another murder reached us, perpetrated at the close of the day yesterday at Winston by P. Shultz on the person of C. Holder, son of Michael Holder. The above unfortunate being was an apprentice of mine, living with me within the time of two years.

Thurs., Dec. 2. This morning I visited a family, Schreiver, who lately moved near to Shoretown, his wife's m.n. Fansler. He was sick of feaver and flux, distressed about his soul, he wished me to come to see him. I conversed and prayed with him, directing him to Jesus the Saviour.

Fri., Dec. 17. Frank was executed this afternoon, and I humbly believed he had obtained mercy.

Wed., Dec. 22. [V]isited William Leinbach, who has moved with his family on the Hauser's Mill. He and family desire to connect themselves with Bethania congregation.

([Bethania Report:] As a general thing the attendance on the Sabbath at Bethania and Bethabara is small. The meetings in the country, on the other hand, are scarcely ever otherwise than good, and are a source of encouragement.)

Friedberg Diary, with Hope, Muddy Creek, Macedonia, 1858
[Extracts transcribed; handwriting is that of Christian Lewis Rights.]

Mon., Jan. 4. Went to Salem, had to go by way of Waughtown to escape the mud. The roads are almost impassable, but the weather is remarkable warm for this season of the year, and rain almost every other day.

Thurs., Jan. 7. [S]carlet fever . . . is prevailing considerable in this neighborhood at this time, principally among the children.

Mon., Feb. 8. A neighbor, Harrison Swaim, narrowly escaped being killed by the limb of a tree falling on him.

Fri., Feb. 12. This morning about 6 o'clock it commenced snowing, and continued without intermission until 4 o'clock P.M., when it changed to sleet and continued all night.

Sat., Feb. 13. It continued sleeting till 9 o'clock A.M. The snow and sleet is about 12 inches deep. The ground underneath is dry, and the probability is that it will lay a considerable time.

Sat., Mar. 6. At Flat Rock school house there was an examination, and when the people started home Paulina Mock was thrown from a buggy and it is feared is seriously injured. About 2 o'clock it began to snow, and was still snowing at dark. The past week we have had the coldest weather there has been this winter.

Mon., Mar. 8. Snowing in the morning; about 3 o'clock P.M. it quit. The snow is about 2 inches deep. I went in my sleigh to visit Gottfried Fishel; he is very sick—erysipelas. From there went to John Kanauss's; his oldest boy is sick. It is a very sickly time. Dr. Shelton remarked to me the other day that he had had more practice in the last 2 months than in six months put together before. Sr. Rosalia [Rosina] Rominger is likewise very sick.

Wed., Mar. 10. Alice is sick, went for Dr. Shelton. Sleighing good in the morning, but by 10 o'clock it became very warm, and the snow is melting fast.

Fri., Mar. 12. I went to Macedonia, found a good congregation waiting for me. Preached from Psalm 1. Afterwards a subscription was taken up for the support of the minister for this year amounting to eighteen dollars, then had an election for a Committee. The three brethren Daniel Sheek, Edward Lee, and Thomas Calvin Riddle were elected.

Thurs., Mar. 18. A number of the brethren repaired the church roof, put a new roof on the woodshed and well-house, also repaired the roof of the smoke house.

Mon., Apr. 25 [26]. In the morning it rained, and in the afternoon considerable snow fell. The weather for a week previous to last Friday had been unusually warm, but suddenly on that day after a slight shower the wind blew up cold, and on Saturday morning we had considerable frost, enough to nip the potato tops and kill some of the beans in the gardens.

Sun., May 2. Owing to family circumstances I did not go to Hope.

Mon., May 3. At 1/2 past 7 o'clock P.M. Sr. Rights gave birth to a daughter.

Sun., May 9. During the past [week] there has been a Gypsy camp on the Widow Eader's land, and a great many flocked to see them and have their fortunes told. ([Friedberg Report:] I alluded to it in my sermon, and remarked: if they were only half as much concerned about their souls and would come to me during the next week, I would tell them some things (without looking into their hands) that would be greater importance than any communication from the old Gypsy crone. There was considerable hanging of heads throughout the congregation about that time, and a brother remarked to me next day that a good many wondered: how Rights knew *they* were there.)

Wed., May 12. Anniversary or Congregation Feast. [T]here was an election for a new Committee. The Brethren elected are Daniel Spach (Sen.), Christian Spach, Jesse Mock, Henry Perril, William Shore, Solomon Hage, Samuel Tesh, and John S. Kanauss. After the election, Lovefeast, and in conclusion arrangements were made to cover the church, and a subscription paper circulated among the members to buy the nails and shingles. About 90 dollars were subscribed. The Brethren Benjamine and Christian Spach were appointed to buy the shingles. Finally arrangements were made to get wood, repair fences, etc. Next year Bro. Jesse Mock is to attend to it, and each member to pay 60 cents per year. The paling fences are to be kept up by companies.

Sun., May 30. Committee meeting. Brother Wm. Shore elected Treasurer for the next 2 years.

Sun., July 4. Preaching at Hope in the morning for the whites, in the afternoon for the negroes.

Fri., July 9. Preaching at Macedonia. Afterwards a meeting of the members was convened to consult what is to be done with Joseph Hodge and William Hood for being intoxicated. It was agreed that they be cited to appear next time there is preaching and make due acknowledgement.

Fri., Aug. 6. Preached at Macedonia. . . . Joseph Hodge and William Hood appeared on trial and confessed they had done wrong and promised to do so no more and [were] suffered to remain in the church.

Sun., Aug. 15. At Macedonia. At night before service gave an invitation to persons wishing to join the church to come forward, when the following three presented themselves, viz.: the married Jonathan Brown and his wife Anna Malinda Brown, and the single Stephen Morgan Smith.

Tues.-Fri., Aug. 24-27. Night meeting at Friedberg. [On Thursday] celebrated Hope anniversary. On our return home one of the carriage wheels ran off. After some trouble succeeded in getting it on again, and on arriving at home found the people already for prayer meeting.

Sun., Aug. 29. At 9 o'clock prayer meeting. Preaching at 11 o'clock, 3 o'clock, and at night. During the meetings of the past week seventeen persons professed to have found peace in believing. The interest in the meeting continues unabated. Crowds flock in every evening, and all seem to be serious and very attentive.

Mon., Aug. 30. Visited bro. William Holland. He and Sr. Holland and four children are sick with typhoid fever, as also a young man living with bro. Thornton and bro. Jacob Cook.

Fri., Sept. 10. Stopped at brother Holland's. He is getting worse and says he will die, and Sr. H.'s departure is looked for every hour. Truly this is an afflicted family.

Sun., Sept. 26. On this night we closed the series of our meetings; they have lasted five weeks. 51 professed to have found peace in the believing.

Sun., Oct. 24. Baptism and confirmation at Friedberg. Services commenced 1/2 past 10 o'clock by preaching, then there was an intermission of half an hour, when we again assembled, at least as many as could find room (a great many had to remain outside), when the following persons were confirmed and baptized, viz.: Baptized: Single Men John Floyd, Felix Delap, the Married Esther Caroline Crouse, Susan Foltz, the Single Derilda Miller. Confirmed: John Burke, Harrison Crouse, Jonathan Spach, Jesse Hardman, Sandford Earnest, Alexander Padgett, Lewis N. Spach, Archibald Sink, Elias Seides, Timothy Fishel, Lewis Mock, Alexander Mock, William Johnston, Emmanuel Spach, Wesley Spach, Theophilis Spach, John Crouch, Anderson Rominger, Edward Mock, Wesley Lashmith—20; Louisa Evans, Emma Shore, Mary Earnest, Mary Burke, Mary Fishel, Harriet Chitty, Susan Fishel, Maria Spach, Elizabeth Foltz, Catharine Sink, Loretta Padgett, Cornelia Ann Walk, Theresa Weasner, Martha E. Smith, Nancy Swaim—15. Received: Maria Kanauss. In all 41 persons. The Salem Band of sacred music was in attendance and did good service on the occasion. At night we had service again.

Sat., Dec. 5 [4]. At night prayer meeting in Brother Benjamine Spach's new house. Intending to move into it next week, he proposed to have a prayer meeting in it before it was permanently occupied.

Fri., Dec. 17. The negro Frank belonging to I. G. Lash was hung at Winston.

Friedland Reports, 1858
[Extracts transcribed; handwriting is that of John Chapman Cooke.]

Sun., Jan. 31. I have nothing of important to communicate from Friedland. It remains in all its circumstances as usual, without anything having happened to give interest to its character except that the attendance has been better of late than usual. The services have been regularly maintained, as also the Sunday Schools to which there have been attached 48 children, although they do not all attend regularly. The average attendance is 25, and this is the only redeeming feature in the appearance of Friedland.

Sun., Mar. 28. Palm Sunday. [E]lection for 2 Committee members. Philip Spach was elected but declined serving. Wm.

Gibbins was then elected and Jonathan Lowder, which together with Alexr. Snyder is the present Committee.

Sun., Apr. 4. (Easter.) Sunday School, 25 children. [At] 10 o'clock burial ground service, a very large assembly. [At] 11 o'clock preached from Matt. 28:6. The Church was crowded inside and outside, the most respectable and well behaved company I have yet seen at Friedland.

Sun., Apr. 18. Compared notes of the week with those of the Committee and found that we have now 27 communicant and 13 Society members who have attached themselves to us as members of the renewed Congregation at Friedland.

Sun., Apr. 25. [At] Committee meeting proposed the festival of May 12th. This was disagreed to, and instead of which it was agreed to have the regular festival kept in future on the 18th of February. Added 3 names to the Society members.

Sun., May 9. It was agreed by the Committee that all persons who may wish to be registered on our books shall appear before the Committee and satisfy them as to their qualifications for membership.

Sun., May 16. Proposed to begin the services on Sundays at 10 o'clock from June 1st to continue throughout the summer when it will again be at 11 as formerly. Agreed to.

Sun., June 27. After the morning service I was taken very ill with swelling of the head and face with fever, and was obliged to go to bed where I lay in agony until the gathering in my head broke 6 days afterwards and the swelling began to reduce. Very ill all the week with various symptoms, either one of which was very severe.

Sun., Aug. 29. On the following Wednesday [Sept. 1] night, Alexr. Schneider, communicant and Committee member, ran away from his creditors, having sold his property and turned it into cash, so that nothing is left to satisfy his debts. He took all his family with him and has gone west. On the previous Sunday he stated his wish to have a certificate of membership, which I unsuspectingly gave him.

Sun., Sept. 5. [H]eld a consultation meeting to take into consideration the condition of this remnant of a congregation. We find that nearly all of the Old Members have disappeared. Within the last 2 years they have either deceased or removed from Friedland, and the remainder is so few that they can scarcely be counted. In view of this state of things Bro. Lowder proposed that the Committee, now consisting only of himself and Br. Wm. Gibbons, be discharged and the congregation disorganized, as the remains are but nominal and there is no encouraging prospect of a better state of things. This proposal was not acted upon, and the case stands as it was.

The following week in company with Bro. Lowder I made a visitation which extended into Davidson County. The result was not satisfactory. The old branches of the church have become infirm, and their children have forsaken their footsteps, and there is not a family but what in general the younger branches are attached to either Baptists or Methodists. At present I believe that there is not more than 6 bona fide communicant members belonging to Friedland, by which I mean they who attend the church and take any interest in it. And if the nominal number decreases during the ensuing time as they have during the two previous years, Friedland Congregation will be quite decimated. When I first came to Friedland the following persons were in communion: Elizth. Sides (since deceased); John G. Sides, Florina Sides, Phillippina Sides (these removed); Philip Kerner, John Kerner, Elias Kerner, Nathl. Kerner (these live some distance off, are relatives of the Sides family, and on Sunday used to put up at their house; when Bro. Sides removed they had no stopping place, and in consequence have withdrawn; I believe they now attend the Methodists in their neighborhood); also Alexander Snyder, Mary Snyder together with Catharine, Belinda and Phoebe Anne Snyder (Society members removed); also the families of Styers and Schultz (removed). And in fact Moravianism has nearly disappeared from Friedland.

Sun., Sept. 12. During our residence at Friedland we have endeavored to promote the Sunday School as much as possible, and for this purpose we procured a quantity of Testaments and also a collection of miscellaneous interesting little books from Bro. Keehln, which we distributed as rewards, but we found that one after another, after they had received their rewards, slacked off, and many of them, when they had got all they could get, quit altogether and did not return. Taking these people altogether, both great and small, I have come to the conclusion that they are the meanest people I have yet seen in Christendom. The last time Bro. Bahnson preached here he took occasion to speak to a person in order to arouse him from sleep. This person is related to the 3 Miss Nissens, who were and still are on the Old Book as communicant members. It seems they have taken offense at this, and since then have not put their feet in the church, also the young people of Williard's family, who are companions of the persons spoken to.

Sun., Nov. 1 [Oct. 31]. Our Sunday School is in fact composed of children whose parents belong either to the Baptists or Methodists, and as they have no Sunday Schools the parents allow them to come in order to receive the advantage of such education as we give them, but it is no part of their intention that they shall embrace the faith of our church, and in this view of the subject, our Sunday School is but a nursery for other denominations.

Sun., Nov. 28. I intend to serve the Communion on the Sunday following Christmas and am making a strenuous effort to have a general Lovefeast on the same occasion.

Sun., Dec. 19. Announced my intention to preach my farewell sermon on the following Sunday, which produced a general murmur of disapprobation.

Sat., Dec. 25. Christmas day. A crowded church. Read the Scripture lesson from Luke 2. Preached from Acts 10:38. After which a general Lovefeast. Full meeting. After which the Holy Communion, 10 communicants present. In consequence of the short days, bad roads, and no moonlight, several communicants who had long distances to go could not remain.

[New] Philadelphia Reports, 1858
[Extracts transcribed; handwriting is that of George Frederic Bahnson.]

Fri., Feb. 12. Bro. Bahnson rode in a sleigh to Philadelphia in order to give the members an opportunity to vote for a delegate to the approaching Synod, but on his arrival at the church, he and his companion were the only persons that had turned out. There could of course be no election.

Sun., Feb. 21. The Rev. Thomas Fry preached at the usual time. Afterwards Bro. Bahnson presided at the election of a delegate to the Provincial Synod that will convene tomorrow. Bro. Thomas Spach was elected.

Sun., Feb. 28. Bro. Bahnson preached on Zech. 13:1. The house was well filled, though as usual principally by young persons, some of whom do not always behave with becoming propriety, but require an additional word of exhortation, which is not withheld either.

Sun., Mar. 14. Bro. Thomas Fry preached not at the usual time, but according to previous arrangement at 11 o'clock in the morning, so that Bro. Bahnson coming out for preaching at the usual hour met him returning from the church. They attempted to revive the Sunday school, which had gone into winter quarters during the cold season. On the part of some parents there is a lamentable apathy, while the minds of others are influenced by very silly prejudices. The brethren, though, are determined to go on in the good work no matter how few may come, and doubtless they will succeed.

Sun., March 28. There seems to be rather a better spirit among some of the people in these parts; they attend preaching very well and besides meet statedly either in the church or at friends' houses for offering up prayer and praise. May the good beginning be favored with a promising continuation and be crowned with a happy end. . . .

Sun., July 25. Bro. Bahnson preached on 1 Tim. 2:4. There was present a very large audience, more numerous than at any preceding time, so that not all could enter the church. It was owing in a measure to the fact that a preacher from a distance had been expected. After preaching Bro. B. baptized 3 infants. The conduct of some persons present on a former occasion of a similar kind having been reprehensible, owing to severe unbiblical statements made by a certain sort, Bro. B. took occasion to remind all present of their duty to maintain strict decency and order on such a solemn occasion as the administration of a sacrament, etc.

[Handwriting is now that of Maximilian E. Grunert.]

Sun., Oct. 3. A protracted meeting was commenced around a stand erected near the church. Besides bro. Frye, the brethren Emil Schweinitz, Holland and Grunert attended. Bro. Alspaugh was likewise present.

Mon., Oct. 4. The meeting was continued for some length of time of evenings, and although the accounts do not agree, it appears that upwards of 30 professed to have found the Lord Jesus.

1859

[Charles Darwin published *On the Origin of Species*, proposing the theory of evolution. The unification of Italy began as Sardinia defeated Austria and annexed most of northern Italy.

Oregon was admitted as the thirty-third state in February. In August the first commercial oil well was drilled in Titusville, Pennsylvania. In October John Brown's raiders seized the federal arsenal at Harpers Ferry, Virginia. Federal troops under Robert E. Lee captured Brown and put down the rebellion.]

Memorabilia of Salem Congregation, 1859
[Extracts transcribed; handwriting is that of Francis Raymond Holland.]

The year has been marked by health and plenty and temporal prosperity in every section of our country. While in Europe immense armies have stood in battle array and many thousands have been slain, peace has reposed upon our banners. But while a bountiful Providence has smiled upon our land, and while no complications with foreign powers have seriously threatened our peace and safety, it would be vain to deny that there is danger at home. There is plainly a weight lying on the spirit of all good men and a dread of judgment coming upon the land. Our prayers have been joined to those of our fellow Christians in the North and South, that the Lord in mercy would stay the madness of sectional strife, and make of those who are brethren by a common origin and history, and by every consideration of interest, duty, patriotism, and religion, a truly united and happy people.

Throughout the year, general good health has prevailed in our village and neighborhood. Early in spring the measles made their appearance among the children, but were so mild in character that they did not prove fatal in any case. The number of deaths in our congregation this year is less than it has been in any year since 1852. It is true death has been restricted to no age. Of the deaths that have occurred, four were those of infants; one a maiden of 14 years; two young men, one aged 18, the other 23 years; the father of a family at the age of 65; and a widowed mother and grandmother nearly 80 years of age. Besides these, an unmarried sister who had been greatly afflicted for a number of years departed this life in the Lunatic Asylum near Raleigh at the age of 49 years.

Social prayer meetings have been held throughout the year in a number of private houses, and since Easter a band of young men have assembled once a week in an upper room for prayer and supplication.

An increased interest in the Sunday School cause has manifested itself among us. To this, a series of lectures on Sunday Schools and early religious training, delivered in the month of May by Mr. Wm. R. Hunter of South Carolina, contributed in a considerable degree. Our own Sunday School has been regularly kept, and is attended by 200 scholars, taught by 27 teachers.

It is certainly a pleasing circumstance that during the year upwards of 50 brethren and sisters belonging to this congregation have been regularly engaged as teachers and managers of Sabbath Schools in Salem and vicinity. In these schools upwards of 450 children and youth have been instructed in the life giving truths of the gospel.

Besides all this, much good seed has been sown into the hearts of the numerous pupils in the Salem Female Academy, an institution which has throughout another year enjoyed the kind fostering care, protection, and blessing of our gracious Lord and Savior. The number of pupils, as for many years past, has been fully equal to the extent of the accommodations, being limited to 210 boarders, besides day scholars.

The spiritual instruction of the colored population in our town and vicinity has received a large share of our earnest attention. It having been considered by the P.E.C. most proper to view the colored congregation as forming a part of the Salem Church and to put them permanently under the pastoral care of the minister of the Salem Congregation, accordingly in the month of June the pastor of this congregation took charge of them. Several brethren and sisters having been found cheerfully willing to assist in the Sunday School, the number of scholars in attendance has since that time been much more numerous than before. The preaching at 3 P.M. on the Sabbath days has also been numerously attended. A meeting for familiar catechetical instruction, held in the chapel on Tuesday evenings, has also been proportionally well attended, the number present averaging about 50. On Oct. 23, 2 adults were baptized, and 2 confirmed. The service on this occasion took place in the large church. The colored communicants belonging to this congregation are 30 in numbers, viz., 10 brethren and 20 sisters. During the year 7 infants were baptized. The Sunday School numbers about 75 regular scholars, and the stated hearers are about 150.

A commendable degree of interest has been taken in the various benevolent operations of the church. The Young Men's Missionary Society and the Female Missionary Society have manifested their usual activity. The Home Mission Society has continued to cultivate its field of labor in the mountains of Virginia. The Bible and Tract Societies have not been inactive. The regular monthly distribution of tracts in town and neighborhood was faithfully performed by the female members of the Tract Society. Besides the semi-annual collections for foreign missions, collections for sundry benevolent purposes were on several occasions made, and a liberal spirit was manifested. As nearly as could be ascertained from the sources of information at hand, not much less than $1,000 has been contributed for the various benevolent objects of the church. May the Lord increase the number of cheerful givers and add to their means of doing good!

The centenary Jubilee of the congregation at Bethany on June 12 and 13 was an occasion of great interest to this congregation, and the celebration was numerously attended by brn. and srs. from this place.

On June 15, the ordination of Br. Robert Parmenio Leinbach, appointed as minister of the Friedland congregation, was performed here by Bishop Wolle of Bethlehem, Pa.

In consequence of external changes in the condition of the congregation, chiefly arising from the abrogation of the so-called lease system, a thorough revision of the Church Rules and Regulations was made in order to adapt them to these altered circumstances, and the revised Rules, having been duly adopted, were subsequently printed and since the month of June have been in force.

Salem Diary, 1859

[Extracts transcribed; handwriting is that of Francis Raymond Holland.]

Mon., Jan. 3. Br. Holland conducted the opening exercises of the Boys' School and of the public school. The latter is taught by Sr. D. Vogler. The Directors requested Br. Holland to give, say, half an hour's religious instruction in this school every week, which request, D.V. [God willing], shall be complied with.

Fri., Jan. 7. Was told not long since by two communicants in *good* standing, that they had never experienced to their knowledge a change of heart which brought with it "peace in believing"! How many more such there may be, the Lord only knows! May He have mercy upon us!

Mon., Jan. 10. Congregation Council met at 7 P.M., 39 members present. Resolved that the present Church Committee should continue in office till the new rules be completed and adopted. Resolved to appoint a committee to investigate and report upon the best plan, etc., of enlarging the church or building a new one.

Fri., Jan. 14. Visited the prisoners in jail at Winston. One of them confined on charge of murder declared that he endeavored to pray to God. Some token for good. "The way of the transgressor is hard."

Sun., Jan. 23. Coldest day thus far this winter. Thermometer sunrise 10° above zero; 3 P.M. 24°.

Fri., Jan. 28. Several cases of measles have occurred in the Female Academy. Prayer meeting at Philip Reich's. May the prayers offered for both father and son in that family be answered, and they be rescued from the impending ruin of intemperance, from which they express their anxiety to escape.

Mon., Jan. 31. Prayer meeting as usual at 7 P.M., well attended. Br. Holland invited the Brn. and Srs. to extend some aid towards the rebuilding of the parsonage at Ebenezer, Wisconsin, which has been lately consumed by fire.

Sun., Feb. 6. After sermon a church door collection in aid of our missions to the heathen was taken, amounting to $100.25.

Mon., Feb. 7. The collection towards the rebuilding of the parsonage at Ebenezer, Wisconsin, amounts to $127.25 of which $15 is to be applied towards relieving Br. Kaltenbrunn *personally* on account of losses sustained by the fire. Br.

Joseph Hall took an active part in this matter by voluntarily calling on the members in town for contributions. Forwarded to Br. Goepp a check for $126 for Br. Kaltenbrunn; paid $1.25 for said check.

Tues., Feb. 8. Prayer meeting at Sr. D. Vogler's. A small company had been invited by Sr. Vogler with the view of specially interceding for an erring brother of hers in the west.

Fri., Feb. 11. Prayer meeting at Christian Hege's. A pleasant meeting. Company rather too large. These social prayers are held quite frequently. It is important to preserve their *social* character, therefore the company should consist chiefly of friends and neighbors specially invited.

Fri., Feb. 25. Prayer meeting at Br. E. A. Vogler's. Social prayer meetings have been kept once or twice every week for a number of weeks past.

Sun., Feb. 27. At 7 P.M. Br. Holland preached in the Methodist Church at Winston by invitation of the pastor, Rev. Mr. Smoot. The services in our own church as well as in the Methodist Church were well attended this day.

Mon., Mar. 7. Heavy rain during the forenoon. Great quantities of rain have fallen of late. The measles, of which there have been many cases in the Academy and quite a number in town, appear to be on the decrease. They have been mild in character.

Sun., Mar. 20. At 7 P.M. Br. Smoot, the Methodist minister stationed at Winston, preached in the church.

Fri., Apr. 1. Prayer meetings were held this evening at Br. E. A. Vogler's and at Sr. Denke's. On yesterday (Mar. 31) there was prayer meeting at Father Fries' in the German language, kept by Br. Bahnson. Prayer meetings are kept weekly in the Sisters House and Female Academy.

Sun., Apr. 3. [A] church door collection was taken in aid of the Home Mission congregation at Chaska, Minnesota (under the charge of Br. Martin A. Erdman), who are about to erect a house of worship. The collection amounted to $51.67. At 2 P.M. Br. Holland preached at Pleasant Fork School House, where a Sunday School has this day been re-organized. Forwarded by Br. Holland to Br. Goepp a draft for $51.16, being the amount of the collection (less exchange) for Br. Erdman.

Thurs., Apr. 7. A public meeting for the reorganization of the Forsyth Co. Sunday School Union was held at 2 P.M. A new Board was elected, and the hope was indulged that a new impulse would be given to the S.S. cause, especially by the employment of an agent to canvas the county and organize the schools. Collection $5.25.

Mon., Apr. 11. Br. Holland was engaged today in speaking individually with the female candidates for confirmation. The narratives they gave of their spiritual experience were on the whole very cheering. It appears that some experienced a change of heart last summer, and others at different times, up to within the last few days. Among the means blest to their awakening and conversion were mentioned the instruction for the Great Girls, the usual services in the church, Br. Bahnson's closing address to the candidates last year, and the services in the Methodist church at Winston during the revival last summer.

Sun., Apr. 17. Palm Sunday. Confirmation and baptism at 3 P.M. Service conducted by Br. Holland. Twenty-one persons were confirmed and three baptized under a solemn sense of the Savior's presence.

Mon., Apr. 25. At 10 A.M. the Salem Bible Society held its annual meeting, which was very thinly attended. A remittance of $100 was ordered to be made to the parent society at New York. Collection: $14.

Tues., Apr. 26. At 7½ P.M. Congregation Council met to take into consideration the draft of new Church Rules, prepared by the Salem Elders' Conference, acting as a committee for that purpose. After some progress made, Council adjourned to meet again on Thursday evening.

Thurs., Apr. 28. Congregation Council. Adjourned to meet Tuesday evening.

Tues., May 3. Congregation Council met according to adjournment at 7½ P.M. to take into further consideration the draft of the new rules. After several hours spent in discussing the subject of the "Elders' Conference," a committee was appointed to report to the Council next Tuesday evening.

Fri., May 6. Prayer meeting this evening at Br. E. A. Vogler's. Br. Siewers of Bethany, happening to be in town, was present, and took part in the exercises. A delightful meeting. The Young Men who were confirmed on Palm Sunday have assembled once a week, and invited some of their companions to join them in a prayer meeting.

Sat., May 7. Mr. Wm. R. Hunter of S.C., a member of the Presbyterian Church, delivered the first of a series of lectures which he intends to deliver here on S. Schools, the religious training of the young, etc. Short notice had been given, nevertheless a goodly number of children and others assembled at 3 1/2 P.M. in church and were favored with a most interesting and excellent address.

Sun., May 15. [At] 3 P.M. Mr. Hunter delivered the last of his series of lectures. Subject: prayer. His lectures appear to have produced a good impression. His remarks on Sunday Schools and early religious training (constituting the drift of his lectures, into which many narratives, etc., were introduced) were certainly very good. He distributed books and cards to all the children and young people. The 1st Ps. was committed to memory by nearly all, including the pupils of the Female Academy, for reciting, which he gave to each a small book. The children of our S. School voted him the contents of their penny box, amounting to $7. Besides, he received in donations in Salem upward of $100 to aid him in his benevolent labors of lecturing and organizing Sunday Schools.

Tues., May 17. Congregation Council at 7 1/2 P.M. Finished the revision of the Church Rules, which were finally adopted without a dissenting vote.

Fri., May 20. Infant school examination, commencing at 1 P.M. Well attended by parents and friends. The scholars acquitted themselves very creditably, especially in singing. The teacher, Miss Sophia Pfohl, certainly deserves great credit for the patience, kindness, and faithfulness with which she teaches this school.

Thurs., Fri., May, 26, 27. Examination of scholars in Salem Female Academy. Number of scholars, including 68 from Salem, is 345. The exercises, it is said, gave general satisfaction and were not different in character from those of many years past, with the exception that fewer classes were examined, and music and singing occupied the greater part of the time.

Sun., May 29. At 2 P.M. Br. Holland organized a S.S. at Waughtown. Br. and Sr. Fulkerson and Sr. Maria Crist have undertaken to teach in it on Sunday afternoons.

Tues., May 31. Congregation Council this evening held the first election of members of the Board of Elders under the amended Congregation Rules. At the first ballot E. A. Vogler had a majority of votes, but declined, owing to his filling several other offices in the community, which he supposed would interfere with this. After several ballotings Br. Emil Schweinitz was elected, and finally the Board was completed by the election of the Brn. Grunert and Bahnson.

Wed., June 1. Congregation Council met at 8 P.M. and proceeded to elect the Board of Trustees. The Brn. F. Fries, E. A. Vogler, T. F. Keehln, J. Fulkerson, G. Sides, and Charles Cooper were duly elected.

Mon., June 6. Weather yesterday and today has been very cool. Thermometer 42° at sunrise. Slight frost in low places.

Thurs., June 10. Examination of Salem Boys School.

Sun., June 12. Whitsunday. Centenary Jubilee of the Bethany Congregation. Many brn. and srs. from Salem went up to attend the festival. In consequence the attendance at church was not more than half as large as usual.

Mon., June 13. Second day of festival at Bethany. Many went up from Salem. The exercises were solemn and edifying and very numerously attended. The weather on both days was very favorable.

Wed., June 15. At 8 P.M. ordination of Br. R. Parmenio Leinbach to be a deacon of the Brn.'s Church by Bishop Peter Wolle, who arrived in our midst last Friday evening from Bethlehem, having been requested to come hither for the purpose of ordaining the above named brother.

Thurs., June 16. Br. Holland attended the prayer meeting in Br. Charles Cooper's chair shop, or ware room. This prayer meeting has been conducted and held regularly by a number of young men, among whom are the 3 young brethren confirmed on Palm Sunday last [Charles Henry Cooper, Lewis David Eberhardt, and Edwin Gustavus Sussdorf]. There was a delightful spirit prevailing among that little band of 10 or 12 individuals.

Sun., June 19. Br. Holland took charge of the Colored Congregation this day in compliance with the request of P.E.C. Preached for their Church at 1 P.M. from 1 Tim. 1:15.

Sun., July 2. At 10 A.M. Litany and preaching by Br. Bahnson. The Rev. Mr. Smoot of Winston, being from home for a season, had requested Br. Holland to occupy the pulpit of the Methodist Church in Winston during his absence. Br. Holland preached there at 10 A.M.

Mon., July 4. The day was very pleasantly celebrated. In the morning firing of guns, ringing of bells, and martial music. At 10 A.M. Br. Holland preached from Prov. 14:34: Righteousness exalteth a nation, etc. In the evening the square was beautifully illuminated. The National Declaration of Independence and the Mecklenburg Declaration were read, and an address delivered by Br. Bahnson. A large concourse of people was present, and the evening passed off quietly and pleasantly.

Sun., July 17. Br. Comenius Chitty, one of the [Sunday School] teachers, who has for a long time been faithfully engaged in the school, being about to leave for Nazareth Hall, where he will assume the duties of teacher, was commended to the favor and care of God by singing a few benedictory verses and prayer.

Mon., July 18. The weather has for some weeks been intensely warm. In consequence of the diminished attendance on Monday and Wednesday evenings, it has been resolved to discontinue the weekly prayer meeting and Bible lecture, say, till Sept. 1.

Mon., Sept. 12. Prayer meeting on Monday evening resumed this evening. Br. Holland communicated some account of the wonderful revival in Ireland from the *Fraternal Record.*

Wed., Sept. 14. Bible lecture resumed this evening: 1 Samuel, 9th ch. A merciful preservation was experienced last night, inasmuch as thro' the carelessness of some inmate of the Sisters' house who had left several imperfectly extinguished firebrands in a corner of an outbuilding, fire was communicated to the contiguous woodworks, and had even commenced burning in a pile of bake wood. At 1/2 past 9 P.M. one of the aged sisters, feeling thirsty, concluded to go into the yard for fresh water (altho' her pitcher contained water as usual), when perceiving the smell of fire, search was made and the fire discovered in time to be extinguished by the sisters with the water, slops, etc., at hand. Had it remained undiscovered but a few minutes longer the consequences must have been deplorable, and there is no telling where it would have stopped.

Mon., Sept. 19. Protracted meeting at Muddy Creek since Saturday. Br. Bahnson has been over since the commencement of it. Br. Holland went over today. The meetings were well attended.

Sun., Oct. 23. At 21/4 P.M. there was adult baptism and confirmation; 2 colored people were baptized and 2 confirmed. The service was held in the large church, and numerously attended by all classes except white *brethren.*

Mon., Oct. 31. Congregation Council at 7 P.M. Committee on church enlargement reported a plan for the enlargement of the church edifice. Council voted that it is expedient that the church building be enlarged. Yeas 19. Nays 15. The subject was referred back to the committee with a view to their reporting a more detailed plan by the first meeting of Council after New Year.

Sun., Nov. 6. At 3 P.M. Br. Grunert preached to the colored congregation, and Br. Holland kept [communion] preparatory meeting, in which the single sister Eliza Starr was admitted to membership on certificate from the Methodist Protestant Church, and Christina Parnell, formerly a single sister, was excluded from the congregation for the sin of fornication.

Mon., Nov. 21. About 5 P.M. an alarm of fire was raised in town. A board kiln near Fries' steam saw mill had caught fire. The contents of the kiln were consumed, but providentially the fire spread no further. A heavy rain had fallen during the whole afternoon, and the wind moreover blowing away from the neighboring buildings, there was but little danger of the fire spreading, and the flames were without difficulty confined to the place of their outbreaking.

Thurs., Nov. 24. Thanksgiving day. In common with the citizens of at least 25 states of the Union, the people of N.C. were invited (by proclamation of the governor) to observe this day as a day of special thanksgiving to God.

Sun., Nov. 27. At 3 P.M. Br. Holland addressed the colored people in their place of worship and at 4 attended to the funeral of a negro boy (belonging to Fr. Fries) named George, who had met with his death accidentally ([Salem Report:] from the discharge of a pistol in his own hand). This was the first interment on the new cemetery for the colored people.

Wed., Nov. 30. Home Mission Society held its semi-annual meeting. Br. Friebele, the home missionary at Mt. Bethel, was present. Not much interest manifested in the cause.

Fri., Dec. 16. At 7 P.M. Br. Holland kept a prayer meeting for the communicant members of the congregation, when the exclusion of S. Zacharias Rights, and Alexander C. Vogler and his wife Antoinette m.n. Hauser for breaking 7th Commandment, was announced to the congregation.

Single Sisters Diary, 1859

[The following is the final entry of the Single Sisters Diary, which was begun Apr. 5, 1786. It is also the only Diary entry in English. Transcribed in full.]

Mon., Sept. 5. The kitchen department given over to the Academy, an entire change takes place in Sisters House. Several of the oldest sisters obtained their dinner from the school, but the others rented their rooms and boarded themselves. A kitchen and a wash-house were formed out of part of the old wood-shed, for the use of the sisters. The former kitchen and wash-house being sold to the school, and a division fence erected.

The custom of 3 or 4 sisters living in the same room, and only having a limited amount of furniture was altogether abolished, and each individual occupant furnished her room according to her own taste.

Female Missionary Society of Salem, 1859
[Extracts of minutes transcribed.]

Sun., Aug. 7. After singing and prayer Bro. Bahnson addressed the meeting stating among other things that as nearly all the colored people attending our church were not, as originally, residents of the neighborhood, but belonging almost exclusively to members of the Salem congregation, therefore the African church could in no wise be considered in the light of a mission church, but constituted rather a part of our own church here at Salem. On this account the pastor of the church had consented to be charged with the colored congregation likewise. This society would therefore be at liberty to apply its funds elsewhere.

On motion the following appropriations were made:

1. $10 toward erecting a monument to the memory of former missionaries in the state of New York, viz. the brethren Buttner, Powell, and Bruce.

2. $30 toward building the new schoolhouse at Springplace.

3. $25 toward the mission on the Musquito coast.

Inquiries were made concerning the grave of Sr. Anna Gambold, but without satisfactory results.

Diary of the African Church in Salem, 1859
[Extracts transcribed; handwriting is that of George Frederic Bahnson.]

Sun., Feb. 20. Bro. Bahnson preached on Genesis 50:20, pretty good audience. There might always be many more than really come, the colored population of Salem increasing very fast.

Sun., May 29. Bro. Bahnson preached on Heb. 2:3. Not as many as could have been expected. Groups of Negroes are seen standing at the corners and dispersing at the approach of the minister. Many owners not feeling their solemn responsibility, but acting a very indifferent part. Not much can be done at present to bring the colored people to the house of God.

[Handwriting is now that of Francis Raymond Holland.]

Almost all the Negroes attending this church belonging to Salem, it was considered most proper to view the Negro congregation as forming a part of the Salem church, and put it permanently under the pastoral care of the minister of Salem, on which account Bro. Holland will take care of it.

Sun., June 19. Br. Francis R. Holland assumed the pastoral charge of the colored congregation, preaching at the usual hour, 1 P.M., from 1 Tim. 1:15: This is a faithful saying, etc. At the close of the service he announced that the S. School would in future precede the sermon, and the latter be held at 3 P.M.

Sun., June 26. At 2 P.M. the Sunday School was organized by taking down the names of 46 persons, and forming them into 8 classes to be instructed by as many brn. and srs. from among the white members at Salem. Sr. Denke, who has for many years taught the colored children, and who for several years past has had the entire labor of the S.S. resting on her, will continue her faithful services by taking charge of one of the classes. 3 P.M. preached from Proverbs 10:5.

Sun., July 3. The Brn. Henry Cooper, Gustavus Sussdorff, Herman Hoffman, and Lewis Eberhard and the Srs. M. Denke, Rebecca Stauber, Martha Vogler, and Leana Schaub were present, and entered with zeal upon their work as teachers in the S. School. About 60 children and adults are now enrolled as members of the S. School. At 3 P.M. preached from Ps. 1:1-2. Gave an invitation to such as felt desirous of serving the Lord to attend a catechetical meeting to be held in the chapel on Tuesday evenings at 8 o'clock.

Tues., July 5. About 20 attended instruction this evening. They were very attentive, and it really appeared as if some of them were quite in earnest in seeking the one thing needful.

Sun., July 17. S. School was very numerously attended. About 80 scholars were present. Learnt partially the words and practiced the singing of "Will you go?" in [the] American S.S. Union collection.

Sun., Aug. 21. Attendance very small owing to a camp meeting at Maple Springs 4 miles from Salem. Br. H. gave some account of our missions to the heathen.

Tues., Sept. 13. Between 30 and 40 persons attended the instruction this evening. Last Tuesday evening all but 4 had absented themselves, owing to a circus exhibition which was going on at the same time. They were addressed on the subject of worldly amusements, and a number of them frankly admitted the improper nature of exhibitions such as they had witnessed last Tuesday evening.

Sun., Sept. 25. After sermon the congregation was informed that their minister had appointed the Brn. William Hamilton and Harry Vogler to act as Helpers or elders, for 12 months. After the congregation was dismissed, the communicants remained for a meeting preparatory to the Holy Communion, to be celebrated next Sunday. Alexander (at A. E. Vogler's) and Pinkney (at Fries'), who have applied for membership, were invited to be present as spectators. Two females, who also applied some time ago, appear to have had their minds unsettled by the proselyting zeal of some of the colored members of the Methodist church at Winston. Consequently they did not show themselves today.

Sun., Oct. 2. Lovefeast and Communion. Br. and Sr. Friebele, who had formerly served the colored charge, were present, being at Salem on a visit from Mt. Bethel, Va. There were 20 colored communicants present.

Tues., Oct. 18. Finished the course of lectures preparatory to baptism and confirmation. These lectures, which have been held every Tuesday evening in the chapel since the beginning of July, were well attended—from 30 to 40 being present on an average—and from some indications the hope may be cherished that they have not been unblest to some souls.

Sun., Oct. 23. This was the day appointed for baptism and confirmation. Hezekiah Pinkney, the servant of Francis Fries, and Mary, an aged black woman, the wife of Cyrus, living beyond the paper mill, were confirmed; and Alexander, the servant of E. A. Vogler, and Julia Catharine Jarvis, a free brown girl living at Br. Thornton's, were baptized. The meeting was held in the large church, and was numerously attended by the colored population of Salem and vicinity. A good number of white sisters and some 20 or 30 white brethren were also present. Great attention and solemnity prevailed. Upon the whole, it is believed that a better state of religious feeling is gradually beginning to prevail among the colored people around and in our midst.

Sun., Oct. 30. Sunday School as usual. After the school was closed, 5 infants were baptized into the death of Jesus. The church was well filled by an attentive congregation.

Sun., Nov. 20. Sunday School was well attended. Preaching also. Men and boys more sleepy than usual. Corn shuckings of night, the cause, as they allege.

Sat., Nov. 26. George, a boy aged about 12 years, belonging to Fr. Fries, died today. He had concealed an old pistol in the barn near the steam saw-mill, and yesterday afternoon while carelessly handling it, it went off, inflicting a mortal wound, the ball passing through the liver and coming out at the back. He had afterwards stuck the pistol behind a board, and to the end declared that he had fallen on a sharp iron and thus hurt himself!!

Sun., Nov. 27. At 3 P.M. Br. H. addressed a small congregation in the church, and at 4 conducted the funeral of George. He was buried in the new cemetery for the colored people, and is the first interred there.

Sun., Dec. 18. Celebration of Christmas at 2 P.M. The S.S. scholars were rewarded with cakes, pictures, little books, and wax candles. Some of the colored brn. had decorated the church quite prettily for the occasion. All seemed to enjoy themselves very much. The house could not quite contain the crowd of colored people assembled. The announcement was made that there would be no service next Sunday. Several members requested to be allowed to meet at the usual time and hold a singing meeting. Permission granted.

Sun., Dec. 25. Having during the previous week requested Br. Grunert to conduct the services for the colored people today, he kindly consented. The number present, owing to the want of very general notice, was rather small.

Thurs., Dec. 29. The Tuesday evening meetings have been continued with one exception thus far. The attendance at all the services has been good. Upon the whole the condition of the colored people appears hopeful. The number of communicants belonging to the church is 30, viz.: 10 brn. and 20 srs.; 7 infants and 2 adults were baptized.

Salem Congregation Council, 1859
[Extracts of minutes transcribed.]

Mon., Jan. 10. 39 members present.

Br. Francis R. Holland, the newly appointed Pastor of the Congregation presided.

1. The time having expired for which the present Congregation Committee had been elected; the question was laid before Congr. Council, whether they would now proceed to elect a new one or retain the present one until the new rules and regulations of the Congregation that are now being framed shall have been completed and laid before Council, when it would of itself become necessary to elect a new Committee.

The motion was made, seconded, and unanimously adopted, that the present Committee remain in office until the new rules shall have been accepted by the Council.

3. The motion was made and seconded to appoint a committee to take into consideration the expediency of either enlarging our present Church or of erecting a new one, and report to the Congregn. Council at some future period. This motion was based upon the fact that for several years already the Church, especially on the side occupied by the female portion of the audience, has been inconveniently crowded, not only on festive occasions, but frequently also on ordinary Sundays. The motion was adopted and the Chairman requested to nominate 5 brethren to constitute said Committee. Br. Holland asked for time for deliberation before making the appointment.

Tues., Apr. 26.

1. Minutes of last meeting having been read, the Chairman (Br. Holland) remarked in reference to § 3 that he had nominated a Committee consisting of the Brrn. Robt.

Schweinitz, E. A. Vogler, Lewis Belo, Fr. Fries, and S. Thos. Pfohl. Said Committee has met and acted on the subject, but is not yet ready to report.

2. The object of the present meeting being to lay before the Congregation Council the new Church Rules as framed by the Elders Conference and Church Committee for further action, the Rules were upon motion communicated to the Council.

[For the remainder of this meeting and for the next six meetings, held Apr. 28 and all five Tuesdays in May, Congregation Council debated the proposed new Rules and Regulations. The first section, treating of the "Principles of Faith and Practice" of the Church, were, on amendments, adopted "with but one dissenting voice." The first four paragraphs of the second section, treating of the General Synod, the Provincial Synod, the Unity Elders Conference, and the Provincial Elders Conference, were "retained as an appropriate introduction to the second part of the Rules."

[The fifth paragraph, treating of the proposed Board of Elders (superseding the old Elders Conference), "gave rise to a long discussion" that extended over three meetings. A committee was appointed to act upon a resolution that "it is the sense of this Council that a change be made in the constitution of the (Salem) Elders Conference." The committee, consisting of the Brn. Nathl. Vogler, Adam Butner, Edwd. Leinbach, and Fr. Fries, with Br. E. A. Vogler as chair, made its recommendations in a report that encompassed the entire new Rules and Regulations as proposed by the Elders Conference and the Church Committee. The Board of Elders, the committee reported, "shall be composed of the Pastor or Pastors of the Congregation, the Principal of the Salem Female Acady. and *three* other Brethren to be elected by the Congregation Council." Congregation Council accepted the committee's report "by an almost unanimous vote."

[The sixth paragraph of the second section of the proposed new Rules and Regulations treated of the proposed Board of Trustees, which would supersede the old Church (Congregation) Committee or Town Committee (or Town and Church [Congregation] Committee), as it was also called, depending on the matters it was dealing with at the time, or simply the Committee, or its earliest form, the Aufseher Collegium. Congregation Council defeated two amendments to its committee report on the Board of Trustees, but did adopt a sentence that stated that "no one shall hold a seat in the Board of Elders and in the Board of Trustees at the same time."

[Congregation Council then considered its committee report on the section of the proposed new Rules and Regulations that dealt with Congregation Council itself. Several minor amendments were adopted, but the sentence stating that "this Council shall be composed of all brethren, communicant members of the Congregation" gave rise to a series of efforts to strike out the word "*communicant*." The efforts failed, the last time "only two votes being given in favour of striking out."

[Having approved new Rules and Regulations by sections, Congregation Council also twice voted to adopt them as a whole, the first time with "but one dissenting voice," and the second time "by a large majority of votes, only 2 votes being given against." Time now came to debate the signing of the new Rules and Regulations by individuals:]

Tues., May 31. Present 38.

The question having been bro't before the Council whether it was required that every member of the Congregation sign these rules as now amended and altered, the following resolution was laid before the meeting, viz.: "Whereas the question has arisen in this body whether it is necessary for such members of the church as have previously signed the rules of which the present are merely an amendment, to subscribe them again *as now amended*, therefore Resolved that any member of the Church who has heretofore bound himself by his signature to the observance of the Church Rules is by such signature also considered as bound for the observance of these Rules as now revised, amended, and adopted by a constitutional majority (2/3) of the Congregation Council present (see Conclusion No. 2 of the Rules of 1850), but every male member of the Church becoming of age, or any new member that is admitted to the Church must sign them before he can claim the privileges of a member of the Church."

The above Preamble and Resolution after having been duly seconded was adopted by a unanimous vote.

A Committee of three, consisting of the Brrn. F. R. Holland, R. de Schweinitz, and Thos. Pfohl, was appointed to superintend the printing of these rules, with authority to add such notes or explanations as they may think proper.

2. A motion was then made, seconded, and adopted now to proceed to the election of three Brethren for the new Board of Elders. . . .

Wed., June 1. Present 24 members.,
1. . . . Council next proceeded to elect 6 Brrn. to constitute the Board of Trustees.
2. The Secretary of the Congregation Council having resigned his place, Br. Augustus F. Pfohl was appointed to act in that capacity in future.

Mon., Oct. 31. Present 38 members.
Chairman stated the object of the meeting, to be for the purpose of hearing the report of the Committee appointed some time since upon the enlargement of the Church. Bro. R. de Schweinitz, the Chairman of the Committee, verbally reported the plan which to them appeared the most feasible and practicable. After considerable discussion it was moved and seconded, "that it is the sense of this body that an enlargement of our Church is desirable." Before the calling of the votes it was asked, Is the question of the enlargement agitated for the purpose of admitting the blacks to our Church? That subject having been discussed at some length and the question having been called, the Council decided by a vote of 19 to 15 that it was desirable to enlarge the Church.
The motion next prevailed that the report be again referred to the Committee to elaborate their plan, make estimates, and at the same time invite further plans from any or all members of the Church and not to report before the 1st of Jany. next.

Elders Conference/ Board of Elders
of Salem Congregation, 1859
[Extracts of minutes transcribed.]

Wed., Jan. 12. Brn. Bahnson and E. Schweinitz absent.
4. It was thought advisable to change the times for taking up missionary collections at the church doors (see Dec. 1, 1858) to Feb. and Aug.

Wed., Jan. 26.

3. Br. Martin Hauser of West Salem, Ill., solicits also a collection for the benefit of the church building for the English congregation there. No action was taken for the present, in as much as br. Fogle is expected from there in a few days.

Wed., Feb. 9. br. R. Schweinitz absent.

2. In the matter of the collection for West Salem br. M. Hauser will be informed that the feeling in the congregation is such as to make a collection for that object inexpedient.

Wed., Mar. 9. br. E. Schweinitz absent.

5. The minutes of several meetings of the Committee were communicated. Some amendments proposed to the draft of the new rules, now before that body, were concurred in by the Conference.

6. It was mentioned that br. Rudi Blum had entered the state of holy matrimony, without giving notice. Br. Holland will inquire of him whether he considers himself a member of the church or not?

Wed., Apr. 6.

5. The Church Committee having adopted the draft of new rules proposed by the Elders Conference, as amended, returned the same to the Elders Conference for further action, and these amendments having been concurred in, it was resolved to call a meeting of the Congregation Council on Tuesday after Easter, Apr. 26, for the purpose of laying this draft before that body. It was thought proper to invite all the members to sign these new rules, if adopted, but not to insist, if any of those who have signed the former ones would object to affix their signatures.

Board of Elders of Salem Congregation, 1859
[Extracts of minutes transcribed.]

The revised rules of Salem Congregation, as adopted by the Council, provided for a Board of Elders, to consist of the pastor or pastors, the principal of Salem Female Academy, and 3 brethren to be elected by the Council. This election, held on

May 31st, 1859, resulted in the choice of the brethren E. A. Schweinitz, M. E. Grunert, and G. F. Bahnson, and on . . .

Thurs., July 14. . . . the Board met for the first time.

Present the brn. F. R. Holland, Robt. Schweinitz, G. F. Bahnson, and M. E. Grunert. Br. E. A. Schweinitz was absent.

Br. Grunert was requested to act as secretary of the Board. Agreeably to the requirements of the rules, the first business was the drawing of lots to determine the time of service for the elected members respectively, which resulted as follows: br. Grunert for 1 year, E. A. Schweinitz for 2 years, and G. F. Bahnson for 3 years. The stated meetings of the Board will be held every other Wednesday at 10 A.M.

These preliminaries having thus been disposed of, the regular business was proceeded with.

3. Br. Joshua Boner has resigned some time ago his office as organist and director of church music. The Board acknowledged that the time is past when the duties of this office can be expected to be performed without a salary. The brn. Josh. Boner and E. W. Leinbach were named as the only two persons at present available, and the former was appointed by the Board. The chairman will notify the Board of Trustees of this appointment, requesting them to fix a salary, upon which br. Boner will be informed of his election.

Wed., Aug. 3. Br. R. Schweinitz absent.

2. To §3 the chair remarked, that the Board of Trustees did not know what amount to offer, and that br. Boner upon being asked what compensation he would expect, demanded at least $200, a sum which the Trustees declare they cannot give. The Board finally agreed upon asking br. E. W. Leinbach for what sum he would be willing to serve as organist. Br. Holland will speak with him.

4. Several members of the church band have gone to the Piedmont Springs, Stokes Co., to assist there in making music for the entertainment of the guests, especially at their dances. They will be spoken to.

Wed., Aug. 10. Br. R. Schweinitz absent.

2. The persons mentioned in §4 have promised to close their engagement as soon as possible, and not to do so again.

3. The names of several brn. and srs. on the catalogue were mentioned, whose membership was somewhat doubtful, and with few exceptions retained for the present. The following were struck off: [blank] Vogler, Wm. Ed. Wagoman, Ge. Munsch, and Reuben Reich.

Wed., Aug. 24.

5. The organist business came up again. It was remarked that it appeared from private information that the Board of Trustees *as such* did not yet dispose of br. Boner's offer (see minutes of Aug. 3, §2), and that consequently for the present nothing could be done until that case was decided.

Wed., Sept. 7. Br. R. Schweinitz absent.

2. The question came up whether attendance at the circus could or should be made a matter of church discipline. Moral suasion appeared to be the only suitable way, until public opinion is changed to a higher degree for the better.

3. Br. Francis Carmichael is reported to have been bound over to court for assault and battery. The facts in the case will then become known.

Wed., Sept. 21.

2. Br. Holland stated that he had received the following communication from the chairman of the Board of Trustees, viz.: "The Board of Trustees are willing to pay a reasonable sum per year to a person who will act as organist, and at the same time consider it his duty, in consideration of the sum paid, to instruct others that may be willing to enter a class, so as to qualify them to act as organists, or to perform the different vocal or instrumental parts in our church music."

Br. Pfohl at the same time resigned his office as "so called director of church music."

The Board did not consider the above communication all that could be desired, no definite sum having been named, and other duties having been connected with the organist office, resolved, however, to accept the proposition, and br. Boner will accordingly be spoken to again. If he, as is most likely, refuses, br. E. W. Leinbach will be approached.

4. Christina Parnell must be excluded for fornication. This being the first case under the new rule which makes mentioning the name of the individual in a meeting of the communi-

cant members obligatory, some discussion followed respecting the time of such announcement. The next [communion] preparatory meeting will, as a general thing, appear the most proper occasion.

Wed., Oct. 19.
2. The organist business is settled, br. E. W. Leinbach having accepted the offer. It appeared unnecessary to appoint a particular director of music.

Wed., Dec. 7.
3. Several young brethren have applied for permission to decorate the church at Christmas. Pleasing as it is to have the church decorated on the occasion, the Board nevertheless hesitated to give its consent. When in former years the church was decorated, it gave rise to protracted evening gatherings of young people of both sexes in the chapel, and caused various complaints at the time. The originators are well meaning persons, but cannot exercise a controlling influence. At all events the warden is to be consulted, and even if there should be no objection from that side, the superintendence of the preparations by married persons of weight must be secured.

5. Various members appear anxious to have occasionally German singing meetings. Such will be held from time to time on Friday evenings in the chapel.

7. To Alexander and Antoinette Vogler, who were married on Oct. 26th, a child was born a few days ago. They must be excluded.

8. Zacharias Rights, for years suspected of lewd practices, was detected some time ago, when about to meet a Negro girl. The Board resolved to notify him that he was excluded, and would take his acquiescence as an acknowledgment of his guilt.

Aufseher Collegium (or Town & Church Committee or Congregation Committee), 1859
[Extracts of minutes transcribed.]

Tues., Jan. 11. Not present the Brrn. F. Fries, E. A. Vogler, and W. Peterson.

1. Several members of the Committee have attended to the matter of the lots in the upper part of Church Street and recommend that all lots on Main Street between Cemetery and North Street receive a depth of 180 ft., and that Church Street be 50 feet wide from the lot of Edwd. Leinbach to the Winston line, which recommendation was adopted.

3. It was resolved in the course of the present year to cover the Warden's house with shingles instead of tiles.

Tues., Jan. 25. Not present the Brrn. F. Fries, Theod. Keehln, and Wm. Peterson.

3. The Warden was authorized to give about 50 of our love-feast mugs that have been used for some time already to New Philadelphia Congregation if they should make application for them.

Tues., Feb. 22. All present.

3. Br. Edwd. Belo makes application to purchase the field lying on the east side of the Cedar Alley, between the lot of Sister Kremer and the graveyard. Committee, being apprehensive that selling said field might eventually lead to its being used for the purpose of erecting a dwelling house on it and perhaps to the opening of the Alley as a public street, unanimously voted against the application of Br. Belo. Should, however, the Inspector of the Fem. Academy, who now occupies the ground, be willing to let Br. Belo have it, Committee would not object to rent it to him under certain conditions hereafter to be spoken of more fully.

6. Upon application Committee is willing to put up gas pipe and fixtures at Diacony expense in the Post Office with the understanding that 6% on the cost be added to the yearly rent paid by the Postmaster.

Tues., Mar. 8. All present.

5. The Rules and Regulations of the Salem Congregation as revised and adapted to the present condition of the congregation by the Elders Conference were next communicated to the Committee.

The following suggestions were made by the Committee, viz.:

In Article 19 of the first part of the rules to insert "also gambling, purchasing and selling of lottery tickets."

2ndly, change the time of electing members of the Church Committee from January to May and let it take place on the first Thursday in May, because on the first Monday of January the election of Town Commissioners takes place, and it might perhaps be preferable not to have another election so soon again. Excitements arising at town elections might have an injurious effect upon the election of the Church Committee.

Having now heard the Rules for the first time, Committee wish to have time given them for reflection till their next meeting, before they are returned to the Elders' Conference.

Tues., Apr. 5. Not present Brrn. Theod. Keehln and Wm. Peterson.

1. Regarding the new Congregation Rules it was tho't expedient by Committee that a proviso should be entered stating that if for any cause the election of new members of the Committee does not take place at the appointed time, old members should retain their office till an election can be effected. And further it was proposed that the time of the annual election be changed from the first Thursday to the first Tuesday in May.

The above amendments having passed unanimously, the Rules and Regulations of the Salem Congregation were unanimously adopted by the Committee and ordered to be returned to the Elders Conference for further action.

3. It was resolved this year to make charges for waterwork expenses only against persons occupying houses situated within those limits of town to which the water from the spring is taken and not to make it, as heretofore, a charge against members of the congregation residing in all parts of the town.

4. Committee resolved to appropriate a sufficient piece of ground situated east of and adjoining the new Cemetery for a new Negro Graveyard. This burying ground is to belong to the Negro Church established at this place and to be placed under the same rule and control as the former negro graveyard.

Br. F. Fries expresses his willingness to put a fence around this piece of ground at his own expense, provided a portion of it is allowed him where he can bury such negroes as belong to him or are in his employ.

N.B.: The Church Committee as heretofore existing having been superseded by the *Board of Trustees* as established by the new Church Rules adopted May 17th, 1859, for further proceedings regarding the *secular and financial* matters of the Salem Congregation, see *Minutes of the Board of Trustees.*

Board of Trustees of Salem Congregation, 1859
[Extracts of minutes transcribed.]

Tues., June 14.

A new body of "Rules and Regulations" for the government of the Salem Congregation having been adopted by the Congregation Council on May 17th, according to which the Town Committee (or Aufseher Collegium) as hitherto existing was superseded by a *"Board of Trustees"* to consist of six elective members and the Warden (so long as such an officer shall yet exist), the Congregation Council had on June 1st elected the Brrn. Francis Fries, Elias A. Vogler, Theod. Keehln, Jacob Fulkerson, John Gottlieb Seitz, and Charles Cooper as members of said Board.

These Brrn. met for the first time on the evening of Tuesday June 14th and organized by electing S. Thos. Pfohl (the Warden) as President and Secretary for 1 year, viz., to the first Tuesday in May next.

Agreeably to the new rules the elective members of the Board then proceeded to determine by drawing of lots when the term of service of each of the present members is to expire, and the following was the result: The Brrn. Cooper and Fulkerson are to serve till the first Tuesday in May 1860; the Brrn. Fries and Vogler till 1st Tuesday in May 1861; and Brrn. Keehln and Seitz till 1st Tuesday in May 1862.

1. The minutes of the meeting of the Committee held on Apr. 5 were then read.

Board agreed to let Br. F. Fries have a part of the new Negro Graveyard for his separate use on the conditions offered by him, viz.: that he make a fence around the whole graveyard at his own expense. The size of the graveyard is to be determined by a committee to be appointed by the President.

Tues., July 12. Not present Br. Fr. Fries.

1. Board had a conversation respecting the Waterworks established here, and gave it as their opinion that since this body has no longer the care of them, the most advisable plan would be for such individuals and establishments as are dependant upon them for a supply of water to keep them in proper repair and condition until a regular water company be formed.

2. Board on their part have no objections that the meetings of the Young Men's Literary Society be kept in the garret room of the Boys' School house, provided the School Committee is willing.

Tues., July 26. Not present Br. F. Fries.

1. The Board of Elders think it desirable that a regular Church Organist be procured, and request this Board to name the salary they are willing to pay him. Trustees do not wish to name a sum, as they do not profess to know how such services should be rated, but prefer that the Elders, with whom lies the appointment, should ascertain from the organists what compensation they would require.

3. The revenue law of 1858-1859 of this State containing in §25 amongst the exemptions "the property specially set apart for and appropriated to the exercise of divine worship or the propagation of the gospel," it would appear as if thereby the whole of the Diacony property were exempt from taxation; in as much as since the separation between Church and Town Expenses has taken place, the funds of the Diacony are now applied exclusively to *Church purposes.*

Board think it advisable to apply for legal council in the case before declining to list the property.

Mon., Aug. 8. All present.

2. In case the Sons of Temperance consent to have their hall used as a reading room for the citizens and young men of Salem, this Board is willing to give its consent to have the hall so used, provided no improper assemblies collect and make disturbances. This body retains the right to withdraw this consent and to insist on the strict conditions with the Sons of Temperance to have the hall used for no purpose other than the meetings of said society.

3. The Inspector of the Female Academy has determined to care for the boarding of the School himself, and for this purpose wishes to rent such part of the Sisters House premises as he thinks will be necessary for his purpose. . . .

Tues., Aug. 9. All present.

1. The Board after having in the morning examined the Sisters House premises, and after a conversation with the trustees of the Academy concerning the application of the Inspector as stated in the minutes of yesterday, came to the following determination, viz.:

The part thus cut off from the Sisters House lot . . . on which the kitchen building, bleaching place, and part of the garden are situated, is to be given over to the Academy under the rules laid down in such transfers of lots by the Congregation Council, i.e. that the Inspector purchase the ground from Salem Diacony. All other lands hitherto held in rent by the Sisters House, whether included in the present garden or in fields, to be hereafter rented to the Academy.

Of the lower story of the Sisters House, the part lying north of the first door, embracing the rooms now occupied by the Sisters Cathar. Stauber, Justina Stockburger, Lydia Transu, and the kitchen girls, and also the two cellars in that part of the house are to be rented to the Academy, together with the privilege of using the entry in that part of the house.

Academy will further rent the granary, ice house, and smoke house. The kitchen building including the wash house, the barn, stables, spring house, butcher house, small brick house at the back of the garden, etc., as also the kitchen apparatus, farming tools, stock of cattle and hogs, and provisions of every kind, etc., to be sold to the Academy.

In order to provide the necessary convenience for such sisters as would desire to prepare their own victuals, it was resolved to arrange a kitchen in the present woodshed and also in the so called meat-cellar, and to furnish a place for washing wherever it is most convenient, and to make the necessary accommodations in the middle cellar for storing up of provisions by the inhabitants of the different rooms. As there are a few of the sisters now living in the house that are incapacitated thro' age or feebleness from providing for themselves, altho' they are not entirely destitute of means, the Inspector was requested to furnish them with their dinners out of his kitchen at such rates as he will see fit to charge, which favour on his part is, however, not to be made a precedent in the case of others that might become enfeebled hereafter. Board named the following individuals as those that should be thus provided for, viz.: the Sisters Elisabeth and Justina Stockburger, Christina Christman, and Sally Waterson and perhaps also Christina Brösing if she should desire it.

2. Sister Lucinda Bagge desires to make her flower garden over to the Academy; it is in consequence hereafter to be considered as forming part of that piece of ground sold to the Academy for a pleasure ground.

Tues., Aug. 23. Not present the Brrn. J. G. Seitz and Theod. Keehln.

1. Board resolved for the present not to sell the Sisters House furniture, with the exception perhaps of a few articles that the Inspector might need for the office and kitchen.

5. Board having satisfied itself that an institution of the nature of the Salem Diacony is not exempt from taxation (see revenue law of N.C. 1858-59, §25), the Warden will list its taxable property as heretofore.

Tues., Sept. 20. Not present the Brrn. J. Fulkerson and E. A. Vogler.

1. The following communication from Br. Holland, Chairman of the Board of Elders, was laid before the Board of Trustees, viz.:

"The Board of Elders, having some time ago appointed Br. Joshua Boner organist, desires the Board of Trustees to take some definite action in regard to the salary, so that in case a new appointment should be necessary, it may be made without delay."

Board of Trustees, being convinced of the necessity of making some effort towards reviving and supporting our Church Music, which for want of persons able to perform on different instruments is at this time, as far as the instrumental parts (brass instruments excepted) are concerned, at a low ebb, resolved that instead of now fixing upon a stated salary, the following answer be returned to the Board of Elders for their consideration and for further action, viz.:

"The Board of Trustees are willing to pay a reasonable sum per year to a person who will act as organist and at the same time consider it his duty, in consideration of the sum paid, to instruct others who may be willing to enter a class so as to qualify them to act as organists or to perform the different vocal and instrumental parts in our Church Music."

Tues., Oct. 4. Not present the Brrn. C. Cooper, Theod. Keehln, and J. G. Seitz.

1. The Board of Elders, approving of the idea of the Trustees regarding the organist, have made the proposition as amended to Br. Joshua Boner, who, however, declined to accept it; whereupon they offered it to Br. Edward Leinbach, who is willing to act as organist for $100 a year and to instruct a number of persons in music, say 3 or 4 lessons a week, for which service he would ask an additional $100 a year. Board of Trustees, by a unanimous vote, resolved to pay him the above salary.

4. Sister Lucinda Bagge having been appointed successor of Sister Maria Petersen in the office of superintendent of the Sisters House, Board was of opinion that $100 per year would be a reasonable salary in her case, as her predecessor (who lived in the house free of charge for board and rent) had received $65 a year.

5. The yearly accounts and statement of Single Sisters Diacony for the fiscal year ending April 30, 1859, was next laid before the Board, from which it appeared that the accounts closed on that day with a deficit of $326.28. At the same time it was stated that the property of various kinds sold by the Sisters House to the Academy amounted according to the valuation of the Brrn. chosen for that purpose to $5,400.30, of which sum $4,000 have been paid already, and the balance may be expected shortly.

Tues., Nov. 1. Br. Theod. Keehln was called off in the beginning of the session.

1. In reference to §4 it was remarked that Sister Luc. Bagge has been approached respecting the salary and that she declines to accept more than $50 for the first year of service.

4. The yearly accounts of Salem Diacony from May 1, 1858, to Apr. 30, 1859, were then laid before the Board, from which it appears that the receipts from all sources amounted to $6,698.41 and the disbursement to $4,340.87¼, but in as much as the extraordinary receipts for land, amounting to

$3,482.07, were added to the Land Fund, the accounts closed with an apparent loss of $1,124.53 1/4.

Board next examined the notes due the Diacony contained amongst the assets, and found that, exclusive of about $2,000 that are to be deducted from the debts of Charles Brietz . . . , about $950 are to be considered as irrecoverable and about $670 as doubtful.

Board will at its next meeting examine more thoroughly the debts due on account.

Tues., Nov. 28. Not present Br. Fulkerson. Br. Theod. Keehln present only part of the time (then called away).

1. . . . Board turned its attention to . . . the application of Br. Edwin Clemmons for a building lot on the south side of Mill lane. Board is not disinclined to lay out some lots in that locality, but think that, in as much as the building of a railroad from High Point to that place is in agitation, it would be desirable to defer laying out lots on that lane till the railroad has been located, as it is not improbable that it might pass over that ground.

3. Board next went into an examination of the debts due on account to the Diacony and found that about $1,500 may be considered as lost and about $900 as doubtful. It was proposed in order to simplify the ledger to balance off all the accounts that are lost or doubtful by one account under the name of "Deperate [Separate] Debts," which general account could then be balanced off by profit and loss as soon as the means for doing so are at our disposal, which is not the case at this time.

A "Book of Accounts" separate from the ledger might also be kept in which all accounts could be entered that possibly might be made available hereafter and in which the yearly charges against the individuals might be entered without, however, giving credit in the ledger for sums due by them.

4. Mr. Thos. Wilson has taken the outlot in rent formerly held by Henry Hughes. As the latter is still indebted to the Diacony for rents, etc., it was suggested that hereafter no transfer of outlots from one person to another be countenanced by this Board, until the person holding them in rent has paid his debts due the Diacony.

Provincial Financial Board, 1859
[Extracts of minutes transcribed.]

Wed., Feb. 2. Fr. Fries absent at Raleigh.

1. A bill of Alexander Vogler for writing table (see §6, March 18, 1858) and some repairs of furniture, whole amount $14.50, was presented, and Board on motion ordered Treasurer to pay the same.

Wed., Feb. 16. Fr. Fries absent at Raleigh.

3. Br. and Sr. Cooke, who will leave Friedland in spring, must either find a dwelling here or at the North. As it is desirable that they should remove to their proper home at the North, and their private means are very limited, Board, on motion, appropriated $60 for their traveling expenses, in case they removed to the North.

Wed., Mar. 30. Fr. Fries and E. A. Vogler absent.

1. Treasurer stated that he had paid $95 to Br. Rights for the purchase of a new horse, but that Br. Rights, having succeeded in getting the horse for $85, would be very thankful if the $10 could be used by him for the purchase of a new set of harness. Board, on motion, appropriated the $10 for this purpose.

2. Chairman was requested to examine a buggy belonging to Amos Rominger, associating with himself some expert, and if in their opinion expedient, to purchase the same for no more than $40.

3. The following bills were read and passed. Bill of Henry Minung for $26, repairs of buggy injured at Mt. Bethel; G. F. Bahnson for $9 for buggy umbrella and common umbrella destroyed at Mt. Bethel and traveling expenses to Mt. Bethel.

Sun., Apr. 3. All the members present.

1. Br. Bahnson reported that Amos Rominger's buggy was not fit for use.

2. Treasurer reported that the Steward of Philadelphia congregation demands 6% for the small capital of said congregation, invested with Sustent. Diacy., or will otherwise withdraw the money, to which Board had no objection.

3. As Br. Parmenio Lineback has been appointed minister at Friedland, P.E.C. propose that $300 per annum be secured

to him, as his salary, inclusive of all contributions, etc. Board agreed to this proposition.

On motion it was further resolved that Treasurer commission Br. John G. Sides to make the necessary repairs at the Friedland parsonage, provided the cost does not exceed $50, forthwith. . . .

4. Board agreed to secure $200 per annum to Br. Thos. Frye as minister of Phila., Hope, etc. If a serviceable buggy for his use can be bought for $65, Board authorized the purchase of the same.

Wed., Apr. 13. Fr. Fries absent.

1. Treasurer reported that Jno. G. Sides, after an examination of the parsonage at Friedland, is of the opinion that the cost of the necessary repairs will far exceed $50. New weather boarding, window frames and sash, etc., are required. Br. Sides was, on motion, authorized to make the absolutely necessary repairs; the windows are not to be enlarged.

Thurs., Aug. 18. All the members present.

1. John G. Sides' bill for repairs at Friedland parsonage, amounting to $89.11, was presented and passed.

2. Br. Lewis Rights asks for $75, being the amount he falls short of $300 income for the year 1858. On motion, his request was granted. The chairman mentioned that Friedberg congregation had adopted such measures that $300 are secured to the minister for the current year.

3. Br. S. T. Pfohl, Treasurer, submitted the account and statement of Wa. Sustentation Diacony from June 1, 1857, to May 31, 1859, comprising a period of two years. The total amount of receipts was $5,069.81, and of disbursements $5,209.91, leaving a deficit of $140.10. On May 31, 1859, the amount of assets was $38,232.81, of liabilities $939.08; of the above assets $32,443.14 are invested in bonds and notes, $786.24 accrued interest, $3,000 invested in Sustentation house, and $2,003.43 cash in hand. It was mentioned that in the above amount of receipts only one year's contribution of Salem Female Academy was included.

5. On motion it was resolved that all Moravian Church publications be procured for the Provincial Archive, and the bills presented to Board.

6. On motion it was resolved that $1,000 of the cash in Treasurer's hands be invested in N.C. State Bonds, and that the property of Wa. Sustentation be listed for taxation, as the clause in the revenue bill, which seems to exempt it, was not intended to apply to it.

7. The very painful and peculiar position of Br. C. F. Kluge (for nine years a faithful servant of this Province), as regards the amount of pension he at present receives, was brought by the Chairman, according to the recommendation of P.E.C., to the notice of the Board. A motion was made that Wa. Sustentation annually pay $25 toward Br. Kluge's pension, provided the Pa. Sustentation undertakes to pay the same sum, so that said brother by this means receive the full sum of $320 per annum to which a married resting couple is entitled at the North. After some discussion the final decision of this motion was postponed to the next meeting of the Board.

8. Br. Bahnson requested Board to order gas fixtures and pipes to be introduced into his house. Br. Fr. Fries was requested to make an estimate of the cost and report to the Board.

Thurs., Oct. 27. All the members present.

1. The resolution offered at last meeting, as contained in §7 of minutes of Aug. 18, 1859, was taken up. After some discussion the following preamble and resolution were unanimously passed: Whereas, since the General Synod of 1857, no general Sustentation Fund of the Unity can be said to exist, and the Provinces of the Unity have received their respective shares of the property of the Unity, and whereas we deem it right, proper, and just that Br. and Sr. C.F. Kluge, who have served in both districts of the American as well as in the German Province, should receive the full pension to which a resting married couple is entitled at the North, and whereas the pension they receive from the German province amounts to only $274 per annum, therefore resolved: "That Wachovia Sustentation Diacy. pay annually towards the pension of Br. and Sr. C. F. Kluge the sum of $25, provided Pa. Sustentation Diacy. pay a like sum for the same purpose."

2. The Treasurer reported that Henry Hughes had transferred all his rights and title to the house and lot in Bethabara, and the meadow and upland joining John Henry Shore's plantation, to him (S. T. Pfohl) in consideration of the note which

Hughes had given for this property having been returned to him. As this property is to be disposed of, it was deemed best to make it known that it is for sale, but to be in no haste about closing a bargain for the same, as the land and lot are by no means without value. James Webb has been sued. S.F.A. has paid a contribution to Sustent. Diacy. of $1,000 for 1859.

Bethania Reports, with Bethabara, 1859
[Excerpts transcribed; handwriting is that of Jacob F. Siewers.]

Fri., Jan. 21. Rainy. About 4 P.M. a dreadful storm arose, and floods of rain poured down; the wind drove the water everywhere into the house. The street was one sheet of water.

Sun., Jan. 23. Very cold. Went out to Samuel Stauber's. He is also down with pneumonia, and Sophia is thought to be beyond help. The distress of this family is truly great. It being very cold, I dropt the meeting, and staid at Stauber's. Towards evening I returned home and Sr. S. and myself went out to the Stauber's. Sophia, the doctor says, is dying. We all united around her bed in prayer. About 1 A.M. [Jan. 24] she breathed her last. On the Tuesday previous, I conversed with her and urged the necessity of preparing for death, and entreated her not to postpone this important work; for life was uncertain and it was our duty and gain to make our peace with God. Little did I think she would leave us so soon. Br. Stauber is better.

Sat., Jan. 29. Visited at Samuel Stauber's; they are all improving.

Sun., Mar. 13. After dinner heads of families met to deliberate on the manner of celebrating the Centenary of the Congregation next June 12th, Br. Bahnson being present and assisting. We came to no definite result.

Sun., Apr. 24. Easter Sunday. Met in the church at 5 A.M., proceeded to the graveyard. Prayed the Easter morning Litany; more Negroes than white persons present.

Mon., Apr. 25. After dinner heads of families met in the School House, and the following conclusions were unanimously had: The Centenary Festival: The Moravians in all our settlements are invited. The celebration to be in the church. The lovefeast to be the closing meeting on Monday. The Sacrament to be administered the following Sabbath.

Mon., May 9. Went to Salem for materials to paint the church; remained overnight at H. Fogle's.

Fri., May 13. They have whitewashed the church and finished scouring, preparatory for painting.

Sat., May 14. Painting in the church.

Mon., May 16. Went to Salem to prepare paint for church. Returned; painted the whole week.

Thurs., June 9. Finished the painting of church.

Sun., June 12. Whitsunday. Centenary Celebration. In the morning the brass band played several tunes on the church steeple. At 10 A.M. the congregation assembled in the church; the back of the pulpit had the number 100 enclosed within a tasty wreath, the front 50 enclosed with a wreath. The numbers having reference to the centenary of the settlement and the jubilee of the present church consecration. The service was opened by a musical piece from the choir, after which br. Bishop Wolle offered a prayer, and was followed by br. Bahnson on Psalm 118:24: "This is the day," etc., Br. R. Schweinitz closing with prayer. At 2 P.M. after prayer br. M. E. Grunert preached on Psalm 116:12-13, br. L. Rights closing with prayer. After a short interval the service was resumed by br. G. F. Bahnson reading an historical account of the Church of Bethania from its commencement, drawn from the Church Diary. At night the congregation gathered back of the church, and after singing a hymn, went in procession to the graveyard, accompanied by the brass band. The grounds were illuminated by 100 torches. Br. Bahnson prayed the Easter Morning Litany and singing a number of hymns, the band leading, after which the company returned to town. Thus ended the festivities of this day, there having been about 1,500 persons in attendance during the day.

Mon., June 13. Second Day. The services were opened by Bishop Wolle at 10 A.M. speaking on the daily Word and the verse in connection therewith, "I will be sanctified," etc., Ezek. 20:41. Number 761,7. Br. F. Holland next preached on Isaiah 44:3-5, followed by br. T. Fry in prayer. Afternoon during a public lovefeast br. Bahnson concluded the reading of his report of the Church History, and then read a congratulatory letter from the breth. of the U.E.C. and also one from br. F. F. Hagen, former pastor of this congregation, closing with an address to the congregation. At early candle light br. L. Rights preached on Eccles. 7:10: "Say not thou," etc. There was a collection taken during the lovefeast, amounting to some 43 dollars. There were about 900 persons present during the lovefeast. The evening service was well attended. Thus closed the festivities of Church at Bethany. May the Lord accept the praise and thanksgiving, hear and grant the prayers and petitions offered, and bless and renew his covenant with this congregation, is the prayer of the Pastor.

Sun., July 31. Preached at Bethania on Matt. 13:3-9. Rode to John Grabs's and preached at 1 P.M. on Matt. 8:2-4 to a full house. Rode to William Wolf's and preached at 5 1/2 P.M. at his school house on the same to a good assembly. The house is small, and not more than half were accommodated. There were 2 Methodist preachers there, br. Folp and Bowman, the first closed the meeting with prayer. I had a bad cold and spoke with difficulty.

Sat., Aug. 13. Went to Bethabara to the celebration. Forenoon service at 10 A.M. Read the transactions of the Fathers of the Renewed Brethren's Church, as drawn from the Diary kept at Herrnhut. Afternoon during the lovefeast finished the reading. It commenced raining towards the close of the meeting and rained very hard. After it abated, the Lord's Supper was administered, 16 persons partaking.

Sun., Aug. 14. Sabbath. Celebrated the 13th at Bethania. Forenoon after singing and prayer, discoursed on Romans 8:9 to a good audience. Owing to the threatening appearance of the weather we met at 1 P.M. by request and read the Church's records of the 13th. There was no lovefeast, no preparation having been made. The Sacrament was then administered, 39 communicants partaking. It commenced raining before 1 P.M. and appearances were very unfavourable, causing so few to attend.

Sun., Aug. 21. After praying the Litany, preached to a very small audience on Hebrews 11:7. Maple Springs camp meeting is now the great attraction, so much so, in fact, that I was advised to drop the meeting at Bethabara as they would all go to camp meeting. Went to Salem.

Sun., Nov. 6. Preached at 10, after praying the Litany, on Matt. 7:13-14, good audience. Afternoon preached at Bethabara at 1 P.M., good attendance. After preaching . . . gave notice that a prayer meeting would be held at early candle light.

[The meetings continued through Fri., Nov. 11.]

There were corn huskings every evening around Bethabara, Sunday excepted, and yet these meetings were well attended, and the audience on the increase.

Thurs., Nov. 17. Sr. S. and myself went to br. Pratt's, and I united in marriage Emily C. Pratt with Standford Long Nickols, both being mutes and formerly scholars of the State Institute for the Deaf and Dumb.

Thurs., Nov. 24. Thanksgiving day. Preached at Bethania at 10 A.M. on Eccles. 12:14 and at Bethabara at 1 P.M.

Thurs., Dec. 1. Attended Conference at Salem. In the evening attended to a prayer meeting in the Sisters House Chapel by request of Miss Bagge.

Fri., Dec. 16. Visited Mrs. Rachel Leinbach, who had applied for readmittance to the congregation. She gave satisfactory evidence of her sincerity.

Sat., Dec. 17. Called the Committee together and proposed Rachel's application. No objection.

Friedberg Diary, 1859
With Hope, Muddy Creek, and Macedonia till June,
then with Hope
[Extracts transcribed; handwriting is that of Christian Lewis Rights.]

Sat., Jan. 1. [T]he subscription for the support of the minister for the present year was renewed, but in consequence of the rain last night the waters were up so that a good many could not attend.

Thurs., Feb. 17. Committee meeting. ([Friedberg Report:] Among other business a complaint was made by Brother Sandford Earnest against his sister Catharine Swaim for abusing (cursing) her father, Brother Christian Earnest. The Committee requested brother Rights to make inquiries.)

Fri., Feb. 18. Went to Brother William Thornton's; they are moving to Brother John George Spach's, Sr. Thornton's father's. Bro. Thornton has sold his plantation to a Mr. John Yonce for $1,000. Before leaving we exchanged horses. I gave him old Bounce and 85 dollars for a horse said to be 8 years old and recommended by the man that raised him, Mr. Christian Yonce, for his good qualities. Poor Bounce. It went hard to give her up. For many a weary mile through cold and heat, wet and dry, we have jogged on together.

Sat., Feb. 19. Visited Sister Catharine Swaim, Harrison's wife. A com[plaint] was lodged in the Committee against her by her brother, saying that she abused her father Christian Earnest. ([Friedberg Report:] She admitted that she made use of some pretty hard expressions, but that her father returned the compliment in kind, and that all parties in the quarrel were governed by anything else than the law of love.)

Mon., Feb. 21. Visited Brother Earnest, Catharine Swaim, and Sanford Earnest, requesting them to meet the Brethren William Shore and John Kanauss and myself at Friedberg to-morrow at 1 o'clock with a view of compromising the difficulty. The Brethren Shore and Kanauss were appointed by the Committee as arbitrators.

([Friedberg Report:] *Tues., Feb. 22.* The Brethren William Shore, John Kanauss, Christian Earnest, and Sandford Earnest met according to appointment, but Catharine Swaim did not come. It was then agreed that Brother Earnest should state the difficulty to the Brethren, and then they go and see Sr. Swaim. Brother Earnest then gave *his* side of the question. The Brethren then called on Sr. Swaim. Her story *had a side too*, and about sundown they came back to Friedberg about as wise as they were when they set out, and the quarrel no nearer made up. She said the reason she did not come [was that] her husband would not let her, which I expect is true, and he has sworn if Earnest ever comes on the place he'll shoot him.)

Sun., Feb. 27. ([Friedberg Report:] Called the Committee together, and the Brethren Kanauss and Shore reported their failure to effect a reconciliation, and gave as their opinion that both parties are to blame. The Committee say they must make up before they can be permitted to come to the Lord's table, and if a reconciliation is not effected in a reasonable time, they be excluded altogether.)

Fri., Mar. 4. Communion at Friedberg. Between the 1st service and the Lovefeast there was a meeting of the heads of families wherein Brother William Shore read a statement of the income for the support of the minister for the past year, after which he addressed the meeting, urging upon the members the necessity for making a strenuous effort to raise the required sum the present year, and threw out suggestions how it might be done.

Sat., Mar. 5. Attended the examination of the school in Flat Rock District, taught by Mr. White.

Mon., Mar. 7. Just after leaving Bro. [Henry] Perril's it began to thunder and lighten—the first this year—and while yet a mile from home it began to rain. The darkness was intense, relieved occasionally by a flash of lightning, only to add to the gloom a moment after. Sam, the new horse, did admirably, and if I could not see the road he could, and presently we came up safe at our own door pretty well drenched.

Fri., Mar. 10 [11]. Preaching at Macedonia from [blank]. Afterwards Committee meeting. Andrew Cope was charged with being drunk. He came forward, acknowledged his sin, and promised to abstain in future; and the Committee agreed to leave him in the church for the present.

Thurs., Mar. 14 [17]. Today we had the first lettuce out of our garden.

Thurs., Mar. 24. At 2 o'clock P.M. the members of the Wachovia P.E. Conference, viz., the Brethren G. F. Bahnson, Emil A. de Schweinitz, and Robert de Schweinitz, came to confer with Friedberg Committee in regard to the amount paid the minister for his last year's labors. Brother Bahnson opened by reading a hymn, and after singing prayed, and then explained the object of the visit. Brother Wm. Shore, on the part of the Committee, informed the Conference what steps had been taken in order to bring about the desired object.

Sun., Apr. 3. I preached at Hope . . . and informed the Committee perhaps brother Thomas Fry would become their future pastor, and that Brother Leinbach would remove to Friedland.

Thurs., Apr. 7. Attended the monthly Conference at Salem, and it was made out that Brother Thomas Fry take New Philadelphia, Hope, and Macedonia, and Brother Rights retain Friedberg and Muddy Creek, and that Bro. Rights is to announce tomorrow that on the next regular monthly appointment at Macedonia he preach his farewell sermon and brother Fry take his place.

Fri., Apr. 8. Preaching at Macedonia. Afterwards Committee met. It seems a difficulty has arisen between the brethren David B. Wheeler and Daniel Sheek in regard to a settlement as parties in the Committee for the building of the meeting house at Macedonia. It originated on this wise: After the house was finished, there was still owing to Mr. Ellis the builder the sum of $17.50, and as the money subscribed and paid in had all been spent, David Wheeler gave his note to Ellis for the unpaid balance, and Daniel Sheek was security in the note. Mr. Ellis subsequently traded said note to Mr. Adolphos Moss in Clemmonsville. Some months ago Brother Sheek told me of this note—the first I knew of it—and requested me to bring it to the notice of the congregation with the request that efforts be made by subscription or contribution for its payment. So after the sermon I did mention it, and requested the members to try and raise the money and pay it off, as Brother Sheek had told me that Mr. Moss wanted the money, and Brother Sheek stated further in the conversation that he thought he had paid enough to be exempted, as he had paid in the neighborhood of $60 in money out of his own pocket besides what work he had done. I mentioned this also to the members, and here the matter rested for that time. At a prayer meeting some time after, brother Calvin Riddle mentioned it again and proceeded to take up a collection, when Brother Wheeler got up and stopped the proceedings by saying that when the proper time arrived the means could be raised and that he was not uneasy but that it would be paid off, and hereupon Brother Riddle desisted. Sometime in February, I think, a man called at Friedberg and requested of Sr. Rights if I was at home. She told him I was in Salem. He seemed to regret it very much, and after sitting awhile rose to leave and in going out remarked: Tell Rights that Wheeler from Davie County was here and called to see him on particular business. From Friedberg Brother Wheeler went to Brother William Thornton's, where he staid overnight, and [in] conversation [said] to Bro. Thornton that Daniel Sheek had never paid anything out of his own pocket towards the building of that meeting house (Macedonia), and that there was still something over two dollars of the subscription in Sheek's hand that never had been accounted for. Brother Thornton said: How do you know. Wheeler then drew from his pocket what he said was a correct estimate of the income and disbursements, and according to this statement it was as he had said, and he said it was correct. Brother Thornton asked him: How did you get it. He said: I went to Sheek and examined, made the estimate and drew it off just as you see it. Brother Thornton said to him: What did Sheek say. Wheeler's reply was: "He never said one word." A few days after, brother Thornton [was] at Friedberg and stated to me what Wheeler had said. On Friday, 10th March, being the day for the Macedonia appointment, before preaching, Sheek handed me a letter from Mr. Moss written to him (not to Wheeler), stating he looked to him for the payment of that note and that he must have his money on the next week. Brother Sheek requested me to urge it upon the members once more. I did so after preaching but found that no one seemed disposed to do anything in the matter. I finally told them the debt was just and must be paid and offered to be one to give $5.00 towards it. This brought out Brother John Hall. He gave $5.00, and a few more gave something, and in this way with considerable trouble about enough was made up to pay off principal and interest. I said in my remarks that unless something was done that day to pay off that note I should not come into Davie anymore. Wheeler read a statement professing to be a list of the expenses of building, and his whole cost for material, building, and all was but $61, which would still leave some $3.50 in Sheek's hand exclusive of the note, and called upon the[m] to come up now, the proper time was here, and pay that note, his note, but from appearance he might be calling yet without getting anything. On Saturday, Apr. 9, I called on brother Sheek and asked him to let me see his accounts of receipts and expenditures. He cheerfully complied, and it was ascertained that Daniel Sheek had paid, over and above what he had received and besides what work he had done like the rest, $57.01 1/4, leaving the note out of the question. I then told him my object and what the report was, and that it was generally believed through the neighborhood that he still had some money not accounted for. It seemed to surprise him, and he asked who started it. I said Wheeler. He seemed surprised, and said it was the first he had heard of it, and said that Wheeler had called on him one day during the winter with a view, as Wheeler said, to make a final settlement of the meeting house question, and that he gave him the book, and told him to make the calculation himself, and that Wheeler brought it out precisely as the present statement specifies, and in that statement Wheeler himself wrote paid by Daniel Sheek $57.01 1/4, and in the statement shown to brother Thornton and the one read at the church this item is entirely left out.

	$	cts.
Total Cost	139	01 1/4
Paid by subscrip.	64	50
	74	51 1/4
Ellis note, unpaid	17	50
	57	01 1/4

leaves $57.01 1/4 either paid by somebody, or there must be a debt to that amount still owing, and brother Daniel Sheek says he has vouchers to show that he did pay it. Brother Wheeler admitted to the Committee that he might have been mistaken, but said he made it a point to make no apology even if he did injure a man if he did it ignorantly, that he did not see that he had injured Sheek, and further that he cared nothing about it no way, and then went on to read a paper abusing the church in general and the pastor here at Macedonia in particular, and finally it was agreed to lay the matter over till next time. After several others were excluded, viz., Joseph Hodge for drunkenness, [blank] Mock [blank], and Jacob Tanner and Wm. P. Ward are also accused of drinking but this is laid over.

Thurs., Apr. 21. Maundy Thursday. Meeting at Hope. [T]here was an election for a Committee. Ten votes were cast. Brother Christian D. Sides was re-elected with 7 votes. Brother William Thornton received 6 votes, and Brother Calvin Transou 6 votes.

Sun., May 1. The funerals of Frederick William, Cyntha Cornelia, and Benjamine Franklin Holland were preached at Hope by Brother Bahnson. . . . There were a good many persons present. ([Friedberg Report:] Notwithstanding the Dunkards had their annual visitation meeting on this day only two miles from Hope, and the report had gone out that one of their best preachers, from Virginia, was to hold forth at 11 o'clock, still we were constrained to have the service in the grove before the house, as there would not have been sufficient room in the church for the funerals.)

Wed., May 4. This day part of the Friedberg church we covered new. There were about 75 hands. They covered the front side and about half of the back side. ([Friedberg Report:] about seventy-five hands were present, and a perfect Babel they made it. About sundown Brother Bahnson looked in, said, "Good evening," and rode off again.)

Thurs., May 5. Church covering continued, and a new lightning rod put up.

Fri., May 6. Today the brethren covered the Lovefeast kitchen and the back porch, and laid a floor in the back porch, and finished cleaning up. I went to Macedonia and preached from 1 Peter 1:3. Afterwards Committee meeting. David Wheeler and Daniel Sheek came to an understanding.

Sun., May 8. In the afternoon went to Hopewell, and was about beginning the service when Rev. Mr. Swicegood arrived, and I gave way and he preached. ([Friedberg Report:] he expressed his regret at having made the mistake, thinking my time was the 3d Sunday, and asked me to preach, but it being his charge, I declined.)

Thurs., May 12. Friedberg congregation anniversary. Brother and Sister Bahnson present. Brother Bahnson kept the morning meeting and afterwards preached John 10:14: I am the good Shepherd. Afterwards Lovefeast, during which Brother Bahnson gave a brief outline of his western trip and the condition of the Indians. Then there was a meeting of the heads of families. Brother Mock read a statement of his year's work, and it was found that were some six dollars wanting to make up deficiencies. A subscription was circulated, and the amount raised. The grave diggers agreed to take away the dirt or put it all in for the same money as formerly. A vote was taken, Francis Fishel and Christian Earnest candidates. Francis Fishel was re-elected. Brother Rights's subscription was also circulated and some added.

Tues., June 7. Preaching at Macedonia. . . . Afterwards elected two additional Committee men, Richmond Sheek and Joseph Hodge, then tried to settle some difficulties between Calvin Riddle and David Wheeler but failed. ([Friedberg Report:] an effort [was] made to expel David R. Wheeler from the Church on the ground that he was a mean man and a stumbling block to the Church and the world, a difficulty having sprung about between Wheeler and Riddle as to who should have the key of the Church, Wheeler having it in possession, and Riddle demanding it. Wheeler refused to give it up.)

Sun., June 12. Whitsunday. I went to Bethania to celebrate the Centenary Jubilee, it being a hundred years since the consecration of the first and fifty years since the consecration of the last church.

Wed., Aug. 3. The Brethren Daniel Spach, Sen., Wm. Shore, David Spach (Daniel's), and Chr. Spach's black boy Hamilton cleaned out the [well?]. They took out 18 toads; some of them were dead. Brother David Spach went down.

Sun., Aug. 7. [A]t 9 o'clock P.M. left Salem for High Point with our son Theodore. He is going to Nazareth Hall. He is 13 years old today. It was hard to give him up, but hope it will be for his good. On the way a plank broke at a bridge, but we escaped without injury.

Mon., Aug. 8. Theodore took the cars at 4 o'clock A.M., and I returned to Salem by ten.

Mon., Sept. 12. Went to Salem, and from there to Davie County after Bro. Stephen Morgan Smith. Arrived at his father's after night, and learned that he was at Macedonia at a prayer meeting. I went over, and as the meeting had begun I did not go in immediately but sat down on a bench outside, and directly someone began to pray. I recognized the voice; it was Stephen. And it occurred to me how little does he think that this may be the last prayer that he may *ever* offer here or at least for some time. I afterwards went in, spoke and prayed, and after the meeting was dismissed spoke with Br. Smith, and then returned to Brother Hall's.

Tues., Sept. 13. Went to Salem with Stephen M. Smith.

Wed., Sept. 14. Went to Br. Chr. Spach's to bid Wesley farewell.[1] We united in singing and prayer.

Sat., Dec. 11 [10]. Meeting of heads of families [at Friedberg], and a subscription for a new graveyard fence.

Private Dairy of R. P. Leinbach, 1859
[Serving Friedland; extracts transcribed.]

[In March 1859 Br. and Sr. Cooke made plans to move to Bethlehem, Pennsylvania. From March 20 to mid June, Friedland was served by Thomas Frye, the minister of New Philadelphia. To fill the pastorate at Friedland, Provincial Elders Conference called Robert Parmenio Leinbach, a native of Salem who had been educated at Nazareth Hall in Pennsylvania.]

Wed., June 15. Evening 7 o'clock, I was ordained by Br. Peter Wolle at Salem, N.C.

---

[1]Both Stephen Morgan Smith and Wesley Spaugh were going to the theological seminary in Bethlehem, Pennsylvania.

Thurs., June 16. Married by Br. Bahnson and immediately set out for Friedland.

Sun., June 19. Br. Bahnson introduced me to the congregation. At 2 P.M. Mr. Eli Hine's child was buried, Br. Bahnson officiating.

Sun., July 3. Commenced Sunday school with about 18 scholars.

([Friedland Report to Ministers Conference:] Having been in charge of this congregation but a brief period, and then only during the busy season, which did not admit of much visiting, our report must naturally be but meagre and unsatisfactory. The number of members, according to Br. Cook's last year's list, amounts to 49, of whom 34 are communicants. We have visited some 8 or ten families and have always been kindly received. Not knowing the average attendance at church, we are unable to form any estimate at the present time. Sunday School was opened last Sunday morning with about twenty scholars. The school will if possible be organized next Sunday. The prospects of a flourishing school are very encouraging. There appears to be desire on the part of the parents to send their children, and with proper encouragement the latter will by and by be brought together in considerable numbers. Friedland July 6, 1859.)

Thurs., July 7. Went to Salem to [Ministers] Conference.

Sun., July 10. Taught several songs in Sunday School. This seemed to attract scholars, as they came in large numbers. Sunday School officers were elected: Pres. Rev. R. P. Leinbach, Vice Pres. Br. Em. Reed, Treasurer Br. Gibbins, directors the brn. Lowder, Steward, Sills and Hege. My dear wife was unwell this afternoon. Went down to the School House to hear Br. Long preach. Closed the services with address and prayer.

Sat., Aug. 13. Br. and Sr. Bahnson came down about 10 o'clock. At 11 he kept the first meeting, delivered a very appropriate address giving a brief historical sketch of the day commemorated, as also some very practical remarks. After a brief delay, lovefeast followed. Our good old Moravian tunes were sung by Moravians only from Salem. Communion succeeded. Br. Bahnson behind the table. I served out the elements. After the first prayer, which was very earnest, Mrs. Steward, a non-communicant but present by request, gave vent to a passionate outburst of feeling, rushing to and embracing her daughter and others present. Mrs. Eli Weevil, a

Methodist sister, sought to relieve her overcharged feelings in a succession of shrieks. After some disturbance they were quieted. The clouds threatening rain, most of the people remained until after the storm. In consequence of this little fuss in communion, the members desired a prayer meeting in the evening, thinking to revive the flame. Tho' it rained, quite a number came.

Sun., Aug. 14. Br. Long preached for us and did his utmost to revive yesterday's revival or more properly excitement. Fortunately it was in vain. Rain in the afternoon again. My heart was often sick and sad about the state of affairs here. We were such a small band in the midst of these people, it seemed so pitiful and so different from what we were used to. It was truly disheartening. I had been invited by Br. Long to assist him in his service, but excused myself on the plea of damp weather. Was glad I did not go.

Tues., Aug. 16. A day I shall never forget. We went to visit Br. Reed's. My poor dear wife was there taken with severe chill and fever. She could scarcely return to Friedland. She was very sick, tho' I little dreamed what it was. It was the beginning of consumption, which today, Feb. 15, 1860, is far gone towards its fatal termination. She and I came to Salem next day, where she is now, sick in her father's house, which she will not leave until she is conveyed to her last resting place!

Sun., Sept. 11. As a general thing attendance at church was very good. Every Sunday some new faces showed themselves, drawn doubtlessly by the reputation of the Sunday School, which was growing.

Mon., Sept. 19. Sister Lucia[1] and myself went to Friedland to bring up various articles [to Salem]. On our return we found my wife had a high fever. On this day the Dr. gave her some strong medicine which checked the fever for a while.

Sun., Dec. 4. Went to Friedland, very rainy, and found no one there. Built a fire, dried my clothes and then returned.

Wed., Dec. 14. It having been agreed upon to celebrate Xmas with as much eclat as possible, it was resolved to have Xmas cakes, candies and candles distributed to the scholars.

---

[1]Lucia Josephine Foltz Shultz, sister of Sophia Constantina Foltz, wife of R. P. Leinbach.

Br. Gibbins found us a gallon of molasses. Sister Anne[1] and Mother and mother Foltz found the flour and baked the cakes.

Sat., Dec. 24. At 2 o'clock we had our lovefeast. Thro' the kindness of Sr. Justina Stockburger, who made our candles, and Aunt Regina, who trimmed them, they cost us nothing but the price of the wax. The children and parents seemed all much pleased with the feast. The decoration gave general satisfaction.

[New] Philadelphia Reports, 1859
With Macedonia and Muddy Creek after April
[Extracts transcribed; handwriting is that of Thomas Frye.]

Sun., Mar. 20. Went to Friedland, was introduced to that congregation by Br. Bahnson, and preached for the first time in that church to a tolerably large congregation, though not so attentive as we could desire. . . .

Sun., Mar. 27. Was the time appointed for the baptism of Calvin T. Jones. . . . Br. Bahnson, who was invited before, officiated. He also before the ordinance of baptism preached from Acts 2:38 on the subject of baptism to the great satisfaction of all present so far as we've learned save one man who "loves much water in baptism."

Sun., June 12. Preached my farewell sermon at Friedland from Acts 15:29 to a small but attentive congregation.

Sun., Aug. 21. Attended at Muddy Creek with Br. Bahnson, who was going to preach and just as he had given out a hymn and we commenced singing two unmannerly dogs present commenced fighting, but there was a man of good order in the assembly who soon parted them by the application of his cane after which we united in singing and prayer, which after it was over Br. Bahnson preached an appropriate sermon to a large congregation of tolerably well behaved people from Matt. 22:14 which we hope will result in good.

[*Tues., Sept. 27.*] Late at night Mr. Petticord sent for me to instruct him and sing and pray with and for him, notwithstanding his peculiar notions of immersion and dunkardism and denunciation of Moravian and Methodism.

---

[1]Anne Elizabeth Clauder, wife of musician Edward W. Leinbach, brother of R. P. Leinbach.

1860

[Garabaldi's "Red Shirts" conquered most of Sicily and southern Italy. In the Far East, British and French troops seized Peking and burned the royal palace in a dispute with China over trade agreements.

In April the Pony Express began deliveries between St. Joseph, Missouri, and Sacramento, California. In November Abraham Lincoln won the presidential election. South Carolina seceded from the Union on December 20.

North Carolina gave its electoral votes to John C. Breckinridge. The federal census counted the state's population at 992,622, including 330,000 slaves.]

Memorabilia of Salem Congregation, 1860
[Extracts transcribed; handwriting is that of Francis Raymond Holland.]

[W]hile the Lord has dealt bountifully with us in granting health and plenty, and continuing to us all the elements of material prosperity, the apprehensions which rested like a gloomy cloud upon the minds of the thoughtful and observant at the beginning of the year have not only remained undissipated, but have become more dark and gloomy; and we cannot conceal from ourselves the mournful fact that we are now, through the madness of political strife between two different sections of our country, in the most fearful and perilous crisis which has occurred in our history as a nation. The triumph of a sectional majority in the election of their candidate to the presidency has strained to the utmost the cords which during three-fourths of a century have bound together our growing republic—if indeed it has not already caused them to part asunder forever.

This year, like several of its predecessors, has been distinguished by remarkable revivals of religion in various parts of the world. Our own church in several portions of her widely extended mission field has also shared the blessing. In Australia an awakening has taken place among the degraded aborigines, for whose benefit our brethren have been laboring a number of years, which has resulted thus far in the baptism of the first convert of that nation, and which promises yet greater results. In Jamaica an extensive and remarkable work of grace, such as has probably never been witnessed to the same extent in any of our missions, has taken place. In Mosquitia the field of labor has greatly extended itself, while new invitations are still given to come and preach the gospel, and the self-denying labors of the missionaries have been crowned with an encouraging degree of success.

In regard to our own congregation we have great cause, notwithstanding our numerous shortcomings and aggravated offences, for thankfulness that we have been favored with so many tokens of the loving-kindness of tender care of our merciful God and Savior, who has granted us the help of his Spirit and the support of his grace. The different festivals of the church have been duly celebrated, and at stated seasons the table of the Lord has been spread in our midst. Doubtless many a soul has at such times experienced a season of refreshing from the presence of the Lord. Though we cannot speak of striking results or of a great ingathering into the church, yet we can confidently indulge the hope that the seed sown has in some instances fallen upon good ground.

The colored division of the congregation has enjoyed the stated ministrations of the word and sacrament, and all the services have been marked by a good attendance and orderly deportment. The evening meetings during Passion Week, which were this year for the first time held for the colored people in their own house of worship, were particularly well attended, and evidently not without a blessing. The church edifice presently used by the colored people, having become too small to accommodate the increasing number of hearers, measures were taken for the erection of a new and more commodious one. To the application for subscriptions a liberal response was made, and the prospect is entertained that in the course of next summer the house will be erected and completed. During the year eleven persons were admitted to full membership, viz., 6 by baptism, 4 by confirmation, and 1 by certificate. Three communicants have departed this life, 4 non-communicants, and 2 children. Two children were baptized, and 4 couples married, The number of communicants is 39. The Sunday School numbers from 50 to 60 scholars, and the stated hearers are at least 150.

During the year our institutions for education have continued in the even tenor of their way, enjoying the gracious blessing and protection of the Lord. Among the very large number of pupils in the Salem Female Academy, very good health has prevailed. One pupil, however, was removed by death, viz., Miss Caroline Robinson of Alabama.

On June 17th Br. James Haman of West Salem, Ill., was ordained a deacon of the United Brn.'s Church, and on Sept. 16th the brn. Jacob F. Siewers, John A. Friebele, Thomas Fry, and Robert Parmenio Leinbach were ordained presbyters, by Br. G. F. Bahnson, Bishop.

During the year the various benevolent operations of the church have been sustained, at least to the same extent as in former years. The Female Missionary Society, the Young Men's Missionary Society, the Home Mission and other Societies have manifested their usual activity.

It remains to be recorded that throughout the year our place and neighborhood have been exempted from distress by fire and water, hail-storms, tornadoes, and other providential visitations. Several brethren experienced a merciful preservation of their lives on occasion of the bursting of the steam boiler at a saw-mill in town on Jan. 23d.

Salem Diary, 1860
[Extracts transcribed; handwriting is that of Francis Raymond Holland.]

Sun., Jan. 8. Holy Communion today. Small attendance on the brn.'s side. It is said that much bad feeling has arisen in consequence of the party spirit manifested at the borough election last Monday. Probably the political excitement of the last congressional election has had much to do with it.

Tues., Jan 10. Streets of Salem this evening were generally lighted with gas. Several lamps were ready and lit before the close of last year, but this evening, it is believed, was the first time that all the lamps at present to be put up were lit.

Sun., Jan. 22. The Rev. Mr. Bernheim, a minister of the Lutheran Church, preached. Br. Bernheim's object in visiting Salem was to collect funds towards the building of a Lutheran college at Mt. Pleasant, Cabarras Co., N.C. According to br. B.'s statement the Lutherans have contributed very liberally towards this object, and with a little assistance from public-spirited individuals they hope to place the college on a sound and permanent foundation.

Mon., Jan. 23. Br. Bernheim left at 10 A.M., collected in Salem and Winston $90, exclusive of $50 subscribed by Smith, a Lutheran member residing near Salem.

Shortly after 8 A.M. the steam boiler at Fries' saw mill exploded, dangerously scalding and wounding the colored fireman. Five or six other persons employed on the premises had a most providential escape. The boiler was thrown across the street, falling just behind a passing wagon driven by Br. Wm. Ackerman. Considering all the circumstances, it is wonderful that no more persons were injured.

Sun., Feb. 5. Br. Parmenio Leinbach this evening commenced keeping meetings—to be held weekly—for the factory people. A room for this purpose has been granted by Mr. Patterson, the proprietor of Wachovia Mills.

Mon., Apr. 16. The gas fitters being engaged in the church this week, there will be no evening meetings.

Mon., Apr. 30. Prayer meeting 7 1/2 P.M. Commenced reading from *Fraternal Messenger* Br. Connor's report of the revival at Gracefield [Gracehill?], Ireland.

Thurs., May 3. Annual meeting of Forsyth Co. S.S. Union. Only 9 or 10 persons present.

Sun., May 6. The congregation was . . . informed that Br. Bahnson, in consequence of the nomination of Bishop made by the Provincial Synod of 1858, having been confirmed by lot, would set out for Bethlehem (D. V. [God willing]) on tomorrow to receive an episcopal consecration. We joined in commending our brother to the favor of the Lord by singing several benedictory verses.

Sun., May 13. Litany and preaching by Br. Holland. In the evening Br. Grunert kept an address in memory of Count Zinzendorf, it having been on May 9th 100 years since the decease of this distinguished servant of Christ in the Brn.'s Church.

Sun., May 20. Br. Holland preached at 3 P.M. at "Double Bridges" school house on the road to Bethabara. A Sunday School has recently been organized there. The Brn. Henry Fockel and John Hege, members of Bethabara Congregation, have been active in building the house and organizing the school. A numerous congregation had assembled, and great attention prevailed.

Wed., June 6. The evening meetings having latterly been poorly attended, the Board of Elders agreed at their last meeting to drop them for the present. This evening a prayer meeting was kept for the young men in the chapel. About 15 or 20 were present.

Sun., June 10. At 8 P.M. Br. H. preached for the factory people in a room fitted up by Mr. Patterson in one of his buildings, where service has been conducted for some time past by Br. P. Leinbach and others. The room was well filled.

Sun., June 17. At 8 P.M. Br. Bahnson ordained Br. James Haman a Deacon of the United Brethren's Church. Br. Haman, being at present here on a visit to his mother, will leave in a few days for his field of labor at West Salem, Ill.

Mon., June 18. Commenced taking subscriptions for the erection of a new church for the colored people to be erected on the old Negro graveyard lot.

Tues., June 19. Visited Br. David Blum and notified him that on account of his persistent refusal to pay his church dues he is considered as having withdrawn himself from the membership of the church.

Wed., June 20. Board of Elders met. The trombone band asks for an exemption from paying church dues as an acknowledgment of their services in playing at funerals. Board considered the request reasonable and will communicate it to Board of Trustees. The minister was directed to see whether the old custom of announcing deaths from the steeple by the band could not be revived.

Wed., July 4. The day was celebrated in various ways, according to the taste of different individuals. At 10 A.M. there was preaching by Br. Holland to a large audience.

Mon., Aug. 6. Monthly missionary prayer meeting at 71/2 P.M. Remembered especially: the mission in Australia, from which the cheering intelligence has been received that a work of grace is going on among the natives, of whom one, a youth named Pepper, after giving such evidence as leads to the hope of his being truly converted, has applied for baptism.

Wed., Aug. 8. The Board of Trustees, at their meeting last evening, voted an appropriation of $500 towards the erection of a new church for the colored people. They also agreed upon a plan of the building, which it is estimated can be built for about $2,400. Improvements in the plan may, however, be suggested and carried out, with the consent of the Board. The subscriptions thus far amount to about $1,800, viz., from individuals $900, Salem Female Academy $250, Female Missionary Society $150, Salem Diacony $500.

Fri., Aug. 17. The Children's festival celebrated this day. The festival was well attended, as usual, and nothing can be cited to distinguish it favorably or unfavorably from the festivals of years past, possibly of those within the memory of the present generation.

Sun., Aug. 26. Celebration of Single Brn.'s festival. The different meetings for this division of the congregation were very well attended, but few being absent. This was also the case in regard to the Lord's Supper, from which only seven of the Single Brn. at present in Salem were absent from any cause whatever, and of these four were known to be detained by sickness. May the services of this day have proved a blessing and encouragement to all who attended them!

Mon., Aug. 27. Br. Holland was invited by the Board of Trustees to meet with them this evening in order to concert measures for erecting the new church for the colored people. A committee was appointed, consisting of the Brn. S. T. Pfohl, T. F. Keehln, and Holland, who are to contract and make all necessary arrangements for the erection of the church.

Sun., Sept. 16. At 7 P.M. the Brn. Jacob F. Siewers, John A. Friebele, Thomas Fry, and Parmenio Leinbach were ordained presbyters of the Church of United Brn. by Br. G. F. Bahnson, Bishop.

[Handwriting is now that of George Frederic Bahnson.]

Sun., Sept. 30. A collection taken at the church doors after the morning services amounted, with other small sums added, to $47.00. It is destined for the benefit of the church built at Egg Harbor City, N.J.

[Handwriting is now that of Francis Raymond Holland.]

Sun., Oct. 7. Br. Holland, having returned from a visit of 2 weeks at Mt. Bethel, Va., was unable to keep any meetings today on account of hoarseness, etc., from a cold recently contracted. Br. Bahnson preached morning and evening, and Br. Grunert attended to the colored charge.

Sun., Nov. 4. Preaching at 10 A.M. by Br. Sylvester Wolle, principal of the Bethlehem Female Boarding School, who is at present making a visit of several weeks duration at Salem.

Mon., Nov. 5. 7 P.M. monthly missionary prayer meeting. Remembered and commended to the Lord: *our Country.*

Tues., Nov. 6. Presidential election passes off quietly and orderly.

Sun., Nov. 18. At 7 P.M. the Rev. Mr. Mann, minister of the Methodist Episcopal Church at Winston, preached.

Sun., Nov. 25. At 10 A.M. Litany and preaching by Br. Bahnson. At the same hour Br. Holland preached in the Methodist Church at Winston. At 1 P.M. Sunday school, which was very well attended. Mr. Schaefer of Petersburg and Mr. Kemp of Baltimore, both actively engaged in S. Schools at their own homes, having dropped in to see the school, upon request addressed the scholars.

Thurs., Dec. 13. Br. Wm. Holland, father of the writer of this diary, fell asleep in Jesus at 1/2 past 11 o'clock P.M., aged 70 years, 9 mos., 24 days.

Mon., Dec. 24. At 41/2 P.M. was the Lovefeast for little children, well attended. The church has been tastefully decorated with wreaths, and garlands of evergreens. The Lovefeast at 7 P.M. was very numerously attended. Very good order prevailed throughout.

Diary of the African Church in Salem, 1860
[Extracts transcribed; handwriting is that of Francis Raymond Holland.]

Sun., Jan. 22. Communion, 36 colored communicants present, 5 or 6 being Methodist.

Sun., Feb. 5. Wet afternoon. S.S. at 2 P.M. About 40 scholars present. Opened with prayer by Benj. Atwood, the only male teacher present. The srs. Rebecca Stauber, Leana Shaub, and Martha Vogler taught their classes as usual. Sr. Denke could not attend, owing to the slippery state of the streets.

Fri., Apr. 6. Good Friday. At 2 P.M. a good congregation assembled to hear the account of the day. Br. Leinbach conducted the service. On Monday evening Br. Bahnson had read, on Tuesday Br. Grunert, on Wednesday evening Br. Bahnson. Good order and attention prevailed.

Sun., Apr. 8. Easter. A large congregation assembled on the graveyard at 9 A.M. when the Easter Day litany was prayed. Immediately afterwards a sermon was preached in church on the history of the day. The house was too small to contain all the people.

Sun., Apr. 22. At 2 1/4 P.M. Communion lovefeast and immediately thereafter the Lord's supper; 25 colored communicants partook. Seven candidates for membership were present as spectators, viz.: Giles and Peter (Fries), Ben (Zevely), Jane (Clemmons), Susan (Waugh), Katy (Lash), and Epsey (Hege).

Sun., May 6. Br. Holland preached at 3 p.m. on the miracle of feeding the 5,000. Announced to the Congregation that Henry (Webb), having brought a certificate of membership from the Methodist Church at Winston, wants in future be considered a member here. Also that, in addition to William (Hamilton), the brn. Alex. (Vogler) and George (Fries) have been appointed elders for one year from today.

Sun., June 17. Br. Holland preached on the summary of the law, Matt. 22:37-40. Attendance rather small. It is reported that Henry Fries has hired hands to cut wheat today on the pretext that it might spoil if the harvesting were deferred!! This in part accounts for the slim attendance today.

Sun., June 24. Baptism and confirmation in the large church. Two adults, Ben (Zevely) and Peter (Fries), were baptized, and 4 confirmed. The latter were Epsey (Hege), Katy (Lash), Betty (Shepperd), and Ned (Lemly).

Sun., July 15. Lord's Supper celebrated this day, 27 colored communicants present. Father Byhan also partook with us. The newly received members, with the exception of Betty (Shepperd), were all present as partakers for the first time.

Sun., July 22. Br. Massa Warner being here on a visit from Philadelphia and intending to remain till sometime in September, has consented to superintend the S. School. He accordingly made a beginning today. The brn. Gustavus Sussdorff, Lewis Eberhard, and Ben. Atwood, after an absence of some weeks, today again took charge of their classes.

Sun., Aug. 26. Br. H. preached on Matt. 9:36, etc. During the month, the Tuesday evening lectures were regularly kept with the exception of one evening. The singing on Thursday evenings was also attended to by Dr. Keehln and wife.

Sun., Sept. 2. Br. Massa Warner, intending to return to Philadelphia this week, closed his labors in the S.S. to our great regret. There being camp meeting at Maple Springs, the attendance today was small. Preached on the Scripture point of Timothy taught by his mother, putting frequent questions to the children, which were readily answered. Both adults and children by this means were kept quite attentive.

The services for the remainder of the month [of September] were regularly kept, except on the last Sunday in the month, when they were omitted, owing to the lovefeast [in the white church] kept on the festival of the Holy Angels.

Sun., Oct. 28. Preaching by Br. Holland. Attendance on this last day rather small, owing to "big meeting" at Winston, where also the Lord's Supper was celebrated, and which in compliance with the customary invitation was also enjoyed by a number of our communicants.

The lectures on Tuesday evenings were regularly kept throughout the month [of November]. Also the singing on Thursday evenings, conducted by Dr. Keehln. The attendance at all the meetings has been good, and the deportment quiet and orderly.

Salem Congregation Council, 1860
[Extracts of minutes transcribed.]

Mon., Jan. 9. Present 36 members. Chairman of Committee on enlargement of the Church stated that not having held any formal meeting he had therefore nothing further to report, and at the same time would beg leave that said Committee be discharged from further duties. Motion made, seconded and carried that they be discharged.

Board of Elders of Salem Congregation, 1860
[Extracts of minutes transcribed.]

Wed., Jan. 25.

2. The present Negro church (building) and the desirableness of having a better one, was spoken of.

Wed., Mar. 28. Br. Bahnson absent.

1. Br. Holl. reported that he had spoken with D. Blum, who appeared somewhat inclined to look at the matter in a different

light, and declared he had never said that he would not pay in future if the past was cancelled. The Board thought that before going further, this answer should be reported to the Board of Trustees.

4. The new Ode for Great Sabbath was presented for inspection.

Wed., May 9.

The Congr. Council having re-elected br. Grunert, and having elected br. Fulkerson to fill the vacancy created by br. Bahnson resigning his seat, the Board met for the first time as now constituted.

Wed., May 23.

2. A communication from the Board of Trustees was read, stating that they cannot exonerate Dav. Blum from paying his just church dues. Br. Holland will inform him now that unless payment is made, this Board cannot but look upon him as having withdrawn from the church.

6. The funeral sermon of Bettie (Fries), lately deceased, and a good member of the Negro church, will be preached on Sunday after next in the large church, the Negro church being too small. The Board could see no sufficient reason why funerals of Negro church members, under the circumstances, should not be kept at the large church, especially when a considerable number of white people may be expected.

Wed., June 6. Br. Fulkerson absent.

2. Dav. Blum has finally declared that he will not pay his dues. He has consequently withdrawn from the membership of the church, and the case will be mentioned to the members on the next suitable occasion.

Wed., June 20. Br. Rob. Schweinitz absent.

1. Br. Holland reported that Dav. Blum is not satisfied, and declares that he does not withdraw, etc. The Board thought that the public announcement need not be immediately, but the Board of Trustees is to be informed.

2. Br. Holl. stated that the leader of the so-called "Church Band" called on him to state the difficulty of getting the members together on every funeral occasion: that they would be ready to do so, however, if they could be, in consideration of

their services, exonerated from their church contributions. It was suggested that this might be a good opportunity for re-introducing the good old custom of announcing the departure of a member of the church by the performance of hymn tunes from the steeple, which has been given up for several years. The matter must be laid before the Board of Trustees, recommended by this Board to their favorable consideration.

Wed., July 25. Brn. R. Schweinitz and Fulkerson absent.

1. It was . . . stated that the church band, encouraged by liberal subscriptions towards purchasing new instruments, will in future perform the tunes prescribed for the announcements of departed members of the church.

Wed., Aug. 8.

2. The Board considered the case of those town girls, who are not children any more but continue going to school. The discussion, which took a wide range and touched the necessity of setting the schooling of all the town girls upon a different footing, resulted for the present in the passage of the following resolution, viz.: Those girls that are 14 years old and over are to go to a different Bible class and not to the town girls' room anymore before meetings.

Wed., Aug. 22. Br. Fulk. absent.

1. The reading of the minutes brought the town girls up again. The spirit prevailing among them was lamented, as evidenced by their conduct in and out of meeting, although it might be difficult to bring specific charges against individuals. It is also a matter of regret that when the great girls' room and great girls' Choir were abolished, nothing was devised in place of it. Those older girls who are not yet communicants cannot be properly attached to the single sisters, and the suggestion was made to have a particular festival or prayer day for them about the 4th of June. No action was taken.

Wed., Oct. 31. Br. Fulk. absent.

3. Br. H. brought to the notice of the Board the rule laid down by the Board of Trustees some time ago and communicated to the Congregation Council on May 1st, refusing peremptorily the burying of any person on our graveyard who at his death is not a member of the congregn. This rule has

produced already much bad feeling in the case of Julius Kern, and other cases may occur at any time. The Board thought it advisable to draw the attention of the Board of Trustees to this matter.

The absence of several brethren on Nov. 7th prevented a meeting on that day, and a conference with the Board of Trustees having been suggested, such meeting took place on Friday Nov. 9th, in which the graveyard rule was fully discussed and the lovefeast question spoken of. (Minutes to be found in the minutes of the Board of Trustees.)

Tues., Nov. 13.

A called meeting of the Board was held, caused by David Blum's departure the night before, and the request for a grave on the graveyard. The Board passed a recommendation to the Board of Trustees, to grant this request, which was subsequently done after rescinding the rule.

Wed., Dec. 12.

2. In regard to the bad conduct of the young men, the Board thought that a statement publicly made of complaints made for being disturbed, connected with an admonition to those whom it may concern, would be proper; also that the front benches on the men's side, which now stand north and south, be placed again as formerly, parallel to the others. Concerning this latter arrangement br. Holl. will speak with br. Pfohl.

3. The Board did not see proper to abolish the Christmas lovefeast without having the opinion of the Congregation Council, and even if this should be in favor of the measure, it would be very doubtful whether the majority of the members of the church were of the same opinion.

4. The second week in January will be very generally observed as a week of prayer for the coming of the Kingdom of God, and prayer meetings on every evening will be held here also.

Fri., Dec. 21.

The meeting was called for the purpose of considering the application for readmission of Alex. and Antoinette Vogler. Granted.

The following names were taken off the list as absentees, viz.: James Payne and Eugene Clewell. Dietrich Tavis has withdrawn from the church.

Fri., Dec. 28.

2. The propriety of having a prayer meeting daily in the afternoon during the week of prayer beginning Jan. 6th was acknowledged, particularly for the benefit of such as may be unable to attend at night.

Board of Trustees of Salem Congregation, 1860
[Extracts of minutes transcribed.]

Wed., Jan. 25. Full Board.

1. The "County Board of Valuation" having beginning of this year assessed all the land belonging to Salem Diacony not included in the [incorporated] town plot at $40 per acre (formerly $20), thereby increasing the valuation of the land given in by $30,000, Board of Trustees consider this valuation too high, in as much as a not inconsiderable part of the land thus valued consists of cleaned land (partly worn out) and is furthermore cut up by a number of public roads. It was therefore resolved that we apply to the County Board for redress at its next meeting on the first Monday in April, according to §13 of the revenue law of N. Carolina of 1858-59.

2. Board next entered into a free discussion on the expediency of selling the different fields and outlots now held in lease or rent by sundry individuals in the vicinity of town, but without arriving at any conclusion for the present, resolved to meet again for further consideration of this subject on next Monday evening.

Mon., Jan. 30. Full board.

1. Application was made by Br. Jacob Rothhaas for permission to have his grandchild (a daughter of Mr. and Mrs. Thomas Faircloth, not members of our church) buried on our graveyard, which permission was rather reluctantly granted on condition that he pay $5 for keeping the grave in order and that he furnish a tombstone.

The above application gave rise to the following resolution which was unanimously adopted by the Board:

"Whereas one of the means that induced the Diacony to encourage the laying out of the Cemetery to the east of the Moravian Church Graveyard, and to take for the ground a mere nominal price, was to make the Moravian Graveyard exclusively a Congregation burying ground; and whereas this has not heretofore been formally spread on the minutes of this Body:

"Therefore resolved that from this time forward the said Moravian Graveyard in Salem be kept for the interments of members of said Moravian Church and none other, with the single exception of teachers or pupils in the Salem Female Academy or in the Congregation Town Boys' School."

This resolution is to be communicated to the Congregation Council at its next meeting.

2. Board next again took into consideration the sale of fields and outlots near town. But altho' unanimous in the opinion that such fields and lots should be sold, and that it would be to the advantage of the Diacony to do so, it was finally resolved for the present to lay the subject on the table, for the reason that it would be preferable before those fields and lots pass beyond the control of this Board to ascertain the locality of the contemplated railroad from High Point to Germanton, this Board being of opinion that if such a road is really built and should pass thro' our lands, then the Diacony should for the benefit of the community in general and of our town in particular grant the right of way thro' its lands, which object might in a measure be defeated if the fields and lots were now sold to private individuals.

Tues., Feb. 7. Not present Br. Francis Fries.

2. It appearing from the action of the last Congregation Council that the idea of enlarging our Church has been abandoned for the present, and as the building stands in need of repairs at different places, the Brrn. Cooper and Pfohl were requested to examine its condition more fully and then report to this Board.

At the same time the subject of introducing gas lights into the Church was bro't before this body, and the above named committee was also requested to take this matter into consideration and report on the subject.

The question was also asked whether in case the Church is supplied with gas, the same should be done with regard to the Pastor's dwelling?

3. Br. Charles Clauder who has thus far tended the organ bellows for $12 a year, asks for an increase of salary, and Board resolved to raise it to $15 with an extra compensation of $5 for his attendance at rehearsals of music.

Mon., Mar. 5. Not present Br. Fulkerson.

3. The committee appointed on Feb. 7 to take into consideration the introduction of gas lights into our Church and Chapel reported that in their opinion the arrangements could be made very conveniently and without a very great expense. . . . Board resolved that this plan be carried into execution. It was further resolved to introduce gas fittings into the Diacony houses occupied by the Pastor and the Warden.

5. A letter from Br. Wm. S. Leinbach, now living near Bethania, in which he intimates that a remuneration for services rendered to the congregation as a musician during a course of 36 years, would be thankfully accepted by him, was communicated to the Board. Altho' Board fully appreciate the services that Br. Leinbach may have rendered in this line, still they do not feel authorized to grant the petition before them, as that would open a door for applications from a number of individuals who have in former days devoted their time and talents in a similar manner for the benefit of the Congregation.

7. Br. David Blum having, upon application from this Body, refused to give a note for his Congregation or Church account now due and amounting to about $130 and likewise refused to contribute anything in future, on the plea that Diacony was largely indebted to him by transactions had in 1843 to 1845, which assertion is, however, not admitted as correct by this Body, Board resolved that this declaration on his part be reported to the Board of Elders for their further action according to the rules of the Church. But in as much as the family, i.e., his wife and younger children, appear attached to the Church and to appreciate their privileges of membership, it was resolved that we exonerate Sister Blum from paying her portion of church dues, as under existing circumstances it might be impossible for her to do so.

Tues., Mar. 20. Not present the Brrn. J. Fulkerson and Theod. Keehln.

3. A communication from the Board of Elders was next laid before the Board, in which they state that it appears desirable to them that some rules should be made for the regulation of burials in the new cemetery for coloured people, which has been recently laid out and appropriated to that especial purpose, in conformity to a resolution of the Church Committee, adopted in their meeting of Apr. 5th, 1859, and embraced in §4 of the minutes of that date.

In compliance with the request of the Board of Elders, and in accordance with certain suggestions contained in their communication (which see amongst the documents) Trustees passed the following resolutions respecting the burial of coloured people on their new cemetery:

Resolved, 1st that the right of burial on this graveyard, free from extra charges, be granted to all persons of colour that are members of the African Church at this place or whose master or mistress is a member of the Moravian Church at Salem, with the understanding, however, that the grave must be neatly sodded and the superfluous earth (remaining after finishing the grave) must be removed from the cemetery immediately after burial and not suffered to remain on the graveyard.

Resolved, 2ndly that other persons of colour may also be interred on this graveyard by complying with the conditions respecting the finishing off of the grave and the removal of the superfluous earth, as stated in Resolution 1st, and by paying the sum of $5 for each permission to bury on said graveyard. No permission is, however, to be granted before the stipulated price of $5 has actually been paid into the hands of the Pastor of the African Church, and by him handed over to the Warden, who will open an account upon his books for that purpose.

Tues., Apr. 17. Not present the Brrn. F. Fries and C. Cooper.

1. [T]he "County Board of Valuation" had upon representation from this Board reduced the valuation of the Diacony lands from $40 to $30 per acre, thereby making a difference of upwards of $16,000 in the total valuation.

2. The town of Winston applies for a building lot for the purpose of erecting a school house, selecting for that purpose either the N.W. corner of Cherry and North Street or the second lot north of Col. Gibson's on Church Street, offering to

take it either in lease with the understanding that they hereafter pay whatever price lots in neighbourhood will bring, or pay cash for it now. In case a railroad should cross the lot they would be willing to grant the right of way.

Tues., May 15. Not present the Brrn. F. Fries (absent at the north) and Chs. Cooper.

The term of service of the Brrn. Charles Cooper and Jacob Fulkerson as members of this board having expired on the 1st Tuesday of this month (see minutes June 14, 1859) and the Congregation Council having on that day elected the Brrn. Charles Cooper and Joshua Boner as members of the Board of Trustees for the term of three years, Board met and organized, agreeably to the revised rules, electing S. Thos. Pfohl as Chairman and Secretary for 1 year to the first Tuesday in May 1861.

1. [T]he application from the town of Winston for a lot (see last minutes §2) was again renewed, the locality now, however, being changed to a lot that would be situated on the east side of the continuation of Cherry Street, and immediately west of the lot in Winston now occupied by Hezekiah Thomas. Board upon further consideration resolved unanimously to grant the application, and appointed the Brrn. Pfohl and Theod. Keehln as a committee to attend to the laying out of the lot.

2. A communication from the Board of Elders respecting the case of Br. David Blum was next communicated, in which they say that Br. Blum, upon being spoken to regarding his refusal to pay his church dues, "proposed to pay punctually all future claims, but asks that the old claims should be dropped." Board of Trustees cannot understand how such an exception could be made in the case before them, without laying themselves open to similar applications from others that may also be more or less in arrears, and can therefore not entertain the idea suggested by Br. Blum.

Tues., June 12. Not present the Brrn. F. Fries and J. Boner.

1. A communication from Br. Fr. Holland as Pastor of the negro congregation in reference to the erection of a new church for the use of the coloured population of Salem and vicinity was laid before the board. Said communication contains in substance the following proposals, viz.:

1st: That the Board of Trustees grant the old negro graveyard as a site on which to build the new church.

2d: That the Board authorize the erection on said lot of a neat and durable church of such material and dimensions and after such plan, as having been submitted to the Board, shall be sanctioned by them.

3d: That the proceeds from the sale of the lot at present occupied by the church be applied towards the new building.

4th: That the Board make such further donation from the funds at their disposal as they may see fit towards the furtherance of the object in view.

5th: He proposes to collect by subscription the means required, in addition to the donation applied for, to render a faithful account of the monies received, and submit them to the order of the Board of Trustees, so that this Body may become the legal agent in carrying out the design.

Board after deliberation unanimously gave their sanction to the first and second proposals, substituting, however, the word *permit* for *authorize* in the latter; were, however, not prepared to adopt the 3d and 4th without having a more definite idea of the value of the property, and without first having viewed the premises and determined upon the size of a lot that might be sold with the old church. All the members present signified their willingness that this body give a liberal contribution from the funds entrusted to them towards the object contemplated.

Tues., June 26. Not present the Brrn. Fries, Cooper, and Keehln.

2. Since the last meeting of the Board the lot for the Winston Academy has been laid off. As said lot and another one of the same size lying to the north of it [#94 and 95] would form a complete block between four streets, the Company interested now make application for the north lot also. Board is willing to sell both the lots to them, thereby giving them a front of 200 feet on the east side of Cherry street by a depth of 183 ft.

It was proposed that the Commissioners of the town of Winston be requested to give names to their streets running from east to west for the purpose of designating the locality in that town more conveniently.

Mon., July 2. Not present Br. F. Fries.

3. The subject of laying out more building lots was next again taken up, and after some deliberation Board resolved, in

order to be able to act advisedly in the matter, to go on next Friday morning to view the several localities to the east and west of Winston, where it is thought desirable to lay out more lots.

Tues., July 10. (A.M.) Extra meeting of the Board. Not present the Brrn. Fries and Keehln.

Board met for the purpose of considering the application of the family of Mr. Julius Kern to bury his remains on our Moravian burying ground under the plea that he had formerly been a member of our Church, had separated from it only because he moved away from here and joined himself to another church merely for the purpose of being an active member of a Christian congregation, and that it had been his intention after his return to this neighbourhood to join this congregation again, but had been prevented from so doing by his decease taking place only a few days after his return.

Board, after hearing a full statement of the case, do not feel freedom to depart from the rule respecting burials on our Moravian Graveyard recently made and publicly announced to the Congregation Council (see minutes of Board of Trustees, Jan. 30, 1860, §1), as they consider a strict adherence to it the only way of obviating the difficulties under which they have laboured for many years with regard to such burials, stating at the same time that the only question to be decided on such applications will be that of *Membership of the Church*, which question can best be answered by the Pastor of the Church himself.

Tues., July 10. P.M. Not present the Brrn. F. Fries and Joshua Boner.

2. Board, according to previous arrangement, on Friday last viewed the localities designated in minutes of July 2, 1860, §3, and concluded to lay out another street running northwardly behind Mr. Gibson's lot [#134], on the east side of which street 3 lots of about 108 ft. front could be laid off between Belews Creek [Street] and North Street. ([Margin note:] See Oct. 30, 1860, §2.)

Board further resolved to continue Cherry and Elm Streets to the street running north of the lots laid out for the Winston Academy (which street is hereafter to be designated as Fourth

Street) and for the present to lay out lots only on the east side of these two streets.

Fri., July 27. Not present the Brrn. F. Fries and Theod. Keehln.

1. A letter from Br. Holland in reference to the new Negro Church led to a long discussion, and Board, without coming to any definite conclusion, resolved to resume the subject at its next meeting. Some of the members will in the meantime make an estimate of the cost of a plain but neat and substantial building of the size required.

Tues., Aug. 7. Not present Br. F. Fries.

1. A communication from the Board of Elders, stating that a request had been made by the Trombone Band to be exonerated from paying their church dues on account of services rendered on funeral occasions, and which request was now recommended by the Board of Elders to the favourable consideration of the Board of Trustees, was laid before the latter Board. Trustees resolved that the regular performers of the Trombone Band be exonerated from paying the Church dues so long as they announce the death of a church member by blowing from the steeple and also render the usual services at funerals. The amount for which each of them shall be exonerated shall be the annual contribution required from an unmarried brother. This regulation to go into operation from August 1st.

Board further granted a donation of $15 to the Salem Brass Band towards the purchase of new instruments, with the understanding that the death of a member of the church be announced by blowing of church tunes from the steeple, as had been customary heretofore.

2. A plan and estimate of cost of a new Negro Church was laid before the Board by the Brrn. Vogler and Seitz. According to this plan the building would be 40 by 60 feet and the hall 18 feet high with an ante-room of 10 feet and a gallery of the same depth, 10 windows of $3_{1/2}$ by $9_{1/2}$ ft. and two smaller ones in the recess of the pulpit. The building to be surmounted by a cupola or belfry of sufficient size to answer its purpose. The church to be constructed of brick, walls and ceiling plastered, and the space from the floor to the windows ceiled with boards. The estimated cost of such a building would be about $2,300.

The plan here submitted was based upon one sent in by Br. Holland at the last meeting of the board, but which was tho't to be too expensive for the means at command. At the same meeting Br. Holland also sent in a communication stating that he had succeeded in procuring subscriptions from individuals to the amount of $900, from Female Missionary Society $150, from Salem Female Academy $250, further pledges from individuals in case the money is needed $400, making in all $1,700.

In addition to the above he relies on a handsome contribution from this Board, on a donation from the Sustentation Fund, on a further appropriation from the Female Missionary Society of a good portion of their invested capital, provided it be needed, and on the promise of several individuals (who have already subscribed liberally) to do more if necessary, in order to erect a substantial, ample, and creditable edifice. So that he is of opinion that $2,500 could be raised.

Board approved the plan laid before them, and appropriated $500 from the part of the Salem Diacony towards the erection of that Church, 5 members voting for it, and Br. E. A. Vogler refraining from voting, because he had understood that in consequence of the action of the Provincial Elders' Conference making the care of the negro congregation part of the duties of the Pastor of the Salem Congregation, it would be expected that in future the expenses of said church would fall upon and have to be defrayed by Salem Diacony, against which construction he, for his part, would protest, and consequently was not prepared to vote a donation towards the erection of the new church until a proper understanding was had on the subject.

Mon., Aug. 27. Not present the Brrn. F. Fries and E. A. Vogler.

Br. Fr. R. Holland present by invitation.

Board met for the purpose of taking the necessary steps towards the erection of the New Negro Church, as, according to the statement made by Br. Holland both verbally and in previous communications to this body, there is every reason to believe that the necessary amount will be contributed to defray the expenses of the building. Board therefore elected S. Thos. Pfohl as Treasurer, to take care of the money subscribed for this purpose, Br. Holland signifying his willingness to collect the subscriptions and pay them over to the Treasurer.

As it was tho't expedient to give the execution of the plan into the hands of a more limited number than the whole of this body would constitute, a building committee was appointed for that purpose, consisting of the Brrn. Holland, Thos. Pfohl and Theod. Keehln, with power to have the building erected either by contract or otherwise, as they may think most expedient.

Tues., Sept. 4. Not present Br. F. Fries.

1. [I]t was resolved that this Board request the Provincial Elders' Conference to inform us what action they have taken in regard to the Negro Congregation of this place and what their views are with regard to the expenses necessarily connected with its maintenance, no official information ever having been made to this body, if their views really are that in future the Diacony of Salem will have to bear the expenses of that Church also.

Mon., Sept. 24. Not present the Brrn. F. Fries and Theod. Keehln.

1. A communication from the Prov. Elders' Conference in answer to the questions addressed to them in relation to the Negro Congregation (see § 1 of last minutes) was read to the Board.

In this communication, after some historical details, the Prov. Elders' Conf. return the following answer to the questions proposed, viz.:

1. The coloured congregation has been given over to Br. Holland as part of his charge.

2. Prov. Eld. Conf. does consider that it is henceforth to be looked upon as part of Salem Congregation.

3. Salem Diacony can, however, NEVER become responsible for the financial maintenance of the coloured congregation, without the consent of the Board of Trustees of Salem Congregation.

This communication gave rise to various remarks on the part of the Board of Trustees, indicating that the opinion of the members did not in every point touched upon agree with that of the P.E.C., but in as much as no demand for pecuniary assistance was now before them, it was not tho't necessary to enter further into the matter at this time.

Tues., Oct. 16. Not present the Brrn. F. Fries and J. G. Seitz.

1. At an informal meeting of the Board held on the 2nd inst., 4 members inclusive of the Chairman being present, permission had been granted for the erection of a speaker's stand and arrangement of seats for an audience in the woods between Col. Gibson's lot and Aug. Fockel's plantation for the purpose of keeping a mass meeting of the Whig and Union Parties. The use of the two lots on the muster ground still held by the Diacony was also granted for the purpose of preparing a barbecue and giving a special entertainment on the occasion. The committee of arrangements will see to it that dead timber that may be cut down for the purpose of making seats will be sold after having been used by them and the proceeds paid over to the Diacony.

Application was now made for the use of the stand and seats for a Democratic mass meeting to be held on next Tuesday, which application was granted by the Board, the committee of arrangements of the Whig and Union Parties having given their consent already.

5. Mr. I. G. Lash wants an ice house built on the Bank lot, for which he is willing to pay an additional rent. Board resolved that his wish be granted.

Mon., Oct. 22. Not present Brrn. F. Fries and C. Cooper.

1. The yearly accounts of Salem Diacony, as also the statement of assets and liabilities of the same, from May 1, 1859, to Apr. 30, 1860, were laid before the Board. The receipts in that time amounted to $4,305.12 and the expenditures to $6,468.51, showing an apparent deficit of $2,163.39, occasioned, however, by deducting $2,135 of principal and interest from the debt of Charles Brietz.

The receipts from the sale of Town lots, viz., $764.05 were added to the Town Lot Fund, which now amounts to $11,316.99.

As there appears a credit of $335 on the School account (accumulated in the course of several years), it was proposed to transfer as much of that credit to Repair account as has been charged on the latter to Apr. 30 for repairs at the Boys' School premises, viz., $177.83. The balance of expenses for repairs at said premises will appear in next year's account. The item of

$50 paid on Church account for training of musicians for service in Church music led to the remark that some of the Board had understood that no instruction had been given during the summer and had only been again commenced within a few weeks, contrary to the agreement with Br. Edwd. Leinbach, whilst the salary had been regularly paid him for the whole time. Chairman was requested to speak with him on the subject and ascertain how the case stands.

2. The accounts of the Single Sisters Diacony, owing to the sale of part of the property to the Female Academy, showed receipts amounting in all to $10,200.32 and the expenditures to $5,155.39, leaving an excess of receipts of $4,944.93, which amount is to be added to the reserved fund. (The above expenditures include the cost of the new kitchen and wash house and alterations necessarily connected with the new arrangement.) The cash remaining in the hands of the agent or Warden, after the winding up of the former arrangement and after payment of all debts, amounting to $5,900, has been put out on interest at 6% into hands that are considered as perfectly reliable. The notes due the Single Sisters Diacony now amount to $10,061.16, of which, however, $2,400 draw no interest.

Tues., Oct. 30. Not present Br. F. Fries.

2. The town lots to the west of Winston will now be laid out as soon as the corn has been gathered in. Board is of opinion that the front of the lots between the back street (nameless) of Winston and Elm Street (which will be only about 145 ft. in depth) should correspond with those of Winston situated on Salt Street, as it is presumed that the owners of the front lots would buy those lying immediately behind their lots, and as there appears to be some idea of abandoning this back street of Winston and giving the land to the occupants of the lots on Salt street.

Br. Charles Brietz, having now procured a lot, will not wish to purchase one back of Gibson's, as he had contemplated doing. It was consequently resolved for the present not to lay out any in that neighbourhood.

3. Board then had a conversation respecting the sale of the fields on the Shuman plantation, but came to no decision on the subject, and will resume the consideration at its next meeting.

4. Board came incidentally to speak of certain irregularities that have crept into our Lovefeasts within the course of the past summer, it having become customary for strangers staying at the hotels indiscriminately to attend them, contrary to existing regulations made by the Congregation Council. Considerable misbehaviour by a number of them has been remarked, and Board thinks it proper to lay this subject before the Board of Elders and to ask them whether they do not think it better that a change be made and some of the customary lovefeasts, such as Great Sabbath, Christmas, etc., be omitted if the evil cannot be remedied.

Fri., Nov. 9. Joint meeting of the Board of Elders and the Board of Trustees. Not present the Brrn. F. Fries and C. Cooper.

S. Thos. Pfohl was appointed Secretary for the occasion.

1. This joint meeting of the two Boards had been called at the instance of the Board of Elders in order to take into consideration a rule or regulation adopted by the Board of Trustees regarding burials on our Moravian Graveyard, by which rule burials were strictly and exclusively confined to persons belonging to the Moravian Church and to pupils and teachers in the Salem Female Academy or in the Congregation Town Boys' School.

Various objections were raised on the part of the Board of Elders against this rule, based chiefly upon the grounds that under a rule like this cases could not but occur that would most deeply wound the sensibilities of families or members of the Congregation, thereby causing a hardness of feeling against the Congregation itself and eventually estranging them from it.

On the part of the Board of Trustees it was urged that in making this rule it had been the desire of the Board to draw a line of distinction at the only point where in their opinion it could be done, and that for years already the Board had laboured under the greatest perplexities whenever an application for interment of one not a member of the Church was before them, not having any distinct rule by which to regulate their actions in the premises, and in consequence frequently laying themselves open to the accusation of favouritism on the part of others.

After a long and friendly interchange of ideas the subject was left in the hands of the Board of Trustees for reconsideration.

2. The Board of Trustees having drawn the attention of the Board of Elders to the attendance of strangers at Lovefeasts, a conversation on this subject ensued, which, however, led to no definite results.

Tues., Nov. 13. Not present the Brrn. F. Fries and E. A. Vogler.

2. Board next turned its attention to the rule adopted on Jan. 30, 1860, regarding burials on our graveyard, to practical working of which its attention had been directed by the Board of Elders as stated in the minutes of Nov. 9th.

Board of Trustees, convinced by the reasons assigned against the rule, as also by their own observation as regards the impressions produced by its enforcement, and not wishing to uphold any regulation that might possibly prove injurious to the welfare of the Church, the motion was made to repeal the rule adopted on Jan. 30, 1860, regarding burials on the Moravian Graveyard (see minutes of Jan. 30, 1860), which motion, after being seconded, was adopted unanimously.

3. The application of the relatives of Mr. David Blum to bury his remains on our graveyard was next laid before the Board, accompanied by a communication from the Board of Elders recommending the granting of the request, as the case of the deceased was a peculiar one (owing to difficulties that many years since had taken place between him and the then authorities of the Church, and to more recent occurrences by which according to the rules of the Church he had to be considered as having withdrawn from the membership of the Church), and as a refusal to grant this application might seriously disturb the peace and harmony of the Congregation, as well excite needless prejudices against the Church. Board upon deliberation and after viewing the peculiar circumstances of the case granted the request by a unanimous vote.

Tues., Dec. 11. Not present the Brrn. F. Fries and C. Cooper.

1. Application was made for a lot in Winston for the purpose of erecting a Presbyterian Church on it. The locality asked for is on the western side of Cherry Street, fronting and

thereby shutting up 4th Street, as it is not tho't necessary to continue that street further than Cherry. Board granted the application. . . .

Provincial Financial Board, 1860
[Extracts of minutes transcribed.]

Tues., Jan. 17. All the members present.

1. An application of Br. J. F. Siewers, minister of Bethabara Congregation, for the meadow and upland heretofore held by Henry Hughes was laid before the Board. On motion the application of Br. Siewers was granted on the following conditions: The meadow and upland are given to the Bethabara minister for his use and benefit for a term of two years, provided the Bethabara Congregation makes the hay, keeps up the fences and cultivates the upland free of all expense to the minister, and the use of the land, etc., be considered in lieu of the $50 heretofore annually paid to the minister by Sustent. Diacy. Board resolved that the house and lot in Bethabara returned by H. Hughes should be sold, and recommended Wm. Flynt as a suitable agent to effect a sale. A payment of $3 to Joseph Butner for ditching the meadow was sanctioned by Board.

2. As some of the Country Congregations are indebted to Salem Congr. Diacy. for communion bread and congregational accounts furnished them for a long series of years, and as these congregations have no means of paying, it was resolved that Sustent. Diacy. assume these debts, and from the 1 of Jan. 1860 pay the sum of One Dollar per annum, for which all the Country Congregations are to be furnished with communion bread from Salem. The debts thus assumed by Sustent. Diacy. are:

for Bethany	$20.75
for Bethabara	36.33
for Friedland	2.70
for Hope	0.20
Total	$59.98

Wed., June 13. Absent Francis Fries.

1. The Treasurer stated that the house and lot in Bethabara had been sold for $60 cash to Dr. Beasly.

2. Br. J. F. Siewers, to whom the resolution of Board concerning the land and meadow (see Minutes of Oct. 27, 1859 [Jan. 17, 1860], §1) had been communicated, on the part of Bethabara Congr. some time ago made the following proposition: "Bethabara Congr. promises to pay the minister $25 in cash, to make the fences, and to have the hay made on shares, the minister to get the half of it stacked in the meadow and to rent out the upland, the minister to get 1/3 of corn delivered at Bethany." Board, considering this proposition to be perhaps more advantageous to the minister than the original resolution, agreed to it.

3. Br. J. F. Siewers has made application to P.E.C. for assistance. Bethany Congr. agreed to pay him $178 per annum. On the 20 May 1860, 3 years had expired since his arrival at Bethany, and on that day the Congr. owed him $166. As Br. Siewers is entitled to $300 per annum and has received only $178 from Bethany and $50 for Bethabara, he has fallen short of getting the above amount by the sum of $72 annually. Hence Board resolved that $186 be granted to Br. Siewers, which sum makes up the deficit to Jan. 1, 1860. At the same time Board urge upon Br. Siewers the absolute necessity of using every means in his power, especially by bringing this whole matter before the Bethany Committee, to collect the arrears due him and to have the whole matter of the minister's salary properly regulated according to the enactment of the Provincial Synod.

8. Br. Bahnson proposed that an annual appropriation be made for a Provincial library, chiefly for the use of the country ministers. The consideration of this matter was postponed till after the annual accounts have been submitted by Treasurer.

Wed., Aug. 8. Fr. Fries absent.

1. The Treasurer of Wa. Sustentation Diacy. submitted the annual accounts and statement to May 31, 1860, to Board. The sum total of receipts, including a contribution from S.F. Acady. of $1,000, was $3,471.08, and of payments $3,583.14, leaving a deficit of $112.06. On May 31, 1860, the assets amounted to $37,627.32, of which sum $32,690 are at interest. The actual liabilities were $445.65.

Thurs., Nov. 15. Fr. Fries absent.

1. Br. Parmenio Lineback proposes, instead of having his old carriage repaired, to exchange it, with the consent of the Board, for a good second-hand carriage, which can be got for $75. He hopes to be able to sell his old carriage for $20. On motion it was resolved that the Brn. S. T. Pfohl and E. A. Vogler examine the old carriage and the one proposed to be purchased, ascertain their respective value, and report to the Board.

Bethania Diary, with Bethabara, 1860
[Excerpts transcribed; handwriting is that of Jacob F. Siewers.]

Sun., Jan. 8. After praying the Litany preached at 10$1/2$ A.M. on Matt. 2:1-12 and gave notice that an invitation had appeared in the *New York Observer*, from the Lodianno Mission of the Presbyterian board in northern India, recommending the observance of the 2d week in January as a period of united prayer that the Lord would pour out His Spirit upon all flesh, that in consequence there would be a prayer meeting held in the church at early candle light. After dinner went to Mickey's S. House, and preached at 1 P.M. on the above. In the evening held the above meeting, a short discourse on the Doctrinal Text of the day, Acts 16:14, with prayer.

[Br. Siewers kept prayer meetings throughout the week at Bethania "at early candle light."]

Fri., Jan. 13. The weather and roads are so unfavourable that the meetings have been slimly attended.

Sat., Jan. 21. Rode to Bethabara and met the Heads of Families, all present but J. Hege. The object of the meeting being the election of a new Committee and grave digger, we proceeded to ballot. The following brethren were elected: Abraham Shemel by 5 votes, John Hege by 4 votes, and Thomas L. Spach by 4 votes. On the 3d ballot br. Christian Hauser was elected by 4 votes. Br. William Pratt was elected grave digger by 5 votes. There were but 7 br. present. Br. Spach then read the church accounts and gave a satisfactory statement of the appropriation of the funds by receipts in hand from the various persons dealt with. Br. Pratt and Christian Hauser agreed to drop their claims on the church. Br. T. Spach had a claim of $10.83 against the church for Sacrament wine and

other matters, and br. Chris. Hauser a claim of $2 cash out-
lays. This sum was equally divided among the members, all
agreeing to pay their part, excepting br. John Shore, who pled
that he had not attended the church for several years, hence
would not pay any past debts. They then each contributed 50
cents for a fund to defray current expenses.

Sat., Feb. 11. Finished the church accounts to be laid before the Heads of Families tomorrow.

Sun., Feb. 12. At 10 1/2 A.M. preached at Bethania on Luke
23:42-43. At 2 P.M. administered the Lord's Supper to 44
communicants. Afterwards Heads of Families met, 19 present
without the chair. They then proceeded to ballot for a new
Committee. On the first ballot the following brn. were elected:
Sol. Pfaff 13 votes, H. H. Butner by 12, Daniel Butner by 15
votes, Joseph Transou by 12 votes, William Leinbach by 10
votes. The Committee then proceeded to elect the 6th member
and br. Martin Holder received 14 votes. Br. Transou was
prevailed on to accept the office of Steward for one year, and
was elected after being nominated. As the Steward is entitled
to a seat in the Committee by his office, it was moved and
seconded and unanimously carried that L. S. Grabs be elected
in his place. The following brn. were then nominated and
elected as sextons: Daniel Butner, Levin S. Grabs, R. Oehman,
Wesley Kearney, and J. B. Chitty.

There was no meeting held in the evening.

Fri., Feb. 17. Afternoon Sr. S. and myself visited at Pratt's;
he had called to see me in the morning while I was from home.
He is much distressed in mind for fear of a dissolution of the
Union, and war as the consequence. Ever since the Harpers
Ferry tragedy his mind seems almost wandering.

Sat., Feb. 18. Afternoon the newly elected Committee met at
the parsonage, and transacted their business. The letter from
the brethren of the P.E.C. was read to them, but no definite
action had on it.

Sat., Mar. 3. Rode down to Bethabara and met the Heads of
Families at 1 P.M. Read the letter from the P.E.C. concerning
the duty of congregations to provide support for their ministers. Also the proposition from P.E.C. in reference to a certain
meadow. They agreed to pay $2 per family to the preacher, and
they would try and make up $25 annually. They further agreed
to fence the meadow, and hire out the hay making on shares,
the minister to have half. The upland John Shore undertook to

cultivate and give one-third of corn to the minister and deliver it.

Thurs., Apr. 5. [Maundy Thursday.] At 2 P.M. reading, and after an interval administered the Lord's Supper, 53 communicants partaking. Towards the close the meeting was disturbed by several rising and going out, and finally abruptly broken up. Fire had got out of some fields and was spreading in the woods around some of the adjoining plantations.

Sun., Apr. 8. Assembled in the church. The hymn "Hail, All Hail Victorious Lord and Saviour" was sung by the congregation, and a prayer offered. We next proceeded to the graveyard, where, arriving before sunrise, we prayed the Easter Morning Litany, the Brass band of this place taking part in the solemnities. A larger number of black folks attending than usual. At 10 A.M. preached on John 11:25, good attendance. The meetings held the past week were very well attended. After dinner went to Bethabara and after praying the Easter Morning Litany, preached on the above text.

Fri., Apr. 20. Went with br. Thornton from house to house, and he sold some $9 worth of books of the Tract Society publications.

Sat., Apr. 28. Rainy. This afternoon little George Winkler, Emelia's son, arrived here from Salem. He had been sent by his mother to Old Fries's plantation for tomato plants, returning took the wrong road and came here. I took him home in my conveyance.

Sun., Apr. 29. Widows Festival. At 10 A.M. held the morning blessing; there were but 8 attending the services. Immediately afterwards preached on John 21:15-17 to a small congregation. At 2 P.M. we had the lovefeast, and shortly after, the Lord's Supper. The weather being unfavorable, few widows attended. Meetings were held all around us, and at Stauber's School house a Missionary and Campbellite Baptist preached today. The latter has had meeting there yesterday and the day before.

Mon., May 7. John Shore and son kindly ploughed the parsonage orchard for me, and with help I planted it in corn.

Fri., Sat., May 18, 19. Worked on the lot opposite the parsonage and elevated the front square by filling it up to prevent the water from flowing over it, both from the front and alley.

Sat., May 26. Towards evening by request, after a shower of rain, buried the newborn infant of Mr. Richmond, who resides at present in this place. This is the sixth infant he has lost.

Sun., May 27. After dinner went to go to Spanish Grove, and passing through Pfafftown, took br. Peter Pfaff along, but we were brot to a halt near the head of the oil-mill, the rain falling in torrents, accompanied with severe lightning, thunder, and wind. I was so wet from the rain drifting into the front of the carriage, we abandoned the route and whenever the wind lulled a little, returned, and thus after several halts we got back to Pfafftown.

Sat., June 2. Mrs. Richmond is said to be very low, and Sr. S. went in the evening to see her and resolved to stay with her overnight. About 3 A.M. I was awakened and requested to offer a prayer at her bedside, with which I complied, and during which she breathed her last.

Mon., June 11. My brother sent his servant Rich to plough my corn, in consequence of which I did not go to the Home Mission meeting.

Mon., June 18. Visited at E. Beck's; his wife has a little boy, and is doing well. There were 14 years between the last children.

Fri., June 29. Ephraim Transou and family arrived here last night on their return from Texas, having left here last September. They lost their elder son, whose widow came back with them. They do not give a very flattering description of that state.

Sat., June 30. Miss Steiner and Miss Vogler from Salem called here and spent the day with us, and Sr. Denke on her return also called and took vesper here; our Margaret after a stay of a month with us returned with above company to Salem.

Fri., July 6. Returned home towards evening with Flavius Lash, who had arrived from Nazareth Hall. We had very dark and threatening clouds before us, which caused me to push the horse rapidly forward, and we had hardly time to get the horse and carriage under shelter before a most terrible storm of hail and rain burst upon us. How thankful we were that we had reached home in safety. The ground was covered and white with hail. There were several panes of glass broken, above in the house where there are no shutters, and some 16 panes broken in the church windows. The trees before the house and church no doubt saved the windows from a general smash. The water poured into the house from various quarters.

Sat., July 7. This morning we became first fully aware of the damage the hail caused. The corn around and in town, looks pitiful, all our garden vegetation, oat crops, peach and apple trees, and grape vines show the power and fury of the storm. Last evening everything looked so promising, and now all is desolation.

Sun., July 15. After meeting br. Levin Grabs informed me that there was very little hope entertained for the recovery of Peter Pfaff.

Mon., July 16. This morning went to Pfafftown, and found br. Peter Pfaff sitting in his front porch, apparently as well as ever. He had obtained some ice from L. Grabs and upon applying it the strangulation was removed. He felt a little weak, otherwise well.

Tues., July 17. Today the candidates for the Legislature and the Sheriff's office spoke in town. Remained at home.

Wed., July 18. Remained at home. I have been these days . . .

Thurs., July 19. . . . at home engaged in reading Chalmers . . .

Fri., July 20. . . . . likewise Lectures on the Romans.

Sat., July 21. This morning my brother arrived from Salem, and communicated the happy intelligence of Elisabeth's safe delivery of a son. Mother accompanied John home to remain some days with E.

Thurs., Aug. 2. Election Day for Governor, Legislature and Sheriff.

Fri., Aug. 17. Visited at John Shore's, afterwards went to Bethabara and took home my share of the potato crop raised in the garden, nearly 4 bushels.

Sun., Aug. 26. At 10 A.M. preached at Bethania on 1 Tim. 1:15 to a small audience. After dinner went to Spanish Grove and preached to a full house.

Sun., Sept. 2. Owing to the camp meeting at Maple Springs, I dropt the appointments here and at Bethabara, and went with Sr. S. to Hope with a view of meeting Br. Rights and accompanying him to Macedonia, where a protracted meeting was being held. Brother R. arrived about 11 A.M. and by his request I preached on John 3:16 to a small audience. We took dinner at Christian Sides, and about 4 P.M. left for John Hall's by Clemmonsville, where we after some detention at the ferry arrived at sunset and were kindly received.

Tues., Sept. 4. Still cloudy and rainy. Went with P. Lein-back in his buggie to meeting and preached at 11 A.M. on Luke 15:11, after which I returned, and after dinner started home.

Sun., Sept. 16. Children's Festival. Morning blessing at 9 1/2 A.M. Preaching at 10 A.M. on John 14:6. Afternoon lovefeast, 53 present. Some 13 children sang 5 pieces from the choir. After lovefeast Sr. S. and myself went to Salem. At candle light in a public meeting br. Bahnson ordained the following brn. presbyters of the Moravian United Brethren's Church, namely Thomas Fry, John Friebele, Parmenio Leinbach, and Jacob F. Siewers.

Sun., Sept. 23. Protracted meeting at Mickey's School House. There was a large congregation here today and their behaviour good.

Fri., Sept. 28. Sr. S. and myself went to the Mickey's School House and found a good audience, the house full. Closed these meetings with the prayer that the Lord would bless the efforts made this week by his servants and make them effective in the conversion of souls.

Mon., Oct. 15. After night, while going down the cellar for a candle, I made a false step and fell. Fortunately I threw out my hands and caught on the floor of the entree, thus breaking the fall and saving myself from a great danger, but hurting myself seriously in my back.

Sun., Oct. 21. [W]ent to the Dutch meeting house, where I was invited to preach a child's funeral. The parties not appearing on account of sickness, and the Lutherans holding at the time a protracted meeting here, I was solicited to make a discourse to the converts and penitents, with which I complied.

Mon., Oct. 22. Went with Sr. S. by br. John Alspaugh's invitation to Mount Tabor and preached there at 2 P.M. on Gen. 32:24, etc., to a full house.

Thurs., Oct. 25. I understand the protracted meeting at the Dutch meeting house closed last Tuesday evening, having lasted 11 days, 40 converts having professed.

Sun., Oct. 28. No service at Bethania—protracted meeting. The church could not contain the audience.

Tues., Nov. 6. Presidential Election.

Fri., Nov. 30. The weather beginning to be cold and a number of panes of glass being broken in the church and parsonage windows by the hail storm last summer, I went in company with Sr. S. to Salem to get glass, putty, and a diamond to repair them.

Mon., Dec. 3. [A]t br. Edwin Schultz's gave him the small edition of br. Peter Wolle's tune book, and as he can sing by notes, he promises to become a good help to aid in introducing our tunes in the country.

Tues., Dec. 4. Sr. S. and myself visited at br. and Sr. Pratt's; their daughter Caroline, who was married to Mr. Nichols, had a daughter some weeks ago and is suffering very much from a sore breast.

Sat., Dec. 15. Last night snow fell to the depth of 5 or 6 inches. Made roads or paths in the yard and around the church.

Mon., Dec. 24. At early candle light held the usual Christmas Evening meeting. Opened by a piece from the choir by the children, 15 or 16, mostly girls, then a hymn was sung by the congregation, followed by prayer and short address. Lovefeast for the children was then served, the choir singing several pieces. Candles brot in, whilst the choir was singing, "Christ the Lord, the Lord most glorious." Closed by rising and singing, "Praise the Lord God from whom all blessings flow."

Tues., Dec. 25. Christmas. Sr. S. and myself went to Bethabara. Preached at 2 P.M. to a good audience on Luke 2:14. At early candle light held the lovefeast, full house. Returned home.

Sun., Dec. 30. Snow and rain, no service.

Mon., Dec. 31: Cloudy and miserable under foot. I did not go to Bethabara. About 8 P.M. we had the lovefeast at Bethania; there were several pieces sung by the choir. In spite of the high water and miserable roads there was quite a number in attendance. At $9 1/2$ the Memorabilia was read, and at $11 1/2$ the last meeting took place. After 12 a prayer was offered, and the Text of New Year's Day read. Thus closed this eventful year, with heavy clouds lowering around the destiny of our Beloved Country. May God, our God in Mercy spare us from the fearful results of Disunion and Civil War, and cement us again in peaceful Brotherhood, and Christian Bonds as a nation.

Friedberg Diary, with Hope, 1860
[Extracts transcribed; handwriting is that of Christian Lewis Rights.]

Sun., Jan. 1. On account of its being the Sabbath the annual custom of renewing the subscription for the support of the minister was deferred till another time.

Tues., Jan. 3. The coldest morning we have had for several years, according to the thermometer. At Salem they are housing ice, the second crop this winter.

Tues., Jan. 24. ([Friedberg Report:] Buried Mr. David Hage at Friedberg. He was in Hickory and Moravian, but I don't suppose he has heard a sermon in ten years except at the funeral of his son five years ago. I preached from Isaiah 55:1-2: Ho, every one that thirsteth, etc. Some of the friends seemed to take exception because I said some people raked and scraped and delved all their days, never went to meeting nor contributed a cent for the cause of God, and when they were dead it was expected that the minister should preach them to heaven. They said it was too personal.)

Sun., Jan. 29. ([Friedberg Report:] Our Sunday School seems to be reviving with the beginning of the year. It has been better attended during the month than for some time previous, and preaching has been well attended, not only by our own people, but by strangers living at a distance. The graveyard subscription is progressing, and by Easter it is hoped the new fence will be made. On account of the bad weather I did not go to Macedonia, but learned that the typhoid fever is prevailing considerably in that neighborhood.)

Fri., Feb. 17. Preaching at Macedonia. . . . ([Friedberg Report:] I left Brother Hall's about sundown for home. When crossing the river, Harry predicted I would not get home, for said he, "It will [be] dark as pitch," and dark it was. At Hope my horse turned off from the road and got me into the pine woods, and it seemed as though I could neither find a road nor get through for the trees. After feeling round, I found where it appeared to be trodden. I got in the sulky, and went some distance when the horse stopped. I got out and felt round and found him with his nose against Brother Ball's gate. I went to the house and remained till morning.)

Mon., Mar. 12. ([Friedberg Report:] Set off for Good Hope afoot, as I had engaged a hand to plough and my horse was needed at home. After walking 4 miles, half way, I passed my friend, Dr. Shelton. He asked where I was going. I replied to Good Hope. What, walk there and back? Certainly. How comes that? I remarked, I and my horse have concluded to divide the labor; I do the preaching and he the ploughing, and when I get rich like you, I'll keep two horses. The Dr. laughed and called to his boy to bring me a horse, and an excellent animal he was. I mounted him and went on my way.)

Tues., Apr. 3. Today we had a good turnout, 80 persons being present, and the new fence around the graveyard was nearly completed. The palings and railings were all planed off, and the work is neatly and substantially done.

Sat., Apr. 7. Great Sabbath. Attended the Communion at "New Philadelphia" with Bro. Thos. Fry. On my return I was thrown from my sulky, but was not much hurt.

Fri., Apr. 14 [13]. Preaching at Macedonia. . . . Afterwards there was an election for a portion of the Committee, the 2 years for which three of the Brethren had been elected having expired. The same brethren were re-elected, viz.: Calvin Thomas Riddle, Daniel Sheek and Edward Lee. The Committee, therefore, are the Brethren Joseph Hodge and Richmond Sheek, elected in July 1859, and the Brethren Edward Lee, Daniel Sheek and Thomas Calvin Riddle, [elected] this day, April 14th [13th], 1860, for two years from this time.

Sat., May 5. In the afternoon Committee meeting. ([Friedberg Report:] After the business on hand was finished, the Chairman [Br. Rights] reminded the Brethren that this was the last time they would meet, as the 2 years for which the present Committee was elected would expire on the 12th of May, when there would be a new election; and then proceeded in a brief review of the labors of the past two years, and concluded by tendering his thanks to the Brethren for the promptness manifested on their part in meeting here for the transaction of business when called upon, and the spirit of "Brotherly Love" and forbearance exercised towards him and one another, when we were here together; and whatever the issue of the election might be, his wish and prayer was that the labors of the new Committee might prove as harmonious as that of the present had been. Brother William Shore arose and said that although it was getting late and some of the members had a considerable distance to their homes, yet he desired to say a few words in reply to what had already been said. He for one esteemed it a privilege to have been permitted to be an humble co-laborer in this body and could say with truth that the meetings of the Committee had been a blessing to him. He had felt again and again that the Lord was in our midst and that it was a good thing for "Brethren to dwell together in Unity," and whether it would [be] his lot to be again associated with this body or not, he would ever desire to cherish the pleasing associations connected with our meetings here. The Brethren then united in singing "When Brethren dwell in unity," closing with prayer.)

Sat., May 12. Congregation anniversary. ([Friedberg Report:] Election for a Committee, which resulted as follows: Edward Foltz, communion steward, Solomon Tesh, lovefeast steward, Daniel Spach, sen., chapel servant. Committee: Christian Spach, Jesse Mock, William Shore, Solomon Hage, Henry Perril, John Kanauss, and Benjamine Spach, sen. It was determined by the Church Council that hereafter the number of Committee members should be seven instead of five, which makes the whole number ten.)

Sat., May 26. Mr. Edward Spach put up a lightning rod at the west end of the Church.

Sat. June 2. Friedberg Committee meeting. This was the first Committee meeting since the election and a good deal of business was transacted. Brother William Shore was again elected treasurer. He tendered his thanks to the Brethren for this renewal of their confidence, as he has held the office for four years, and [he] urged upon the Committee to [do] all in their power to further the welfare of Friedberg Congregation. Brother Rights mentioned that since our last meeting brother George F. Bahnson had been consecrated a Bishop of the United Brethren's Protestant Moravian Church at Bethlehem, Pennsylvania, on Sunday, May 13th, 1860, and that since his return to Salem, it has pleased the Lord to remove by death another member of his family. Whereupon it was resolved that the Committee in behalf of the Congregation tender to Brother Bahnson its congratulation upon his recent consecration as a Bishop of the United Brethren's Protestant Moravian Church, and especially as for the time being Bishop and President of Wachovia or the Southern Province, and the Committee further desires to tender its sincere sympathy in view of the recent bereavement in the removal by death of a beloved daughter out of Brother Bahnson's family, and that Brother Rights is hereby requested to tender to Brother Bahnson a copy of this resolution, and the same be recorded upon our minutes.

Fri., June 15. Preaching at Macedonia. . . . Then Committee meeting. Joseph Hodge, William Ward and Jacob Danner are accused of having been intoxicated, and the Committee [resolved] that they be spoken with and requested to appear on the next meeting day and clear up the matter or be excluded from the Church.

Sun., Aug. 5. I learned that Sr. Libengood had been bitten by a snake, and after preaching [at Hope] visited her. She is still suffering from the effects of the bite but is improving. At night brother Edmund de Schweinitz from Philadelphia preached at Friedberg. . . .

Mon., Aug. 6. I carried our daughter Alice to Salem and put her in the Female Academy.

Sat., Aug. 18. Celebrated the children's festival [at Macedonia]. There were about 50 children and 70 persons in all.

Sun., Sept. 16. Celebrated the 33d anniversary of the Friedberg or Charity Sunday School. The Sunday School was organized on Sunday, Sept. 16th, 1827.[1] In the evening we went to Salem where the Brethren Seivers, Fry, Frebely and Leinbach were ordained Presbyters by Bishop G. F. Bahnson.

Sun., Sept. 23. Opened the Sunday School and distributed some papers and cards among the children, a present from a lady in Salem.

Sun., Oct. 21. ([Friedberg Report:] The house [at Pleasant Fork] was crowded almost to suffocation, and by the time the services closed my clothes were saturated with perspiration, and before I reached home I was taken with a chill and pain in my side from which I have been suffering ever since.)

Sat., Dec. 15. Yesterday evening about 8 o'clock it commenced snowing and snowed all night, and as that is our communion day there were but few present. The snow is between 3 and four inches deep.

Mon., Dec. 31. A disagreeable morning. Snow during the night. Started for Hope by way of the South Fork bridge. The waters were up. Middle Fork it was nearly breast deep to my horse. There were only about a dozen present at the meeting.

----

[1]Friedberg's Congregation Council authorized the forming of a Sunday School on Sept. 16, 1827. The organizational meeting was held Sept. 30, 1827, with 17 members joining and a constitution adopted. See *Records of the Moravians in North Carolina*, v. 8, p. 3827.

Private Dairy of R. P. Leinbach, 1860
[Serving Friedland; extracts transcribed.]

Sun., Jan. 1. Snow on the ground. Very cold and hard to get along. Got as far as Shepperd's, and found myself compelled to turn back. Found out afterwards there had been no one there.

Fri., Jan. 13. Afternoon visited, in company with Mother and old Mrs. Fries, Mrs. Wright down the country, who had long been afflicted with an awful cancer in the face and who, tho' of notorious character, speaks like a most orthodox Christian.

Sun., Feb. 12. During the whole winter the Sunday service was below par. Singing school in the neighborhood contributed to thin our audience sadly. Indeed the attendance here cannot be depended on. Every novelty draws the people.

Mon., Feb. 13. Went down to Friedland after our furniture, bedding, etc.

Tues., Feb. 14. Went out for remainder. Monday a new fence was built around the graveyard. By some misunderstanding members of other denominations assisted.

Sun., Feb. 19. Never can I forget with what a very heavy heart I used to go down to Friedland on Sunday morning. Sickness of my dear wife at home and the state of affairs down there—discouraging in the extreme—combined to render my situation far from enviable. My labors were not heavy—far from it—but circumstances rendered them very trying.

Tues., Mar. 27. Br. Bahnson and myself started out on visitations, going first to Nissen's, where Sally, who had joined the missionary Baptists, told Br. Bahnson the time might perhaps come "when he too would have himself immersed."

Sun., Apr. 22. The Sunday School has been in a languishing condition for some time past. Last Sunday there was not a single female teacher present—all gone to the Baptist singing school. Mother Lowder and Sr. Sally Weevil assisted in teaching.

Sun., May 27. ([Friedland Report:] Conduct in Sunday school improved. The previous Sunday upwards of 600 verses had been recited. This Sunday several hundred were again added to the list.)

Sun., June 10. There having been complaint of the S.S. teachers as well as scholars in regard to conduct, I determined

Public Meeting at Winston,

On December 29th, 1860.

A Meeting of the citizens of Forsyth County, irrespective of party, will be held at Winston, on Saturday the 29th of December, inst., at 11 o'clock, a. m., to take counsel together on the alarming condition of the country. South Carolina has seceded from the Union. Commissioners from Alabama, and Mississippi are now at our State capital inviting North Carolina to do the same thing. A great question is now before the people,—no less than Union or Disunion.

Believing that there is safety in the voice of the people, all our fellow-citizens, without regard to party, are earnestly invited to attend.

MANY PEOPLE.

December 20th, 1860.

With South Carolina already seceded in December 1860, notice was given to citizens of Forsyth County, North Carolina, of a meeting to debate the fate of the Union.

to separate them in different rooms in the house. The plan works very well as far as conduct is concerned, but as was anticipated, the number of scholars has diminished, those who coming merely to see and be seen absenting themselves.

Sun., June 24. Audience good and attentive except some young folks who excited my ire by the[ir] misconduct, in consequence of which I finished off my remarks by a general attack on all misdoers in church. ([Friedland Report:] Not many present in Sunday School, as Br. Long preached down at the School House. He closed his year's labor there with something of disgust.)

Sun., July 1. ([Friedland Report:] Preached to a large and orderly congregation composed for the most part of young people. The older members of the congregation have not as yet returned to their allegiance, and 'tis somewhat uncertain whether they ever will.) All this time my poor dear wife has been steadily growing worse. She suffers very much from heat and difficulty in breathing.

Tues., July 31. During this interval of time, my dear wife has gone to her rest, and her remains have been committed to the earth, there to remain until the trump of the Archangel shall summon them to join her beatified spirit, now and "forever" with [the] Lord. I did not go out for several Sundays. Br. Bahnson, in a spirit of true brotherly kindness, attended to the congregation for me.

Sun., Aug. 12. As the Sunday School has for some time been in a languishing condition, it was deemed expedient for various reasons to bring it to a close.

Sun., Aug. 26. Preached from Heb. 7:28. Called next day to see James Voss, who had been severely wounded in the head by Moses Smith with a hoe. The patient was asleep but Mr. Martin told me he had positively refused to see a minister.

Tues., Aug. 28. Sodded my dear wife's grave with sod bro't from Friedland garden.

Sun., Sept. 2. Buried James Voss, who died Saturday morning from the effects of his wound. Preached from Amos 4:12 to the largest audience I ever saw at Friedland.

Sun., Sept. 16. Preached from Rom. 7:13. In the evening was ordained Presbyter by Br. Bahnson together with the Brn. Fry, Siewers, and Friebele.

Thurs, Fri., Oct. 11, 12. Attended court—summoned as witness.

Sun., Nov. 24 [25]. It was so cold in the church my teeth almost chattered.

Sat., Dec. 1. Went to Friedland. Took down lime for white-washing. . . .

Sun., Dec. 2. During the sermon was very much disturbed by the misconduct of two young men, Smith and Hitchcock.

Sun., Dec. 16. Had intended not to go down, knowing no one would be there, but my conscience gave me no peace, so I went and found no one but br. Lowder. The walling of the cellar had been broken open to get out some rabbits.

Tues., Dec. 26 [25]. Christmas. Preached from Luke 2:11 to a very large congregation. ([Friedland Report:] Many no doubt had come in expectation of seeing our Xmas celebration and partaking of lovefeast, as they came from a distance. In this they were, however, disappointed.)

[New] Philadelphia Reports, with Macedonia, Muddy Creek, 1860
    [Extracts transcribed; handwriting is that of Thomas Frye.]

Sun., Apr. 8. Easter Sunday. At 9 o'clock we assembled to attend to the usual services on the Graveyard, after which I preached . . . to a good congregation notwithstanding the meetings at Bethel, Tabor, Sharon, and the Baptists at Ridenses [Ridings'?].

Wed., June 20. Went to Davy Co. to visit the Brethren in company with Br. Bahnson, whom I met at Esq. Douthid's. After visiting a few and finding them busily engaged in reaping their wheat, so that we thought best to return home until some other time.

Sun., July 1. Preached at Macedonia from John 5:39 to a very large assembly of people, so much so that the house and galleries were crowded, and it was said some 50 persons could not get in the house, yet all conducted themselves well, and at night we had prayer meeting with a large number of people.

Sun., July 15. Br. Bahnson preached [at Muddy Creek] . . . to so large a congregation that half of them could not have gotten in the house. Wherefore we had to repair to the almost rotten stand, and notwithstanding the very uncomfortable situation of the place the people were for the most part very attentive, and the sermon, which was excellent, we believe had its desired effect in many respects, for it was calculated to stir up and warm the hearts of Christians and arouse the backslider and awake the unregenerate to repentance. After preaching Br. Farabee, an Episcopal Methodist, closed by prayer.

Tues., Aug. 21. Mr. Nelson came for me and my wife to come to his house to see to laying a little Negro boy who had just died on his cooling board because no one would go for fear of taking the disease.

Sat., Sept. 1. Met at Phil. in order to settle the difficulty between Brn. Norman, Kiger, Crater and Spach, which we are glad to say was completely settled, each asking the others' forgiveness and agreeing together that he who should ever name it again should be looked upon as guilty.

Sun., Sept. 16. Preached at Muddy Creek . . . to a large concourse of people on a funeral occasion of three youths of Couler, children of Israel Olaver's, after which I returned home and from thence to Salem to celebrate the 16th of Sept. and at 7 o'clock of that evening was ordained Presbyter with three other Brethren, namely Brn. Siewers, Frebelle, and Leinbach, of the United Brethren's Church by Br. Bahnson, Bishop in the Southern Province of the United Brethren.

Sun., Dec. 2. Went [to Macedonia] to preach again, but as Br. Jacob Sheak, Episcopal Protestant Methodist preacher, was there I invited him to preach, who preached from Eph. 3:15, after which I dismissed the people after the usual form, after which the Committee met and presented me with a list of the names of the Macedonian Church members and also held a consultation on the subject of building a new brick church to enlarge their tract of land, for which the Brethren Hall and Lee were appointed.

1861

[In March Victor Emmanuel II became king of a united Italy. Czar Alexander abolished serfdom in Russia. The first transcontinental telegraph line began operation.

Kansas became the thirty-fourth state on January 29, but ten other Southern states joined South Carolina in secession. On February 8 the Confederate States of America were formed, and Jefferson Davis became their provisional president the next day. Abraham Lincoln was inaugurated the sixteenth U.S. president on March 4, and the Civil War opened on April 12 as South Carolina troops opened fire on Fort Sumter.

Following Governor Ellis's message to President Lincoln— "You can get no troops from North Carolina"—North Carolina seceded on May 20. Union troops captured Forts Hatteras and Clark on the Outer Banks at the end of August.]

Memorabilia of Salem Congregation, 1861
[Extracts transcribed; handwriting is that of Francis Raymond Holland.]

In some respects, the year 1861 has been a year unexampled in the experience of us all. Notwithstanding the apprehensions of public danger, which rested like a gloomy cloud upon the minds of the thoughtful and observant at the beginning of the year, the nature and extent of our national troubles have probably exceeded our worst anticipations. The present year has witnessed the commencement of a fearful and calamitous war between two different sections of our once united and prosperous country. When and how the dreadful strife will end is known only to God. Preparations on a gigantic scale have been made by both parties to the contest, which betoken an obstinate prosecution of the war on the one part, and an energetic and determined resistance on the other.

Already some of the fairest portions of our country have been ravaged by the desolations of war. Fields have been laid waste, houses demolished, villages consumed, and districts that smiled as the garden of the Lord [have] been trampled down and made desolate by the footsteps of contending hosts. Battles have been fought and victories won; but sad and numerous have been the instances of individual suffering and distress, few of which have ever been published and some of which cannot easily be imagined. Heartsickening it is to contemplate even in imagination the horrors of the battlefield: the groans and agony of the dying, wounds long left bleeding and undressed, loss of limbs, and maimed and mangled bodies. Then there are the days and nights of loneliness and suffering in the crowded hospital or amid the yet greater privations of the camp. Mournful beyond expression is the loss of precious lives, every one of which is of inestimable importance to some few loving hearts (at least), though its loss may never sensibly affect the public. How many families have thus been shrouded in mourning and gloom, how many hearts left desolate and now weeping over loved ones they will greet no more on earth! And saddest of all is the thought of multitudes of precious souls ushered in a moment into the presence of their Judge without any evidence of having been prepared to meet their God! For although there be devout men—faithful soldiers of Christ as well as of their country—in our armies, the moral condition of all large armies is too well known to be a secret, and gives but too little hope that the generality of those composing them are prepared to die.

As a congregation and community we have indeed special cause of thankfulness for exemption from suffering and distress. In various portions of some of the neighboring states, neighbor has been arrayed against neighbor in deadly strife; from portions of the country the inhabitants have had to fly, leaving their homes where plenty abounded, and having to submit to the severest privations and hardships. Some have witnessed the destruction of their property; and in many families there has been bitter mourning for husbands and fathers or sons and brothers fallen in battle. From all this, *we* as a congregation have been thus far exempted. In a most remarkable manner have the lives of those more immediately connected with us been preserved, both on the field of battle and when disease cut down its victims on their right hand and on their left; so that thus far the absent members of this congregation, as far as we know, have all been spared. Those who, from our midst, went forth to minister to the sick and dying, having accomplished their errand and been blest with great success in their labors, have been brought back in safety to their homes.

Owing to our having been for more than half a year deprived of the usual intelligence from the different Provinces of our church, we are unable this evening to take our customary survey of its condition and activity in Christian and heathen lands. Our mission among the Cherokees, the only one in communication with this Province, has naturally been affected by the unsettled condition of the country and the warlike preparations of that people; and our brethren there are entitled to our especial sympathy and prayers.

We have heard that Br. Levin T. Reichel, who had been deputed by the U.E.C. to make a visitation to our mission stations in Labrador, has safely returned to Europe after having accomplished the object of his mission. Of those brethren who are separated from us by the line which divides the North and the South, we have reason to believe that the bonds of Christian charity and brotherly love toward us are not broken, and that, like us, they would rejoice in the restoration of peace and good will between the lands lying so closely side by side.

After having been thrice called upon by public proclamation to observe days of "fasting, humiliation, and prayer," viz., on Jan. 4th by proclamation of the President of the U. States, and on June 13th and Nov. 15th by the President of the Confederate States, we were invited on Dec. 5th by the proclamation of the Governor of this State to the pleasing duty of thanksgiving for the many and undeserved mercies conferred upon us. The services on all these occasions were numerously attended; and we trust that the confessions, supplications, and thanksgivings of his people came up with acceptance before the Lord.

On Monday, July 22d, a daily prayer meeting was commenced, to be held every morning at 8 o'clock, especially for the purpose of interceding for our country, and for those of our friends and connexions who in obedience to the call of the state had gone forth as soldiers from our midst. This meeting was held regularly till Dec. 21st, a period of 5 months, when it was deemed advisable to close it at least for the present. The attendance for some time past had greatly diminished.

The colored division of the congregation has enjoyed the stated ministrations of the Word and sacrament; and the services have been marked by a good attendance, orderly deportment, and in some cases by the exhibition of deep feeling. On Apr. 14th 9 persons were admitted to full membership, viz., 6 by baptism and 3 by confirmation. Three communicants have departed this life, 5 non-communicants, and 1 child. Three children were baptized, and 1 couple married. The S.S. numbers about 75 scholars, and the number of stated hearers is about 200. The number of communicants is 44.

On Aug. 24th the cornerstone of a new church for the use of the colored congregation was solemnly laid with fervent prayer that in the house to be thereon erected the gospel might be preached in its purity and simplicity, with demonstration of the Spirit and of power, and that multitudes of precious blood-bought souls might therein learn the way of pardon, peace, and eternal life. On Dec. 15th the newly erected edifice was solemnly dedicated to the worship and service of the triune God—Father, Son, and Holy Ghost. A numerous congregation by its presence testified the interest felt, on the part of white and black, in the success and prosperity of the cause for which the house was solemnly set apart.

Our institutions for education, at a time when so many colleges and schools have been all but broken up, have of course not remained unaffected. Nevertheless we have cause to rejoice in the gracious favor and protection of the Lord. In the Female Academy, for the first time in many years the number of scholars has not equaled the extent of the accommodations, although the decrease is less than might have been anticipated. The health of the pupils, upon the whole, has been good. Such epidemics as have prevailed were mild in their character. One pupil only was removed by death, viz., Miss Martha Eudora Hobbs of Mississippi.

The various benevolent societies of the church have held their customary annual and other meetings, and endeavored to carry on their operations according to the opportunity afforded them. The several foreign mission societies have not been unmindful of their work of faith and labor of love. The Home Mission Society has continued to cultivate its field of labor in the mountains and has had reason to rejoice in its somewhat improved condition and prospects. The Tract Society responded to the call for means to print tracts for the soldiers by an appropriation of $125 for this object, which was increased by a church door collection to $240. The Bible Society supplied the volunteers from this county with Bibles and Testaments to the extent of the supply on hand.

Salem Diary, 1861

[Extracts transcribed; handwriting is that of Francis Raymond Holland.]

Fri., Jan. 4. Day of fasting, humiliation, and prayer, appointed by proclamation of the President on account of the disturbed and distracted state of the country. The services were well attended.

Sun., Jan. 6. [At] 7 P.M. prayer meeting, the first of the series of special prayer meetings, designed to be kept throughout the week.

Sun., Jan. 13. Prayer meetings were kept during the whole of the past week at 1 P.M. and 7 P.M. each day. They were numerously attended, and a solemn spirit appeared to prevail.

Wed., Jan. 16. At 7 P.M. Br. Holland in keeping Bible lecture, having been disturbed by several persons talking while the congregation was kneeling in prayer and similar disturbances having ~~frequently~~ occasionally[1] occurred for several months past, abruptly suspended the service and left the church, thus leaving it to the congregation to devise measures to keep order or not as they might see it.

Thurs., Jan. 17. At 7 P.M. a meeting of the fathers of families—54 being present—took place in the chapel, upon an invitation sent round at the instance of several members during the day. Br. Bahnson presided. Br. Holland was not present. Resolutions were unanimously adopted, which if carried out will put a stop to disorderly conduct in church. The meeting pledged itself to support all the officers of the church in the maintenance of good order.

Sun., Jan 20. At 10 A.M. public service. After the litany had been prayed, Br. Holland communicated to the congregation the resolutions adopted on Thursday evening last, and then preached on Gen. 28:17: "How dreadful is this place," etc.

Sat., Jan. 26. This afternoon, Mr. W. R. Hunter, who as a travelling lecturer on S. Schools had visited our place and delivered a series of lectures in May 1859, again unexpectedly made his appearance. At 7 P.M. he lectured on "Education, its importance in a national point of view."

---

[1]The word "occasionally" is penciled in above the penciled out "frequently."

Sun., Jan. 27. At 7 P.M. Mr. Hunter lectured on "The influence of belief in forming individual and national character." A collection taken up to aid Mr. Hunter in prosecuting his useful labors amounted to over $100.

Sun., Feb. 17. The Lord's Supper was celebrated this day. The German Communion was held at 3 P.M. instead of 7¾ P.M., in order to give a better opportunity for those who usually attend this meeting, most of them being aged, to avail themselves of the privilege. The Communion service in English was held at 7 P.M.

Sun., Apr. 28. Widows' festival. The meetings were kept in their usual order, but quite a number of the widows were prevented from attending them all, some by family circumstances, others, it is said, by anxiety and apprehension on account of the present disturbed and distracted state of the country and the fear that their sons will soon have to leave them and take up arms in defence of the state.

Wed., May 29. Annual close of Salem Female Academy. The exercises this year were limited to one day on account of the numerous departures of scholars for their homes during the last few weeks, the present unsettled and alarming condition of the country having caused many persons living at a distance to prefer having their daughters at home. A company of volunteers, 105 strong, commanded by Capt. Reeves, passed thro' town on their way from Surry Co. to the eastern part of the state.

Thurs., June 13. Was observed as a day of fasting, prayer, and humiliation upon the recommendation of the President of the Confederate States. We conformed with the request of the Congress of the same. At 10 A.M. there was public service, which was numerously attended. Br. Holland preached from Hosea 11:8. The day was generally observed.

Mon., June 17. Two companies of volunteers raised in Forsyth County, and who had been encamped near Salem for several weeks, left for the seat of war. Their immediate place of rendezvous is Danville, Va., where a sufficient number of companies will join them as speedily as possible, in order to organize a regiment. The parting scenes were most painful and affecting. The companies halted near the church, the line extending in front of the Academy, from the portico of which short addresses were delivered by Br. Bahnson and Br. Michael Doub of the Meth. Church, the latter of whom has a son in one of the companies. A fervent prayer was then offered by Br. Bahnson, the large concourse present sang "The grace of our Lord Jesus," etc., and the soldiers then filed off amid the tearful adieus of the multitude. Many of the relatives and friends accompanied them as far as the bridge, where they bade them finally, farewell.

In Company A (Forsyth Rifles) are the following communicant members of this congregation: The Single Brn. William J. Pfohl (1st Sergt.), Samuel C. James (2d Sergt.), Henry W. Barrow (2d Corporal), J. F. Schaffner, Gustavus E. Sussdorff (ensign), Benjamin F. Atwood; besides the following persons whose parents are members of this congregation: Alfred H. Belo (Capt.), Edw. A. Brietz (2d Lieut.), James A. Reich, Alexander Rights, P. T. Shultz.

In Company B (Forsyth Grays), Capt. Wharton, the following persons are communicant members of this congregation: The md. Br. Wm. Francis Carmichael and Single Brn. Thos. Byron Douthit, Lewis B. Eberhard, Sam'l. G. Hall, Joseph H. Reich, James Edw. Shulz, Cornelius A. Shultz, Julius R. Vogler; besides the following whose parents are members: David Murchison, Augustus B. Butner, Reuben L. Chitty, Augustus A. Clewell, Francis Edwd. Keehln, and Henry Shore (suspended from communion).

Besides these, a number were stated hearers in our church. May our heavenly Father screen them from temptation, shelter them in the day of battle, guard them from all danger, and may the blessing and peace of Christ our Savior be with them, and may they, if consistent with His all-wise and gracious will, be brought back speedily, in peace and safety!

Sun., June 23. At 10 A.M. Litany and preaching conducted by Br. Bahnson. The litany, changed to correspond to our altered government, was used, as thus changed, for the first time today. Also the prayer to be used in time of war.

Mon., June 24. The 3d company of volunteers from Forsyth, commanded by Capt. Miller, started this morning for Danville. They were addressed and prayed with by Br. Bahnson in their camp before starting. The men composing this company are principally, if not altogether, from the country, and many are connected with our congregations at Bethania and Bethabara.

Mon., July 15. At 8 P.M. a meeting of the Tract Society was held, at which $125 was appropriated to aid in republishing tracts in this state, and to issue an edition of the New Testament for the use of the soldiers.

Sun., July 21. At 8 P.M. Br. Holland conducted the evening service, and announced a daily prayer meeting at 8 A.M. to intercede especially for our friends and relatives absent in the present calamitous and lamentable war. The suggestion to meet thus daily for prayer came from a member of the congregation, and is hailed with great satisfaction by the pastor.

Mon., July 22. At 8 A.M. prayer meeting was held, which was very well attended. Immediately after the same the Boys' School was re-opened, under the tuition of Br. Albert I. Butner and Sr. Kremer. 20 scholars only were present.

Tues., July 23. Prayer meeting at 8 A.M. In the afternoon the report reached us that a bloody battle had been fought on Sunday near Manasses Junction, Va., between the Confederate Troops and the soldiers of Lincoln. The former are said to have gained a decided victory. As it is pretty certain that the regiment to which our young men belong was on the spot, the anxiety is very great on their account.

Wed., July 24. Prayer meeting at 8 A.M. The anxiety to hear whether any of our young men have been killed or wounded continues very great. Br. David Clewell left for Richmond yesterday evening, hoping to be permitted to get through to Manasses and render assistance.

Thurs., July 25. Prayer meeting at 8 A.M. In the evening letters were received stating that none of our young men were injured in the late battle. Their regiment was stationed in the centre behind entrenchments, and tho' exposed to a cannonade, no one was struck by the balls and shells thrown at them.

Fri., July 26. Prayer meeting at 8 A.M., in which we returned thanks for the preservation of those near and dear to us, and besought the Lord to comfort the afflicted and bereaved whose friends or relatives have been killed or wounded.

Sat., July 27. 8 A.M. prayer meeting.

Sun., July 28. At 10 A.M. public service, conducted by Br. Bahnson. At the opening of service, we offered up our thanksgiving and praise for the great victory gained by the Confederate States troops on Sunday last. At the close a collection was taken at the door for supplying the soldiers with tracts and testaments. It amounted to $115.

Sat., Aug. 3. The morning prayer meetings have been held through the week, and were well attended.

Sun., Aug. 11. Celebration of the 13th. The different meetings were held as usual, with the exception of the lovefeast at 2 P.M. In this meeting the ode or Psalm was sung, but no cakes and coffee served. This course was rendered advisable on account of the scarcity and high price of coffee, there being but little for sale in town, and the price having ranged from 33 to 37 cents per lb. The lovefeast was not so well attended as usual.

Sun., Aug. 18. Celebration of the children's festival. Lovefeast was served to the children only. The usual meetings were all kept and pretty well attended.

Sat., Aug. 24. At 5 P.M. the cornerstone of the new church for the colored people was laid by Br. Bahnson in the presence of a large congregation of white as well as colored persons. For particulars see Diary of Colored Congregation.

Tues., Aug. 27. Capt. Kinyoun's company of volunteers from Yadkin left this morning for High Point.

Sat., Aug. 31. The prayer meetings at 8 A.M. have been held uninterrupted up to this date.

Sun., Sept. 1. The Single Brn.'s festival was celebrated today. Owing to the absence of so many single Brn. in the army, the number present was but small. At the Holy Communion 17 communicants partook.

Tues., Sept. 3. The morning prayer meetings will be discontinued during the remainder of the week owing to the church cleaning which commences today.

Fri., Sept. 13. Capt. Spear's company of volunteers from Yadkin arrived this evening, and . . . .

Sat., Sept. 14. . . . Passed on to High Point.

Mon., Oct. 14. Br. Holland performed a marriage ceremony near Pfafftown in the encampment of a company of volunteers. Br. R. de Schweinitz took Br. Holland thither and back in his conveyance.

Wed., Oct. 16. This morning Capt. Stowe's company of volunteers passed through on their way to Raleigh.

Fri., Nov. 15. Day of Humiliation and Prayer, by appointment of the President of the Confederate States. At 10 A.M. service was conducted by Br. Bahnson, and well attended. At 7 P.M. singing meeting, closed with prayer.

Thurs., Dec. 5. This day having been appointed by the Governor as a day of thanksgiving, there was preaching, etc., at 10 A.M. by Br. Holland.

Sun., Dec. 15. At 10 A.M. Litany and preaching by Br. Bahnson. At 2 P.M. was the consecration of the new church erected in the course of the year for the colored congregation. The house was well filled, and the exercises were marked by great attention on the part of the large congregation. The utmost order and decorum prevailed.

Sat., Dec. 21. The daily prayer meetings, which have been held at 8 A.M. since July 22, were brought to a solemn close, at least till after the Xmas holidays. About dark there was an alarm of fire. The gas works had caught fire, and a portion of them was burnt down.

Sun., Dec. 22. At 10 A.M. public service. The congregation returned thanks for the merciful preservation enjoyed last evening. The air having been calm, the buildings near the gas works were all preserved. There was no evening meeting, as it was uncertain whether the church could be lit up with gas. By evening, however, the gas was again in use in the street lamps, etc.

Tues., Dec. 24. The weather was mild and beautiful, and the Christmas Eve celebrations conducted in the usual manner, [and] was numerously attended by the congregation. But few strangers were present this year.

Wed., Dec. 25. At 10 A.M. preaching by Br. Holland. In the evening the younger pupils of the Female Academy recited a "Xmas Dialogue" in their chapel before a numerous audience.

Tues., Dec. 31. The usual meetings were held. The evening was clear and mild, and the church was well filled at 8 and at 11 1/2 P.M. With thankful hearts to the Lord, we closed this troublous year. He has signally protected and blest us; and in comparison with many other parts of our country, we may say that we as a congregation have not known his judgments.

Diary of the African Church in Salem, 1861
[Extracts transcribed; handwriting is that of Francis Raymond Holland.]

Sun., Mar. 10. After preaching, an "enquiry meeting" was kept, inasmuch as several have been deeply convicted of sin, and have presented themselves as seekers of religion. On the 24th of last month already, unusual feeling was exhibited on the part of several young men, one of whom wept bitterly in his distress on account of his sins. Last Sunday the "mourners" were specially remembered in prayer in a meeting held after the close of the preaching. Today five persons were received as candidates for confirmation, viz.: Wm. (Siewers), Sultana (Waugh), Mary (Waugh), Susan (Waugh), and Rachel (Hege). Some 5 or 6 were present as inquirers.

Sun., Mar. 24. Palm Sunday. At 7½ P.M. commenced reading "the acts of the last days of the Son of Man" to a crowded and attentive congregation. On Monday, Tuesday, and Wednesday evenings the reading was continued.

Fri., Mar. 29. At 1½ P.M. the history of the day was read to a very attentive congregation.

Sun., Mar. 31. Easter. At 9 A.M. the Easter morning litany was read in the old graveyard, adjoining the church, and immediately afterwards public service was held in the church, which, as usual on other Easter days, could not contain the crowd.

Sun., Apr. 14. Six adults were today solemnly baptized into the death of Jesus, viz.: Lewis (Hege), William (Siewers), Jefferson (Siewers), Richard (at J. Boner's), Mary Magdalene (at T. F. Crist's), and Rachel (Hege). Three were confirmed, viz.: Sultana (Waugh), Susan (Waugh), and Mary (Light). The services were held in the large church, and were numerously attended by a very attentive and quiet congregation.

Sun., May 26. 2½ P.M. service conducted by Br. H. As the evenings have become very short, the Tuesday evening lecture has been discontinued for the present.

Sun., June 30. After preaching, a meeting for the members, in which Katy (Lash) was excluded from membership for her sin of fornication.

Sat., Aug. 24. At 5 P.M. the corner stone of the new church was laid by Br. Bahnson with appropriate religious ceremonies. The following is a copy of the document deposited in the corner stone:

> In the name of God the Father, Son, and Holy Ghost, this corner stone of a church for the use of the colored members of the United Brethren's or Moravian Church at Salem was laid with fervent prayer to God that in the house to be erected on this spot, the blessed gospel of our Lord Jesus Christ might be preached from generation to generation in its purity and simplicity, with demonstration of the spirit and of power; that the Holy

Sacraments of the Christian Church might be administered therein according to the institution of Christ, and in conformity with the rights [rites] and usages of the United Brethren's Church; and that multitudes of precious souls, redeemed with the blood of Christ, might therein learn the way of pardon, peace, and eternal life.

This corner stone was laid on the 24th day of August, Anno Domini 1861,

Jefferson Davis being Provisional President of the Confederate States of America;

Henry T. Clark, acting Governor of the State of North Carolina;

George F. Bahnson being Bishop of the United Brethren's Church in the Southern Province of North America;

Emil A. de Schweinitz, Administrator of the Unity's Estates in Wachovia;

Robert W. de Schweinitz, Principal, and Maximilian E. Grunert, Assistant Principal, of the Salem Female Academy;

Francis R. Holland being pastor of the Congregation at Salem;

Samuel Thomas Pfohl being Warden of the Congregation at Salem;

Jacob F. Siewers being Pastor of the Congregations at Bethany and Bethabara;

Christian Lewis Rights being Pastor of the Congregations at Friedberg and Hope;

Thomas Fry of the Congregations at Friedland and Philadelphia;

Robert Parmenio Leinbach of the Congregations at Macedonia and Muddy Creek;

John A. Friebele of the Home Mission Congregation at Mt. Bethel, Virginia;

Gilbert Bishop and Jacob Mack, being Missionaries of the United Brethren's Church among the Cherokees west of Arkansas;

The Provincial Elders' Conference consisting of the Brn. George F. Bahnson, Emil A. de Schweinitz, and Robert W. de Schweinitz;

The Board of Elders of the Salem Congregation consisting of the Brn. Francis R. Holland, Robert W. de

Schweinitz, Emil A. de Schweinitz, Maximilian E. Grunert, and Jacob L. Fulkerson;

The Board of Trustees of the Salem Congregation consisting of the Brn. Saml. Thos. Pfohl, Charles A. Cooper, Joshua Boner, John Gottlieb Sides, Theodore F. Keehln, Elias A. Vogler, and John Nathaniel Blum.

The Scripture texts for the day in the text book of the Protestant Church of the United Brethren for the year 1861 were the following:

"I am the Lord: that is my name: and my glory will I not give to another, neither my praise to graven images." Isaiah 42:8.

> O majestic Being,
> Were but soul and body
> Thee to serve at all times ready:
> Might we, like angels
> Who behold thy glory,
> With abasement sink before thee.
>
> Hymn book [of 1851] No. 558, v. 3.

"Christ Jesus, being in the form of God, thought it not robbery to be equal with God: but made himself of no reputation, and took upon him the form of a servant, and was made in the likeness of men." Phil. 2:6-7.

> Whence can my weak spirit fetch
> Thoughts profound enough to reach
> This unfathom'd condescension.
>
> [1842 Hymnal, No. 188, v. 2.]

Historical Sketch of the Origin and Progress of the
Colored Congregation at Salem

Already previous to the year 1822, the desire had been expressed, especially at the annual meetings of the Society for the Propagation of the Gospel, that on the part of the U. Brethren's Church, more might be done toward the religious instruction of the African race in the vicinity of Salem than had been hitherto attempted. After individuals of this race had, it is true, from time to time become communicant members of the church, nevertheless it appeared desirable that such additional opportunities should be afforded as would be more likely to prove attractive and profitable to these people than those they had hitherto enjoyed.

In the year 1822 a number of sisters belonging to the Congregation at Salem, for the express purpose of spreading the gospel among the colored people of this vicinity, formed themselves into a Society under the name of the Salem Female Missionary Society.

The formation of this Society led to the resolution on the part of the Provincial Elders' Conference to institute regular preaching for the colored people, and to form from among them a separate congregation. Br. Abraham Steiner was appointed to take charge of this field of gospel labor. On March 24th, 1822, he kept the first service, which was attended by about 60 hearers, among whom were four communicants. On Sunday, May 19th, the Lord's Supper was administered for the first time, three communicants, besides the minister, being present as partakers, viz.: Budney, his wife Phebe, and John Emanuel. The meetings for public worship were kept, as regularly as circumstances admitted, once a fortnight, on Sabbath afternoons, at various places in the neighborhood of Salem.

On Sunday, Dec. 28th, 1823, the new church, which had been erected mainly through the exertions of the Salem Female Missionary Society, was solemnly consecrated to the worship of the triune God. This house, situated a short distance South West of this spot, on the adjoining lot, is at the present date still used for the purpose to which it was at first consecrated. But having been for some time already too small and inconvenient, the erection of the new and larger building, in the corner stone of which this document is deposited, was resolved upon and undertaken in reliance upon the help and blessing of the Lord. The means for this purpose were liberally contributed by the individual members and friends of the Congregation at Salem, as well as by the several church Boards.

In the year 1859 it was resolved by the Provincial Elders' Conference in future to consider the colored charge as forming a part of the Salem Congregation.

Accordingly since that time they have been served by the pastor of said Congregation.

The following brethren have had the pastoral care of the colored people:

Br. Abr. Steiner from 1822 till 1832
Br. John R. Smith from 1832 till 1838
Br. Sam'l. Thos. Pfohl from 1838 till 1841
Br. Gottlieb Byhan from 1842 till 1852
Br. John A. Friebele from 1853 till 1857
Br. George F. Bahnson from 1857 till 1859
Br. Francis R. Holland from 1859 till ____.

Since 1857, circumstances having frequently prevented the brother in charge from being present, Br. M. E. Grunert has, for such occasions, cheerfully attended to the Sunday services.

In the Sunday School, which has been kept with great regularity since the year 1822, a number of sisters have served as teachers with exemplary zeal and fidelity. From 1822 till 1849 the school was under the superintendence of Sr. Sarah Steiner, and since 1849 under that of Sr. Mary Denke. The teachers at present engaged are the Srs. Mary Denke, Rebecca Stauber, Anna Johanna Stauber, Martha Vogler, Leana Shaub, Olivia S. Warner, and Caroline Siewers.

From the year 1822 till the present time:

78 persons have been received into full membership;
196 infants and 32 adults have been baptized;
109 persons have been buried;
16 marriages have been solemnized.

The present number of communicants is 44.

(Here follows a list of the communicants.)

The number of stated hearers is about 200.

Besides this document, there were deposited in the corner stone a Bible, Church Catechism, Historical Sketch of the Brn.'s Church, and Text book for the year 1861.

The order of services was as follows:

1. Singing.
2. Address by Br. Bahnson.
3. Reading of the foregoing document by Br. Holland.

4. Singing, during which the box to be deposited in the stone was soldered up.

5. Prayer by Br. Bahnson.

6. Doxology.

The weather was fine and a large assembly was present.

Sun., Sept. 29. Holy Communion; 48 communicants partook, including some Methodist members at Winston.

Sun., Nov. 17. S. School and preaching. A number of persons being convicted of sin and expressing their desire to be prayed for and with, several prayers were offered after the sermon, br. George (Fries) and Henry (Webb) leading in prayer. There was a general melting of hearts, and many tears were shed.

Tues., Nov. 19. The regular evening lecture was held. It was well attended. The inquirers were addressed and remembered in prayer.

Sun., Dec. 8. Preaching in the old church for the last time.

Sun., Dec. 15. Consecration of the new church. Br. Bahnson offered the first prayer, Br. Holland preached, Br. Grunert followed with an exhortation, and Br. R. de Schweinitz closed with prayer. A large congregation was present, completely filling the house.

Sun., Dec. 22. Christmas celebration. The S. School scholars sang a number of Xmas hymns, and the children were rewarded with cakes and wax candles. Br. Holland read Luke 2 and preached a short sermon. Br. Grunert closed with prayer.

Board of Elders of Salem Congregation, 1861
[Extracts of minutes transcribed.]

Wed., Jan. 16.

2. The meetings kept twice a day during the past week were remarkably well attended, especially at night.

3. Complaints were made about some young men who had a carousal at the hotel. Gust. Sussdorf appears to be deeply penitent. Sam. Hall will be spoken to. The "literary society" appears to be going down, and to be more a stumbling block than a benefit.

Wed., April 17. Br. Fulk. absent.

2. The lovefeasts for the colored people were spoken of. Hitherto sr. Denke has taken the responsibility and has had her outlays refunded by the members or other friends. It would appear proper to cause the members to elect a steward, whose office it would be to collect such funds as may be required for church purposes, among which firewood for warming the church was mentioned.

3. The prayer for the President and the Union in our litany was spoken of. For a considerable time it was prayed every Sunday, and its repeated omission of late has been remarked upon. The Board did not come to a determination whether or not it should be regularly used under the circumstances. (Note: It was omitted afterwards.)

4. The troubles in the town girls room continue and increase. Requests to have daughters placed, even while children, into rooms in the Academy become numerous, mothers have come to the room and abused Miss Petersen before the girls, etc. A change in this arrangement seems absolutely required.

Wed., May 1. Br. Fulk. absent.

2. The day for the election of church officers is Tuesday next. It was thought best to postpone it for a week on account of the general muster falling on that day. (It was postponed for 2 weeks.)

Wed., May 15. Br. Fulk. absent.

3. The scarcity and high prices of coffee and sugar at present may interfere with our lovefeasts. If they must be discontinued from purely financial reasons, the suggestion ought to come from the Board of Trustees.

4. The Sunday school and other meetings for the colored people were spoken of. It is known that there is opposition to them, but nothing had been heard directly or officially.

Wed., June 12. Br. Fulk. absent.

2. The election, held on May 21st, resulted in the re-election to this Board of br. E. A. Schweinitz.

3. The meetings for the colored people have gone on as usual.

4. Tomorrow will be observed as a day for humiliation and prayer, in accordance with the proclamation of the President of the Confederate States. The service at 10 A.M.

Mon., July 22. Br. Fulk. absent.

2. Br. Rob. Schweinitz gave the reason for the present called meeting. Sr. Theresa Petersen has resigned her office as teacher of the town girls' room, and it is now necessary to make arrangements for filling the place. In the present uncertain state of affairs the Academy will be far from full in the beginning of the session at least, and he therefore proposed not to appoint a separate teacher for the present, but instead of giving up rooms in the Academy, to divide the town girls temporarily into them. The Board, having no suitable candidate to offer for the situation in question, although recognizing the unsatisfactory nature of temporary arrangements, was gratified to see this provision made, at least for a time, in this difficult matter.

3. Br. R. Schweinitz also informed the Board that P.E.C. had determined the present compensation of $130 a year, paid by the Diacony from the tuition money received from the parents of the girls, being considered insufficient, that they would not keep the town girls for that sum any longer, but proposed that the whole of the tuition money should in future be paid to the inspector, instead of the diacony. P.E.C. desires the Board to notify the Board of Trustees of this. The Board fully acknowledged the justice of the demand, but regretted the unfortunate time, as the diacony has pledged itself to come this year to the aid of the boys' school for $250. The matter was postponed.

4. On Aug. 13th the Ode will be sung as usual, but no cake and coffee provided.

Wed., Aug. 7. Br. Fulk. absent.

3. There are again several girls past the age of 14, and not received into the Choir at the last sisters' feast. According to the rule adopted Aug 8, 1860, such are left to themselves. The Board agreed that the only way to remedy existing evils was to return to the old plan of a great girls' room and superintendent. Br. Holl. will speak with br. Pfohl, whether a room can be got for that purpose, and with sr. Bagge, to request her to consider provisionally the charge of the girls.

4. The children's feast falls upon a Saturday, and will, therefore, be kept on Sunday 18th. In the lovefeast, the children *only* will get coffee and cakes.

Wed., Aug. 14. Br. Fulk. absent.

2. Br. Holl. reported that sr. Bagge would assist as much as possible in organizing and sustaining the great girls' room, altho' she can not take the sole charge of it. Her proposal is to take a room in the sisters house, at present occupied by Henriette Leinbach, Martha Vogler, and Leanne Shaub. By putting the first into another room, and making the other two superintendents of the great girls, the object would be most easily accomplished. The Board thought if sr. Bagge would be generally present, especially in the beginning, the two sisters mentioned would do well enough, and that, in consideration of their services, they should be rent free. Sr. Bagge would be the proper person to address them on the subject, and also to announce the measure to the respective parents and girls, but without begging them to avail themselves of the benefits of the arrangement, in as much as attendance at the room cannot be enforced.

For future, girls will be received among the sisters on the first festival after they have become 17 years of age.

Wed., Oct. 9. Br. Fulk. absent.

2. The proposed exhibition of tableaux for the benefit of the volunteers was spoken of. Although convinced that the plan was gotten up without any bad intention, yet as opinions have been asked concerning their propriety, and in consideration of the consequences, br. Holl. also having on Sunday last solemnly protested against it. The Board cannot but disapprove of the same, agreeably to the spirit and the letter of our rules. But things having gone as far as they have, it was thought unnecessary to do anything further in the matter.

Wed., Oct. 9. 2 P.M. Br. Fulk. absent.

The Board met again, information having been received, meanwhile, that a protest had been prepared by some members of the church for insertion in the public paper against the action of those church members who continue to prepare for the exhibition of those tableaux, and also that the impression prevails more or less in the congregation that br. Holl. was standing alone among the ministers in his views. The Board thought that said protest should not be published, and then unanimously passed the following preamble and resolutions, viz.:

Whereas, the opinion of the Board of Elders has been asked in reference to the public exhibition in contemplation, in which communicant members of the church are engaged as actors, and

Whereas, both the resolutions of the General and Provincial Synods and the rules of Salem Congregation express their disapprobation of all amusements of this kind, therefore

Resolved that we, the Board of Elders, consider them inconsistent with the principles and regulations of our church, and entirely disapprove of their being introduced among us.

Resolved, that the pastor be requested to communicate these resolutions to the congregation this evening.

Wed., Nov. 13. Br. Fulk. absent.

3. Friday next has been appointed by the President as a day of fasting and prayer, and our acting Governor has endorsed the proclamation. There will be a service at 10 A.M., and a singing meeting in the evening.

4. The new Negro church is almost finished.

Wed., Dec. 11. Br. Fulk. absent.

After the reading of the minutes the consecration of the Negro church was more fully discussed. Br. Bahnson will open the exercises by a dedicatory prayer, br. Holl. preach the sermon, br. Grunert follow in an exhortation, and br. Rob. Schweinitz close with prayer. Masters and mistresses, as well as contributors to the building, will be invited, and accommodated with seats, as far as there will be room.

4. The languishing condition of the Boys' school came up. It was thought advisable to hold a joint meeting with the Board of Trustees before the subject is brought forward in the Congregation Council.

Board of Trustees of Salem Congregation, 1861
[Extracts of minutes transcribed.]

Tues., Jan. 22. Not present Br. F. Fries.

3. It was mentioned that Br. Edwd. Leinbach had been spoken to regarding the instructions in music given to a class of boys and young men, and that he stated that during the summer months he had not kept the class, as he felt a need of relaxation from such duties during the hot season, and as the scholars did not attend regularly.

5. Circumstances that have transpired render it necessary in the opinion of the Board to commission one of its members to state to the Forsyth Literary Society that altho' we wish to encourage every laudable endeavour to improve in useful knowledge, we nevertheless can do so only as long as the deportment of the members is correct, but that if they should make themselves guilty of improper conduct and of proceedings foreign to the object of the society, we should feel ourselves reluctantly compelled to refuse them the further use of the room in which their meetings have thus far been held.

Br. Theod. Keehln was requested to lay our views before the society.

Tues., Feb. 19. Not present the Brrn. F. Fries, E. A. Vogler, and J. G. Seitz.

1. Difficulties having arisen amongst the Winstonians with regard to the location of the lot for the Presbyterian church, the Commissioners of the town desiring the continuation of Third Street to the Winston line, the lot will not be laid out till they have come to an agreement among themselves.

2. The sale of the lots in Winston to be laid out on Elm and Cherry Streets will take place on Friday, the 8th of March.

4. Br. Andrew Kern having recently died in Florida, his father, Br. Gottfried Kern of Nazareth, makes application thro' Br. Holland to have his remains interred on our graveyard, which request was granted the more readily, as the deceased, altho' not living in any of our Congregations, had never separated from our connection and had in former years served as teacher in our Boys' School.

5. Application was also made by Mrs. Selma Kern for permission to bury the remains of her deceased husband, Julius

Kern (now buried in the Cemetery) on our graveyard, which request was also granted by the Board.

6. The School Committee, being again under the necessity of procuring another teacher for our Boys' School, have directed their attention to Br. Albert Butner, who for a number of years has been engaged in teaching (part of the time in our own school). A letter in reply to one addressed to him holds out the prospect that he would accept of such an appointment, provided a sufficient salary could be secured. As he could not support his family on the salary that has been paid to the present teacher (viz., $400), and as the School Committee, owing to the small number of scholars, is not able to pay more, it now makes application to the Board of Trustees for assistance for at least one year, in the expectation that perhaps by that time the School under an experienced teacher might increase sufficiently to bear its own expenses.

Board of Trustees, being fully impressed with the importance of making an effort to procure an experienced and if possible a permanent teacher for our Boys' School, resolved unanimously to give $250 for the purpose required, which amount it is expected will stand to the credit of School account by the 1st of May of this year.

Fri., Feb. 22.

Some of the members of the Board met at the former Negro Graveyard and determined that the new Negro Church be erected to the east and outside of the graveyard, the front of the building to be placed where the east fence of the graveyard now stands. This appears to be the most favourable place for erecting the Church; the graveyard would thus form the entrance or yard to it. Such of the members of the Board as could not attend on the spot had given their sanction to this locality.

Sun., Feb. 24. Not present Brrn. F. Fries and Theod. Keehln.

Application having been made by our sister Annette Smith to have the remains of her husband Dr. Elisha Smith interred on our graveyard, the Board granted the request.

It was stated at the same time that the remains of Br. Andrew Kern had been taken to Nazareth, Penna., for interment.

Tues., Mar. 19. Not present the Brrn. F. Fries and J. Boner.

2. The town commissioners of Salem and Winston . . . by mutual consent [have] run the dividing line between the two corporations at right angles with Main Street (instead of due east and west as heretofore). . . .

Tues., Apr. 2. Not present the Brrn. F. Fries and C. Cooper.

1. The Town Commissioners make application to rent the hall of the Sons of Temperance for their use, the temperance society, being in a manner defunct, not having kept any meetings for some time already, altho' they have not as yet surrendered their charter. Some of the members base a desire to draw the rent for the room in case the commissioners get the use of it upon this circumstance, that they still hold the charter.

Board took no action on the question, because some of the members wish to speak with some of the former Sons of Temperance on the subject before coming to a conclusion on this matter.

2. The attention of the Board having been directed to the fact that the Town Hall [in the former Potter's shop on Main Street] has become a place of resort to young persons assembling for improper purposes, it was resolved that after Br. Brietz shall have vacated the part of the building now held in rent by him, the doors be kept locked and the keys be given to Br. Wimmer, now living in the former Potter's dwelling, who as police officer is to be requested to see to it that all nuisances in the house and on the lot be discontinued.

Thurs., May 30. Not present Br. Theod. Keehln.

1. The term of service of the Brrn. F. Fries and E. A. Vogler having expired, Congregation Council had filled the vacancy by electing the Brrn. E. A. Vogler and Nathl. Blum as members of the Board of Trustees for the ensuing three years.

Board met and organized by electing Br. S. Thos. Pfohl as President and Secretary for one year.

3. The Chair reported that the few remaining Sons of Temperance at this place consider their society as defunct and that they relinquish their claim to the Hall, which according to agreement (see minutes of Committee Aug. 13, 1849) is now at the disposal of this body representing the interests of the Salem Diacony. Board consequently now resolved to rent the former

Temperance Hall to the Town Commissioners of Salem for their use, charging them at the rate of $30 a year for rent. (See minutes Apr. 2, 1861, § 1.)

Tues., June 25. Not present the Brrn. C. Cooper, and Theod. Keehln.

2. A note of $3,000 belonging to the Single Sisters Diacony having been paid up within a few days, the question was laid before this body, in what manner the money could be safely invested again? Board was of opinion that to loan it to the County of Forsyth, which is at this time desirous to borrow money on coupon bonds (the coupons receivable in pay for public taxes) for the purpose of equipping its volunteers, and which expenses the State of North Carolina in Convention assembled has concluded to refund to the counties, would be as safe an investment as could be made under the existing difficulties under which the country is now labouring.

Tues., Aug. 6. Not present the Brrn. Theod. Keehln and E. A. Vogler.

1. Br. Edwd. Hege asks whether part of the old field to the east of Henry Blum's and some woodland adjoining it on the north, say about 10 acres in all, could be bo't and at what price? Board think it not advisable to enter into the sale of land under the present disturbed state of the country and consequent scarcity of money.

3. The annual accounts of Salem Diacony from May 1, 1860, to April 30, 1861, together with a statement of the assets and liabilities of the same on Apr. 30 of the present year were laid before the Board. The receipts from the usual sources in the course of the fiscal year amounted to $3,731.51 and the disbursements to $4,023.26, thus showing an excess of disbursements of $291.75, owing to the unusually heavy expenses on Church account occasioned by the introduction of gas pipes and fittings into the Church and Chapel. The proceeds from sales of Town Lots, amounting to $978.83 have been added to the Lot Fund, which has now increased to $12,295.82.

4. The accounts and statements of assets and liabilities of the Single Sisters Diacony for the last fiscal year to Apr. 30, 1861, were next communicated. The receipts amounted to $769.08 and the disbursements to $603.09, being an excess of

$165.99 of receipts, which latter sum added to the Reserved fund raises the same to $5,993.30.

Tues., Sept. 3. Not present the Brrn. Theod. Keehln and E. A. Vogler.

2. The question was asked, whether the Board in electing a building committee for the New Negro Church had intended that said committee should strictly and exclusively confine themselves to the plan of the building laid before the Board and adopted by the same on Aug. 7th, 1860, or whether some latitude would be allowed them, and particularly whether Board insisted upon it that the steeple of the church should be built as represented on that plan? Board unanimously gave it as their view that the building committee is at liberty to deviate from the plan then proposed if they see proper to do so, and that as regards the steeple there was no objection that the plan first proposed, but against which some objections were raised, be substituted for the one then laid before the Board, viz., on Aug. 7th, 1860.

4. The attention of the Board was drawn to a well that was dug near the Waughtown road on the first rise beyond the bridge and which being open and uncovered might become dangerous to children or to cattle. Br. Fr. Fries, who had it dug for the purpose of making brick at the place for the Female Academy, will be requested to have it filled up.

Mon., Sept. 30. Not present the Brrn. J. Boner and Theod. Keehln.

3. A large number of chestnut trees having died in our woods within the last few years, Br. Fr. Fries asks permission to cut them in order to make rails of them or use them for burning of coals, and is willing to pay for the timber. Board grants him permission to do so. . . .

4. Br. Wm. Schulz has transferred the field held in rent by him beyond the creek to the Inspector of the Female Academy, who intends to use it for the purpose of making a pond for ice on it. Board sanction the transfer.

Tues., Oct. 29. Not present the Brrn. C. Cooper and J. Boner.

1. In as much as the 4th section of the Tax Law of the Confederate Government ordering a war tax of 50 cents upon

each one hundred dollars in value to be levied on certain properties enumerated in the Act contains among other regulations the provision: "That the property of colleges and schools and of charitable or religious corporations or associations actually used for the purpose for which such colleges, schools, corporations or associations were created, shall be exempt from taxation under this act," and Board of Trustees being of opinion that the property of the Salem Diacony is clearly covered by this exemption and not required to pay the war tax, by a unanimous vote [Board] instructed the Warden not to list or give in the property of the Diacony.

2. Board resolved shortly to view the premises of the Old Negro Church, preparatory to the laying off of a lot for said building, which can be sold so soon as the new church shall be completed.

Wed., Nov. 20. Full Board.

2. The Old Negro Church standing on the lot that has now been laid off, being the property of the Salem Female Missionary Society (which Society, however, has no claim upon the lot), will have to be disposed of, as that Society has resolved to contribute the proceeds towards the erection of the new negro church. In order to ascertain its value the Board has appointed two person who assessed it at $250, a sum too high according to the opinion of the Board.

After mature reflection Board resolved to adopt the following plan, as in its estimation just and equitable to both the Diacony and the Salem Female Missionary Society, viz.: that we value the lot at $100 . . . and the Old Church at $150 and consequently begin the sale at $250 for house and lot; should more be realized, the excess above $250 to be divided pro rata between the parties interested, viz., the Diacony to receive 2/5 and the Salem Female Missionary Society 3/5 of the amount paid over and above the $250. The sale to take place on Saturday 30th inst. Possession can be given as soon as the old church is vacated by the congregation worshipping there. The terms of the sale are to be cash at the time of the delivery of the property.

Fri., Dec. 20. Not present the Brrn. C. Cooper and Theod. Keehln.

1. In reference to §2 of the last minutes, mention was made that the Old Negro Church and lot sold for $350, of which sum,

according to agreement, Diacony received $140 for the lot and the Salem Female Missionary Society $210 for the Church.

2. A communication from the Trustees of the Salem Female Academy was laid before the Board of the following import, viz.: That for many years there had existed an understanding between the Town Committee and the Trustees of the Salem Female Academy that the daughters of members of the Salem Congregation should be schooled by the Academy for the annual sum of $130, and that for their especial benefit two teachers should be salarized. At the time when this agreement was made the sum paid may have been a fair compensation for services rendered by the Academy, the number of town girls being small and the salary of the teachers likewise. But after the number of children increased and the salary paid to teachers was raised also, the Academy was at greater expense than the sum paid for them amounted to, while at the same time the school fees received by the Warden from the parents and guardians of the girls of Salem Congregation over and above the $130 were not paid to the Female Academy but retained for the benefit of Salem Diacony. In view of these facts the Trustees of Salem Female Academy can therefore not do otherwise than consider the compensation received by Salem Female Academy considerably out of proportion to what said Academy is doing for the town girls, and consequently make to the Board of Trustees of Salem Congregation the following proposition, which they consider fair, viz.: "That the school fees, as charged at present for our town girls, or daughters of members of Salem Congregation, be hereafter paid directly to the Principal of Salem Female Academy, so that said Academy may receive for services rendered the full sum which is really paid for them by parents and others." It is proposed that this new arrangement should begin with the new year.

Board, after some conversation on the contents of this communication, resolved to postpone final action, as the Board of Elders desire a consultation with them regarding the situation of our Boys' School, and as it was not considered impossible that subjects there to be bro't forward might have some tendency towards this matter.

Provincial Financial Board, 1861
[Extracts of minutes transcribed.]

Mon., Feb. 25. Fr. Fries absent.

1. The Brrn. S. T. Pfohl and E. A. Vogler (Committee appointed, see §1, Nov. 15, 1860) reported that the Friedland carriage could be properly repaired for about $30, and that the second-hand carriage proposed to be bo't is too light and small in their opinion. On motion $30 was appropriated for repairing the old carriage. Br. Parm. Lineback was recommended to employ Br. H. Minung for this purpose.

2. The following bills for work done at and articles bo't for the Sustent. house were presented by Br. Bahnson and ordered to be paid:

Julius Mickey's bill for drain, etc., $12.73; official postage $2.42; C. Houser's bill $2.50; A. Fogel's bill for hauling and work $2.50; E. A. Vogler's bill for box of window glass $3.25; L. Hine's bill for whitewashing 1860 $5; in all amounting to $28.40.

3. An application of Br. L. F. Kampmann, Insp. of Theol. Seminary, for $17 amount of fees paid to a Lecturer on Elocution, whose lectures were attended by the students from our Province at present in the Theol. Seminary, was on motion granted and ordered to be paid.

Wed., Apr. 3. Fr. Fries absent.

1. The Bethany carriage, which was recently damaged by the running away of the horse, has been repaired by Br. H. Minung at the very low cost of $2.50.

2. Chairman communicated a letter from Br. Lewis Rights, in which he makes a statement of his financial affairs, from which it appears that owing to sickness, etc., he has incurred in the years 1859 and 1860, over and above what he received from his congregation, a debt of $200. This debt presses heavily upon him, as he has no means to liquidate it. His congregation paid him in 1859 and '60 not quite $300 yearly. Board considered Br. Rights' case and were unanimously of the opinion that he should be relieved from this debt. Therefore, on motion $200 were granted to Br. Lewis Rights.

3. Br. S. T. Pfohl, Tr., mentioned that he had paid a contribution of $5.25 towards the melodeon for the Church at Bethabara. This instrument, bo't from private subscription at Salem,

is to be at the disposal of P.E.C., if it should no longer be used in the Church at Bethabara.

Thurs., July 26. Fr. Fries and E. A. Vogler absent.

4. Br. Pfohl, Tr. of Sustent. Diac., submitted the annual accounts and statement to May 31, 1861, to Board. The sum total of receipts, including a contribution from Salem Female Acady. of $1,800, amounted to $4,303.95. The total disbursements amounted to $3,022.17, leaving a surplus of $1,281.78. On May 31, 1861, the assets amounted to $38,906.90 and the actual liabilities to $443.45. On motion $372.42 of the surplus were appropriated for the reduction of the book value of the 11 acres near Bethabara, and $250 for Macedonia Church. The balance of the surplus, $659.36, was added to Fund Acct. The amount of the Provincial Fund was on June 1, 1861, as last year, $32,926.83, of Fund Account including above balance, $4,914.20.

Wed., Sept. 25. Fr. Fries absent.

Br. Thos. Pfohl having requested a meeting of the Board for the purpose of deciding about an appropriation for the new Negro Church at Salem, it was on motion resolved to grant the sum of $250 for this object.

Wed., Nov. 27. Brn. F. Fries and E. A. Vogler absent.

1. Br. E. A. Vogler having sent in a verbal resignation of his position as a member of the Financial Board by Br. Robert de Schweinitz, the Chairman had a conversation with him on the subject and reported that Br. Vogler adhered to his determination and that he (Br. Vogler) had likewise, in Br. Fr. Fries' name, resigned his (Br. Fries') position as a member of the Financial Board. Board proceeded to fill, according to the Resolution of Provincial Synod of 1858, the two vacancies caused by these resignations. The two brethren, Henry Lineback and J. N. Blum, were nominated and approved by the Board, and the Chairman was requested to notify them of their appointment.

2. The question having arisen, whether Wa. Sustent. Diacy. was at present indebted to Pa. Sust. Diacy., the Treasurer informed the Board that the last account received by him from the North, had been in Jan. 1861, and that the balance due had been paid by him during the course of last winter.

Bethania Diary, with Bethabara, 1861
[Extracts transcribed; handwriting is that of Jacob F. Siewers.]

Fri., Jan. 4. Preached at Bethania at 10 1/2 A.M., after singing the hymn 611, on Jonah 3:1-10 to a good audience. After dinner went to Bethabara, rang the bell, and preached to br. Christian Hauser and Thomas Fetter and a little boy. [A]t night held a prayer meeting at Bethania. ([Margin note:] Fast and prayer recommended by the President.)

Sun., Jan. 6. Preached at Bethania at 10 1/2 A.M. on Matt. 2:1-12, good audience. Afternoon went to Bethabara and preached at 1 1/2 P.M. on the same. After an interval of 1/2 an hour we held a prayer meeting and a discourse on the subject of the day, according to the program of *The Moravian* of November 1.

Sun., Jan. 13. At night held the closing meeting of the week of prayer. The evening meetings were well attended. May the Lord in mercy grant His abundant blessing on this week's united prayer.

Sun., Jan. 27. I did not go to Spanish Grove. The roads are so bad and I feared to ride so far on horseback, owing to my back being weak. I, however, visited an old Negro woman, Else, who sent for me; she lives about a mile from Saml. Stauber's. Conversed and prayed with her. Afterwards spent a couple of hours at br. Thomas Kapp's, who has had a sore throat for some time. Returning, called at br. Samuel Stauber's, visited his Negro woman Sally, conversed and prayed with her, she has the dropsy.

Wed., Feb. 13. Word having been sent us that our little grandchild was sick, we went to Salem this morning.

Thurs., Feb. 14. This afternoon Augustus and Elisabeth's baby died, aged not quite 7 months.

Sat., Feb. 16. This afternoon Rich, my brother's servant, took my horse and carriage to go to Bethania to bring us some clothes. I should have went myself, but Rich was anxious to go, that he might see his mother, who is very sick of dropsy.

Sun., Feb. 17. Rich returned this morning and bro't me the unfortunate news that the horse (whilst he was taking down or putting up the curtains of the carriage) ran away. The wind flapping the curtains frightened him, and he upset the carriage and broke it in such a manner that he could not bring it along.

Wed., Feb. 20. Augustus Pfohl went with me and helped me to fetch my carriage to Salem.

Fri., Feb. 22. Sr. S. and myself returned home today. This being Washington's birthday, the brass band turned out, and hearing that Messrs. Wilson and Patterson, the candidates for the Convention, were at Lash's Hotel, they were invited to the school house, where after some musical introduction, they delivered each a patriotic address on the life, services, and character of the Father of this country.

Wed., Feb. 27. Sr. S. and myself visited at Mother Mickey's. She is entirely blind, but appears to suffer less now in her eyes and head. I conversed with her and we sang a number of our most familiar hymns, English and German. We spent the day there, and before leaving united in prayer on her behalf.

Thurs., Feb. 28. Election day for delegates to the State Convention, which is at the same time to be determined by a vote Convention or No Convention. There were many persons here today.

Thurs., Mar. 7. Sr. S. and myself went to Salem. At night, my brother paying for us, we went to see the Panorama of *Pilgrim's Progress* exhibited by R. J. Greenwood, which we much enjoyed.

Fri., Mar. 8. This evening we again were privileged to see the above painting, and I availed myself of a nearer view on account of my dull eyes, could realize the expressions of the faces of the different characters better, but as a whole lost thereby.

Mon., Mar. 11. Some of the Sunday Sc. scholars went to Salem to the exhibition of Bunyan's Tableaux.

Sun., Apr. 7. Rainy day. After praying the Litany, preached on John 21:15-24. Twelve persons present, 4 males, 8 females, including myself and wife. After dinner went to Bethabara and preached on the same to 3 men and a little boy. This was a disagreeable day.

Sun., Apr. 21. My heart is sick from the distracted state of our Country; may God in mercy stay the arms of violence and restore us to reason and peace.

Thurs., Apr. 25. Sr. S. and myself visited at David Schaus's. Mother Mickey seems much distressed about the prospects of war. Whilst there Peter Pfaff bro't a letter from his daughter, Mrs. Church of Morehead City, which I read for them; its contents but increased her alarm. I conversed with her, we then sang a number of hymns and united together in prayer.

Mon., Apr. 29. I went to Salem and returned with my son Joseph, who by H. Meinung's permission will help me to work in my garden, which is very far back, being disappointed in getting help.

Tues., Apr. 30. This day the band from Salem met with a number of Volunteers and several speakers spoke at Lash's store, the object being to raise volunteers for the State. I understand some 16 volunteered but none of the young men of town. At candle light a town meeting was called and met at the Sch. house, where they organized a company of the elderly citizens including near neighbors, as a home company protection, the young men being included. May the Lord watch over us for good, and prevent the threatening war, and restore peace and brotherly love to our beloved country, is my daily prayer.

Sat., May 11. Drilled the home guard in Military Tactics.

Mon., May 13. Election for Convention, worked in my garden.

Sat., May 25. Garden work. The work I am doing ought to have been done 100 years ago. Then the garden would have been of service to the minister's family.

Thurs., Fri., May 30, 31. Glazing the windows broken last summer by the hail.

Sun., June 2. [W]as told the President of the S. Confederacy, Jefferson Davis, had appointed Thursday the 13th day of June to be observed as a Day of Fasting and Prayer, so I made the appointment.

Tues., June 11. Towards evening br. S. Levin Grabs asked me if I had any objection to Virgil A. Wilson's preaching in the church. I replied that if the Committee had none, I should not, but that under certain circumstances I might reply to him. At early candle light the above preached in the church, opening the service by a hymn, using our book. He delivered a good discourse on the Gospel, its nature, its requirements, faith, repentance, and baptism; that neither by itself would answer, but all together meeting in the individual, would be owned by God and blest by the gift of the Spirit, etc. He stated that the word of God contained no mystery, was adapted to common sense, which was, by the by, the very best of sense. I would here remark, with all his care to instruct his hearers in the simplicity of the gospel requirements, and hence its easy attainment, he never mentioned prayer!! At the close he remarked that the Methodists believed the Baptists might be saved, but the Baptists did not admit that the Methodists would; he also [said] that he did not believe in Methodism, Presbyterianism, Episcopalianism, Moravianism; but *he* believed in Jesus Christ; the former believed in their discipline, but *he* (holding up his Bible) believed in his Bible. I said if I understood him correct (as above) I dissented from him, that the above names chiefly distinguished the different branches of the Christian Church, they built their faith upon the word of God as much as he did, that I objected to his remarks because they were calculated to make incorrect impressions. He then continued his remarks to the close without further interruption.

Thurs., June 13. Prayer and Fast Day. At 10 A.M. preached in Bethania on Jeremiah 18:7-10.[1] After dinner went to Bethabara and preached on the above to a tolerable audience. At 5½ preached at the School House near H. Fogle's by invitation to a small audience. I am told there were only about 12 at Maple Springs.

Sun., June 16. Congregational Festival. Br. Bahnson held the morning blessing at 9½ A.M., preached at 10½ on Matt. 6:33 to a good audience. Afternoon at 2 P.M. Br. B. held the lovefeast, and after an interval the communion. There were present and partaking 44, a number not attending on account of political disturbances, and perhaps on our account. I was very thankful for br. B.'s kindly taking the services off of my hands, not being well.

Sun., June 23. After dinner in company with my daughter Caroline went to Spanish Grove and preached to about 20 females old and young, 2 young men lying outside on the benches refusing to come in. Is this Democratic feeling towards me? I fear it is.

Mon., June 24. At Salem I learned that our aged and venerable br. John Spach had suddenly departed yesterday afternoon.

Sun., June 30. Prayed the Litany according to instructions from the Conference[2] at 10 A.M. and preached on Matthew 9: 1-8.

---

[1]The passage begins: "At what instant I shall speak concerning a nation, and concerning a kingdom, to pluck up, and to pull down, and to destroy it."

[2]Since North Carolina had joined the Confederacy, the Provincial Elders Conference on June 19, 1861, had determined that the prayers in the church litany that refer to the government of the country as well

Sat., July 13. Remained at home. Drilled the young men.

Mon., July 15. It is remarkable, that we have fair and cool weather, and have had for some days. Has the comet in the sky any share in this singular cool weather?

Sat., July 20. Tied up my oats, sunned them and hauled them home, made some 500 bundles.

Tues., July 23. An awful battle is reported to have been fought last Sunday near Manasas, Va., resulting in favor of the South. Heavy losses on both sides.

Thurs., Aug. 1. This was Election day for Clerks; it rained the fore part of the day.

Wed., Aug. 14. The weather is remarkably cool and the night cool enough for frosts.

Thurs., Aug. 15. The weather still continues cool. Should have turned out visiting, but feared I should find no one at home, because there is to be a gathering of Volunteers at Pfafftown. The band of this place has gone out.

Thurs., Aug. 22. At Salem. General muster.

Wed., Aug. 28. Cloudy and drizzling. Afternoon went to Salem and according to promise drilled a number of young men in the School of the Soldier, according to Hardee's *Tactics*, in the Town Hall.

Thurs., Aug. 29. Continued the Drill several hours in the forenoon and afternoon. The object of this instruction is simply to thoroughly instruct, theoretically and practically, a number of young men in the Military Tactics now in use, thus furnishing sufficiently any number required to drill the militia companies correctly in those elementary lessons, without which the musters now required so frequently by law are to say the least a waste of time and a mere farce. For it is impossible to drill a company profitably, in the Company and Battalion exercises, if they are unacquainted with the Elementary Drill. The Captains and Lieutenants are not able to drill a numerous district Company in Squads of 4 or 5 men at most (even generously allowing that they understand their duties) without a number of efficient aids. The manner I adopt is to inform the men the why and the wherefore during the Exercises, that they may become intelligent aids in instructing others, and to

---

as the prayer in times of war should be amended to be "consistent with our present circumstances." See *Records of the Moravians in North Carolina*, v. 11, p. 6062.

remedy the defects of the more than useless musters now prevailing. Returned home in the rain. ([Margin note:] This short chapter is intended to explain the course I am pursuing, the object I have in view; whatever *is said* or *may be said to the contrary* notwithstanding. J. F. S. s.)

Sat., Aug. 31. This morning at a quarter past 5 A.M. we experienced an earthquake, the house tottered, the windows were shaken, accompanied by a rumbling noise.

Wed., Sept. 4. Towards evening we went to Salem. Drilled in the Town Hall.

Thurs., Sept. 5. After dinner a short drill. Returned home.

Wed., Sept. 11. Towards evening went to Salem. At night drilled in the Town Hall till 9 1/2.

Thurs., Sept. 12. Drilled fore and afternoon. Returned home. Like to have had a serious accident at the ford on Silas creek.

Sat., Sept. 14. Thomas Spach called here this morning. His Father kept his accounts in German with the written German alphabet, which he could not read. I copied them for him in English.

Sun., Sept. 15. After praying the Litany at Bethania at 10 A.M. preached on Gen. 4:3-8 to a small audience, the whole country having gone to Maple Springs camp meeting. Towards evening Sr. S. and myself went to Salem.

Mon., Sept. 16. At night, according to agreement, drilled at the Town Hall.

Mon., Sept. 23. It was cool enough for frost this morning. Went out to the Methodist protracted meeting near Constantine Stoltz's, and by request preached for them on Matthew 13:1-9.

Sat., Sept. 28. Started for Friedberg, having promised br. Rights if I could I would lend him a helping hand [in a protracted meeting]. [C]alled at br. Ephraim Transou's, having heard that they had lost a son [Owen] in the army of Virginia. This heavy affliction I hope and trust may be blest and sanctified to their souls. Conversed and prayed with them.

[Reaching Friedberg, Br. Siewers participated in the protracted meeting over the next several days.]

Mon., Sept. 30. At night br. Rights conducted the service by an exhortation, and several females were under conviction and prayed for mercy, among which was br. Rights' Alice. What a pleasing sight to a Father, to be instrumental in leading his own child to seek the Saviour, a sight that creates joy in Heaven, joy to Jesus, and participated in by the angels of God. The services were well attended, and good order prevailed. May the good Lord continue to bless the labors of this faithful servant of his, to his own soul as well as to his flock. Amen.

Wed., Oct. 2. Returned home, took br. Rights' daughter along to the Salem Academy.

Sun., Oct. 13. At 1/2 past 10 A.M. prayed the Litany at Bethania, and preached on John 10:14 to a small congregation, there being preaching in Pfafftown for the Volunteer Company encamped there by br. Michael Doub. At candle light discoursed on the 40th Psalm, closed with prayer, remembering especially the young men of our community who are to leave for the Army in a few days to the mercy and care and protection of our Lord and Savior.

Mon., Oct. 14. This morning called at br. Daniel and Herman Butner's, desiring to speak to William and Frank Butner, but they had already left.

Tues., Oct. 15. Thomas Conrad having departed this life yesterday morning, his funeral was to take place today at 1 P.M., but owing to the Volunteer Company of Cap. Stow's leaving Pfafftown today, the Corps[e] did not arrive here until after 3 P.M. A larger congregation than I was led to expect assembled here, and I preached on Matthew 6:13-14. After which the burial service took place.

Wed., Oct. 23. Sr. S. and myself, having heard of the death of br. Ephraim Transou's son Rubin, went to Pfaff Town to see this heavily afflicted family.

Sun., Oct. 27. After dinner went to Spanish Grove, and preached to 2 men and some 12 or 14 females, several boys being outside. Joseph Conrad went out and bro't them in, but they soon again went out. After meeting I gave them some instruction.

Tues., Oct. 29. Sr. S. and myself visited at the widow Sr. Mariann Butner's, whose aged mother-in-law, the widow Butner, has her 91st birthday today.

Sun., Nov. 3. At 101/2 A.M. preached at Bethania on Luke 16:1-13. After dinner went to Bethabara and preached on the above to a small audience. Sr. S., who had accompanied me with the intention of instructing the Sunday School children in singing, was disappointed in not finding any scholars at church. The road being quite heavy she staid at br. Christian Hauser's. I went to the double bridge S. House and preached on the above to 8 persons all told.

Wed., Nov. 6. Afternoon went to Salem. Election for President and Vice, and members of Congress. Took the returns down to Winston.

Fri., Nov. 15. Fasting, humiliation, and prayer day at Bethania 10$1/2$ A.M. One brother present and some 13 or 14 sisters. Opened by singing no. 611 and offering a prayer at the Table on our knees. Rising, the brother [had] left, and I had a small audience of sisters. Preached on Isaiah 58.[1] After dinner went to Bethabara and preached on the same to 3 men and some 15 females.

Thurs., Dec. 5. ([Margin note:] By the Governor, Thanksgiving Day.) Preached at Bethania on Psalm 116:12-13 at 10$1/2$ A.M. to a tolerable audience. Coming out of meeting, a letter was handed me from br. Ephraim Transou requesting me to take his name from the Church Book, and to consider him no longer a member of the Moravian Church, for reasons which need no explanation, adding that it includes his family. Dated Nov. 17th, 1861.

Tues., Dec. 24. At early candle light, a good audience having assembled, the meeting opened by the brass instruments. After singing a hymn, followed by prayer on our knees and a short discourse on the subject of our Saviour's birth, the lovefeast prepared for the children was served, during which the choir of children sang 4 hymns. Closed by singing the Doxology. Mr. Baldwin, Baptist minister now resident of this place, and Mr. Sennecar, Lutheran minister, who has been preaching in this neighborhood for some time, I am told, were present.

Tues., Dec. 31. At half past 11, the last meeting is usually held. At 12 midnight the organ and brass instruments played the Tune 146. Then we all knelt down and offered a prayer. After which the Daily Word and Doctrinal Text for the 1st of January was read from the Text Book of 1851, which was agreed upon to be used, another failing to be obtained.

---

[1]Isa. 58:6 states: "Is not this the fast that I have chosen? to loose the bands of wickedness, to undo the heavy burdens, and to let the oppressed go free, and that ye break every yoke?"

Friedberg Diary, with Hope, 1861
[Extracts transcribed; handwriting is that of Christian Lewis Rights.]

Fri., Jan. 4. In accordance with the recommendation of the President of the United States setting apart this day as a day of humiliation, fasting and prayer in view of the political difficulties by which we are surrounded, there was preaching here at Friedberg at 11 o'clock from Ezekiel 7:25-27 and again at night from Matt. 24:1-13. The church was well filled.

Wed.-Fri., Jan. 16-18. Visited among the Hope members. A considerable excitement was created from a fear that owing to the high waters I had been drowned.

Sat., Feb. 9. Brother Bahnson in his round of visitation called at Friedberg yesterday evening and remained overnight. This morning I accompanied him to Brother Daniel Spach's, jun., where by agreement we were to meet Brother Solomon Hage, who was to conduct him through Fishel Town, but on arriving there brother Hage had not yet come, and we proceeded on to Brother Sandford Fishel's and from there were on our way to Jacob Fishel's, when Bro. H. overtook us, and the brethren proceeded on their mission, and I returned home.

Mon., Mar. 4. Inauguration of President Lincoln.

Fri., Mar. 29. Good Friday. Services at Friedberg: reading, Lovefeast and Communion. Several of the old brethren told me afterwards that they had never seen as many persons at Friedberg on this day as were here today, and among them was brother John Hall from Macedonia, soliciting subscriptions for their new church.

Sun., Mar. 31. Easter Sunday. At the ringing of the bell at 1/2 past 9 o'clock we formed before the church and went in procession to the graveyard and prayed the Easter Morning Litany. Then returning we went into the church, or as many— which was about half—as could get in, and I preached from the doctrinal text for the day, 2 Tim. 1:10: Jesus Christ hath abolished death, etc. ([Friedberg Report:] Several respectable strangers, I was afterwards told, that came from a distance could not get in, and it is agreed on all hands that there have not been as many persons here for many years, if ever, on this day, and the conduct of the people was commendable throughout.) In the afternoon went to Hope, where we likewise went in the graveyard, and then I preached from Luke 24:8.

Thurs., June 13. President Davis fasting and prayer day. Preached from Judges 10:15-16: And the children of Israel said unto the Lord, we have sinned, etc.

Mon., June 17. Went to Salem to see two companies of the Volunteers leave, but they were gone before I got there.

Sat., Sept. 28. Commenced a protracted meeting at Friedberg.

Tues., Oct. 1. [Meeting continued. A]n invitation was given for those that desired to be prayed for, and seven came forward. Out of that number 5 professed to have found peace.

Fri., Nov. 15. Fast day. Preaching. ([Friedberg Report:] Hardly anyone came. Praying for the Southern Confederacy is not popular here.)

Sun., Dec. 1. Preaching at Hope from Luke 12:31. ([Friedberg Report:] After the congregation was dismissed an old gentleman present took me to task for a sermon I preached at Friedberg some weeks before when he was present, and we discussed the matter at length. He professes to be a Christian, but does not think it necessary to belong to any church.)

Wed., Dec. 25. Christmas. Preaching at Friedberg from Matthew 2. Afterwards Lovefeast for the children, then a closing meeting during which the [children] sung "Hark the Angels Singing," repeated a dialogue, recited verses, etc. It was a beautiful day, and the church was densely crowded, and good order prevailed throughout.

Sat., Dec. 28. By request of Brother Francis Fishel went with him to Reedy Creek to see his sister, Mrs. Hanes. She is very low with typhoid fever, expects to die and seems to be in despair as regards the salvation of her soul. She says she is lost, that there is no alternative for her but to be damned. I conversed and prayed with her, and tried to prevail with her to try and pray, but all seemed unavailing.

Private Diary of R. P. Leinbach, 1861
[Serving Friedland till June, then Macedonia and Muddy Creek; extracts transcribed.]

Tues., Jan. 8. Evening prayer meeting at Piney Woods meeting house. A number of young men were present who had given trouble at different times to different ministers, but their conduct then was certainly very exemplary.

Tues., Jan. 29. Visited Br. Ph. Spach's. G. Sides from Texas was there. Had some interesting conversation. 'Tis rather strange with this br. P. Spach; he never comes to church. Nor do any of the family of Reed's.

Sun., Apr. 28. In consequence of Br. Bittle's sudden resignation of his office of "Town School teacher," I was applied to by the board to take his place for a month until the regular close. By permission of the Conference I did so, attending, however, to my duties as minister of Friedland. The visiting was of course out of the question.

Having received and accepted a call to take charge of the Macedonia congregation, I preached my farewell sermon at Friedland on Sunday, May 26, from 1 Cor. 1:3 to a numerous audience. It was a source of comfort to me that there seemed to be real regret manifested on the part of the people. I had labored under great discouragements at Friedland. I was almost fresh from the North, had always been accustomed to town or city congregations, and mostly in a comparatively flourishing condition where, if we did not wield the controlling influence, we at least kept our own. Here at Friedland—my first post—I found everything down, the premises in neglected condition, the congregation anything but prosperous and rather overawed by the surrounding Baptist element. I lived there but two months when my dear wife was taken sick. It required some time for me to feel my way and to obtain an influence. The fact of my having been at the North and just coming from Salem prejudiced the people against me, and I was just beginning to become efficient when I received the call. Owing in part no doubt to domestic trials and rather unusual difficulties, I have become thoroughly disheartened and had conceived the opinion (the greatest obstacle to success) that I could achieve nothing at Friedland. I was, moreover, satisfied that nothing but the adoption of the so called "new measures" would ever revive the congregation, and I was not prepared and not able to take an active part in them. I was satisfied there was some degree of spiritual life, but was satisfied I was not the person to bring this out to advantage so as to accomplish any great good. I wanted something more done than merely keep the congregation together. I believed a person more experienced could bring this latent spark into open flame. Under this impression I was willing to leave this handful of precious faithful souls in the care of Br. Fry.

Thurs., June 6. Conference. Sent a trunk of books over to Br. Hall's by opportunity.

Fri., June 7. Packed up my things for Macedonia. Feelings of deep anxiety of course filled my breast. Going to a new place, untried by anyone, new class of people—'twas a serious and prayerful time with me.

Sat., June 8. Accompanied Br. Bahnson over to Elm Hill, which was to be my home.

Sun., June 9. Preached my introductory sermon at Macedonia. Having been somewhat physically reduced, my throat (which always sympathizes with the body generally) was not in good order, and having to speak in the open air, I soon became hoarse. Hence did not speak long. The audience was large and very respectable, and I regretted my inability to acquit myself to more satisfaction.

Tues., June 11. Called on br. Calvin Riddle by request. Remained all night with him. Bed bugs allowed me no rest. I soon found this was truly a new country, and many novel experiences were to be made. There was none of the German element to which I had always been accustomed.

Thurs., June 13. Prayer and fasting by recommendation of Pres. Jefferson Davis. Before the sermon br. D. Wheeler came to me and asked for his paper certificate of church membership. He stated that there had been difficulty between himself and other members. I begged him to postpone the matter, as I was a stranger and did [not] wish such an act to be my first official work. He consented, and I have heard nothing more since. ([Macedonia Report:] During the sermon Lieutenant Lane of the first company of Davie volunteers entered the church. After the congregation was dismissed he by request entertained the assembly by recitals of events from the seat of war. He was out drumming up recruits.)

Sun., June 23. Organized the Sunday School. Br C. Riddle electrified the congregation by expressing his unwillingness to serve in any capacity in the Sunday School for reasons which he promises to assign me anytime at my convenience. Br. Wheeler was elected superintendent, Br. W. Laster vice president, Br. D. Sheek secretary, and Br. Richmond Sheek treasurer.

Thurs., June 27. Called on Br. Riddle and learned from him that the reason he would not serve in the S. School was because Br. Wheeler would probably be connected with the school.

I spoke to him about making up his difficulty with Br. Wheeler, and he expressed a perfect willingness to do so. The following Sunday after having preached from Luke 19:41-42 I brot the two brn. together, and to the surprise of all they shook hands after years of bitter hostility. Br. Wheeler again carries the keys notwithstanding the fuss that was made on that score formerly.

Sun., July 14. Preached from Acts 17:31 on the Judgment. In the afternoon I preached again at Ward's Schoolhouse, from Psalm 130:3-4. The attendance was very good, could not all be accommodated; hence I spoke under the door, women inside, men out. Arrangements were made to continue the preaching, the neighbors promising to furnish benches and to cut out a road.

Sun., July 21. Preached over at Muddy Creek to a very good audience. Remained all night at Mr. James Eckels. There are good congregations at Muddy Creek, kind and very intelligent people; but 'tis more difficult to gain attention there than any place I have been preaching at. I fear there are too many who love to imbibe spirituous liquor more than to partake of spiritual food.

Wed., July 24. Went up to Br. D. Sheek's and Br. R. Sheek's, called on Br. Jonathan Miller. We had just heard of the fearful battle of Manassas, having a number of friends there. Br. Sheek and I concluded to go to Salem and obtain the full accounts.

Sun., July 28. In the afternoon at 3, I preached at Walnut Grove, or Ward's Schoolhouse. Took supper at Evefelter Laster's. He belongs to no church, tho a professor, and seems satisfied to live thus. I reasoned with him but could not altogether convince him it was his duty to belong to a church.

Sun., Aug. 4. Preached from 1 Kings 22:23. As there had been some dissatisfaction expressed with our manner of standing in prayer, I was waited upon by Br. Calvin Riddle, who made a request that at the kneeling posture might be adopted. Some knelt and some stood—uniformity was desired. I promised to lay the matter before [Ministers] Conference, which I did. The Conference instructed me to allow them to do as their consciences dictated, to kneel or stand; but as for the minister, he was to conform to the Moravian custom of standing in prayer in the pulpit. I stated before preaching what the Moravian custom was, but at the same time told them to do as their conscience required. That evening was prayer meeting for the volunteers. I spoke first, was followed by Br. Riddle, who indulged in a series of personal remarks in regard to people who were too proud to kneel. Indeed the whole tenor of his remarks was so shamefully personal that a number of the members of the church were offended, and Br. D. Sheek spoke to Br. R. about it, telling him he had hurt my feelings very much. He answered, "When I speak I mean to hurt people's feelings, and you need give yourself no uneasiness, as I am going to join the Methodists, who have offered to make me licensed exhorter." Br. Riddle has always been a leading member here, had had things his own way, had been opposed to having a stationed minister, and now that there was one here who did contrary to his wishes, I supposed he was trying to have affairs conducted on his principles. Finding I would not yield by kind means, it seemed he strove to *compel* me. I have since learned that he has confessed this to have been his object. I called to see him in reference to this matter, told him there was a collision between his ways and our ways, and that if he wish to remain a member of our church he must conform to our rules. I told him he had set the weight of his influence against me in my official capacity. He disowned any intention to wound me or give any personal offense, asked my pardon, said Br. D. Sheek had misrepresented his words— but that his religious principles he could not give up. These principles are opposition to infant baptism and to standing in prayer. I put the question thus: Will you conform to our Moravian rules? If not, there's no use in your remaining. I told him I should refer the matter to the Committee the next [Sun]day.

Sun., Aug. 11. After preaching I called the Committee together. Br. Riddle was not there. The brethren Lee and D. Sheek were for making short work. Brn. R. Sheek and D. Hodge were opposed to severe measures. They both stated that they were ignorant of Moravian rules. I told them a very prominent rule was "observance of the rules," and that Br. Riddle had given me to understand what tallied with his notions was all right, what did not he should not observe, i.e., his religious principles he should not give up. They still seemed undecided, plead that Br. Riddle had meant nothing, neither in regard to the principle of kneeling in prayer, nor had he any idea of saying anything disrespectful towards the minister in charge, notwithstanding that many had regarded his address as highly so.

Br. D. Sheek then repeated Br. R.'s words in regard to the matter: "When I speak I mean to hurt people's feelings." It was clearly evident that such had been his intention: he had spoken those words, then denied them, and denied all motives that were attributed to him, and which he has since confessed himself to have been ruled by.

Thereupon all the brn. agreed that if, as it seemed, he was inclined to rule, regardless of his duties as a member, towards the church and towards his minister, regardless of the laws of truthfulness, why the sooner he was out of the church the better, and therefore he "ought to go." This was the resolution of the Committee, but it was not communicated to him, owing to various reasons. The report was spread abroad that he was thrown out of the church. Meanwhile I had various duties to attend to.

Tues., Aug. 13. I went down to Friedberg to celebrate the 13th of August. Before service began, they sang some most beautiful tunes; the effect was most pleasing and admirably adapted to attune the heart to the worship of the Triune God.

Sun., Aug. 18. Preached at Muddy Creek to a good audience. Mr. Alex Ellis has commenced giving lessons to a singing class which at least helps to fill the house even if it does not materially swell the singing as yet.

Tues., Aug. 20. [Provincial Elders] Conference approved of the decision of the [Macedonia] Committee.

Fri., Aug. 23. Friday afternoon Br. Riddle called to see me. He spent several hours with me. He was willing, it appeared, to do everything reasonable provided he could have his own way. He wished to represent the difficulty as a personal one. I told him it was not. He asked me, then, if the trouble was not personal, why did it come upon him. I told him he was the author of all this trouble; if he would chime in with our rules there would be no difficulty anywheres else. He went off after receiving from me another assurance the difficulty was not a personal one.

Sun., Aug. 25. We had a good congregation, large and very respectable. After preaching, Br. Riddle got up and requested the congregation to remain for his sake. In many words and in pretty strong language he stated his determination to withdraw from the church, that he could not abide infant baptism and standing in prayer. He hoped we might remain united, that God's blessing might rest upon us, offered up a prayer whilst men and women were sobbing like children. I replied in a few words, stating that I had extended all privilege in regard to prayer but that was not satisfactory, that others were allowed to do as they chose, but that was not enough; they wished me to do as they wished regardless of my pledges and obligations to the contrary. Thus the matter closed. Owing to mental anxiety and physical depression, I felt myself too weak to preach in the afternoon and recalled the appointment.

Mon., Aug. 26. I handed Br. Calvin Riddle the desired certificate.

As there was to be protracted meeting at Bethlehem,[1] I was requested to call in the services for that Sunday. Having understood that there was to be protracted meeting at Friedland at the same time, I resolved to go down there. I went over to Salem and from there down to Friedland. I cannot describe the feelings with which I wandered over that loved spot.

Thurs., Sept 5. I attended [Ministers] Conference. Saturday I returned home, where I learned that Henry Hall, a member of the congregation and a soldier at Manassas, had the typhoid fever and that his father was going on to see him.

Sun., Sept. 8. I went up to Macedonia. There were but few present. I felt awkward and much embarrassed. There was a general feeling that all was not well and the sequel proved it; for after preaching some ten persons applied for certificates of membership. I took down the names and in due time I wrote them and sent them to the owners. Br. Wheeler was much affected, talked very much to the purpose, sometimes had the members weeping, sometimes laughing. He called on them to unite with him in prayer, which they did. My feelings during this severe trial may be more readily imagined than described. I had been discouraged at Friedland because members would not come flocking in; 'tis bad enough to be unable to build up a church. But I was yet to learn what it was to tear one down, at least in part. I spoke a few words at the close of his appeal. I told them it was to me an incomprehensible matter; at Friedland the Methodists came to my meetings, and some had even spoken of joining the church. Here I did as I had done there, and now my own members were leaving me because I was not Methodistic enough.

Fri., Sept. 13. . . . I learned that Henry Hall had died at Manassas the previous Friday at 4 o'clock A.M.

---

[1]A meeting place in northern Davie County, known in the previous century as Timber Ridge Meeting House.

Sun., Sept. 15. I preached at Muddy Creek from Acts 18:30-31. After dinner I called to see Old Sr. Cooper, who is almost if not quite 100 yrs old.

Sun., Sept. 22. Went home with Br. D. Sheek by invitation, remained all night at his brother Richmond's. Our church difficulty is not yet over. Yesterday three more members applied for certificates. The season of trial I shall not soon forget. There was danger of losing br. R. Sheek, and I therefore made it my business to spend as much time there as possible.

Sat., Oct. 19. Called to see Br. Daniel Sheek, who had returned from Manassas a few days before. Found him weak and sick.

Sun., Oct. 20. We arrived [at Friedland] about suppertime. I preached in the evening from Isa. 55:6, [and] called on Br. Mock to follow me with prayer. Before he was half thro' the storm broke out, and when we rose from our knees there were three or four girls prostrated before God, pleading for mercy for their souls. There were a number of young persons (young men also) down on their knees that evening, and some of them the most wicked of the wicked. It was a joyful sight to see old Friedland once more waking up. Our meetings were kept up until Thursday, when we started home.

Mon., Oct. 28. Evening about dark Br. Henry Hall's corpse arrived from Manassas. I went on to Salem the same evening to notify Br. Bahnson of the fact, inviting him over to attend the service and to procure the services of the Salem Brass Band.

Tues., Oct. 29. Afternoon Henry was buried up at Macedonia. Br. Bahnson preached the funeral sermon to a crowded house. The band was present and performed suitable pieces for the occasion. 'Twas a sad and impressive time with all.

Mon., Nov. 11. Made arrangements for confirmation instruction for the three young girls who professed to have attained unto the pardon of their sins: Amanda Miller, Margaret Cook and Elizabeth Sheek.

Tues., Nov. 12. This afternoon I went up to keep instruction, but soon became convinced that it was morally impossible for those children to comprehend the catechism. Br. Sheek told me Sr. Lucy Fry, who had left the church with a number of others, was anxious to be readmitted.

Sun., Nov. 24. [At Friedland t]here did not seem to be such a spirit among the members as there had been; there had not been praying enough done. I learned that there had been quite a number of deaths in the neighborhood since my last visit. Four children had died out of one family, several more, all of diphtheria. There was a child buried there at Friedland on Monday morning, but I was not called in to officiate and knew nothing of it until it was buried. I went there but came too late.

Mon., Dec. 2. Went over to Muddy Creek to take over two quilts I had begged of Br. R. de Schweinitz for old Sr. Cooper.

Sun., Dec. 29. Preached from Isa. 40:8. As there was singing in the immediate neighborhood under the conduct of Mr. Calvin Riddle, we had but a small congregation.

[New] Philadelphia Reports, with Macedonia and Muddy Creek till June, then with Friedland, 1861
[Extracts transcribed; handwriting is that of Thomas Frye.]

Fri., Jan. 4. Went to Macedonia to attend to the fast and prayer proclaimed by the President of the U.S. The congregation was small, [it] having rained on Sunday before so that it was not published. Still there were some forty present.

[Sat., Jan. 5. At Macedonia] we measured one side of the land which Br. Sheek offers to give to the Church. Our brethren seem to be in good earnest to build a new church if they can get help.

Tues., Mar. 12. Went to Macedonia according to previous appointment with Br. Bahnson . . . , after which the Brethren proceeded to elect a committee for the building of a new brick church. The Brethren elected were Br. Hall, Br. Danl. Sheek, Br. Jonathan Miller and Father Sheek as an advisory Committee, after which a subscription paper was presented to which was subscribed some $2.35-2.40 by 5 men.

[Sat., Mar. 31. Great Sabbath.] Had Lovefeast and Communion at which Br. Alspach and wife were present, who both manifested great interest in the participation of the Lord's Supper, being the first time in which they have partaken in the Moravian Church. We also had two Lutheran Sisters who were so well pleased with our mode that they told Br. Kiger if they lived near enough they would become Moravians, and so said a young man from Davy County of the Methodist Church who partook with us.

Sun., Apr. 28. Preached at Phil. from Luke 15:18 to a crowded house of people. Serious attention and solemnity appeared to pervade and tears were freely shed, so that we were encouraged for the better. Saw Br. Norman, who still said that he does not wish to live in the church while three or four of the Brethren remained in it. We therefore called the Committee together, who decided that if they wished to have their names taken off that it should be done.

Sat., May 4. Preached at Macedonia from Isa. 55:6 to but some 28 hearers, there being a muster in the neighborhood for volunteers.

Sun., May 19. Delivered my farewell address at Muddy Creek from Acts 20:27.

Sun., June 2. Delivered my farewell address [at Macedonia] from Acts 20:27.

Thurs., June 13. Fast and prayer at Phil., only some thirty present.

Sun., June 23. Preached at Friedland from 1 Cor. 14:24-25 to a good and well behaved people of Methodists, Baptists and Moravians and outsiders.

Sun., July 28. Preached at Phil. . . . [W]e returned thanksgiving and praise to God for his great mercy in granting us the victory over our enemies at Manasses.

Sun., Oct. 20. Had prayer meeting at Friedland. . . . On Tuesday some of the Brethren sent for Br. Rights, after asking whether I was willing, who I think arrived on Wednesday and performed a noble part to our help in preaching and prayer meeting, etc. On Thursday we closed for the present, the result of which was 18 or 20 converts, some even of which are called iron shells. There are 10 of our converts applied for membership.

1862

[Despite the war, the United States Congress approved the Homestead Act to encourage settlement of the West. The Land Grant Act paved the way for western state university systems. Union forces took New Orleans, but neither side won total victory in the East. The battle on Antietam Creek at Sharpsburg on Sept. 17 resulted in the bloodiest day in American history.

In February the Burnside expedition captured Roanoke Island, making Confederate use of North Carolina ports difficult. Federal troops burned Winton later that month and occupied New Bern. In September, Zebulon B. Vance, colonel of the 26th North Carolina Regiment, was elected governor. In Guilford County William Sidney Porter (O. Henry) was born.]

Memorabilia of Salem Congregation, 1862
[Extracts transcribed; handwriting is that of Francis Raymond Holland.]

In an unprecedented degree, this year has been a year of affliction and bereavement. To all of us, whatever may have been our personal or domestic state, this year has been a trying and a startling one. The desolating tide of an obstinate and bloody war has continued to roll over our land. All around us—to the east and west, north and south—has the fearful conflict raged. Upon a moderate estimate, it is computed that not less than 200,000 men on both sides have perished or been permanently disabled during this year. Were these ghastly victims of war to march past us, two and two, in close ranks and at quick time, not less than two whole days from sunrise to sunset would be required for the dismal procession to sweep past a given point! And could we this evening take a glance at all the cold, desolated homes that contain so many bleeding hearts all over our once united and happy country, what language would be adequate to describe our emotions!

Though we have great cause for gratitude as a congregation for exemption from the suffering and distress occasioned in many parts of the country by the presence of large armies, as well as for the distinguished preservation vouchsafed to nearly all the young men from this congregation in the scenes of danger through which they were called to pass, yet have we in various ways felt the pressure and sad effects of the war more sensibly during this year than in the preceding one. Not only have we had to encounter greater embarrassments in respect to outward and temporal affairs—embarrassments which have given rise to anxious thoughts for the future—but our eyes are no longer unfamiliar with the sight of sick and wounded and disabled soldiers, nor our ears with the cry of the bereaved! More especially of late have we been called upon to sympathize with brn. and srs., friends and neighbors, in the sore afflictions and bereavements that have been permitted to come upon them through the casualties of war.

While the many victims of cruel, relentless war thus prove that death has in this year reaped a rich harvest, various diseases were also commissioned to do their works and permitted to make unusual and startling inroads into many places and districts of [the] country. The town of Wilmington in our state suffered in an almost unexampled degree for several months from the ravages of yellow fever, while in many other places various contagious or epidemic diseases have carried off an unusual number of victims. In this congregation the number of deaths has been considerably greater than the average for many years past (being only equalled by those in 1857), and taken together with those of individuals in our town and neighborhood not connected with us by membership, the number largely exceeds the aggregate of any former year. Our church books contain the record of 52 funerals (including persons of all conditions) on occasion of which the services of the church were asked and performed.

With comparatively few exceptions they were the youthful, including a number of children, who were removed from this mortal state of existence into the eternal world. According to age they are as follows:

Under 5 years	10
From 5-10 years	8
From 10-20 years	7
From 20-30 years	13
From 30-40 years	7
From 40-50 years	1
From 50-60 years	3
From 70-80 years	1
Over 80	2

During the year we have continued to be deprived of intelligence from the different Provinces and mission fields occupied by our Church beyond the limits of the Confederacy. From the mission among the Cherokees, the painful intelligence was received in a letter from Sr. Bishop that at New Springplace on Sept. 2d the assistant missionary, Br. Ward, a native Cherokee, had been put to death in cold blood by a party of Indians who also took the missionary, Br. Bishop, prisoner, conveying him some distance to their camp. After having interred the remains of Br. Ward and waited for a number of days in vain for tidings from Br. Bishop, Sr. Bishop and Sr. Ward with their children left the mission station, retiring for greater safety into the state of Arkansas. Today intelligence has been received that Br. Bishop and his family had arrived at Bethlehem, Pa., in a very destitute condition, but nothing further concerning Br. Mock, the other missionary. The fate of the remaining missionaries as well as of the stations and flocks is of course unknown.

During the year our institutions for education have continued in regular operation. The number of pupils in the Female Academy has this year again been fully equal to the extent of the accommodations. It is certainly a proof of the kind care, protection, and blessing of our gracious Lord and Savior, that among this large number of pupils not a single death has taken place.

The colored division of the congregation has throughout the year enjoyed the stated ministrations of the Word and Sacrament; and the services have upon the whole been marked by a good attendance. The deportment of the congregation has been very quiet and orderly. The meetings during the Passion Week and at Easter were, as usual, quite numerously attended and—there is reason to hope—not without a blessing. On Sept. 28th nine persons were admitted to full membership, viz., 2 by baptism and 7 by confirmation; 12 persons have departed this life, viz., 5 adults and 7 children; 5 infants were baptized, and 4 couples married. The Sunday School—and the exercises of which consist of singing and oral instruction in the Scriptures—has been kept with exemplary faithfulness by a number of sisters. Their patient and unselfish labors have been attended with an encouraging degree of success. The number of communicants in this, the colored division of the congregation, is 52; and the number of stated hearers about 200.

Salem Diary, 1862
[Extracts transcribed; handwriting is that of Francis Raymond Holland.]

Wed., Jan. 1. The Texts of the day, "Lord, lift thou up the light of thy countenance upon us" (Ps. 4:6) and "My grace is sufficient for thee; for my strength is made perfect in weakness" (2 Cor. 12:9), were calculated to encourage us to prayer and confidence in God our Savior during the year upon which we have been permitted to enter. We know not what this year may bring forth, nor who of us shall live on earth to see the end of it. In public affairs, the future seems gloomy; and as regards our congregation, we have cause to cry mightily for an outpouring of the Holy Spirit.

Fri., Feb. 28. Day of Humiliation and Prayer, by proclamation of President Davis. Public service at 10 A.M.

Sun., Apr. 13. Palm Sunday. At 10 A.M. preaching by Br. Holland. At 3 P.M. 14 young persons were confirmed and 1 baptized. They were all females. At 7 1/2 P.M. reading the "Acts of the Last Days of the Son of Man."

Sat., Apr. 19. At 2 P.M. the usual lovefeast meeting was held. The ode [was] sung, but no cakes and coffee served, owing to the impossibility of procuring the latter article.

Sun., Apr. 20. Easter. At 5 1/4 A.M. the Easter Morning Litany was prayed on the graveyard. At 10 A.M. preaching.

Fri., May 16. Day of Humiliation and Prayer, by proclamation of President Davis. Service at 10 A.M., conducted by Br. Holland. Tolerably well attended on the srs. side, poorly by the men.

Thurs., May 22. At 2 P.M. Infant School examination. Hailstorm, very severe, near Salem to the south and southeasterly. Here but few hailstones fell, but they were very large. Some as large as hen's eggs.

Wed., May 28. Close of annual session of Salem Female Academy. No examination this year—musical entertainment in the evening.

Sun., July 6. At 10 A.M. Litany and preaching by Br. Holland. In the sermon recalled to mind the character and martyrdom of John Huss.

Sun., Aug. 10. Celebration of the 13th. At 2 P.M. Lovefeast ode sung, but no refreshments served, owing to the impossibility of purchasing coffee and sugar. At 3 P.M. Lord's Supper in German, and at 71/2 P.M. in English.

Sun., Aug. 17. Children's festival. Several individuals having contributed sugar and coffee, a lovefeast was prepared for the children.

Sun., Aug. 24. Rev. Alfred A. Watson, a minister of the Episcopal Church, recently stationed at Newbern and now chaplain of the 2nd Regt. N.C. troops, preached at 10 A.M. Br. R. de Schweinitz read the litany in the absence of Br. Holland, who visited Macedonia on this day.

Fri., Aug. 29. At 71/2 P.M. a meeting was held for the Single Brn. and Youth to state to them the reason which had led the Board of Elders to decide not to celebrate the Single Brn.'s festival this year. The absence from home of nearly all the single Brn. is this reason. In this meeting it was also mentioned that the boys who had attained the age of 14 years would now be included in the Choir of Youth.

Sun., Sept. 7. Married People's festival. Lovefeast ode sung at 2 P.M. No cake and coffee served. At 31/2 Holy Communion, pretty well attended, considering that a number of married brn. are from home, sickness prevailing in some families, and the minds of some in suspense, as no particulars have yet been received concerning our people in the recent battle at or near Manasses.

Mon., Sept. 15. At 71/2 P.M. prayer meeting. After an interval of about 2 mos. the weekday evening meetings were resumed. There is to be prayer meeting on Monday evenings and Bible lecture on Wednesday evenings.

Thurs., Sept. 18. Day of thanksgiving, by appointment of the President "for mercies vouchsafed to our people and for recent successes of the Confederate army." Public service at 10 A.M.

Wed., Sept. 24. At 4 P.M. funeral of Mary Jane Yates, child of Mr. Chas. Yates and his wife Sr. Mary Yates. The child died of diphtheria yesterday evening. This is the sixth death by means of diphtheria in Salem within a little less than a month.

Thurs., Oct. 2. At 2 P.M. the Male Missionary Society held its annual meeting. But a small number of members present. No lovefeast this year.

Sun., Oct. 5. At 10 A.M. litany and preaching. Preaching by Rev. J. D. Scheck, a Lutheran minister who visits our place on a collecting tour. He is one of the agents of the Lutheran

Synod of N.C. to procure funds for the erection of an institution at Louisville, Forsyth Co., N.C., in which the daughters of deceased and disabled soldiers are to be furnished with a gratuitous education.

Tues., Oct. 14. Br. Scheck left, having collected for his object in Salem about $400.

Sun., Nov. 9. Congregation festival celebrated this day. Owing to the difficulty of obtaining sugar, milk, etc., the lovefeast was omitted. Instead the ode used for several years past was sung at 2 P.M., the usual time of lovefeast. At 3 P.M. the Lord's Supper was celebrated in the German language, Br. Grunert officiating; and at 7 P.M. in English. The attendance of sisters was very good, brethren only tolerable.

Sun., Nov. 23. At 10 A.M. litany and preaching by Br. Bahnson. At 11 A.M. the young man Augustine L. [Lewis Augustine] Hauser departed this life. About 6 weeks ago he returned from the army in bad health, having from exposure, etc., in camp contracted the disease which carried him off. How many men in the prime of life have fallen victims to disease in this abominable war, besides the thousands who have been slain in battle!

Wed., Dec. 24. At $4 1/2$ lovefeast and candles for the little children. At 7 P.M. lovefeast for the congregation. Owing to the scarcity and high price of coffee, sugar, flour, etc., the amount required was this year raised by voluntary contributions among the members.

Female Missionary Society of Salem, 1862
[Extracts of minutes transcribed.]

Sun., Jan. 5. A letter from Bro. Holland was read in which he returned thanks for the liberality thus far manifested towards the erection of the church for the colored people, and asked for a future appropriation, the debt upon the building amounting to about $200. Thereupon it was on motion resolved that the amount at present in the hands of the treasurer, together with the collections to be made during the coming half year, be appropriated to the benefit of the Negro church.

Diary of the African Church in Salem, 1862
[Extracts transcribed; handwriting is that of Francis Raymond Holland.]

Sun., Apr. 13. Palm Sunday. No preaching today. At 7 1/2 P.M. commenced reading the acts of the last days of the Son of Man to a numerous congregation.

Sun., Apr. 20. Easter. Litany at 9 A.M. and preaching by Br. Grunert.

Sun., June 1. Holy Communion; 33 colored communicants partook.

Sun., July 13. S.S. Br. Holland preached. Several persons have of late professed to have sought and found the pardon of their sins, viz. Jake (Keehln), Philip (Lagenour), and Aggie (Lemly). They hope soon to be received as full members!

Sun., Sept. 28. S.S. Baptism of 2 adults, viz. Michael, servant of Mr. Sam'l. Lagenour, and Jacob, servant of Dr. Keehln. Seven persons were confirmed, viz.: Margaret (John Reich), Caroline (Sam. Lagenour), Rachel (J. H. Blum), Aggie (A. H. Lemly), Julia (A. Waugh), Emily Cornelia (John George Spach), and Ellen Susanna (J. G. Spach). The two last are daughters of br. William, servant of Br. John George Spach of Friedberg. There was a large congregation present, both of whites and colored people.

Sun., Oct. 19. At 2 P.M. Communion Lovefeast. After a short recess Holy Communion was celebrated; 45 colored communicants present. Seven whites also partook of the communion, among them a wounded soldier of a Louisiana regiment who has been here for several weeks with some of his wounded companions to recruit their health.

Sun., Dec. 21. Christmas celebration, conducted by Br. Grunert.

The Congregation at the close of the year consists of 52 communicants.

Board of Elders of Salem Congregation, 1862
[Extracts of minutes transcribed.]

Wed., Feb. 12. Brn. E. Schwtz. and F. absent.

[B]r. Holl. laid before the Board a communication from br. F. Fries, in which he offers to lend a bell to the Negro church permanently, upon certain conditions. The Board thought it would be better to thank br. F. for his offer, but without entering into any compact to leave him entirely free to remove the bell, as his property, at pleasure.

2. The Board was led to adopt the following rule: The new Negro church is not to be used for any other purpose except the meetings for worship and religious instruction of the colored people.

Wed., Feb. 26. Br. F. absent.

2. Br. Fries declines in another communication to enter into the views of this Board with regard to the bell.

Wed., Mar. 26. Br. F. absent.

2. On funeral occasions the singing of a verse before the church will necessarily be omitted in future, unless the singing is supported by a brass band.

Wed., May 7. Brn. R. Schwtz. and F. absent.

[T]he results of the election held yesterday by the Congregation Council was stated to be the re-election of the br. Fulkerson as a member of this Board for 3 years.

Wed., June 4. Br. E. Schwtz. and F. absent.

2. Br. Holl. mentioned that sr. Bagge wished to know, whether she would be sustained in keeping up the rules of the sisters' house in regard to male visitors in the evening. The Board will certainly do so, altho' it would appear as if there was nothing improper in the case mentioned.

Wed., July 2. Br. F. absent. (also br. R. Schwtz.)

The minutes having been read, br. Holl. proposed that the Wednesday evening lectures, which are very poorly attended, be discontinued during July and August. The Board assented, and also fully approved of the Sunday evening meetings having been kept all along at 7 1/2 P.M.

Wed., Aug. 13. Br. F. absent.

2. In regard to the lovefeast in the children's festival the Board thought that if br. Cooper could possibly get the materials, the usual refreshments should be given to the children, but as last year, to them only.

3. The Brethren's festival will not be celebrated in the usual way. The reception of those youths who belong to the Choir can take place in a special meeting (say on the evening of Aug. 29th).

Wed., Oct. 15. Brn. F. and Grunert absent.

Resolved, that the chapel is not to be used as the place for keeping a corpse during the funeral.

Wed., Nov. 26. Br. F. absent.

Br. Holl. read a circular, received by him from Mr. W. R. Hunter, containing an appeal for pecuniary assistance to enable him to continue his present work of distributing tracts, etc., on the railroad between Petersburg and Weldon, principally among soldiers, without charge to the Evangelical Tract Society at Petersburg. The Board resolved to have that circular printed in the *People's Press* with the request to those interested to leave their contributions with the pastor.

2. Br. Holl. laid before the Board an anonymous communication, purporting to come from the ladies of Salem, requesting the use of the church for a prayer meeting for females on Dec. 1st at 12 o'clock, to keep which br. Bahnson has been invited. The Board thought that the ladies had misunderstood the call upon females throughout the Confederacy in the public papers to pray unitedly for peace at that hour, and that where no female praying circles existed, closet prayer was recommended, but that under the circumstances it would better to let them have their way. Br. Holl. will answer the communication briefly, explaining the matter, and address it to one of the sisters who are said to have brought it to his house in his absence, but also give notice of the intended meeting, as requested.

3. On Christmas Eve candles will be distributed to the children, as usual; the refreshments cannot be procured. The Board was of opinion, however, that the infants would get their cake, and some sort of tea in their meeting at 3 o'clock.

Wed., Dec. 10. Br. F. absent.

3. The plan of having occasional service in the empty Prot. Methodist church in Winston, mainly for the benefit of those members of Salem congregation who live in that neighborhood and come to our church but rarely, was discussed.

Tues., Dec. 30. Br. F. absent.

2. The following was agreed to:

"*Ordered*, that no corpse is to be brought into the church during the funeral."

Board of Trustees of Salem Congregation, 1862
[Extracts of minutes transcribed.]

Fri., Jan. 10. Joint meeting of the Board of Elders and Board of Trustees.

Not present the Brrn. N. Blum and C. Cooper.

1. The Chairman (Br. F. R. Holland) stated the object of the meeting to be an open and free interchange of ideas in regard to the condition of our Boys' School, whose income, owing to the small number of scholars, is not sufficient to pay the salary of the teachers, and is at this time only enabled to continue to the end of the present session (June 30, 1862) by a contribution of $250 from Salem Diacony, and by the collection of debts still due for tuition from former sessions.

The members of the two Boards are all impressed with the importance of retaining the services of the present efficient teacher, Br. Albert Butner, and as there is no prospect of a material increase of scholars from the members of our Congregation, nor any likelihood of a great accession from strangers during the continuance of the civil war, there appears for the time being no other alternative, if the school is to be continued on its present plan, than to make extra exertions, principally on the part of the Salem Diacony, to assist the financial department of the school.

2. Meeting resolved that until after Easter next no Lovefeasts, either Communion or Congregation Lovefeasts, shall be kept, owing to the extraordinary prices of coffee and sugar, occasioned by the blockade of the southern ports, the former now selling at 75¢ and the latter at 20¢ per lb., with the probability of still higher rates and greater scarcity hereafter.

Tues., Jan. 21. Not present the Brrn. Joshua Boner and Theod. Keehln.

1. In reference to the proposal of the Board of Trustees of Salem Female Academy contained in their communication (see minutes Dec. 20, 1861, §2), this Board after discussion

resolved that we agree that the school fees, as charged at present for our town girls or daughters of members of Salem Congregation be hereafter paid directly to the Principal of Salem Female Academy, and that consequently the payment of the $130 per annum on the part of Salem Diacony be discontinued. This Board would, however, propose that the time when this arrangement is to go into operation be changed from New Year (as proposed by the Trustees of the Academy) to May 1st 1861 or to the beginning of the school session after the public examination of last year, as it would simplify the change in various ways.

As this Board, in granting $250 in aid of the Boys' School when we only had a credit of $219.50 on our school account, had calculated to make up the deficiency thro' the receipts of the town girls' school fees, we would request the trustees of Salem Female Academy to make us a donation of $30.50, being the balance of our appropriation remaining unprovided for if our proposition of altering the time first proposed should be accepted by the trustees of the Academy.

Tues., Feb. 18. Full Board.

1. In reference to the resolution contained in §1 of the last minutes another communication from the Board of Trustees of Salem Female Academy was communicated, suggesting that for the sake of rendering accounts less complicated, the whole arrangement intended be postponed till after the examination in May next, and that from *then* parents pay directly to the principal of Salem Female Academy. In this case the Diacony or School account would receive more than the donation asked for. Board unanimously agreed to accept this proposition.

3. The offer of Mr. Henry Lash to buy the old pottery lot and buildings, and if sold publicly to bid not less than $1,000 led to a long interchange of ideas, but without arriving at a final result, Board resolved to meet again on this subject on Monday evening next.

Mon., Feb. 24. Full Board.

Board, having met according to agreement for the purpose of considering the expediency of disposing of the old pottery buildings and lot (see §3 of last minutes), entered upon that subject immediately. While on the one hand it was urged to be desirable to get rid of buildings that stand in need of repairs in order to keep them in a habitable condition, and that it would consequently be more prudent to take even less than they had formerly been held at than to expend money on buildings that after they should have been purchased by anyone would only be removed in order to make use of the locality for the erection of a new building, it was on the other hand maintained that *now* was not the proper time to dispose of them, as owing to the civil war and consequent stagnation in many kinds of business, town property especially had greatly diminished in value, and that even if a reasonable price could be obtained, the safe investment of the money received would at this time be attended with considerable difficulties, if not rendered almost impossible. Another subject that exercised an influence upon the minds of some of the members of the Board was the Town Hall situated upon the lot and connected with the other buildings in question. Altho' this body is under no obligations to furnish a place for public meetings of the citizens, it might still produce disagreeable consequences if the public should be deprived of such a place at times like the present when no other could be furnished or be found in town. It is but reasonable to suppose that if the present Town Hall was to be sold, frequent applications would be made for the use of our Church for purposes that should, if possible, be kept out of that building.

Finally the motion was made and seconded, "Not to sell the buildings and lot of the old pottery at this time," which motion was adopted by 4 votes against three.

Thurs., Apr. 24. Not present the Brrn. Theod. Keehln and E. A. Vogler.

1. Upwards of twenty of the members of the Congregation having for nearly a year served as volunteers in the Confederate army, it was resolved that the customary Church expenses due at the end of the present month be not charged to them during their absence. This resolution also embraces such as have left for the same purpose at a later period, they also being exempt from the time of leaving.

Tues., May 13. Not present the Brrn. C. Cooper, Theod. Keehln, and N. Blum.

1. Congregation Council having on Tuesday 6th inst. re-elected the Brrn. Theod. Keehln and J. G. Seitz, whose term of

service had expired, the members present organized by the election of S. Thos. Pfohl as President and Secretary.

3. Edmund Blum asks for a reduction of his annual charges for Church expenses, saying that he does not derive the full benefit from the church on account of the distance at which he lives from it (about two miles). Board can not enter into an alteration of the established rates, because by acceding to a request like the one before us, we should become involved in endless difficulties with the members of the church.

Thurs., June 5. Not present the Brrn. Theod. Keehln and N. Blum.

1. The postmaster at Salem, Br. O. A. Keehln, having notified the Warden that he intended temporarily to remove the post office from the present locality to the Bookstore, as he could thereby save the wages of one hand, and stating at the same time that he would continue to pay the customary rent for the office as heretofore and that it was his intention to move back to the present locality as soon as the war was at an end and the book trade could be carried on properly as heretofore, the matter was laid before the Board in order to learn the views of the members and to ascertain whether any steps can be taken on the part of the Board to prevent the contemplated removal of the post office.

Altho' the fondly cherished hope of a former Town Committee, that by furnishing a properly arranged post office building in a central part of the town the convenience of the public as far as the locality of the office is concerned had been *permanently* secured, would be at once destroyed by the contemplated action of the present Postmaster—a hope more or less based upon a communication from an officer of high standing in the General Post Office Department—this Board as such nevertheless does not consider itself possessed of any power or authority to dictate to the Postmaster at what particular place he shall keep his office, the question of locality appearing to them to lie between the Postmaster and the community in general for whose convenience or accommodation the office has been established.

Thurs., Aug. 28. Not present the Brrn. Theod. Keehln and E. A. Vogler.

1. A communication from the School Committee was received, stating that application had been made by Sister Kremer for an increase of her salary as teacher in our Boys' School, but that although the Committee consider her request under present circumstances a reasonable one, the state of the School funds did not allow them to make even the smallest increase of expenditures, and they consequently request such assistance from funds at the disposal of this body, if any, as the case may seem to them to require. Board after some consultation on the subject found it expedient to lay the subject over to a future meeting and in the meantime to request from the School Committee a statement of its present financial condition and probable income during the next year, i.e., till end of June 1863.

3. The annual accounts of Salem Diacony from May 1, 1861, to April 30, 1862, together with a statement of its assets and liabilities on the latter day was laid before the Board.

The receipts in the course of the financial year amounted to $4,591.01 and the disbursements to $4,561.09, showing an excess of receipts of $29.92. The sale of Town lots amounted to $866.19 which sum added to the Town lot fund raised it to $13,162.01.

The accounts of Single Sisters Diacony for the same time showed the receipts to have amounted to $697.46 and the disbursements to $513.94, being an excess of receipts of $178.77. The use to be made of this income was left undetermined for the present.

The Lovefeast account this year closes with a debt of $171.16, which had been accumulating for a number of years.

Thurs., Sept. 25. Not present the Brrn. Joshua Boner and Theod. Keehln.

1. In reference to §1 of the minutes of last time it was stated that the School Committee upon examination find the financial condition of the School to be the following, viz.:

The Treasurer has now in hand in cash and accounts due from former sessions $187, which, however, is not sufficient to pay the balance of salaries of teachers for the present session amounting to $363, and he consequently would require $176 more to be enabled to pay salaries till end of December of this year, the amount due for school fees not being available till after the expiration of the term. For the second session the salaries to be paid at present rates will amount to $400, from which deduct the probable income for tuition from the first session, calculated according to the present number of scholars at $250, will leave a further deficiency of $150 at the end of the second session, and consequently a total deficiency of $326 for the year ending June 30th 1863. The amount of salaries as paid at this time is $800 a year, viz., to Br. Albert Butner $600 and to Sister Eliza Kremer $200, which salaries are paid quarterly. The number of scholars at present amounts to 30, of which 12 pay at the rate of $12 and 18 at $20 per year, being an income of $504 for the present school year. Board after a long deliberation on the subject finally concluded to lay over the main question about an appropriation to a future meeting, meanwhile authorizing the Warden to pay over the balance now standing to the credit of School account in the books of the Diacony, amounting to $33.90 to the treasurer of the School, in case it should be needed to pay the quarterly salary due at the end of the present month.

3. The account of the Treasurer of the Building Committee of the New Negro Church (see minutes Aug. 27, 1860) was next communicated, from which it appears that the cost of the erection of the Church together with the fencing of the lot and other arrangements connected therewith amounted to $2,845.97 and that after paying all accounts $1.28 remain in the hands of the Treasurer for the use of said Church.

Tues., Nov. 11. Full Board.

1. After the minutes of last meeting had been read and approved, Board again entered upon the consideration of §1 relating to the financial condition of our Boys' School, and finally came to the conclusion that owing to the present disturbed condition of the country by reason of the existing civil war and the depressing influences exercised thereby upon the community in general, the Board is willing to pay the deficiency of the present school year ending June 30, 1863. Board, however, trusts that the Treasurer of the School will use his best endeavours punctually to collect the debts due for tuition.

In order to enable Diacony the better to meet this additional expense, it was resolved that $100 from the gain in the Sisters Diacony appearing on the accounts of April 30 of this year be appropriated for the benefit of our Boys' School and the balance of the gain, viz. $78.77, be added to the Reserved fund of said Diacony.

4. The price at which firewood is selling having gone up from $1.75 to $4.00 per cord, Board think it proper *to double* the price that is asked for decayed or dead timber cut from the land of the Diacony.

Tues., Dec. 9. Not present the Brrn. C. Cooper and Theod. Keehln.

1. As application is not unfrequently made to the Warden for building lots in Salem and Winston in localities where none have as yet been laid out, Board concluded not to lay out any more until the present political disturbances and the uncertainty in money matters shall have come to an end, preferring under existing circumstances rather to retain the Diacony land than sell it for a depreciated currency.

3. Application having been made to the Financial Board of the Wachovia Sustentation by a salarized minister for extra assistance towards the support of his family, as owing to the present unprecedentedly high prices of provisions and all other necessaries of life it was impossible with his salary to maintain his family, said Board, consisting with but one exception of individuals living upon salaries, would wish, before coming to any conclusion on the subject, to ascertain the sentiments of the Board of Trustees on the subject, this Board as well as every other that has to determine the amount of salaries to be paid to individuals in the service of the Congregation or its institutions being interested in the question.

Board of Trustees had a long conversation on the subject, and, feeling it to be one of considerable importance to all financial institutions of the Society, was not inclined to come to a decision at once, but laid it over to an extra meeting to be held on Wednesday evening of next week (Dec. 17).

Provincial Financial Board, 1862
[Extracts of minutes transcribed.]

Thurs., Jan. 30. Br. Henry Lineback present.

1. Chairman handed in the resignation of Br. Fr. Fries in writing, and reported that Br. J. N. Blum declined the appoint-

ment. Board proceeded to fill the vacancy by nominating Br. John Siewers and should he decline Br. Jacob L. Fulkerson.

4. It was proposed and finally resolved, that Board empower the Treasurer to pass on and pay such bills as we presented to him, according to his judgment, and to refer such bills as he deem proper to the Board.

Wed., Feb. 5. All present. One vacancy.

1. The application of Br. Lewis Rights for $140, his deficit for the last year over and above his salary, amounting in all to $302, was presented. After considerable discussion, Board granted the application, with the proviso that Br. Rights inform the Committee of Friedberg congregation that their contributions are not sufficient to support their minister.

2. Br. John Siewers has declined his appointment, and Br. Fulkerson not yet responded.

Tues., Apr. 22. All present. One vacancy.

1. The Treasurer reported that he had cash in hand to the amount of $5,797 of which $3,410 was capital paid in. He desired the instruction of the Board, how to dispose of this money under existing circumstances. After conversation on this subject, Board resolved that Treasurer be recommended to keep a larger amount of good currency on hand than heretofore, say from $1,000 to $3,000, and to deposit, for the present, the balance in Salem Savings Institute.

2. To supply vacancy in the Board, Br. Theodore Pfohl was nominated, [Br. Fulkerson having declined], and in case of his refusal Br. Joshua Boner.

Thurs., Oct. 9. Br. H. Lineback absent. Br. Joshua Boner present, new member.

1. Br. Pfohl, Tr. of Wa. S. Diacy., submitted the annual accounts for June 1, 1861, to May 31, 1862, and the statement of assets and liabilities on May 31, 1862. The sum total of receipts, including a donation of $1,800 from Salem Female Academy, amounted to $4,267.25, the disbursements to $2,659.82, leaving a surplus of $1,607.43. The assets amounted to $39,934.98, and the actual liabilities to $1,246.75. On motion the following appropriations were resolved upon:

a. A reserve for pensions and stipends of $700.

b. To balance off the amount due on Ferd. Oehman's account $14.67 and the note due from J. H. Barrow $45.56. The remainder of the surplus, $847.20, was added to Fund Account which now amounts to $5,761.40. The amount of the Provincial Fund is as last year $32,926.83.

2. Br. Robert Schweinitz was requested to inquire about the purchase of N.C. State Bonds at Raleigh, whither he intends to go in a few days.

Tues., Nov. 25. All present.

1. Br. Robt. de Schweinitz reported that he had no opportunity when at Raleigh to inquire about State Bonds. The Treasurer stated that he had a large sum of money on deposit in Salem Savings Inst. at present, and requested Board to instruct him in what manner to invest it. After some conversation on the subject, it was ordered that five North Carolina 8 percent State Bonds should, if possible, be purchased, and some 16 shares of Cape Fear Bank stock, if the latter can be had for $125 per share.

Bethania Diary, with Bethabara, 1862
[Extracts transcribed; handwriting is that of Jacob F. Siewers.]

Mon., Jan. 13. This forenoon Benj. Pfaff informed me of the death at Manassas of Br. Nathaniel Pfaff's son John, and that they expected to bury him here tomorrow at 12 noon.

Tues., Jan. 14. At half past 12 P.M. preached the funeral sermon of the above single brother, John Peter Pfaff, born Dec. 22, 1838, aged 23 y., 29 days. The day was cold and disagreeable and the earth covered with sleet snow; notwithstanding, a large audience were present. Br. Nathaniel had the sorrowful satisfaction of being with his son during his last illness to its close, and bro't his remains home.

Wed., Jan. 15. It rained and sleeted during the night, but this afternoon it rained. I took blue pills last night and fear to venture out. Br. William Leinbach paid his church dues for the past 2 years, and told me that his wife desires her name to be taken from the Church Book as she does not desire to be considered a member.

Wed., Jan. 29. Visited the measles patients. Edward [Grabs] has a hard time of it. I never saw them broke out in the manner he has them; his face is swelled.

Thurs., Feb. 27. [At preaching of a funeral f]ound out accidently that the President of the S.C. [Southern Confederacy] had recommended tomorrow to be observed as a day of fasting, humiliation, and prayer. Gave the notice, and reminded the audience of the fact that several of such days had transpired during the past year, and that those especially who professed to take a deep interest in the S.C. did nevertheless show a perfect indifference on such occasions by staying away from church, that I had on one occasion preached to 2 men and 1 little boy.

Fri., Feb. 28. Fast, humiliation, and prayer. Rang the bell at 10 1/4 A.M. S. L. Grabs, the sexton, rang the 2d bell, but no one came. Therefore I did not preach. Afternoon went to Bethabara and preached on Mark 4:38, last clause, "Master carest thou not that we perish." There were some 4 or 5 men, and 15 or 20 females in the church.

Fri., Mar. 7. My hearing is failing very much.

Tues., Mar. 18. Today the 1st draft among the militia for the war in Forsyth Co. takes place; the town in consequence is very bare of men.

Sun., Mar. 23. Afternoon preached at Spanish Grove to a very small audience; there was no fire made and it was quite cold. Returning called at br. Peter Pfaff's, who this day remembered their 60 years marriage.

Mon., Mar. 31. After dinner Sr. S. and myself went to visit Sr. Catherine Conrad (widow), who lives with her son Jonathan. She is in her 87th year, if I am not mistaken, and has been bowed by age and infirmities for some years. We found her sick, as we had learned from her brother Solomon Spoenhauer, who called here this morning. We then left and called at her son Timothy's. Three of his sons are in the Army, the elder at Manassas, the others at Kingston in this State.

Mon., Apr. 14. I heard that Edwin Shultz and one of Thomas Shultz's sons were out squirrel hunting yesterday, and that whilst cutting a tree the ax fell from the helve and cut the knee-pan of the boy's leg nearly off.

Thurs., Apr. 17. Maundy Thursday. Went to Thomas Schultz; his son Samuel was lately badly cut in the knee, but is doing well from all appearances.

Sun., Apr. 20. Easter Sunday. Last night it rained considerably but the congregation met in the church, and after singing and prayer we went to the graveyard, where we prayed the Litany. The attendance was better than heretofore. After dinner went to Bethabara and preached on the same. Returning went to Thomas or Israel Lash's Negro quarter and baptized 3 infants, after explaining what baptism is and the duties of the parents of baptized children.

Fri., May 16. Fast, humiliation, and prayer day. Rainy day. At 10 A.M. entered the church, and as there were but 5 persons present sang a hymn and offered a prayer, concluding with a hymn. Did not go to Bethabara; the roads are in a miserable condition, and no likelihood of an audience.

Mon., Tues., May 19, 20. This day it is 5 years since we arrived here from the mountains.

Wed., May 21. Visited with Pratt's, he has had the flux, but is better. He has three sons in the Army, one in Virginia, and 2 at or near Raleigh; his fourth son, who is on a trip to the salt works, has likewise volunteered.

Fri., May 23. General muster. Joseph rode Pete to Winston.

Mon., May 26. Settled this morning with br. Daniel Butner, and afterwards he requested his name to be taken from the Church Book, assigning as the reason that there were lies in circulation about him.

Wed., June 4. It rained all night, and continues this morning. The creek has risen higher this morning than I have ever seen it, the water flowing over the plank road in various places.

Sat., June 14. Called at H. H. Butner to see Frank, who returned from Halifax, N.C. (where he had the typhoid feaver), last Thursday with Oliver Lehman. He is improving in health.

Sun., July 13. After dinner went to Mickey's School House and for once found an empty house.

Sun., July 20. After dinner went to Spanish Grove, found an empty house, and returned with a heavy heart. After reflection it occurred to me that I had made a mistake; this was the 3d and not the 4th Sunday. I should have went to Bethabara.

Sun., July 27. After dinner in company with Joseph and Frankey Bowden went to Spanish Grove, where I preached . . . to 11 persons, old and young. Went on to Salem. My son Joseph being a Conscript, I took him along, he being ordered to appear in Winston on the 28th at 9 A.M.

Mon., July 28. Joseph left at noon for High Point. I returned.

Fri., Aug. 15. At noon about 75 of the Surry conscripts passed thro' here.

Tues., Aug. 19. This morning Sally Spach came up in the stage from Lexington. Having had the typhoid feaver, she was too weak to walk home to her sister's, called at our house and requested me to take her home, which I did in company with Sr. S. By request held a prayer meeting at Jane Grabs's, her husband having engaged work in a gun factory in Jamestown. A number of the neighbors, chiefly females, being present.

Fri., Aug. 22. Sr. S. and myself visited at br. Samuel Stauber's. He had just returned from Richmond, where he expected to find his son Julius and bring him home, but he had been already buried.

Tues., Aug. 26. Today we received two letters from Joseph per mail, one of the 17th and the other of the 20th.

Wed., Aug. 27. Wrote a letter to Joseph.

Wed., Sept. 3. Went in the country to hunt peaches to put up.

Mon., Sept. 8. Edward Grabs is at his mother's, sick with mumps, visited him.

Wed., Sept. 17. Called at br. Thomas Schultz, he quite recently lost his oldest son Junius in one of the recent battles in North Eastern Virginia. He was not at home, conversed and prayed with Sr. S. and daughter. Went to br. Henry Schultz, he was in the field at work. Permanio, who had been severely wounded in one of the engagements near Richmond, had got home a few days ago, is as yet helpless in his wounded leg, but otherwise is doing well, and may recover. Returning home called at Coller's, they have also lost a son recently at Richmond, conversed and prayed with them.

Thurs., Sept. 18. Visited at Sr. Salome Strupe's. Going out the horse upset the carriage and broke a wheel, but no one was hurt. Walked out to S., she lost her son at the Camp of Instruction of the North Carolina conscripts near Gordensville. He died of measles and flux. Conversed and prayed with them. ([Margin note]: Thanksgiving Day for Victories; *no service here.*)

Thurs., Sept. 25. This morning I had my jaw tooth drawn that has occasioned me so much suffering for the last 10 or 12 days. My whole jaw was affected, and I could scarcely eat anything.

Tues., Sept. 30. At night held a prayer meeting by request at Alexander Grabs's; he and William Stoltz expect to leave in the morning en route for the army as Conscripts.

Wed., Oct. 1. This forenoon the Rev. John Dan. Scheck and the Rev. James R. Sikes called here and took dinner with us. The former is the agent of the Lutherans, to collect funds for building an orphan asylum at Louisville for the children of the deceased and wounded soldiers. He is to preach here in the church on Friday evening the 10th of October preparatory to taking up a collection the day following by visiting from house to house.

Fri., Oct. 3. This evening Alexander Grabs and Wm. Stolz returned from Raleigh, having been detailed.

Sun., Oct. 5. Staid overnight at Salem and heard that my sister Caroline had departed this life at Bethlehem.

Wed., Oct. 8. Visited at br. Henry Schultz's; Permenio, if improving, is very slowly mending. Went to br. Timothy Conrad's; his daughter Sarah has been sick, she tells me, some 7 weeks. I heard she had been sick but was better, but had no thought of finding her in the situation she was in. She speaks with difficulty to be understood, and has green glasses to ease her eyes, which are failing her.

Sat., Oct. 11. We were rejoiced by a letter from our Joseph.

Tues., Oct. 14. Went out after dinner and got a mess of squirrels.

Sun., Oct 26. Rainy day. Rang the bell, but no one came to meeting. Owing to the heavy rain did not go to Bethabara. Remained at home.

Sat., Nov. 1. Went out to Thomas Lash's mill and returning went to John Hege's and took some things there to assist him and family in these tight times.

Sun., Nov. 2. Went down to the Double-bridge S.H. but found no one there; they had just left, giving me out. I had been detained an hour at Bethabara on account of Calvin Hauser's going to Maple Springs to meeting, his Father having to attend to the Post Office in his place.

Tues., Nov. 11. Hauling chips till evening. My brother's Negro Rich, who has been helping me, returned home.

Tues., Nov. 25. Received a letter from Joseph.

Tues., Dec. 2. Visited mother Grabs and mother Lehman, conversed and read some instructive and interesting discourse from Count Zinzendorf's works to them.

Wed., Dec. 3. We heard yesterday that Edward Grabs is sick in Greensborough of typhoid feaver.

Mon., Dec. 8. Visited the sick in town. Edward Grabs was bro't home this evening from Greensboro.

Tues., Dec. 9. Visited the sick in town. Afternoon visited at Henry Schultz's and Timothy Conrad's. Parmenio is no better, but Sarah Conrad can walk again.

Fri., Dec. 12. There is considerable uneasiness manifested on account of the smallpox having appeared at several points not very distant from here. Samuel Stauber returned this noon with several others from Virginia with their deceased sons.

Mon., Dec. 22. Visited at Grabs's, Edward is very low. . . . Called in the afternoon again, poor hopes of his recovery.

Tues., Dec. 23. We were awakened this morning and informed that Edward had just departed.

Fri., Sat., Dec. 26, 27. Remained at home; the latter was a rainy day. I sent the statistics of Bethania and Bethabara this morning [Dec. 27] to Salem by Mr. Shields, who was passing by.

Wed., Dec. 31. [T]he heads of families met and elected a new Committee, resulting as follows: Joseph Transou 11, H. H. Butner 10, William Lehman 10, Solomon Pfaff 10, Nathaniel Pfaff 9, Jacob Werner 7. Br. Levin Grabs was elected steward and principle sexton, and Sr. Sally Stoltz assistant sexton. The Committee being elected, they proceeded to elect br. H. H. Butner as collector and trustee of the graveyard fund. The Committee are to meet on the 2d Sabbath in the coming year. At half past 11 the last meeting was held in the usual manner, closing with prayer and reading the Daily Word of the new year in the edition of 1852.

Friedberg Diary, with Hope, 1862
[Extracts transcribed; handwriting is that of Christian Lewis Rights.]

Sat., Jan. 11. Sr. Rights is sick. Alice and Florence have the whooping cough. The weather is still remarkable warm, and Dr. Shelton says there is more sickness in the country than he has ever known at this season of the [year]. Typhoid fever, pneumonia, measles and whooping cough.

Sun., Jan. 12. Opened the S.S. Afterwards Brother Bahnson preached from Romans 10:12-14, and [read] Brother Frebely's report to the Home Mission Society, and a collection was taken up to aid the cause amounting to $14.20. . . . I went to see some of the volunteers leave for Teague Town.

Sun., Jan. 26. Preaching at Friedberg and then made an attempt to organize a Home Mission Society but failed.

Fri., Jan. 31. The past week has been warm and wet by turns, the warmest January I have ever experienced, and no snow this winter so far.

Sun., Feb. 23. Considerable excitement prevails in the neighborhood on account of a report that there is to be a draft of the militia in Davidson and Forsyth owing to our loss on Roanoke Island of 23 hundred men taken prisoners. Also in the loss of Fort Donelson in Tennessee. The battle there was fought the 14th, 15th, and 16th. Our loss was five hundred and the federal loss in killed, wounded, and prisoners 23 hundred. ([Friedberg Report:] the strange part about it [the draft] is that the very men that were the strongest in favor of the war 12 months ago are the very ones that don't want to go now when their country needs their service.)

Sat., Mar. 1. A Regiment met at Wagoner for the purpose of drafting for the war. Those drafted out of the neighborhood were [blank].

Mon., Mar. 17. This morning the drafted men of Davidson County have to meet at Lexington in order to be carried to Raleigh tomorrow as their place of destination for the present time [and they] are getting more gloomy than ever. A number of the drafted men in our neighborhood have the measles.

Tues., Mar. 18. Draft in Forsyth. Those drafted immediately in this neighborhood are Levy Covis, Henry Earnest, John Foltz, Augustine Crouch, John Crouch, Amos Heartel, James Spach, Obadiah Spach, Lemuel Mendenhall, and Hiat. Of this number only Lemuel Mendenhall, John Crouch, James Spach and Obadiah Spach are members of the church.

Sun., Mar. 30. The congregation was not large today from the fact that almost every family has the measles or is expecting them—Solomon Hages, Jacob Fishels, John Weasners, Jesse Fishels, Wm. Weavers, Jesse Millers, and George Fishels. They are, however, as yet of a mild type.

Tues., Apr. 1. Visited among the measle folks.

Wed., June 4. On yesterday and [today] there was a heavy rain, and the waters are higher today than they have been for many years. Some of the plank were taken off of the South Fork bridge, and the bridge over Muddy Creek between Friedberg and the Muddy Creek Meeting is carried away, and also the bridge at Jordan Rominger Mill is damaged so that it is impassable, and the river must be very high.

Sun., July 13. [T]here was Communion, as a number of our members are included among the list of the conscripts that expect to leave for the camp of instruction at Raleigh next Tuesday. It was a solemn time. There were 120 persons partook of the Communion.

Tues., July 15. I went to Lexington to see the conscripts leave, but they did not get off.

Wed., July 16. Started with Brother Alexander Mock and Jordan Rominger to Raleigh.

Thurs., July 17. Arrived in Raleigh at 11 A.M. and started immediately for Camp Carolina three miles from the city near the Weldon Rail Road.

Fri., July 18. Left Raleigh for home.

Sat., July 19. Arrived at home.

Mon., July 28. Today the Forsyth conscripts have left for Raleigh by way of High-Point.

Wed., July 30. Today the Davidson conscripts succeeded in getting off to Raleigh. This was their third trial.

Thurs., Sept. 18. Thanksgiving by President Davis. ([Friedberg Report:] In accordance with the recommendation of President Davis, there was service in the church at 11 o'clock, tolerably well attended.)

([Friedberg Report:] *Fri., Sept. 19.* Brother Fry paid us a flying visit. In the evening Sr. Spach, Christian's wife, sent me word to come over if I was able, Brother Spach was gone to Thomasville. I went and found her much distressed. They had received a letter from Jefferson, Va., stating that their son, brother Solomon Augustus Spach, had died there on the 9th inst.)

([Friedberg Report:] *Tues., Sept. 30.* I was sitting on the porch [at Br. Shore's] when the gate opened and a man came slowly through the yard. I remarked to brother Shore, there is a sick soldier, for he had a knapsack. He came right up to me, caught me by the hand, and said, how do you do, brother

Rights. It was brother Solomon Tesh. He was wounded at Harpers Ferry, and was on his way home on furlough.)

Mon., Oct. 6. Visited Brother Jesse Kanauss. He has come from the hospital at Richmond, where he has been confined for some time by rheumatism. He seems to be very weak.

Thurs., Oct. 9. Visited Brother Solomon Tesh. He has taken the typhoid fever since his return.

Tues., Nov. 25. In the evening visited at Brother Christian Spach's. Brother and Sr. Spach are both dangerously sick with typhoid fever. I found Sr. Spach evidently near her end. We united in prayer, and while so engaged she breathed her last at 3/4 past six o'clock P.M. I remained until 10 o'clock and then started for home. In the meantime it began to rain and was very dark, but being provided with a torch all went well for a while, but suddenly my light went out leaving me in pitchy darkness. I tried to steer the right course, but there were so many logs and brush heaps in the way that I soon lost it, and after wandering about for several hours in the rain I gave it up and took shelter against the body of a large pine and waited for day. After standing awhile I began to get very cold and after feeling round I found a spot of some twenty paces clear of bushes, and so I thought I would play sentinel for the sake of variety, and came to conclusion that I could stand two hours pretty well, but half a night, especially as it was the first lesson, was rather hard. In the morning I found myself within two hundred yards of where my light went out, having made a complete circuit.

Private Dairy of R. P. Leinbach, 1862
[Serving Macedonia and Muddy Creek; extracts transcribed.]

[*Fri., Jan. 17.* W]e went to lay out the [Macedonia] graveyard. The Brn. Hall, Miller, E. and H. Lee, R. and D. Sheek, and Messrs. J., S., and E. Douthit were present.

Sat., Jan. 25. Sr. Lucy Fry was, by consent of the Committee, re-admitted into the church.

Tues., Feb. 11. The Brn. put posts around the Graveyard at Macedonia.

Sun., Mar. 16. River too high to go over to Muddy Creek. ([Muddy Creek Report:] 'Tis a wonderful community. The people attend preaching very well, and after preaching one can scarcely get rid of going home with them.)

Sun., Mar. 23. ([Macedonia Report:] There is great excitement in consequence of the draft. Some of our people are very much afraid of the Yankees. The war and the times fill all men's minds. They are the last and indeed only subject of conversation before they enter the church, and immediately resumed on coming from the house of God.)

Sun., Mar. 30. ([Macedonia Report:] Macedonia seems to be rapidly growing in importance. It occupies a sort of central position, geographically, politically, and financially. The young folks come here to see each other; the older ones to talk politics and discuss the news. The district holds its muster close at hand, and the tax gatherers have fixed upon it as a spot very suitable as for the "receipt of custom.")

Fri., Apr. 18. Went to Macedonia to hold Easter meetings. Reading; and communion was administered. On account of the high water I could not go over to Salem, and hence we were compelled to forgo Communion bread, and substituted light bread. There were 5 brn. and 16 sisters present. The Lord was in our midst. I enjoyed a real blessing. Two new members were received into our midst, the Srs. Ann Cook and Nancy McBride.

Sun., May 4. Ploughing and working out [of doors during the week]. Had received money at Salem to pay my board, but it being Confederate money, mine host would not receive it.

Sun., June 8. Preaching at Macedonia: 1 Peter 4:6. Our community was greatly excited by the news of the great battle at Richmond—the Seven Pines. A number of our young men were wounded and several killed.

Sun., July 6. Preached at Muddy Creek. Dr. Shuman was to be buried at Salem at 5 P.M. I was anxious to attend. I left Squire Ellis' house at 3 and by hard riding I succeeded in reaching the church by 5 o'clock. Having a good horse belonging to my brother, I was able to accomplish it.

Wed., July 9. Went to Br. H. Jones. He was much exercised about the conscript bill.

Fri., Aug. 3 [1]. Read the account of the outpouring of God's spirit upon the church at Herrnhut [in] 1727 from Greger's *Brüder Geschichte.* 'Twas a blessing to my soul.

[The Private Diary of R. P. Leinbach interrupts. The following are excerpts transcribed from the Macedonia Reports; the handwriting is that of R. P. Leinbach.]

Sun., Nov. 9. Whilst out visiting I learned that Br. G. Sheek had sold the land for which the Church holds a title bond.

Sun., Nov. 30. The people seem to be considerably exercised about the smallpox, of which some cases have appeared.

Sun., Dec. 14. Br. D. Wheeler, who has been carrying the keys and has usually made fire, has absented himself entirely. He unlocks the church and bookcase doors, and then returns home again, leaving us to make fire or sit in the cold.

Wed., Dec. 17. Mr. J. McBride refuses to sell the land he has bo't from Br. G. Sheek, which was intended for the church.

Sun., Dec. 28. There were but seven adults in church. I kept a prayer meeting and then dismissed the congregation. Fear of smallpox seems to keep a good many away. One of our neighbors, Mr. Wm. Jones, is reported to have died of that disease, and the people seem to be panic stricken.

[New] Philadelphia Reports, with Friedland, 1862
[Extracts transcribed; handwriting is that of Thomas Frye.]

Sun., Feb. 9. Gave Br. and Sr. Kiger certificates of their standing in the church, [they] having moved off some 12 or more miles from Phil. and wish to unite with some church.

Sun., Feb. 16. Went to Friedland to preach, but the key was not there, so that we had no preaching. The weather being unfavorable and a number of the people having measles, there were but few present.

Sun., Feb. 23. Preached at Phil. from Matt. 10:32-33 to rather a small audience to common on account of measles.

Sun., Mar. 16. Preached at Friedland from Luke 6:45 to a large number of attentive hearers. All seemed as solemn as Judgment.

Sun., July 13. At 6 P.M. had prayer meeting for our young men who soon will leave us for the camp of instruction.

Sun., July 27. [A]t 5 P.M. had prayer meeting for our young men who desired us to meet with them and talk and sing and pray with and for them for perhaps the last time. It is their desire that we should tell our Brethren to remember them in their prayers, that the Lord might protect and shield them from all the deadly implements of war, and grant them health and feed and clothe them, and finally that they may return to their parents and wives and children and loved ones and enjoy gospel opportunities as before.

Sun., Sept. 21. [A]t 4 P.M. had prayer meeting for our young men who are gone into the army.

Tues., Sept. 30. [V]isited Mr. Crater, who will leave us to-morrow for the army.

Sun., Oct. 5. Preached at Phil. from Nahum 1:7 to a larger audience than common since our young men left us to go to the army. Had a good meeting; tears flowed freely.

Tues., Dec. 23. Was sent for to pray for the young Mr. Burk late in the evening, whose left leg was amputated about the knee. Sung and prayed with him and instructed him. Stayed all night. Next morning before I left I talked with him again, and it seemed that he was satisfied that he could get no relief but in Christ Jesus.

Fri., Dec. 26. [C]alled by to the young man again. Found him rejoicing in the hope of a blessed immortality. His mother told me that he talked to them all almost equal to the minister of the Gospel.

1863

[France expanded its sway in southeast Asia by gaining control of Cambodia. France also tried to enlarge its influence in the Western Hemisphere by occupying Mexico City in June, and the United States was too involved in its own Civil War to react effectively. Japan's emperor tried and failed to ban foreign traders.

President Lincoln's Emancipation Proclamation declared that as of January 1 slaves in the Confederacy were "thenceforward and forever free," though the war continued. General Lee's army invaded Pennsylvania but was turned back at Gettysburg July 1-3. Vicksburg fell to General Grant on July 4, giving the Union full control of the Mississippi. Draft riots in New York City protested money payments instead of personal service. West Virginia was admitted as the thirty-fifth state.

In North Carolina following the battles of Gettysburg and Vicksburg, William Holden began a peace movement.]

Memorabilia of Salem Congregation, 1863
[Extracts transcribed; handwriting is that of George Frederic Bahnson.]

It is true, as a general thing, the year at whose close we are standing was to many of us such a one as we should not like to pass through again. To not a few among us it was a year of trials and afflictions, and without scarcely any exceptions, all of us felt the heavy pressure of the times in which we are living, and we felt it the heavier on account of the great contrast which has come upon us. For while we were *once* living in a land flowing with milk and honey and yielding even to the poor the necessaries of life, not only have plenty and abundance left us in general, but want and destitution have taken their place. Since the often dark days of the first struggle for independence, more ominous clouds have never lingered around our national horizon, and at this very time the questions, *what shall we eat, what shall we drink, wherewithal shall we be clothed*, are anxiously asked by many who never had occasion to do so before.

The fearful struggle between the alienated and enraged portions of a once united country is still going on in all its fearfulness, scattering far and wide misery and destruction and desolation. Desperate battles were again fought during the course of this year, and thousands [were] hurried into premature graves and called before their God "in a day when they looked not for him, and in an hour that they were not aware of." At times many of us were filled with anxiety on account of sons, brothers, or other near and dear relatives who are in the army. But although that number, by no means inconsiderable before, was increased during the course of the year, and affectionate fathers and doting mothers had to send their dear sons into unknown and thick dangers, we have most abundant cause to call upon our souls to bless the Lord this evening for the wonderful protection he did most mercifully vouchsafe to our beloved ones; for the number of those among us who had to give up their sons either on the field of battle or in hospitals is strikingly small; and while we heartily sympathize with them, we cannot but return thanks to a gracious God for having preserved so many who were exposed to similar dangers and attacks of death. . . .

It is true at times the clouds poured down more than was desirable, so that the waters rose to a very considerable height in their respective courses. This was the case at the close of the month of June, so that on the 29th our creek was swollen to an almost unprecedented depth. Part of the tolerably high bridge was swept away, and for a couple of days foot passengers had to be taken across in a little ferry boat procured for the purpose. The damage done to the growing crops was very considerable. Upon the whole, the lowlands were interposed with very injuriously by the high waters and proved in many instances almost a failure. But the upland, yielding in some instances unexpectedly large returns, the harvest was a pretty good one and would have gladdened the hearts of the needy, had not the cruel and unfeeling spirit of speculation and extortion stepped in and proved *one* of the sad causes why the very necessaries of life are made to command almost fabulous prices such as, we sincerely trust, will fill our children's children with perfect astonishment and amaze. Great destruction was the result, and doubtless a larger number of persons old and young will suffer this winter from want of food, clothing and shoes. Our own neighborhood is believed to be better provided for than perhaps any other, for which we have great reason to be thankful; but even then the poor and such as are not in favorable outward circumstances find salt at $12 and corn at $8 per bushel, and everything in proportion—a very great hardship indeed. ([Margin note:] County prices are mentioned here. Market prices: $20-25 for salt, $10 and more for corn, bacon between $2-3 per lb. and not to be had.)

Nevertheless we have abundant cause (in this respect also) to bless the Lord and not to forget all his benefits. No footprint of an enemy has been seen in our parts, while elsewhere the fairest portions of the land, our own state not excepted, have been overrun and destroyed. We still possess our peaceful homes, while elsewhere, even in our own state, large numbers of families had to turn their backs upon the cherished spots they had called "sweet home" and to secure as well as they could habitations among strangers. And although we cannot know how soon things may change, we will put our trust in the Great and Good Being, who never sleepeth nor slumbereth, but as the King of Kings keepeth his own Israel in perfect safety under the shadow of his wings.

Among the personal notices, we would mention that at the close of the month of October Bro. Holland left with his family on a longer visit to Bethlehem, Penna. For the present Br. Bahnson has resumed the pastoral office of the white congregation, and Br. Grunert has kindly consented to minister to our colored people in holy things.

[A separate addendum in the hand of Br. Maximilian Grunert:]

In the colored division of the church the Sunday school and the customary services were kept through the year as regularly as circumstances would allow. Among the 14 children baptized, 9 were children of members. One adult was baptized on her sickbed upon her earnest request. Seven persons were buried on their graveyard, one of whom was a communicant member. Six have been received into the church by confirmation, and one admitted to membership from another church. The number of communicant members is 58.

Salem Diary, 1863

[Extracts transcribed; handwriting is that of Francis Raymond Holland.]

Thurs., Jan. 1. Not having received any textbook for the year 1863, we have adopted that of 1857, the days of the week corresponding to those of this year.

Mon., Jan. 5. At 7 P.M. monthly missionary prayer meeting. We have been so long cut off from all sources of missionary intelligence and our attention has been so intensely and exclusively directed to matters around us immediately affecting ourselves, that it is to be feared the interest in missions has greatly declined. It may, however, only lie dormant, and be awakened with the returning opportunity to participate actively in the work of sending the gospel to the heathen.

Tues., Jan. 6. At 7 1/2 P.M. lecture in the chapel for the colored people. This meeting, which has been kept during the fall and winter, say, about 6 months every year for several years past, continues to be pretty well attended, and affords an opportunity for familiar instruction in the Holy Scriptures, sometimes partaking somewhat of a catechetical character.

Sun., Feb. 8. At 10 A.M. Litany and preaching by Br. Bahnson. At the same hour Litany and preaching by Br. Holland in the Protestant Methodist Church at Winston. The trustees of that church having very courteously consented to our using their house every two weeks for a service of our own, the commencement was made today. It is hoped and believed that this measure will prove beneficial to our members residing in Winston, Liberty, etc.

Sun., Feb. 22. Br. Robt. de Schweinitz went to Winston at 10 A.M. but owing to the bad weather and shocking state of the roads—a heavy fall of rain and sleet having taken place—no congregation had assembled. Br. Holland has been confined to the house for several days with a severe cold.

Sun., May 10. General suspense is prevailing in regard to the fate of relatives and friends engaged in the recent battle [of Chancellorsville] near Fredericksburg, Va. At 5 1/2 P.M. Father Zevely departed this life in the 83rd year of his age.

Mon., May 11. Intelligence has today been received from the 21st Reg't. N.C. troops and the 1st Battalion, from which it appears that all the members of this congregation in those bodies are safe, though the loss in killed and wounded, especially in 21st Reg't., is very severe. We have great cause of gratitude for the very distinguished preservation thus far vouchsafed to our young men.

Wed., May 13. Intelligence was this day received, through a letter from Br. Joseph H. Reich to his parents, that Br. Charles I. Clauder had fallen on the battlefield near Fredericksburg on Sunday morning, May 3. He was found dead by the litter bearer with his testament lying open on his breast, and is thought to have expired very soon after he fell. Before the battle he had seriously admonished his cousin, Br. Jos. Reich, to be instant in prayer, and directed him, in case of his death, to send messages to his relatives here urging them all to prepare to meet their God.

Wed., May 27. Close of annual session of Salem Female Academy. Musical entertainment in the Academy Chapel; no public examination.

Sun., June 28. At 10 A.M. Litany and preaching by Br. Holland. Br. Grunert preached at Winston to a pretty numerous audience. For several days past heavy showers of rain have fallen.

Mon., June 29. The creek below town was swollen to an almost unprecedented height by the heavy rain of last night in addition to what had fallen before, and part of the bridge was swept away, and the damage to the growing crops along the bottom must be very great. For several days foot passengers were conveyed across the creek in a boat.

Mon., July 6. 8 P.M. missionary prayer meeting; called to mind the martyrdom of John Huss.

Mon., Aug. 17. 7½ P.M. Congregation Council took into consideration the proposal of the Board of Commissions of the Town to give back to the Council the waterworks, together with the money in hand, etc. Council resolved that a company be formed to keep up the waterworks, under certain conditions specified in the resolution.

Fri., Aug. 21. Day of prayer and humiliation by appointment of President Davis. Public service at 10 A.M. conducted by Br. Holland.

Wed., Sept. 10 [9].[1] The 21st Reg't. N.C. Troops, in the Confederate States' service, passed thro' Salem on their way

---

[1]The *People's Press*, published Thursday, Sept. 10, 1863, reported (p. 2, col. 5) that dinner was served on Salem Square on Wednesday, which was the 9th.

into the western part of the state, probably to put down the Union demonstration in the counties of Yadkin and Wilkes, etc. Dinner was served to the regiment, numbering between 300 and 400, in the square. Many of the men being from this neighborhood, there were affecting meetings and sad partings with friends.

Sun., Oct. 25. At 10 A.M. Litany and preaching by Br. Holland. 1 P.M. Sunday School. At 7 P.M. evening service . . .

[Handwriting is now that of George Frederic Bahnson.]

. . . at the close of which Br. and Sr. Holland and family, about to leave on a longer visit to Bethlehem, were commended to the kind care and protection of our gracious Lord and Savior.

Wed., Oct. 28. Br. Holland left this morning with his family. Our best wishes accompany him. May the Lord bring them in safety to their widowed mother at Bethlehem.

Mon., Nov. 2. The band of the 21st Regiment arrived here today. Several Salemites are among them.

Sun., Nov. 15. A beautiful day. The [Chief] Elder's Festival as also the congregational festival were celebrated. At 2 o'clock Br. Emil Schweinitz kept the lovefeast—no coffee nor cake though. At 3 P.M. Br. Grunert administered the holy communion in German; the number present was very considerable in the big church. At 7 P.M. communion in English by Br. Robert Schweinitz, Brn. Emil Schweinitz and Grunert assisting.

Thurs., Dec. 10. The Governor of N.C. having recommended a day of humiliation and prayer, public service was held at 10 o'clock, and pretty well attended. Br. Bahnson preached on Luke 13:3. May the Lord in his infinite mercy "stay his wrath, which has been heavy upon us and open the way for the speedy restoration of peace to our desolated land, on such terms as will best promote his glory and both the spiritual and temporal welfare of his creatures."

Sun., Dec. 20. Br. Bahnson preached on Phil. 4:4. It was an uncommonly cold day, of which we have had several. The brethren, as far as their attendance at church could show it, appeared to stand in much greater dread of the cold than the sisters.

Thurs., Dec. 24. At 4 1/2 Br. Bahnson kept the lovefeast for the little children and at 7 o'clock a meeting for the whole congregation. We had to dispense with the coffee and cakes.

There was nevertheless a very large congregation present, who behaved very well.

Fri., Dec. 25. Preaching was pretty well attended, but the trial of a loose white woman and some negroes, which took up much more time than had been anticipated, attracted a crowd of people into the commissioners' hall, some of whom would have gone to church.

Thurs., Dec. 31. Rainy and very unpleasant. At 4 1/2 Bro. Bahnson kept a meeting for the children. At 8 o'clock he read the Memorabilia, and at 11 1/2 kept the closing meeting. For many years there have not been so few people in these meetings.

Diary of the African Church in Salem, 1863
[Extracts transcribed; handwriting is that of Francis Raymond Holland.]

Tues., Jan. 6. At 7 1/2 P.M. lecture in the chapel.

Sun., Feb. 15. S. School. No preaching. Weather bad, and Br. Holland feeling unwell.

Sun., Mar. 29. Palm Sunday. No S. School nor preaching today. At 7 1/2 P.M. commenced reading the acts of the last days of the Son of Man. A large congregation was present.

The Tuesday evening meetings in the chapel were discontinued in this month, owing to the growing shortness of the evenings, which has always had a great effect in lessening the number of attendants. They were already interrupted last month by the inability of Br. H. to attend to them owing to the obstinate cold he had taken.

Sun., Apr. 5. Easter Sunday. Easter Morning Litany prayed at 9 A.M., followed by preaching.

Sun., Apr. 19. At 2 P.M. Communion Lovefeast, followed by the Holy Communion. Nearly 50 colored communicants present.

Sun., May 31. Sunday School as usual. Preaching by Br. Holland, after which 7 children whose ages varied from a few months to over 6 years were baptized into the death of Jesus.

Sun., Aug. 2. Confirmation. Sophy (Waugh), wife of Calvin (Taylor), was confirmed. Calvin Taylor was received as a communicant from Methodist Church.

Sun., Aug. 23. Lovefeast and Communion; 45 colored communicants present, including several of the Methodist Church.

Sun., Oct. 18. S. School. Preaching by Br. Holland. The preaching today was better attended than on the 2 preceding Sundays, the protracted meeting at Winston which has been held for several weeks past, having come to a close.

[Handwriting is now that of Maximilian E. Grunert]

Sun., Nov. 1. Br. Holland having left Salem during the last week on a visit to Pennsylvania, br. Grunert preached to the congregation on the subject of the day, taking Rev. 7:9ff. for a text. At the close he announced a meeting for the members of the church to be held next Sunday after preaching, and gave notice that he had been charged with the care of this congregation during br. H.'s absence, adding a few words of encouragement. The number present was about 15 men, 23 women, and upwards of 20 children, besides a number of whites, mostly the teachers of the Sunday school, which had, as usual, preceded preaching.

Sun., Nov. 8. Found a good congregation, engaged, as usual, in singing after the Sunday school, and preached on Eph. 3:19. They were very attentive. When the congregation was dismissed, the members (about 30) remained, and took the front seats. It was pleasing to hear them heartily join in singing "How pleasant is love's harmony," etc. Addressed them in a familiar way on the necessity of keeping their hearts, and walking uprightly. Henry led in prayer afterwards. After the meeting one man and two young women expressed their desire to join the church by confirmation.

Sun., Nov. 22. S. School and preaching on Matt. 24:35. The attendance was moderate. A good number of the members remained after the service to attend the confirmation instruction which followed. Sol. (Lemly), one of the candidates, however, was not present. Another woman applied for admission. They evidently were interested in the subject.

Sun., Nov. 29. 1st Sunday in Advent. After S. School a sermon was preached on Matt. 3:1 (last clause). The congregation having been dismissed, confirmation instruction followed. An elderly woman, Rhoda (Reed), was present, who has before this already expressed her desire to be added to the church by holy baptism. The 3 female candidates for confirmation expressed their great desire to be admitted soon, and were promised to be confirmed next Sunday, with a view of their partaking of the Lord's supper on the Sunday following. Jemima said she felt the Savior very near. Sol. is to consider yet what he thinks would be best for him. Jeff. led in prayer at the conclusion.

Sun., Dec. 6. 2nd Sunday in Advent. Found a goodly number of colored people and also many white sisters and a few brethren assembled to witness the confirmation. Before the service began, a point had to be settled. Judy (Rights) had applied for membership to br. Holl., had attended the instruction, together with a number of others, but no one had spoken to me about her. And now she is sitting in the front seat together with the other candidates, expecting to be confirmed. There sat also Rhoda (Reed), altho' *she* had been put there by kind sisters. After a little conversation with Judy I concluded that it would be best to gratify her; and consequently the following 5 were confirmed, viz: Solomon (Lemly), Judy (Const. Rights), Jemima (Lemly), Mary and Amanda (N. Blum). They appeared to be sincere. May the Lord confess them before His Father and the holy angels.

Sun., Dec. 13. 3rd Sunday in Advent. Lovefeast and the holy Communion. There were 40 colored communicants present; several white sisters also partook. Considering the muddy and slippery roads, and the threatening aspect of the weather, the attendance may be called good, although several Methodists were among the number. Some feeling manifested itself, and the new members were moved particularly. The Savior evidently was present to bless his people.

Sun., Dec. 20. 4th Sunday in Advent. Christmas celebration. There was a suitable decoration on the platform before the pulpit. After the address a number of pieces were sung by the Sunday school teachers and scholars, and cakes and candles distributed among the children. Good order prevailed; Dr. Keehln was kind enough to see to that. The number of white visitors was less than last year.

The congregation at the end of the year numbers 58 communicants (Jesse (Meinung) included).

Salem Congregation Council, 1863
[Extracts of minutes transcribed.]

Mon., Aug. 17.

Present 19 members. Council was called together by the Board of Elders on account of the reception of the following communication from the Board of Commissioners of the Town of Salem.

Mayor's Office, Aug. 7th, 1863.

At a meeting of the Board of Coms. held last night, a motion was made and unanimously carried that from and after this date the said Board will no longer furnish from the Waterworks water to the cisterns in Town as heretofore.

It was further agreed to that the said Board will at any time give up and make over to any person or persons all their right, title, and interest in the said Waterworks including Taxes levied and now ready for collection from the consumers of the Water, to any person or persons the Cong. Council may direct.

By order of Board of Coms.

J. G. Sides, Mayor

The following views were accordingly expressed by various members.

The Council being of the opinion that the Board of Trustees is no longer the proper body for the future control of the water works, they are therefore unwilling that it should resume the future control of said Works.

A considerable number of our citizens residing in the central portion of our town, together with the Sisters House and S.F. Academy, being either entirely or in a large degree dependant upon this water, it is to them a matter of vital importance that the Waterworks must be continued in operation. The present condition of the country rendering it impossible and inexpedient for a company to extend or increase the supply of water so as to prove beneficial to every portion of our town, and it being thought probable that at some future time a company would be formed having that object in view, this Council will give over the present establishment to some company which will maintain the present supply, together with all the cash and materials on hand, with the condition that should a company be formed at any time with a view of more extended supplies, it will be transferred to such company. The Board of Trustees being at present unwilling to make a right and title to the land through which the troughs are laid and upon which the House is located, and inasmuch as the various Boards and institutions of the Church are more largely dependant upon the water obtained from that source, it was deemed proper that the S.F.A., Administration, Cong. Diacony, and Sust. Diacony should assume the control of the said Waterworks.

These views were therefore embodied in the following resolutions and unanimously passed by the Council:

Resolved, that Cong. Council hereby authorize the Town Comsrs. to make over their right, title, and interest in the Waterworks and all appurtenances thereto belonging, together with the money in hand, to the S.F.A., Cong. Diac., Sust. Diac., and Administration and such other persons as now depend on the Waterworks for their daily supply of water, with the understanding that the above named institutions and individuals form themselves into a company for the purpose of maintaining the Waterworks.

Resolved further, that whenever the Cong. Council re-demand the Waterworks for the purpose of carrying out the plan of more extended waterworks the above named institutions and persons shall be bound to again make them over with all the appurtenances to the Council.

Board of Elders of Salem Congregation, 1863
[Extracts of minutes transcribed.]

Wed. Jan. 14. Br. F. absent.

3. The condition of the Sunday School and the older boys were spoken of, but no particular measure could be proposed to prevent the rising generation from running wild.

Wed., Jan. 28. Br. F. absent.

[B]r. Holl. stated that meetings in the Prot. Meth. church in Winston would shortly begin, to be held every two weeks. The Board thought it would be best to inquire of the trustees of that church what rent they thought it right to expect, also to contract with someone to sweep and warm the church regularly.

Mon., Feb. 2. Br. F. absent.

The meeting was called to decide in the case of sr. Sophia Ackerman. She was raised in the sisters house from a tender age, but has for the last few years been living in a family, and lately in the employ of the school. She has been sick now for a number of weeks, and the probability is that she will continue to be so for a long time. The Board has no objection to her admission into the sisters' house sick room.

NB: The Board was of opinion that sisters who have no other home, when disabled by sickness, ought to be admitted there as their proper home, but preferred to decide every particular case on its own merits.

2. Br. Holl. mentioned that several members, living in the country, had expressed a desire for occasional afternoon communions in English. Laid over.

Wed., Feb. 11. Br. F. absent.

After the reading of the minutes it was remarked that Sophia Ackerman had died before the removal could take place.

2. Br. Holl. made on Sunday last a beginning with Moravian meetings in Winston, and found the attendance quite encouraging.

Wed., May 6. Br. F. absent.

3. On Whitsunday the English communion will be held in the afternoon and the German in the evening in place of the usual meeting. The Board thought that twice a year was a sufficient number of times to meet the wishes of our members in the country in this respect. (See Feb. 2, 1863, §2.)

Wed., May 20. Br. F. absent.

The minutes having been read, mention was made of the action of the late Cong. Council (met on the 7th, adjourned to 12th), by which br. Grunert was re-elected a member of this Board, and the brn. J. Boner and C. Cooper again elected into the Board of Trustees.

Wed., June 3. Brn. R. Schwtz. and F. absent.

2. Br. Holl. read a communication from br. E. W. Leinbach, resigning his office as organist. It is not likely that he could be prevailed upon to continue, nor that br. J. Boner, the only

other individual who could undertake it, would consent to accept. Br. Holl. will see about it.

Wed., June 17.

With regard to the organist business br. H. reported that he had incidentally spoken with br. Leinbach and br. Boner, and after a lengthy discussion it was determined that br. L. be spoken to officially, with a view of agreeing with br. B. upon some plan to divide the duties, and perhaps get help from some of the sisters.

The communion in July will be omitted, principally on account of the scarcity of wine at the present time.

Wed., July 1. Br. F. absent.

The minutes having been read, br. Holl. reported that neither br. Boner nor br. Leinb. were willing to serve; the latter, however, having spoken of reappointment with new negotiations about salary, the Board considered it its duty to reappoint him.

Wed., July 29. Br. F. absent.

After the reading of the minutes br. H. mentioned that br. Leinbach having given as his ultimatum, $300, the Board of Trustees had rejected this proposal. As there is no other candidate for the organist's place, the Board is now compelled to let the matter rest. It was yet resolved that br. L. be requested to continue to act as director of the music.

Wed., Aug. 12. Br. F. absent.

3. A meeting of the Congrn. Council will be held on Monday next, the Town Commissioners having declared their determination not to keep the waterworks any longer, and their readiness to surrender the property to any party which said Council might authorize to receive it.

Wed., Sept. 9. Br. F. absent.

2. The meetings in Winston are but little encouraging; it was thought best, however, to keep on a little longer at least.

Thurs., Oct. 29.

Br. Holland left yesterday with his family on a visit to Pennsylvania, and as, owing to the war and other circumstances, his return is doubtful, a temporary arrangement, which is to last no longer than the end of next May, has been adopted, in accordance with which br. Bahnson was in the chair at this meeting. Br. Fulk. was absent.

1. Br. Bahnson has taken charge of Salem congregation, and br. Grunert will supply the colored charge.

Wed., Dec. 9. Br. F. absent.

3. The deplorable condition of the boys' school was considered, but no measure for relief could be proposed. (Br. Alb. Butner returned shortly after and took charge.)

4. On Christmas eve there can be no lovefeast, unless the members should again, as last year, take up a collection. The little children, however, the Board thought, should get something.

Board of Trustees of Salem Congregation, 1863
[Extracts of minutes transcribed.]

Tues., Jan. 6. Full Board

1. Owing to unforeseen circumstances the Board had not been able to meet on Dec. 17th, and now took up the unfinished business referred to in §3 of last minutes. It was evident to the Board that at present prices of provisions, etc.— wheat, e.g., selling at $5 per bushel, flour at $28 to $30 per bbl., corn $3 per bu., pork $25 to $30 per 100 lb., beef 12¢ to 15¢ per lb., butter 50¢ per lb., salt $12 per bu., and wood at $4 per cord—families who with established salaries could with former prices only maintain themselves, would under now existing prices not be able to do so; and that consequently it would become necessary to render them some extra assistance at this time, they not being in the same situation as mechanics and others, who in order to meet these heavy outlays raise their own prices in proportion. After considerable discussion the motion was finally made, seconded, and unanimously adopted (the Chair refraining from voting), "That owing to the above stated causes a bonus or donation be given to the Pastor and Warden to aid them in support of their families, the amount to be paid to each to be calculated at the rate of $40 for each member of the household or family exclusive of servants or hired helps." Br. W. Meinung, who draws a pension

from the Diacony, also to receive the sum of $40 towards his maintenance.

2. Br. John Wimmer having met with the misfortune of losing a leg and arm in the present war and being thereby rendered incapable from doing any thing towards the support of his family, it was resolved that the rent for his dwelling in the old pottery be no longer demanded of him.

3. A teacher in the Academy would rent a room in the Sisters House that has now been unoccupied for about 1/2 a year; her intention, however, would not be to live in it but merely to use it as a locality for storing away her furniture, etc. Board think it would be most advisable not to rent it to her under such circumstances, as the room might be required for one that stood in need of a place to live in.

Sat., Jan. 17. Not present the Brrn. J. Boner, Theod. Keehln, and J. G. Seitz.

Upon application the privilege was granted to Mr. H. D. Lott to bury his infant child upon our graveyard, he and his wife having for several years already very regularly attended our meetings and frequently communed with the Congregation. Another one of his children being very sick at this time, it was understood by the Board that in case of its death the same privilege be granted if it should be desired.

Wed., Apr. 8. Full Board.

1. The privilege of cutting dead timber for firewood on the Diacony land being as it would appear abused by some of our neighbours taking the liberty of not only cutting for their own use but of cutting and selling it to others, it was resolved again to engage the services of a *forester* whose duty it should be to have an especial eye upon this wood cutting, to grant permission to cut, to designate the part of the woods where the applicant should cut, and to see to it that a correct statement of the number and measurement of trees cut by each one be rendered to the Warden, and that no wood be cut without his permission. Board resolved to tender the appointment to Br. Traug. Christ and to compensate him according to the time he spends in the discharge of his duties.

2. The Trustees of the Salem Female Academy having omitted at the proper time to make an appropriation for the support of our Boys' School, the Principal of that institution

now proposes that the school fees of the town girls be paid to the Warden for another year, viz. to Apr. 30, 1863, in order to give the benefit of the excess of receipts to the Diacony for the use of the Boys' School. The proposal was accepted by the Board.

Mon., May 4. Full board.

. . . Board again entered upon the consideration of the application of Mr. Wm. Wheeler for the lot [#162] on the muster ground. . . . [S]ince the meeting of April 10th Br. Levin Belo had come forward with the statement that he had several years since made application for the lot in question, but had been informed that it was not for sale. If it should now come into market he thinks his application should have the prefer-ence, or that if it is to be disposed of it should be done at public sale. This gave rise to the remark, that justice would require a proceeding of this kind, not only towards Levin Belo but all others that had heretofore asked for the lot. Against this it was urged on the opposite side that it would not be prudent under the existing difficulties in money matters either to take the depreciated Confederate currency now in general circulation, which cannot be invested in any stock other than Confederate bonds, or publicly to make it a condition of sale on the part of a *Church Board* that such notes would not be accepted. A step of this kind might, however, be avoided by a private understanding with an individual that payment must be made in a certain kind of currency to be determined upon between the parties. It was further maintained on the same side that no one who had applied for the lot during this time when it was held under reserve for certain purposes and consequently not in market could reasonably expect by such application to have established a standing claim on it for all time to come.

After a further remark, that all difficulties in the case might be avoided by postponing or declining action in regard to the lot till the state of the country and its finances would again be settled, when a sale could be kept, if it was at all tho't expedi-ent to sell the lot, the motion was made and seconded that the lot in question be sold to Mr. William Wheeler.

The Board having first excused Br. E. A. Vogler from voting on account of his connection with some persons more or less interested in the case, the vote was taken on the motion and decided in the affirmative by 5 for and 1 against it.

In next dwelling upon the price to be asked for the lot it was stated that calculated at first class rates the amount would be about $325, to which, however, should be added $64.34 refunded to Charles Shober as expenses for digging a well on it before he again surrendered the lot to the Diacony, as also the value of the timber and the fence on the lot.

The motion was finally made and seconded that $500 be asked for the lot and that payment must be made in Carolina Treasury Bills fundable in 1863 in 6 percent N. Carolina State Bonds. Before, however, the vote was taken an amendment was proposed and accepted that the price of the lot be put at $600 in the currency stated above, which amendment was passed by a vote of 4 for and 3 against it.

Tues., May 12.

The Congregation Council having this evening re-elected the Brrn. C. Cooper and Joshua Boner, whose term of service had expired, and all the members of the Board of Trustees having been present at the Council with the exception of Br. Theod. Keehln, they met immediately after adjournment of Council and organized by electing S. Thos. Pfohl as President and Secretary.

1. Mr. Wm. Wheeler having in the course of last week paid the $600 in the currency required, and the Warden having $280 of the same kind on hand already, it was resolved that $1,000 N. Carolina 6 percent bond be purchased for the Diacony, as it was presumed that the $120 still lacking towards the amount can be procured by paying a premium for them.

2. The Warden asked the question, whether he should take Confederate bills in payment of the annual Church accounts now due? Board was of the opinion that he *should* take them, as it would not in their estimation be proper for a body acting in the name and behalf of a Church to refuse to receive them.

3. It was further resolved not to bring any charges for Church expenses against the families of such married brethren as are serving in the Confederate army.

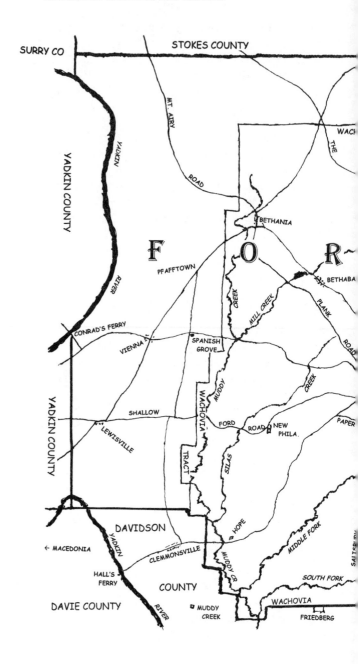

Tracing of a map of Forsyth County, North Carolina, drawn by
townships (not shown here). The block in the center is the

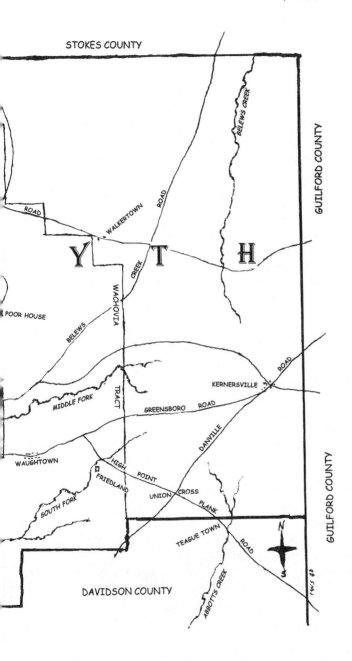

STOKES COUNTY

GUILFORD COUNTY

BELEWS CREEK

ROAD

WALKERTOWN

CREEK

WACHOVIA

Y T H

POOR HOUSE

BELEWS

TRACT

MIDDLE FORK

KERNERSVILLE

ROAD

GREENSBORO ROAD

DANVILLE

WAUGHTOWN

HIGH POINT

FRIEDLAND

UNION CROSS

PLANK

SOUTH FORK

TEAGUE TOWN ROAD

GUILFORD COUNTY

N

S

DAVIDSON COUNTY

ABBOTTS CREEK

r in 1863. The 37-inch by 45½-inch original features the county's
Salem Congregation, holding the towns of Salem and Winston.

Tues., June 23. Not present Br. Theod. Keehln.

1. The Soldiers' Relief Society having about the beginning of the present month taken possession of the Town Hall with the consent of the members of this body for the purpose of establishing a *way-side hospital and lodging place* for soldiers passing thro' town on their way from and to the army, the question came up what rent should be charged for the use of the hall. Board in consideration of the benevolent object of the society unanimously resolved that no charges be made for the use of the hall.

Wed., July 22. Full Board.

2. Application having been made by several persons for building lots in Salem and Winston with a view of securing the lots named in order to build dwelling houses on them whenever the state of the country shall render building practicable, Board, on the one hand not willing to recede from the resolutions adopted not to sell lots for a depreciated currency that could not be profitably invested at this time, and yet desirous of favouring such applicants as far as it can be done consistently with their duty towards the Diacony, passed the following resolution by a unanimous vote:

"Resolved, that whenever any one applies for a building lot with the intention of erecting a dwelling house on it for himself and family so soon as the state of the country shall render it practicable, said lot, desired for the above stated purpose, shall be considered as secured to the applicant, provided at the time when the present troubles shall be ended and the financial difficulties settled there exists no special reason why said lot should not be sold. In case no hindrance exists the lot shall be sold to him at private sale for such sum as shall be agreed upon between the parties."

This arrangement would in future do away with the public sale of lots in general as practiced hitherto.

4. Br. Edwd. Leinbach, after resigning his situation as Church Organist, has been re-appointed as such by the Board of Elders and is willing to undertake it again, provided a salary of $300 a year be paid him. Board of Trustees think the charge too high in proportion to the amount of services required of an organist, and is consequently not inclined to pay the sum demanded.

3. Board gave it as their opinion that the Salem Diacony is exempt from paying the Confederate taxes, as the 16th section of the Act contains the following words: "The income moneys of hospitals, asylums, churches, schools, and colleges shall be exempt from taxation under the provisions of this act." The Warden will consequently not list any thing for Salem Diacony, but the Single Sisters Diacony, not being embraced in said exemptions, will have to be listed.

6. The firm of F. & H. Fries ask whether we are willing to take a N. Carolina state bond in payment for the town lots held by them? (There being 6 lots that would amount to not far from $1,000.) Board agrees to take such a bond at par, allowing them the interest due on the bond at the time the transfer takes place.

Tues., Sept. 15. Not present the Brrn. Theod. Keehln and N. Blum.

1. Our neighbour Frank Reich, who without having received permission from this Body, some years since erected a dwelling house and other buildings on a field of the former Shuman plantation held in rent by Br. Joshua Boner, having died recently, it will in the settlement of his estate become necessary to dispose of this property situated on lands of the Diacony. Board in order to avoid difficulties that might otherwise arise out of the irregular proceedings of F. Reich, resolved that, inasmuch as it is in contemplation, as soon as circumstances will admit also to sell lands situated beyond the limits of the corporation, a suitable lot be laid off (say of about 1/2 acre, more or less) and sold at third class rates, for which a note with approved security is to be given, because we do not wish to take Confederate currency.

This transaction is, however, not to stand as a precedent for other cases, but is only agreed upon in the present instance as affording a means of effecting a settlement of the estate of a person deceased.

2. The yearly accounts of Salem Diacony from May 1, 1862, to April 30, 1863, together with a statement of the assets and liabilities on the latter date were next communicated, from which it appears that the total

receipts amounted to	$6,788.28	and the
disbursements to	3,833.48	being an
excess of receipts of	2,954.80	of which amount,

however, $2,714.35 having been received from the sale of town lots have to be added to the Lot Fund, leaving $240.45 open for disposal by the Board. It was resolved to place the latter amount to the credit of Repair account.

3. The accounts of the Single Sisters Diacony for the same time were next communicated and shewed the

receipts to have been	$681.35
and the disbursements	541.22
leaving an excess of receipts of	140.13 which

amount Board resolved to add to the Reserved Fund.

Tues., Dec. 16. Not present the Brrn. Joshua Boner and Theod. Keehln.

1. The minutes of last meeting having been read and accepted, Board again spoke of the matter contained in §1 of the minutes, and for the information of the Administrator, Mr. Christian D. Sides, clearly defined the position of the different parties interested in the following manner:

The Administrator can only sell the house and lot in fee after having previously bo't the lot from the Proprietor; and as we do not want to take the kind of money current at this time, we agree to take his (C. D. Sides's) note, and make him a deed for the lot as soon as he calls for it. With regard to the field held in rent by Reich (the house lot now to be laid out excepted) we consider that Reich is possessed of no interest that could be sold by the Administrator, except the [fence] rails that may be around the field, as the Proprietor by renting a piece of land to an individual from year to year retains all his rights and privileges to the same and is at liberty again to take possession of it as soon as he sees proper to do so.

2. A communication from the Prov. Elders' Conference dated Oct. 19th, 1863, was next laid before the Board. Said communication states that Br. Francis Holland having left for a protracted visit to Bethlehem, the temporary vacancy thus occasioned has been filled by giving the charge of the Salem Congregation to Br. G. F. Bahnson and of the coloured people to Br. M. E. Grunert.

5. The square on our graveyard on which the married and widowed Sisters are buried being nearly filled, it will become necessary in the course of the coming spring to enlarge the graveyard on the north side by taking in sufficient ground to add another square in length. The fence on the north side is

still sufficiently substantial to bear removal, so that only two sides of new fencing will be required.

6. The two daughters of our departed Sister Mahela Butner have offered gradually to pay the rent still due on the room occupied by their mother for about ten years, which on account of straitened circumstances bro't on by long continued ailments she had not been able to do, which rent now amounts to upwards of $100. Board appreciates the motive that induces these two sisters to make this offer, but in as much as one of them has for a number of years been almost the only support of her infirm mother and a sister then a mere child, and as the rent has never been taken in account in the books of the Diacony, is not inclined to accept the offer made [by] them.

Provincial Financial Board, 1863
[Extracts of minutes transcribed.]

Thurs., Jan. 15. All present.

1. Treasurer reported that he had bought 5 N.C. 8 percent Bonds, with interest, for $6,135.55.

2. The Board of Trustees having granted to the minister of Salem Congr. $40 for each member of his family, exclusive of servants, as extra assistance on account of the hard times, Board granted the same to Br. Bahnson. The sum of $40 was likewise granted to the widowed sisters receiving Sustentation. Sr. C. Van Vleck, who is a pensioner of Pa. Sust. Diacy., is to receive the same amount and should the latter hereafter refuse to pay it, Wa. Sust. D. would have to bear the loss.

Tues., Apr. 28. Br. Robert de Schweinitz absent.

1. An application of Br. Lewis Right was considered, in which he asks for $150 for the year 1862, being the amount of his deficit over and above the salary received from his congregation, which was $285.90. On account of the hard times, Br. Rights' application was granted.

2. Br. Bahnson stated that on account of the high prices of grain, he wishes the horse belonging to the Sustent. Diac. in his keeping to be disposed of. An offer to buy the horse for $250 has been made by Danl. Grubb Jr. Board has no objection to the sale of the horse for the above sum, provided the payment be properly secured by note to Treasr. of Wa. Sust. D.

As Br. Bahnson has made arrangements to procure a horse when needed by him for official purposes, the allowance of $75 per annum for official use of horse and carriage will continue.

Tues., Aug. 11. Br. Joshua Boner absent.

1. The Treasurer, Br. S. T. Pfohl, submitted the annual accounts for June 1, 1862, to May 31, 1863, and the statement of assets and liabilities on May 31, 1863. The sum total of receipts, including a donation of $1,000 from S.F. Acady., amounted to $3,671.45, and the disbursements, including a premium of $1,000 paid for State Bonds, to $4,083.08, leaving a deficit of $411.63. The total assets on June 1, 1863, after deducting the deficit were $40,006.68, and the actual liabilities $530.08. The Provincial Fund was as last year $32,926.83, and Fund Account $5,349.77.

2. At Br. Bahnson's request, it was resolved on motion: "That from September 1, 1863, Br. Bahnson keep an account of the wood used by him, which at the end of 12 months, shall be submitted to the Board, which shall then pay the same in lieu of his allowance for wood."

Mon., Nov. 30. All the members present.

1. On account of the very high prices of provisions and all necessaries of life, the assistance for the year 1863 was fixed at $80 for each member of a family, exclusive of servants, and this amount will be paid by Treasurer to President of P.E.C. and to the widows who receive their pensions from Wa. S.D.

Bethania Diary, with Bethabara, 1863
[Extracts transcribed; handwriting is that of Jacob F. Siewers.]

Thurs., Feb. 5. Last night or rather this morning it commenced snowing and continued nearly all day, the wind high and drifting the snow through every crevice, the snow being from 6 to 8 inches.

Thurs., Feb. 12. Went out to the widow Butner's; the old mother is 94 years of age. It was thought that she had a paralytic attack, found her to all appearance as usual.

Sun., Feb. 15. Today Oliver Lehman left for the Army; he expects to join the Band in the 33d Regiment of N.C. troops.

Mon., Feb. 16. Alvin Butner, Benj. Chitty, Julius Shaub, James Grabs, Doc. Mock and others went to Winston to the enrollment, orders having been published for them to appear with 3 days rations. The roads are very muddy.

Sun., Feb. 22. This morning the ground, although soaked with rain, was covered with snow or rather sleet. The bell was rung at the usual time for preaching and but one person appeared; after waiting some time we decided to drop the service.

Mon., Feb. 23. Wrote a letter to my son Joseph.

Tues., Feb. 24. Went out to visit the widow Sr. George, m.n. Strupe. She was not at home, being at her son-in-law's who has to leave home tomorrow as a conscript.

Wed., Feb. 25. Br. Alvin Butner left early this morning as a conscript for the Army. It is said that 150 leave on this enrollment from this county.

Mon.-Sat., Mar. 9-14. At home working in my garden, sawing wood and repairing fences.

Fri., Mar. 27. ([Margin note]: Prayer and fast day.) At Bethania held a discourse at 10, very few present. Went to Bethabara, no one there.

Wed., Apr. 8. Gazeil Grabs, our neighbor, desiring to go to the funeral of John Walls, her sister's husband who was bro't from the Camp on the Rappahannock and is to be buried tomorrow, asked me for Pete, and I could not well refuse her.

Sat., Apr. 11. Sr. S., myself and Betzy Hauser went to Sr. Mary Shore, widow. Baptized the sons of Augustine and the daughter of Edward H. Shore. The fathers are in the army ([Bethania Report:] at Fredericksburg) and by letter requested me to administer baptism to their infant children. ([Bethania Report:] Poor Mother Shore is nearly blind. She is unable to read or do any work, and suffers much from rheumatism.)

Mon., May 11. Wesley Kearney kindly ploughed my orchard with Pete. Aug. Oehman dropt corn for me and I covered it. It was very warm.

Sat., May 16. Fair. Received a letter from Joseph, he's well.

Thurs., May 21. My Caroline is sick.

Sun., May 24. Preached at Bethania at 10 A.M. on Acts 2:1-18. After preaching the members of the Committee remained. The application of Sr. William Leinbach desiring to attach herself to the congregation again was bro't forward. She was admitted without objection. Brn. H. H. Butner, Joseph Transou, Sol. Pfaff and William Lehman and Jacob Werner present.

It was resolved that the Congregation Festival be observed on Sunday the 14th of June, and that a lovefeast be provided.

Thurs., May 28. Caroline is very sick, the feaver is of a bilious feature.

Sun., May 31. My daughter is on the mend.

Sun., June 7. I learned that the above infant [Leonora Paulina Hine] was buried on our [Bethabara] Graveyard this morning. The parents would not have me to preach the funeral.

Sat., June 27. Visited Virgil, he is in a deep sleep or stupor. ([Bethania Report:] Virgil a boy of about 13 years of age and belongs to T. Lash; he has typhoid in its worst form.)

Mon., June 29. Assisted Alick to make a coffin for Virgil, giving him the proper instruction.

Tues., June 30. Between 12 and 1 P.M. held a discourse at Thomas Lash's Quarter in Town, and afterwards performed the burial service for Virgil, who departed the 28th, aged about 13 years. Typhoid feaver.

Sun., July 12. During the service [at Mickey's School House] a storm arose with heavy rain, lightning and crashing thunder. Several trees were struck close by; some of the children commenced crying, and I was requested to wait awhile. The water courses had risen in the meantime so much that I feared to cross Bear Creek on my return home, but I ventured and crossed it in safety. The corn on the road seemed almost entirely prostrated by the storm.

Tues., July 14. Br. Thomas Lash was kind enough to let me have the help of one of his servants, Alexander, to help me renew my gate and one panel of my fence, the posts having fallen down from decay. The bake-oven roof was also about to fall down; the posts supporting it were rotten.

Sun., July 19. Evening meetings have to be dropped for the want of candles.

Thurs., July 23. We were very agreeably surprised by a visit from br. and Sr. Holland from Salem with their little daughter.

Fri., July 24. Preached at 4 P.M. at Lash's quarter in Town the funeral service of Frances, daughter of Sandy and Betzy, servants of the above, on 1 Cor. 1:30. Her age about 14 years. Departed [the] 22d.

Mon., Aug. 3. Visited the sick, and helped Wesley Kearney with his cider making.

Thurs., Aug. 6. Made a cooper's plane for my brother.

Fri., Aug. 21. ([Margin note]: Fast and prayer.) Rang the bell at 10 A.M.; no one coming, there was no service. Visited the sick in Town. William Grabs returned from Greensboro sick; he has typhoid feaver.

Sun., Aug. 23. Visited Snow and Chitty. Snow is getting better, but Chitty is worse; he will take no medicine, alleging it's only his headache.

Mon.-Wed., Aug. 24-26. B. Chitty has been visited by Doc. Mock; he pronounces his case typhoid feaver in the last stage and very doubtful of recovery.

Sat., Aug. 29. Doc. Horten sent for; little hope for Benj. [Chitty].

Sun., Aug. 30. ([Bethania Report:] At 12 was called to the bedside of Benj. C.; he was evidently dying, speechless but conscious. After singing a portion of the hymn "Rock of Ages, Cleft for Me" and prayer, I imparted to him the last blessing in the name of the Lord. At 1 preached the funeral of Virgil and Frances, children of Sandy and Betzy Lash, at the negro Church under the oaks to the largest negro congregation I ever addressed. They were attentive and their behaviour good. At about 4 P.M. I was called to Benj. C. and discovered he was dying. He breathed his last softly without a movement. This is a sore bereavement for us all. He was greatly beloved by all who knew him far and near, and I shall miss his harmonious and manly voice in our assemblies.)

Tues., Sept. 8. Took Alexander Grabs to Florence, Guilford county.

Fri., Sept. 11. Alick's daughter Letitia having died the previous evening, I made the coffin.

Sat., Sept. 19. Visited in company with Sr. S. the widow Sr. Mary Shore. Her son Edward Shore is at home a paroled prisoner [of war], saw Joseph at Fort Delaware, he was making coffins.

Sun., Sept. 20. They have commenced a Sunday school [at Bethabara], Sr. Elisabeth Kraus and Sr. Hine as the teachers. The former Sr. will also keep an infant school in the middle back room of the Parsonage during the week.

Thurs., Oct. 15. Gathering corn in garden and shucked it.

Fri., Oct. 16. Carried my corn on the loft of the Church.

Mon-Thurs., Oct. 19-22. Rainy. The home guard met at Pfafftown. Worked about my premises.

Fri., Oct. 23. This morning Bowser's son called on me desiring that his grandfather Henry Miller, who died that morning, might be buried at Bethabara, and that Helsabeck might preach the funeral. I told him the rules of the Church and directed him to the Committee. After dinner 3 cavalry deserter hunters called before the house, Rail, Ben. Turner, and Henry Spiess, the first asking me for the Church key. I gave it to him, and he and Turner searched the Church for deserters, saying they had orders to search the Church.

Tues., Oct. 27. Went to Salem with Johnson to see br. Holland before he left for the North.

Mon., Nov. 2. Commenced this afternoon to put new bottoms on my boots, fearing that if our shoe-makers were to leave for the Army I would have to do my own work.

Tues., Nov. 3. Worked on my boots.

Wed., Nov. 4. As above. Election for ([margin note:] Congress.)

Wed., Nov. 11. Sr. S. and myself visited at Br. William Leinbach by invitation; his son Edgar leaves tomorrow for the army again. We sang a hymn, read a chapter, and offered a prayer in his behalf.

Thurs., Nov. 12. Worked in my yard, put the fence in good repair on the side of the Srs. Strup, etc. The firing of cannon heard.

Sat., Nov. 14. Today firing of cannon heard in westwardly direction.

Wed., Nov. 18. [A]t the Bethabara bridge the back spring of our carriage broke in the plate, but we got home safe.

Thurs., Nov. 19. Alfred Stoltz being at home on furlough, he kindly mended it for me without charge.

Sat., Nov. 21. After a long dry spell, we have been blest with a regular rain all day. Filed and set some saws for neighbors.

Mon., Nov. 23. Wash day. Afternoon went down to br. John Shore, and brot up my rent corn, about 7 bushels.

Tues., Nov. 24. Put my corn up on Church garret. I received a letter this morning from Sallie Spach desiring to connect herself with the Methodist Church.

Sat., Nov. 28. Bought 3 bushels of potatoes at $3 per bus. and put them away.

Sun., Dec. 6. The [Bethabara] heads of families were to meet here today. The members of the Committee being present, the subject of the graveyard was introduced, persons having been buried there contrary to the rules. Committee resolved that in future no one is to be buried here who is not a member of the Church, or a resident member of a family that has obtained the privilege of burial by contributing to the keeping up the burial ground, but by consent of the Committee and paying $10 for an adult grave and $5 for a child's grave. The minister in charge of the Congregation is to conduct the Services. The Committee respectfully request the P.E.C. to give their sanction to the above in written notice to be put up for the public.

Sat., Dec. 12. Our dog Rat died last night. We had kept him here on Joseph's account, who claimed him as his pet.

Friedberg Diary, with Hope, 1863
[Extracts transcribed; handwriting is that of Christian Lewis Rights.]

Mon., Jan. 5. Visited Sister Nancy Scott. Her oldest child is badly burnt by his clothes taking fire, and she has just heard that her husband [Alexander] has died in the army.

Mon.-Wed., Mar. 9-11. Plowed. Found it hard work, and at night I would be so tired that I could hardly walk from the field to the house.

Thurs., Mar. 12. Brother Levy Padgett left for the army.

Sun., Apr. 19. Opened the Sunday School, then kept instruction, then preached from 1 Cor. 1:30. In the afternoon preached at Pleasant Fork to a good congregation from 1 Cor. 1:18, then called at Sandford Earnest's and prayed with him, and then went to Winston and preached in the Episcopal Methodist Church from 1 Cor. 1:18.

Sun., June 28. In the afternoon, about 3 o'clock, it began to rain and rained with short intervals until sometime in the night, and the prospect is good for a freshet.

Mon., June 29. This morning it had stopped raining, and Southfork was very full and still rising. Ripple's Bridge and Todd's Bridge are washed away, and all the fencing and considerable quantities of wheat along the bottom are gone too. The bridges on Middlefork are also gone or so wrecked that there can be no crossing. Southfork and Middlefork, it is said, were higher than was ever known. The bridge at Salem is gone, at Lagenauer's mill between Clemmonsville and Stafford, and Johnson's are gone or impassable, and on Muddy Creek a great deal of wheat was carried off, so that the freshet of yesterday may be called the *big freshet,* and it is only a matter for thankfulness that such freshets come but once in a century.

Mon., Sept. 21. Went to Lexington to attend the enrollment. Found myself conscripted and the enrolling officer gone.

Tues., Sept. 22. Went to Lexington again, but the enrolling officer had not returned from Raleigh. Returned home and went to Salem. Got home about 12 o'clock, having rode fifty-two miles since sunrise.

Sun., Sept. 27. Preaching at Friedberg from Acts 12:11, and at the close of the sermon communicated some extracts from letters received from brethren in the army, Solomon Tesh and Ephraim Weasner. In regards to the revival that is in progress in their brigade, they have erected a brigade stand, and have had preaching three times a day for more than a week, and from 40 to 50 inquirers each day, and the interest was still on the increase. Several of the officers had made a profession of religion likewise. One of the brethren asked: "What are you doing at home?" My answer was: Nothing; people have no time to attend to religion; they must make money.

Mon., Nov. 16. Visited Mrs. Roberts and Brother Fry. ([Friedberg Report:] By request visited an old lady, Mrs. Roberts, wife of Josiah Roberts. Some weeks ago she had her hand crushed in a cane mill, and all her fingers and thumb had to be amputated. She is in a low condition, and it is doubtful whether she will ever get well.)

Sun., Nov. 29. [I]n the afternoon preached the funeral of David Fishel, jun. He died at Richmond on the 7th of last February. Also baptized his infant daughter. . . .

Thurs., Dec. 10. Fasting, humiliation, and prayer day by the Governor, Vance. Preached at Friedberg in morning from Malachi 2:9, and in the afternoon at Hope from the same text.

Private Diary of R. P. Leinbach, 1863
[Serving Macedonia and Muddy Creek, plus Friedland after October; extracts transcribed.]

[The Private Diary of R. P. Leinbach lapses for the first half of the year. The following are extracts from the Macedonia Reports he filed with Ministers Conference.]

Sun., Jan. 4. Another case of smallpox reported. Fresh panic. When anyone is taken sick 'tis at once a case of smallpox, and the neighbors keep aloof until the patient is recovered. Tho' the people have almost all been vaccinated, they seem to put little faith in its efficacy.

Fri., Jan. 23. About two hundred Confederate artillery horses crossed the river. About half of them remained all night with their drivers. They were going on to South Carolina to recruit and get ready for summer service. When they were gone I was horrified to find my carriage bridle was missing. 'Tis probably by this time actively engaged in Confederate service.

Sun., Jan. 25. There being scarcity of wood at the church, Tuesday was appointed to come together and collect some. None were present but Br. R. Sheek and myself, and after working a few hours, the rain drove us home. But we succeeded in getting the keys from Br. Wheeler, which is regarded as a very fortunate event. Br. D. Sheek carries them now, so we'll have fire again.

Wed., Feb. 4. [In the] morning Lucinda, infant daughter of Br. Jonathan Miller, died. At the same time his wife and little boy were very sick of the same disease. The little girl was buried Thursday (5th) morning during a very heavy snow storm. The little boy died Friday night, and was buried the following Sunday morning. The mother lingered until Wednesday (11th) night, when she departed this life, and was buried the following Friday (13th) morning. The previous Monday (9th) night Sr. M. McBride, wife of Mr. Jno. McBride, was taken sick of the same disease and died the following Thursday night (12). Tuesday (10th) night little Amanda, about 12 yrs. of age, was taken sick and lingered several weeks. At the same time there were four other persons who more or less exhibited the same premonitory symptoms of the disease, myself among the number. In consequence of which I was unable to attend to the funeral of several of these persons. These were supposed to have been all poisoned by an old negro woman belonging to Br. Jonathan Miller.

Mon., Feb. 23. [T]he symptoms of the disease growing worse, I went to Salem, hoping to obtain relief from change of location, as the disease had been pronounced miasmatic by one of the physicians.

Fri., Feb. 27. Little Amanda died and was buried Saturday afternoon. The corpses all showed signs of decay immediately after death and required speedy interment.

Fri., Mar. 1. My health having improved, I returned home, and . . . .

Sun., Mar. 8. . . . Preached at Macedonia to a very small congregation.

Fri., Apr. 3. In consequence of a previous arrangement, I went down to Friedland to keep Easter meetings there.

Sun., Apr. 5. After we had returned from the graveyard there was preaching at Friedland. It was supposed there were about 400 persons present. We formed in procession, the singers four deep in the lead, singing whilst going to the graveyard and returning from it. The presence of half a dozen armed soldiers at the graveyard after preaching caused a general panic among the young men, who were mostly about home engaged in different occupations to keep out of the war. As most of them had no exemption papers to produce, they found it most convenient to get home without passing the graveyard, preferring the by-paths thro' fields, woods, and meadows.

Sun., May 10. [At Macedonia, m]uch anxiety was felt about the safety of the young men of the congregation who were said to have been engaged in the battle of Chancellorsville.

[The Private Diary of R. P. Leinbach picks up again.]

Wed., July 1. River Home. For several months I have been employed tending several patches of corn. My expenses have been considerable, tho' trifling in comparison with what they might have been but for the kindness of Br. and Sr. Sheek. I have been compelled to purchase turning plow, a shovel, and bull tongue and a calf tongue. I had thought seriously of purchasing a hoe harrow and may do so still. April, May and June have passed away and find me now engaged still trying to help my corn along. The affairs of the congregation are truly discouraging. All our young men are gone, several have been killed, some died. The old people do not interest themselves in the affairs of the church as they should do. All men's hearts are troubled because of the war. The attendance at divine service is but indifferent. We have commenced Sunday School and there seems to be considerable disposition among the scholars to attend. I take all the Testament-reading boys and girls in one class, and what comes besides I portion out to others—Br. R. Sheek or some one else.

Fri., July 3. I transplanted several stalks of corn; it remains to be seen how they will thrive.

Mon., July 6. I remained at home, as it was too wet to plant, and tacked some leather soles on my wooden bottoms to prevent the mud adhering to them so much.

Tues., July 7. Heard that Henry Jones had been killed in Penna. The militia is to be taken out for state defence. Our army is said to be in Penna. I wonder much how this business is going to turn out. They are said to have taken Chambersburg, York, Gettysburg, Harrisburg, and goodness knows what all. I fear it will but expedite the final agony and hasten that which is written in the book of destiny, and might possibly have been prolonged awhile by mere defensive movements. I should not wonder if the Northern administration had purposely allowed this movement to unite and rouse their people to a more effectual resistance. During the summer I have done very little reading or studying. It has required all my efforts to keep up with my crops. It has now been raining so much that it is too wet for upland corn to do well except in certain kinds of ground. In spiritual matters, my poor heart experiences the lukewarmness and indifference to which all seem at this time to be subject. The war, the war seems to absorb all men's minds, and the scarcity bro't on by the war renders men more callous instead of causing them to feel their dependence on the Supreme Being.

Wed., July 8. My thoughts are often with the dear friends of the past. What are they doing? How are they coming on? Herman, Clement, Leibert, Granville, Coz Gus, and all the rest. And my cherished friend and scholar J.H.S. I wonder whether he is still in the land of the living. Oftentimes memories fond and gushing come thronging thickly on me. In dreams I traverse old scenes, am among old friends and acquaintances, and live over again old times. But what a vast gulph separates us now. With them, no doubt, all is comparatively well. How is it with us?

Thurs., July 9. Uncle Harry tells me corn planted in the new of the moon becomes very tall, and the ears are higher and not so large as that planted in the full.

Sat., July 11. For two days the sun has been shining very dimly as thro' a fog or haze; his whole disc is visible of a pale blood red color and quite powerless. Some of the neighbors are hauling in their wheat, whether dry or not. My corn is said to be very high and standing among the weeds and crab grass. I dread seeing it. Next week will be a week of heavy work, if the weather permits. Vicksburg is said to be in possession of the Federals. No doubt there is great joy at the North. Lee is said to have defeated them at Gettysburg. Ist das wirklich der fall? [Is that really the case?]

Wed., July 15. Tho' the moon has fulled, there is no change apparent in the weather. 'Tis said that when the moon changes in the morning, it betokens wet weather; when in the evening, clear and settled weather. The moon changed this evening at 5 o'clock, and there has been rain all round us. Some 5 or 6 S. Carolina cavalry soldiers staid all night. Very glum side. I learn that Gen. Bragg has withdrawn from Tennessee, and that state and Alabama must be open to the Federals. Charlestown has been attacked, and from what this cavalry soldier says, they have got at it from almost the only vulnerable point, and he thinks they may take it. Should they, the days of the Southern Confederacy are almost numbered. Lee has retired to Hagerstown. No doubt he was worsted in the late engagement.

Thurs., July 16. In the evening, however, a storm came up and such rain and such hail I have never witnessed. It stormed fearfully. We had just finished supper at Br. R.'s when the storm broke upon us in all its fury. It penetrated the kitchen roof as also the house roof. Next morning I went to examine my corn, and what a spectacle. The corn in the black ground had been about ten feet tall, but it was all blown down, matted together fairly. The rest was not so bad. Some of the stalks were broken, shorn off.

Fri., July 17. The river was up very much beyond crossing. Port Hudson is gone. Went up to examine my wheat—in much better condition than I expected to find it. Br. D. Sheek says his corn is almost ruined—$5,000 will hardly cover damages.

Thurs., July 30. There has been so much rain that everything is damp and mouldy.

Mon., Aug. 10. Plowed most of the day. Tuesday and Wednesday morning plowed. Thermometer about 90° in the shade. Thursday evening thrashed part of my wheat; storm came up; finished the remainder next morning. Saturday prepared sermon.

Sun., Aug. 16. I have again taken up my Greek. I trust I may progress further than ever before; am also reading history of Germany.

Wed., Aug. 26. [W]ent to Salem with a load of wheat. Thursday morning procured some cotton thread for Cope's women by waiting almost one hour amidst a crowd of men and women.

Sun., Aug. 30. ([Macedonia Report:] The militia officers are among the regular attendants at service. Macedonia appears to be the place and Sunday the day selected for the discussion of their military affairs. They come to church, tho' mostly not attached to it, and our members are beginning to betake themselves to the woods.)

Sat., Sept. 5. Saturday went up to Smith Grove with Br. Richmond. Camp meeting at Smith Grove. Elder Wytsche presided. I have not heard so stirring a preacher in a long time; would I could hear him once again. Saturday night walked home and then went up again. Staid all night at Br. R.'s tent.

Wed., Sept. 16. Today cutting tops. There has been a perfect time in the neighborhood. The home guard has been scouring the woods for deserters and conscripts. A number have come in and surrendered themselves. ([Macedonia Report:] Among them Andrew Cope.) Br. Richmond Sheek is to be enrolled tomorrow. He is my mainstay here and if [he] should leave, there's but little encouragement for me.

Thurs., Sept. 17. Worked up in the corn, tying up tops. Cornelius helped me and showed me how. These times put us all to work, and compel me, alas, often to neglect my business, I mean my pastoral labors. Would that I could again go 'round as I used to. As there is so much sickness here and no person coming in to help nurse, I agreed to go down to Br. Chrn. Spach's for Br. D. and have some wheat exchanged for the new white wheat.

Sun., Sept. 20. Preached at Muddy Creek. . . . The people urged me so much at meeting to come to see them I hardly knew what to answer them. The truth is I must work or I cannot manage. Also if I want pants, where shall I get them? Homemade jeans cost $5 and upwards, wheat $7.50 a bushel, corn some are offering $10. Iron 60 cents per lb., leather $10 per lb. Salt $25 per bushel. Hat for $16. Wool rolls $5 per lb. Bacon $1.25 per lb. Beef sells in Salem at $.50 per lb. Horse shoeing costs $5. And at such prices how is it possible for a person with a salary of $300 a year to get through, even when he does not pay more than $162 for board and lodging. I have raised 22 bushels of wheat, some corn, some peas, and cut some tops. I don't know how I shall come thro'. And yet the good folks seem to think I have nothing to do but come to see them.

Mon., Sept. 21. Went to see Mrs. Thos. Cooper and others immersed at Conrad's mill. ([Macedonia Report:] At the Baptist Church at Union Hill.)

Mon., Sept. 28. Morning about 7 o'clock Sr. Hall died. She had been in a dying condition for 10 or 12 hours. She was buried this (Tuesday) afternoon between 12 and 1 o'clock. There was no funeral preached.

Fri., Oct. 2. On the road I stopped and consulted Dr. Wharton about my health. He told me my system was in a relaxed condition and prescribed tonics; said I was affected by atmospheric influence.

Mon., Oct. 12. Had my horse shod all round. Tuesday was to have taken Br. R. Sheek to Salisbury, but he concluded to go in to the salt petre business, he having been detailed for the business.

October, 1863. In consequence of Br. Fry's illness, he resigned the charge of Friedland, and it naturally devolved on me, and furthermore in consequence of Sr. Hall's death, I must seek another home. I tried to persuade Br. R. Sheek to build me a cabin on his land somewhere and board me, but he declined the honor. Mr. E. Hine also declined taking me, so there was no other course but to return to Salem, where I found a home with my brother, still, however, attending to Macedonia. I preached my first sermon at Friedland Sept. [Oct.] 25 from Numbers 10:29, after which I went home with Br. Gibbins. I was glad to assume charge of Friedland again. So many hours had I spent in prayer for that dear old place that I knew that sooner or later a blessing must come upon it, and I only found out during my stay in Davie how much my heart clung to that dear sanctuary, my first love! ([Friedland Report:] The congregation seems to be considerably disturbed by the exigencies of the times. The home guard had been called out to secure the persons of deserters, etc., and as some of the children of members were discovered by said home guard there was considerable feeling against members who were serving in the Home Guard.)

Mon., Oct. 26. Monday and Tuesday morning my horse was used in the sugar mill for grinding cane.

Sun., Nov. 1. And here I am now, my last Sunday at Br. Hall's. I shall probably move my things to Salem this week. I have almost all of my corn, some of my wheat, my chattels, and sofa to take over to town, and some oats to sow yet if I can make things work right. It is desired that I should live at Friedland, but that appears to be impracticable. Nous verrons [we shall see]. How I am to feed my horse this coming year remains to be seen, as my expenses are heavy and my income small, and the future looks dark and lowering. "Forsetan et haec olim meminisse juvabit." [Perhaps it will be pleasant some day to recall even these things. Virgil's *Æneid*, i, 203.]

Sun., Oct. [Nov.] 8. Preached again at Friedland from Prov. 32:6 [22:6]. The deep sense of contentment and joy in again ministering to this dear people cannot be expressed in words.

Sun., Nov. 22. Preached at Macedonia; found a number of window panes wantonly broken. Thursday . . . [a]fternoon went to Br. Jno. Knauss. Friday returned. My object was to procure hay. As I was to remain at Salem I required it, and as the farmers were required to give the tenth and some had already been pressed, there was a poor prospect of obtaining any.

Sun., Nov. 29. Next morning [Nov. 30] went to South Fork in search of hay. Was fortunate enough to secure the promise of some at Br. Chr. Spach's. Remained with him that night. We have a very pleasant evening singing and playing on the piano. He and I tuned two keys of his instrument, which required considerable labor on our part, inexperienced as we were in such matters. I engaged my hay at $3.00 per hundred lb. Confederate money. I partially engaged some at Mr. Eli Foltz's at $1.80 in old bank bills, or $2.00 in state money.

Thurs., Dec. 3. The last month of this terrible year has commenced; thousands who saw the year's beginning will not see its close. Today I brought 22 bushels of corn of Br. Jno. Knauss' boys for which I paid $10 per bushel, making the sum of $220. I had no money of my own and was compelled to borrow it of my brother. Two hundred and twenty dollars for twenty-two bushels of corn! Great country. Great war! I have now 32 bushels of corn which have cost me more than $300. I raised about twenty bushels, which would be worth almost $200 more. How is [it] possible for this state of affairs to continue this much longer? Another year like this will ruin me completely. Oh! for faith to put my whole trust in the Lord. I was out at Friedland this afternoon with Anne. How much my heart yearns towards the dear old place; I wish circumstances would admit of my living there now. It appears I could do more good, could realize more fully my condition and position. The Lord will provide in his own good time. The land looks much better than I had expected to find it, and I intend with God's blessing to do all I can this winter both spiritually and temporally for the dear old place. I feel thankful to the Lord that he has been pleased to place me there once more. I have prayed for it. I have visited its shores in my dreams. And now I am again stationed there. But how different now from the time I first went there. Then mental improvement was still an object. Now I look at my books, my commentaries, my lexicon, my Schiller, and wonder why they are here to mock me. I might as well pack them all up and put them away. The cry now has become corn, wheat, bread and meat. Bragg has been whipped at Lookout Mountain, has retreated, and was said to have been again worsted at Ringgold. Tennessee is expected soon to go back.

Fri., Dec. 4. Went to Br. Chr. Seides' mill after a load of rough edge plank to make a shelter for my conveyance and hay. John thought it was too heavy at first, but drew it up Atwood's hill[1] in fine order.

[*Mon., Dec. 7.*] Got some moss. . . . 'Twas clear and very cold.

Tues., Dec. 15. [W]ent after laurel. 'Tis said Gen. Grant has left Georgia and is pursuing Longstreet towards Richmond. I am told A. Lincoln has issued a proposition to the seceded states offering pardon to all who would return to their allegiance. Congress is in session, and will no doubt pass very heavy conscription bills.

Tues., Dec. 22. Working at the decoration. Next morning I went down to High Point after brother James. 'Twas an event for me, as I had not seen a locomotive for five years, and there was no telling how many years it might be until I should see another.

---

[1]This is not at the present-day Atwood Road, but nearer to Salem on the Shallowford Road, where it is now called First Street and crosses the Atwood land at Peters Creek at the foot of what is still a steep hill, rising in the West End section of Winston-Salem.

Sat., Dec. 26. [W]ent up to Miss Hagen's to play chess; spent the evening there with some company.

[New] Philadelphia Reports, with Friedland, 1863
[Extracts transcribed; handwriting is that of Thomas Frye.]

Wed., Feb. 11. James Rominger, one of our conscripts, was brought home from a hospital in Virginia in a distressed condition. On Thursday morning I heard of it and went immediately to see him. Found him very near exhausted and entirely deprived of reason, yet at the request of his wife we prayed with him, and after some hours we returned home, and early next morning went to see him, and found him dead.

Sun., June 7. Preached at Friedland from Prov. 13:15 to a very large assemblage of people, and amongst the rest I had 7 soldiers, all Georgians of General Stewart's Cavalry, who seemed to listen to preaching with interest. After preaching conversed with them, and found them all apparently very fine young men.

Mon., Aug. 17. Very sick. Unable to get about until Saturday. Some better so as to be up the best part of the day and write some.

Fri., Aug. 28. Br. Rights happened to hear that I was sick and paid me a visit.

Sun., Sept. 13. Have not preached in four weeks and still unable to preach.

[Thomas Frye's Reports from (New) Philadelphia end here.]

1864

[Austria and Prussia joined in seizing territory from Denmark. In Mexico, the French installed Austrian Archduke Maximilian as emperor.

Nevada was admitted to the Union as the thirty-sixth state. General Sherman marched through Georgia, taking Atlanta in September and Savannah in December.

On April 24, in one of the few Confederate victories in North Carolina, Plymouth was recaptured, but the sinking of the *Albemarle* by Union forces dashed hopes of relieving the Federal blockade. Zebulon Vance defeated William Holden 4 to 1 in the governor's race, meaning no separate peace for North Carolina.]

Memorabilia of Salem Congregation, 1864
[Extracts transcribed; handwriting is that of George Frederic Bahnson.]

In general this year partook of the same sad and melancholy character which the preceding one exhibited; only that the horizon is surrounded by clouds, if possible, more ominous and threatening than at the beginning of the year. With some hope of approaching peace we entered upon this year, and now we are about to close it while the coveted blessing appears to be as far off as ever.

Bloody and fearful have been the contests carried on during this year. Large numbers of the young and robust have fallen on the bloody battlefields, cities and towns were destroyed, many homes desolated, want took the place of plenty, and this day thousands are homeless and houseless, on whom at the beginning of the year comfortable or even luxurious habitations smiled a joyous welcome.

Widows and orphans sit this evening in sadness and sorrow whose husbands and fathers gladdened their hearts in days now gone by forever. Some of the most fertile portions of our country were visited by fire and sword as by a devastating tornado, and smiling farms and residences changed into a desert and fruitful fields into a howling wilderness, and with sensations of almost insufferable grief and anguish of heart, once happy families gaze upon the ruins of their earthly all.

Houses of the Most High in which his blessed word had been proclaimed and his holy sacraments administered were destroyed or desecrated and put to most disgraceful uses.

The call to arms was resounded again and again during the course of this year with steadily increasing loudness and vehemence, and multitudes of the young as well as of those further advanced in life are at this moment, altogether contrary to what they were expecting at the beginning of the year, in the tented field and necessitated to rush to the battleground whenever the signal shall strike upon their ears.

Throughout the length and breadth of the land only comparatively few families can be found whose fathers and sons or other connections are not from home, and in whose behalf the minds of parents, wives and relatives are not filled with anxious fears and sad forebodings. From our own midst not a few were thus compelled to leave for the army, and our church catalogue contains between 60 and 70 names of such as are absent, we sincerely trust, only for a season. While thus on the one hand many of those who provided for their own, either wholly or in part, were disabled from continuing so to do, the currency of the country depreciated more and more, and the necessaries of life, much of which was claimed for supplying the government, became scarcer and rose higher and higher in price until their value has become almost fabulous.

And still there is no end to be seen by human foresight or sagacity, for the gory pall of devastation and bloodshed is still fearfully hanging over our beloved land.

This is a sad but by no means untruthful picture of our condition as a nation. The Lord has a fearful controversy with us as a people, and his anger is burning still; and to all appearances the storm of battle and the horrors of war are drawing nearer to where we dwell.

Our hearts must overflow with gratitude when we call to mind our general experience as a church and congregation. Not one of our congregations in this District was interrupted in its regular or particular meetings and solemnities during the course of this year.

It was to us a matter of deep regret that the present unfortunate state of the country cuts us off from almost all intercourse with the rest of our Church, but we felt convinced that many of our brethren and sisters, this side and beyond the ocean, remembered us in their prayers, and entertained for us feelings of brotherly love and sympathy, and that their petitions were joined with ours that the fearful scourge now visiting us might be speedily removed.

In general this year was not a very healthy one, an effect produced by a variety of causes. Still the mortality was not as large among us as has been the case sometimes, but we were reminded in the very midnight hour of last year, that in the midst of life we are in death. Some of our members were visited by severe and tedious afflictions by which one of our sisters was confined to the house for the greater part of the year and could not come to the courts of the Lord at all. All of these, however, are to all appearances recovering by the Lord's goodness.

([Margin note:] On the 7th of Dec. a Provincial Synod met here at Salem, but owing to the present condition of the country it resolved to meet again soon after the declaration of peace and meanwhile to leave things as they are without entering into any further examination of the spiritual and temporal condition of our Province or electing any of those boards which are to be chosen every 6th year at a Provincial Synod.)

([Addendum:] In the colored division of the congregation 6 adults were baptized and 3 confirmed during the year. Two communicants have departed this life. Four children of members were baptized. At the close of the year the number of communicant members on the list is 63.)

Salem Diary, 1864
[Extracts transcribed; handwriting is that of George Frederic Bahnson.]

Fri., Jan. 1. A bright though a cold day. Weeping may endure for a night, but joy cometh in the morning [Ps. 30:5]. God grant that the bright sunshine following upon a dark and gloomy light may be an emblem of times of peace and prosperity that may be in store for us.

Mon., Jan. 4. Most unexpectedly Henry, the son of Bro. Bahnson, arrived at home. He had been paroled at Point Lookout.

The whole week we had very cold weather, a little sprinkling of snow but very little. People were busy hauling in ice; it is about 2 inches thick. Colds are very prevalent.

Sun., Jan. 10. An exceedingly cold day. Only 10°. At 10 A.M. Bro. Bahnson prayed the litany and preached on the gospel lesson. Considering the cold weather and the cold church (in spite of the furnace) the audience was quite encouraging.

Sun., Jan. 17. Quite a good audience present, but as the Presbyterian minister was holding forth at Winston, some of our members thought it their duty (?) to encourage him and attended there. O for true church patriotism.

Mon., Jan. 18. Intelligence was received that the single Bro. Arthur Van Vleck, a northern prisoner at Richmond, had departed this life on the 21st of Dec. last.

Wed., Jan. 27. The weather was uncommonly pleasant and warm. Fire was scarcely needed. People sat with open windows and began to work in their gardens, planting potatoes, onions, etc.

Wed., Feb. 3. The Salem Band arrived yesterday on furlough.

Tues., Feb. 9. Bro. Bahnson commenced lectures on the catechism, preparatory to confirmation. He kept them in the chapel, any person being allowed to attend. This evening there were but very few persons present, owing to a free concert given by the Salem Band in the courthouse, which was attractive to old and young.

Sun., Feb. 21. The waterworks were frozen so that water was rather scarce.

Mon., Feb. 22. Bro. Bahnson kept prayer meeting at 7 1/2 o'clock P.M. Some boys in memory of Washington's birthday were out with a drum and torchlights. Their parents had better come with them to prayer meeting.

Sun., Feb. 28. In the evening Bro. Bahnson kept a singing meeting with prayer. The singing, though without the assistance of the organ—for we have no regular organist at present —was very good.

Mon., Mar. 7. During this week the examining board of surgeons with the enrolling officers were busy at Winston, conscripting a good many persons who had heretofore been exempted. At first the conscripts were treated very harshly. They were marched about under guard, kept like prisoners in the guardhouses, and not allowed to go home without a guard,

While home on furlough in early 1864, the band of the 26th North Carolina Regiment gave concerts. The pencil inscription reads: "Feb. 9th, 1864, at Winston Court House. The next Tuesday afternoon same Programme with 2 exceptions in the Academy."

nor to give security for their appearance. After a while, though, milder measures were adopted. We learn to see strange sights in our once free and highly favored land. Lord have mercy upon us.

Thurs., Mar. 17. Bro. Bahnson kept the annual meeting of the Salem Tract Society. It was not possible to do much this year. We have only sent our contributions to the Rev. W. W. Crowder, agent of the Tract Society at Raleigh. May they have done some good to immortal souls and spread the knowledge of the Lord.

Tues., Mar. 22. We had an uncommonly severe snow storm with very severe cold. Peach trees had been in blossom and spring flowers had come out very prettily, but a white funereal sheet covered everything. The wind being pretty high, the masses of snow were drifted very considerably. It was a sharp day. It continued snowing all day long, so that the depth of the snow was probably one foot on an average. The drifts are of course much deeper. It was impossible to have meeting in the evening, the first time, it is presumed, in many years that an evening meeting had to be dropped during Passion Week.

Wed., Mar. 23. A beautiful, fair, and sunshiny day. There was now a chance for making paths, and the snow ploughs were kept busy. It is supposed that this is the deepest snow we ever had at Salem towards the close of March. It will render fighting between the two hostile armies impossible for some time. Meanwhile, though, the soldiers may be much inconvenienced by this deep snow. It will no doubt cause some suffering among the poor people at home with whom wood and other necessaries are scarce.

Fri., Mar. 25. Good Friday. Rain all day and at times very hard. In the evening the choir could not sing, the members suffering with wet feet.

Sun., Mar. 27. Easter. A beautiful day. The dampness of the ground rendering it highly imprudent to go to the graveyard, Br. Rob. Schweinitz prayed the Easter morning litany in the church. A number of furloughed soldiers were present at these meetings. Several of our Salem "boys" are among them. They all look well and hearty, even such as have returned from captivity at Point Lookout.

Mon., Mar. 28. A very fine day. As our Bible association had been unable to do anything during the course of the year, the annual meeting was dropped. In the afternoon about 100 negroes of both sexes went out fishing; they seemed to be a very happy crowd. It seemed almost increditable that there are so many darkies in Salem, but alas! it is even so.

Sat., Apr. 2. Almost all the ministers residing at Salem went to the funeral of our departed brother Thomas Frye, late minister at [New] Philadelphia. He had been ailing since last August and departed this life on Thursday the 30 [31] inst.

Fri., Apr. 8. By recommendation of the Congress and the President of the Confederate States, this day was observed as a Day of Prayer and Humiliation. At 10 A.M. Bro. Bahnson preached on the daily word appointed for today, a very suitable text, Isaiah 59:2. It is the eighth day of this kind since the beginning of our national troubles. Lord grant that the next one may be a day of thanksgiving and praise for our deliverance. The attendance at church was better than on any one of the preceding days. Lord, own thy word.

Wed., Apr. 20. The weather cannot settle down in conformity with the season. It is very cold and unpleasant for this time of the year. Garden and field labor is lamentably retarded.

Wed., April 27. The warmest day of the season, 84°. Vegetation is thriving wonderfully. Though the frost seems to have killed all the peaches, some other trees bloom very promisingly.

Sun., May 1. Widows' festival. No organist being present, the musical pieces generally sung on this occasion had to be omitted. It is a great pity that there is no regular organist in such a congregation as this. Still this is not the only thing which is not as it ought to be.

Thurs., May 5. Ascension. A beautiful day, 80°. May warm weather continue, although it will not be as welcome as it usually is, for it will bring with it fearful bloodshed and carnage. Glorified and almighty Savior, bring this fratricidal struggle to a desired end.

Sun., May 8. Single Sisters festival. At 2 P.M. Bro. Bahnson kept the "real" lovefeast (cakes with unsweetened Confederate coffee).

Sun., May 15. Whitsunday. A very pleasant day after the rain of yesterday. Bro. Grunert kept the first meeting, which was not very well attended. It is a great pity, but at present the fearful war occupies the minds of people almost exclusively, and things of greater importance are set aside. O Lord, send thy spirit to breathe into the hearts of all men thoughts and desires of peace, good will, and concord.

Wed., May 25. Bro. Bahnson kept Bible lecture, remembering in his prayer the Synod of the Northern Province, which was to convene today. The meeting was not attended by many. The mail coming in the evening is perhaps one cause, as every person is on the stretch for news. But it is certainly a very poor plea.

Thurs., May 26. An entertainment closed the present session in our Female Academy. A number of strangers were here, but not as formerly.

Sun., May 29. The audience was rather small. The Presbyterians had their communion and other solemnities at Winston, by which, in all probability, some of our "cosmopolitan" members were drawn from their own sanctuary. It is to be regretted that they possess no more patriotism.

Mon., May 30. Bro. Bahnson kept prayer meeting, rather poorly attended, though some of the pupils of the Academy were present. Our own people are too much engaged with the news expected from the mail, arriving at the time of the meeting. Alas this "cruel" war does seem to exercise no influence for good in a religious point of view. Lord, put an end to it.

Mon., June 13. Very cool.

Wed., June 15. A warm day for once.

Sun., June 26. An uncommonly hot day. It is almost unbearable, 98°.

Mon., June 27. The heat was almost insupportable, and gardens suffered much from drought. Towards evening we had a pleasant shower, though but a small one. People have been busy cutting wheat, others are at it. The yield is pretty fair. Corn generally looked well. O Lord, grant us a bountiful harvest and grateful hearts to employ thy goodness as shall be pleasing in thy sight.

Mention should have been made sooner of the fact that Bro. Holland, according to an understanding with the P.E.C., resigned his office of pastor of this congregation by extending his long visit to Penna. beyond the close of the month of May. Bro. Bahnson consented to continue to fill the vacated office, and Bro. Grunert to minister principally to the colored portion of this congregation.

Fri., July 1. A very hot day, thermometer up to 96. A little sprinkling in the morning, then clear and hot. After dinner very suddenly the alarm of fire was given. Bro. Shaffner's house was in flames. Very soon all that could go were on the spot, and everything was done that could be performed by human exertions. Providentially there was a perfect calm. To save the dwelling house was impossible, the fire having gained too much headway and everything being as dry and inflammable as tinder. A large number of sisters and other females were present and worked with a will. Had it not been for them, not near as much water as was needed could have been procured. The shop and the warehouse were providentially saved, though standing very close to the burning dwelling. Part of the house being a log building, the logs old and very large, the flames raged fearfully and could not be subdued, until the whole fabric had been torn down. The fire consumed everything with uncommon rapidity, the heat and dryness of the season being partly the cause, as well as the fact that it was partly a frame building. Still, by very great and continued exertions a considerable quantity of things was saved, though many were naturally lost. It was a melancholy sight to see the home of a family of our congregation reduced to a heap of black and smoldering ruins, and general sympathy was felt for the afflicted family.

It is a sad circumstance that Bro. Shaffner had unwittingly been the cause of the calamity, humanly speaking. He and his wife had taken some must out of an old chimney that had not been used for years. Swallows had taken up their abode in it and thrown down a little soot on the must. Unfortunately, Bro. Shaffner resolved to burn a little straw to consume what little soot there might be, thinking and telling Sr. Shaffner that there could be no danger, as the chimney had a cover on top and had not been used for many years. To make, as he thought, assurance doubly sure, he sent out a boy to watch the sparks, who reported all safe. Without dreaming of any danger, the family went to dinner, and found out nothing until their daughter Sarah thought that she heard a strange crackling noise, and on going out saw that the roof was on fire. They attempted to put it out by pouring some water on the roof, but soon discovered that the fire had spread beyond their reach. Thanks to the mercy of God no serious accident happened to anyone that helped on the occasion.

When the house had burnt down it was noticed that the swallows had built two nests in the chimney which Bro. S. attempted to burn out, and this may explain the reason why sparks flew on the roof sufficient to set it on fire. Providentially the house nearest their own and belonging to Bro. Alex Meinung is standing empty, and they will move into it, thus finding a shelter ready prepared for them.

Mon., July 4. What a glorious national festival day this used to be. Now all is gloom and uncertainty. O that a merciful God would bring back happy years that are passed! O mihi procteritos referet si Jupiter annos! How long, great and gracious Jehovah, O how long!

Wed., July 6. Bro. Bahnson kept prayer meeting. Referred to John Huss, and his martyr confession of the truth.

Thurs., July 7. Governor Vance addressed the people in the square. Such an audience has not been seen here for many a day. The speech occupied three hours, but no one complained of its length.

Sun., July 10. Very warm and uncommonly dry. Vegetation is almost fatally injured by the drought.

Wed., July 20. After a long drought we had a refreshing shower, thanks to the Lord.

Mon., July 25. The exercises in our Boys' School commenced again today. There will be a large number of scholars, coming up fully to 35. As a general rule no more will be taken.

Wed., July 27. Cool and cloudy but no rain, though we need it very much. In the evening we had a tolerably nice shower.

Thurs., Aug. 4. Governor's election as also of other officers of the state government. All went off very peaceably and without any disturbance whatever.

Fri., Aug. 5. Were blessed with a pretty nice shower, much needed.

Wed., Aug. 10. No prayer meeting because there was no gas!

Sun., Aug. 14. Celebration of the 13th of Aug. At 2 P.M. a comparatively small number sang the ode prepared for the 13th of August. The gas having given out, the communion in English was celebrated at 3 1/2 P.M. It was unexpectedly well attended. Bro. Bahnson kept Lovefeast and communion. At 7 1/2 Bro. Grunert kept the communion in German. The evening happening to be cloudy, it grew rather dark before the meeting closed.

Wed., Aug. 17. Children's festival. At 2 P.M. Bro. Bahnson kept the lovefeast (we had bitter Confederate coffee and very small cakes). The children seemed to enjoy it very much.

Sat., Aug. 20. Today the home guard were called out to hunt deserters, our teacher, Bro. Albert Butner, being summoned to join them. There will be no exercises in our Boys' School until he shall return. The writer of this would never have expected to be compelled to make such an entry as this in the Salem Church Diary. Tempora mutantur! [Times change.] Lord, have mercy upon us and restore us again to thy favor.

Wed., Aug. 31. Today some of our married Sisters, whose husbands are at present at Kinston with the First Battalion, went to that place. May they be kindly watched over and protected. It being desired to have a general lovefeast on the approaching festival of the married people and widowers, a subscription had been taken about. It amounted to some $130. The smallest cakes costing at this time at least 18 cents, and everything else being in proportion except sugar, which is out of the question, a lovefeast for 500 persons would cost at least $125 if not more. We all pray for a speedy change for the better. May the Lord grant it.

Sun., Sept. 11. At 2 P.M. Bro. Bahnson kept lovefeast; it was of course well attended but not crowded. A very pleasing feeling prevailed. We partook of so called Confederate coffee without sugar (it sells at from $12-15) and small cakes by no means of the first quality. Nearly $140 had been collected for defraying the expenses and will hardly be sufficient. Hard times indeed.

Sun., Sept. 18. Cloudy and rainy. The audience was only tolerably large. Rainy weather on Sundays has always exercised its effect upon church going, but it does so still more now, clothing in general and shoes in particular being less able to bear it than in common times.

Thurs., Sept. 22. At 10 A.M. the Rev. Chas. F. Deems, financial agent of the N.C. orphans endowment fund, delivered a lengthy but very eloquent address in behalf of that enterprise, and took up a collection for that object. It amounted on the spot to more than $20.00 and more will be collected.

Wed., Oct. 5. Bro. Bahnson kept prayer meeting. Rather unpleasant weather; the streets are not lighted. This and other causes reduce the number that attend evening meetings.

Fri., Oct. 21. Today a number of our married brethren had to leave for the army. Yesterday the report was spread that a number of escaped prisoners of war were seen at Bethabara.

Some of our citizens turned out in pursuit of them, but found none. It seems to have been an idle rumor.

Wed., Oct. 26. Still more of our members are hurried off to the army. May the Lord graciously watch over them and bring them back in safety. Some 30 men from Guilford Co. who had attempted to go north were carried through town with numerous guards on their unwilling return to military duty.

Sun., Oct. 30. So many men having been sent to the army, it was a pleasing sight to behold some that are left at home.

Wed., Nov. 2. There is a good deal of sickness in town, and some are very seriously affected, and they who recover do so exceedingly slowly. Neither medicine nor food suitable for the sick is as plentiful as we used to have both; on the other hand trouble is more general and has of course a depressing effect upon all, whether sick or well.

Sun., Nov. 13. [Festival of November 13th as well as congregation anniversary.] At 2 P.M. the ode was sung, no attempt having been made in these troublous and sad times to procure the necessary things for a lovefeast. Very unjustifiably, orders had been issued that a portion of the home guard should assemble at the courthouse on this very day. Hence some of our members had to wend their way to that place at the very time when we assembled ourselves in the house of God.

Wed., Nov. 16. The president having recommended this day as a day for "public worship," Bro. Bahnson preached at 10 o'clock from Genesis 15:1. The audience was not numerous, but the Lord was in our midst. May He have pity upon our poor and bleeding country.

Sun., Nov. 27. We entered upon the happy season of Advent. May the Lord be allowed to enter the heart of old and young. Owing to the fact that one sister could not get ready to sing from the choir, the beautiful piece generally sung on this day had to be omitted in preaching. In the evening Bro. Bahnson kept meeting. The usual piece, "Hosiannah," was sung to the delight of all those who can remember how this beautiful and time-honored piece was sung in their infancy and boyhood, perhaps at places very distant from their present abode.

Mon., Nov. 28. A very pleasant day. The weather has moderated very much. It was a real spring day, 75°, rather too warm for comfort.

Wed., Dec. 7. The Provincial Synod met at 10 o'clock. All the members present except two. A good spirit prevailed, but owing to the circumstances in which we live, an adjournment took place until after the war, unless compelled by circumstances to meet sooner. Everything was left in statu[s] quo.

Mon., Dec. 12. Srs. Yates and Warner left for the North.

Sun., Dec. 18. Cloudy, damp, and drizzly. The evening was very dark and rainy. No lamps are lighted in the streets, which are very muddy. Shoes are bad and scarce, gum shoes not to be had. . . .

Sat., Dec. 24. Christmas Eve. At 4½ P.M. Bro. Bahnson kept the lovefeast for the little children, and at 7 P.M. the usual meeting for the congregation. The times allowed only candles for the children, the materials for a lovefeast being at present out of reach. The meeting was nevertheless well attended and very proper decorum observed.

Sat., Dec. 31. Cold and rainy. At 4½ Bro. Bahnson kept the usual meeting for the children. At 8 P.M. he read the Memorabilia and at 11½ he kept the last meeting, ending the year which had been fraught with trials, difficulties, and bereavements, and is still presenting a ominous aspect. May the Lord help and support us.

Diary of the African Church in Salem, 1864
[Extracts transcribed; handwriting is that of Maximilian E. Grunert.]

Sun., Jan. 3. The day was cold. Found, on coming to the church, that the Sunday school had been a lame affair, owing, in part, to a funeral in the large church. The congregation was small, and the house cold. Preached on Luke 13:6-9.

Sun., Jan. 10. Another cold day. The attendance was better, and the house warm. After the Sunday school a sermon was preached on Matt. 13:33. The members remained for a private meeting, in which the case of Jesse (Meinung) was mentioned, who, without giving notice, had joined last fall the Methodists on trial as a probationary member, being unable to get a recommendation. Unless he, in this way, had broken up his connection with this church, late developments would have made his exclusion necessary. It is very gratifying that all the members have borne a good Christian character at a time when, through examinations by magistrates, the sins of many others became known.

Sun., Jan. 24. The church was nearly filled with an attentive congregation, attracted by the notice that Ben (Wheeler's) funeral sermon would be preached, and favored by a beautiful day. The text was Matt. 24:44.

Sun., Feb. 14. The attendance was moderate; some paid the strictest attention, others slept. Towards 9 P.M. was called to the bedside of sr. Mary, wife of Lewis (Hege), who was thought to be sufficiently conscious to converse. Found her in a low condition with typhoid fever, and altho' partly awake, yet evidently unable to understand me. Engaged in singing and prayer with the company present.

Sun., Feb. 21. The attendance was rather poor. Convinced myself of the necessity of having some sort of church officers to visit the members and also inform the ministers of what is going on.

Sun., Feb. 28. At the close [of preaching] the members of the church remained, and were informed that the office of helpers, or elders, was about to be revived in order to help the minister. After a few more remarks the following three were named to serve for 1 year, viz.: Alek (Vogler), Ben (Zevely), and Lewis (Hege).

Sun., Mar. 6. All the members of the church having been invited to commune with the Methodist church in Winston, the attendance was very small.

Sun., Mar. 20. Palm Sunday. The church was filled in the evening to hear the reading of the acts of the last days of the Son of Man, not, however, at the opening of the meeting, when the number present was but small. The constant coming in of men and women during the address, the former having in part heavy wooden soles, was very trying. This being over, the attention was very encouraging, and the singing powerful. The reading was continued on Monday, Wednesday, and Thursday evenings, and on Friday at 2 P.M., when about 50 or 60 met. The impression produced on me by their conduct was very favorable.

Sun., Mar. 27. Easter Sunday. At 9 A.M., after singing a verse in the church, the Easter Morning Litany was prayed on the old graveyard. A sermon followed on Rom. 6:5.

Sun., Apr. 10. The weather being unfavorable, and the number present at the close of the Sunday school but small, the usual sermon was omitted, and a prayer meeting held instead. A few remarks were made on Psalm 23, and a few of the brethren led in prayer.

Sun., Apr. 17. The meeting was less satisfactory than usual, the congregation being small, and a considerable number slept, some from the very beginning of preaching.

Sun., May 22. But a very few persons had assembled, the crowd having gone to Belo's pond, where a "dipping" was to take place. After singing and prayer they were dismissed.

Sun., May 29. It seemed difficult to supply the Sunday school with teachers.

Sun., June 5. Sunday sch. was not well attended, preaching somewhat better; it seemed, however, difficult to fix the attention of the audience.

Sun., June 26. S. School was pretty well attended. Afterwards we had a lovefeast, gotten up by the colored members among themselves, and after a short recess the Holy Communion, of which 39 colored and a few white people partook. They evidently enjoyed themselves.

Sun., July 10. The attendance was tolerable, in fact pretty good, but with the heat, and consequent drowsiness, not much spirit prevailed.

Wed., Aug. 3. Br. Fulkerson came to say that his black boy, Wesley, aged about 21, a faithful and steady hand, had died last evening quite unexpectedly of apoplexy.

Sun., Aug. 28. Meeting was pretty well attended; some of the children had to be reminded, however. It is too long for them to have to sit still during school and meeting, and yet should they be sent off before the latter commences?

Sun., Sept. 18. A rainy day. Sunday school poorly attended. Preaching on Luke 10:20 better [attended], although several who had expected a funeral sermon left again.

Sun., Sept. 25. At 2 P.M. we had a meeting with prayer and an address in reference to the Lord's supper which followed. There were no particular evidences of deep feeling manifested, as was the practice years ago; and yet I thought to perceive an earnestness of purpose to live unto the Lord, especially among the men. About 40 (39) communicated. Heard afterwards, that some of the members did not partake on account of the coldness prevailing in the church!

Sun., Oct. 2. After Sunday school and singing a sermon was preached on Luke 19:41-42. Some seemed affected; in fact, it was known for some time already that several were seeking the Lord. This became more evident in a prayer meeting which followed, where five or 6 came forward and occupied the front seats, desiring to be prayed for, which was done. Some of the brethren starting a lively tune, the meeting became to a considerable degree methodistical, and difficult to describe. I endeavored to point out that bodily exercises, as groaning and often repeated forms like "Lord, have mercy," profited nothing; that the point was to repent truly of sin and to come to Christ as the only helper who gives rest unto our souls, etc. Whether I was understood and said the right thing under the circumstances, I cannot tell. The good brethren who felt quite at home and were delighted, calmed down, and the meeting finally closed with an invitation to the mourners to come to see me, and meanwhile to endeavor to keep on wrestling with God.

Sun., Oct. 9. When the congregation had been dismissed, a number remained for additional exercises. Two were there rejoicing in hope, they expect to join the church. Four or five are yet as before. I tried to speak with them, but their answers were less satisfactory as could be wished. Encouraged them and directed them as best I knew. They were commended also to the Lord in prayer.

Wed., Oct. 12. Mike (Vogler) called with a black boy Charley, lately bought by br. Ed. Clemmons, who has lately professed a saving change and now desires to join the church. Conversed with him a long time; he seems to be uncommonly ignorant, and the description he gave of his experience showed that he was really in earnest. Encouraged him as well as I could.

Sun., Oct. 16. A prayer meeting followed [preaching], in which the same individuals were present as mourners, who had already two weeks ago been seeking. Some of the best members are so much filled with the idea that this is the only way, that it is difficult to reason with them and to preserve the usual quiet character of our meetings. Douglas, at present at Wm. Winkler's, also rejoices in hope that his backslidings are healed.

Sun., Oct. 23. Sunday school was poorly attended; indeed the teachers, who in other years began to practice for Christmas before October already, and had during these months a better attendance than for the rest of the year, are doubtful whether anything in that line can be done. [Following preaching,] we had afterwards a prayer meeting, very much in the same way as the last few Sundays. Br. Lewis (Hege) asked permission to make some remarks, and did so, for the most part in a pleasing way, which showed his understanding of the way of salvation.

Sun., Oct. 30. Six candidates for church membership presented themselves . . . for instruction, which was also attended by a considerable number of others, mostly members. They seem to like this practice, and evidently understand gradually more of the doctrines of religion.

Sun., Nov. 13. Owing to the meetings in the large church there was no preaching today. The request had been made by several members to have a prayer meeting among themselves instead, and permission given, provided that at least one of the teachers was present.

Sun., Nov. 20. An invitation having been given to all the colored people to attend a meeting in the Presbyterian church in Winston this afternoon, and our people signifying their wish to go there, no meeting was held in our church.

Sun., Nov. 27. Instruction following [preaching]. The ignorance of most of the candidates is very great; but not very much ought to be expected of them.

Sun., Dec. 4. Was better pleased in instruction than last Sunday.

Sun., Dec. 11. Sr. Olivia Warner, who for a number of years has taught the adult men with zeal and faithfulness, is about leaving for Pennsylvania. It will be almost impossible to fill her place. It is true that but few availed themselves of the privilege of her instruction regularly, but these few evidently profited.

Sun., Dec. 18. The day appointed for baptism and Holy Communion. The following 8 persons were admitted to church membership, viz., by holy baptism: Charles (Clemmons), Nathan (Starbuck), John Henry Jones (free, yet indentured to Hr. Hughes), Lucinda (Mickey), and Julia (O. A. Keehln); by confirmation: Douglass (A. H. Shepperd's estate), Mary Monterey (Waugh), and Emma (Hege). It was an interesting occasion and well attended, although the weather and roads were very unfavorable. A good number of white sisters was also present. After a short interval, between 50 and 60 persons partook of the Lord's supper. Left the church with the impression that the Lord had been very gracious to his people today.

Sun., Dec. 25. Christmas. The celebration took place at 2 o'clock. After singing, reading on the narrative, and an address, we worshipped the newborn King, and asked him to grant unto us the benefits of his incarnation. A number of pieces was then sung, which had been practiced for the occasion. There was no decoration, nor distribution of cakes or candles. The audience was quite large and orderly.

The congregation at the close of the year consists of 63 communicants, Jesse (Meinung) and Pinkney (Fries) having been dropped. Several others are nominal only.

Board of Elders of Salem Congregation, 1864
[Extracts of minutes transcribed.]

Wed., Jan. 13. Br. F. absent.
The unhappy life of John and Sally Chitty was spoken of. As to their differences in pecuniary matters, br. B. will speak to br. E. A. Vogler, her trustee. To produce between the parties a feeling of love appeared to the Board, after former attempts by br. Holl., a little-promising undertaking.

Wed., Feb. 24. Br. F. absent.
[B]r. Bahn. stated that Augustus Reich (John's) was among the candidates for confirmation, and that his wife, heretofore a member of the Lutheran church, desired to connect herself with us at the same time. The Board rejoiced to hear that he seems to be much affected. There is no objection to the application.

Wed., Mar. 2. Br. F. absent.
[B]r. Bahn. read a letter from John Boner (Tho.'s), printer in Raleigh, in which he states his desire for confirmation, although he will not be able to attend the usual course of instruction. The Board thought that this should not prevent his being admitted if br. B. finds him otherwise a suitable candidate.

2. Augustus Reich may have to leave for the army before Palm Sunday; if so, he will be confirmed sooner.

3. Br. Bahn. will request br. Josh. Boner to assist in playing the organ during Passion week.

Wed., May 4. Br. F. absent.

The election of Church officers will take place on Tuesday next, having been forgotten this week.

Wed., May 18. Br. F. absent.

After the reading of the minutes it was mentioned that br. E. A. Schweinitz has been re-elected a member of this Board for 3 years by the late Congregation Council.

4. The subject of Memoirs, as handed to the pastor at funerals, was spoken of. In the opinion of the Board the minister is undoubtedly at liberty to omit passages, which in his judgment are not suitable. In the case of persons who die unconnected with any church, it might be even proper to limit the personal matters to the merest outline of dates and names.

Wed., June 1. Br. F. absent.

4. The fact that not only the weekday evening meetings, but the Sunday services also, are less attended than for years, is undeniable. It may be that occasionally there is a particular attraction in Winston, but as a general thing, the cause is that our people neglect church. No measure was proposed to counteract the evil.

Thurs., June 16. Br. F. absent.

The meeting was called to have the opinion of the Board in regard to the funeral of Harrison James, deceased today in the Winston jail. The Board thought that in case a burial on our graveyard, and also on the cemetery, should be refused, it would not be proper to have public exercises at the church.

Wed., June 22. Br. F. absent.

[T]he burial services of Harrison James, which were finally conducted by br. Parm. Leinbach and Mr. Jenkins in Winston and on the county graveyard, gave rise to some further discussion.

Wed., Aug. 3. Brn. R. Schwtz. and F. absent.

4. The Board was of opinion that sponsors at baptisms ought to be baptized persons.

Wed., Sept. 14. Br. F. absent.

The Rev. C. B. Deems will be here on Sept. 22d to present the claims of the proposed Orphan Asylum for soldiers' children. If the weather permits, the square will be the place for the occasion. But if it has to be indoors, the Board was of opinion that altho' the church would not well be refused, he nevertheless should be spoken to beforehand to avoid what would give offense.

2. As to invitations to lovefeasts, the Board came to the understanding that some discretion in granting and refusing applications was necessary, so as not to admit the curious, nor to refuse such as would appreciate the service.

3. Some little boys have not conducted themselves in church as they ought. As to schoolboys, they will be required to take the front seats. In the case of others, the Board regretted the inefficiency of the doorkeepers, but at the same time did not consider their sitting in front as a remedy for the evil.

Wed., Nov. 9. Br. F. absent.

2. The subject of guests at the communion came up again. The Board acknowledged the impropriety of persons communing with us who have joined another church after having been birthright members here, unless they make application. Yet in consideration of the probability of a public notice to this effect being misunderstood, and also that a small matter might thereby appear of more importance than it really is, it was thought better not to say anything in public.

3. Several brethren of the colored division of the church have applied for permission to have a prayer meeting among themselves in their church when they cannot have their regular services on account of communion or other services in the large church. The Board seemed to have misgivings to grant such permission, unless some white brother or sister of character were present.

Board of Trustees of Salem Congregation, 1864
[Extracts of minutes transcribed.]

Tues., Feb. 2. Not present Br. Theod. Keehln.

1. With regard to §1 it was stated that since the agreement then made respecting the lot to be laid off for the house of

Frank Reich, the Proprietor of the land has expressed his doubts whether under the circumstances of the case the Administrator of the estate could lawfully hold the deed for the lot, and he (the Proprietor) proposed that the resolution of the Board then formed be so altered as to require the purchaser of the lot to give his note with approved security, and that no deed be made to him until the note is paid. By this means the Diacony would, besides having personal security on the note, also retain the title to the lot as additional security. This proposition of the Proprietor was accepted by a majority of the members of the Board.

2. In reference to §6 of last minutes it was stated that the two sisters Butner, altho' grateful for good intentions of the Board in remitting the rent due for their mother's room, are not willing to accept the offer made them, but prefer gradually to pay the same.

10. The Principal of the Salem Female Academy wishes to take in rent a small room situated in the north end of the Sisters House wood shed for the purpose of fixing it up as a lodging place for some negro men that he has hired. Board is willing that he take the room in rent, but objects to the use that is intended to be made of it, not considering it proper or becoming that a negro house or room should be kept so near the Sisters House.

Fri., Mar. 4. Not present the Brrn. C. Cooper and Theod. Keehln.

2. The application of John Nissen to buy the pottershop and lot [#48] was again spoken of, but no further action could be taken on it tonight, as obstacles that had presented themselves last time already have not yet been removed. The chief hindrance to go into a sale of this property at this time being the use of the town hall as a wayside hospital for soldiers (see minutes, June 23, 1863, §1) and the occupation of the dwelling part by Mr. John M. Wimmer, a cripple for life, Board [is] not feeling inclined to enter into further consideration of the subject until both could be provided for otherwise.

3. Congress having recently passed an act by which after Apr. 1st all Confederate money of the denomination of $10 and upwards will be either withdrawn from circulation or taken only for a short time longer at a discount of 33.3 percent, the question was asked whether the Warden should continue to

take it in payment of debts? Board thinks it might be taken as yet, because it can be converted either into Confederate 4 percent bonds that will be received as payment for taxes during the present year, or the money itself might perhaps be taken by the County as payment in advance for taxes, a measure of this kind being in contemplation at this time.

4. No regular organist having for some time been employed by the Congregation, it frequently happens that the organ is not played in meeting, and Board understanding that there are several single sisters with decided musical talents and who are already skillful performers on the piano, who would be inclined occasionally to attend to the organ, provided someone could be found to give them the necessary instruction in *organ* playing, and Board being willing to pay for such instruction, appointed the Brrn. Boner and Pfohl as a subcommittee who will try, perhaps in company of the Brrn. Grunert and Ed. Leinbach, to make such arrangements as may be necessary to arrive at the desired end.

Wed., Mar. 16. Not present Br. C. Cooper (sick).

1. The sale of the house of Frank Reich took place on the 5th inst., the house and lot being bo't by Augustus Fockel, who has given his note with Robt. Schweinitz (Principal of Female Academy) for security. Reich's interest or improvement on the land (9 3/4 acres) was bo't by Wm. H. Wheeler, the conditions of the sale stipulating expressly that the purchaser is under obligation to fill up the holes where the clay for making of brick on this land had been dug out.

2. John Nissen having now succeeded in finding a suitable locality for the "wayside hospital" and for a family (altho' not for Mr. Wimmer), Board took up his application for the purchase of the pottershop and lot. Since the last meeting of the Board Theodore Pfohl has also made application in the name of his son William, now in the army, for the purchase of the property if it is for sale now. This second application, giving a very different appearance to the case before the Board, led to a long and earnest conversation, in the course of which every member present seemed to feel that it might be most advisable under now existing circumstances not to depart from the resolution of the Board not to sell this property whilst the present trouble of the country continues, which resolution had been passed on Feb. 24, 1862. . . .

As moreover the lot is a very desirable one and has heretofore been applied for already by a number of persons, it would appear as not acting with due consideration especially towards our young men that are still without a house and lot, if we should proceed to sell this (one of the few on Main Street still held by the Diacony) whilst they are absent in the army risking their lives in defence of our country, and are thereby prevented from attending to their interests at home.

Another subject spoken of was this: whether in case we determine to sell at all, the building should be limited to the two applicants now before us?

Without coming to any decision on the case (it being late already), Board adjourned with the understanding that we meet again on Tuesday after Easter, being the 29th inst.

Wed., Mar. 30. Not present the Brrn. C. Cooper (sick) and E. A. Vogler.

1. Board next again took up the application of John Nissen for the purchase of the pottery building and lot, when after some further conversation on the subject, in which, however, no new ideas were advanced, but for reasons stated at length in the minutes of last meeting, a proposition was made "that the property be not sold till after peace is established to the country," which proposition after being seconded was passed by a vote of three for and two against it.

6. The time in which Confederate money can be invested in 4 percent bonds at its full value expiring according to law with day after tomorrow, the question was asked whether the money on hand belonging to the Diacony should be so invested or kept back in order to exchange it for "new issue" at the discount of 33.3 percent?

It being improbable that the State would take the Confederate 4 percent bonds in payment for taxes, and no probability existing that such bonds could be sold for any reasonable amount hereafter, and it further being uncertain whether Diacony, as a Church institution will be liable to pay a Confederate tax on its property, Board resolved that the money of the Diacony now on hand liable to be affected by the Currency Law be not funded into 4% Confederate Bonds, but kept for exchanging into money of the "new issue" at the discount required.

Thurs., May 12. Not present the Brrn. C. Cooper (sick) and Theod. Keehln.

1. Congregation Council having on the 10th inst. re-elected the Brrn. Nathl. Blum and E. A. Vogler, whose time of service had expired, as members of this body, Board met and organized by electing S. Thos. Pfohl as President and Secretary.

5. The Warden stated that he had discontinued taking the Confederate $5 notes in payment of debts due the Diacony, as they will be subject to a deduction of 33.3 percent after July 1st, and as people in general are now already disinclined to take them at par. Board sanctions the action of the Warden.

Tues., May 24. Not present Brrn. C. Cooper (sick) and Theod. Keehln.

4. Board resolved to give to Br. Charles Cooper, who has for a number of years served the congregation in the capacity of principal sexton (Erster Saaldiener) at a salary of $25 a year, an extra allowance of a like amount ($25) for his services, and to remit his Church account for the last year. In addition it was resolved that on account of long continued sickness in his family, especially of himself and wife, that no charges be bro't against him for certain trees that he had been permitted to cut for firewood behind the graveyard.

Fri., June 17. Not present the Brrn. C. Cooper (sick) and N. Blum.

The application to bury the remains of Harrison James on our graveyard was laid before the Board. The deceased, whose mother is a full member of our church, altho' he had never more closely connected himself with it, was serving out a sentence of two years imprisonment in the jail at Winston for robbing the mail at the Post Office at this place, and died yesterday. Board, altho' deeply commiserating the condition of his poor mother, could not but unanimously refuse the application, under all the circumstances connected with the case.

Tues., July 19. Not present the Brrn. N. Blum. Theod. Keehln, and C. Cooper (sick).

1. [T]he remark was made that Br. Chr. Ebert had erected a hog pen in the yard back of the part of the [pottery] shop rented by him and had built it under the windows of the building in which the wayside hospital is kept and near the

back door of the same. The town commissioners have notified him to remove it as being a nuisance in its present locality. Should he refuse to comply, it may become the duty of this body to take further steps in the matter.

2. A communication from the Provincial Elders' Conference was laid before the Board stating that when Br. Francis R. Holland, Pastor of the Salem congregation, left on a longer visit to Pennsylvania, it was the understanding between him and the Prov. Eld. Conf. that he should have leave of absence till the end of May, and that a longer stay should be considered as a resignation of his office. The time having now expired and P.E.C. not having received any communication from him, the pastorate is now vacant, and P.E.C., on taking the matter into consideration, have, owing to the present state of the country, not considered it advisable to make a permanent appointment, but concluded to continue the temporary arrangement, which has existed since Br. Holland left us, until peace shall be restored to the country, when further steps can be taken for a final disposal of this important matter.

3. Br. Charles Cooper has on account of sickness in his family resigned his office as principal sexton (Erster Saal-diener); but Board of Elders not being willing to accept his resignation, he having for a number of years held the office and devoted himself faithfully to it, and thinking that before long circumstances in his family may again become more favourable, Board of Elders prefer to make only a temporary appointment of another Brother until such time that Br. Cooper can re-enter on his office, and request the Board of Trustees to give such substitute a compensation for services he may render without depriving Br. Cooper of the salary that he has been drawing. Board of Trustees agree to the request, and resolved that the Br. to be appointed receive during the time of his service the same salary that Br. Cooper had been drawing, and that in the meantime the salary of the latter be continued.

Tues., Sept. 27. Not present the Brrn. E. A. Vogler and Theod. Keehln.

3. The annual accounts of Salem Diacony and Single Sisters Diacony from May 1, 1863, to April 30, 1864, together with the statement of the assets and liabilities of both on the latter day, were laid before the Board.

a. From the accounts of Salem Diacony it appears

that the receipts amounted to $6,237.47
and the disbursements to <u>5,578.19</u>
showing an excess of receipt of $659.28
after the receipts for town lots and land, amounting to $1,384, had been added to the respective funds.

   b. Single Sisters Diacony had

paid out $958.08
and had received <u>711.90</u>
and consequently was deficient 246.18

This result was owing principally to the amount of taxes ($231.27) and the high prices of articles in general.

   c. Board resolved that of the excess of receipts of Salem Diacony $246.18 be applied to cover the loss of the Single Sisters Diacony and $413.10 (the balance) towards a debt of $455.78 standing open in the accounts of Salem Diacony for Church repairs (building a 3d gallery in church, etc.). The credit of $52 on School account is to be paid over to the Treasurer of the Boys' School, and by decision of the Board the tuition of Isaac Boner (son of sister Soph. Boner) is to be defrayed for the present by the interest accruing from the Education Fund.

   4. Board authorized the Warden to borrow on account of Single Sisters Diacony a sum of money sufficient to pay the Confederate taxes of the present year, which in the case of said Diacony will amount to $899.64. The increased outlays of this Diacony render it necessary that Board take into serious consideration in what manner its condition can be placed upon a somewhat better footing, the expenses for taxes alone in the present year exceeding by about $350 the whole of its yearly income.

Tues., Oct. 25. Not present the Brrn. E. A. Vogler and Theod. Keehln.

   2. Board next took into consideration the present condition of the Single Sisters' Diacony (see §4 of last minutes) and resolved upon the following measures to increase its income and to diminish its expenses, viz.: Salem Diacony is to pay the $2,400 that it owes the Sisters' Diacony and for which no interest has been paid thus far, and in order to make it available immediately, that amount of certificates held by Salem Diacony in Salem Savings Institute at 5 percent is to be transferred to Single Sisters Diacony. Further, the board of the

sicknurse towards which $50 a year had been paid by the Single Sisters Diacony will hereafter be defrayed by the Single Sisters Poor Fund, as also all expenses for wood and for lamp lard used in the sick room, for which reason Salem Diacony will transfer certificates in Salem Savings Institute to Single Sisters Poor Fund for the $900 due the latter and held by Salem Diacony without interest.

Mon., Dec. 19. Not present the Brrn. Theod. Keehln and E. A. Vogler.

2. The Financial Board, having recently made an extra appropriation for the present year to such persons as are financially dependent upon Wachovia Sustentation, ask the Board of Trustees whether they would not on behalf of the Salem Congregation undertake to do something in this respect for Br. Bahnson, who has, ever since Br. Holland left for the North, acted as its Pastor, the Wachovia Sustentation all the time paying his salary as President of the Provincial Elders Conference? Board of Trustees, in consideration of the services rendered by Br. Bahnson, and in further consideration that no Pastor's salary has been paid by the Congregation since Br. Holland left, resolved unanimously that the amount that would have been paid as salary to a Pastor of Salem Congregation from Nov. 1, 1863, (when Br. Holland's salary terminated) to Dec. 31, 1864, viz., $746, be given as a donation to Br. Bahnson towards the support of his family.

Provincial Financial Board, 1864
[Extracts of minutes transcribed.]

Wed., Mar. 30. All the members present.

1. The Treasurer, Br. Pfohl, desired to have the opinion of the Board, whether he should fund before April 1, 1864, $690, which he has in cash in Confederate notes. Of this amount, $200 are $100 notes. On motion, it was resolved: That the $200 be funded unless they can be exchanged for notes of lower denominations, and the balance ($490) be kept and exchanged for new issue, at the rate of $3 for $2 established by law.

Wed., Sept. 7.

1. Br. Lewis Rights, who received for the year 1863 $450 from his congregation, applies for an additional sum of $300 in order to defray the expenses of the said year. Br. Parmenio Lineback received for 1863 from Macedonia $120.75, Muddy Creek $46, Friedland $1.50, sum total $168.25. Both applications were on motion granted in consideration of the hard times. Br. Jacob Siewers has not bro't in his statements of receipts from his congregations since 1860. On motion, Board resolved to pay for Br. Frye's coffin. It was mentioned that the buggy and harness belonging to Sust. Diac. formerly used by Br. Frye had been returned, and that Br. L. Rights had taken the buggy and Br. P. Lineback the harness. The horse Sr. Frye still retains for the feed. Br. Frye received for 1863 from Friedland $30 and from Phila. $75.20. There is therefore a balance of $54.80 due his estate for 1863 and 1 quarter to March 31, 1864, for the current year, having received $90 of this sum during his lifetime.

2. Br. Thos. Pfohl, the Treasurer, submitted the annual accounts and statement of Wa. S.D. from June 1, 1863, to May 31, 1864. The total receipts, inclusive of a donation from S.F.A. of $1,500, amounted to $3,893.16, and the disbursements to $2,889.90, showing a surplus of $1,003.26. From this the appropriations and payments resolved upon as above §1, $604.80, are to be deducted, leaving a balance of $398.46, of which $225 were on motion appropriated to Pension Fund, leaving a surplus of receipts of $173.46 to be transferred to Fund Account, which thus will amount to $5,523.23. The Prov. Fund is as last year, $32,926.83. The total assets $42,192.42 and actual liabilities $1,022.38. On motion Treasurer was requested to purchase writing paper for the use of the country ministers.

Wed., Nov. 30. All present.

2. The extra assistance for the year 1864, on account of the times, was fixed at $125 for each member of a family, exclusive of servants, and this amount will be paid by Treasurer to the widows who receive pensions. Br. Bahnson, who is entitled to the same, being at present minister of Salem Congr., it was resolved that Financial Board request the Board of Trustees of Salem Congr. to pay this amount to Br. B. as Salem Congr. Diacony does not pay any minister's salary at this time.

3. Br. Bahnson's bill for firewood from Sept. 1, 1863, to Sept. 1, 1864, amounts to $248. Since Sept. 1864 an additional charge for the current year has come to it of $32, [for a total of] $280, which amount will be paid by Treasr. according to resolution of Aug. 11, 1863.

Bethania Diary, with Bethabara, 1864
[Extracts transcribed; handwriting is that of Jacob F. Siewers.]

Fri., Jan. 22. Returning from S. St. [Samuel Stoltz] called at his son Constantine's, and learning that his father-in-law had been hurt by a fall from his horse, I went over to William Hoffman, and found him unable to walk without crutches. Today I heard that Soln. Spoenhauer had likewise sustained serious injury from a fall.

Sat., Jan. 23. Left this morning early to visit S. Spoenhauer and found him at his son in-law's, Mr. Coe (shoe-maker). He fell some 10 days ago from his stone steps, it being icy, and dislocated his hip; he appeared very glad to see me. I conversed with him and at parting offered a prayer. Returning called at William Anderson's, he has a son lying helpless of supposed white-swelling.

Sat., Jan. 30. We visited at br. William Leinbach's, his son Edgar has to return to the Army tomorrow. We sang some hymns, read a chapter from the Scriptures, and prayed with the family. ([Bethania Report:] He claims having been born again whilst in the Army, and I see no reason to doubt it.)

([Bethania Report:] *Sun., Feb. 14.* Afternoon went to Mickey's S. House. The house has been put in order again, glass in the windows and a stove, etc. A school has been commenced. The door was locked. . . .)

Wed., Mar. 9. This evening by request held a prayer meeting at Thomas Johnson's, Esq. His son William was conscripted and has to leave tomorrow; the room was crowded. It is reported that Reinhold Oehman, Egbert Lehman, and the Millers left last night.[1]

---

[1]The memoir of Egbert Thomas Lehman, written at the time of his death in 1932, states:

> His honest convictions kept him from entering the army. After an unsuccessful effort in 1864 to cross the line, he returned home in deep snow and later

Thurs., Mar. 10. We had today a heavy rain, commencing about midnight; the bottoms are all overflowed. This was the last day of the enrollment of our Regiment.

Fri., Mar. 11. Cloudy weather. By request of Samuel Strupe wrote a petition in behalf of his son James.

Sun., Mar. 13. This morning Benson Daub, and the wife of Joseph Daub, m.n. George, called requesting me to write a petition for Joseph Daub, who is confined at Fort Branch under sentence of death for attempt to desert. I wrote it this afternoon, and Rev. Soln. Helsebeck is to take it on to President Jef. Davis tomorrow.

Tues., Mar. 15. Afternoon Sr. S. and myself went to Salem on account of the illness of our little grandson. At Thomas Wilson's, Esq., the breech-strap of the harness tore, and the horse became unmanageable, but we succeeded in stopping him at between Spach's and Swink's and sustaining no injury. . . .

Tues., Mar. 22. It commenced snowing before day and continued with storm all day. Afternoon made paths in my yard to the well and in front of house and church; but the drifting snow by night had filled them up again.

Wed., Mar. 23. Engaged the whole forenoon in clearing the snow from our usual walks; this kind of work is very tiresome.

Thurs., Mar. 24. A large quantity of snow had drifted on the Church garret, which I had to remove.

Fri., Apr. 8. Rainy day. Preached on Isaiah 59:1-15. ([Margin note:] Prayer and fast day.)

Mon., Apr. 11. Fair day. Went out in the woods with Joseph Transou and his servant and cut a tree and split it up for palings.

Thurs., Apr. 21. Took off the palings of the fence next [to] the alley and put slabs next to the ground and thoroughly repaired the fence. The hogs were breaking in the yard continually.

Sat., Apr. 23. Repaired my garden fence. I have used up all my nails by patching the fence opposite the Parsonage. The hogs and cows are so troublesome; food for them is very

---

made another attempt, which led him on a trip of several hundred miles across the mountains, part of the way with a sprained ankle. He reached the state of Indiana, where he remained a year.

scarce, and the green grass too inviting for them to respect property.

Mon., Apr. 25. Having promised the horse to Alexander Grabs, he failing to get his brother to take him part of the way to Florence, I started with him to Salem this morning. The bottoms on the creek all under water.

Wed., May 11. Working at a medicine case [cabinet] for Doctor Mock.

Sun., June 5. I did not go to Bethabara, was told whilst passing through there that they were all going to Mr. Banner's funeral to be preached next Sabbath at Beck's School-house by Sol. Helsabeck.

Thurs., Fri., June 16, 17. E. Schaub gave me a one-horse load of hay and another for helping him.

Mon., June 20. Sr. S. and myself walked down to br. William Leinbach's, whose son Benjn., 17 years of age, has to leave today for Winston and the Army. We conversed with them, read a Psalm, and united in prayer with them in behalf of their son; the family are much distressed. He had attended instruction so far, and I regretted that he had to leave before he was confirmed. Br. Philip Pfaff's son Artimeus has also to leave today.

Tues., June 21. This morning br. Wesley Kearney was to leave for Winston and the Army. Thus far he had been exempt as a shoe-maker.

Mon.-Sat., July 4-9. Worked at Thomas Lash's water-wheel.

Tues., July 19. Government salt wagons passed through here today.

Thurs., July 21. Sr. S. and myself visited at Mary Ann Butner's, having heard that she was unwell, found her about the house and much better. Her son James had returned from the Army on sick furlough; he had been in the Hospital some time.

Fri., July 22. Working about home. Working on my carriage.

Fri., Aug. 5. Returned home, met a soldier, Mr. Herman, Dawson's son-in-law, took him home, poor fellow is very weak, chronic diarrhea.

Mon., Aug. 8. Made a pair of new shafts for my carriage.

Tues., Aug. 23. Forenoon put a pair of shutters to Sr. Betzy Hauser's front window, fitting them and hinging. Filing saw.

Sun., Aug. 28. Went to br. Timothy Conrad's, his son Wiley is at home on sick furlough, has had the typhoid feaver.

Tues., Sept. 6. Sr. S. and myself went to br. Nathanial Pfaff's, his son leaves tomorrow, his furlough having transpired.

Thurs., Sept. 15. After dinner commenced turning Soln. Theiss's molasses rollers for mill, which I had agreed to build and be paid in molasses.

Thurs., Fri., Sept. 29, 30. Rainy. Finished the mill at last, much detion [delay?] by bad weather.

Mon., Oct. 10. Went down to Jacob Theiss's and engaged 4 pigs at $1 bank bill apiece, to be kept 2 weeks longer.

Wed., Oct. 12. ([Bethania Report:] We visited at br. Alexander Transou, his son Amos has returned from the Army sick.)

Mon., Oct. 17. Jacob Theiss sent me word to come after my pigs, the sow having died. I went and bro't them home.

Thurs., Oct. 20. Working at pig pen.

Fri., Oct. 21. Finished my pen.

Sun., Oct. 23. Today Sol. Theiss and Naaman Reich left for the Army by Greensboro.

Mon., Oct. 31. Held a prayer meeting at br. S. Levin Grabs's. He leaves tomorrow for the Army by Greensboro.

Fri., Nov. 4. Went for molasses, 12 gallons.

Mon., Nov. 7. Afternoon Sr. S. and myself went to visit mother Mickey at D. Schausses, conversed and prayed with them. D.S. and son-in-law are in the Army.

Sun., Nov. 13. After meeting, hearing that br. William Leinback had been seriously hurt yesterday, Sr. S. and myself walked out to his house and found him quite cheerful, conversing with some friends and neighbors who had likewise heard of his having been hurt. He had went to Alexander Transou's, who was grinding cane, and stood at one of the posts of the mill. The leaver, coming round unnoticed by him, caught his head against the post, between which there was a space of the thickness of a hand only. He screamed, and providentially the horse stopped, or it must have crushed his head. He had a small bruise at his temple, and complained of stiffness and soreness of his neck.

Wed., Nov. 30. Working about the yard. I've been for the last weeks under the weather. What is the matter I do not know. I am weak and unfit for any employment.

Tues., Dec. 6. The misses Joseph Doub paid us a visit today. I was engaged in preparing for hog killing. At noon

Samuel Strupe was kind enough to kill and butcher Caroline's pig; it weighed 130 lbs. Sr. Levin Grabs kindly assisted.

Wed., Dec. 7. Sr. S. and myself went to Salem. Synod opened at 10 A.M., afternoon session at 1 1/2 P.M., resulting in adjourning the Synod until after the war, or as soon as circumstances required.

Sat., Dec. 31. According to notice given, the heads of families were requested to tarry here a short time with the view of electing 2 new members of the Committee in the place of Jacob Werner and br. Sol. Pfaff. There appearing so few present, it was remarked that the members of the Committee present were sufficient to transact the business on hand. The others were dismissed, [leaving] H. H. Butner, Joseph Transou and William Lehman.

([Bethania Committee minutes:] *Dec. 31, 1864.* Br. Siewers then informed the Committee that application had been made to bury the bodies of Isaac Shore, Sanders Shore, William Shore, and Nerva Hauser on our Graveyard, who had died in Virginia and were about to be disinterred and bro't here. Also an application from Sr. Lauretta Tice inquiring what amount in Confederate money the Committee would ask for the burial of the young man Hine, who was killed up about the mountains. Committee had no objections to the burial of the 4 first named persons, neither to the desire of their being buried in one grave side by side, provided the surface order and distances were retained. Some conversation took place on the currency, and it was unanimously decided that the payment be made in gold and silver, as the only reliable money in these times, and that the regular price of ten dollars should not be departed from. As to Sr. Lauretta's question, the Committee unanimously decided they would on no terms take in Confederate money in payment for burial on our Graveyard.)

Friedberg Diary, with Hope, 1864
[Extracts transcribed; handwriting is that of Christian Lewis Rights.]

Sat., Jan. 2. The coldest day we have had for many years.

Sun., Jan. 3. On account of high water and ice I did not go to Hope, but went to Salem in the afternoon.

Sun., Jan. 31. January from the 1st to the 19th was excessively cold, but since that time it has been like spring, dry and warm.

Sat., Feb. 27. A child of Christian Disher, deceased, was buried today on the graveyard. I had to attend the enrollment at Lexington and did not preach the funeral.

Tues., Mar. 22. For several days it has been very cold, and this morning it began to snow and snowed rapidly all day. There was keen driving east wind which made the snow drift considerable, and where not drifted was about 12 inches deep.

Wed., Mar. 23. Today I was engaged in clearing the snow from the garret.

Fri., Apr. 8. Fast day. Preached at Friedberg: Esther 4:16.

Sat., Apr. 16. Prayer meeting for the country at 4 o'clock in the afternoon at Friedberg.

Sat., Apr. 23. Was engaged in writing petitions and at 4 o'clock had prayer meeting in the church, well attended.

Sat., May 7. Sisters feast, 56 present. Afterwards Committee meeting. Brother Daniel Spach, Sen., resigned his office as general chapel steward, which he had held for 30 years, and the Committee elected brother Jesse Mock his successor. A motion was made and passed returning the thanks of the Committee to Brother Daniel Spach for the faithful performance of his duties as general chapel steward for the last 30 years.

Sat., May 21. Attended the enrollment at Lexington.

Mon., May 23. [W]ent with Sr. R. to see Brother Em. Spaugh, who came home on Saturday from Point Lookout, where he was a prisoner of war for some time. He is very feeble from scurvy. ([Friedberg Report:] He gives a pitiful account of the condition of the prisoners there affected with the disease. Amos Miller, brother Jesse Miller's son, died a few weeks [ago]. Before he left from it, his whole plea was to go home, and in his last hours in his delirium he imagined he was there, and he seemed overjoyed at once more being with his friends.)

([Friedberg Report:] *Mon., June 21.* Visited Brother Charles Rothrock, who has returned from the army wounded, and as it was getting dark when we came home, Sr. Rights in going out the back door fell head foremost down the steps. The children made an alarm, and I ran over from the stable, where I was putting away the horse, and found her lying speechless, and the blood running out at her mouth and nose. By applying cold water to her face she came to, and with considerable difficulty succeeded in getting her into the house, and though much bruised she sustained no serious internal injuries.)

Sun., July 17. Preached . . . at Pleasant Fork in the afternoon. . . . Here they have an interesting Sunday School in progress this summer conducted principally by brother Jacob Timothy Fishel, and he deserves praise for his perseverance in getting it up and the manner he carries it on. It is the best Sunday School I know of.

Sun., Oct. 15 [16]. In the afternoon I preached at Pleasant Fork from Acts 4:10-12. The Sunday School will be suspended, as brother T. Fishel will leave on Thursday for the army, and J. Knouse and a number of others.

Sun., Nov. 13. Brother Ephraim Weasner was with us; he has been gone 27 months.

Private Diary of R. P. Leinbach, 1864
[Serving Friedland, Macedonia, and Muddy Creek; extracts transcribed.]

Sat., Jan. 2. Started for Davie County. The thermometer had been down to 11°. I have been in the cold so much that my eyes are becoming inflamed. I must stay at home a few days and let them recover.

Sun., Jan. 10. From having been exposed so much to the cold, my eyes are becoming inflamed and trouble me considerably. Br. W[alk] has recommended me to use "Schähl Krauk" (sullen thyme), which on trial I find relieves them.

[*Wed., Jan. 20.*] I learn there are strong efforts being made to call a convention of the people. Wed. afternoon I went down to South Fork to see about getting up my hay; overtook Br. J. Walk, who agreed to come on to Br. Hege's next morning. Went on to Br. Hege's, who gave me a load of hay, and Br. W. brot it up for the sum of $6 Confederate money. As I was coming on I met Br. Rights, who had been looking for me for several days. He had some propositions to make concerning a school at Kernersville which sound very plausible. Nous verrons.

[*Thurs., Jan. 21?*] Yesterday my hay was put up. The little shed is packed close, and now John can eat to his heart's content.

Sun., Jan. 24. Went to Friedland. Found Br. Berry, a blind Methodist preacher, there who preached for us. After preaching I went to Kernersville in company with some of our Kernersville friends and brn. I saw Dr. Kerner, found this plan not so plausible as might seem.[1]

[*Mon., Feb. 1.*] [C]alled on Noah Killian's; his children sing remarkably well.

[*Tues., Feb. 2.*] [M]orning went to Teague Town to meet the Band Boys, who are coming home on furlough.

Sun., Feb. 7. Preached at Macedonia from Psalms 50:22 to a large congregation. ([Macedonia Report:] Their appetite for spiritual food becomes clogged with weekly services; they require a month's time to digest it.)

Mon., Mar. 7. I started off to cousin D.H. in order to purchase a pig.

Tues., Mar. 8. I came away with it, having promised to pay one dollar in silver for the animal. Tuesday night I remained at Br. J. Knauss and during the night my pig strayed away—or was stolen—and I have heard nothing of the quadruped since.

Mon.-Wed., Mar. 14-16. I was engaged at Friedland in sowing oats. 'Twas the first time I was ever thus engaged, and there's no telling how it is going to work.

Tues., Mar. 22. Snow and storm all day—snow to the depth of 10 and 12 inches. Wednesday morning borrowed a sleigh and took some folks out sleigh riding.

Thurs., Apr. 7. Conference in the morning. Warm discussion in reference to baptism and Macedonia congregation.

([Ministers Conference minutes:] *Thurs., Apr. 7.* As the children of several members of Macedonia congregation have passed the age of 2 years without having been baptized . . . , the question came up, what was to be done in the matter. Shall the period be lengthened out, and the delinquent members yet be urged to comply with the law of the church; or shall these parents be on that account excluded; or lastly shall nothing be done, and the people allowed to go on as heretofore? As a general thing it was acknowledged that the rule not to baptize children over 2 years is unnecessary in our congregations, and is, when strangers apply for baptism of their children beyond that age, either disregarded, or cramps the

---

[1]The previous summer the General Assembly had passed an act to incorporate the Kernersville High School.

minister's conscience, who feels that he is forbidding them, contrary to the will of Christ. Conference seemed inclined to let the rule stand, but to allow the minister to baptize older children if he will take the responsibility. In Macedonia, the case is very peculiar, and br. L. could only be encouraged to exert himself by representing to the people the benefits of which they thus deprive themselves and their children, to overcome the prejudice in their minds. To proceed against them now with church discipline was not urged.)

Sun., Apr. 10. After preaching I was compelled to exclude Ph. Smith from the [Friedland] congregation and to read it out in Vorbereitung [preparatory meeting]. ([Friedland Report:] announced the exclusion of Phebe Smith, daughter of Jacob and Anne Smith, in consequences of having been married too late.)

Thurs., May 5. Ascension Day. Not having a text book I did not know the nature of the day in time to advertise service.

Mon., May 9. The Brn. Louder and Reed came about noon and set fire to the brush on the new ground. When I came down [to Friedland], I found it burning brightly. That evening I went home with Br. Louder. The next morning Mother Louder presented me with flax jeans for pantaloon pattern.

Tues., May 10. Remained all night at Br. Steward's. The family presented me with some very nice cotton jeans for pantaloons.

Sun., May 15. Whitsunday. My birthday: 33 years old. "At 30, man suspects himself a fool. Knows it at 40." My kind mother presented me with a very nice piece of cotton cloth for pantaloons. I preached over at Muddy Creek, riding over and back the same day. 'Twas a mortification of the flesh. I had intended going over in the buggy with two horses, but the road was too heavy.

Sat., May 28. Sr. Gibbins presented me with a pair of flax pantaloons—just the very thing to work in.

Wed., June 1. Took a ride in the afternoon. A most unusual event. Miss S. Blum.

Fri., June 3. Felt like resting—and did rest. Rain the evening before and rain all day more or less.

Sat., June 4. Rain again. Called to see Uncle Henry Blum in the afternoon. Sehnsucht sehr stark—was kömmt hervor. [Longing very strong—what comes of it?]

Sun., June 5. All this time, i.e., for the last month, Grant has been fighting beyond Richmond. For more than 20 days he has been trying to get that place. We shall see yet how he will succeed.

Tues., June 7. ([Friedland Report:] There were several persons buried at Friedland about this time, all of whom except Br. Reed's child were outsiders. The members are beginning to see that their graveyard will soon be filled up with strangers, and no one to attend to keeping up the graves.)

Fri., June 17. Visited [blank] and enjoyed myself vastly.

Mon., June 20. Today W. Cooper went to the army. I was down to see him off.

Mon., June 27. Henry and I were hauling Father's hay home, which he had bo't of the Confederate government. 'Twas very warm work.

Sun., July 3. ([Friedland Report:] At Macedonia I baptized the infant daughter of Henry and Elizabeth Lee (m.n. Fry). I made use of the occasion to give some of the reasons why we believe in infant baptism, at the same time enjoining upon the members the duty of bringing their children to be baptized. It was the first time I had ever baptized a child in the Macedonia Church, and as there were a number of persons present opposed to infant baptism, I was anxious to make the best use of the occasion. I was afterwards told that there were views presented which were entirely new to many present.)

Thurs., July 6 [7]. Today Gov. Vance is to speak.

Sun., July 17. Rode to Muddy Creek. Preached from Rom. 12:11 and afterwards administered communion. . . . A colored brother of the Methodist Church wished to commune with us but did not, as the church was too full. ([Friedland Report:] A colored member of the Methodist Church was present, who desired to commune with us, but as the church was too full to admit of his sitting downstairs, the matter fell thro'.)

Mon., July 17 [18]. Went to Friedland; hauled up my oats; ploughed my peas and put some hens' guano among my corn.

Sun., July 31. ([Friedland Report:] After preaching [at Macedonia], I spoke to Br. Em. Riddle about baptizing his youngest child, but as none of the others had been baptized he concluded this one could also do without. He seems to be very firm in the matter.)

Thurs., Aug. 11. More or less rain these days. I was busy patching and mending my old shoes. James came up from Raleigh.

Fri., Aug. 12. Edward took John and went over to the river to tune pianos. Was busy cobbling again. Fine rain.

Mon., Aug. 15. Cobbling again. Fixing myself some plough boots. Very heavy rains.

Sat., Aug. 20. Went on to Muddy Creek to Sr. Davis's; two of her sons are in the army, and her husband is guarding a bridge near Lexington.

Sun., Aug. 21. Preached at Muddy Creek on the Parable of Lazarus. The number of men present was very small, as almost all had gone off to hunt deserters. Staid all night at Sr. Davis's after visiting Squire Ellis, Sr. Holland and D. Essic.

Tues., Aug. 23. Got some $50 of Br. Pfohl. Last fall I applied for an increase of salary. 'Tis now almost Sept. and I have thus far received about $70.00. Often during these hard, sad times, do I dream of Bethlehem and Auld Lang Syne. Last Wednesday was the Children's Festival. How many years is it now since the Holy Spirit worked so powerfully upon [my] heart at Children's Festival; and how the Lord has led and guided me since that time, and made me one of his servants. How does my soul rejoice at God's bidding, and yet seek to hide itself in shame and confusion of face at the thought of its own vileness and unworthiness. How often does my heart swell with gratitude unto God, that he has been pleased to return me to Friedland. I am much attached to the place and people, and trust that in God's own time I may be permitted to live there once more.

Mon., Aug. 29. Took br. James to High Point. Remained all night at Friend Thomlinson's. Returned next day. How the sight of the cars stirred up memories of the past.

Thurs., Sept. 1. Took dinner at Hausertown with the Misses Millers. Bought 150 pounds weight of bran and shorts[1] for John at $18.00.

Tues., Sept. 6. Returned from . . . [Wesley] Boner's. He is at home on sick furlough. He gives a bad account of affairs at Charlestown.

Thurs., Sept. 8. Went to Friedland to dig potatoes. Mr. Hine came and helped me.

---

[1]Shorts: a mix of bran and the coarse part of meal, suitable for eating by Br. Leinbach's horse John.

Fri., Sept. 9. Busy still with my potatoes. They are very fine; when the plough passes thro' the row proper 'tis a beautiful sight to see them roll out.

Sat., Sept. 17. One of the most important days of my life, inasmuch as I made a speech which bound two lives in one. [The remainder of the day's entry is in a different color ink and is interlined with the next day's entry.] It was a lovely afternoon, and after spending some time at Mr. Blum's, a walk was proposed. We strolled into the woods, and sat on a fallen bough. Miss B. was telling me of her plans—teaching and then returning to the Single Sisters House. I told her of mine, and that I wished her to join her lot with mine and become my helpmate and companion. What a look of agony she gave me! She never answered me at all. It seemed as if I had suddenly deprived her of all joy and enjoyment and placed a heavy burden on her heart. We returned slowly, stopping under an oak awhile where I sealed my proposal.

Fri., Sept. 23. Rain. [The next sentence is in a different color ink and is interlined.] My Darling has fully consented to be mine, but what a week of solicitude she has had.

Sun., Sept. 25. Preaching at Friedland. ([Friedland Report:] Several of the home guard present with their muskets and accoutrements.)

Sun., Oct. 2. ([Macedonia Report:] [A]fter preaching administered the communion to about 18 souls, among whom was Calvin Riddle, who was at home from the army on furlough. In consequence of the severity of his wounds in both thighs, he was compelled to remain outside in the wagon, where I brought him the elements. It was the first time he had communed with us since leaving the Church, and he seemed to be very much affected.) Afternoon called on C. Riddle; staid at Br. Lee's.

Sun., Oct. 16. Preached at Muddy Creek from Mal. 3:8. Congregation rather down. ([Muddy Creek Report:] The men were almost all gone from home, out on military duty.) Took dinner at Br. Essic's. Most of the people gone from home, engaged in this wicked war.

Mon., Oct. 24. Went to Friedland . . . to Br. Louder's. The next morning I was presented with two chickens and some butter by Mother Louder and a promise of a bushel of wheat from him. I called on Br. Em. Reed, who, I was informed, was to go to Greensboro. Found him making some shoes for his family.

Mon., Oct. 31. Spent evening with my Dearest.

Thurs., Nov. 3. [T]he days, weeks and months roll round, and our country is still involved in war. My heart sickens when I contemplate the sad prospect round me. There is so much suffering in the land wherever I go in these different counties about here. I come across women and children who are suffering for bread, clothing, shoes, etc. How and when must and will this cruel war end. And with all this dark aspect of affairs, I have one bright hope which sheds light on my dark path, a noble, truehearted Being has consented to unite her lot with mine whenever times are more propitious—perhaps before.

Tues., Nov. 8. Went to Friedland after a load of corn; returned in the rain.

Wed., Nov. 9. In the afternoon went to Friedland again.

Thurs., Nov. 10. Returned home with corn and wheat, which I took because I dreamed it had been stolen.

Sat., Nov. 12. Went to Friedland to celebrate the 13th of November. Found, to my consternation, the parsonage had been robbed and a number of articles removed. The communion cup, jug, table spread, ribbon and pins, plates, cups and saucers, knives and forks, a pitcher, coffee pot, coffee mill, baptismal service, smoothing iron, etc., were gone. My axe, hatchet, bed tick, shorts, humstring,[1] hair brush, plough share, boot leg, some wheat, some potatoes, etc., were abstracted from me. As we could not celebrate the Lord's Supper and there were but few persons, I only kept Lovefeast. Returned home.

Mon., Nov. 21. Had two teeth filled with composition, which Dr. Hunter was kind enough to do gratis.

Tues., Nov. 29. Returned from Davie Co., having been buying corn of Br. R. Sheek's at $25 per bushel and hauling it besides. The country is in a miserable condition: suffering, trouble, hunger, starvation almost, and yet taking out more men. Such are some of the terrible consequences of Secession!!!

Spoke today with Br. Chas. Anderson about the church at Muddy Creek. Alas! alas! I am so situated that I cannot do anything for the unfortunate neighborhood. This secession and

---

[1]Perhaps meaning a humstrum, defined by the *Oxford English Dictionary* as a musical instrument of rude construction or out of tune, or a hurdy-gurdy.

its consequent war has almost compelled me to say with Othello: my occupation's gone. From attending to my pastoral and ministerial duties, I must betake myself to farming, shoemaking, saddling or at least harness mending and wagoning. There is but very little time I am ever able to devote to reading the Bible as I should do.

Wed., Nov. 30. Ploughed in the last of my wheat at Friedland. In the afternoon Bill Brendle came to the church, and but for the opportune arrival of some of the sisters of the congregation passing by, he would have carried off my boots. He had them on his arm already—in the very act. ([Friedland Report:] Stealing and robbing are going on all around. Sheepfolds, hog lots, calf pastures, corn fields, hen roosts, smoke houses are all exposed to robbery. Even the sanctuaries are not exempt from the depredations of thieves and burglars. White women are kept by negroes, who must steal in order to keep them. Such are some of the mildest of the countless terrible evils brought upon this devoted country by *secession.*)

Thurs., Dec. 1. Bro't the last of my potatoes up today from Br. Steward, where I had taken them for safekeeping. Henry Belo was buried this afternoon on the Cemetery; he had been slain last May at the battle of the Wilderness. I was so exhausted from my labors and wagoning, that I laid down this afternoon and slept about two hours. Had a letter of congratulations from James the other day.

Wed., Dec. 7. Synod was convened at Salem. The Brn. Louder and D. Sheek represented the Friedland and Macedonia congregations. I was elected secretary. Synod adjourned in the afternoon, requesting the PEC and Financial Board to continue in the performance of the functions of their respective offices.

Sat., Dec. 10. The sleet was so deep and frozen so hard that it did not thaw much, and walking was very difficult and fatiguing. The winter has commenced very severe.

Sun., Dec. 11. Undertook to go to Friedland, but the roads were in such a bad condition, I found it impracticable and turned back. Wrote 4 letters in the afternoon to go north with Mrs. Yates.

Tues., Dec. 13. The snow and ice not gone yet, roads very bad and rough. How do the weeks, months and years roll round. Last Sunday I wrote to Robert P. Krause, and H.A.B. How much it reminded me of old times. Herman is at Bethlehem, professor of theology, and here I am at Salem, cobbler, harness mender, farmer, everything almost but what I should be. Truly the Lord's ways are not as our ways, nor his thought as our thought. Last evening I was reading to my Friend from H.W.B. How much it was enjoyed. Why is it, that I have at times such strange, unaccountable longings. At such times nothing but prayer will avail. I feel much better; by tomorrow I trust I shall be all right. 'Tis the longing after the Infinite. The greatest part of the week I have been busy with my corn shucking and putting it away.

Thurs., Dec. 22. Bro't James and T. Wolle from H. Point. Horses balked at Fiedler's bottom. Had to hitch stage horses in. Stage tongue broke. Came home horseback.

Fri., Dec. 23. At home—tired.

Sat., Dec. 24. Fed Yanks. Christmas Eve. Went to meeting in the evening.

Sun., Dec. 25. Christmas Day. Mother's birthday. Preached at Friedland. A very large congregation present.

Mon., Dec. 26. I spent afternoon with my Darling, then attended Dialogue together.

Tues., Dec. 27. Sherman is, according to latest accounts, still at Savannah. There was some fighting at Wilmington.

Sat., Dec. 31. The last day of the year 1864. 'Tis a dreary day, raining and snowing alternately. 'Tis my Sunday for Macedonia, but I shall probably not go over. 'Tis a time for memory and tears. Went as far as Mr. Lewis Hanes', where I remained all night. I had been very undecided. Several times I changed my mind about going, and at last about 2 3/4 I started off and reached Mr. Hanes' before night sometime.

[New] Philadelphia Reports, 1864
[Extracts transcribed; handwriting is that of Emil A. de Schweinitz.]

On account of Br. Thomas Frye's failing health, Philadelphia was attended to by brethren from Salem since the beginning of October 1863. Br. Frye having departed this life on the 31st day of March 1864, the congregation has been regularly served since that time by the Brn. Bahnson and E. A. de Schweinitz.

Sat., Aug. 13. The congregation assembled at 2 P.M. for the celebration of the day. The number of communicants was small, only 15 being present. The assessment of taxes in the district and other hindrances caused the absence of several brethren.

Sun., Aug. 28. All the brethren, with the exception of those belonging to Home Guard, were present.

Sat., Nov. 12. Congregation festival. In the afternoon the congregation assembled for the celebration of the day. But a small number were present. Several Brethren were absent on home guard duty, and others were prevented from coming. The first meeting was held at 2 P.M. and [was] followed by the Holy Communion. There was no lovefeast. Only 10 communicants.

Sat., Dec. 24. Xmas Eve. At 2 P.M. the Christmas Eve meeting and lovefeast were kept. The children received candles as usual. The sisters' side of the church was filled, and on the Brn.'s side none were wanting that were able to come.

1865

[Argentina, Brazil, and Uruguay invaded Paraguay, killing or forcing into exile three-fourths of its population, and seizing much of its territory. Russia expanded into Turkestan, east of the Caspian Sea.

The Civil War at last came to an end as Confederate forces surrendered. Union troops occupied the South, which could expect harsher treatment after the assassination of Abraham Lincoln. The 13th Amendment abolished slavery.

In North Carolina the fall of Fort Fisher in January led to the Federal occupation of Wilmington, the Confederacy's last port. General Sherman's army entered North Carolina and defeated Joseph E. Johnston's army at Bentonville. In the meantime, General Stoneman's raiders entered the state from Tennessee and wreaked havoc as far as Guilford County. In April Raleigh was occupied, and General Johnston surrendered the last major Confederate force on the 26th. U.S. president Andrew Johnson appointed William Holden as provisional governor, but Jonathan Worth defeated him in the fall election. In December Shaw University opened at Raleigh "for Freedmen."]

Memorabilia of Salem Congregation, 1865
[Extracts transcribed; handwriting is that of George Frederic Bahnson.]

[T]his evening we stand at the close of a year which proved uncommonly (peculiarly) remarkable to us, perhaps more so than any one of those which preceded it. As a community and Christian congregation, as a portion of our beloved Brethren's Church, we have passed through the last year of the first century of our existence. Before those of us who may be spared shall meet again in a manner similar to this, it can be said: for 100 years has been in Salem the tabernacle of the Lord [Ps. 76:2]; yea blessed be his name, the Lord has thus far to his flock kept without separation.

But not only as the last year of the first century of our existence as a church, does the year that is now fast passing away claim our particular consideration, for it was in itself one of the most memorable of our lives. We entered upon it, as was proper, with the deepest gratitude for past mercies and favors experienced during very trying times and with the firm hope and assurance that the Lord would continue to watch over and protect us and send deliverance in his own good way, but at the same time the horizon appeared overcast, dark, and gloomy while ominous and threatening clouds continued to arise in every direction. The fearful civil strife between portions of a once united people had been going on for years, devastating the fairest portions of our beloved land, decimating its once highly favored indwellers, sowing broadcast mourning and lamentations, sundering the most sacred ties uniting man to man, interfering most fatally with the happiness of numberless families, depriving parents of children, children of parents, wives of their husbands, and reducing smiling landscapes into howling deserts. Not only did there appear to be no prospect of a speedy termination of this lamentable and fearful state of affairs, but the appalling war cry was drawing nearer to our own parts, and fear and apprehension of greater evils would involuntarily fill the hearts of men looking for the things that were coming to pass.

But while threatening clouds and darkness thus surrounded us, and our little faith and confidence were at times ready to fail, the Lord our ever merciful Guide and Protector was preparing to make us realize the blessed truth of his own word: He that dwelleth in the secret place of the most High shall abide under the shadow of the Almighty. He shall cover thee with his feathers, and under his wings shalt thou trust; his truth shall be thy shield and buckler [Ps. 91:1,4]. Many rumors of a very disquieting nature reached us from time to time, until it was positively announced (reported) that a large portion of the Federal army under Stoneman would be in our midst on Monday, April 3d, but thanks to the Lord, we were soon assured that the number of raiders had been overestimated and that all had turned towards Danville, Va. Thus our homes were mercifully spared this time, although perhaps many a father had risen in the morning fearful that before evening he would have no place where to shelter his dear ones with himself. In the evening of the day which we had so much feared we returned sincere thanks unto the Lord for his gracious protection.

In his unsearchable wisdom, he had, however, determined that our dreaded anticipations should to a great extent be realized. After we had enjoyed the solemn meetings on Palm

Sunday we were greatly startled the next day, April 10, by the intelligence that the same portion of the federal army, looked for on the 3d, would pass through Salem today, and indeed towards evening, about 4 o'clock, they took us completely by surprise, as they appeared all at once in our midst. Before we could realize it, soldiers were seen at every corner of the streets, had taken possession of the post office, and secured our whole town. Some of our brethren had gone out to meet Genl. Palmer, the commander of the troops, coming our way, and our Mayor, Bro. Josh. Boner, addressed him personally. When commending our town and community to his protection, not only on our own account, but also of our large female boarding school, the General assured him that persons and property should be safe, that no destruction of any kind would be allowed, and that we might feel perfectly secure from harm during their stay with us. Other persons had gone out to reconnoiter, of whom two were captured and taken to the federal camp; they were, however, released the next morning.

Genl. Palmer established his headquarters in the house of our Bro. Josh. Boner. In very great, comparative, silence about 3,000 cavalry passed through our town, pitching their tents on the high ground beyond the creek. Had it not been for the noise their horses and swords made, it would have been hardly noticed that so large a number of, at the time, hostile troops were passing through our streets. The strictest discipline was enforced, guards rode up and down every street, and very few indeed, comparatively, were the violations of proper and becoming conduct on the part of the soldiers. The night was as quiet as any other, except that there was a great deal of riding to and fro in main street, and some of us could not divest themselves of apprehensions that they and their houses would be in imminent danger, in case the cotton factories in town should be molested.

Providentially, government stores were in town in considerable abundance, so that individuals were not called upon to contribute anything except bread and the like, for which the men would generally ask politely and return thanks in the same manner. Fears were, however, entertained by some, whether their good behavior would continue to the last, and no doubt many a fervent prayer ascended to the throne of a prayer hearing and answering God, and not in vain. For no outrages, except the pressing of horses, of any kind were committed, and even the cotton manufactories were spared by the federals. Without any fault on the part of their officers, some of whom had been scholars in Litiz and spoke feelingly of that happy time, entrance was effected into one of these establishments and a considerable damage done.

During the afternoon of the 11th a large number of the Federals came back from the railroad, which they had tapped in several places. They brought with them about 50 prisoners. By some mistake they came into the graveyard avenue and passed through the graveyard and part of the cemetery, having shifted their camp to a place above town, but passing through those hallowed grounds, almost all of them dismounted and led their horses; some even uncovered their heads. Before dark they had all left, passing through Winston towards the river, and though other soldiers, said to be less disciplined than that portion of Palmer's Brigade which had been here, have been near our town, they were not allowed to enter it. Nevertheless prudence dictated a measure of precaution, especially against stragglers from Johnston's army, and for some time our own people kept watch during the night, and by the Lord's kind assistance all evil was averted.

The Confederate army under Lee having surrendered, portions of them passed through our town every day. They were of course under no discipline and rendered watchful care necessary. This applied particularly to a corps called Wheeler's cavalry. During Passion Week our main street was more or less alive with them, which circumstance interrupted our meetings very much. On Wednesday, in the first meeting we were able to keep, we offered up our humble but heartfelt tribute of thanksgiving and praise to Him, who had so mercifully protected our beloved Salem. Most persons were, however, afraid to leave their houses, especially in the evening, and so it happened that on Maundy Thursday there were but 6 male communicants present, besides the ministers.

On the 20th of April a number of Confederates made their appearance, pretending to be in search of government cloth, to find which they had intended to search individual houses. As had been agreed upon, the different bells were at once rung, and in a very short time, a by no means inconsiderable number of men, many of them soldiers themselves who had come back on parole, assembled near the square, armed as well as circumstances permitted and fully determined to resist the entrance into private houses. Our unbidden visitors soon changed their language and withdrew after a short time without offering any molestation at all. ([Margin note:] On a former occasion some soldiers came to town as they alleged in search of horses, and had the hardihood of taking two of our citizens prisoners, but on being remonstrated with and asked for their authority, they begged off and left us.)

As the Lord our God thus exercised his gracious guardian care over us who had remained at home, our numerous brethren sons and friends who were away from us were also mercifully protected by him. While we could discover no way in which hostilities might be speedily terminated, we were all at once surprised by the intelligence that General Lee had surrendered on the 10th of April to General Grant and Gen. Johnston on the 27th to Gen. Sherman. Thus the fearful war was really ended and much bloodshed spared. Our loved ones returned one after the other, and when we consider how many of them there were, and to what dangers, hardships, and privations they were exposed, and how wonderfully they were taken care of and almost all allowed to return to the bosom of their families, surely we must exclaim with one heart and one voice: Bless the Lord, O my soul, and forget not all his benefits [Ps. 103:2]. As an eagle stirreth up her nest and fluttereth over her young, spreadeth abroad her wings, taketh them, beareth them on her wings, so the Lord alone did lead them [Deut. 32:11-12], and kept them safe beneath the shadow of his wings, as the almighty King of Kings. O that neither they nor we would forget the gratitude we owe our Lord, and present to him spirit, soul, and body as a sacrifice well pleasing in his eyes.

In consequence of the manner in which the long contest between the South and the North terminated, the colored people were declared to be free, and during the course of the year the required number of states consented to the 13th article [amendment] of the constitution, which abolishes forever throughout the U.St. involuntary servitude except for crimes committed. Too little time has elapsed to allow us to judge of the results of this measure, but we humbly trust that He who caused it to be adopted will also see to it that it may work for good to those who are more immediately affected by it.

On the 14th of May the 10th Regiment of Ohio Volunteers began a longer stay here at our place. Col. Saunderson established his headquarters in the house of our Bro. Edw. Hege. They left again on July 13th, and although upon the whole they had conducted themselves tolerably well as a body, still little regret was felt at their departure, in as much as it had appeared, very plainly, that their presence was anything but *necessary* or pleasant and their moral influence was anything but beneficial. A few of the officers and men attended our place of worship, but the majority of them cared for none of these things.

On Tuesday the 10th of January we had heavy rain accompanied by very severe thunder and lightning. The watercourses rose in a very short time and caused a general freshet. The bridge across our creek was undermined and its pillars washed away; the water covered the race bridge. Almost every bridge in the neighborhood was destroyed, also some on the railroad, so that travelling was considerably interrupted, as was also the mail, which could not come across our creek. The damage done to fences was also very great. ([Margin note:] We were then not aware that we should be left without any regular mail for months.)

On Saturday, the 21st of January, we had a very heavy sleet, a good description of which was given in the following manner: Saturday morning last exhibited the heaviest sleet that we remember ever to have witnessed. Everything exposed was icy, and the numerous shade trees skirting our sidewalks presented a charming appearance, every twig being encased with the beautiful frostwork of the previous night. And the forest surrounding our town stood forth in its silvery beauty, only wanting a bright sun to illumine the sparkling and wondrous creation of the frost king. During the morning, however, a drizzling rain augmented the weight of ice, until crash after crash indicated that destruction was abroad among the beautiful shade trees. For some time indeed outdoor locomotion was both difficult and dangerous on account of the falling branches. In some portions of our town the streets and sidewalks were impassable because of young trees bent to the ground and broken limbs lying across the way. The old sycamores around the square were considerably mutilated, and many of the smaller trees broken off or greatly damaged. The ancient cedars of the avenue leading to the graveyard presented a grand appearance. They stood forth like pyramids, and you could see through them from one end to the other of the avenue. They as well as those in the graveyard were somewhat injured, though they escaped comparatively well. But by far the most lamentable destruction occurred among the fruit trees in town and country, as in all probability several years' growth will not restore them to their former usefulness. The forest trees were also damaged to a considerable extent and the roads blockaded by the fallen timber, which, however, furnished many loads of firewood, gladdening the hearts, especially of the poor who needed not to have it cut first.

The high prices of the necessaries of life which had prevailed during the war were not so much reduced by the cessation of hostilities as had been fondly expected. The wheat crop also failed to a very great extent, and the scarcity of money was more or less severely felt by the whole community. Still we have abundant cause to laud and magnify our ever gracious God, that peace, with many of its blessings, has been restored, and we will indulge in the sweet hope that ere very long we shall be admitted to all the privileges which we once enjoyed as a portion of a highly favored nation. When we take into consideration how other states and neighborhoods fared during the last fearful years, how other communities were deprived of large numbers of young men that had joined the army, and how fearful the condition of some parts of our country continues to be at this moment, and that during this eventful year in our midst not a single home was destroyed, not a single family called upon to mourn for a beloved one lost by the war, that not a single regular member of our congregation was permanently injured during the campaign of *this* year, that our Salem stands this evening as intact and secure as it did before the war began, language is utterly at fault to express the depth of gratitude (and adoration) that ought to fill every heart and soul towards him, whose wondrous works we are this evening called upon to consider.

On the 10th of March we had the last of numerous days of humiliation and prayer, and on the 7th of December, the day appointed by the President of the U.St. as a day of thanksgiving and praise to Almighty God for all his blessings and especially for the restoration of peace and we trust of increasing harmony and concord, we added our mite to the general offering of gratitude of our reunited country.

On Sunday the 13th of August we commemorated in spiritual union with many of our sister congregations, this side and beyond the great waters, that particular visitation of grace which our mother congregation at Herrnhut experienced at the holy communion in the church of Berthelsdorf in 1727. Almost all of those whom the war had taken away from their homes in our midst had returned in safety, so that peculiar sensations of gratitude filled our hearts at the solemn meetings of the day, and it is hoped that very many of us experienced a visitation of grace similar to that vouchsafed to our forefathers.

In conclusion we would mention that a Provincial Synod was held here from the 14th to the 21st of November. The brethren Geo. F. Bahnson and Christian Lewis Rights were elected members of the P.E.C. Bro. Emil Schweinitz continued the 3d member. The P.E.C. appointed Bro. Bahnson, President of the Conference, and called him as pastor of the Salem congregation and appointed Bro. Grunert to assist as much as his other duties will allow.

Salem Diary, 1865
[Extracts transcribed; handwriting is that of George Frederic Bahnson.]

Sun., Jan. 8. The audience was encouraging. Some residents of our town miss preaching as regularly as others attend it and have done so for years. May God have mercy upon them ere it shall be too late. Some of our wealthiest men belong to this miserable class, and seem to feel perfectly at ease. Judgment day will show whether they are right or the Bible.

Tues., Jan. 10. Severe rain—thunder and lightning part of the forenoon. The watercourses rose in a very short time, and caused a general freshet. Our bridge was undermined and sunk together after the rain had receded. Almost every bridge in the neighborhood was destroyed, also some on the railroad so that travelling was somewhat interrupted. Nothing could come across our creek today, hence we had no mail at all. Great damage was done to fences everywhere. Our bridge will be useless for some time and the ford must suffice. A destructive fire at Charlotte destroyed millions of commissary and other public stores. Truly there is trouble in the land. O that men would seek the Lord in sincerity and truth.

Thurs., Jan. 19. Very unpleasant weather. Cold, rain and sleet. The trees were coated with ice, which caused not only limbs of a large size, but whole trees to be thrown down. It was dangerous to be in the streets. They and the square were strewn with large branches of trees, and one could hear trees fall in the woods with a great noise. Some of our streets were [so] blocked up, that vehicles could only pass with difficulty. The oldest inhabitants could not remember such a destruction of trees of every kind. Many fruit trees were ruined entirely as also shade trees. No mail arrived nor left. The watercourses were also very high.

Wed., Jan. 25. Bro. Bahnson kept Bible service. The brethren's side is almost empty. Only one single brother and a boy present in all. Were it not for the sisters the chapel would be empty. Query: Do the sisters need such meetings more than the brethren? Answer: No. Rumors of peace caused the hearts of all to rejoice. May they only be something more than idle rumors.

Fri., Jan. 27. The coldest day we have had this season. The ice, it is said, is 4 and 5 inches thick. A holiday was given to the schoolboys, that they may go on the ice with their teacher. People were everywhere busy filling their ice houses.

Tues., Feb. 7. Heavy sleet or very fine snow fell to a considerable depth. Very cold. Walking very unpleasant. The practice of making paths everywhere is dying out.

Wed., Feb. 8. Some sleighing, but no evening meeting.

Mon., Feb. 20. We have an uncommonly disagreeable winter —cold and wet. It is impossible to do anything by way of preparing the soil for gardening. There is a good deal of sickness, and that of a painful and tedious character.

Sun., Feb. 26. The weather became pleasant during the day. . . . The attendance was pretty good, considering all things. There is no doubt that not a few are kept from the house of God by want of shoes and other things.

Wed., Mar. 1. Bro. Bahnson kept lecture, speaking on the Passover and institution of the Lord's Supper. It was rather poorly attended. The times are very discouraging. People's minds are so much taken up with the war, that they care much less than they should for the one thing needful.

Sat., Mar. 4. Today something came to light that startled our whole community and made the ear of everyone who heard tingle. Yesterday soon after dinner widow Vierling, who acts as nurse, Sr. Grunert, Carrie, and Annie Grunert were taken with vomiting, but no suspicion of any kind was aroused at first.

But when little Annie most unexpectedly breathed her last, before midnight, it was strongly suspected that poison had something to do with the death of the little child. A post mortem examination proved arsenic in the stomach. Such poison had been bought some time ago by a negro man belonging to Bro. Hn. Butner in Bethany. Jane, the girl belonging to Sr. Grunert, and the negro man were arrested and brought to a preliminary trial. Jane finally confessed that in order to get back to Bethany she had repeatedly attempted to poison her mistress, and also on Friday by strewing arsenic on some rolls that were put into soup prepared for her. Providentially Sr. Grunert took a dislike to the soup and ate but little. Little Carrie took it, but did not eat much either, and gave it according to her request to little Annie, who ate the last, and thus put into her stomach a large quantity of arsenic, enough, it was said, to poison ten men!! Jane stated that the plan of poisoning her mistress had been suggested to her by John, a negro belonging to Bro. Fulkerson. John with Jane and Squire, the old negro from Bethany, were all sent to jail, although it appears now that the poison Squire bought for Jane was not used at all, but had been kept by her just as it was. There was a fearful indignation, especially towards Jane and John, and the adoption of lynch law was strongly urged by some, but, thank God, rejected.

Thurs, Mar. 9. At noon the 1st Battalion of N.C. Troops arrived here. It contains a number of our Salem boys. They all looked remarkably well. Dinner was prepared in the square for such as have no friends in town. The battalion was sent on to hunt deserters in this county and in Yadkin. Surely we live in evil times!

Fri., Mar. 10. This day having been recommended as a day of humiliation and prayer with thanksgiving, there was public service at 10 A.M. conducted by Bro. Bahnson, who preached on the occasion from James 5:16. The attendance was rather better than "little faith" had anticipated.

Wed., Mar. 22. Today the Battalion left again, having been engaged in hunting deserters both in this county and in Yadkin. Several deserters had been shot in our neighborhood by order of Capt. Wilson. It is said that his orders were to proceed in this way. But the bodies being left unburied by the roadside, people felt a considerable degree of indignation against such measures.

Sun., Apr. 2. Quite a pleasant day, but one of fearful excitement throughout our town. The report had reached here that Stoneman was coming at the head of 4,500 men accompanied by 4 cannons, and consternation became the order of the day. Some people were busy all last night and all day, despite of its being the Lord's day, in moving things of every kind and description to safer places. The Academy was a favorite spot. Cotton was stored in a number of houses, increasing the danger by fire to a very high degree.

Mon., Apr. 3. Cloudy. Surely it could be said this morning, "thou knowest not what a day may bring forth." It was the general expectation that the raiders under Stoneman would come here sometime during the day. But thanks to the mercy and favor of Him whose tabernacle Salem still is, the intelligence was received that in the first place the number of raiders had been very much exaggerated, and in the second, that they had turned towards Danville, probably with the intention of tapping the railroad. Thus our homes were mercifully saved for the present, and we humbly pray for the whole war.

Tues., Apr. 4. Reports reached us today that Richmond and Petersburg had been evacuated; also that the raiders were on their way to Hillsville, Va.

Sun., Apr. 9. Palm Sunday. Bro. Emil Schweinitz preached at the usual time. At 7 P.M. Bro. Bahnson began the reading of the Acts of the Son of Man, in the usual solemn manner.

Mon., Apr. 10. Rainy, but more clear after a while. This day was to Salem a very remarkable one whose experience calls for the most heartfelt gratitude and thanksgiving to Him who never leaves nor forsakes his own, and who thanks to His neverfailing mercy allows us still to exclaim: In Salem also is his tabernacle! A rumor had reached us that a portion of the federal army, raiders under Gen. Stoneman, would reach us today. But we could scarcely credit it, till after 4 o'clock they made their appearance. Bro. Robt. Schweinitz, the Mayor [Joshua Boner], and others had gone to meet them, and were assured that all private property should be respected. Gen. Palmer and staff took up their quarters at Bro. Josh Boner's, and in very great comparative silence and with the strictest order, about 3,000 cavalry passed through town and pitched their camp on the high ground beyond our creek. Had it not been for the noise their swords and horses made it would have been scarcely noticed that as large a number of troops was passing through town. The strictest discipline was observed, guards rode up and down every street, and the violations of mild and gentlemanly conduct were very few indeed. The night was as quiet as any other, except that there was a good deal of riding to and fro in the main street. Providentially, government stores were here in considerable abundance, so that individuals were not called upon to contribute any thing except breads, for which they would ask politely and thank in the same manner. Fears were of course entertained by some whether they would continue this good behavior to the last, and no doubt many a fervent prayer ascended this evening. The meeting was of course dropped.

Tues., Apr. 11. While the conduct of the federals continued to be very good in town, they did not treat all our neighbors as gently as they did us. Horses were taken everywhere and represented by them as a measure of necessity. It was understood that even the factories should be spared, and nothing be touched except government stores, but some soldiers opened the factory of Hy. Fries, and a mob entered, destroying the inside very thoroughly and carrying off a great deal of property. The old factory being used for grinding was preserved. Several persons had been taken prisoners by the federals, among them our teacher, Albert Butner, but they were soon paroled. No outrages of any kind were committed in private homes. Some of the officers had been at school in Litiz, and spoke feelingly of that happy time. During the afternoon a large number came back from the railroad, where they had caused destruction. They passed, by mistake of some kind, into our graveyard avenue, and finding it closed above, turned into the graveyard itself. But most of them dismounted, leading their horses through that hallowed spot. It is said that some even took off their hats. They did not in any way spoil the walks. Before dark all left, passing through Winston towards the river. We thanked God and took courage.

Wed., Apr. 12. The night passed very quietly. A kind of home guard was organized so that between 20 and 30 persons will be patrolling the streets, which will be necessary on account of stragglers. At 7 1/2 Bro. Bahnson kept reading meeting after having offered up a tribute of gratitude to Him who extended his hand once more over his Salem. We could have no gas. We had but poor light, and also but a very small congregation. But almost everybody is afraid to go from home.

Thurs., Apr. 13. Maundy Thursday. A very beautiful day, but parties of southern soldiers passed through town almost continually. At 2 1/2 P.M. Bro. Emil Schweinitz kept the meeting, and at 4 P.M. Bro. Bahnson continued the reading of the acts of the day. In the evening Bro. Bahnson presided at the celebration of the Lord's Supper. It was very well attended by the sisters, but of brethren there were but 11 present, 5 of whom are ministers. Still the Lord was in our midst distributing his rich blessings.

Fri., Apr. 14. A beautiful day. On account of the insecurity caused by the soldiers, no brothers went either to Bethabara or [New] Philadelphia. Our meetings here were only interrupted by numbers of soldiers passing through and rendering it necessary for brethren to remain at their homes. At 9 A.M. Bro. Grunert celebrated the holy communion in German. About 8 brethren were present. The meetings at 10 A.M., 2 1/2 and 7 1/2 P.M. were kept by Bro. Bahnson. The attendance was of course not as good as usual. May this congregation never pass through such a week again, although we have most abundant reason to thank the Lord that all turned out as it did.

Sat., Apr. 15. Rainy till in the afternoon. No meeting at 2 P.M. Bro. Emil Schweinitz kept the evening meeting at 7 1/2 P.M.

Sun., Apr. 16. A very pretty day. At 5 1/2 A.M. Bro. Rob. Schweinitz prayed the Easter morning litany. The procession to the graveyard consisted principally of females. There was a large number of them. At 10 A.M. Bro. Bahnson preached to a good audience on Luke 24:32. The remains of Dennis Shay, a member of one of the regiments of Palmer's brigade, were interred in the cemetery. Owing to the reports that Johnston's army would pass through very soon, the usual funeral solemnities were omitted. In the evening Bro. Bahnson kept the meeting. Very few were in.

The meetings in the week were dropped for the present.

Sun., Apr. 23. A very pretty day, but rather unusually cold. Bro. E. A. Schweinitz preached from John 20:26-29. For reasons, the litany was not prayed, but an extemporaneous prayer substituted. The audience was uncommonly good. It did one's very heart good to see so many male hearers. Many of our sons and brethren had returned during last week. Genl. [Lee] had surrendered the Army of Northern Va. This took place on April 10, and all the men that surrendered were at once paroled. May the Lord soon bring a desired end [to] this horrible war. S.S. as usual. At 4 P.M. Bro. Bahnson kept a meeting for our widowed sisters, and also the meeting at 7 1/2 P.M. was kept by him. More men in than for a long time.

Wed., May 3. At 4 o'clock was the funeral of Single Sr. Sarah Elizabeth (Henrietta) Friebele, eldest daughter of Bro. John A. Friebele and his first wife Sr. Henrietta Peterson. It will be an unexpected blow to Bro. Friebele, with whom we cannot communicate, as we have had no regular mails since the 10th of last month. We sympathize deeply with him.

Sun., May 14. A very pretty day. Bro. Bahnson prayed the litany (omitting, as Bro. R.S. did last Sunday, that part which refers to governments, etc.) and preached from James 1:16-21. A report that federal soldiers would arrive shortly kept many from church. S. School as usual, but very few in, both teachers and scholars. Several hundred federal cavalry arrived during the afternoon, and took up camp above town near Bro. Aug. Fogel's house. At 3 P.M. Bro. Bahnson preached in German. Text: John 21:16. Not as many in as sometimes. At 7 1/2 P.M. he kept singing meeting with prayer. Almost as many federal soldiers in as other persons. The arrival of the former causes naturally some excitement and disturbance. The negroes, having been declared free on May 5 by proclamation of some federal general, were seen strutting about in their newborn freedom. Some, but not very many, have left their former masters and set up for themselves. Whether they are fit to do so successfully time will show. There might be some doubts. The federal camp is just in front of Bro. Augustus Fogel's dwelling house. Officers occupy the houses of the Brn. Jas. Lineback and Ed. Hege. The stars and stripes are again hoisted in our midst; may they bring back good old times.

Sun., May 21. A very pretty day. At the usual hour Bro. Grunert prayed the litany and preached from John 16:24. The audience was very good. Not a few federal soldiers and officers are in the habit of attending our meetings. Their behavior is on the whole very good indeed. S.S. as usual. The Rev. Mr. Clark, chaplain of the 10th Ohio Vol. Cavalry, addressed the school in a few remarks of a very proper character. He also preached to the negroes from 1 Cor. 7:21, communicating to them formally that in virtue of the proclamation issued Jan. 1, 1863, by the late Abr. Lincoln they were free and no longer in bondage, exhorting them to be industrious, honest, truthful, kindly disposed, and to strive above all things for that higher freedom with which the son of God maketh those free that come to him in repentance and faith. In the evening Bro. Bahnson kept the meeting. A fearful storm came up, with exceedingly vivid lightning, sweeping wind, and plenty of rain. Some of the people were compelled to remain in church till nearly 9 o'clock. The rain which fell today and yesterday was very much needed, and all should feel truly thankful for it; though it put some to a little inconvenience at the time.

Thurs., May 25. Ascension day. At 9 A.M. Bro. Bahnson kept the usual meeting; it was attended as it usually is. Bro. Emil Schweinitz preached at the usual time from 1 Pet. 3:22 to a rather small audience. One of the federal soldiers was killed today by the accidental discharge of a pistol in the hands of a drunken comrade. By request Bro. Bahnson preached in the evening at 7 1/2 in the German language. A number of Germans belonging to the 10th Ohio Regiment were present.

Sun., May 28. Very pleasant and cool. At the usual time Bro. Bahnson prayed the litany, and the Rev. S. G. Clark, chaplain of the 10th Ohio Regiment, preached an evangelical sermon from Matt. 13:33. At the usual time was S. School. At 3 P.M. Bro. Bahnson kept a meeting preparatory to the holy communion, and at 7 1/2 the usual evening service.

Sun., June 4. Whitsunday. Hardly any federals were in this morning. At 3 P.M. Bro. Bahnson kept the holy communion in the German language and in the evening at 7 1/2 in English. The minds of our people are very much disturbed by a variety of causes. Lord, renew our days as of old, and baptize us with the spirit and with fire.

Sun., June 11. The Older Girls celebrated their annual festival. At 10 A.M. Bro. Bahnson prayed the litany. For the first time since more than 4 years, the prayer for the President of the U. St. was uttered. The text was John 3:3. The attendance was pretty good; very few soldiers were in. At 2 P.M. there was a lovefeast in the chapel for the Older Girls. All was in the old style, as far as creature comforts were concerned, coffee and sugar having been procured. At 7 1/2 Bro. Grunert kept the evening meeting. For some cause or other we had no gas, and darkness reigned rather unpleasantly. Not a vestige, though, of anything like disorder was exhibited.

Sun., June 18. Paroled prisoners return every day, and among them some of our young men. May they all arrive in safety and that very speedily.

Sun., July 2. The heat is unusually great, and diseases begin to show themselves. Dead horses are not removed sufficiently far from town by the soldiers, and spread a very unpleasant and unhealthy smell.

Tues, July 4. This day we celebrated by ringing of bells, firing of cannon, and the like. A large crowd was in town from the country. Not a few colored people had come in, probably expecting great things. At 10 A.M. the square was well filled with people, the Declaration of Independence was read by Mr. Hy. Thomas and an address delivered by Col. Saunderson. Upon the whole the crowd behaved well, and was drawn in the afternoon to Winston, where a large union meeting took place.

Sunday, July 9. Excessively hot. Bro. Bahnson prayed the litany and preached from John 3:6. Quite a number of soldiers were in. Upon the whole, though, the effect of the heat was seen in the non-attendance of others. S.S. We had a very grateful shower late in the evening, refreshing all vegetation and cooling the atmosphere very pleasantly.

Last Wednesday there was to have been prayer meeting, but no sexton making his appearance to ring the bell, the few who had come together dispersed, and these meetings will be dropped for the present. Because the soldiers are here, sisters living in town do not like to venture out, and as the brethren cannot be convinced that these meetings are needed by them also, the attendance has been anything but encouraging.

Thurs., July 13. Everybody, or at least a vast majority of the people, rejoiced that the 10th Ohio Vol. Cavalry left this morning. In more than one respect their presence had been productive of unpleasant results. May they have been the last of northern troops quartered upon us. On Monday they had been paid off and since then many had not seen a sober moment. They were as a body most fearfully profane and a poor specimen of the vaunted superiority of northern morals. Though professing to be the friends and liberators of the colored people, they treated some of them with unheard of barbarity, hanging them up by the thumbs, etc. The officers of the regiment were, with very few honorable exceptions, extremely immoral men, and the privates followed suit. Their influence upon the community was evil, and only evil, and that continually.

Fri., July 14. This evening about 10 o'clock Dr. Keehln was attacked in main street by 6 soldiers, knocked down and robbed. That is supporting the civil law with a vengeance. Today we received a batch of documents from Germany, informing us of things that took place years ago (e.g., the Continental Provincial Synod) of which we had heard nothing. May the Lord prevent the repetition of such things.

Sun., July 16. During the week a number of rather unwelcome northern soldiers lingered about here. A great many females around here—and even some of our single sisters in town—have become somewhat familiar with them. Marriages—not a few—have taken place through the country. Foolish virgins!!

Mon., July 17. Our Boys School resumed its exercises.

Sun., July 23. The absence of gas is sensibly felt, and there is, alas, very little hope for any very soon.

Tues., July 25. Had a very welcome shower, refreshing all vegetation and cooling the heated atmosphere. Fevers had begun to attack a number of persons. Wheat has been a failure —some people have scarcely realized their seed sown last year. But corn promises to be very abundant.

Fri., July 28. Very hot, 98° and upwards on some thermometers. Heat oppressive.

Sun., Aug. 6. There was no meeting in the evening, as it is just now impracticable to light up the church properly, there being no gas to be had.

Sun., Aug. 13. We celebrated a happy festival [of August 13th]. . . . At 2 P.M. Bro. Bahnson kept the lovefeast, and at 4 o'clock he administered the holy communion in the German and at 7½ P.M. in the English language. The number of participants was greater than for a considerable number of years.

Thurs., Aug. 17. Children's festival. At 2 P.M. Bro. Bahnson kept the lovefeast. It may be worthy of being noticed, that at the lovefeasts on the 13th and 17th we could, at the first time for several years, use genuine coffee, which sells at present at $0.60 per pound.

Sun., Aug. 27. Single Brethren's festival. Bro. Bahnson kept their meeting at 8½ A.M. Quite a number of them were absent, although this festival had not been celebrated for four years. Our peculiarities are not appreciated as they should be, nor are their objects understood. It is a great pity indeed. At 2 P.M. Bro. Bahnson kept the lovefeast for the Single Brn. It was of course much better attended by them than the morning meeting. At 7½ Grunert kept the evening meeting, after which

Bro. Bahnson administered the holy communion to 18 Single Brn.

Tues., Sept. 19. Today Bro. Rob. Schweinitz left with his family on a visit to Bethlehem.

Thurs., Sept. 21. Today was the election of members of the state convention. Lash and Starbuck had the majority in our county.

Sun., Sept. 24. The weather was unusually hot, so that the oldest people do not remember so warm a September. A good deal of sickness prevailed.

Sun., Oct. 1. The semi-annual collection for our foreign missions was taken up, amounting to about $39.00. There were apparently not many people in preaching. Money is very scarce, and people are rather unwilling to own it publicly. At 7 P.M. Bro. Bahnson kept a liturgical meeting that was very well attended. The gas, which should have burned, left us in darkness. The people were very orderly, though, and a few candles sufficed. After the public service, teachers and others partook of the cup of the covenant.

Mon., Oct. 9. Bro. Bahnson kept prayer meeting in which he read the beginning of the memoir of our departed colored Bro. Arch Monteith; it is very interesting indeed.[1]

Sat., Oct. 14. Since the 18th of Sept. we had had no rain till today. It rained more or less all day, having commenced during the night, and everybody was glad.

Mon., Oct. 16. Bro. and Sr. Siewers with their daughter Caroline left for West Salem. May the Lord go with them.

Sat., Oct. 21. At 7 P.M. Bro. Rob. Schweinitz and family came back from a visit to Bethlehem.

Thurs., Oct. 26. Bro. Emil Schweinitz returned from a visit to Bethlehem.

Fri., Nov. 17. The Provincial Synod, which had convened on the 14th, had been continued day by day and closed its session this evening for the week to meet again, D.V. [God willing], on Monday.

Tues., Nov. 21. This evening the Provincial Synod adjourned sine die. A change had been made in the constitution,

---

[1]Archibald Monteith was a helper at the mission station of Carmel, Jamaica. He died July 5, 1864, and his memoir was published in two issues of *Periodical Accounts*, September and December 1865. The memoir begins: "I was born in Africa, about the year 1799; the country of the Iboes was my home."

abolishing the office of President without any other office, and electing two members to constitute the P.E.C. with the addition of the Administrator as the 3d member, the P.E.C. to appoint its own President. The Brn. Bahnson and Lewis Rights were elected members, and at the first meeting of the new P.E.C. Bro. Bahnson was appointed President.

Mon., Nov. 27. Bro. and Sr. Cooper had arrived on Saturday from Moravia, Iowa, to be stationed at Friedland. Bro. Henry Cooper kept the meeting.

Thurs., Dec. 7. Very unpleasant in the morning. This being the day recommended by the President of the United States as a day of public thanksgiving and praise, divine worship was conducted at 10 A.M. by Bro. Rob. Schweinitz, Bro. Bahnson being prevented by indisposition. The attendance was not very large.

Sun., Dec. 10. In the evening Bro. Emil Schweinitz kept singing and prayer meeting, in which he announced to the congregation that Bro. Bahnson had received and accepted a call to be permanent pastor of this congregation, and that Bro. Grunert will assist as much as his other duties will allow him to do. He is called as Mitprediger [assistant pastor] in addition to his being Mitinspektor [assistant Inspector of the Female Academy].

Mon., Dec. 11. Bro. Bahnson kept prayer meeting. According to a plan adopted that another ministerial brother is to offer up the concluding prayer, Bro. Emil Schweinitz did so.

Diary of the African Church in Salem, 1865
[Extracts transcribed; handwriting is that of Maximilian E. Grunert.]

Sun., Jan. 1. At 2 o'clock a respectable and soon increasing congregation met. The exercises consisted in singing, prayer, and an address, after which I called upon Peter (Fries) to lead in the closing prayer. No white people were present.

Sun., Jan. 8. The congregation was not quite as large as usual, a number of the regular attendants having gone to Friendship, where the funeral sermon of a black boy was preached.

Sun., Feb. 5. Those from a distance seem to come almost better than those quite near. There is some encouragement in seeing those who have walked for several miles to enjoy the meeting.

Sun., Feb. 19. The Sunday school is often very poorly attended, yet the teachers keep on. Srs. Rebecca and Hannah Stauber have given up, compelled by failing health. Sr. Maria Crist has taken charge of the class of men, sr. Hermina Foltz of the boys, sr. Hannah Blum of the older [girls], and sr. Christine Petersen of the little girls.

Sun., Mar. 5. 1st in Lent. No meeting, owing to the funeral of a member of br. Grunert's family.

Sun., Mar. 12. Sunday school and preaching on Matt. 26:49-50.[1] The attendance was not very large.

Sun., Mar. 19. [T]he 3 brn. Alek (Vogler), Ben (Zevely), and Lewis (Mickey) were reappointed elders or helpers for another year.

Sun., Mar. 26. The members had prepared a lovefeast. The holy communion followed, of which 42 colored communicants (not all members of our church) and about 10 white guests partook. Afterwards a pretty general shaking of hands took place.

Sun., Apr. 9. Palm Sunday. The meeting was at 7 P.M. After address and prayer the reading of the acts of the last days of the Son of Man was commenced. The congregation was large.

Mon., Apr. 10. Owing to the arrival this evening of Gen. Palmer with 3 regiments of Federal cavalry, no meeting could be held. The excitement, etc., in consequence prevented the meetings on Tuesday and Wednesday evenings also.

Thurs., Apr. 13. Reading at 7 1/2; the congregation was very small.

Fri., Apr. 14. Good Friday. Meeting at 2 P.M.; well attended.

Sun., Apr. 16. Easter. Prayed at 9 A.M. the Easter Morning Litany in the old graveyard, read afterwards the acts of the Resurrection and preached on the subject of the day to a large audience.

Sun., Apr. 23. A good many men but comparatively few women were present.

---

[1]The passage reads in part: "And forthwith he [Judas] came to Jesus, and said, Hail, master; and kissed him. And Jesus said unto him, Friend, wherefore art thou come?"

Sun., Apr. 30. A number of our people attended the quarterly meeting in Winston, yet there was a tolerable congregation.

Sun., May 14. No meeting, as a regiment of U.S. cavalry came to town this afternoon, and the colored people wished to see them.

Sun., May 21. 5th after Easter. The church was crowded with colored people, and a few whites, it having become known that the Rev. Mr. Clark, chaplain of the 10th Regt. Ohio Cavalry, would speak. The services were opened with singing, whereupon br. Grunert offered prayer. Mr. Clark then read his Text, 1 Cor. 7:21,[1] and after a few remarks on the circumstances of the church at Corinth, proceeded to read two general orders from Genl. Schofield, dated Headquarters of the Army of the Ohio, Raleigh, N.C., etc., which the Provost Marshal had desired him to communicate to this congregation. In the first it was made known that according to the proclamation of the President of the Un. States the slave population of this state was now free. The second contained a number of regulations establishing temporarily the relations of this freed population. He then proceeded to give them good advice, told them that now they would have greater responsibilities, and encouraged them to industry, honesty, and piety, etc. Br. Bahnson closed with a few remarks, the Lord's prayer and singing. May this great change turn out to the eventual wellbeing of these people, and the furtherance of the kingdom of God among them.

Sun., May 28. The S. School was numerously attended, showing the necessity of more teachers. For preaching a very large congregation had assembled, which was addressed on the subject of our Lord's Ascension. The stopping of the meeting for colored people in Winston had bro't a good many into our church today. Some 40-50 remained for a private meeting for the members of the church.

Sun., June 4. Read after preaching to the congregation a letter, addressed to them by br. F. R. Holland, and received a few days ago.

Tues., June 13. This evening Rev. Mr. Clark, chaplain of 10th Ohio Cavalry, preached on Luke 13:24 to a very large

---

[1]"Art thou called being a servant? care not for it; but if thou mayest be made free, use it rather."

audience, especially towards the close. Br. Grunert took part in the exercises.

Sun., June 25. At 2 a meeting was held intended for the communicants only, but largely attended by others also. These having been dismissed, the Lord's supper was administered to about 50 persons, a pleasant and blessed service.

Sun., July 23. The heat being very great, there was neither a large attendance nor for the most part much attention.

Sun., Aug. 20. S. School was numerously attended. Several large cards, and also books, granted by the Sunday School Union, Philadelphia, and which had come to hand during the past week, were used for the first time. Sr. (John D.) Siewers, and Reg. Vogler entered as teachers. Today a funeral sermon was preached in memory of Anna Laws(on?), who had died in June 1864 near Bethabara, of which congregation she had been a member from infancy; of her daughter Sophia, died Feb. 1865, a communicant member of the church; and of her son Jake, who had been shot during the war near his home near Bethabara by order, I believe, of Capt. Wilson, C.S.A. The text was 2 Tim. 3:15. The congregation was quite large.

Occasion was taken to point out to the colored people the necessity of taking a decided stand, and for that which is good; the view also of cursing and taking the Lord's name in vain, which is indulged in, by some at least, to a fearful extent, was specially mentioned and testified against.

Sun., Sept. 24. The S. School was kept at 1 o'clock as usual. At 2 a meeting was held with prayer and an address in reference to the Lord's supper. After a short recess the Holy Communion was administered to 28 colored persons, and not even all of these were members of this church. The Lord made it a blessed hour to a number at least, as they told me afterwards. But it is evident that a number were prevented from coming by nothing, and that considerable coldness prevails.

Sun., Oct. 1. After meeting, the case of Alek (Vogler), who some 10 days ago had a difficulty and was somewhat tipsy, was disposed of. On his expressing willingness to ask pardon, myself and the helpers thought, the matter might be dropped now.

Sun., Oct. 15. The Sunday School was encouraged by receiving a donation of books from the North thro' Mr. John Tinson, superintendent of the Sunday school of the North Baptist church, Camden, N.J., who several weeks ago had paid us a visit. Afterwards br. Jacob Siewers preached on the words, "Adam, where art thou?" [Gen. 3:9].

Sun., Nov. 19. After S. School a circular from the Super-intendent of the Freedmen's Bureau in Charlotte was read to a large congregation, explaining various matters and giving good advice. Br. Friebele being present, he was called upon to address the congregation, which he did at some length. The exercises closed with the singing of the doxology.

Sun., Nov. 26. [After the service] Br. Henry Cooper, who was present, made some additional remarks. As he had been active in the S. School years ago, the Negroes were glad to see him again. The congregation was moderate.

Sun., Dec. 3. S. School and preaching. . . . Afterwards meeting for the members, some 17 attending. Urged the necessity of stirring up the members to be more awake to their duties.

Sun., Dec. 10. The number of children present was un-common, probably preparatory to Christmas. After preaching, the rule about burying on the Negro cemetery was explained, viz.: Members and their children free of charge; others may obtain permission upon paying $2.50 per grave, and are then expected to keep it in order. The congregation was pretty good.

Sun., Dec. 24. At 11/2 P.M. the Christmas celebration took place. The day being very unfavorable, slippery, icy, and wet, but few were present, perhaps 90. Little books and cards were distributed among the S. School scholars, after the programme had been gone through.

[Inserted in the Diary is a loose leaf sheet dated Dec. 31, 1865. It states:]

The colored division of the church has passed this year through a severe ordeal. The sudden change from a state of servitude to freedom could not but have a very great influence upon those affected by it. Although of those connected with the church a limited number only left this neighborhood, yet it would appear as if the restlessness created by the emancipation and the desire to find comfortable homes of their own selection had withdrawn attention measurably from the care for their souls. No less than six communicant members have departed this life. With unwearied care a number of white sisters have continued their efforts to instruct the ignorant, and the regular ministrations of the word were sometimes well, at other times indifferently, attended. The number of communicant members at the close of the year is somewhat uncertain; as many as fifty are yet on the catalogue.

Board of Elders of Salem Congregation, 1865
[Extracts of minutes transcribed.]

Wed., Jan. 11. Br. F. absent.
The want of brethren willing to teach in Sunday school is severely felt.

Wed., Feb. 8. Br. F. absent.
Br. Bahns. mentioned that he had been asked by one of the colored brethren, whether something could not be done to have the order of the Mayor revoked, by which the social prayer meetings, which they for years had held among themselves, were forbidden. The Board was of opinion that these meetings might have been allowed to go on; but that if, as is alleged, the State laws prohibited them, this Board, of course, could not enforce permission. Br. Bahns. will speak with the Mayor on the subject.

Wed., Feb. 22. Br. F. absent.
[B]r. B. stated that the Negroes had commenced again to meet for prayer at Dr. Zevely's, sr. Z. having become responsible for the meetings.

Wed., Apr. 19. Br. F. absent.
3. Under existing circumstances to pray publicly for the President of the Confederate States was not considered proper. The 2 prayers in the Litany, in which that functionary is mentioned, may be left out, or an extempore prayer offered in place of the Litany at the discretion of the brother who officiates.

Wed., May 3. Br. F. absent.
The [Congregation] Council has re-elected br. Fulkerson as a member of this Board.
3. The want of any provision in the sisters house to assist helpless old sisters in preparing food, etc., was spoken of in connection with the situation of sr. Christina Lick.

Wed., June 7. Br. F. absent.

3. Jane Smith has become a mother. The father of her child is not known. She must be excluded; the announcement need not to be at once.

4. As we are again under the government of the United States, and have also a Governor appointed over us, the original prayer in the Litany for those in authority will be used again. It was suggested to use it every Sunday for the present.

Wed., July 26. Brn. R. Schweinitz and Fulk. absent.

As there is no gas, and great scarcity of other light, the Sunday evening services will be held at an early hour, for the present at 7 P.M.

Wed., Aug. 9. Br. F. absent.

[T]he remark was made that by next Sunday the chandelier would be hung up again in the church; the English communion will, then, be had at night.

3. As there is now again some probability to obtain the services of a regular organist, it was resolved that the Board of Trustees be asked what sum they would feel justified to appropriate as a salary under present straitened circumstances.

Wed., Aug. 16. Br. F. absent.

[I]t was mentioned that br. A. Meinung had begun last Sunday to help out in playing the organ.

Wed., Aug. 23. Br. F. absent.

2. As sr. L. Bagge intends going shortly on a protracted visit to Bethlehem, it appears necessary to charge someone meanwhile with the superintendence of the sisters' house. Srs. Betsy Blum and Hanne Lisel Shultz were proposed, and in case they both should decline, Rebecca Stauber.

3. Various plans were proposed to introduce again singing of our tunes in the boys' school. Nothing, however, seemed unobjectionable, and finally it was agreed upon to ask br. Meinung whether he would be willing to teach the boys in their school room for half an hour a week as was done formerly.

Wed., Aug. 30. Br. F. absent.

[I]t was mentioned that both sr. Blum and br. Meinung are willing to undertake the charges mentioned.

3. As there is now a prospect to get gas into the church again, the weekdays' evening meetings will not begin till then, provided it does not last too long.

Wed., Sept. 27. Brn. R. Schwtz. and F. absent.

3. The Board of Trustees is willing to pay $100 a year to an organist, with the understanding that the payment is made when the diacony will have sufficient funds to do so. The Board would not make an appointment at present.

Wed., Nov. 29. Brn. R. Schwtz. and F. absent.

6. The appointment by the P.E.C. of br. Bahnson as permanent minister of Salem, as a necessary consequence of the action of the late Provincial Synod in abolishing the office of President of the P.E.C. as a separate salaried charge, was laid before the Board.

Mon., Dec. 4. Br. F. absent.

[T]he president stated the object of the meeting, namely to pass upon the appointment laid before the Board last Wednesday, and in connection with it the appointment of br. Grunert as Assistant Minister with certain defined duties, agreed upon between P.E.C. and himself. The Board consented to both the appointments.

Sat., Dec. 9. Br. F. absent.

The meeting was called for the purpose of passing upon the application by the Board of Trustees to have a meeting of the whole adult congregation, communicants under age being also invited, before which the financial condition of the diacony and sustentation is to be laid with a view of obtaining aid, agreeably to a resolution of the late Provincial Synod. The Board agreed to have such a meeting given out for next Thursday evening.

2. Br. Bahns. stated that the Board of Trustees had agreed to the appointments spoken of at the last meeting, of which the congregation will now be informed.

Board of Trustees of Salem Congregation, 1865
[Extracts of minutes transcribed.]

Thurs., Jan. 19. Not present the Brrn. E. A. Vogler and Theod. Keehln.

1. The question in relation to the Pottershop and Lot, having now appeared as unfinished business on the minutes since Sept. 27, 1864, Board resolved, altho' again not full, to proceed in the case. The motion was consequently made and seconded: "That the Pottershop and Lot be now put into the market, i.e., let it be known that the house and lot is now for sale." The reasons urged for now disposing of this property and contrary to the so frequently renewed resolutions of this body not to part with it as long as the war continues were the dilapidated condition of the buildings, the uncertainty when the war will end, and the almost certainty that when it terminates the country will financially not be in a better condition than at this time.

After an interchange of opinions and ideas on the subject, the vote was taken and resulted in the adoption of the resolution by four against one. It was next resolved that the property be put up at public sale on Saturday, March 18th, and that a notice to that effect be put up forthwith at the house in order to give publicity to the resolution now passed, so that should any one who may have had an idea of purchasing this property be at a distance from here, he can be informed of it by his relations or friends.

Tues., Mar. 14, 1865. Not present Br. Theod. Keehln.

1. Next Saturday the 18th inst. being the time appointed for the sale of the Pottershop and Lot, Board proceeded to determine certain points preparatory to said sale. . . . 4th. The purchaser is to give a note with approved security. The note to be due twelve months after date, whenever demanded, payment of principal and interest to be in specie, gold or silver. The deed for the lot [is] not to be made until the note has been paid. Possession of the property can be given as soon as the terms of the sale have been complied with. 5th. Board by a majority of vote resolved that the minimum price of this property be put at $2,000. Should no sale be effected on the day appointed, it is understood that the property remains in

market at the same price and can be sold privately to any one that hereafter is willing to comply with the conditions.

Thurs., Apr. 13. Not present Br. Theod. Keehln.

Board was called together for the purpose of deciding an application from Br. C. L. Banner to rent the Parsonage, now unoccupied, in order to live in it with his wife and daughter during the continuance of the unsettled condition of the country, the seat of war having now gradually approached nearer to us and a Federal force having in the course of the present week made a stay of 24 hours in Salem, during which time Banner's house had been visited by straggling soldiers that had committed some depredations on his property, thereby greatly alarming his family. He intends bringing only one or two servants with him, and if at any time the house should be needed for a minister, will cheerfully give it up.

Board advise Br. Banner not to leave his possessions and move to town with his family but to remain at home, as no private property had been molested by the enemy in town during their stay, and are of opinion that if Br. Banner had himself remained at home, instead of hiding in the woods, thus leaving his family unprotected, no injury would have been done to his property.

Fri., Apr. 14. Not present the Brrn. C. Cooper and Theod. Keehln.

The advice of the Board has been communicated to Br. Banner, but he requests a re-consideration of his application of yesterday, stating that his wife and daughter are in such a state of excitement and alarm, owing principally to an occurrence that took place at the house of his neighbour, that he considers it his duty to provide another home for them for the present. Board upon this second application granted the request of Br. Banner, not from the conviction that it would conduce to the safety of his property, but in order to quiet the minds of his family.

The house applied for being more or less taken up with boxes containing goods belonging to Br. Holland that could as yet not be sent to him, and also with furniture of different kinds, Br. Banner can only have the use of such part of the house as will not be required to keep the boxes and furniture, neither can he use any part of the garden, that being already planted by Br. Bahnson and others. Owing to the total derangement of the currency at this time, the question about the rent to be paid by Br. Banner was for the present left undetermined.

Tues., May 9. Not present Br. E. A. Vogler.

Congregation Council having on the 2nd inst. re-elected Br. J. Gottl. Seitz and chosen Br. John D. Siewers in the place of Br. Theod. Keehln, Board met and organized by electing S. Thos. Pfohl as President and Secretary.

With reference to minutes of May [Mar.] 14 it must now be stated that the pottershop and lot was bro't by Mr. John I. Nissen, who has complied with the conditions of the sale and taken possession of the property, Mr. John Wimmer having left the house.

Br. Banner has not found it necessary to remove his family to town as contemplated.

3. The financial crisis expected for some time already having now, by the fall of the "Southern Confederacy" and consequent worthlessness of all Confederate currency and stocks, burst upon the country, and other kinds of paper currency being at present of very uncertain value, it will be most advisable in closing the books of the different Diaconies (the time for which has now arrived) not to take or make any payments, but simply to enter the different charges and credits on the proper accounts, deferring all cash transactions till the value of the currency has again been properly adjusted. The amount of Confederate notes in the hands of the Warden and belonging to Salem Diacony at the time when it ceased to be of any value is $314.55.

Tues., June 20. Not present Br. C. Cooper.

1. Br. Christian Thos. Pfohl applies for two town lots in Winston situated on corner of Cherry and (Winston) First Street, with the intention of building a dwelling house on them so soon as circumstances will permit. The lots applied for are under resolution of the Board of Trustees of July 22, 1863, §2, now to be considered as secured to the applicant under the further provisions contained in said resolution.

2. The Warden and Forester having on account of depreciated value of the Confederate currency sold the green limbwood broken down by the ice in January last at 30 cents for a

one-horse load and 60 cents for a two-horse load, it would appear as not altogether just to demand the same prices now since the Confederate currency has come out of circulation and a better one is beginning to take its place. It was consequently resolved to reduce the price of this kind of wood respectively to 20 cents and 40 cents for the future and also to extend the benefit of this resolution to such persons as have not yet paid for their wood.

4. No dividend having been received within the last fiscal year from the Bank of Cape Fear on the two shares of stock into which the legacy of $200 from Br. Em. Shober, given in trust to the Warden with the proviso that the profits arising therefrom should "be applied in aid of keeping up an efficient nightwatch in Salem," have been converted (See minutes of Town Committee [Aufseher Collegium] Oct. 9th, 1848, §5), Board is of opinion that it can not reasonably be expected that Diacony should out of its own means pay interest on the $200 thus invested when they have not yielded any profit. The whole of the profits arising from this fund have regularly been paid to the Town Commissioners since the incorporation of the town.

5. On July 1st next 11 coupon bonds of $100 each on Forsyth County belonging to Single Sisters Diacony will become due; but as no new investment of the money could be made, and as moreover it might perhaps not be desirable under present circumstances to take the kind of money that would be offered in payment, it was resolved for the present not to demand the money, but to leave it with the County even tho' no interest will be derived from it after the bonds are due.

Wed., Sept. 13. Not present the Brrn. Joshua Boner and N. Blum.

2. Board of Elders is desirous of again appointing a regular church organist, and wishes to know whether it can offer him a salary of $100 a year (the same that had been paid some years since). Board of Trustees does not object to the salary, but does not know when it will be able to pay it under the present state of affairs.

3. In consequence of the abolition of negro slavery in the United States, the words "or whose master or mistress is a member of the Moravian Church at Salem" are to be stricken out from Resolution 1st of the Rules respecting the burying of negroes on the new Negro Graveyard, so that hereafter only

members of the Negro Church are to be interred in that graveyard free from extra charges. (See minutes of Board of Trustees
Mar. 20, 1860, §3.)

Tues., Oct. 24. Not present the Brrn. N. Blum and J. D.
Siewers.

1. By suggestion of the Pastor of the Negro Congregation
Board resolved that for the present only $2.50 instead of $5 be
charged for a grave on the negro graveyard for a person not
belonging to the church, as it is presumed that the negroes will
not be able to pay the full amount, their earnings being now
used up for arranging their household affairs.

2. The accounts of Salem Diacony for the year ending
Apr. 30th, 1865, together with a statement of its assets and
liabilities on that day, were laid before the Board, from which
it appears that the disbursements exceeded the receipts by
$151.63 after having deducted $1,800 from House account,
and added $200 to Salem and $183 to the Winston Town Lot
Fund. Through Profit and Loss account $769.89 had to be can-
celed, that amount having been lost on Confederate money
partly as discount in exchanging old for new issues, or as cash
on hand at the end of the war when money became worthless.

The financial condition of the country being such at
present that no income whatever is derived from the capital
invested by the Diacony, amounting to $30,791.65, and the
Warden consequently not being able to meet even the common
expenses for church purposes, Board resolved to make an
appeal in the name of all its elected members to the members
of the Church to exert themselves in paying a least part of their
Church dues, if they are not able to pay them in full, and
thereby enable the Warden to defray the necessary expenses. A
printed copy of this appeal is to be handed to every contributing member of the church, together with his yearly
church accounts.

3. The accounts of the Single Sisters Diacony were next
communicated to the Board and showed a deficit of $837.95
occasioned by the enormous amount of taxes, viz., $1,100.97,
that had to be met by this Diacony, when the whole of its
income during the fiscal year amounted to only $804.23 and
after its expenses had been materially curtailed, according to
the resolution of this Board of Oct. 25, 1864, §2.

Tues., Nov. 7. Not present Br. Joshua Boner.

1. A subscription taken up last year to defray the expenses of the lovefeast at the married people's festival having been signed by the individuals in the expectation of paying the sums subscribed in Confederate currency, not having been collected immediately, was charged on the yearly accounts; it was resolved that, since the sums subscribed have now to be paid in a better currency, to reduce it in each case to 1/4 of the sum subscribed.

3. The members of the so-called "Church band" (composed of the blowers of wind instruments at funerals, etc.) ask to be furnished with some firewood from the Diacony land for their use when practicing on their instruments on winter evenings. They expect to cut it themselves. Board is willing that they should have it.

Wed., Dec. 6. Not present Br. Joshua Boner (at Raleigh).

3. A communication from the Prov. Elders Conference was laid before the Board of the following import, viz., that Prov. Elders Conf. had made the following appointments: Br. Bahnson to be minister of Salem and Br. Grunert to be what is called in German "Mit Prediger," with the understanding that, being Vice Principal of the Salem Female Academy and having, as such, a variety of duties to perform, he can only take upon himself the following obligations:

1st to attend to the coloured congregation, not promising, though, that he can visit such members as live out of town, but confining his principal activity to the church building.

2nd to attend to the Sunday school as long as it shall not interfere with duties to the coloured congregation.

3d to preach once a month.

Br. Grunert wishes the Board of Trustees to understand his position, lest more be expected of him than he is able to perform.

A communication was also received from the Board of Elders of Salem Congregation to the following effect: In regard to the appointment of Br. Grunert, the Board of Elders would beg leave to say that they should regret it very much if the "Parsonage" were rented out to strangers, or occupied by any one but a servant of the church. The reasons are various, but among the rest its contiguity to the church building. They would therefore suggest that Br. Grunert have the privilege to move into it, which he desires to do. There would appear to be little or no objection to this, for on the part of Salem Female Academy there is a willingness to rent out the house occupied at present by Br. Grunert and allow the Sustentation fund to receive the net profit of the rent, which would probably amount at least to as much as would be procured by renting out the parsonage.

Tues., Dec. 19. Not present Br. J. Boner.

The minutes of last meeting were read and approved.

A numerously attended meeting of the communicant and adult members of the Congregation, spoken of last time, took place on Thursday, 14th, when the financial condition of Salem Congregation and of the Wachovia Sustentation was presented to those present. It appearing from statements then made that Salem Congregation has failed to make up by contributions the necessary church expenses, including the salary of the Pastor, sundry other salaries of persons employed by the church in various ways, expenses for lighting, warming, cleaning and repairing the church and keeping the graveyard in order, amounting to about $900 a year, the accounts showing for the last 8 years a deficit of about $360 a year on an average, which loss was canceled by Salem Diacony. But in as much as owing to the financial embarrassment under which the South is labouring at present, its resources are now rendered unavailable and may remain so for an indefinite time, not to mention the heavy losses that it will eventually sustain; it becomes absolutely necessary that the members of the Congregation exert themselves more, in order by their individual contributions to meet all the church expenses. As according to the rules of Salem Congregation it is made the duty of the Board of Trustees "to fix the amount of church contributions to be annually paid by the members," the meeting had resolved that the matter be referred for arrangement to said Board, the members present pledging themselves, with but a few dissenting voices, to abide by and carry out whatever arrangement the Board of Trustees should see proper to make in the matter. In order to assist Wachovia Sustentation in its present need, it was resolved by the meeting that a subscription for voluntary contribution be opened and taken round by some Sisters to be appointed for that purpose, and that in addition, a monthly collection be taken at the Church door for the benefit of Wachovia Sustentation.

Pursuant to the above resolution of the meeting of last Thursday, Board of Trustees now proceeded to make such alterations in the contributions of the church members as circumstances seemed to require, and resolved that the following be the established rates, viz.:

a married couple pays ....$8.00 a year
married brethren whose wives are not
 member of the church, widowers
 and single brethren over 21 years of age pay ....$4.00 a year
and married sisters whose husbands are not
 members of the church, widows and single
 sisters over 18 years of age pay.......................$2.00 a year
(instead of heretofore respectively $4.25 and $2.25 and $1.10) by which rates according to the number of members at this time belonging to the Church about $1,000 will be raised in a year.

It was further resolved that in order to make payments more convenient for the contributions and to afford a more constant supply of money to the Warden, these contributions be hereafter collected *quarterly*, instead of yearly, as heretofore, and that a separate Collector be appointed for the express purpose of attending to this matter.

More than one half of the fiscal year, beginning May 1st of each year, having already expired, it was resolved that as soon as practicable the dues for the 6 months already passed be collected according to the former (old) rates and that the new regulations begin with the 2nd half of the fiscal year on Nov. 1st, 1865. The quarterly collections are also to include the lovefeast account, but rents, interest, poor fund, school account, and other incidental charges are not to be embraced in them, but will be collected once a year as heretofore. It is further understood that Congregation dues and Lovefeast charges are no longer to be entered on the personal accounts of the church members in the books of the Diacony, but must be paid in cash, and will only be entered to the credit of the respective Church and Lovefeast accounts when the amount due has been actually received.

On Lovefeast account a debt of upwards of $230 has accumulated in the course of years, which by the action of the Board of Trustees of Nov. 7, 1865, §1 (see minutes), will be considerably increased. It was consequently resolved that hereafter the actual cost of each lovefeast be ascertained immediately after it has taken place and the amount be divided among the members of the Church.

Provincial Financial Board, 1865
[Extracts of minutes transcribed.]

Thurs., Nov. 9. All present.

2. Board authorized the Treasurer to procure textbooks for 1866, per mail from Bethlehem.

3. The annual accounts of the Treasurer of Wa. Sustent. Diac. from June 1, 1864, to May 31, 1865, were submitted. The total amount of receipts were $3,417.84 and of disbursements $4,192.29, showing a deficit of $774.45. The assets amount to $41,508.33 inclusive of N.C. Coupons and deposit in Salem Savings Institute. The actual liabilities are $3,362.72. The Provincial Fund is $32,926.83 as heretofore, and Fund Account $4,748.78. Smaller funds amount to $470. Of the assets the present value of a large amount is very uncertain and very considerable losses must be looked for.

Tues., Nov. 28.

The Financial Board met this evening for the first time to organize [following Synod]. Members composing the Board are the three members of Wa. P.E.C., G. F. Bahnson, Lewis C. Rights, and E. A. de Schweinitz, and the three members elected by the Provincial Synod held this month, viz.: Brrn. E. A. Vogler, Sam. Thomas Pfohl, and Robert de Schweinitz. Br. G. F. Bahnson was appointed Chairman, Br. S. T. Pfohl Treasurer of Wa. Sustent. Diacy., and Br. E. A. de Schweinitz Secretary.

2. A resolution was offered and passed unanimously that "the Treasurer be authorized to sell coupons of Old N.C. State bonds, not exceeding $500 in value, in view of the approaching end of the quarter, to meet his most pressing liabilities and necessities."

Bethania Diary, with Bethabara, 1865
[Extracts transcribed; handwriting is that of Jacob F. Siewers.]

Mon., Jan. 9. After night it rained very hard. Alexander Grabs bro't up sick from Florence by Wm. Stoltz.

Tues., Jan. 10. Lightning and thunder, showery all day. The water courses are very high.

Wed., Jan. 11. At home. I have been suffering since New Year more or less from neuralgia.

Fri., Jan. 13. Opened the ditch on the back street to drain the lots and cellars opposite the parsonage.

Fri., Jan. 20. Hauling leaves for the ditch on back street, which after covering with plank, were put on top and then filled up again with earth.

Sat., Jan. 21. This morning every object around was encased with ice, the heaviest sleet I remember of, and as the rain gently falling served to thicken the crust of ice, it began to break the branches of the trees and caused a constant cracking and crashing all around. Our streets were at places impassable for vehicles.

Fri., Jan. 27. The thermometer fell to 8 degrees this morning but it was wind-still and exceedingly cold. The Committee were called together. Present: H. H. Butner, Joseph Transou, Levin Grabs, Willm. Lehman, and Nathaniel Pfaff. The cause of meeting being to reconsider the terms on which several of our neighbors desire to bury their dead on our Graveyard.

([Bethania Committee minutes:] It appeared that a strong feeling of dissatisfaction prevailed on the conditions of the Committee. It was urged that the widows, at least some of them, had not the gold or silver to pay for the burial of the dead and no how during the war. Br. L. Grabs, Joseph Transou, and Nathaniel Pfaff and Harmon Butner declared their willingness to stand security for the payment of the above. The Committee then agreed to wait for the payment until after the war, and that gold or silver or its equivalent would be exacted and required.)

Sat., Jan. 28. Br. S. Levin Grabs and Joseph Transou resigned their seats in the Town Committee. The latter br. returned the Graveyard funds to me.

Fri., Feb. 3. Mrs. Benj. Hauser called to know about her son's burial at our graveyard.

Tues., Feb. 14. Today I was to preach the funeral of Nerva Hauser and Isaac Shore, Br. Bahnson was requested to preach the funeral of Alexander Shore, and Rev. Solomon Helsebeck was to preach the funeral of William Shore. The above four persons were brought here from Virginia to be buried on our graveyard. Owing to the burial of br. Thomas Spach at Bethabara, I went there, and br. Bahnson officiated at Bethania in my stead. Preached the funeral of br. Thomas Spach at Bethabara on Gal. 3:1, good attendance. [B]r. S. was our Steward, a member of the Committee and for some time manager of the Sunday School held there in the church. He was the most active member of the congregation, but am sorry to add, that for the last 12 months he was but once present in the church if my recollection serves me right. The cause, I suppose, was an objection to my views on the war, he being a strong advocate thereof.

Wed.-Sat., Feb. 15-18. At Salem. Our little grandson Frederic departed on Monday evening the 13th at about 6 P.M. On the 17th our little grandson was buried. The delay was owing to the weather. Returned on the 18th.

Mon., Feb. 20. Whilst I was gone to Salem, the cattle and hogs broke down the fence on the lot opposite, which I repaired today.

Wed., Mar. 8. My 60th birthday. Augustus Oehman helped me in hauling leaves in my stable, and afterwards a load of chips. Afternoon he went to Thomas Kapp's mill for my corn and corn chop, but he got mired the other side of the ford, and the horse breaking the swingletree, he left the carriage. I went to work to replace it by a new one but could not finish it.

Thurs., Mar. 9. Finished my swingletree and went and hitched the horse. Martin Briggs, coming along, was neighbor to me and helped me turn the wheels which were nearly hub deep in mud, and so Pete pulled out.

Fri., Mar. 10. Prayer and fast day. Prepared for service, rang the bell, but only one person coming, I dropt it.

Mon., Mar. 13. Commenced spading in my garden.

Thurs., Mar. 23. This was a remarkable stormy day, the fences in town were shattered and blown down. Repairing my fences.

Sat., Mar. 25. At home working about my premises.

Sun., Mar. 26. [C]alled at br. Peter Pfaff's, the old man is braking fast. Br. Sol. Pfaff was there likewise, having returned yesterday from Raleigh.

Fri., Mar. 31. Planting in my garden. Afternoon went out to br. Thomas Kapp's, got 2½ bushels of corn, too many before me to get my chop. Great excitement about the Yankey-raid.

Sat., Apr. 1. Great excitement, reports of a strong Yankey-raid in the adjoining county.

Sun., Apr. 2. Preached in Bethania at 10 A.M. on John 19:1-7. I did not go to Bethabara, the excitement I thought filled all hearts.

Mon., Apr. 3. Went out to br. Thomas Kapp's and got 2½ bushels corn chop, 1 peck corn meal, and 1 peck coarse hommony for little chicken's food. Afternoon worked at a martin-box.

Tues., Apr. 4. Wash day. Finished my box and put it up.

Sat., Apr. 8. About home sawing and splitting wood. Afternoon some exciting news came that the Yankeys were advancing.

Sun., Apr. 9. Palm Sunday. Preached in Bethania at 10 A.M. on John 19:28-30. During the day various reports were bro't to town. In the evening we held the usual reading of the Acts of the Son of Man.

Mon., Apr. 10. At early candle light we met in church and continued the reading, and when near the close, the announcement that the Yankeys were in town broke up the meeting. When I went in front of the parsonage I perceived the street full of cavalry, and heard that the town was in the possession of Gen. Stoneman's command estimated at 4 or 5 thousand horsemen. In a short time, I saw our Pete taken by the well. I went up street, and finding the General's quarters, I stated my case to him. He replied that if I could identify my horse, I should have him. This I stated was out of the question as I could not see well in the night, and among so many horses there was no chance of finding mine. He was very busy and I left. After some time he sent for me, and said that they had pressed a Negro of the town to pilot them to the Shallow-ford on the Yadkin, and if he knew my horse and Dr. Mock's, he should bring them back in the morning, and to do this he wrote an order for our horses and told us to give it to Nathan. But our search for Nathan was fruitless; the soldiers had taken him off. The army left between 11-12 o'clock, doing us no further harm, for which we felt thankful to the Lord.[1]

Tues, Apr. 11. The state of the minds of all was such that upon consultation it was determined to drop the meetings of the week; every family was fearful of leaving home.

Wed., Apr. 12. Sr. S.'s limb being very sore and painful, I went after dinner to br. Thomas Kapp's to get a little whiskey and upon returning about 5 P.M. I found the town in possession of a detachment of Gen. Stoneman's army numbering some 125 or 150, but on ascertaining that I was a citizen of the town I was permitted to pass on. Before night they left for the Shallow-ford.

Thurs., Apr. 13. Maundy Thursday. The surrender of General R. Lee, commander of the Army of Virginia, having occurred on the 10th unto Gen. Grant, commander of the U. Sts. forces, the soldiers of Gen. Lee's commenced passing through the town, calling nearly at every house for something to eat. This continued during the week. The meetings were in consequence dropt.

Fri. Sat., Apr. 14, 15. Continuation of the passage of the Army.

Sun., Apr. 16. Easter. Counselled the members of the Committee; they agreed to drop the meetings. The travel of soldiers continues.

Mon.-Sat., Apr. 17-22. The travel continues, 6 and 7 hundred per day.

Sun., Apr. 23. Preached in Bethania at 10 A.M. on John 11:25-26.

Mon.-Sat., Apr. 24-29. Worked in my garden.

Sun., Apr. 30. Preached in Bethania at 10 A.M. on John 20:26-31. Sr. Edwin Pfaff was immersed by Virgil Wilson this day at Pfafftown. Preached in Bethabara on the above.

Mon., Tues., May 1, 2. Working in my garden.

Mon.-Sat., May 8-13. Working in my garden and getting wood.

Tues., Wed., May 16, 17. Hauling wood.

---

[1]In the Bethania Memorabilia of 1865, Christian Lewis Rights wrote: "Gen. Stoneman made his quarters with Br. Elias Shaub, and after remaining some three hours to rest and partake of refreshment, the whole body moved on towards Salisbury. The greatest inconvenience from this unexpected visit to the citizens in town and the surrounding country was in the loss of horses."

Thurs., Fri., May 18-19. Sawing and splitting wood and work about premises.

Mon.-Wed., May 22-24. Working in my garden, etc.

Thurs., June 1. Humiliation, Prayer, and Fast Day. The day was observed. Preaching at 10 A.M. on 2 Sam. 3:31-38. Good attendance from the country.

Sun., June 4. Whitsunday. [B]aptized the infant son of William, formerly Lash's servant, and Matilda, formerly belonging to Edwin Speace; name William Isaiah. Administered in the church.

Mon., June 5. Cut down the limbs of the trees before the church that were injuring the roof. Afternoon br. Reinhold Oehman arrived from the West.

Thurs., June 15. A request had been made for an appointment for the Rev. Mr. Clarke, chaplain of the 10th Ohio Cavalry Regiment, at present stationed in Salem, to preach here in the church at 10 A.M. Mr. Clark preached here as above on Matthew 13:33 to a large audience of white[s] and blacks.

Fri., July 14. Hauling fire wood from the church land.

Mon., July 17. Wm. Lehman went with me, and traced the lines of the church land.

Sun., July 30. After dinner Sr. S. went with William Ackerman's son to Salem. She had not been down there for some 4 months. He bro't up br. Wesley Kearney from Salem. Egbert Lehman also returned this morning, also John Kapp.

Thurs., Aug. 3. Did not go to [Ministers] Conference, was tired of walking and the weather very warm.

Fri., Aug. 4. Got br. H. H. Butner's horse and went to Salem, and bro't mother home by night.

Wed., Aug. 9. At night 3 mountain boys called on us, 2 of David Easter's and 1 Edwards', took supper and lodged in the hay loft.

Thurs., Aug. 10. The young men left after breakfast for home. Walked to Salem. Started to br. Thornton's, met him 6 miles from Salem and returned with him. His description of the Fry horse caused me to abandon the idea of getting him. Br. Bahnson proposed my taking him on trial. Returned home as far as Bethabara with John Shore's wagon.

Mon., Aug. 14. Visited the sick. There are 4 sick at Lash's cabins with typhoid feaver.

Tues., Aug. 15. Made a new horse trough and repaired the stable.

Thurs., Aug. 17. Went to Salem this morning with Elias Schaub. Br. Thornton brot the horse up, and I took him in charge and returned by night.

Sat., Aug. 19. This morning I heard of little Lizzy's death, one of mother's most promising S.S. scholars, at about 2 A.M. She was the daughter of Sandy and Betzy. I visited them day before yesterday and had no thought she would die. Conversed with her, she was about 10 years of age.

Wed., Aug. 23. Went to Samuel Stoltz's to buy some corn, but he had none to spare.

Tues., Aug. 29. Received a letter from Jacob, with one from Joseph.

Wed., Aug. 30. Met Alfred Stoltz on the way to the North.

Thurs., Aug. 31. This morning Mr. Snow left with Logan for the mountains.

Sat., Sept. 2. Visited the sick at Lash's quarter, conversed and prayed with them. At early candlelight Sr. S. and myself went to Lash's quarter, and I held a prayer meeting by request of one of them.

Tues., Sept. 5. Visited the sick at Lash's quarter. Paid Wm. Leinbach's an evening visit. Beautiful moon light.

Thurs., Sept. 7. This morning I went early to br. Willm. Leinbach's and got his horse, brought him home, and went to Salem. The horse done tolerably well until the last mile, then I feared he would not hold out; but I was enabled to attend [Ministers] Conference. Partly to give the horse rest, and partly to enable Margaret to get ready to go home with me I postponed my return to morrow.

Fri., Sept. 8. This morning I left Salem with my daughter Margaret for home, and after clearing the village I determined to walk and spare the horse, being satisfied that the horse had not strength sufficient to travel well. I left him walk his own gait the whole way. We arrived at Bethany about 1/2 past eleven A.M. Having fed the horse, I took him home and spent the afternoon there taking supper with the family.

Sat., Sept. 9. This morning the cows having broken into our lot opposite us, I had to repair it. Gathered my corn in the lot for fear the cows would destroy it, as the fence is and has been in bad condition for several years, and I have had considerable trouble on that account.

Sun., Sept. 10. Children's Festival. Afternoon the children had their lovefeast (in the old style). The children sang a hymn,

"Hark my soul," etc., and during the partaking of cake and coffee I addressed the children. . . .

Mon., Sept. 11. Visited Sr. P. Stoltz, but was prevented from speaking with her as I would desire. Conversed some with Mary K., giving her good counsel. This morning a young man came to request me to preach the funeral sermon of his brother who died of a wound received at or near Winchester, Virginia, during the war; his name is Bevel and has a brother living in Winston, Forsyth Co. He desired the service at the [New] Philadelphia Church, as most convenient to the relatives. I promised to do so, nothing preventing, if Br. E. Schweinitz, the pastor, was willing, on the 2d Sabbath in October.

Thurs., Sept. 14. This morning Augustus Fogle came up from Salem and bro't a letter from br. Bahnson with a call from the Northern P.E.C. and approved by the Southern P.E.C. to New Salem, Illinois, as pastor of the English part of the congregation.

Sat., Sept. 16. Went in company with my daughter Caroline to Salem. Called at br. Bahnson's and informed him of my acceptance.

Wed., Sept. 20. I had received an appointment from the Postmaster General, as Postmaster of Bethania which I could not accept and had to decline and recommend someone in my stead.

Thurs., Sept. 21. The election of delegates for Convention took place today. Lash and Starbuck 74, Johnson and Teague 21. Total 95 votes.

Tues.-Fri., Sept. 26-29. Preparation for leaving.

([Margin note:] *Sun., Oct. 1.* At 10 A.M. preached my farewell sermon on Heb. 2:3. Afterwards the following Brethren were elected as Committee of Bethania: Joseph Transou by 12 votes, Nathaniel Pfaff by 13 votes, Elias Schaub by 10 votes, Thomas B. Lash by 8 votes, William Lehman by 8 votes, Thomas Kapp by 10 votes. Steward: S. Levin Grabs by 13 votes. Reinhold Oehman unanimously as grave digger. There being 14 brethren present.)

[Handwriting is now that of Christian Lewis Rights.]

Sun., Oct. 15. Sunday. A missionary Baptist minister (Mr. Devon) preached at Bethany today.

Wed., Oct. 25. Brother Chr. Lewis Rights and family, the future pastor of Bethany and Bethabara, arrived this evening.

Tues., Nov. 14. Went to Salem to attend the adjourned Provincial Synod of the Southern Province. Wednesday, Thursday and Friday attended the Synod.

Sun., Nov. 19. [At Bethabara] elected a Committee: Christian Hauser, steward, Henry Fogle, John H. Shore, and Lewis Hine.

Mon., Nov. 20. Went to Salem to attend the Synod. Considerable discussion in reference to protracted meetings, etc.

Tues., Nov. 21. Synod continued. Constitution amended. P.E.C. elected: Brother Bahnson, Emil de Schweinitz, and Chr. Lewis Rights. Then Synod adjourned *sine die.* Afterwards the P.E.C. organized, and brother Bahnson elected chairman. A resolution was passed by the Synod that a Committee of three delegates be appointed to wait upon the different churches and inform them of the financial condition of the Church, the Sustentation fund having sustained a loss of about Twenty Thousand Dollars by the war, and try and influence [them] to make more exertions to maintain their ministers. The delegates for Bethania are E. A. Vogler, John G. Sides, and Allen Spach, and William Leinbach and they are to be here on the 3d Sunday in December and also at Bethabara in the afternoon.

Sun., Dec. 10. This morning a messenger came to inform me that brother H. Butner had had another severe attack of his old complaint during the night and it was thought he was dying. I went down and found him unconscious, but Dr. Mock, who was present, said he would recover again. At 1/2 past 10 the Rev. Mr. Conder of the Lutheran denomination preached a sermon on baptism from Eph. 4.5: One Lord, one Faith, one Baptism. The sermon lasted about two hours and a half, and was listened to with marked attention by a large congregation. In the evening visited brother Butner, found him better and prayed with the family.

Sun., Dec. 17. At 10 o'clock the brethren E. A. Vogler and Allen Spach came to our house, brother Sides having come up the evening before, as the committee appointed by the President in accordance with a resolution of the Prov. Synod, Brother Wm. Leinbach, the delegate from Bethania, being likewise included in the committee to lay before the congregation the financial condition of this Province and to urge upon the members the necessity of making the necessary efforts to support their minister.

Before preaching, the delegation visited the Sunday School and were entertained by the children by the singing of several hymns, and then the School was closed by singing the verse "from us all while we remain," in which all joined with a zest which made one feel that it was good to be there. And the church bell ringing for service, the congregation assembled, and although the morning was unfavorable, the attendance was quite good. After singing and prayer and an address by Brother Rights, the committee was introduced, and brother E. A. Vogler proceeded to lay the work before them. He was listened to with great interest, and when he was through the matter was freely talked over in a brotherly spirit, and the final conclusion was to meet on Christmas day and take up subscription and see what can be raised.

In the afternoon the brethren visited Bethabara in conjunction with brother Lewis Hine. Here too the people seemed to be interested in the matter and agreed to meet day after Christmas and see what can be done.

Mon., Dec. 25. On [account] of the unfavorableness of the weather it was proposed to postpone the meeting of the [Bethania] heads of families in order to devise some plan for the support of the minister till New Year's night.

Tues., Dec. 26. [H]ad a meeting [at Bethabara] for the purpose of determining upon some plan to raise something towards the support of the minister. A subscription was started and $51.50 were subscribed.

Sun., Dec. 31. [In Bethania] the heads of families met in the School House and after some consultation it was agreed to start a voluntary subscription and see what could be realized. The sum of $185 was subscribed. As the evening was so unfavorable several of the members were not in town. During the lovefeast and the last meeting several pieces were sung from the choir under the direction of brother William Leinbach, who has been found willing to lend a helping hand in this interesting department of Moravian worship. The brass band was also in attendance.

Friedberg Diary, 1865
With Hope till October, then with Macedonia and Muddy Creek
[Extracts transcribed; handwriting is that of Christian Lewis
Rights.]

Sun., Jan. 1. [T]he subscription was renewed. My income
for last year was $185.00.

Tues., Jan. 9 [10]. Last night it began to rain and rained
until about 2 o'clock this afternoon accompanied by thunder
and lightning. The rain came down in torrents, and Southfork
was said to be higher than it has been in thirty years.

Thurs., Jan. 11 [12]. I went to Salem. The bridges on Southfork are all washed away and also on Muddy Creek, and the
Salem bridge is down, and it is said a great many Rail Road
bridges are washed away. This will be remembered as the great
freshet in January 1865.

Sat., Jan. 21. The heaviest sleet that there has been known
for years. A great many limbs and trees are broken off.

Sun., Jan. 22. On account of the ice no one came to meeting.

Wed., Feb. 1. A beautiful warm day like spring. The roads
are getting dry.

Tues., Feb. 7. Snow and ice.

Sun., Apr. 9. Palm Sunday. Owing to the unsettled state of
the country, the Committee thought best to omit the evening
readings during the week.

Tues., Apr. 11. This morning some wagons drove up and
reported that a body of the Federal Army were at Salem, came
there yesterday evening, and that the town had been surrendered. The wagons belonged to Mr. Augustus Reich and Mr.
C. L. Banner, and their black men said they were trying to save
their horses. Of course there is great excitement in the country.

Thurs., Apr. 13. Owing to the excitement in the country I
did not go to Hope but went to Salem. Found that the Federal
army had gone by way of the Shallowford towards Salisbury,
where there was heavy cannonading yesterday and last night.
The Federals had done no damage in Salem more than the
breaking up of the machinery of Mr. Fries's Woolen Factory
and taking all the horses in and round Salem and Bethany and
robbing Mr. John Alspaugh of several hundred dollars in gold
and his gold watch and brother Henry Perril of his horse. At

Salem I encountered about 2 hundred of Wheeler's Cavalry, Confederate, and they took the Salisbury road near Friedberg, where they stole a number of horses during the night. Heard at Salem that Gen. Lee had surrendered his army at Amelia Court House in Virginia. When I came home I found that Federal Scouts had taken supper at our house.

Fri., Apr. 14. Good Friday. Services at Friedberg: Reading, Lovefeast, and Communion.

Sun., Apr. 16. Easter Sunday. At 1/2 past 9 o'clock read the Litany on the graveyard, then preached from John 21:9. In the afternoon service at Hope.

([Friedberg Report:] *Wed., Apr. 26.* Visited Brother Trougott Spach, who has just come back from Petersburg. Found him quite sick.)

Sat., Apr. 29. Heard today that Gen. Johnston of the Confederate Army had surrendered near Greensboro in this state to Gen. Sherman of the Federal Army on the 26th inst., which ends the war in this part of the country. Lee surrendered on the 9th of April.

Sat., May 6. The Single Sisters celebrated their festival today. There were 46 present. From 9 till 11 o'clock, speaking in the room; at 11 an address in the Church; afterwards lovefeast and Communion and another closing meeting constituted the services of the day. The sisters seemed to enjoy themselves, although our coffee was made of rye and sweetened with homemade molasses. The cakes were furnished by Sister Solomon Hage and were excellent in quality and ample in size, and during a four-years war we have never dropped a lovefeast nor was there ever a stint in the size of the cakes.

Sun., May 7. After preaching [at Hope] went to brother Christian Sides; found his son William very sick with typhoid fever. He was taken sick on his way home, and between Kernersville and Waughtown he gave out and had to lay down by the side of the road. His companion, a Georgian, went on to his father's, and told him to send for him, and brother Sides went and brought him home.

Sat., May 27. Communion at Friedberg. ([Friedberg Report:] Brother Eli Sides, who has been a prisoner of war at Camp Chase in Ohio and came home a few days ago, was present.)

Sun., May 28. Preached the funeral of Alson Pinckston, infant son of Alexander and Louisa Mock, from 1 Cor. 13:12. ([Friedberg Report:] The child died the 24th of November 1862 during the father's absence in the army. For the last 12 months he has been at Hope in Indiana, where he attached himself as a member.)

([Friedberg Report:] *Mon., May 29.* Visited Brother Harrison Crouse, who has just returned from Point Lookout, where he was a prisoner. He is suffering very much with acute rheumatism, and has no use of his lower limbs.)

Sun., Aug. 6. Theodore came home today.

Sun., Aug. 13. Celebrated the festival of the day. [T]here was Lovefeast with good coffee and Communion.

Sun., Oct. 22. Preached my farewell sermon at Friedberg from 2 Tim. 4:6: The time of my departure is at hand. . . .

Wed., Oct. 25. Moved to Bethany.

Sat., Oct. 29. Brother Bahnson introduced me to the Bethany Congregation as the Pastor by an appropriate and feeling address. I then preached from Romans 15:30. In the afternoon there was a welcome Lovefeast kept by brother Grunert, during which he gave the people of his former charge a faithful address. There was a good congregation in attendance, and quite an interest was manifested in the services, and the people seemed particularly pleased to meet with the two brethren who had been their former pastors. For myself, it was one of the saddest days of my life, and I was thankful when it was over. Immediately after dinner brother Bahnson had an interview with the Committee, and reminded them of the duty to the minister and the congregation.

[The handwriting is now that of R. Parmenio Leinbach.]

([Friedland Report:] *Sun., Nov. 5.* Br. Bahnson introduced Sr. L. and myself to the Friedberg congregation. Preached my introductory sermon from Rom. 1:16.)

Sun., Dec. 10. The delegates from Synod were here: Brn. John Siewers, Elias Vogler, Nathaniel Blum. After the meeting with church members was over I practised the scholars in singing. 'Twas 4 o'clock when I sat down to dinner.

Fri., Dec. 15. In the morning went to Salem after my surplice.

Sat., Dec. 16. Communion Day at Friedberg. About 100 communed. 'Twas bitter cold—5 fires kept going. Lizzie Watson, a girl whom we had staying with us, left us one day and carried off several burial sheets, large and small, communion tablespread, ribbons, etc. We have replaced all the things. It has cost us about $10.00.

Mon., Dec. 18. The brn. J. Burk, Levi Padgett, Edward Foltz out gathering moss this evening. A number of brn. working at the decorations.

Sun., Dec. 24. It rained very hard all day. Not a soul came to meeting. The trees were covered with ice.

Mon., Dec. 25. Christmas Day. The house was crowded. After preaching came the Children's Lovefeast, during which the Sunday school children sang the hymns "Golden Rule," "Happy Day," "No rest here," "I want to be like Jesus." This meeting was followed by another, in which the children recite verses, and receive cards with another verse for the next year.

Fri., Dec. 29. Br. Wm. Shore and H. Rominger were here today to put in window panes. I am much exercised these days about a schoolhouse to be built on Br. Daniel Spach's land. I want it to be built on Church land and make a parochial school of it so as to be under the control of the Church, whereas the brn. think differently and prefer to have it a public school house. It's a clear case what will become with the house. It will be used as a preaching place by other denominations, and here they will have their protracted meetings right under our noses.

Private Diary of R. P. Leinbach, 1865
[Serving Friedland, Macedonia and Muddy Creek; extracts transcribed.]

Sun., Jan. 1. [W]ent on to Macedonia, stopping at Hall's awhile. There was but a small congregation present.

Tues., Jan. 10. Rain all day. The cellar was flooded; the creek rose; water was higher than had been known for many years. The Salem Bridge was broken down, and bridges all over were washed away. Sides and Hanes bridges on Muddy Creek were almost the only ones remaining on that romantic stream. The river was very high. Several bridges were washed along the railroad track. Was busily engaged these days in mending my boots and shoes.

Wed., Jan. 11. Pumping and carrying water out of the cellar.

Tues., Jan. 17. [A]t Rev. Mr. Ferrabee's. He gave me good advice about manner of speaking.

Wed., Jan. 18. Returned home. Learned that Fort Fisher had been taken by the Yankees.

Fri., Jan. 20. Was awakened about 2 o'clock in the morning by a messenger from Mr. Hine's, requesting me to come down to see him. He was very sick with measles and did not expect to recover. ([Friedland Report:] Eli Hine had contracted the measles while in the army at Kinston.) Found him better; conversed and prayed with him.

Sat., Jan. 21. It rained all day and froze as it fell. Trees and limbs broke down and fell to the ground from the weight of ice. The roads were everywhere much obstructed by the limbs of trees.

Sat., Jan. 28. Went to the river. The weather was most intensely cold. Thermometer 8 and 10 in the morning. The wind was very fierce. Could not cross the river on account of the ice.

Sat., Feb. 11. Took Mother to Edith Rothrock. Coz J. Fishel had been shot as deserter near her house and was there. This winter I have been very busy; but the time has passed pleasantly and under the circumstances I may say happily. I have always had pleasant times in anticipation, which has sweetened every toil. Political matters are slowly culminating. Sherman is near Branchville. Peace propositions and armistice died out.

Mon., Feb. 13. We were all busy preparing a box to send to Julius. 'Twas an immense thing.

Tues., Feb. 21. ([Macedonia Report:] Called to see Radford Miller, son of Br. Jonathan Miller, a member of the Junior Reserves. He was very sick and did not expect to recover.)

Wed., Feb. 22. ([Macedonia Report:] Called again to see R. Miller. He had been engaged in the first attack on Fort Fisher, where he had signalized himself as much by his daring wickedness as by his bravery.)

Thurs., Feb. 23. Called to see Calvin Riddle, who had been taken suddenly sick.

Sat., Feb. 25. Rode out to Liberty for sundry purposes; had John cleaned. Sherman is said to be near Charlotte. He's a wonderful man. 'Tis rumored that part of Stoneman's Command is near Statesville. The people along the N.C. Railroad are said to be terribly exercised about the Yanks. I suppose they think the day of retribution now has come. The prisoners are removed from Salisbury. Over in Davie some of my friends are much reduced in spirit; they think negroes and general property as well as personal are all gone, that the Federal Government will sell them all out, and let them and their children starve, or do worse. They are generally suffering much anxiety—i.e., the Secesh. It has been raining and drizzling all day; snow is pouring down. No mail for the last day or two. The stage has twice been stopped to release deserters.

Tues., Feb. 28. Was working in my oats all day long. Thrashed and put it up. Had my type[1] taken.

Wed., Mar. 1. Saw Dr. Kee[hln]. Times are very sad and distressing. He tells me he was stopped by deserters some time ago. Some of Morgan's men were here and said a number of them were coming down to this country and would live off of the Union people. Nous verrons. ([Margin note:] N.B.: The war is closed and they have not come yet. Jan. 1866.) All the ports are said to be open now again.

Fri., Mar. 3. Elizabeth and Johnny Sheek were over [from Davie County]; took them to see the curiosities.

Thurs., Mar. 9. The Battalion came to town.

Sat., Mar. 18. Our community was shocked on hearing that David Huff and 4 other men had been shot by order of Capt. Wilson. I was sorely distressed for poor David Huff and his deeply afflicted family, as I believed him to have been innocent of the charge of instigating the expedition for the release of J. Huff, a deserter. To what are we coming? I cannot learn the crimes of the others. "Vengeance is mine, I will repay," saith the Lord.

Wed., Mar. 22. This morning the Battalion went off to H. Point. I should not like to be in the place of their infatuate commander.

Sat., Apr. 1. Went over to Mr. E. Davis after oats on my way to Macedonia. Took dinner at his house. On my arrival at the River, I found ten or twelve army wagons on the other side, fleeing from the "Yankees." They were said to be up at Yadkinville. I went on over and found the whole community marvelously exercised about the Yankees. The people of means were busily engaged all Saturday night and Sunday in burying and hiding away their provisions and moveables. There was to have

---

[1]Tintype. R. P. Leinbach's brother, Henry A. Leinbach, was a photographer in Salem.

been a large congregation, but so great was the panic that but few were present at meeting.

Sun., Apr. 2. Spoke at Macedonia on Eccles. 8:8 to a small congregation. Went to Br. Sheek's, and whilst others were being terribly exercised I slept after dinner, for I was completely and thoroughly exhausted. Staid all night at Br. D. Sheek's.

Mon., Apr. 3. Returned to Salem. The country still in a tremendous panic. Everybody everywhere about half-witted— excepting, of course, myself. There were scouts along the road all the way from Greensboro to Shallowford. Entre[n]chments were thrown up at Puryear's plantation and grand preparations, on a small scale, made to repel some 4,500 Federal cavalry. Tuesday *400* Confederate Cavalry arrived at Salem, but the Yanks, no doubt hearing of the state of affairs, wisely turned towards Virginia. After my return home I broke up the Irish potato patch.

Sun., Apr. 9. Preached at Friedland—Palm Sunday.

Mon., Apr. 10. A day not soon to be forgotten by the people of Salem. A portion of Gen. Stoneman's command of raiders made their entree into the town of Salem. John was out on a scout, and was returned about 5 P.M. with the intelligence that the Federals were about the Double Branch. I got on him with my saddlebags stuffed, and went down to Br. Louder's, where I spent a rather uneasy night. Next morning, after tying John out under a pine tree, I started off afoot to see what was going on at Salem. I found the town full of Yankees. They had built a fence across the road at Shepherd's and cut down trees so as to form a species of breastworks from Em. Reich's to Banner's. Contrary to all expectations, they did not interfere at all with private property except horses, and those they swept wherever they came across them. In the evening I went back again. My horse had been neighing to half a dozen other horses around who like him were "bushing it" from the Yankees, who were all thro' the country hunting horses, but fortunately mine had escaped. I found several Philadelphians among the number of Federals. There were a great many men from Ohio, and among them I made the acquaintance of one Capt. Hunter of Champagne County, Ohio, who seemed to be a particularly fine man. The general and staff (Palmer) took up their quarters at the Mayor's office. There were troops on the creek hill, troops in town, troops at the commissary's, troops everywhere. Sentinels were posted all over town and around it, so that no one could get out without a paper. I procured one without any difficulty, and returning to Br. Louder's found all right, tho' my horse had kept up a neighing with 4 or 5 neighboring horses all day long.

Wed., Apr. 12. I learned up at Br. Gibbins' that the Federals would be out again after horses, and so I went back and "bushed" my horse all the morning; at noon Br. Louder sent me word that the Yankees were all gone. But now a new source of trouble arose. A number of Confederate or Rebel Cavalry came to Salem and went all thro' the country scouring around for cloth, which the Federals had given out, and stealing horses wherever they could find them.

Thurs., Apr. 13. Maundy Thursday. I started off this morning with Br. Louder to go to Salem, but on the road I learned the Rebels were cruising and raiding all round for horses and that there was too much danger in going to Salem, so I flanked the town by way of Laughenour's mill[1] and left my horse at Br. F. Burkhardt's and came to town. All was quiet in town, tho' there were cavalry men about. Attended Communion that evening; there were six *Brethren.* There appeared to be a gloomy pall settled over the whole community. It was reported that Gen. Lee had surrendered his army to Gen. Grant, and this was confirmed by the reports of such men as came in from time to time.

Fri., Apr. 14. This morning I walked out to Br. Burkhardt's after my horse. Several cavalry men had tried to stay there the previous night, but Sr. B. would not take them in. Had she done so, probably my horse would have gone with them. Every road I came to I watched first very narrowly to see whether any cavalry men were out. I felt more like some criminal escaping from justice. After more or less roundabout riding I arrived at Br. Louder's, where I learned that he had not undertaken to go to Salem, but had turned back and gone back home. As it was Good Friday, I went on to Friedland to keep the meetings of the day. Alas! what a time it was to celebrate the day. The country was in a pitiful condition; bands of soldiers straggling thro' the country, some stealing, others borrowing, some taking openly; the people uneasy and anxious, some few at work, others

---

[1]Laughenour's mill was on the site of the first Salem mill, about two miles southwest of town on Salem Creek.

hiding their horses, and none able properly to appreciate the solemn season which we were striving to observe. Contrary to expectation, there was a goodly number of souls present. I preached on the subject of the day, after which I read the history of our Saviour's suffering and death, and followed with the administration of the Lord's supper. About 14 souls communed.

Sat., Apr. 15. Was at Br. Louder's all day in dread of horse thieves. Came to town about 10 A.M. in company with some soldiers—McCayne and Brubaker of Huntsville.

Sun., Apr. 16. Easter Sunday. Walked to Friedland, went on the graveyard and preached on subject of the day. Walked back in the evening. Capts. Barlow and Rogers came to town to impress, or more properly, to steal horses. It was reported that Vaughn's army was coming thro', and in consequence John was taken and put in Aunt Regina's cellar for safekeeping. Puss was in Father's leather cellar, and Pet in James' basement story. ([Friedland Report:] On account of the danger of traveling the highways, I remained at home the two following Sundays, and always carried arms with me whenever I used my horse during the week.)

Mon., Apr. 17. Was downtown all day.

Tues., May 2. Two years since Ferd. Hall and C. Clauder were slain.

Sun., May 7. Went to River but could not cross. The ferry boat had been sunk. A notice posted up aside of the road read as follows: "Wheeler's cavalry has damaged my boat, so that it has sunk, so no crossing. J. Hall." To which someone had added: "Bad as he is, the devil may be abused, be groundlessly charged and causelessly accused. Pilgrim." On our return, we had to go all the way to Uncle G. Spach's before we found any-one at home. They too had had a terrible time down there with the horse thieves, several horses in the neighborhood having been stolen.

Sun., May 14. Went to Friedland, preached from 2 Kings 5:1. On my return, I found the town fully occupied by Federal Cavalry. The 10th Regiment Ohio Cavalry, of Gen. Kilpatrick's command, was sent here for the protection of the citizens of the county. The Colonel's headquarters were at Mr. Hege's, whilst the doctor of the Regiment and others were located at Br. James' domicile.

Mon., May 15. My birthday. Thirty-four years old. Another year has passed away, and with it the Southern Confederacy. What a fall!!! The rumor is that Jeff Davis has been caught in female attire in Washington, Ga., and in that apparel was taken on to Washington. Nous verrons. Davis, etc., bushing it, and Sherman's army in N. Carolina, a regiment in Salem and a part next door neighbors—will wonders never cease! Went to Friedland and hoed my potatoes. 'Twas very warm and dry. For weeks we have been looking for rain and none comes. The ground is hard and ploughing in places very difficult.

Tues., May 16. Hoeing potatoes. At Capt. Hine's last night.

Fri., May 19. At home. Resting. The whole week I have been unwell, felt very weak, limbs aching. Every labor so fatigues me. But we live in the midst of exciting times. Lincoln assassinated; Davis captured in his wife's clothes; Booth slain; Vance arrested; and thus goes the Confederacy.

Sat., May 20. Flag raising at Winston. Went to Br. Foltz's.

Sat., May 27. At Salem. The 10th Ohio still encamped above here. The tents, horses, wagons, campfires look quite picturesque. I have become acquainted with a number of the men and am very much pleased with them. One of the number, Jonas Thatcher, a member of the Methodist church, is a very consistent man, and calls in from time to time.

Sun., May 28. Br. J. Thatcher and his bunkmate accompanied me to Friedland. In the afternoon Rev. Mr. Clark, chaplain of the 10th Ohio Cavalry, preached for us from Hebrews 1:2 to a very large congregation. He was a very friendly man, and everyone seemed to be much pleased with him.

Thurs., June 1. Preached at Friedland on the occasion of fast and prayer day proclaimed by Pres. Johnson in consequence of the murder of Abraham Lincoln by John Wilkes Booth. Psalms 39:4.

Fri., June 2. At home. Mr. Thatcher with me. I rode his horse yesterday.

Mon., June 5. Went to Moxville, took Br. R. Sheek. A number of us took the Oath administered by Capt. Sug.

Fri., June 23. Henry Siddall came home today. Poor Julius still at Point Lookout.

Sat., June 24. Mother is quite sick with flux.

Sun., June 25. My hand or rather finger gives me trouble. Mr. Swink took me down to Friedland. I first had prayer meeting followed by preaching. Sergeant Thatcher was present and offered up a prayer. Much feeling.

Thurs.-Sun., June 29-July 2. These days I am doing nothing but nursing my hand. It has commenced running.

Tues., July 4. James went to High Point and bro't Julius home at last. Mother still sick. She has been lying on the lounge now for several days. She is much better than she was a few days ago. The Yankees are celebrating the day in full style—drinking, fighting, shooting cannon, blowing their hands and fingers off, and behaving badly generally. Col. Saunderson made a very able speech this morning. My friend Thatcher, Co. C, 10th Ohio Cavalry, keeps himself out of all such scrapes. He calls regularly to see me.

Thurs., July 6. Mother still continues very weak. The prescribed remedies do not appear to produce any results. Still sleeping and unconscious. Mrs. Belo is to stay tonight, together with the members of the family. Drs. Keehln and Shaffner are attending upon her, but their united skill appears unable to do anything for her relief.

Fri., July 7. About 3 A.M. Julius came up, aroused us with the expected but dreaded intelligence that Mother was dying. We hastened down, but she had slightly recovered herself. The doctor was sent for; he told us she would probably last until morning, perhaps until ten o'clock. In the hours of early dawn, Br. Bahnson was sent for; he came and imparted the blessing of the church in the German language. About a quarter before eight she quietly and gently breathed her last. As she had been in life, so she was in death—quiet, peaceful, gentle. We have lost the best of mothers.

Sun., July 9. ([Friedland Report:] Rev. Mr. Clark, chaplain of the 10th Ohio Cavalry, preached the funeral sermon of David Huff, who had been shot by members of the 1st N.C. Battalion and buried at Friedland. His text was taken from Numbers 23:10, and was treated with ability and feeling, but when he left the spiritual and went on to the political part of his discourse, he seemed to bid farewell to reason. He dipped into secession, negro slavery, treatment of secessionists, and in short all possible affiliations of secession. I remonstrated with him afterwards on the subject, but he protested against there having been any mention made of politics at all.)

Mon., July 10. It is reported that the 10th Ohio Cavalry, which has been encamped near Salem for a long time, is under marching orders. Tho' I am much attached to some few of the men, I should be truly glad to see them leave.

Tues., July 11. Married Elijah Simms of the 10th Ohio Cavalry to Miss Augusta Fetter at the house of the bride's mother.

Thurs., July 13. The 10th Ohio Cavalry has really left town this morning, sack and pack. Br. Thatcher is still remaining here a day or two. He was to leave his favorite, Bell, here in my hands, but I don't know how to manage the matter. I cannot procure another horse to carry him to Lexington.

Fri., July 14. I have made arrangements by which I shall be able to retain Bell.

Sat., July 15. Mr. Thatcher went off today at noon. He left Bell in my hands. Last night I took a blue pill at a friend's suggestion, and it has worked me pretty considerably. I was in bed all the afternoon in consequence.

Sun., July 16. I undertook to go to Muddy Creek, but was too feeble and did not get farther than Br. Foltz's where I climbed on the hay loft and remained until the family returned home. I remained there all night. . . .

Wed., July 19. Went to Friedland after a load of oats. On my arrival there I found to my consternation that a quantity of it had been abstracted. I had written to Br. Gibbins, requesting him to to come and haul it up for me, but when I discovered it was being stolen I resolved to take it all home. I hauled another load in the afternoon, tho' Br. Gibbins, according to request, bro't it all into the hay loft for me. I was much exercised these days for my potatoes at Friedland, fearing someone might come and remove them, or rather a portion of them. Someone has taken about 9 bushels out of Mr. Moses Steward's patch and thoroughly emptied Mr. S. Weevil's. As I am able to do so very little on account of my hand, I have time to knock around, and yet I am not stout nor strong, and mental application is as difficult as physical.

Sat., July 22. Birthday. ([Margin note:] Spent the afternoon with my darling. What a happy time we had. My darling dressed my finger for me.)

Mon., July 24. Br. Julius and I went up to Shamel's, leaving Bell there.

Tues., Aug. 1. At home writing. My hand is just becoming so that I am again able to use a pen. I received a letter today from cousin Mary Irwin. It did me much good to hear from my old friend, and about my old friends and acquaintances again.

Times are changing somewhat. Money is scarce and goods comparatively plenty. Wheat has turned out very badly; indeed it is almost an entire failure. Our flour must be brought from the North. Corn bids fair to do very well; the fields look very pretty, so fresh and green. Potatoes are also promising handsome yields.

Fri., Aug. 4. Helped get Edw.'s potatoes out. The Yankees had thinned them out so, there were not more than about 30 bushels. Sorted and put mine away in James' cellar.

Sun., Aug. 6. Preached at Macedonia to a full house. Remained all night at Br. Richmond Sheek's. About 1 o'clock A.M. the fleas drove me out into his oats shed, where I slept until day. This is now the second time they have played me such a trick. On my return home in the evening, we hauled a load of apples from the field. I found an elegant present from coz Mary awaiting me. It consisted of a dressing gown and a pair of slippers.

Sun., Aug. 27. Commenced our protracted meeting at Friedland. Sr. Rights was with us all day, and someone abstracted her umbrella during service.

Thurs., Aug. 31. The meeting continued again all day long. We had intended bringing the meeting to a close this morning by prayer meeting and communion. But so many mourners came forward it was impossible and we kept up meeting all day late into the night. Several previous evenings the meetings had not gone so well. We ascribed them to the influences of the manner in which the service had been conducted by Br. Berry. But on Friday [Sept. 1], under Br. Rights' conduct, everything worked very well.

Thurs., Sept. 14. Went up to coz George Shamel's after Bell.

Fri., Sept. 15. Returned home. She is much improved, tho' she will not work well.

Sat., Sept. 16. Was out riding with company with Miss Sallie Blum.

Tues., Sept. 19. Received a call to go to Friedberg. Br. Siewers has received a call to go to West Salem, Illinois. Br. Rights has received and accepted a call to go to Bethany. I am very much exercised about it, as the Friedlanders are so loath to give me up and the condition of the church at present is a very interesting one.

Sun., Sept. 24. Prayer meeting at Friedland, and preaching from [blank]. I announced the changes that were to be made;

my poor people seemed to be really distressed, tho' they were hardly more disturbed than I was.

Mon., Sept. 25. Saw Br. Rights in town; had long conversation with him. He was greatly exercised about the changes. Had he known the feelings of his people, he would have declined the call.

Mon., Oct. 2. Went down town and found folks busy baking cakes and fixing generally.

Tues., Oct. 3. This evening I was *married to Miss Sarah Ann Blum* at half after seven in the evening by Bishop Bahnson. There were a number of people at church (being public), and all our relatives and a few particular friends were down at the house. All seemed to enjoy themselves very much.

Wed., Oct. 4. At home in the morning; took a ride out to Liberty.

Thurs., Oct. 5. At home enjoying the happiness of realizing that I was a married man.

Mon., Oct. 9. Went to work at the sugar cane business. Several of our sisters helped us in the sweet cause. Allen and Silvia had helped some the week previous, and I still kept the former. I am living at my dear wife's home, and a sweet home it is for me.

Thurs., Oct. 12. Still working at the sugar cane. We have been engaged in stripping cane using Mr. Hege's machines, invented by Br. Const. Hege.

Sun., Oct. 22. In the afternoon [at Friedland] baptized 18 young souls and confirmed 9. . . .

Sun., Oct. 29. Preached my farewell sermon at Friedland from 2 Cor. 4:11. A good deal of weeping going on.

Thurs., Nov. 2. Moved to Friedberg. The brn. J. Walk, W. Shore, Em. Spach, J. Mock, and J. Knauss came up to convey our goods, altho' the weather was very unpleasant, as it was raining most of the time. 'Twas rather an inauspicious day and times, but our hearts were light, and we felt that He who had helped us "hitherto would help us all our journey through." On our arrival at Friedberg we found a number of the brn. and sisters waiting to receive us and having in waiting for us an excellent supper, the fragments and remains of which were principally left with us, serving to supply our table for several days. The rooms had been nicely whitewashed and cleaned, and we found everything in pretty good order. Some repairs will be required, as during the war nothing could be done.

Friedland Reports, with Hope, 1865
[Extracts transcribed; handwriting is that of Charles Henry Cooper.]

Sat., Nov. 25. After a prosperous journey I arrived at Salem.

Sun., Dec. 3. The day previously published as the time of my commencement of public duties at Friedland, I appeared for the first time before that congregation. Bishop Bahnson being physically disabled from attending on the occasion, br. R. de Schweinitz kindly consented to accompany me. On arriving at the church we found many already assembled. It was a source of pleasure to hear the Lord's people speaking in hymns and spiritual songs, singing and making melody to the Lord even before the general service began. Br. Schweinitz introduced the new pastor by singing and a most appropriate prayer and address urging the people to do their utmost to raise their Church to the highest prosperity in every respect. In the hospitality which we then and since have experienced we bear them witness that their love is not in word only but in deed and in truth.

Thurs., Dec. 7. Thanksgiving day. I preached at Friedland. Text from the daily word, Ps. 118:21. Subject: National sins and afflictions and judgments, and national deliverances and blessings.

Mon., Dec. 11. Today we moved to our new home at Friedland.

Fri., Dec. 22. Weather cold but did not hinder the brn. Gibbins and Reed from carrying out their charitable agreement to come together on this day to build me a hog pen. This they carried out in a praiseworthy manner.

Sat., Dec. 23. I visited several members who had been at and taken part in worldly amusements. Other cases of misdemeanors like those above alluded to, of recent occurrence, show how strong are the temptations against which our younger members have to contend. . . .

Sun., Dec. 24. The day appointed for beginning labors at Hope, but prevented on account of inclement weather. I proceeded no farther than br. C. Sides', who thought it unnecessary to go to the church, as in all probability no one would be there. After dining with him and having a profitable conversation about Church affairs, and fixing the 1st Sabbath in every month as the Hope preaching day (the Lord willing), I returned with my brother, who accompanied me, to Salem.

Mon., Dec. 25. Started early for Friedland, but not venturing to cross the creek at Salem, which was swollen by recent rains, I proceeded by Lackenour's mill and did not reach my post till late in the day. I, however, found a large congregation awaiting my arrival.

Sun., Dec. 31. Though it rained fast this evening a very attentive little company gathered in the church. All seemed to enjoy the solemnities of the last service ever to be held in this church in the year 1865.

[New] Philadelphia Diary, 1865
[Extracts transcribed; handwriting is that of Emil A. de Schweinitz.]

Sun., Jan. 8. The weather had been unfavorable and rainy for the greater part of the week since New Year, but cleared away fair on Sat., Jan. 7. Sunday morning was very cold, and the roads, which had been very cut up, were frozen quite hard, so that it was very difficult to get along especially on the hills on both sides of Atwood's creek. Br. Schweinitz reached Phila. a few minutes before 11 A.M. and found a very good audience assembled.

Sun., Jan. 22. Started in my buggy for Philadelphia as usual. But after proceeding some little distance, I found the roads so obstructed by trees and large limbs, and the ice falling from the trees in such continuous showers, that I was forced to return to Salem. In passing thro Salt Street my buggy became entangled in the branches of a tree which had fallen across the street, and had to be cut out by a negro before I could proceed.

Tues., Jan. 31. Heard that Br. Timothy Transou was very sick. Rode out on horseback in afternoon to see him. Found him suffering from a long continued attack of cramp-colic. Prayed with him at his request. Returned home about 5 P.M. In order to induce the doctor to visit him that night, I accompanied him after supper. We got there about 8 P.M., found Br. Transou suffering great pain. The doctor's opiate quieted him very soon. Got home again by 10 1/2 P.M.

N.B. On this day the widowed Br. Martin Rominger of Phila., aged 77 years, was married to Emma [Emily] Davis, a young woman of 22 years. I was called upon to perform the marriage ceremony, but not being at home Br. Bahnson married them.

Thurs., Feb. 2. Visited Br. Tim. Transou in company of Dr. Z. and my brother Robt., who drove us there, because he wanted to see if Laura Transou was ready to return with him. Found Br. Tr. much improved.

Sun., Feb. 5. Br. Martin Rominger and his young wife created a good deal of curiosity among the female part of congregation.

Sun., Feb. 26. Took dinner at Br. Thomas Spach's. In the afternoon drove over to Sr. Frye's with him. Found her still confined to bed but improving. Her son is very ill. Br. Solomon Hege, who is their doctor, was there and intended to spend the night with his patients.

Sun., Mar. 5. There was meeting at Mt. Tabor, and several of the younger members had gone there to hear the new Methodist circuit preacher deliver his first sermon.

Sat., Mar. 18. Went to Phila. to preach the funeral of the boy John Crater, son of the widowed Sr. Sarah Crater m.n. Ketner and her deceased husband Levi Crater. The little boy had had his little finger smashed and nearly cut off by an accident. He seemed to be doing well for about 10 days, was about as usual without complaining. On Sunday, March 12th, he began to complain, and was seized with spasms the next day. The doctor was called, but the lockjaw had taken hold of him, and he died on Thursday evening, the 16th of March, after great suffering. He was a very good little boy, obedient and affectionate. His death caused great grief, not only to his widowed mother and grandparents, who were very much attached to him, but to all who knew him. The church had been occupied by a company of soldiers one night during the preceding week, but no damage was done except a few grease and tallow spots on the floor and pulpit.

Sun., Apr. 2. Dined at Br. Martin Rominger's, where I had an opportunity of becoming acquainted with his young wife. Afterward visited Sr. Frye, who is up again, and Sr. Burkhardt, whose husband is on duty with the home guard. The news of a raid of the ~~enemy~~ U.S. cavalry,[1] which was reported as approaching rapidly, caused considerable uneasiness and excitement.

Owing to the disturbed state of affairs, on account of a raid of Federal cavalry, which took place on Mon., April 10, Salem and the surrounding country being occupied by them for upwards of 24 hours, and the swarming of Confederate cavalry in rear of Federals, and the return of disbanded and paroled soldiers from Genl. Lee's army, it was considered unsafe for a good horse to be on the road. I could not get one to go to Phila. on Good Friday afternoon, April 14, as had been my intention. A few members had, however, assembled, who ascribed my not coming to the true cause.

Sun., Apr. 16. Easter Sunday. Left Salem at 8 A.M. with broken down cavalry horse. Found roads heavy from yesterday's rain. Arrived at Phila. a little before 10 A.M. Found a much larger congregation assembled than I had expected on account of state of affairs. Heard a good account related about the way the members fared during Federal raid. Several lost their horses and had 2 broken down cavalry horses left in their place. Br. M. Rominger suffered most severely. Prayed Easter morning litany at 10 A.M. in graveyard. On my way back [to Salem] met a good many paroled soldiers from Genl. Lee's army going home.

Sun., Apr. 30. The return of the paroled soldiers from Genl. Lee's army causes the increase of attendance among the men. Quite a number of strangers were present. Squads of Confederate cavalry have during the past weeks caused considerable uneasiness and alarm to the farmers, altho' they have not committed any depredations near Phila., as in some other districts.

Sun., May 14. Found regiment of Federal cavalry in town [Salem] when I returned.

Sun., May 28. Quite a number of Federal soldiers were present, some of whom seemed on very friendly terms with the neighbors. Br. M. Rominger has had some trouble with two soldiers and reported them to headquarters.

Sun., June 25. Several Federal soldiers attended church in the morning.

---

[1]The word "enemy" is struck out, and "U.S. cavalry" inserted.

Sun., July 30. Sr. Charlotte Frederica Butner m.n. Burkhardt celebrated her jubilee, being 50 years old today. According to invitation I went out after dinner and found the whole family including Br. and Sr. Burkhardt and children and Mr. and Mrs. Riddle, their daughter, gathered together. Sr. L. Bagge and Hannah and Reb. Stauber from Salem, former companions of Sr. Butner in the Great Girls room of the Sisters House at Salem, were also present. Between 3 and 4 P.M. we sat down to a vesper-table, loaded with various kinds of cake. Before partaking of which, after a few words in reference to the occasion, I called on the assembled company to commend Sister Butner to the continued fatherly care, love and mercy of our precious Lord and Savior, whose she is and who has mercifully led her safely on her pilgrimage for 50 years, by singing some appropriate verses, according to our Moravian custom (we sang No. 594, v. 5 and 8, and No. 863). The afternoon was spent quite pleasantly, and I returned home about 7 P.M.

Sat., Aug. 12. Celebration of Aug. 13th. The custom of celebrating such festival days in the week, altho' it prevents outsiders from coming, always likewise prevents some of the members from attending.

Thurs., Dec. 7. Day appointed by President of U.S. as a day of National Thanksgiving for Peace. The morning was rainy, but it cleared away about 11 A.M. Preached on Ps. 118:21 to a quite a good congregation, considering the state of the weather.

1866

[Prussia and Italy defeated Austria in the Seven Weeks' War and seized territory.

The Federal occupation of the South continued, and the Ku Klux Klan was organized to hamper African American voting. Congress took control of Reconstruction and advocated "Freedmen's rights."

In March the North Carolina legislature adopted a "Black Code," giving African Americans limited rights, but not allowing them to vote or testify against whites.]

Report, 1866
[Transcribed in full.]

To the Brethren of the P. E. C.:

In accordance with the Resolution passed by the Synod of our Church, held at Salem in November last [1865], found on Page 13 of the printed Abstract of the Minutes of said Synod, We the undersigned, who were members of the various committees therein specified, have visited the different Congregations to which we were assigned and now beg leave, after united consultation to submit the following Report.

We ventured upon the work, rather weak of faith in the success of the undertaking, but in reliance on a higher power than Man, on one "who is able to make his strength perfect in our weakness."

We well knew that the present was a most inauspicious time, as the whole country is completely prostrated—no money scarcely to be had, and every one trying hard to secure some wherewith to pay the heavy taxes now due and expected. To make a Cash collection at this time was considered entirely impracticable, and therefore the Subscription Lists were so arranged as to leave the payments to be made at such time within the Year as the subscribers' circumstances would best allow.

We tried to set before our people the true condition of our finances—our present straitened circumstances—and the absolute need of action on their part. We appealed to them that after the most marvellous and undeserved care of protection that had been vouchsafed to us all living in this section of the country, it was our bounden duty, and we should embrace with willingness the opportunity of devoting a small portion of what a kind Providence had spared to us to his service. That our efforts and appeals were not altogether without some effect the sequel will show.

We commenced our labours on Sunday the 10th day of December [1865] on which day we visited the Congregation at *Friedberg*. Knowing the commendable church pride possessed by this next to Salem the largest congregation of our Province, we selected it as the first point to go to, knowing that they could and would do their duty, and that we would ourselves be encouraged and be able to encourage others by referring to the action of their brethren at Friedberg. At our latest advices, Friedberg Congregation had subscribed $300.00 and agreed to farm the open land belonging to the Church for the benefit of their Pastor. We understand there has also been some grain subscribed, but what amount we are not able to state. They likewise on the day of our visit started another list for the benefit of our Sustentation Diacony, which received on the spot about $40.00.

The next Congregation we visited was that of *Bethania*. This congregation had unfortunately permitted political matters to estrange many of the members during the war, and public services at the church were attended by a very few. On the day of our visit, however, although the day was a very inclement one, we were gladdened by meeting quite a number, and there seemed to pervade the assembly an earnest wish and desire to bury past differences in oblivion, and all together to take a new start, and seemed willing and anxious to do their whole duty.

Another encouraging feature we met at this place was their Sunday School, in which the children seemed to take much delight. We learn the subscription at Bethania amounted to about $265.00.

Bethabara, where the first Moravian Altar in all this country was erected, now 112 years ago, was our next point. This congregation has for a number of years past done almost nothing toward the support of its minister. On learning our financial condition and the resolution of the Synod, a universal desire was manifested that their services at Bethabara might be continued, and the pledge given that "they would do what they could." The subscription list received the signatures of a number of friends not members of our Church, and amounted to $51.00. The lists at Bethania and Bethabara combined amounted to about $315.00.

We visited *Macedonia* on the 7th of January [1866]. It was a very rough, cold, and disagreeable day, yet we found a good congregation and the church was pretty well filled. This congregation has services but once a month, and we candidly confess that we did not expect to receive much encouragement, but here as elsewhere our faith was put to shame.

Though we were to say among strangers, we soon were made to feel that we were among Brethren and Sisters, and the desire was expressed that instead of having their services lessened, they wanted them increased, and the promise which we have so often received in our rounds, "we will do what we can," was freely made. The subscription list received on that day some $75 or $80, and with the additions which we know will be made by some who were absent on that day and who we know have the cause at heart, we put down Macedonia at $100.00.

Here at Macedonia we think a good field is open for our Church and one which should by no means be neglected, but looked after more closely as soon as possible.

Friedland Congregation was visited on Sunday the 14th of January, but our visit and object had in a manner been anticipated by Bro. Lowder, who had been at work and who met us on our arrival and announced to us the result of his labours, which we found so gratifying that we could but commend the promptness of himself and his congregation.

A subscription amounting to $100.00 besides the farming of the land by the young men of the congregation had all been arranged, and Br. Cooper, their pastor, spoke in the very highest terms of the kindness and liberality received on all sides from his charge. But what is worth more than all this— we found the congregation fully alive, and one could not be in their midst long before we find, that though to say comparatively poor in this world's goods, *they are rich,* and are "laying up their treasures in Heaven where neither moth nor rust corrupt, nor thieves break through and steal."

Some of us have since visited this congregation at one of their prayer meetings, and from our own experience can say, "It was good to be there."

On Sunday January 21st we went to *[New] Philadelphia.* This congregation since the death of our good old Bro. Fry has been without a stationed minister, but was fortunate indeed in having regularly every two weeks the services of Bro. E. A. de Schweinitz of Salem. He declined receiving remuneration for his services, and thus the congregation had but little to pay for several years past. The congregation is but small yet the subscription list received on that day $60.00.

Hope was visited on Sunday February the 4th. This is we believe the smallest of our congregations at present but we hope will not long remain so.

The day was a very cold and chilly one, and on our arrival at Hope we were chilled if possible still more to see the forlorn, forsaken, and dilapidated appearance of things in and about the church and parsonage. Part it seems had been used as a stable or shelter by cattle, and part a fit abode for owls and bats. Fences [were] all down, the graveyard unenclosed, and in the church-hall some 3 or 4 young people [were] sitting shivering in the cold.

We betook ourselves to gathering sticks and making fires, and before long were comparatively comfortable.

By and by persons began gathering in. Some of the Brethren from Friedberg came over, and by the time Bro. Cooper (who had stopped on the way to visit Bro. Christian Sides, one of the oldest members and who was confined at home on a sick bed) arrived, the church was filled. An excellent sermon by Bro. Cooper was earnestly listened to by an attentive audience composed mostly of young people. We remarked to the audience that we were comparatively strangers, and we were aware that Hope had but few members, yet the unusual proportion of young persons composing our hearers had particularly arrested our attention. We told them that we did not believe that Hope was a hopeless case, and from the time we entered that church-hall our chilliness had doubly worn off, and we felt that renewed exertions ought to be made here, and learning that many of those present were not members of any church, we thought it well worth the effort if even but one of the many young immortal souls before us could be saved, for "there is joy even among the angels of heaven over one sinner that repenteth."

The land belonging to Hope, though only a few acres, we were told produced well and was well worth tending, and a Brother expressed his willingness to farm it provided the fences were rebuilt, and it was agreed upon to meet the next Saturday and repair them. Besides this a subscription of $46.50 was at once made up.

In summing up the amount of the subscription lists we find them to foot up to $961.50, but as there were a number absent at every place, we think we can safely put the total at $1,000.00 besides the farming of the lands belonging to the churches, and which will be of considerable benefit and importance to the ministers.

Finally in reviewing the results of our visits we feel deeply humbled and grateful. We have been every where met so kindly, and been every where so agreeably disappointed [in our original fears]. It has been to us, instead of a task, a pleasure and a delight, and whilst the work has been blessed to our own souls, we hope and pray it has not been without benefit to our congregations and their members.

Whilst the time was very inopportune as regards money matters, it was a good time in another point of view. We believe that the feelings of our own hearts were shared very generally; and that all feel that notwithstanding the marvellous and undeserved care and protection which has been so graciously vouchsafed to our people in the times of trial and trouble through which we have passed, we have all been neglectful, ungrateful, backsliding children, and feel that it is high time to awake from the lethargy and lukewarmness into which we have all fallen. Might we all take fresh courage, "and work whilst it is called today before the night of death cometh, in which no man can work."

Thinking over what the result of our mission has been, even now whilst all has been so cold and dead, what could be done if we would awaken our zeal, and we be visited by a gracious outpouring of God's Spirit upon our congregations? Some of them are now earnestly praying for it! Would that all would as one man opportune our prayer-hearing answering God for this blessing!

The congregations at Hope and Macedonia we would at this time particularly recommend to your most favourable consideration and attention. Hope neighborhood has so many young people that would attend service there, and Macedonia has a live spirit, and the projected new church which they intended to build when the war came on, we believe would soon become a fixed fact if they could have the services of a regular stationed pastor.

Can not another Brother be added to our now devoted and active country ministers to take charge of Macedonia and Hope?

We in conclusion would say that we believe that the future is full of promise, and that rich blessings are yet in store for our little Zion.

Be encouraged! and may the prayers of the whole church sustain you in your labours.

E. A. Vogler)
J. N. Blum)   Visited Friedberg and Macedonia
J. Siewers)

E. A. Vogler)
J. G. Sides)   Visited Bethania and Bethabara
A. A. Spach)

E. A. Vogler)
J. L. Fulkerson)   Visited Friedland and Hope and Phila.

Jesse Mock present at Friedberg
D. Sheek present at Macedonia
W. Leinbach present at Bethania
L. Hein present at Bethabara
J. Lawder present at Friedland
T. Transou present at Philadelphia.

We feel that in duty to you, to the Synod, and to the Church, we can not, we dare not dismiss this report without adding a few words more, and trust that the Brethren of the P.E.C. will not consider us as transcending our duty.

Love to our Church and love to our common Lord alone prompts us to venture to do what we feel a bounden duty.

We have now enjoyed a free interchange of views and opinions with the different congregations, and we believe perhaps saw matters from a different standpoint and had their views more freely given to us than would have been done to our Brethren in the ministry.

You well know and remember what an intense interest was felt in the Synod's deliberations on the subject of protracted meetings and the manner of conducting them and other meetings, etc. We candidly believe and say it, that a different conclusion, and one which was apprehended by some, would have proved fatal to our Church in this Province.

To speak further, in all candour we must say, and that with deep regret, that we find that there is not that feeling of confidence that the churches have the hearty cooperation and approbation of the governing Board that would be desirable and ought to prevail.

Offenses have been given—wounds, deep and sore made— that will take a long time to heal. This is an unpleasant subject and we will not pursue it further; less we could not say, and will close by most earnestly begging, yea entreat, plead, and beseech our Brethren of the P.E.C. that they be very careful and cautious, and if perchance some things may and do occur in some of the services of either of our congregations that does not suit their individual feelings and opinions, that they will deal gently! We have been in great danger!

In all love and respect, do we speak of what we do know, and testify of what we have seen.

Your friends and brethren,

E. A. Vogler	Wm. S. Leinbach
J. L. Fulkerson	Jesse Mock
John N. Blum	Timothy Transou
A. A. Spach	
J. G. Sides	

Memorabilia of Salem Congregation, 1866
[Extracts transcribed; handwriting is that of George Frederic Bahnson.]

Not a few circumstances contributed to make this year—to some of us, measurably—one of temporal trials and hardship. It is true the political horizon had become to some degree more clear. Feelings of harmony and concord had begun to unite us again as *one* nation. But nevertheless the sky was not yet quite cloudless, and at this very moment questions of great importance concerning our real status are undecided, so that hope and fear are still alternating in our minds. And although free intercourse between the various portions of our widely extended country had been fully restored, trade and commerce did by no means reach the same favorable extent to which they had been brought years ago.

As a general thing the necessaries of life—no matter of what description—were unusually high in price, and the means for procuring them were in many instances very much circumscribed. Mechanical pursuits, which had formerly yielded a satisfactory remuneration, were brought to an almost complete standstill, and the question so frequently forced upon many during the course of the last few years, *what shall we eat, and what shall we drink, and wherewith shall we be clothed,* continued to intrude itself here and there. By the emancipation of the colored people, the temporal wealth of our section of country had been interfered with if not permanently, at least for the present time. Moreover the season did not prove very propitious for the products of the soil in our parts. A hard winter had in part injured the wheat crop, and its condition not improving very much, the consequence was a very considerable failure of this necessary means of subsistence. A pretty severe drought threatened the corn with a similar fate, but the Lord was pleased to send fructifying rains, so that in this particular the fears and apprehensions entertained were to a high degree relieved.

In our own community sickness prevailed at times to a somewhat alarming extent, and although after all comparatively few cases of death ensued, some of us were nevertheless severely tried by the severance of family ties. No less than 6 married couples were thus separated, 4 married Brn. and two married sisters having been called hence. But though in every instance the blow was felt severely, still, most providentially, only in *one* case a large family of children were left fatherless.

One hundred years having elapsed since the small and insignificant beginning of our Salem was made in the midst of primitive woods, as a matter of course a joyous Jubilee had to be celebrated. With singular unanimity, zeal and perseverance, hard labor was employed for weeks to give to our venerable house of worship a festive appearance. This was very suitably planned and executed with perfect success. The grand and imposing and at the same time exceedingly suitable decoration is still lingering before our minds' eye. All who took such zealous part in adorning the courts of the Lord are deserving the thanks of the congregation. (But we would mention here for future reference that the Brn. E. A. Vogler, Jas. Leinbach, Alex. Meinung, John Siewers and Henry Fries constituted the committee whose duty it should be to devise and superintend the decoration. They associated with themselves the Sisters Addie Herman, Jane Welfare, Eliza Kremer and Maggie Pfohl.) All who were peculiarly gifted with musical talents, under the guidance of our active organist, busily and successfully prepared themselves to heighten the festivity of the approaching Jubilee. A large number of members, offering their services as sextons under the direction of the chief sexton, who survived these festive days only by a few months, made themselves ready to see to it that our house of worship should be made to accommodate the largest possible number of people, and present a scene of order and decorum. While these outward preparations were going on, the servants of the Lord, assisted by His spirit, called for a spiritual making ready to bid welcome in our midst our gracious Covenant God and precious Savior. On account of the decoration which was going on, our church edifice could not well be used for two Sundays, on which account service was held in the chapel of the Academy.

And thus the 18th of February was reached. Invitations had been sent to ministers in the neighborhood, as well as to our brethren at the North. But although a few of the former attended, of the latter none could be present, except a brother, Bro. Holland, who had been pastor of this congregation but a few short years ago and who on this solemn and festive occasion preached the sermon on the first day of the Jubilee. On the evening of the 18th of February at 7 o'clock the festivities of the Jubilee were ushered in by a solemn close of the first century which has elapsed since the commencement of our now flourishing town and congregation here at Salem. A large audience had assembled.

Early in the morning of the 19th sweet melodies floating through the air reminded us that the day of Jubilee had arrived. At 9 o'clock the first service of the day was held. At 10 o'clock preaching followed. At 2 1/2 P.M. a concise account of the settlement of Salem and of some of the principal subsequent events was communicated. After this the colored people had a meeting. At 8 P.M. a very large procession, estimated to consist of some 1,500 souls, went up to the graveyard. The avenue leading to the graveyard as well as that sacred spot itself was illuminated with pine fagots placed on numerous stands, prepared for the occasion. The gate and the graves of the first settlers were also handsomely and appropriately decorated, and the latter marked by crosses of evergreen. When all assembled within the graveyard, singing and praying of a portion of one our litanies took place, and thus ended the first day.

On Tuesday the 20th many friends and members, whom high waters caused by severe rains had kept away yesterday, considerably increased the multitude that thronged our house of worship. The first service was preaching at 10 o'clock; this was followed at 2 o'clock by a very happy lovefeast, of which it is supposed about 1,200 persons partook. The services proper of these festive days closed in the evening at 7 o'clock with the Lord's Supper, at which about 500 communicants feasted sacramentally upon the Lord's body broken on the tree and the atoning blood shed for their souls' salvation.

Thus ended this ever memorable Jubilee, the festivities of which were not marred by a single unpleasant occurrence, but all the meetings were marked by peculiar order, decorum and solemnity.

During the course of this year some changes took place among the ministers of this congregation. Br. Robert Schweinitz accepted a call to become principal of the boarding school for boys at Nazareth, Pa., and left us with his family in July. Br. Grunert was appointed his successor as principal of our Female Academy. Bro. Albert Lawrence Oerter, minister in Canal Dover, Ohio, accepted the call to become assistant minister at Salem and vice principal of the female boarding school. He arrived here with his family in August.

Bro. Allen Spach was also appointed principal sexton in the place of our departed Bro. Chas. Cooper, who had filled that office for a long number of years.

A highly commendable spirit was manifested in this community shortly after our Jubilee to try to prevent as far as possible the public sale of that liquid poison which has destroyed the bodies and souls of more victims than all other scourges from which mankind can suffer taken together. As unfortunately such persons were still found who for filthy lucre's sake would give their neighbors drink and *put their bottle to them and make them drunken*, an appeal was made to our county court not to grant any licenses for the sale of spirituous liquors in Salem if a vast majority of the voters should be in favor of such a prohibition. The court acceded to this proposition, and on the 17th of March the votes were taken. To the honor of our community 81 were cast in favor of prohibition of the sale of intoxicating drinks within our corporate lines, and only 15 persons could be prevailed upon to vote the other way. If in some way or other this prohibition is disregarded, He that revealeth all secrets will in due time bring it to light, and by no means clear the guilty.

We cannot close the retrospect of the past year without adverting to a visitation sent upon us towards its close. A cutaneous and eruptive disease, brought here, it is supposed, in articles of clothing sent to one of the pupils in our Academy (Yulce), spread among the scholars, so that very soon a large number were affected, yea after a while it broke out in various families in town, and is at this very moment still prevailing, and showing itself here and there.

Mention should also be made, with grateful feelings of the fact, that 3 times during this year we were threatened with danger of fire, once in our Female Academy and twice in private dwellings; but the Lord preserved us mercifully so that we were more frightened than really injured, although in two of the three cases it might have proved very disastrous under less favorable circumstances.

Salem Diary, 1866
[Extracts transcribed; handwriting is that of George Frederic Bahnson.]

Tues., Jan. 2. This evening our Female Academy experienced a particular preservation from great danger of fire. In the room nearest the side door, wood had caught [fire] about the stove, and the wainscot had already measurably [been] reached when Bro. Rob. Schweinitz, taking home his little son, providentially passing by smelled the smoke and succeeded in putting an end to the threatening danger. The pupils were all in the chapel where they listened to a concert given by the brass band. Had not the Lord mercifully watched over the house, no one can tell how fearful the consequences might have been. Thanks and praise to his adorable name.

Wed., Jan. 3. A meeting of the Congregation Council was held at 7 P.M. to adopt measures for the celebration of our approaching centenary jubilee. There was a very good attendance, and a very good spirit seemed to prevail.

Sun., Jan. 7. Beginning of the week of prayer, which we had also resolved to observe for the first time since 1861, in as much as we had not heard anything about it since that time.

Mon., Jan. 8. Only 13°—the coldest day this winter. People began to fill their ice houses.

Tues., Jan. 9. Still very cold. Bro. Bahnson kept prayer meeting, well attended. Some young people had contributed money that the lamp before the church can be lighted.

Sun., Jan. 14. For years there has not been so good an audience on a common Sunday as this morning. We will thank God and take courage. No doubt the week of prayer had its influence for good.

Mon., Jan. 22. Bro. Bahnson kept prayer meeting, which was well attended. Concluded the memoir of Archibald Monteith. He must have been a most remarkable colored man.

Thurs., Feb. 1. In the evening a meeting of the communicant members took place, relative to the celebration of the approaching Jubilee. Among other things it was resolved that there should be a regular lovefeast to which no one is to be admitted without a printed invitation. Want of room for accommodating all renders this measure necessary.

Sun., Feb. 4. On account of the decorations, no more meetings could be held either in the church or in the chapel.

Sun., Feb. 11. Services took place in the chapel of the Academy. For some particular reason there were hardly any young men present. No other meeting today.

Thurs., Feb. 15. Heard that Bro. Edwin Senseman had departed this life very suddenly on the 8th inst. (Today his burial took place at Hope, Ind.)

Sun., Feb. 18. Bro. Rob. Schweinitz prayed the litany and preached in the Academy chapel. In the evening at 7 o'clock was a solemn meeting closing the first century. Bro. Grunert kept [it]. The decoration is wonderfully grand and becoming. The church was full.

Mon., Feb. 19. Our centenary Jubilee. A happy day. It had been raining all night, and continued steadily part of the morning. Water courses had risen. Our creek could not be forded, and many people were prevented from coming to

Salem. During the forenoon, though, the sun came out prettily. At 9 A.M. Bro. Bahnson kept the first meeting, imploring the Lord in humble prayer and supplication to bless his congregation most abundantly. At 10½ Bro. Holland, who had come here on a visit, preached from Deut. 32:7 after Bro. Parm. Leinbach had offered up the introductory prayer. At 2½ P.M. Bro. Emil Schweinitz communicated a historical sketch of the past century. At 4 P.M. was a meeting for the colored people at which Bro. Grunert preached and the Brn. Rights, Holland, and Hy. Cooper addressed the children of Ham. At 7 o'clock there was a solemn meeting on the graveyard. It was very windy and pretty cold. Bro. Robert Schweinitz conducted that meeting.

Tues., Feb. 20. A very pretty day. The tax collector having come to Winston, the town was crowded with people on that account also, besides that large numbers had come to the Jubilee. At 10 A.M. Bro. Rights preached to a very large and attentive audience. The church had been crowded with all the benches that could be procured, and every seat was filled. Bro. Hy. Cooper offered up the first prayer, and Bro. Rights preached from Deut. 8:2. The conduct of the large multitude had been exemplary during these two days. With this sermon the public services were closed. At 2 P.M. was a lovefeast at which Bro. Bahnson presided. Tickets had been given out, and this arrangement worked very well. It is supposed that there were about 1,200 persons present. Everything went off very orderly without any disturbance whatever. It was indeed a feast of love. At 7 P.M. between 4 and 500 communicants surrounded the sacramental table. Many of them were from our country congregations or other divisions of the Christian church. Bro. Bahnson presided, and the Brn. Emil and Robert Schweinitz, Holland, and Grunert assisted. It was a very solemn meeting, and the Lord was sensibly in our midst. Persons went to communion this evening who had not been at the sacramental table for many years.

Wed., Feb. 21. A request was communicated on the part of the congregation that the meetings should be continued. Of course it was acceded to with the greatest readiness. Bro. Grunert kept an address this evening and closed with prayer.

Thurs., Feb. 22. There was to have been a torchlight procession this evening in honor of Washington's birthday, but owing to the fact that there would be meeting this evening it was postponed. Bro. Bahnson preached from Heb. 13:8. At the close he read congratulatory letters received this day from U.E.C. written by Bro. Matthiesen and another private epistle from Bro. L. T. Reichel and still another from Bro. Jacobson.

Sun., Feb. 25. Today the whole litany was prayed, according to a resolution passed by the Board of Elders. It will make the service somewhat longer.

Sun., Mar. 4. [A] collection was taken up for the mission on the Musquito coast of $130.95. Quite liberal for our "poor" Salem—$39.05 were given by the Female Missionary Society, and $11 had been sent to Bethlehem privately.

Sun., Mar. 11. A colored man from Philadelphia, a minister of the independent colored Methodist church, preached this afternoon in the African church.

Sat., Mar. 17. Today an election was held in town whether any license to sell liquor should be granted or not. Legislature has passed an act leaving this matter to the votes of the citizens of Salem. Fifteen only voted in favor of licenses, among them some old men that should have known better, since they have seen misery in their families—and that for years—caused by the intoxicating cup. (Sam Shulz and Jacob Reich, it is said, were among the 15.) Ten ballots were written by the same person on the same kind of paper. However, 81 votes were given in opposition, a completely overwhelming majority. Hence this curse is removed from our community. We thank God and take courage.

Sun., Mar. 25. Palm Sunday. A very beautiful and, we trust, highly blessed day. Twenty-five persons were added to the church, four by baptism and 21 by confirmation—the largest addition since the existence of Salem.

Sun., Apr. 1. The warmest and most pleasant Easter morning we have had for years. Quite a large congregation assembled at 5 1/2 A.M. and moved in procession to the graveyard, where Bro. Bahnson prayed the Easter morning litany. At 10 A.M. Bro. Robert Schweinitz preached from Matt. 28:1-10. The audience was very large. The first monthly collection in behalf of our Sustentation Diacony was taken up, amounting to $34.85, very good indeed if it can be continued at a similar rate. This can hardly be expected.

Mon., Apr. 2. Anniversary of the Salem Bible Association. The Rev. Hy. Hardie, agent of the American Bible Society, was present. He delivered a stirring sermon in the evening at 7½ o'clock to a large and attentive audience.

Mon., Apr. 9. Many people had come to attend superior court, which has not been in session for years. Several cases were brought forward during the week that were moved to other counties, e.g., that of Jane, the negro girl who poisoned the child Anna Grunert.

Sat., Apr. 21. Bro. Bahnson kept the evening meeting, singing and prayer. Tolerably attended. The evening meetings in the week are not so well attended as they were some time ago. Persons in middle age, the fathers, are principally absent. Some of the young men attend regularly.

Sun., Apr. 22. A pleasant day. Bro. E. Schweinitz prayed the litany and preached. It was a great satisfaction to see how large an audience had assembled, like in the palmiest days before the war.

Wed., May 16. Rainy all day and in the evening. A zealous sexton rang the bell rather unexpectedly, and Bro. Bahnson lectured to a by far larger number of people than he had expected to see.

Sat., May 26. Bro. Bahnson kept the evening meeting, at the close of which he announced to the congregation that Br. Rob. Schweinitz had accepted a call as principal of Nazareth Hall, and Bro. Grunert will enter as his successor. Both brethren were commended to the Lord.

Wed., May 30. There was not evening meeting on account of the entertainment in the Academy. The session thus closed. Some of the young men did not behave very exemplarily.

Tues., June 5. During this week the [jubilee] decoration was removed and the church building underwent a necessary cleaning. No evening meeting.

Wed., June 13. Bro. Bahnson kept the weekly lecture. Very few attended. Now the plea is: too warm! in winter: too cold—so it goes.

Mon., June 18. Very cool morning. Bro. Bahnson kept prayer meeting. Not many men in; they are as usual very irregular, or rather regular in not attending.

Fri., June 22. At 7 o'clock the members of the S.S. gave a very interesting entertainment. It was very well attended and gave universal satisfaction. The object was to procure funds for the library. The collection taken on the occasion amounted to $81.00. Very good indeed.

Sat., June 23. At the usual time Bro. Bahnson kept prayer meeting. These public prayer meetings are not so well attended as those of a social character held every week in private houses. Of course everything new has attraction.

Wed., June 27. At 7 3/4 P.M. Bro. Bahnson kept prayer meeting, remembering, among other subjects, also our dear brethren and sisters in Germany, where according to the latest accounts war has broken out, and the Prussians, it is said, have occupied Löbau and Zittau. We feel of course very anxious about our mother congregation Herrnhut.

Sat., June 30. Soon after 7 o'clock this morning there was an alarm of fire. The ringing of the bell brought the fire company speedily together, but before the engine arrived much of the fire had been overcome. Bro. Irwin Miller's wash kitchen had been set on fire, probably by bacon hung up to smoke to free it from skipper, dropping some of its superfluous fatness and giving fuel to the wood, etc., laid down to produce smoke. The outhouse was very much injured, and some of the bacon spoiled. No other damage was done, altho' it might have turned out very differently.

Sun., July 1. Quite cool in the morning. Fire in the fireplace felt very pleasant.

Wed., July 11. Today Bro. Robert Schweinitz and family left for Pennsylvania. Our best wishes and prayers accompanied them. Brother Rob. Schweinitz has been principal of our Female Academy for more than 13 years, and the Lord accompanied his services with his blessing.

Wed., July 18. Bro. Bahnson kept prayer meeting at 8 P.M. Since the Jubilee there have never been so few present.

Wed., July 25. Bro. Bahnson kept prayer meeting at 7 3/4 P.M. The call of Bro. Albert L. Oerter as assistant minister and assistant principal of Salem Female Academy was announced in the usual way.

Mon., Aug. 6. The Boys School commenced. Bro. Const. Rights entered as teacher. Only 12 boys made their appearance. Several private schools are kept in town. The number of boys in our town school will no doubt increase.

Sun., Aug. 19. The audience was rather small, a camp meeting at Maple Springs being one of the outside attractions. S.S. as usual. New library books were distributed.

Fri., Aug. 31. Bro. and Sr. Oerter with their little son Maurice and Sr. Fetter [arrived]. Bro. Oerter will enter as assistant minister at Salem and assistant principal of our boarding school.

Wed., Sept. 19. Bro. Bahnson began the Bible lectures. There was quite a good audience considering how these week meetings are attended. Only all seat themselves as far as they can from the table, and if owing to an echo in the comparatively empty church, or any other cause, they do not understand every word perfectly, they are apt to blame the minister's voice instead of the place where they sit.

Mon., Sept. 24. Bro. Grunert kept the prayer meeting. It is time that weekday meetings be kept in the chapel.

Mon., Oct. 1. Bro. Bahnson kept prayer meeting in the chapel. The sisters' side was very well filled. He read part of the highly interesting diary of John King of his visit to the negro tribes on the upper waters of Marrowyne, etc.

[The handwriting is now that of Albert L. Oerter.]

Mon., Oct. 22. Br. Oerter kept prayer meeting in the chapel. As the organ was removed during last week, there is now more room.

Wed., Oct. 31. Br. and Sr. Bahnson returned in health and safety from the mountains.

[The handwriting is now that of George Frederic Bahnson.]

Thurs., Nov. 29. This day having been recommended by the general government, as well as by that of our state, as a day of thanksgiving, there was public service at 10 o'clock, pretty well attended.

Mon., Dec. 10. An eruptive disease that broke out in our boarding school some time ago seems to be spreading and excites some uneasiness.

Wed., Dec. 12. The commissioners have taken up the subject of the disease prevailing, and are adopting measures to prevent its spread. Thus far it has been comparatively mild. All affected are recovering.

Sun., Dec. 30. Owing to the prevailing disease and the great cold, snow being on the ground, the audience was very small; had it not been for the pupils of the Academy, the chapel might have held all.

Mon., Dec. 31. Snow—hauling ice, etc. The sky was somewhat gloomy, walking very bad. At 4 1/2 Bro. Bahnson kept a meeting for the children; about 9 were present. At 8 P.M. he read the Memorabilia. Meeting pretty well attended. At 11 1/2 he kept the usual meeting. Very few present; perhaps never was there a smaller audience. Thus the year closed rather gloomily.

Diary of the African Church in Salem, 1866
[Extracts transcribed; handwriting is that of Maximilian E. Grunert.]

Sun., Jan. 21. After S. School br. Wesley Spach preached on Ps. 49:4 and was listened to with attention. Afterwards was a meeting for the members, of quite an encouraging character; although not more than 20 were present. Alek (Vogler) prayed.

Sun., Feb. 4. S. School as usual. Afterwards communion services; 26 colored communicants and 7 white partook. Some were much moved. The services were quite encouraging.

Sun., Feb. 11. S. School and preaching were thinly attended.

Sun., Feb. 18. S. School as usual. Br. Holland preached afterwards on John 14:6. The weather being very unfavorable, the attendance was not large. Quite a number of white sisters were present.

Mon., Feb. 19. Centenary Jubilee of Salem congregation. At 4 P.M. the colored people had a meeting in the large church to give them the opportunity of enjoying the celebration in the sanctuary, beautifully decorated as it was for the occasion. Br. Grunert opened the meeting, after singing, with a few remarks, whereupon br. Bahnson led in prayer. Br. Rights delivered an address, followed by br. Cooper. After singing Br. Holland also spoke, and the time allotted having rapidly transpired, br. Grunert closed. After singing the doxology, the meeting separated. The large congregation was very well pleased.

Sun., Mar. 11. S. School poorly attended. Towards the close the church filled with a crowd that came to hear the Rev. [blank] Williams of the African Methodist Episcopal Church, who was here on a visit. He preached on Psalm 61:4, had 4 parts, and stuck to them. That church will, no doubt, spread over the South, and become *the* African church.

Wed., Mar. 14. Prayer meeting at night. Br. Alek (Vogler) exhorted.

Sun., Mar. 25. Palm Sunday. The meeting was at 7 P.M. Commenced the reading of the acts of the last days of the Son of Man. Large congregation towards the close. The reading was continued on Monday, Tuesday, and Wednesday evenings. On the latter occasion the congregation was small, owing to the rain.

Fri., Mar. 30. Good Friday. At 2 P.M. Wesley Spach read the acts of Friday. The meeting was well attended.

Sun., Apr. 1. Easter. The meeting began at 9 A.M. After singing in the church the Easter Morning Litany was prayed on the old graveyard. Returning into the church, after singing and prayer the acts of the Resurrection were read, and a sermon preached on Luke 24:34. The congregation was very large.

Sun., Apr. 15. S. School as usual. Afterwards the baptism of 2 infants took place. Had some conversation after meeting about the sponsors on such occasions, and about a school for colored children.

Wed., Apr. 18. Prayer meeting at night, somewhat methodistical.

Sun., May 13. At 21/4 was lovefeast; while partaking of it, a number of points were spoken of which seemed appropriate to the occasion. Two young sisters had been dancing; and the neglect of the members' meeting could not be passed over. At the close, upon invitation, 5 females presented themselves as candidates for church membership. Afterwards the Lord's Supper was celebrated, of which about 32 colored people (not all *our* members) and a number of whites partook. The Lord granted us a pleasant and a blessed time; very cordial shaking of hands followed, and I believe that a good impression was made.

Wed., May 16. It rained so hard in the evening, that I did not expect any person at church, and was therefore agreeably disappointed to find not only the 5 candidates, but quite a number of others there. Began confirmation instruction as had been agreed upon last Sunday.

Sun., June 3. Most of the colored people having gone to the funeral of aunt Amie Rights in Winston, the congregation was but small.

Sun., July 1. The S. School was comparatively well attended. Several of the teachers seemed tired of the labor.

Sun., July 22. After S. School we met for adult baptism and confirmation. Laura Margaret (Pender), Amanda Elisabeth (Foltz), commonly called Betty, and Linda Cornelius, or Sides, were baptized, and Dinah Ann Hege (br. Lewis Hege's wife) confirmed. The latter had been baptized among the Methodists.

Sun., July 29. Sunday School as usual. Afterwards lovefeast and the Holy Communion. The new members partook with the church. The whole number of communicants present was not very large, perhaps 30, and a few white brethren and sisters. Br. Grunert, having entered upon another office which requires all his strength, bade them in a "mourners farewell" on this occasion. They certainly pledged themselves to follow the Savior and to love one another.

[Handwriting is now that of George Frederic Bahnson]

Sun., Aug. 5. Br. E. A. Vogler, having consented to be for the present superintendent of the S.S. and leader in prayer meetings, began today. Many promised to attend the S.S. hereafter. Br. Vogler addressed them after S.S.

Sun., Aug. 19. Br. Vogler was present at the S. School as superintendent. Some 50 scholars were present. A good spirit seemed to prevail. After S.S. Bro. V. led a prayer meeting. Several colored brethren offered up fervent prayers.

[Handwriting is now that of Albert L. Oerter]

Sun., Sept. 2. After S.S. (conducted by Br. V.) Br. Bahnson opened service with singing and prayer, and then introduced to the congregation Br. A. L. Oerter, who having accepted a call hither as asst. pastor and asst. inspector of S.F.A., now has the pastoral charge of the colored congregation. Br. O. then spoke on 1 Cor. 3:11, after which Br. V. led a prayer meeting, calling on several of the colored brn. to pray.

Sun., Sept. 23. S.S. and preaching. Text: Ps. 144:15. Practicing Xmas anthems.

Sun., Oct. 14. As we came out of church, we met Br. Mack from Friedberg, who had just arrived, and who, at the request of the members, went into the church and kept prayer meeting with them.

Thurs., Oct. 18. Br. Vogler kept prayer meeting, as there was desire for it among the members, and one in particular seems to be under conviction.

Sun., Oct. 21. At 8 A.M. Br. Vogler conducted a prayer meeting at the church, which was very solemn and well attended; P.M. S.S. as usual, and preaching on Acts 16:31. In the evening Br. Vogler conducted another meeting; the house was crowded. Br. O. could not attend either in the morning or evening.

Sun., Oct. 28. Meetings have been held during the past week either at the houses of some of the members or at the church. Several females are professing to be under conviction. On last Friday evening Br. Oerter was present at the meeting in the church. Br. H. Cooper was also present, and addressed the congregation. Three or four females came forward and knelt at the front seat. (The character of the exercises was rather Methodist than Moravian.)

Sun., Nov. 18. The Wednesday evening prayer meetings are dropped for the present.

Sun., Dec. 16. After S.S. Br. Vogler conducted a prayer meeting, the request having been made by the S.S. of a certain Baptist Church in New Jersey that this S.S. should unite with them on this day in prayer for each other. There was no preaching.

Sun., Dec. 23. After S.S. Mr. John Vassar, an agent of the American Tract Society, addressed the school or congregation in a very interesting manner. He left some Testaments, Primers, etc., for the S.S. Br. O. followed with a short address.

Tues., Dec. 25. Xmas Day. At 2 P.M. the celebration was held. Br. Vogler and S.S. teachers had for some weeks been preparing the scholars. An ode was sung, consisting of a number of Xmas anthems, interspersed with recitations by the children, who did very well. The church had been tastefully decorated with evergreens, an arch rising in front of the pulpit, having in its apex the inscription, "Unto you is born a Saviour, which is Christ the Lord." A lovefeast furnished by Br. Vogler added to the enjoyment of the occasion. The Brn. Bahnson and Emil de Schweinitz were present; the former of whom addressed the congregation before the closing hymn. (Br. O. had opened the exercises with singing, prayer, and reading of Luke 2.) It was a happy day for the congregation, old and young;

many thanks are due Br. Vogler and the S.S. teachers for their faithful labors.

Sun., Dec. 30. But a small congregation had assembled, many being afraid to come to church on account of the smallpox prevailing at present.

Salem Congregation Council, 1866
[Extracts of minutes transcribed.]

Wed., Jan. 3.

[T]he Chairman said that the Church at Salem would on the ensuing 19th day of February celebrate the centenary Jubilee, and that the Council had been called together for the purpose of interchanging opinions in regard thereto, and for the further purpose of devising ways and means for a proper celebration of that occasion.

After being informed how such occasions had been celebrated by different congregations, the feeling of the meeting manifested itself in the desire that we should endeavor to get up a celebration in every respect, both outwardly and inwardly, worthy of the occasion, and that it be one in which every member of our church in Wachovia should be invited to join us.

The meeting had been called for the purpose of discussing the subject, and it was unanimously resolved that so far as we are able we would endeavor to have a nice celebration, with handsome decorations, lovefeast, etc.

Tues., May 1.

Council met for the purpose of filling the vacancies in the Board of Elders and board of Trustees, the term of Br. Grunert in the former and of Brn. C. Cooper and Joshua Boner in the latter having expired.

Bro. E. A. de Schweinitz gave notice that his seat as a member of the Board of Elders would expire within a year, and that he did not desire to be re-elected; because, by virtue of his office as Administrator, he was a member of the P.E.C., to which body an appeal lay from the former Board in certain cases; and to belong to both, at such times, would be rather an embarrassing situation, and a person could not act with the necessary freedom.

Chairman stated that, although the term for which Br. Grunert had been elected to the Board of Elders had expired, yet since his appointment as assistant pastor of the Cong., he was now, according to the Rules, a member of that Board ex officio. Bro. R. de Schweinitz desired the constitution to be so amended that another lay member of the Council would be eligible to a seat on the Board of Elders, and therefore made a motion, that "The clause in the rules which provides that the 'Principal of the Salem Female Academy be one of that Board[']' be repealed," which motion was seconded. Bro. R. de Schweinitz then moved that the Council adjourn to meet on 1st Tuesday after Whitsunday to vote on the proposed amendment of the Constitution and to fill the vacancies in the two Boards.

Tues., May 22.
Council met according to adjournment, 37 members being in attendance. The minutes of last meeting having been read, Bro. E. A. de Schweinitz rose to make an explanation, stating that he had not been sufficiently reported, especially in regard to the remarks concerning his membership in the P.E.C., that it would be preferable and he thought better for the Congregation to have more brethren not in the ministry as members of the Board of Elders, that he had further said that the spirit prevailing in the Cong. at present was such that in his opinion now was the time when the original idea which was intended when the Constitution was changed might be carried out, the intention at that time being to have a large representation of lay Brn. in that Board. Bro. R. de Schweinitz had likewise been incorrectly reported, his remarks being, "That the Constitution be so amended that hereafter, as there was now an assistant minister of the Cong., the Prin. of S.F. Academy should no longer be an Ex. Off. member of the Board of Elders, since retaining that person would increase the number of the Board, besides making an unnecessarily large ministerial representation.["]

The minutes with these amendments were accordingly adopted. The proposed amendment introduced at the last meeting, "That the clause in the Const. which provides that the Prin. of S.F.A. be a member of the Board of Elders, be repealed," was upon motion taken up by the Council.

Bro. R. de Schweinitz stated that he had made this motion for the benefit of the Cong., that it had been the original intention, when the change was made in the Const., to introduce more lay Brn. in the superintendence of the spiritual affairs of the Church, but at that time it was found difficult to find such persons who could be induced to accept the position in that Board. The time had now come when, in his opinion, the vacancies might be more readily filled by lay Brn., and as he had before remarked, the Cong. having a minister and asst. minister, [it] would be proper if the Prin. of S.F. Academy should be excused from serving in said Board as an Ex. Off. member, inasmuch as it would also increase the number of the Board.

Br. Grunert observed that the objection was not applicable as the Const. provided for three lay Brethren to be put into the Board, since there might be three ministerial Brn., should there be two ministers of the Cong. as is now the case.

Bro. E. A. de Schweinitz thought it would be better to have more lay members as it would no doubt be the case that information would be received from them which the ministerial Brethren might otherwise not obtain.

Bro. E. A. Vogler did not see much benefit to be derived from the proposed change, that should the amendment be adopted, the time might again come when we would have only one minister for the Cong., and we would then no doubt desire to have the Const. again altered, and that in his opinion we had better leave it as it stands at present, the Prin. of S.F.A. being at any rate a very desirable member of said Board.

Bro. E. W. Lineback said the ministerial Board was a good one, all good and satisfactory to the Cong., and that if two ministers were good, three would be better. The elective members were considered as representatives of the Cong. and the Prin. of S.F.A. as representing the interests of that institution.

The question being called upon the amendment, the motion was lost.

Board of Elders of Salem Congregation, 1866
[Extracts of minutes transcribed.]

Wed., Jan. 3. Br. F. absent.

2. The "week of prayer," commencing Jan. 7th, will be observed. Evening meetings will be kept every day, with 2 prayers after Sunday.

3. The Centenary Jubilee of Salem Congregation was spoken of. The Board was of opinion that on Sunday, Feb. 18th, no service could be kept, except a solemn close of the century in the evening, that the 19th and 20th should be celebrated, and the Holy Communion close the festival meetings. If the Congrn. Council this evening approves of this plan, the details can be agreed upon hereafter.

Wed., Jan. 17. Br. F. absent.

2. Jos. Hall's establishment is by common report a resort for drinking. It is probable that nothing can be proved, but persons known to love liquor go in and out there frequently. He will be spoken to.

4. An official invitation to preach the sermon on Feb. 19th, the first day of the Jubilee, will be sent to br. Holland, who intends being here at that time. In the evening of that day the congregn. will meet before the church, and march in procession to the graveyard, where suitable exercises will be gone through. In case of rain a simple evening blessing will be held in the church instead. The lovefeast arrangements remain the most problematic: the church is too small, the chances for weather sufficiently dry and warm to keep that service on the square are small, not to mention the additional labor in the musical department. One or more addresses might be interspersed with profit.

Wed., Jan. 31. Br. F. absent.

Jos. Hall says that he does sell liquor, and will continue to do so. The matter was laid over. Br. Holland has written that he will come.

2. A meeting will be held for the colored people in the decorated church on the first day of the Jubilee, after the 2 1/2 P.M. meeting.

3. The Board is requested by the brethren who have the lovefeast in charge to call a meeting of the communicants to consult about the Jubilee lovefeast. Such a meeting will be held tomorrow evening.

Wed., Feb. 7.

3. The meeting of communicant members was held last Thursday with the following results: There is to be a lovefeast, to which the members of all Moravian congregations are to be

invited, also visiting ministers of other denominations, and contributors to the expenses of the celebration in Salem and Winston. Members of other churches who desire to commune with us on this occasion shall also be admitted. All shall come with tickets, furnished by the respective ministers on application; but the country ministers will give out tickets here in Salem only to those of their people that may be here. The tickets will have the name of the holder written on them. The meeting also expressed a wish to have the proposed service on the graveyard.

7. As there are very strange reports current in the neighborhood concerning our Jubilee meetings, the Board thought it best to have a programme printed, setting forth the fact that the public services close with the sermon on the 20th.

Wed., Feb. 14.

2. As burials of strangers on our graveyard appear to become more frequent, their names and numbers will appear on the Church Register, to make it agree with the graveyard plot, while the memoranda will be entered upon the strangers' list.

4. It was proposed that hereafter the whole Litany should be prayed every Sunday. If the congregn. were prepared to expect a somewhat longer service, there would be no objection. As it is, the striking of the hour at 11 is evidently the time at which it is expected that the sermon will close, and everything said after that is little listened to. The matter was held over.

Wed., Feb. 21.

[I]t was resolved to pray hereafter the entire Litany. As to the "Praise the Lord, all ye heathen, etc.," it will be sung by the congregation, or else *said*. The Board did not like the full choir to occupy their seats every Sunday, in order to chant that line.

2. The bellows' blowing is not done regularly by br. Jas. Fisher, but a number of boys come up occasionally for that purpose. The Board would like to hear from br. Pfohl whether in his opinion a change would be proper.

5. The destruction of the Mission premises on the Mosquito coast, by a hurricane in Oct. last, calls for all possible help. The Board thought that on Monday evening next the details of the calamity should be read to the congregn., and on the following Sunday a collection be taken up for that object, instead of the usual semi-annual missionary collection.

6. The Board was of opinion that an attempt should be made to induce our people to bring hymn books to church as a regular practice, in order to make the lining out of the verses unnecessary.

Wed., Feb. 28. Br. R. Schwtz. absent.

2. As people cannot see sufficiently well to read in church with the gas fixed as it is, the Board had reluctantly to admit the necessity of the lining out at night meetings.

Wed., Mar. 28.

3. As to lovefeasts the Board thought that the time had come when the usual lovefeasts should again be kept regularly, unless the congregation should desire the giving up of any.

Wed., Apr. 18. Br. F. absent.

4. The Negroes belonging to the congregn. desire assistance to sustain a school for their children. They feel unable to pay the tuition money themselves in the long run. Sr. Araminta Wagoman has taught them hitherto, and they are perfectly satisfied with her; but having heard that if they would build a schoolhouse, they could get a teacher from the North for nothing, they very naturally wish to obtain either a lot for building, or pecuniary aid to pay the salary of the present teacher. The Board thought this very reasonable, and that such aid ought to come from our own congregation. It was suggested that this Board should start a subscription paper, and some of the Negroes take it round to see what aid could be obtained here.

Wed., Apr. 25. Br. F. absent.

After the reading of the minutes br. Grunert reported that he had a conversation with some of the Negro brethren about their school. They will ask sr. Wagoman for how much she would be willing to teach, say 10 months. After ascertaining how much of that sum they can make up among themselves, they will report how much help is required.

Tues., May 22. 9 1/2 P.M.

The Congregn. Council this evening having elected br. E. A. Vogler, to fill the vacancy created in this Board by br. Grunert's having become one of the pastors of the congregn., and br. Allen Spach, to serve the unexpired term of br. E. A. Schweinitz, who had resigned his seat, the Board met immediately upon the adjournment of the Council, and resolved to hold regular meetings hereafter on alternate Tuesday evenings.

2. The office of principal sexton having become vacant by the recent departure of br. Chs. Cooper, br. Allen Spach was the unanimous choice for that position, and expressed his willingness to accept, provided that br. E. A. Vogler, his employer, was willing to dispense with his services at such times when his presence at funerals and similar occasions was required. Br. Vogler gave his consent.

Tues., June 5. Br. R. Schw. absent.

As this was the first formal meeting of the new Board, Br. B. offered prayer, and remarked that the proceedings of this Board were frequently of such a nature that on account of the persons who were spoken of, and to secure free expression of views, it was indispensable that the deliberations be kept secret.

2. The conduct of several young people in church was spoken of. As to the boys, they will be directed to occupy the front seats, unless they come with their fathers. Several young men have again shown their want of propriety by unbecoming conduct. Various proposals were made how to reach them. No one seemed disposed to give them a friendly warning in private. To address them by a note was also disapproved of, as well as a public reproof. It seemed best, at last, to speak to the fathers of several of them as a first step and then see further.

Tues., July 3. Br. R. Schw. absent.

3. Br. Vogler has written to Lippincott & Co., Phila., about Communion books, and they say that 500 copies would cost between $75 and $80. Br. Blum is not prepared for a job of this kind. The Board thought the above offer very reasonable, and as it appeared desirable to have a greater variety, the addition of which would increase the price of a single copy but a few cents, it was resolved that the brn. Bahnson and Grunert compile a sufficient number.

Tues., July 17.

Br. Robt. Schweinitz, having left this place with his family for Nazareth, Pa., is no longer a member of this Board.

4. The colored people connected with the church apply for help, as they wish to have a permanent school. The Board approved of the principles laid down when this matter was up before. Sr. Ar. Wagoman is now teaching elsewhere. As a first step, inquiry is to be made whether the free-school house on the Commissioners' lot might be obtained for this purpose. Br. Fulkerson will see about that.

6. Several young men continue to misbehave in church. As an appeal to some of the fathers, which Br. Bahnson has made by note, has been unavailing, several members of this Board will make it their business to talk to the young men them-selves.

Mon., July 23. Br. Vogler absent.

Br. Bahnson informed the Board that P.E.C. had given a call to br. Alb. L. Oerter of Canal Dover to become the suc-cessor of br. Grunert as Asst. Principal and Asst. Minister. No objection was made.

The Board of Trustees having determined to sue br. J. Boner, it was resolved that a letter be written to him on the part of this Board to make a last effort to induce him to make a proper arrangement with the Board of Trustees. The Board will meet tomorrow at 5 P.M. to hear the letter. (This took place.)

Tues., July 31.

5. Br. B. read a reply from Br. Boner to the letter sent him in behalf of the Board. The Board ordered that it be returned to the author as lacking the respect due this Board.

6. Br. Grunert having been obliged to give up the care of the colored people, and Br. B. being unable, with the little help he can get, to preach to them regularly, the other members of this Board were requested to come to the help of the cause by taking charge of the Sunday School and occasional prayer meetings afterwards.

7. Br. Fulkerson could not tell whether the Free school house would be granted. As they have some prospects of getting a teacher free of charge if they obtain the permission, and as the house stands on the Commissioners' lot, it appears best to lay the subject before the Mayor.

Tues., Aug. 14. Br. V. absent.

[T]he Boner affair was again spoken of, Mr. Starbuck having busied himself in the matter. Board knows now that the information contained in his letter was satisfactory while the surplus would have been better left out.

2. Br. E. A. Vogler has met the colored people in their church and will do so again.

3. About the school, these people are divided among themselves. The free school house they will probably not get. It is understood that the upper story in Sr. Van [Evan] Boner's shop has been rented to them for that purpose.

7. Br. Bahns. will speak to the brn. E. W. Lineback and A. Minung that they divide between themselves both the organist duties and the salary as they see fit.

Tues., Aug. 28.

After the reading of the minutes, it was remarked to: §2 that the Sund. Sch. for the colored people is looking up; §3 that Ackerman's shop is to be the place for their day-school; §7 that the brn. L. and M. have agreed to the proposal.

Tues., Sept. 11.

Br. Albert Oerter, the new assistant minister, was present and welcomed as a member of this Board.

2. The minutes having been read, Br. B. remarked that he had told br. E. W. Lineback that the presence of an organist was not absolutely required at every meeting, as the brn. L. and M. would then prefer not to be paid organists. The Board was of the same opinion as Br. B.

4. The rules of Salem Congregation, as far as applicable, are the rules for the colored division also. Br. O. will read and explain them.

Tues., Nov. 20.

After reading the minutes, it was agreed that the meetings of this Board be held on Monday evenings after prayer meeting.

Tues., Dec. 18.

3. There will be no tickets for the Christmas Eve lovefeast, which will be only for members. Others may obtain permission on application to the pastor.

Fri., Dec. 28.

2. On account of the prevailing epidemic (smallpox) it was thought best to postpone the celebration of the Holy Communion.

Board of Trustees of Salem Congregation, 1866
[Extracts of minutes transcribed.]

Tues., Jan. 2. Full Board.

2. Our Boys' School being indebted to Br. Albert Butner for part of his salary for last year, which could not be paid because, owing to the scarcity of money parents, etc., were not able to pay the school fees, the question was asked whether, as Br. Butner has now left the school and is on the point of moving away from here, Salem Diacony should take the responsibility of that debt upon itself by giving him a note signed by the Warden, with the understanding that the school pay to the Diacony the amount of the note as the dues now owing to the School are gradually collected. Board was of opinion that such a proceeding was not necessary and could not be expected of the Diacony, in as far as the indebtedness to Br. Butner was not occasioned by a deficiency in the income of the School, but was only bro't about by the inability of the parents to pay what they owed to the school, and that under circumstances so peculiar it might be reasonably expected of Br. Butner to wait patiently till the School was in a capacity to pay him.

3. As it may become necessary to raise some money in the course of a few weeks for the purpose of paying public taxes, the Warden was authorized to sell as many of the coupons of State Bonds now in his hands as may be required to meet that expense.

5. Upon application of some of the members of the Trombone Band (blowers at funerals) the arrangement with regard to some remuneration for their services, which had been agreed upon Aug. 7, 1860 (see minutes), and which had been interrupted by the war, were sanctioned anew, Board agreeing to exonerate as many blowers as would form a complete chorus (say about 5) from paying as much of the church fees as would be required from an unmarried brother.

Tues., Jan. 30. Not present the Brrn. J. Blum and E. A. Vogler.

2. Sister Lucinda Bagge, in order to secure a debt due her by Br. Rud. Christ for the house he lives in, wishes to buy the lot on which the house stands from the Diacony and secure it by a deed, but is not able at this time to pay the money for it. [She] is, however, willing to give her note. As there will not be the least difficulty to obtain this money in the present case, Board is willing to make this an exception from the common rule of cash payments for town lots and also consents to her being furnished with a deed before the note is paid.

Fri., Mar. 23. Not present the Brrn. J. Boner and E. A. Vogler.

1. No steps having as yet been taken towards the quarterly collection of the Church expenses, owing to the scarcity of money and the frequent calls for contributions for religious purposes, it was resolved at the end of April once more to make out the yearly church accounts as customary heretofore, only charging the latter half year according to the new rates as determined upon (see minutes, Dec. 19, 1865) and to begin the quarterly collections with the first quarter of the new financial year.

2. By §2 of last minutes the attention of the Board was drawn to the notes held by Salem and Single Sisters Diacony against the firm of Boner & Christ, which notes are not secured, and Board, thinking it advisable to take some steps in the matter, appointed the Brrn. Pfohl and Vogler to speak to Br. Boner on the subject.

Thurs., Apr. 5. Not present Br. J. Boner.

2. Br. J. Boner, having today been specially requested to attend the meeting of the Board in order to afford an opportunity to have a conversation about the indebtedness of the firm of Boner & Christ, has sent a written communication, in which he in substance repeats the remarks made by him to Br. Pfohl on March 24th, dwelling in an abrupt and ranting manner upon the state of the country, losses by the war, by repudiation and emancipation, and hinting strongly towards the repudiation of all debts old or new, etc., etc., subjects, in the opinion of the Board, foreign to the simple question of doing his duty towards his creditors.

Board had a long conversation on the subject of an answer to this production and resolved that two of the members each prepare an answer and lay it before them tomorrow evening.

Fri., Apr. 6. Not present the Brrn. J. Boner and J. G. Seitz.

The minutes of yesterday's meeting having first been read and adopted, the two answers to Br. Boner's letter, as prepared according to the resolution of the Board, were communicated, and portions of each selected as the answer of this Board.

Fri., May 25. Full Board.

1. Since last meeting of the Board our Brother Charles Cooper, who had been a member of the same for many years, departed this life, and as the term of Br. Joshua Boner had expired, Congregation Council on the 22nd inst. elected the Brrn. Edward Blum and Augustus Pfohl for 3 years. Br. E. A. Vogler, another member of the Board, who also had served in this capacity for a long time, having on the same day been elected a member of the Board of Elders, 1 year of his term in the Board of Trustees being yet unexpired, Br. Charles Hauser was elected for the remainder of this term, viz., to May 1867.

The elected members of the Board of Trustees consequently are the following, viz., the Brrn. Nath. Blum, J. G. Seitz, John D. Siewers, Edward Blum, Augustus Pfohl, and Charles Hauser.

Board organized by electing S. Thos. Pfohl (the Warden) as President and Secretary.

2. The minutes of last meeting having been read, the President next communicated another letter from Br. Joshua Boner in answer to the one sent him under date of April 7th, which answer, however, containing nothing to the purpose, Board resolved not to send a reply, not feeling desirous to continue a correspondence leading to no practical results and proving worse than useless.

3. Board having on Dec. 19, 1864, when the country was flooded with Confederate currency voted an extra appropriation to Br. Bahnson towards the support of his family of $746 (which, however, according to the scaling process since adopted by the state legislature was in reality equal only to $17.76 in specie), which amount, however, Br. Bahnson never drew, not being willing to take it in the currency then customary. His attention having since the end of the war and the total

fall of the Confederate currency been drawn to the fact that it could not be expected that Diacony should now pay the $746 standing to his credit in *good* currency, he has in consequence relinquished his claim to the whole amount, and Board now resolved to substitute $50 of the present currency in its place, amounting in value to much more than the sum originally granted.

4. The value of the coupons of the N. Carolina State Bonds being very fluctuating at this time, owing to the financial condition of the state, it was resolved by the Board that such coupons as became due in the course of our last fiscal year, ending April 30, 1866, be not counted as interest, as had formerly been customary, but be kept attached to the Bonds till they are actually converted into cash.

5. The boards—or trays—belonging to the Salem Congregation, on which corpses are generally laid out previously to being put in the coffin, having occasionally been used for that purpose by the coloured people, Board resolved, in order to avoid disagreeable remarks and feelings in the Congregation, that a set of such trays be made by Br. John Siewers for the use of the coloured people, and that the expenses be defrayed out of the amount standing to the credit of the Negro Graveyard, in the books of the Diacony, which credit has accumulated from the sale of privileges to bury such on the graveyard as were not members of the Negro Congregation.

Fri., June 29. Not present the Brrn. Nathl. and Edward Blum (the latter unwell).

1. Since the former meeting of the Board a "Stay law" has been passed by the State Convention, according to which all proceedings for the recovery of debts are to be deferred to the spring term of the Superior Court in April next. No action can consequently be taken against Boner & Christ for the present.

4. Br. Sylvester Miller applies again for a town lot situated on the corner of Church and (Winston) First Street in Winston, for the purpose of building a dwelling house on it. After a long discussion on the subject, Board resolved that a tier of 5 lots be laid out on Church Street between 1st and 2nd Street. . . .

Tues., July 3. Full Board.

1. Board met at 7 o'clock A.M. on the premises to be laid out into lots (see minutes of last meeting). . . .

2. Board (Br. Chs. Hauser excepted) next went to the Mill lane, where . . . some building lots were also to be laid out. . . .

Tues., July 17. Not present Br. N. Blum.

1. The town lots spoken of [in the last two meetings] have now been laid out. . . . Board further resolved unanimously that none of the lots were to be sold to negroes.

2. The Board of Elders desiring to be informed what action this Board intends to take in the case of Boner & Christ, it was resolved to return as answer, "that according to the treatment we have experienced in this matter, we can see no prospect of coming to a friendly understanding and arrangement, and that nothing remains for us but to resort to such legal measures as may be taken in the case. From present indications, several writs having already been issued against the firm, it would appear as if action on our part might become necessary almost at any moment."

3. With regard to the appointment of a collector of the Church and Lovefeast accounts it was resolved that for the present the Warden undertake those collections.

Mon., July 23. Full Board.

1. Board had been called together to a special meeting this evening for the purpose of laying before it a communication from the Provincial Elders Conference, stating that Br. Albert L. Oerter, minister at Canal Dover, Ohio, had received and accepted a call to fill the vacancy occasioned by Br. Grunert's appointment as Principal of Salem Female Academy, and that Br. Oerter would sustain the same relation to the Congregation as Br. Grunert did before the change took place that removed him to another sphere of activity. Board, not knowing the Brother in question, have no reason to withhold their approval of the choice of those that are probably better acquainted with him.

2. It being necessary according to the law existing at this time that a deed for landed property if of a less value than $500 must be accompanied with a "Revenue Stamp" worth 50 cents, it was resolved that as long as that law is in force, it be made a condition in all sales of town lots or land that the expenses of the Stamp be borne by the purchaser.

Tues., Aug. 14. Not present Br. Chs. Hauser (not at home).

3. The yearly accounts of Salem Diacony from May 1, 1865, to April 30, 1866, together with a statement of its assets and liabilities at the latter date were laid before the Board and examined at length. Owing to a book transaction bro't about by the change from Confederate into National Currency, by which an apparent gain of $696 was occasioned, the yearly accounts closed with a surplus of $820.60, which amount Board resolved to apply towards canceling the following debts appearing among the accounts current debtors, viz.:

Lovefeast acct.	$320.94
Church Repairs	42.68
Bookstore (Acct. Ct.)	397.07
Music acct.	11.95
Wine	45.87
Square, the Balance of surplus	2.09
	$820.60.

Thurs., Sept. 13. Not present the Brrn. C. Hauser and Aug. Pfohl (not at home).

1. The yearly accounts of the Single Sisters' Diacony to Apr. 30, 1866, and statement of its assets and liabilities on that day were next laid before the Board. The receipts amounted to $270.32, and the disbursements to $398.43 and consequently exceeded the former by $128.11. Owing to the precarious condition in which the greater part of the notes and bonds belonging to this Diacony are at this time, the interest has not been calculated or taken into the accounts, with the exception of $45 received from Salem Diacony, which accounts for the very limited amount of receipts of this year compared with the receipts of former years.

2. By request of the Board of Elders the expediency of either repairing or removing the Chapel Organ was taken into consideration.

This organ has now for more than ten years been entirely useless, only taking up the room in the Chapel that might otherwise have been occupied by persons that attend meetings. As owing to our secluded position there is no one at hand that could undertake to repair such an instrument, and as the expense of procuring an organ builder for the express purpose of attending to the work would under our limited means at this time far exceed our ability, it was resolved unanimously to remove the instrument and store it away in a safe place, perhaps on the Church garret.

Tues., Nov. 6. Not present Br. J. G. Seitz (on a journey).

1. Br. E. A. Vogler intends next spring to erect a new store building and asks permission to stack up the timber required in the square near the west fence, and also to put up a temporary lime house, placed so that the lime could be unloaded without driving into the square. The timber he also promises to unload outside and then have it carried into the square. After finishing the building he promises to clean away the rubbish that may have been made in the square. Board gives its consent on condition that wagons are not to drive into the square.

2. Upon application it was resolved that such of the regular trombone blowers (Church band) as are still under age and consequently not liable to pay church expenses, receive as compensation for their services $5 per annum, this amount being about equivalent to the sum total of Church expenses remitted to the blowers. (See minutes Aug. 7, 1860, §1.)

3. The Town Commissioners of Winston having made it a condition that in opening the streets around the block of lots laid out in Winston in July last, the trees standing in the streets be taken out by the root, it was resolved that we charge for the timber only the price paid for *dead wood* on condition that the purchaser comply with the above requirements.

5. It was resolved that the Forester be at liberty to sell dead timber to such people of colour living in town as are members of our Negro Church, if they are able to pay for it.

Tues., Dec. 18. Not present Br. N. Blum.

1. No application having as yet been made for cutting the timber in the streets of Winston under the conditions stated in §3 of the last minutes, Board is willing that applicants not members of our Church be also accepted, should such offer themselves. Should we, however, not succeed in finding any one willing to undertake it, Board is of opinion that the timber should be given gratis to any one who would clear those streets under the conditions stated.

2. Salem Diacony having at present a number of uncashed coupons on old North Carolina State Bonds on hand, the par value of which amounts to $1,350, the Warden laid the question before the Board of selling them now, not knowing what

may eventually be realized from them, and of applying the proceeds towards the payment of debts due by the Diacony. The unsettled political condition of the Southern States exercising a depreciating influence upon the value of the state coupons at present, Board, upon deliberation, resolved not to sell now, but to wait events for some time longer.

Provincial Financial Board, 1866
[Extracts of minutes transcribed.]

Wed., Mar. 28. Br. Lewis Rights not present.

Board met this evening to consider the situation of Br. Lewis Rights, to which its attention has been called. Br. Rights receives no money whatever from his congregations at present, because the scarcity of money is so very great. The subscriptions for his support will no doubt be paid during the course of the year as soon as his people have had an opportunity of disposing of a part of their growing crops. As Br. Rights needs money now, it was moved and resolved to advance him the sum of $75. Of this action of the Board his congregation is not to know anything, in order to prevent a false impression being thereby created.

Tues., Apr. 17. Brrn. L. Rights and E. A. Vogler absent.

1. Br. S. T. Pfohl, Tr. of Wa. S.D., proposed to the Board that the Book Concern or Store, formerly carried on account of Salem Diacy. and now properly devolving on Sustent. Diacy., be given up, as it has proved a very unprofitable concern, and that all Church publications be hereafter procured from the Church Bookstore at Bethlehem. The proposition is that Sustent. Diacy. hereafter pay only for 3 copies of the Monatlische Nachrichten sent direct from Berthelsdorf, for 1 copy of the Missions Blatt, and 1 complete copy of the "Blauen Hefte" to be got from Bethlehem. One copy of the English Church publication "The Messenger" and of the German "Brüderbote" should likewise be subscribed for at Bethlehem. Board unanimously agreed to this proposal, by which a sufficient number of all our Church publications will be provided for the Province at a greatly reduced price.

2. Br. R. P. Lineback's account of receipts from his congregations for 1865, as handed into P.E.C. was laid before the

Board. According to this statement, the sum total of all his receipts for 1865 from his 3 congregations, including the $20 unpaid subscription, amounted to the sum of $40.50. Altho' 1865 was a very hard year, nevertheless Board was greatly surprised at the trifling amounts received and deemed it their duty, before finally passing on any appropriation, to inquire of Br. Lineback whether the Synodal Resolutions of '56 in reference to the duty of members to contribute to the support of their minister had been complied with by the Committees of his congregations. This matter brought up the general subject of the duty of congregations to contribute to the support of their ministers and especially the question, whether the action of the Provincial Synod of Nov. 1865 had not done away with the Resolutions of 1856, by which the sum of $300 per annum was as a general rule in a manner guaranteed to country ministers by Sustent. Diacy. At least such has been the practical effect of those Resolutions. The discussion of this subject was postponed.

Thurs., Aug. 2. Br. Lewis Rights absent.

1. Br. Robert de Schweinitz, a member of this Board, having been called to Nazareth, the first business in order was to fill the vacancy occasioned by his departure. Br. John D. Siewers was nominated and unanimously elected.

Thurs., Aug. 23. Br. Rights absent.

5. The annual accounts of Wa. Sustent. Diacy. from June 1, 1865, to May 31, 1866, were submitted by the Treasurer, Br. S. T. Pfohl. The total amount of receipts was $1,870.90 and of disbursements $2,363.40, showing a deficit of $492.50. A large amount of the assets is of very doubtful value. The whole of the assets amount to $40,979.25, of which not more than one half can at present be regarded as safe.

Bethania Diary, with Bethabara, 1866
[Extracts transcribed; handwriting is that of Christian Lewis Rights.]

Wed., Jan. 24. Visited Thomas Conrad's, Edwin Dull's, Nathaniel Pfaff's and Benjamine Pfaff's, and returned home. I find the young people in this neighborhood are mostly gone to the Methodists and Lutherans. I have no material left to build up a congregation with. If a change had been made 5 or six years ago it might have done some good, but it is too late now; and I find the same state of things at Bethabara, the young people are all gone to the Methodists. ([Bethania Report:] I asked brother Christian Hauser why it was so. He said they went to the Methodist meetings and professed religion and there was no notice taken of them on our part, and so they joined at Maple Springs and Mt. Tabor, and are gone for good so far as we are concerned. Now what encouragement is there for any man to labor with such a prospect ahead, and the Lord requires impossibilities of no man, and yet it might have all been prevented if the right course had been pursued in time, and instead of things in the condition in which they are, the whole current around Bethany and Bethabara might be in our favor.)

([Bethania Report:] *Mon., Jan. 29.* Visited Mr. Michael Hauser's, Joseph Conrad's, and Mrs. Church, a widow. She wishes to join the Church again. Also visited Mrs. Booze.)

Wed., Feb. 14. A beautiful day; was spading in the garden. In the evening it began to rain and after night it cleared off cold from the west.

Thurs., Feb. 15. The coldest morning this winter, thermometer down to five and falling all day.

Sun., Feb. 18. Rain and sleet; about 20 persons were in Church. In the evening went to Salem to participate in the Centennial Jubilee of that congregation. . . .

([Bethania Report:] *Mon., Feb. 26.* Sr. R. and myself visited old Mrs. Bowser. Sung and prayed with her. Coming home we called in at Brother William Leinbach's and took supper. We then united with the family in singing several of our Moravian hymns and closed with prayer. It was one of the most pleasant evenings we have spent in some time.)

Sat., Mar. 10. In the evening I preached for the colored people in their church.

Sat., Mar. 17. Preached for the negroes at night in their church.

Sun., Mar. 18. Opened the Sunday School then preached from Luke 17:11-20. Brother William Shore and Calvin Hauser were present. In the afternoon I preached at Bethabara to a good congregation and closed with a prayer meeting, the brethren E. A. Vogler and Allen Spach participating. I went and took supper with Mr. Joseph Buttner. He and his wife wish to join at Bethabara again.

Sat., Mar. 24. Preached at night to the negroes and although Ezra Hauser had a show in town I had a good congregation.

Sun., Apr. 15. On coming home 1/2 after 9 o'clock found that brother H. Butner had had another severe attack. I went down and staid until 3 o'clock in the morning when he had somewhat recovered again.

Sat., Apr. 28. Preached the funeral and buried the remains of Mrs. Christina Eccles, late Mock, wife of Mr. Harrison Eccles, at Hope. After the funeral I had to hurry home, as I had an engagement to keep confirmation instruction at 5 o'clock, and on leaving Hope came near having an accident. I had turned the buggy round towards Bethany, and when I got in, Sam concluded that he would go to Friedberg, and turned short round and threw Sr. Rights out. One side of the line broke, and he started off in a full run. Fortunately the other side of the line held out, and I reined him against a tree and stopped him. We got home in time and I attended to the instruction. After night I had services for the negroes in their church and baptized three children. The negroes seem [to] take quite an interest in the meetings.

Sun., Apr. 29. At night there was prayer meeting or rather a "Sing Stund," as there is no one to take part but myself in praying. But the meetings in the week and on Sunday evenings are well attended. I open with a hymn, prayer, short address, and then we sing a number of hymns and close with prayer. The singing is delightful. Old and young, even the little children, join in with a will to swell the songs of praise.

Sun., May 13. Preached at 11 o'clock at Spainhour's school house from John 3:2 to a large and attentive congregation. At 4 o'clock I preached at Mr. Woolf's school house near the Pilot Mountain; here too I had a good congregation. After preaching I went home with brother Edward Buttner, where I spent a pleasant night with his truly interesting family. Brother Buttner is very anxious to have Moravian preaching in his neighborhood.

Sun., May 28 [27]. Sunday School celebration at Bethania, text Exodus 2:9. At the close brother Thornton and brother E. A. Vogler made addresses. There was a good attendance and everybody seemed pleased with the exercises, especially the singing. The Brass Band was in attendance and did good service in filling up the interval between the addresses.

Sun., June 3. After returning home about 9 o'clock word came from Sallie Lahman that she wished to see me. I went over and found her weeping bitterly. She said: Mr. Rights, I want you to pray for me; I am such a great sinner. We spent some time in conversation and prayer.

Mon., June 4. Called on Sally Lahman this morning, found her still very much distressed, read and prayed with her.

Tues., June 5. Called on Sallie Lahman. She met me joyfully and said: I have found my Saviour. I said when! Yesterday about noon, now I am ready to be confirmed.

Wed., June 6. Prayer meeting at night in the church. At the close I gave notice if there were any in the congregation that wished to speak with me about their souls they should go to the school house, and I would meet them there. On going over I found three persons, Oliver Lehman, Frank Butner and Egbert Lehman, waiting for me.

Thurs., June 7. ([Margin note:] Revival at Bethania.) [Following the evening prayer meeting:] From having been by myself we were now six, and we again engaged in prayer, and while I was praying James [Butner] found peace, and after a little Egbert likewise, but poor Oliver, it seemed he could not get through. After waiting with him about an hour it was then near midnight. He said he must go home, and he was afraid he would have to give it up. I told him he would get right by morning. I went home, and went to bed. In about an hour I was awakened by some knocking at the door, and on getting up and opening, there stood Oliver. He said he had found peace, and he could not wait till morning to tell the news. After rejoicing together a few moments, he went down the street bareheaded and barefooted to tell some more of his friends what the Lord had done for his soul.

Sun., June 10. Celebrated the anniversary of the Congregation . . . and at the close of the sermon 9 persons were confirmed. . . . At the close of the confirmation brother John Aulspaug (he present by request) prayed. In the afternoon at 2 o'clock there was lovefeast for the whole congregation, and afterwards the Holy Communion was administered to about one hundred and fifty persons. It was truly a solemn time, and the Lord was sensibly in our midst. At night there was prayer meeting.

[Br. Rights' revival at Bethania continued through the week to prayer meeting on *Sat., June 16:*] Thus far about 30 persons have made a profession of religion.

Sun., June 24. At 10 o'clock preached the funeral of Lewis F. Hine, a young man that was shot in Feb. 1864 in Caldwell County by one of the Home Guard from Watauga County in endeavoring to make his way through the lines and go North. The Church was full.

Thurs., July 19. Evening meeting at Bethabara still continues. Some interest appears to be awakening, and the attendance is on the increase.

Sat., July 21. In the evening, meeting at Bethabara. During the week 6 have professed to have found peace in believing and several are still seeking, and tonight the house could not contain more than half the people. Our Prot. Meth. Brethren are taking the alarm; tomorrow there are to be three preachers at Maple Springs.

Mon., July 24 [23]. Being detained, it was late in the evening before I got to Bethabara. I enjoyed the meeting, as I was for once an outsider and took my place among the sinners in the passage, as the house was full and as many outside. I watched some youngsters who had got behind the door and were laughing and talking all the time. At the close I went up to them and gave them a lecture upon the impropriety and sinfulness of their conduct and exhorted them to repent of this and all their other wickedness. They looked as though they would have dropped through the floor, and have behaved very decently ever since. Somebody remarked afterwards that the batteries opened from both sides of the house.

Wed., Aug. 1. Meeting at "Old Town" still going on.

Thurs., Fri., Aug. 2, 3. Meetings at Old Town closed up on Friday evening. Some 20 have professed during the 3 weeks.

Sat., Aug. 19 [18]. Commenced a meeting at Spainhour's school house.

Tues., Aug. 22 [21]. Some 14 had made profession, one man 49 years old and his 2 grown sons.

Sat., Sept. 1. Buried the widow Catharine Reich, late Linebach, at Bethabara. A heavy rain coming up during the services, we could not cross the meadow on account of the high water and had to haul the corpse round the fields to the graveyard.

Sun., Sept. 16. Preached at Stony Ridge School house in Surry County near the Pilot Mountain to a good congregation.

Wed., Sept. 19. Went up on the Pilot Mountain. A Mr. Stevenson preached at the foot of the Pinicle.

Mon., Oct. 8. Went to Long's School House and preached at night.

Sun., Oct. 14. Married people's, widowers' and widows' festival. At the close brother Bahnson addressed the communicants once more, exhorting them to continue faithful to that master whom they had chosen, and expressed his gratification at seeing that so many of the young had come out on the Lord's side, and hoped that the number would still increase. There was a deep feeling in the congregation and tears flowed freely.

([Bethania Report:] *Wed., Dec. 26.* By request I attended a Sunday School celebration at Double Bridge school house. Brother Bahnson was also invited but could not attend. A Lovefeast had been provided under the superintendence of brother Henry Fogle, and while the cakes and coffee were served round, I made an address. As the day was very cold and the arrangements were out of doors, we were rather uncomfortable situated. After the Lovefeast was over we adjourned into the school house, as many as could get in, and then the shutters were closed, and during the singing of some hymns selected for the occasion candles were also here distributed, and everything, considering the unfavorableness of the weather, passed off very pleasantly. At the same time brother Benjamine Linebach had a Lovefeast and candles for his Sunday School children at Pfafftown. A number of persons from Bethania went out and came back well pleased with everything they heard and saw. His school during the summer numbered 80 children. During the year the attendance at the Sunday Schools has been at Bethania 40, Pfafftown 80, Bethabara 75, Double Bridge 50, total 245.)

Friedberg Diary, with Macedonia, Muddy Creek, 1866
[Extracts transcribed; handwriting is that of R. Parmenio
Leinbach.]

Sat., Jan. 6. Have arranged this school house matter. According to the deed it dare be used only for school house and nothing else or deed becomes valueless.

Sun., Jan. 7. We went to Macedonia this morning. The Synodal delegation was there, and a very encouraging subscription taken up at once.

Sat., Jan. 13. The brn. busy putting up a school house.

Sun., Jan. 21. After dinner started off to Muddy Creek. When I got there found they were all gone. It was deemed advisable to drop the service during the winter, as there was no stove at the church.

Sat., Jan. 27. Have been devoting much time for prayer for the church at Friedberg. The remains of the political discords and dissentions are still to be traced, and these must all be worked off before the church can be blessed.

Sun., Feb. 4. ([Friedberg Report:] Preached at Macedonia from 2 Cor. 12:14. 'Twas bitter cold and not many were present. After preaching, a new Committee was elected, viz.: the Brn. D. and R. Sheek and Edw. Lee. Br. Hall was also elected as an addition to the number. Meanwhile, Samuel Smith, in a fit of drunkenness, was trying to ride his mule into the Church. He attempted it twice. The second time I saw him and spoke to him, when he went off. It was said that a young man, D. Smith, had entered the Church on his horse and ridden round the stove some time previous.)

Wed., Feb. 14. Went to Salem to procure "Jubilee Tickets."

Sat., Feb. 17. Committee meeting. ([Friedberg Report:] Some unfavorable reports concerning Br. Jesse Knauss and Widow Bruer having been circulated, he demanded a trial, which came off this afternoon. Nothing having been proved either way, the case was dismissed.)

Sun., Feb. 18. Preached at Friedberg on Malachi 3:8. Close of the first century of the existence of Salem. Celebration of the centenary jubilee commenced. Went to Salem to attend celebration.

Thurs., Mar. 29. The hawks are very troublesome, and have carried off several chickens.

Sun., Apr. 1. Easter Sunday. At an early hour the people began to come in. The day was unusually fine. About 10 the congregation assembled to go on the graveyard. The school came first, then the minister; after him came the females followed by the males. The order of the procession was well observed, and reflected great credit on the managers. The church was afterwards crowded, and many were unable to get in.

Mon., Apr. 2. Out hawk hunting with Mr. John Foltz.

Wed., Apr. 4. Writing and copying church records.

Sat., Apr. 21. Spread leaves, spaded, and planted the rest of my potato patch. Was at work from 5 A.M. until dark.

Sat., May 19. Sarah Ann and myself went to Salem. She had not been up there for three months.

Sat., May 26. Today we had a very heavy rain. It commenced raining early this morning. About 10 A.M. it thundered, and 3 clouds met overhead, and they poured out a perfect torrent of water. Bridges and fences were swept away, meadows overflown, broad swathes made in the corn fields in freshly plowed ground, and wheat, etc., in bottoms submerged. About 1 P.M. it stopped.

Fri., June 1. Killed a copperhead snake out at the gate. I have been much exercised about the condition of the church. The members are entirely too much divided about politics, and some are too much estranged. I have made the prosperity of our Zion the subject of earnest prayer in private. May God hear us.

Sun., June 17. Went over to Muddy Creek. At Friedberg Br. David Wesner preached; in the afternoon the brn. had a truly blessed prayer meeting; the brn. D. Wesner, Nath. Mock, and John Knauss took part or rather were the principal speakers. Br. J. Knauss then spoke in public for the first time in years. These political difficulties had caused brn. to lose confidence in him.

Sat., Aug. 4. Started over to Davie Co. to hold protracted meeting. Saturday evening I began my labors with prayer meeting.

([Friedberg Report:] *Mon., Aug. 13.* Went over to Macedonia to continue the services, but found the people worn out and fatigued, and therefore bro't the meeting to a close Monday evening.)

Sun., Aug. 19. Ever since my entrance upon my duties, I had been painfully sensible that the results of the war had left their sad effects upon this congregation [Friedberg]. Political feeling was now as high as during the struggle, and the bitterness between the two parties threatened to wreck the church, and it was the subject of unceasing prayer with me that God would pour out his spirit upon this congregation, heal these differences of feeling, and unite the church in the bands of holy love once [more]. Riding or walking, on hayloft or in garret, by day and by night—the congregation [remains the] subject of my earnest prayer [to] God, who hears in secret, rewards me openly.

Mon., Aug. 27. ([Friedberg Report:] Whilst we had meeting at Macedonia, a certain Baptist preacher, Rev. Mr. Cornish, had protracted meeting at Muddy Creek, the result of which has been an accession of some 36 members to his congregation. I am told one of the Friedberg members, Sr. Anne Eccles, contemplates joining his church. I have preached over there nearly six years, never had a single convert, and one protracted meeting sweeps out the neighborhood.)

[The Friedberg Diary interrupts. The following is from the Private Diary of R. Parmenio Leinbach.]

Thurs., Sept. 6. Conference at Salem. Saw Br. Oerter; he bro't S.S. song books from Br. Wolle.

Sat., Sept. 8. Protracted meeting commenced at Friedberg.

Mon., Sept. 17. Should have gone to Salem, but did not. Ministers Feast. Meeting again at night. Conversed with Wm. Seides. Quite a good meeting (Br. Knauss exhorted), but the interest abating.

Tues., Sept. 18. Closed the meetings. From all that I can learn, the number of persons professing to have found peace in believing amounts to about 60.

Thurs., Sept. 27. Went to Salem to hear Br. Moran. He preached on Psalm 8. He showed that man's physical[?] structure represented the mineral, animal, and vegetable kingdom, that God valued things in the ratio of the capability of manifesting his glory, that man is the subject of contention between two worlds.

[The Friedberg Diary picks up again.]

Tues., Oct. 2. Visited some of our Muddy Creek members and friends. The Committee of Friedberg wishes them to enrol themselves among Friedberg membership, but they decline.

Sun., Oct. 28. Preached from Heb. 11:23-24. Afterwards baptized one, and confirmed 38 individuals; 3 confirmands were absent on account of sickness. 'Twas a great time for Friedberg.

[The Friedberg Diary interrupts. The following is from the Friedberg Report.]

Sun., Dec. 2. Went to Macedonia. Since last fall the congregations here have much improved in quantity as well as quality.

Tues., Dec. 25. Christmas Day. At an early hour the people, and especially the children, began coming in. We had been practising the S.S. scholars in singing Xmas songs and anthems, and had prepared, to some extent, for a dialogue to be spoken by the smaller scholars, but owing to bad weather and worse roads, they could not practice, and we had almost given up all idea of undertaking to have it in public, but we found the children very anxious to have it, so therefore resolved to undertake, tho' they had never yet all been together. The day was unusually fine, and the church thronged in every part.

The preaching was succeeded by Children's Lovefeast. Then came the Dialogue. The children all did remarkably well and gave general satisfaction. In the same meeting the smaller children recited verses, for which they received tickets with verses printed on them to be learned for next year.

Mon., Dec. 31. For the first time in the new[1] church there was "Watch Meeting" at midnight. In consequence of the bad weather, but few attended.

---

[1]Meaning the "new" Friedberg church consecrated July 28, 1827. Until the December 31, 1866, "Watch Meeting," the congregation's Memorabilia were traditionally read in the midmorning service on January 1.

Friedland Reports, with Hope, 1866
Includes Kernersville beginning with August
[Extracts transcribed; handwriting is that of Charles Henry
Cooper.]

Sun., Jan. 14. Br. Vogler and br. Fulkerson and others from
Salem came out to meet with us today. Br. Vogler then
communicated his report concerning the financial state of our
Province, urging upon his hearers to endeavour to do what
they could for the temporal as well as spiritual interests of the
Church.

Thurs., Jan. 25. It having been previously announced that
br. Leinbach from Friedberg and friend E. A. Vogler and others
from Salem would be present, the attendance at prayer meeting was unusually large, solemn, and interesting. The words of
God, "I will clothe her priests with salvation: and her saints
shall shout aloud for joy," were remarkably fulfilled on this
occasion. So great was the emotion that br. L. was forced to
retire from the stand until it had somewhat subsided.

Sun., Feb. 4. I preached at Hope from Mark 13:34 to a large
and orderly assembly. The financial committee from Salem was
present on this occasion and succeeded in obtaining quite a
good subscription.

Sun., Feb. 11. Meeting at night numerously attended, especially by young people. The effects were not, apparently, as
such favorable circumstances incline us to desire.

Sun., Feb. 25. We had prayer meeting again at night.
Though cast down I was not destroyed.

Mon., Mar. 12. Made my first visit to Kernersville. I stopped
at Dr. Kerner's.

Tues., Mar. 13. In company with br. John Fredric Kerner I
visited people residing in town who are in connection with our
Church. At night I preached in the Methodist Episcopal
Church from 1 Cor. 2:2 to a good audience.

Wed., Mar. 14. I visited br. Phillip Kerner's and then returned home.

Thurs., Apr. 26. We had a profitable prayer meeting at
night. In view of alarming judgments, I exhorted the people to
embrace the cause of God as the only way for present and
eternal safety.

Sat., Apr. 28. We went to see a Mr. Hiatt, who starts for
Iowa on Sunday.

Sun., Apr. 29. The good Spirit was especially present at the evening meeting. . . . We have seldom been so near the shore of eternal deliverance as this time. *We only need more life and work on the part of everyone to ensure success.*

Fri., May 18. I returned to Salem and found father dying. He breathed his last on Saturday, 20th [19th].

Tues., May 22. After the funeral of my deceased parent the day previous we returned to Friedland.

Thurs., June 14. Prayer meeting at night and well attended. Messrs. White and Ellis were present. The former addressed the meeting upon the subject of music and singing schools, one of which they endeavoured to raise here. Subsequent attempts to procure the requisite number of pupils having failed demonstrates the impracticability of such a movement at this time.

Fri., July 6. In the evening br. R. de Schweinitz paid a short and final farewell to old Friedland.

Sun., July 15. I rode to Kernersville and preached to a respectable audience. After service those specially interested remained and determined in the good Providence of the Lord to endeavour to establish a branch of the Brethren's Church at that place. The spirit manifested was truly encouraging.

Tues., Nov. 20. I was taken with a chill this morning and obliged to take [to] my bed, upon which I was prostrated nearly a month. During this time I received many expressions of friendship from brn. and relatives.

[New] Philadelphia Diary, 1866
[Extracts transcribed; handwriting is that of Emil A. de Schweinitz.]

Sun., Jan. 7. Dined at Br. Jno. Butner's. He [is] in trouble about taxes.

Sun., Jan. 21. The Synodal Committee appointed to visit the country congregations was present by appointment, consisting of Brrn. E. A. Vogler, Jacob Fulkerson, and Br. Tim. Transou from Phila. Br. John Siewers, the 4th member, did not appear. After preaching I introduced the Committee, and Br. Vogler then read a statement of the financial condition of Church, calling upon the members and all present to contribute according to their ability to the wants of the Church.

Allusion was made to the peculiar situation of Phila. congregation since Br. Frye's sickness and death, that they had enjoyed the ministration of a brother for whose support they had not to care, hence the congregation was urged to do their utmost now to contribute to Sustentation Diacony. Br. Thomas Spach of Phila. followed Br. Vogler and exhorted the members to give willingly according to their ability. Prayer was then offered up by Br. Thos. Spach and subscription papers circulated. Upwards of $60 were subscribed. Several members were not present who will add their subscriptions. The papers were left in Br. Thos. Spach's hands, to whom the subscriptions are to be paid and by him handed over to Br. Pfohl. After joining in singing once more and the benediction, the congregation was dismissed about 11/2 P.M. A very good feeling prevailed.

Sun., Feb. 4. Invited the congregation to Salem Jubilee celebration.

Sun., Feb. 18. When I had gone about 3 miles the rain began to come down very fast. At the church I found 3 Brethren and 2 sisters and one black man. After having dried and warmed myself, and the lovefeast mugs for the Jubilee at Salem had been packed, I held a prayer meeting, calling upon Br. Thomas Spach to offer up the concluding prayer. The rain poured down as we left the church. Dined at Br. Thomas Spach's and returned home in the rain. At night the solemn close of the century at Salem in the beautifully decorated church.

Mon., Feb. 19. Centenary Jubilee of Salem Congregation. On account of the rain and high water, the members of the Phila. congregation were not present as numerously on this day as they otherwise would have been.

Tues., Feb. 20. 2nd day of festival. Beautiful, mild weather. A large number from Phila. were present and participated in the lovefeast at 21/2 P.M. Some of the Brn. and Sisters remained and partook of Holy Communion at 7 P.M. A very solemn and blessed occasion.

Sun., Mar. 4. After preaching communicated the appeal of Unity Missions Department for aid in view of deficit in last year's account and destruction of mission stations on Mosquito Coast, and announced for the next time a collection to be taken at church door for this purpose.

Thurs., Mar. 8. After dinner drove to Bro. M. Rominger, visited him and wife and their little girl born about 3 weeks since.

Sun., Mar. 18. After sermon, collection for Mosquito Coast mission was taken at church door amounting to $1.85. Dined at Br. John Butner's. In company of Sr. Butner visited Widow Meiers, who wishes to join the Church. She is a communicant member of Protestant Methodist Church, and has 7 children from 15 years downward, all of whom she wants to be considered as joining with her. ([Phila. Report:] The heavy church dues, which she supposed to be required of all members, seemed to be something of a hindrance. Relieved her mind on this subject.) Spoke a few words with Br. Calvin Jones, who offered a lame apology for his irregular attendance at church.

Sun., Apr. 29. When I arrived at church found S. School in operation, which was commenced last Sunday. Thus far about 23 names have been put down.

Sun., May 27. Preached on Romans 9:22 at Philadelphia to a small audience. A great deal of sickness (summer complaint) prevails in the congregation, and the annual Dunker meeting also attracted some of the stated hearers.

Sat., Aug. 11. [At] 2 P.M. celebration at Phila. of Aug 13. [T]he congregation fixed the contributions for Lovefeast and Holy Communion at five cents per head. Except in the case of children of widows, who are to pay only three cents as long as they [are] not communicants.

Sun., Aug. 19. When I arrived at Phila. church found, as I had expected, that the congregation had all gone to Piney Grove, where a protracted meeting has been going on since August 11th in which great interest is taken. Only 3 persons at church. A list of about 8 names was handed to me by Br. Thos. Spach of persons who had professed at Piney Grove and who wished to join at Philadelphia.

Fri., Aug. 24. At early candlelight a prayer meeting at Phila. had been appointed, with special reference to quite a number of young people who had been awakened and professed faith in the Lord Jesus at a recent Methodist protracted meeting at Piney Grove. Br. Grunert accompanied me. We found a good congregation assembled. After the meeting was dismissed I spoke a few words to the converts present and appointed Saturday, Sept. 1, at 3 P.M. at Phila. church as the time for the commencement of instruction preparatory to confirmation.

Sat., Sept. 1. Nine of the candidates were at the church, the others detained by accidents and rainy weather. The list of candidates comprises 15 names. Opened instruction with singing and prayer and closed in same way.

Sun., Sept. 16. The greater part of congregation were at the big meeting at Mt. Tabor, where 3 funeral sermons were preached.

Sat., Oct. 13. There are 3 candidates for baptism and ten for confirmation. They all seem to be sincere. Some, especially of the females, are extremely ignorant of Christian doctrine and Bible knowledge, and one is not able to read. Nevertheless I trust that they all understand the meaning of what they are about doing and are resolved to be the Lord's thro' grace.

Sun., Oct. 14. A beautiful, clear, autumnal day. My wife accompanied me to Phila. today. The church was filled to over-flowing. . . .14 souls in all were added to Phila. communicant congregation. After a short interval the Holy Communion was celebrated. Fifty communicants (besides myself) were present, including a few from other congregations and two Methodist sisters. The 14 new members were of course all present. . . .

Sun., Oct. 28. Took dinner at Br. Martin Rominger's, whom I tried to induce to come to an amicable settlement with Reuben Crater, who has been managing his farm. Their dis-agreement threatens unpleasant difficulties between families nearly related to each other and disturbance of brotherly love in the congregation.

Wed., Nov 7. At 2 P.M. drove to Br. John Crater's to speak with him about the difficulty existing between his son Reuben and Br. Martin Rominger. Br. John Crater had made an appeal to several brethren of the Committee on the subject.

Sun., Nov 11. About 3 P.M. drove to Br. M. Rominger's to bring him to the church. All the members of the Committee were present and Br. John Crater and his son Reuben as well as Br. Martin Rominger and his wife, the latter as a kind of prompter, because the old man is very forgetful. After stating the case and talking over the whole matter, it appeared that the claims of each party were pretty nearly balanced by those of the other, and that by very slight concessions an agreement could be arrived at. Both parties seemed desirous of settling the matter, and Br. Martin Rominger consented to give up his demands if Reuben Crater would do the same. This was assented to by Reuben Crater, and receipts in full exchanged. A complete reconciliation with shaking of hands took place. . . .

Thurs., Nov. 29. Thanksgiving day appointed by President of U.S. and Governor of N.C. The day proved rainy. Before reaching the church was caught in a shower. On account of the bad weather only about 16 persons, young and old, had assembled.

Statistics of the Moravian Church, Southern Province

1857

	Children	Communi-cants	Non-Com-municants	Total
Salem	206	444	68	718
Bethabara	32	34	32	98
Bethany	119	132	63	314
Friedberg	146	167	114	427
Muddy Creek	9	26	4	39
Macedonia		35	11	46
Hope	17	33	12	62
Friedland	59	26	13	98
Philadelphia	28	18	8	54
Mount Bethel	19	41	19	79
Total	635	956	344	1,935

1866

	Children	Communi-cants	Non-Com-municants	Total
Bethabara	15	28	13	56
Bethany	36	126	18	180
Friedberg	148	248	26	422
Friedland	34	77	29	140
Hope	17	25	3	45
Macedonia	15	35	18	68
Muddy Creek	0	14	5	19
Philadelphia	35	51	3	89
Salem	140	462	50	652
Mount Bethel	45	41	0	86
Total	485	1,107	165	1,757

Salem Register, 1857-1866

Infant Baptisms

Winkler, Margaret Anna, born Jan. 19, 1857, to William Parmenio Winkler and Pauline Mariann m.n. Fischer. Baptized Mar. 15, 1857.

Meinung, Ellen Tryphena, born Feb. 5, 1857, to Ernst Heinrich Meinung and Maria Theresia m.n. Hege. Baptized Mar. 29, 1857.

Friebele, Christian Gilbert, born Mar. 2, 1857, to Johann Adam Friebele and Hedwig Josephine m.n. Oehman. Baptized Apr. 12, 1857.

Vogler, Ella Louisa, born Mar. 6, 1857, to Elias Alexander Vogler and Emma Antoinette m.n. Reich. Baptized June 1, 1857, in the parents' house.

Fischer, Harriett Elfreda, born Apr. 1, 1857, to James Fischer and Francisca m.n. Benzien. Baptized June 25, 1857.

Schneider, Edward Martin, born May 16, 1857, to Sandford Schneider and Maria m.n. Griffin. Baptized June 25, 1857.

Hall, Florence Estelle, born May 6, 1857, to William Henry Hall and Ernestina Augusta m.n. Vierling. Baptized July 5, 1857.

Schulz, George Rufus, born Mar. 13, 1857, to William Ferdinand Schulz and Lucia Josephina m.n. Folz. Baptized Aug. 8, 1857, in the parents' house.

Briez, Adelaide Louisa, born July 1, 1857, to Renatus Levin Briez and Maria Sophia m.n. Blum. Baptized Aug. 9, 1857.

Miller, Samuel Augustus, born July 1, 1857, to William Miller and Susan Jane m.n. Strub. Baptized Aug. 30, 1857.

Shore, James William Neil, born Jan. 24, 1857, to William Sandford Shore and Susan Elisabeth m.n. Kennedy. Baptized Sept. 1, 1857.

Shore, Flora Elisabeth, born Aug. 3 1857, to Henry Washington Shore and Lavinia Ann Elisabeth m.n. Boyer. Baptized Sept. 1, 1857.

Siewers, Gertrude Elisabeth, born July 31, 1857, to Johannes Daniel Siewers and Hannah Amanda m.n. Haines. Baptized Sept. 17, 1857.

Ackerman, Ernestine Elisabeth, born Aug. 9, 1857, to Romulus Alexander Ackerman and Serena Rebecca m.n. Snipe. Baptized Sept. 17, 1857.

Lash, Ida Florence, born Sept. 2, 1857, to Henry M. Lash and Eliza Louisa m.n. Blum. Baptized Oct. 27, 1857.

Fries, Henry Elias, born Sept. 22, 1857, to Francis Fries and Lisette m.n. Vogler. Baptized Nov. 6, 1857.

Strupe, John Joseph, born Sept. 27, 1857, to Carlos Strupe and Anna Lucinda m.n. Spach. Baptized Nov. 6, 1857.

Clinard, Edward Clifton, born Nov. 27, 1857, to Livingston Nathaniel Clinard and Charlotte Elisabeth m.n. Schulz. Baptized Jan. 3, 1858.

Ackerman, John William, born Nov. 25, 1857, to William Augustus Ackerman and Jeanette Elisabeth m.n. Spach. Baptized Jan. 17, 1858.

Ackerman, Alice Victoria, born Dec. 26, 1857, to Edward Ackerman and Elisabeth m.n. Davis. Baptized Feb. 7, 1858.

Hein, Mary Jane, born Jan. 6, 1858, to John Lewis Hein and Mary Paulina m.n. Marshall. Baptized Feb. 21, 1858.

Nading, Granville Rudolphus, born Jan. 15, 1858, to William Nading and Ernestine Eleonor m.n. Spach. Baptized Feb. 21, 1858.

Bevel, Charles Armsworthy, born Oct. 28, 1857, to Christian Alexander Bevel and Sarah Catharine m.n Miller. Baptized Mar. 7, 1858, in the parents' house.

Leinbach, Ada Elisabeth, born Mar. 2, 1858, to Edward William Leinbach and Anna Elisabeth m.n. Clauder. Baptized Mar. 28, 1858.

Kühln, Mary Hortensia, born Feb. 12, 1858, to Orestes Aeneas Kühln and Angelica Elisabeth m.n. Bahnson. Baptized Apr. 4, 1858.

Mitchell, Charles Augustus, born Feb. 15, 1858, to Orrin Mitchell and Lisette Caroline m.n Hein. Baptized Apr. 18, 1858.

Paine, Rufus Gilbert, born Mar. 31, 1858, to James Johann Paine and Emma Elvira m.n. Ackerman. Baptized May 9, 1858.

Rights, George Haynes, born July 25, 1858, to Constantin Rights and Elisabeth m.n. Haynes. Baptized Aug. 16, 1858, in the parents' house.

Hall, John Martin Beck, born July 30, 1858, to Joseph Orestes Hall and Louisa Sophia m.n. Smith. Baptized Sept. 5, 1858.

Meller, Ida Adela, born Sept. 27, 1858, to Francis Meller and Caroline m.n. Reich. Baptized Oct. 31, 1858.

Brietz, Charles Joseph, born Sept. 26, 1858, to Charles Gustavus Brietz and Margaret m.n. Morrow. Baptized Nov. 9, 1858.

Crist, Charles Carrick, born Nov. 18, 1858, to Jacob Rudolph Crist and Miranda Rosalie m.n. Keehln. Baptized Dec. 26, 1858.

Snyder, John Paul, born Dec. 6, 1858, to Sanford A. Snyder and Maria Elizabeth m.n. Griffin. Baptized Jan. 16, 1859.

Shore, Charles Edward, born Jan. 14, 1859, to Henry Washington Shore and Lavinia Elizabeth m.n. Boyer. Baptized Mar. 6, 1859.

Lash, Charles Henry Blum, born Feb. 16, 1859, to Henry M. Lash and Eliza m.n. Blum. Baptized Apr. 3, 1859, in the house of the grandfather, David Blum, at Waughtown.

Grunert, Francis Eugene, born Jan. 31, 1859, to Maximilian Eugene Grunert and Emma Theresa m.n. Pfohl. Baptized Apr. 3, 1859.

Butner, Charles Flavius, born Mar. 22, 1859, to Samuel Edwin Butner and Julia Caroline m.n. Eberhard. Baptized May 1, 1859.

Yates, Mary Jane, born Nov. 14, 1856, to Charles Yates and Mary m.n. McMillan. Baptized June 20 [19], 1859.

Yates, Charles Francis, born June 23, 1858, to Charles Yates and Mary m.n. McMillan. Baptized June 19, 1859.

Pfohl, Ellen Augusta, born June 7, 1859, to Edward A. Pfohl and Matilda C. m.n. Phillips. Baptized July 17, 1859.

Bevel, Martha Elizabeth, born May 22, 1859, to Christian Alexander Bevel and Sarah Catharine m.n. Miller. Baptized Aug. 7, 1859.

Starbuck, Ella, born July 25, 1859, to Darius Starbuck and Ellen m.n. Blickensderfer. Baptized Aug. 19, 1859, in the parents' house.

Holland, Sarah Horsfield, born Aug. 10, 1859, to Francis R. Holland and Eliza Augusta m.n. Wolle. Baptized Sept. 11, 1859.

Mickey, Charles Samuel, born Aug. 31, 1859, to Wm. Francis Mickey and Sarah Elizabeth m.n. Ferguson. Baptized Oct. 9, 1859.

Hall, Gertrude Sophia, born Sept. 13, 1859, to Wm. Henry Hall and Ernestina Augusta m.n. Vierling. Baptized Oct. 23, 1859.

Keehln, Emma Rosalie, born Nov. 11, 1859, to Orestes A. Keehln and Angelica Elizabeth m.n. Bahnson. Baptized Dec. 18, 1859.

Fockel, Jane Adelaide, born Nov. 24, 1859, to Augustus G. Fockel and Lucinda Elizabeth m.n. Snyder. Baptized Dec. 23, 1859, in the parents' house.

Brietz, Margaret Louisa, born Dec. 6, 1859, to Charles G. Brietz and Margaret m.n. Morrow. Baptized Jan. 5, 1860, in the parents' house.

Vogler, William Edward, born Dec. 5, 1859, to Alexander C. Vogler and Antoinette S. m.n. Hauser. Baptized Jan. 20, 1860, in the parents' house.

Fries, Louisa Sarah, born Dec. 8, 1859, to Francis Fries and Lisette m.n. Vogler. Baptized Jan. 26, 1860, in the parents' house.

Snyder, George Daniel, born Dec. 11, 1859, to Sanford A. Snyder and Maria Elizabeth m.n. Griffin. Baptized Feb. 17. 1860, in the parents' house.

Hall, Josephine Augusta, born Feb. 19, 1860, to Joseph Orestes Hall and Louisa Sophia m.n. Smith. Baptized Mar. 25, 1860.

Sussdorff, Ellen Louisa, born Mar. 6, 1860, to Christian F. Sussdorff and Louisa C. m.n. Hagen. Baptized Apr. 8, 1860.

Hauser, Mary Frances Gilmer, born Mar. 18, 1860, to Charles F. Hauser and Hermina E. m.n. Benzien. Baptized May 13, 1860.

Lash, Rosa Virginia, born Apr. 3, 1860, to H. M. Lash and Eliza m.n. Blum. Baptized May 17, 1860, in the house of David Blum at Waughtown.

Fetter, Mary Louisa, born Apr. 25, 1860, to Peter Fetter and Sarah Louisa m.n. Stockburger. Baptized May 20, 1860, in the parents' house at Liberty.

Mickey, Rosa Elvira, born May 24, 1860, to Julius E. Mickey and Lavinia M. m.n. Vogler. Baptized July 8, 1860.

Shore, George Edward, born Apr. 2, 1859, to Wm. Shore and Susan Elizabeth m.n. Kennedy. Baptized Aug. 28, 1860, in the parents' house at Liberty.

Pfohl, Henry Augustus, born July 21, 1860, to Augustus F. Pfohl and Elizabeth m.n. Siewers. Baptized Sept. 2, 1860.

Shore, William Thomas, born Sept. 7, 1860, to Henry Washington Shore and Lavinia m.n. Boyer. Baptized Oct. 14, 1860.

Crist, Anna Caroline, born Oct. 3, 1860, to Traugott F. Crist and Maria m.n. Haman. Baptized Oct. 28, 1860.

de Schweinitz, Anna Paulina, born Oct. 28, 1860, to Emil A. de Schweinitz and Sophia A. m.n. Hermann. Baptized Dec. 9, 1860.

Carmichael, Alma May, born Nov. 18, 1860, to Francis Carmichael and Eliza F. m.n. Vierling. Baptized Dec. 23, 1860.

Blum, Adelaide Elizabeth, born Dec. 6, 1860, to Edmund T. Blum and Sarah Catharine m.n. Hartman. Baptized Dec. 26, 1860, in the parents' house.

Bahnson, Lewis Kraepelien, born Nov. 25, 1860, to George F. Bahnson and Louisa A. m.n. Belo. Baptized Dec. 30, 1860.

Atwood, Mary Bell, born Aug. 12, 1860, to Jesse William Atwood and Nancy Florence m.n. Coletraine. Baptized Sept. 15, 1860, in the parents' house. [Recorded out of sequence.]

Yates, Caroline Amelia, born Nov. 29, 1860, to Charles Yates and Mary m.n. McMillan. Baptized Jan. 13, 1861.

Butner, Dora Ellen, born Oct. 20, 1860, to Samuel Edwin Butner and Julia Caroline m.n. Eberhard. Baptized Jan. 13, 1861.

Shultz, Sophia Foltz, born Feb. 4, 1861, to William F. Shultz and Lucia Josephine m.n. Foltz. Baptized Mar. 11, 1861, in the parents' house.

Mickey, William Henry, born Feb. 4, 1861, to William Francis Mickey and Sarah Elizabeth m.n. Ferguson. Baptized Mar. 14, 1861, in the parents' house.

Hall, Augustus Josephus, born Dec. 22, 1860, to William Henry Hall and Ernestina Augusta m.n. Vierling. Baptized Mar. 17, 1861, in the parents' house.

Grunert, Caroline Elizabeth, born Feb. 26, 1861, to Maximilian E. Grunert and Emma Theresa m.n. Pfohl. Baptized Apr. 21, 1861.

Fisher, John Lewis Benzien, born Mar. 4, 1861, to James Fisher and Francisca L. m.n. Benzien. Baptized Apr. 21, 1861.

Leake, George Constantine, born Mar. 14, 1861, to George W. Leake and Charlotte Malvina m.n. Reich. Baptized May 12, 1861, in the house of Charles Cooper.

Kernan, Edward Owen, born Nov. 11, 1860, to Dr. Thomas D. Kernan and Sophia C. m.n. Kremer. Baptized June 9, 1861.

Meller, Edward Francis, born May 24, 1861, to Francis William Meller and Henrietta Caroline m.n. Reich. Baptized June 30, 1861.

Leinbach, Emma Louisa, born June 26, 1861, to Edward Wm. Leinbach and Anna Elizabeth m.n. Clauder. Baptized July 28, 1861.

Snyder, Preston Alexander, born June 14, 1861, to Sanford Alexander Snyder and Maria Elizabeth m.n. Griffin. Baptized Aug. 7, 1861.

Vogler, Mary Anna, born Aug. 30, 1861, to Alexander C. Vogler and Antoinette S. m.n. Hauser. Baptized Sept. 25, 1861.

Strupe, Ellen Sophia, born Sept. 25, 1861, to Carlos Strupe and Anna Lucinda m.n. Spach. Baptized Dec. 2, 1861, in the parents' house.

Peck, Clarence Eugene, born Nov. 20, 1861, to Calvin Peck and Amanda m.n. Ebert. Baptized Jan. 12, 1862.

Ackerman, Charles Alexander, born Nov. 16, 1861, to Romulus Alexander Ackerman and Serena Rebecca m.n. Snipe. Baptized Jan. 26, 1862, in the parents' house.

Hall, Dennis Headly, born Jan. 5, 1862, to Joseph O. Hall and Louisa S. m.n. Schmidt. Baptized Feb. 23, 1862, in the dwelling room of Sr. Hall's mother in the Widows House.

Shore, George Decatur, born Jan. 14, 1862, to Henry Washington Shore and Lavinia Ann Elizabeth m.n. Boyer. Baptized Feb. 23, 1862.

Ackerman, Irwin Sylvester, born Dec. 20, 1861, to William A. Ackerman and Emily m.n. Tesh. Baptized Mar. 9, 1862, in the house of the widow Sr. Rudelphia Ackerman.

Holland, Jane Edith, born Feb. 15, 1862, to Francis R. Holland and Augusta E. m.n. Wolle. Baptized Mar. 9, 1862.

Wimmer, John Walter, born Jan. 18, 1862, to John Mathew Wimmer and Mary Russell m.n. Cloud. Baptized Mar. 23, 1862.

Shultz, John Livingston, born Oct. 8, 1861, to Edmund James Shultz and Cynthia m.n. Thomas. Baptized Apr. 19, 1862, in the house of Br. Clinard.

Keehln, George Leander, born Mar. 27, 1862, to Orestes A. Keehln and Angelica E. m.n. Bahnson. Baptized May 25, 1862.

Winkler, James Lewis, born May 6, 1862, to William P. Winkler and Sarah Ann Elizabeth m.n. Phillips. Baptized June 1, 1862.

Winkler, William Henry, born May 6, 1862, to William P. Winkler and Sarah Ann Elizabeth m.n. Phillips. Baptized June 1, 1862.

Pfohl, Frederick Siewers, born Apr. 27, 1862, to Augustus F. Pfohl and Elizabeth m.n. Siewers. Baptized June 15, 1862.

Roege, William Henry, born June 26, 1862, to Augustus Roege and Christina m.n. Parnell. Baptized Aug. 17, 1862, in the parents' house.

Brietz, John Levin, born Aug. 27, 1862, to Charles A. Brietz and Margaret m.n. Morrow. Baptized Oct. 5, 1862.

Mickey, Mary Elizabeth, born Oct. 21, 1862, to William Francis Mickey and Sarah Elizabeth m.n. Ferguson. Baptized Nov. 16, 1862.

Snyder, Helena Elizabeth, born Oct. 20, 1862, to Sanford A. Snyder and Maria Elizabeth m.n. Griffin. Baptized Dec. 28, 1862.

Butner, Paul Zevely, born Jan. 9, 1863, to Albert Israel Butner and Johanna Sophia m.n. Zevely. Baptized Jan. 26, 1863, in the parents' house.

Butner, Alice Estelle, born Dec. 12, 1862, to Samuel Edwin Butner and Julia Caroline m.n. Eberhard. Baptized Feb. 15, 1863.

de Schweinitz, Paul Robert, born Mar. 16, 1863, to Robt. de Schweinitz and Marie L. m.n. Tschirschky. Baptized Apr. 12, 1863.

Brooks, George Henry, born Apr. 29, 1863, to Charles B. Brooks and Elizabeth C. m.n. Lemly. Baptized June 3, 1863.

Peterson, William Jacob, born May 8, 1863, to William P. Peterson and Paulina D. m.n. Stolz. Baptized June 21, 1863.

Meller, Alice Estella, born Dec. 13, 1863, to Francis William Meller and Henrietta Caroline m.n. Reich. Baptized Jan. 17, 1864, in the parents' house.

Vogler, Adelaide Eugenia, born Nov. 26, 1863, to Elias Alexander Vogler and Emma Antoinette m.n. Reich. Baptized Jan. 31, 1864.

Ackerman, Rufus Augustus, born Sept. 21, 1863, to William Alexander Ackerman and Emily Florina m.n. Tesh. Baptized Feb. 14, 1864.

Carmichal, Robert Lee, born Jan. 13, 1864, to William Francis Carmichal and Eliza Federicka m.n. Vierling. Baptized Mar. 6, 1864.

Schweinitz, Emil Alexander, born Jan. 18, 1864, to Emil Adolphus Schweinitz and Sophia Amelia m.n. Herman. Baptized Mar. 13, 1864.

Vogler, Francis Henry, born Jan. 22, 1864, to Alexander Christopher Vogler and Antoinette Susanna m.n. Houser. Baptized Mar. 13, 1864.

Brietz, Anna Catherine, born Apr. 7, 1864, to Charles Gustavus Brietz and Margaret m.n. Morrow. Baptized May 22, 1864.

Pfohl, Constance Elizabeth, born Apr. 10, 1864, to Augustus Frederick Pfohl and Elizabeth m.n. Siewers. Baptized June 5, 1864.

Shore, Henry Augustus, born May 10, 1864, to Henry Washington Shore and Lavinia m.n. Boyer. Baptized June 26, 1864.

Keehln, Paulina May, born May 22, 1864, to Orestes Aeneas Keehln and Angelica Elizabeth m.n. Bahnson. Baptized July 10, 1864.

Fogel, John Daniel, born June 5, 1864, to Augustus Gottlieb Fogel and Lucinda Elizabeth m.n. Snyder. Baptized July 20, 1864.

Reed, Mary Louisa, born Aug. 29, 1863, to Dr. William O. Reed and Jeanette Florentine m.n. Hagen. Baptized July 22, 1864, in the parents' house at Mount Airy.

Wheeler, Anna Claudia, born May 24, 1864, to Dr. William H. Wheeler and Adelaide Matilda m.n. Shober. Baptized, Aug. 7, 1864.

Atwood, Jesse William, born Aug. 16, 1862, to the late Jesse William Atwood and Nancy Florence m.n. Coletraine. Baptized Aug. 9, 1864.

Fisher, Emma Hermine, born June 26, 1864, to James Fisher and Francisca Louisa m.n. Benzien. Baptized Aug. 17, 1864.

Miller, John William, born July 16, 1864, to Irwin Miller and Olive Victoria m.n. Boyer. Baptized Aug. 28, 1864.

Horton, Hamilton Vogler, born July 20, 1864, to Harrison Horton and Mary Jane m.n. Vogler. Baptized Oct. 23, 1864.

Brooks, Charles Iverson, born Nov. 21, 1864, to Charles B. Brooks and Elizabeth m.n. Lemly. Baptized Dec. 29, 1864, in the house of the child's grandmother.

Hendricks, Robert Lee, born Mar. 23, 1864, to Nathaniel Hendricks and Letitia Isabella m.n. Brown. Baptized Jan. 8, 1865.

Peck, William Calvin, born Oct. 24, 1864, to Calvin Peck and Amanda Lucretia m.n. Ebert. Baptized Jan. 15, 1865.

Butner, John Lewis, born Feb. 19, 1865, to Samuel Edwin Butner and Julia Catherine m.n. Eberhard. Baptized Apr. 16, 1865.

Patterson, Francis Fries, born May 31, 1865, to Rufus L. Patterson and Mary Elizabeth m.n. Fries. Baptized June 30, 1865, in the house of the child's grandmother.

Headley, Samuel Carman, born June 23, 1865, to P. Dennis Headley and Mary Emmeline m.n. Kremer. Baptized Oct. 1, 1865.

Vogler, Mary Alice, born July 27, 1865, to Elias Alexander Vogler and Emma Antoinette m.n. Reich. Baptized Oct. 22, 1865.

Brooks, William Ithiel, born Nov. 8, 1865, to Charles B. Brooks and Elizabeth C. m.n. Lemly. Baptized Dec. 28, 1865, in the house of the child's grandmother.

Rögge, Susan Maria Isabel, born Dec. 8, 1865, to Augustus Rögge and Christina m.n. Parnell. Baptized Jan. 21, 1866.

Hughes, Sarah Odelia, born Dec. 12, 1865, to Henry Hughes and Martha m.n. Collins. Baptized Jan. 21, 1866.

Keehln, Eva Rosalia, born Jan. 27, 1866, to Francis E. Keehln and Sophia Louisa m.n. Reich. Baptized Mar. 18, 1866.

Shaffner, Mary Lisette, born Feb. 13, 1866, to John Francis Shaffner and Caroline Louisa m.n. Fries. Baptized Apr. 21, 1866, in the house of Br. John Vogler.

Shore, Lewis Francis, born Mar. 13, 1866, to Henry Washington Shore and Lavinia m.n. Boyer. Baptized May 13, 1866.

Pfohl, John Jacob, born May 30, 1866, to Augustus Frederick Pfohl and Elizabeth m.n. Siewers. Baptized June 1, 1866, in the parents' house.

Miller, Gertrude May, born May 7, 1866, to Irwin Miller and Olive Victoria m.n. Boyer. Baptized June 10, 1866.

Stockton, Francis William, born Aug. 1, 1866, to Joseph H. Stockton and Julia Elizabeth m.n. Pfohl. Baptized Sept. 23, 1866, in the house of the grandparents.

Starbuck, Henry Reuben, born Aug. 15, 1866, to Darius Starbuck and Ellen m.n. Blickensderfer. Baptized Sept. 23, 1866.

Kernan, Charles Kremer, born Apr. 27, 1864, to Dr. Thomas D. Kernan and Sophia C. m.n. Kremer. Baptized Oct. 11, 1866, in the house of the child's grandmother.

Ackerman, Anna Louisa, born Aug. 12, 1866, to Romulus Alexander Ackerman and Serena Rebecca m.n. Snipe. Baptized Oct. 14, 1866.

Pfohl, Bernard Jacob, born Sept. 13, 1866, to Christian Thomas Pfohl and Margaret m.n. Siewers. Baptized Oct. 21, 1866.

Hendricks, Nathaniel, born Dec. 7, 1866, to Lee Hendricks and Martha Louisa m.n. Fisher. Baptized Dec. 9, 1866, in the parents' house.

Oerter, Albert Eugene, born Oct. 16, 1866, to Albert Lawrence Oerter and Sarah M. m.n. Fetter. Baptized Dec. 23, 1866.

Lineback, Mary Virginia, born Nov. 26, 1866, to Edward William Lineback and Anna Elizabeth m.n. Clauder. Baptized Dec. 26, 1866, in the parents' house.

Adult Baptisms

Tesch, Mary Ann, born Oct. 20, 1834. Baptized Apr. 5, 1857.

Griffin, Martha Sophia, born Oct. 18, 1838, to John M. Griffin and Martha Lucinda m.n. Blum. Baptized Apr. 5, 1857.

Atwood, Jesse William, born Mar. 1, 1831, to William Francis Atwood and Mary m.n. Steelman. Baptized Apr. 5, 1857.

Spach, Maria Elisabeth m.n. Kimmel, born May 15, 1833, to Jacob Kimmel and Nancy m.n. Beckel. Baptized Apr. 26, 1857.

Wimmer, John Matthew, born July 27, 1832, to Peter Wimmer and Mary m.n. Harlan. Baptized Dec. 27, 1857.

Carmichal, William Francis. Baptized Mar. 28, 1858.

Ferguson, Sarah Elisabeth, born Mar. 22, 1839, to Henry Ferguson and Lucinda m.n. Linville. Baptized Mar. 28, 1858.

Hardgrave, Anna Maria, born Aug. 9, 1840, to John Hargrave and Anna m.n Terry. Baptized Mar. 28, 1858.

Peck, Elizabeth, born Aug. 16, 1806, to Barney and Catharine Kimmel. Married to William Peck. Baptized Apr. 17, 1859.

Murchison, Henrietta Amelia, born Oct. 14, 1839, to Roderick Murchison and Henrietta Matilda m.n. Blum. Baptized Apr. 17, 1859.

Schreiber, Elizabeth, born Apr. 3, 1842, to Henry Schreiber and Anna m.n. Taylor. Baptized Apr. 17, 1859.

Atwood, Nancy Florence, born Sept. 22, 1833, to Wm. and Martha Coletraine. Married to Jesse W. Atwood. Baptized July 31, 1859.

Atwood, Benjamin Franklin, born Jan. 18, 1842, to Francis Atwood and Mary m.n. Steelman. Baptized Apr. 1, 1860.

Tesh, Emily Florina, born June 13, 1837, to Henry Tesh and Susanna Barbara m.n. Rothrock. Baptized Apr. 1, 1860.

Boyer, Olive Victoria, born Oct. 2, 1841, to William Boyer and Writter, m.n. Harper. Baptized Apr. 1, 1860.

Ferguson, Rebecca Jane, born Aug. 26, 1842, to Henry Ferguson and Lucinda m.n. Linville. Baptized Apr. 1, 1860.

Jenkins, Huldah Eugenia, born Oct. 6, 1842, to David Jenkins and Mahala m.n. Bryant. Baptized Apr. 1, 1860.

Phillips, Julia Augusta, born Jan. 26, 1844, to Wm. Phillips and Esther m.n. Vickery. Baptized Apr. 1, 1860.

Wells, Mary Jane Lee, born June 4, 1844, in Henry County, Va., to Henry Wells and Mary Ann m.n. Schreyer. Baptized Mar. 24, 1861.

Porter, Jane, born Apr. 10, 1845, in Forsyth County, to Rayford Porter and Eliza m.n. Pearman. Baptized Apr. 13, 1862.

Pfohl, Sarah Eliza, born Sept. 15, 1845, at Columbus, Ga., to Gotthold Pfohl and Jeanette m.n. Crenshawe. Baptized Mar. 29, 1863.

Philips, Susan Rebecca Jane, born Nov. 16, 1845, in Guilford County, to William Philips and Esther m.n. Vickery. Baptized Mar. 29, 1863.

Reddick, Margaret, born Mar. 29, 1835, in Surry County, to Silas Riggs and Martha m.n. Kidd. Married to John Reddick. Baptized June 18, 1863.

Smith, Anna Jane, born May 15, 1846, in Forsyth County, to John Smith and Nancy m.n. Plummer. Baptized Mar. 20, 1864.

Hendrix, Letitia Isabella, born Mar. 8, 1837, in Forsyth County, to Haywood Brown and Revinia m.n. Lumly. Married to Nathaniel Hendrix. Baptized Jan. 1, 1865.

Cook, Mary Elizabeth, born Aug. 7, 1843, near Hope, to Jacob Cook and Nancy m.n. Jarvis. Baptized Jan. 1, 1865.

Kluge, Sarah Caroline, widow Pollock m.n. Bullard, born July 15, 1836, at Grafton, Mass., to John Hall Bullard and Sarah m.n. Dudley. Married to Charles Eugene Kluge. Baptized Mar. 25, 1866.

Philipps, Ada Louisa, born Apr. 6, 1849, to Wm. Philipps and Esther m.n. Wickery. Baptized Mar. 25, 1866.

Fiddler, Mary Elizabeth, born October 1848, to John Thomas Fiddler and Sarah m.n. Crouse. Baptized Mar. 25, 1866.

Wolff, Mary Augusta, born Mar. 5, 1850, to Wesley Wolff and Asley m.n. Shouse. Baptized Mar. 25, 1866.

Nissen, John Israel, born Feb. 28, 1841, at Waughtown to John Philip Nissen and Mary Elizabeth m.n. Vawter. Baptized May 20, 1866.

Marriages

Ackerman, Edward Theophilus, born to Johann Ackerman and Anna Johanna m.n. Spach, married March 5, 1857, to Mary Elisabeth Davis, born Nov. 25, 1826.

Hauser, Charles Ferdinand, born Mar. 9, 1833, to William Hauser and Anna Susannah m.n. Schulz, married July 15, 1857, to Hermina Eleonora Benzien, born Feb. 7, 1830, to Wilhelm Ludwig Benzien and Christina Caritas m.n. Schneider.

Brietz, Charles Gustav, born Aug. 4, 1811, to Christian Brietz and Anna Catharine m.n. Seiler, married July 21, 1857, to Margaret Morrow, born in 1827 to Gabriel Morrow and Anna m.n. Waterson.

Mücke (Mickey), Julius Edward, born Apr. 18, 1832, to Solomon Mücke and Salome m.n. Spach, married Sept. 28, 1857, to Maria Lavinia Vogler, born Dec. 25, 1833, to Timotheus Vogler and Charlotte m.n. Hamilton.

Hall, Joseph Orestes, born Mar. 29, 1834, to James Hall and Sarah m.n. Green, married Oct. 7, 1857, to Louisa Sophia m.n. Schmidt, born May 6, 1835, to Johann Renatus Schmidt and Gertraut Salome m.n. Spönhauer.

Clemmons, Edwin T., born to [blank] Clemmons and Polly m.n. Haines, married Jan. 19, 1858, to Harriett Reecca Butner, born Mar. 29, 1829, to Adam Butner and Christina m.n. Hege.

Carmichael, Wm. F., married Sept. 15, 1858, to Eliza Fredericka Vierling, born Feb. 26, 1839, to Ernest A. Vierling and Johanna Paulina m.n. Reich.

Mickey, Francis W., born July 17, 1835, to Solomon Mickey and Salome m.n. Spach, married Sept. 15, 1858, to Sarah Elizabeth Ferguson, born Mar. 22, 1839, to Henry Ferguson and Lucinda m.n. Linville.

Tice, Isaac, married Dec. 2, 1858, to Anna Maria Hargrove, born Aug. 9, 1840, to John Hargrove and Anna m.n. Terry.

Bahnson, George Frederick, married Jan. 4, 1859, to Louisa Amelia Belo, born to John Fred. Belo (Boehlow) and Mary m.n. Strub.

Peck, Calvin, married Feb. 15, 1859, to Amanda L. Ebert.

Winkler, William P., married Mar. 1, 1859, to Sarah Ann Elizabeth Phillips, born to Wm. Phillips and Esther m.n. Vickrey.

Atwood, Jesse William, married Apr. 14, 1859, to Nancy F. Coletraine.

Pfohl, Augustus Frederick, married Apr. 14, 1859, to Elizabeth Siewers.

Transou, Peter, married May 19, 1859, to Maria Eliese Christina Petersen.

Leinbach, Robert Parmenio, married June 16, 1859, to Sophia Constantina Folz.

Leinbach, James Theodore, married Oct. 17, 1859, to Louisa Caroline Herman.

Pinkston, Jesse Rowan, married Oct. 20, 1859, to Sarah Rebecca Winkler, born to Wm. P. Winkler and wife.

Vogler, Alexander Christopher, married Oct. 26, 1859, to Antoinette Susanna Hauser, born to Wm. Hauser and wife.

Mock, Nathaniel, married Dec. 13, 1859, to Regina Rothrock, born to George and Magdalena Rothrock.

Kenan [Kernan], Thomas D., M.D., married Feb. 14, 1860, to Sophia C. Kremer, born to Charles Kremer and Eliza W. m.n. Vierling.

Mendenhall, William P., married Mar. 15, 1860, to Augusta O. Kern.

Butner, Herman, married Aug. 23, 1860, to Philippina Sides.

Butner, Albert Israel, married Dec. 20, 1860, to Johanna Sophia Zevely, born to Van N. Zevely and wife.

Peterson, William Praezel, married July 11, 1861, to Paulina Delphina Stolz, born to Jacob Stolz and wife.

Ackerman, William Augustus, a widower, born Dec. 16, 1823, married May 2, 1861, to Emily Florina Tesh, born June 13, 1837.

Miller, Irwin, married Mar. 20, 1862, to Olive Victoria Boyer, born Oct. 2, 1841.

Brooks, Charles B., married Aug. 5, 1862, to Elizabeth C. Lemly, born May 9, 1840.

Headly, P.D., married June 11, 1863, to Mary Emmeline Kremer, born Aug. 20, 1842.

Nissen, John I., married Aug. 31, 1863, to Leonora A. Ebert, daughter of Br. and Sr. Christian Ebert.

Wheeler, Wm., married Sept. 1, 1863, to Adelaide Matilda Shober, daughter of Sr. Anna Shober.

Horton, A. H., of Wilkes County, married Sept. 8, 1863, to Mary Jane Vogler, daughter of Timothy and Charlotte Vogler.

Waugh, J. P., of Jefferson, Ashe County, married Sept. 17, 1863, to Henrietta A. Murchison, daughter of Roderick Murchison and Henrietta M. m.n. Blum.

Miller, John Sylvester, married Sept. 28, 1863, to Emma Louisa Shaub, born Mar. 12, 1841.

Beck, William, a widower, of Forsyth County, married Dec. 30, 1863, to Laura Caroline Vogler, born Oct. 23, 1829, to Nath. and Anna Maria Vogler.

Belo, Jacob Levin, born Jan. 24, 1823, married Feb. 18, 1864, to Charlotte Emmeline Vogler, born Feb. 17, 1825.

Keehln, Francis Edward, born Oct. 11, 1841, married Mar. 31, 1864, to Sophia Louisa Reich, born Aug. 9, 1842.

Grunert, Maximilian Eugene, a widower, born Feb. 26, 1823, at Niesky, Germany, married Apr. 26, 1864, to Maria Susanna Butner, born Jan. 21, 1829, at Bethania.

Kerner, Philip, a widower, of Kernersville, married Feb. 8, 1863, to Sallie Gibbins. [Recorded out of sequence.]

Patterson, Rufus Lenoir, a widower, of Caldwell County, married June 14, 1864, to Mary Elizabeth Fries, born Aug. 31, 1844.

Shaffner, John Francis, born July 14, 1838, married Feb. 16, 1865, to Caroline Louisa Fries, born Oct. 8, 1839.

Wolle, Theodore F., married Aug. 15, 1865, to Adelaide Francisca Sussdorf, born Jan. 6, 1841.

Stockton, Joseph H., married Sept. 12, 1865, to Julia Elizabeth Pfohl, born Oct. 3, 1840.

Leinbach, Robert Parmenio, a widower, married Oct. 3, 1865, to Sarah Ann Maria Blum.

Crouse, Daniel Thomas, born Mar. 19, 1836, in Forsyth County, married Nov. 7, 1865, to Mary Ellen Douthit, born Feb. 20, 1841, in Clemmonsville.

Pfohl, Christian Thomas, born Sept. 4, 1838, married Nov. 16, 1865, to Margaret Siewers, born Aug. 25, 1838.

Bahnson, Charles Frederick, born Feb. 15, 1840, in Lancaster, Pa., married Dec. 12, 1865, to Virginia Amanda Johnson, born May 7, 1842, at Farmington, Davie County.

Butner, Augustus Benjamin, born Nov. 28, 1833, married Dec. 19, 1865, to Martha Ann Elizabeth Hall, born Aug. 8, 1843.

Hendricks, Lee, of Forsyth County, married Dec. 26, 1865, to Martha Louisa Fisher, born Sept. 25, 1838.

Jenkins, Robert A., of Thomasville, married June 28, 1866, to Margaret Elizabeth Clewell, born Jan. 5, 1840.

Cooper, William Jacob, born Apr. 7, 1842, married July 3, 1866, to Jane Catherine Blum, born Jan. 29, 1845.

Lewis, Lyman, of Mississippi, married July 24, 1866, to Mary Elizabeth Winkler, born Aug. 24, 1846. [Salem Diary: He resides near Aberdeen, Miss., but originally was from Massachusetts. He had been a soldier in the 10th Ohio Regiment.]

Douthit, Byron, married Aug. 2, 1866, to Julia Jenkins.

Lineback, Julius Augustus, born Sept. 8, 1834, married Oct. 8, 1866, to Anna Sophia Vogler, born Feb. 1, 1846, at Niesky, St. Thomas.

Deaths and Burials

Haman, Adam, born Jan. 7, 1790, in Barbadoes to Adam Joachim Haman and Anna m.n. Hird. Married (1) in August 1824 to Anna Clewell (died 1827). Married (2) Sept. 13, 1832, to Rebecca Schnall. Died Jan. 13, 1857.

Hein, infant son of John L. Hein and Maria Paulina m.n. Marshall. Born and died Feb. 11, 1857. Lived two hours.

Christ, Gustav Adolph Haman, born Oct. 14, 1852, to Traugott Christ and Maria Louisa m.n. Haman. Died Apr. 18, 1857.

Wimmer, Isabella Alice, born Jan. 10, 1854, to John M. Wimmer and Mary R. m.n. Cloud. Died Apr. 28, 1857.

Boner, Mary Francisca, born June 27, 1854, to Thomas Jacob Boner and Phobe Elisabeth m.n. Nading. Died May 2, 1857.

Stow, Eugenia, born in 1842, in Eufaula, Ala., to A. Stow and wife. Died May 5, 1857.

Metts, Elisabeth, born in 1842 in Lawrence District, S.C., to R. H. Metts and wife. Died May 5, 1857.

Meller, Charles William, born May 18, 1850, to Francis William Meller and Henrietta Caroline m.n. Reich. Died May 10, 1857.

Edmonds, Susan, died May 13, 1857.

Swaim, infant son of Joseph Franklin Swaim and Elisabeth Antoinette m.n. Knauss. Born and died June 19, 1857. Lived 3 hours.

Hughes, Ida Maria, born Aug. 21, 1854, to Henry Hughes and Martha m.n. Collins. Died June 25, 1857.

Griffin, Caleb Marion, born Mar. 26, 1849, to John M. Griffin and Martha Lucinda m.n. Blum. Died June 30, 1857.

Vogler, Henry Sylvester, born Oct. 13, 1828, to Nathaniel Vogler and Anna Maria m.n. Fischel. Died July 23, 1857.

Reid, Augusta Florence, born Jan. 13, 1857, in Mt. Airy, N.C., to W. O. Reid [Salem Diary: He is a Methodist minister living in Mount Airy] and Jeanette F. m.n. Hagen. Died July 23, 1857.

Staub, August, born Dec. 12, 1809, in Obersdorf, Saxony. Died Aug. 3, 1857.

Leinbach, Emma Augusta, born Dec. 7, 1825, to Henry Leinbach and Elisabeth m.n. Schneider. Died Aug. 26, 1857.

Sussdorf, Charles Theodore, born June 10, 1856, to Christian Friedrich Sussdorf and Louisa Cynthia m.n. Hagen. Died Sept. 8, 1857.

Mücke, Theresia Rebecca m.n. Beckel, born Nov. 17, 1836, to Johann Beckel and Anna Marie m.n. Spach. Married May 20, 1856, to William Francis Mücke. Died Sept. 14, 1857.

Petersen, Carsten, born Apr. 21, 1776, near Flensburg. Married Dec. 1, 1816, to Agnes Susanna Präzel. Died Oct. 31, 1857.

Byerle, Alexander Frederic, born Aug. 5, 1835, in Davidson County, to John Byerle and Anna Susanna m.n. Folz. Died Nov. 6, 1857.

Blum, John Van Neman, born Feb. 20, 1852, to Edmund Thomas Blum and Sarah Catharine m.n. Hartman. Died Nov. 11, 1857.

Blum, Mary Frances, born Oct. 28, 1829, to William Farrar and Sarah m.n. Ragland. Married Jan. 25, 1849, to Francis Rudolph Blum. Died Nov. 14, 1857.

Spach, Maria Elisabeth, born May 15, 1833, in Davidson County, to Jacob Kimmel and Nancy m.n. Beckel. Married Feb. 15, 1857, to David Spach. Died Nov. 16, 1857.

Fischer, Julia Lucinda, born June 20, 1851, to Jefferson Fischer and Lauretta m.n. Blum. Died Nov. 23, 1857.

Fischer, Samuel Thomas, born May 16, 1857, to Jefferson Fischer and Lauretta m.n. Blum. Died Nov. 27, 1857.

Heckedorn, Catharine, born Sept. 5, 1780, in Pennsylvania. Died Nov. 30, 1857.

Fischer, Amanda Angelina, born May 11, 1854, to Jefferson Fischer and Lauretta m.n. Blum. Died Dec. 9, 1857.

Beckel, Anna Maria m.n. Spach, born July 7, 1800, at Friedberg. Married Oct. 24, 1820, to Johann [Tobias] Beckel. Died Dec. 13, 1857.

Blum, Charles Jacob, born Aug. 19, 1854, in Liberty, to Franz Rudolph Blum and Mary Frances m.n. Farrar. Died Jan. 7, 1858.

Nading, Ernestine Eleanora, born Sept. 21, 1835, to David Spach and Frederica Charlotte m.n. Ebbecke. Married Mar. 30, 1854, to William Nading. Died Jan. 17, 1858.

Blum, Edmund Jacob, born Feb. 20, 1852, to Edmund Thomas Blum and Sarah Catharine m.n. Hartman. Died Jan. 19, 1858.

Winkler, Paulina Maria, born Mar. 6, 1819, in Friedberg, to Thomas and Rebecca Fischer. Married in 1837 to William Parmenio Winkler. Died Mar. 15, 1858.

Bahnson, Anna Gertrude Paulina, born Aug. 10, 1813, near Bethania to Jacob Conrad and Gertrude Elisabeth m.n. Lösch. Married Feb. 20, 1838, to George Fredrich Bahnson. Died May 2, 1858.

Werner, Beatus, born May 10, 1858, to Carl Werner and Catharina m.n. Bryld. Died May 31, 1858.

Paine, Rufus Gilbert, born Mar. 31, 1858, to James Paine and Emma m.n. Ackerman. Died June 18, 1858.

Homann, Augusta Wilhelmina, born Aug. 5, 1807, in Dippoldiswalde, Saxony. Died July 2, 1858.

Meinung, Johanna Elisabeth, born Jan. 1, 1785, to Gottfried Präzel and Maria Elisabeth m.n. Engel. Married Sept. 22, 1808, to Friedrich Christian Meinung. Died July 6, 1858. [Salem Diary: Sr. M. was one of the three Sisters who began our Female Boarding School as the first teachers.]

Vierling, August Ernst, born Sept. 3, 1801, to Samuel Benjamin Vierling and Martha Elisabeth m.n. Miksch. Married (1) Mar. 17, 1825, to Louisa Towle (died 1825). Married (2) June 21, 1831, to Johanna Paulina Reich. Died July 11, 1858.

Boner, Isaac, born Dec. 17, 1776, to Wilhelm and Rahel Boner. Married in 1797 to Dorothea Elisabeth Meyer. Died Aug. 3, 1858. [Salem Diary: He was the oldest male resident in Salem.]

Leinbach, Mira Cornelia, born Oct. 15, 1852, to Wm. S. Leinbach and Sarah m.n. Hauser. Died Oct. 6, 1858.

Conrad, Elizabeth Gertrude, born July 3, 1792, to John Christian and Anna Gertrude Lash. Married Mar. 24, 1811, to Jacob Conrad. Died Oct. 19, 1858.

Payne, Emma Elvira, born Oct. 23, 1826, to John Ackerman and Anna m.n. Spach. Married to James Payne. Died Nov. 23, 1858.

Spach, Anna Johanna, born July 18, 1766, to Adam Spach and Maria Elizabeth m.n. Huetter. Died Dec. 16, 1858. On Oct. 9, 1793, she moved to the Sisters House at Salem, where she continued to reside till her departure. [Salem Diary: She was by over 8 years the oldest member of the congregation.]

Hall, John Martin Beck, born July 30, 1858, to Joseph O. Hall and Louisa S. m.n. Smith. Died Jan. 6, 1859.

Ackerman, Ernestina Elizabeth, born Aug. 9, 1857, to Alexander and Serena Ackerman. Died Mar. 22, 1859.

Lash, Charles Henry Blum, born Feb. 16, 1859, at Waughtown, to Henry M. Lash and Eliza m.n. Blum. Died Apr. 6, 1859.

Reich, Elizabeth, born Nov. 3, 1779, to Henry and Elizabeth Spainhour. Married Nov. 18, 1810, to Mathew Reich. Died Apr. 18, 1859.

Boner, Francis Eugene, born Dec. 18, 1835, to Evan Boner and Sophia Dorothea m.n. Byhan. Died June 18, 1859.

Carmichael, son of Wm. F. Carmichael and Eliza Fredericka m.n. Vierling. Born and died June 27, 1859. Lived but a few minutes, and was interred the same day at evening.

Keehln, Christian David, born Nov. 26, 1793, at Niesky, Saxony. He arrived at Salem in 1818, and entered upon the practice of medicine, which he continued to within a few days of his death. Married July 11, 1819, to Mary M. Landman. Died June 30, 1859.

Brietz, Sarah Elizabeth, born Mar. 21, 1845, in Bethlehem, Pa., to Samuel Ephraim Brietz and Antoinette Louisa m.n. Bagge. Died July 27, 1859.

Siewers, Henry Frederick, born Jan. 12, 1841, to Jacob F. Siewers and Matilda A. m.n. Winkler. Died Oct. 4, 1859.

Spach, Maria, Born near Friedberg. Died in 1859. For several years past she has been an inmate of the Lunatic Asylum near Raleigh, where she departed this life, and where her remains are interred.

Holland, Sophia Elizabeth, born Feb. 24, 1822, to William Holland and Anna Elizabeth m.n. Shumaker. Died Jan. 15, 1860.

Faircloth, Emma Caroline, born Oct. 7, 1859, to Thomas Faircloth and Louisa m.n. Rothhaas. Died Jan. 30, 1860.

Leinbach, Maria Theresa m.n. Lange, born Sept. 30, 1799, at Bethlehem, Pa. Married to Traugott Leinbach. Died Feb. 19, 1860. Being at Philadelphia to undergo a surgical operation, she there departed this life, and her remains were interred at Bethlehem.

Robinson, Caroline, born Feb. 21, 1845, in Autauga County, Ala., to John Robinson and wife. Died Feb. 29, 1860. She was a pupil in the Salem Female Academy.

Haeusler, John, born Dec. 8, 1803, in Wurtemburg. Married June 3, 1830, to Anna Lydia Reich. Died Mar. 2, 1860.

Holland, Sarah Horsfield, born Aug. 10, 1859, to Francis R. Holland and Eliza Augusta m.n. Wolle. Died Apr. 9, 1860.

Bahnson, Ellen Sophia Matilda, born Apr. 5, 1847, to G.F. Bahnson and A.G. Paulina m.n. Conrad. Died May 30, 1860.

Keehln, Emma Rosalie, born Nov. 11, 1859, to Orestes A. Keehln and Angelica Elizabeth m.n. Bahnson. Died June 3, 1860.

Ackerman, Jeanette Elizabeth, born Dec. 13, 1826, to Joseph Spach and Elizabeth m.n. Miller. Married Feb. 2, 1848, to Wm. Ackerman. Died June 22, 1860.

Leinbach, Sophia Constantina, born Nov. 5, 1829, to Geo. Foltz and Verona m.n. Reich. Married June 16, 1859, to R.P. Leinbach. Died July 27, 1860.

Steiner, Caroline, born Apr. 1, 1802, at Hope, Surinam, to Theodore Shultz and Susanna m.n. Loesch. Married to C. Abraham Steiner. Died Nov. 6, 1860.

Blum, John David, born at Schöneck, Pa. Married (1) Nov. 24, 1808, to Sarah Hege (died 1830). Married (2) Mar. 22, 1832, to Louisa Harmon (died 1841). Married (3) Oct. 8, 1843, to Amelia Rothhaas. Died Nov. 13, 1860. On account of certain difficulties and misunderstandings arising out of business transactions, he was considered as having withdrawn from the church, but he still desired to be under the spiritual care of the church, and at his request was interred in our graveyard.

Strupe, John Joseph, born Sept. 27, 1857, to Carlos Strupe and Anna Lucinda m.n. Spach. Died Dec. 3, 1860.

Holland, William, born Feb. 19, 1790, to John Holland and Jacobina m.n. Shumaker. Married Jan. 28, 1814, to Anna Elizabeth Shumaker. Died Dec. 13, 1860.

Waterson, Sarah, born Feb. 16, 1797, in Lincoln County. Died Jan. 25, 1861.

Fockel, Anna Dorothea, born Jan. 16, 1779, at Bethabara, to John Henry Stoehr and Anna Dorothea m.n. Shüz. Married Feb. 22, 1803, to John Christian Fockel. Died Jan. 30, 1861.

Sussdorff, Ellen Louisa, born Mar. 6, 1860, in Winston, to C.F. Sussdorff and Louisa C. m.n. Hagen. Died Feb. 1, 1861.

Bevel, Charles Armsworthy, born Oct. 28, 1857, in Liberty, to Chrn. A. Bevel and Sarah Catharine m.n. Miller. Died Feb. 11, 1861.

Pfohl, Henry Augustus, born July 21, 1860, to Augustus F. Pfohl and Elizabeth m.n. Siewers. Died Feb. 14, 1861.

Leake, Charlotte Malvina, born May 3, 1837, near Salem, to John Reich and Maria Agnes m.n. Shultz. Married Apr. 19, 1860, to George W. Leake. Died Mar. 24, 1861.

Heisler, Maria Antoinette, born Feb. 7, 1838, to John Heisler and Lydia m.n. Reich. Died Apr. 4, 1861.

Olyphant, Ann Jane, born Oct. 27, 1787, at Newport, R.I. Died Apr. 26, 1861.

Hobbs, Martha Eudora, born Apr. 4, 1846, near Jackson, Miss., to Howell Hobbs and wife. Died May 9, 1861. She was a pupil in the Salem Female Academy.

Ackerman, Allen Timothy, born Dec. 21, 1818, near Salem, to John Ackerman and Anna Johanna m.n. Spach. Married Jan. 10, 1843, to Rudelphia Kearney. Died May 22, 1861.

Crist, Anna Christina, born Dec. 30, 1776, at Bethabara, to Jacob Blum and Anna Maria m.n. Born. Married Mar. 17, 1803, to Rudolph Crist. Died May 26, 1861.

Schaffner, Maria Cathrine, born Feb. 11, 1836, to Henry Schaffner and Levinia Elizabeth m.n. Hauser. Died May 30, 1861.

Vogler, William Edward, born Dec. 5, 1859, to Alexander C. Vogler and Antoinette S. m.n. Hauser. Died June 3, 1861.

Leake, George Constantine, born Mar. 14, 1861, near Germanton, to George W. Leake and Charlotte Malvina m.n. Reich. Died June 6, 1861. [Salem Diary: The mother departed this life when her babe was only 10 days old. The care of it was entrusted to its grandmother, Sr. Agnes Reich, wife of John Reich near Salem.]

Hauser, Mary Frances Gilmer, born Mar. 18, 1860, to Charles F. Hauser and Hermina E. m.n. Benzien. Died June 13, 1861.

Hauser, Francis Comenius, born July 23, 1836, to Wm. Hauser and Anna Susanna m.n. Shultz. Died June 14, 1861. In October 1860 he went to Seguin, Texas, as clerk in a mercantile establishment. He died and was buried there.

Bahnson, Lewis Kraepelien, born Nov. 25, 1860, to George F. Bahnson and Louisa Amelia m.n. Belo. Died July 4, 1861.

Murchison, Henrietta Matilda, born Sept. 30, 1812, near Salem, to John David Blum and Sarah m.n. Hege. Married May 30, 1832, to Roderick Murchison. Died July 16, 1861.

Shober, Hedwig Elizabeth, born Sept. 22, 1794, to Gottlieb Shober and Mary Magdalena m.n. Transu. Died Sept. 20, 1861.

Byhan, Gottlieb, born Aug. 4, 1777, at Herwigsdorf near Herrnhut, Saxony, to Frederick Byhan and Elizabeth m.n. Ay. Married Nov. 16, 1801, to Dorothea Schneider. Died Oct. 17, 1861.

Folz, Anna Catharine, born Oct. 15, 1788, at Friedberg, to John Folz and Anna Barbara m.n. Fisher. Died Jan. 12, 1862.

Stockburger, Elizabeth, born Sept. 6, 1781, to George Stockburger and Cath. m.n. Christman. Died Mar. 7, 1862.

Chitty, Sophia Adelaide, born Nov. 10, 1839, to Traugott Chitty and Frederika m.n. Ruede. Died Mar. 9, 1862.

Chitty, Cornelia Rosalie, born Sept. 10, 1843, to Traugott Chitty and Frederike m.n. Ruede. Died Apr. 13, 1862.

Folz, Junius Alexander, born Dec. 15, 1839, to George Folz and Verona m.n. Reich. Died Apr. 25, 1862.

Lash, Louisa Eliza, born July 31, 1838, near Salem, to John David Blum and Louisa Catherine m.n. Harman. Married July 30, 1856, to Henry M. Lash. Died May 13, 1862.

Reich, Lewis Emanuel, born Dec. 21, 1843, near Salem, to John Reich and Maria Agnes m.n. Shulz. Died Aug. 24, 1861, in the military hospital at Lynchburg, Va. His remains were removed hither, and interred in the Cemetery on June 2, 1862.

Reich, John Edwin, born Sept. 16, 1839, near Salem, to John Reich and Maria Agnes m.n. Shulz. Died Dec. 24, 1861, in the military hospital at Richmond, Va. His remains were removed hither, and interred in the Cemetery.

Zevely, Ann Lavinia, born Sept. 26, 1844, to Augustus T. Zevely and Lucinda m.n Blum. Died June 11, 1862.

Atwood, Jesse William, born Mar. 1, 1831, in Yadkin County, to Wm. Francis Atwood and Mary m.n. Steelman. Married Apr. 14, 1859, to Nancy Florence Coletraine. Having been appointed captain of a military company, he left for the seat of war. He was taken ill with typhoid fever, and died July 3, 1862. His remains were interred in the Cemetery on July 5, 1862, and later reinterred in the Graveyard.

Shuman, Frederick Henry, born Oct. 1, 1777, at Gnadau, Germany. Married (1) in July 1802 to Joanna Salome Lineback (died 1821). Married (2) Sept. 11, 1836, to Theodora m.n Shulz. Died July 4, 1862.

Hall, Augustus Josephus, born Dec. 22, 1860, to William Henry Hall and Ernestina Augusta m.n. Vierling. Died July 14, 1862.

Boner, Araminta Elizabeth, born Dec. 12, 1841, to Evan Boner and Sophia Dorothea m.n. Byhan. Died July 20, 1862.

Kremer, Catharine Elizabeth, born May 10, 1840, to Charles Kremer and Eliza Wilhelmina m.n. Vierling. Died Aug. 29, 1862.

Wimmer, Peter Lilburn, born May 6, 1856, to John Mathew Wimmer and Mary Russell m.n. Cloud. Died Aug. 30, 1862.

Crist, Charles Carrick, born Nov. 18, 1858, to Jacob Rudolph Crist and Miranda Rosalie m.n. Keehln. Died Sept. 7, 1862.

Schott, Sarah Lydia, born May 2, 1854, near Salem, to John Wesley Schott and Jeanette m.n. Shore. Died Sept. 22, 1862.

Yates, Mary Jane, born Nov. 14, 1856, to Charles Yates and Mary m.n. McMillan. Died Sept. 23, 1862.

Meinung, Ellen Tryphena, born Feb. 5, 1857, to Henry Meinung and Theresa m.n. Hege. Died Oct. 4, 1862.

Yates, Charles Francis, born June 23, 1858, to Charles Yates and Mary m.n. McMillan. Died Oct. 15, 1862.

Grunert, Emma Theresa, born May 23, 1830, at Friedland, to Samuel Thomas and Anna Elizabeth Pfohl. Married Apr. 22, 1851, to Max. Eugene Grunert. Died Oct. 24, 1862.

Kluge, John Frederick, born July 30, 1862, at Goldsboro, to Eugene and Sarah Kluge. Died Oct. 28, 1862.

Hauser, Lewis Augustine, born Mar. 25, 1841, to Wm. Hauser and Anna Susanna m.n. Shulz. Died Nov. 23, 1862.

Lash, Armenius C., born Dec. 9, 1825, at Bethania, to C. Isaac Lash and Mary m.n. Transou. Died July 30, 1862. He departed this life near Petersburg, Va. His remains were brought hither and interred in our Graveyard on Dec. 6, 1862.

Clewell, John David, born Apr. 15, 1804, at Shöneck, Pa., to Francis Clewell and Anna Maria m.n. Leinbach. Married (1) July 12, 1826, to Johanna Cath. Reich (died 1833). Married (2) Jan. 29, 1839, to Dorothea Matilda Shulz. Died Dec. 13, 1862.

Fetter, Mary Louisa, born Apr. 25, 1860, to Peter P. Fetter and Sarah S. m.n. Stockburger. Died Dec. 15, 1862.

Ackerman, Sarah Louisa, born Mar. 9, 1844, to Allen T. Ackerman and Rudelphia m.n. Kearney. Died Dec. 19, 1862.

Ackerman, Alice Victoria, born Dec. 26, 1857, to Edward T. Ackerman and Mary Elizabeth m.n. Davis. Died Jan. 6, 1863.

Butner, Johanna Sophia, born Nov. 19, 1821, near Salem, to Van N. Zevely and Johanna Sophia m.n. Shober. Married Dec. 20, 1860, to Albert Israel Butner. Died Jan. 15, 1863.

Leinbach, Louisa Caroline, born June 12, 1835, in Philadelphia, Pa., to John G. Herman and Anna Paulina m.n. Shober. Married Oct. 17, 1859, to James T. Lineback. Died Feb. 6, 1863.

Fisher, Mary Rebecca, born May 19, 1840, near Friedberg, to Jefferson Fisher and Lauretta m.n. Blum. Died Feb. 6, 1863.

Ackerman, Sophia Louisa, born Jan. 23, 1837, to John Ackerman and Anna m.n. Spach. Died Feb. 8, 1863.

Lash, Charles Isaac, born Oct. 14, 1799, near Bethania, to Abraham Lash and Christina m.n. Shoemaker. Married Dec. 11, 1821, to Mary Transou. Died Feb. 23, 1863.

Spach, John, born Oct. 21, 1787, near Salem, to Gottlieb and Martha Spach. Died Mar. 11, 1863.

Weatherly, Mary, born Jan. 19, 1849, at Bennettsville, S.C., to T.C. and Margaret Weatherly. Died Mar. 21, 1863. She was a pupil in the Salem Female Academy.

Hall, Sarah Haywood, born Sept. 18, 1802, at Newport, R.I., to Br. and Sr. James Green. Married Sept. 6, 1825, to James Hall. Died Mar. 22, 1863.

Zevely, Van Neman, born Nov. 13, 1780, near Cambridge (formerly Ninety-Six), S.C. Married (1) Oct. 3, 1809, to Johanna Sophia Shober (died 1821). Married (2) Mar. 17, 1822, to Anna Rebecca Holder (died 1825). Married (3) Aug. 20, 1826, to Susan Peter. Died May 10, 1863. [Salem Diary: For many years our departed br. had been engaged as a home missionary in the mountains of Virginia, and great attachment to him still exists among those whom he was the honored instrument of bringing to the foot of the cross.]

Butner, Mahala Elizabeth m.n. Ray, born June 14, 1812, near Bethabara. Married in 1831 to John Butner. Died June 12, 1863.

Miller, a daughter of Irwin Miller and Olive Victoria m.n. Boyer. Stillborn June 18, 1863.

Reddick, Margaret, born Mar. 29, 1835, in Surry County, to Silas Riggs and Martha m.n. Kidd. Married to John Reddick. Died June 19, 1863. Buried in Liberty.

Vogler, Christina, born Aug. 17, 1792, near Salem, to Gottlieb Spach and Martha m.n. Hege. Married Mar. 7, 1819, to John Vogler. Died July 8, 1863.

Rights, Margaret, born June 16, 1793, at Gracehill, Ireland, to George Waterson and Martha m.n. Hammond. Married Nov. 16, 1847, to Joshua Rights. Died July 11, 1863.

Fries, Francis Levin, born Oct. 17, 1812, to John Christian William Fries and Johanna Elizabeth m.n. Nissen. Married May 24, 1838, to Lisette Maria Vogler. Died Aug. 1, 1863. Buried in Salem Cemetery.

Pfohl, Ellen Augusta, born June 7, 1859, at Winston, to Edward A. Pfohl and Matilda A. m.n. Phillips. Died Aug. 3, 1863. Buried in Salem Cemetery.

Belo, Lewis Ephraim, born Sept. 1, 1813, to John Frederick Belo (Boehlow) and Mary m.n. Strup. Married Nov. 21, 1844, to Lisette Henrietta Reich. Died Sept. 11, 1863.

Oehman, John Gottfried, born Sept. 22, 1781, at Weissenstein, Esthonia. Married the single Sr. Rights. Died Sept. 24, 1863.

Meinung, William Lewis, born Oct. 4, 1809, to Frederick Meinung and Johanna Elizabeth m.n. Prezel. Died Oct. 14, 1863.

Benzien, Christine Caritas, born Feb. 26, 1799, at Friedberg, to Martin Snider and Elizabeth m.n. Dixon. Married Apr. 1, 1823, to William Lewis Benzien. Died Dec. 20, 1863.

Rothaas, Maria Magdalena, born Jan. 9, 1790, to Philip Martin and Joanna Vogler. Married in 1818 to Jacob Rothaas. Died Dec. 31, 1863.

Fries, Joanna Elizabeth, born Mar. 15, 1787, to Tycho Nissen and Salome m.n. Meurer. Married Oct. 13, 1811, to John Christian William Fries. Died Jan. 21, 1864.

Rothaas, Jacob, born Sept. 1, 1795, near Salem, to Conrad Rothaas and Anna Elizabeth m.n. Steiner. Married June 9, 1818, to Mary Magdalene Vogler. Died Mar. 14, 1864.

Ackerman, John, born Dec. 16, 1790, near Bethabara. Married Jan. 27, 1818, to Anna Joanna Spach. Died Mar. 14, 1864.

Ebert, Mary Jane, born Nov. 29, 1844, near Friedberg, to Alfred and Rachel Ebert. Died June 13, 1864.

Reid, Mary Louisa, born Aug. 29, 1863, at Mount Airy, to Dr. Wm. O. Reid and Jeanette Florentine m.n. Hagan. Died July 29, 1864.

Brietz, Anna Catherine, born Apr. 7, 1864, to Charles Gustavus Brietz and Margaret m.n. Morrow. Died Aug. 12, 1864.

Rights, Elizabeth, born Aug. 23, 1794, at Friedberg, to Lazarus Hege and Eve m.n. Fisher. Married July 1, 1819, to Matthew Rights. Died Aug. 25, 1864.

Yates, Caroline Amelia, born Nov. 29, 1860, to Charles Yates and Mary m.n. McMillan. Died Oct. 26, 1864. [Salem Diary: She was the last of 3 children of our sister, two having been taken from her two years ago. Her husband is on his way north, and she was to follow him, when this dispensation befell her.]

Peck, Amanda Lucretia, m.n. Ebert, born Sept. 9, 1833. Married Feb. 15, 1859, to Calvin Peck. Died Nov. 6, 1864. [Salem Diary: Bro. Peck is in the army and not allowed to come home. His elder son is idiotic and the babe but lately born. It is a sad case, appealing to the sympathy of every feeling heart.]

Belo, Henry Augustus, born Oct. 29, 1845, to Frederick Edward Belo and Caroline Amanda m.n. Fries. Died May 5, 1864. On Jan. 6, 1864, he left home for the army. He was killed, as is supposed instantly, by a shot wound, and was buried on the battlefield at the Wilderness. His remains were brought to Salem, and re-interred Dec. 1, 1864, in the Cemetery.

Kluge, Charles Edward, born at High Point, to Eugene Kluge and Sarah m.n. Bullard. Died Dec. 3, 1864.

Rogge, William Henry, born June 26, 1862, in Liberty, to Augustus Rogge and Christina m.n. Parnell. Died Dec. 7, 1864.

Byerle, James Edward, born May 15, 1846, near Salem, to John Byerle and Anna m.n. Folz. Died July 19, 1864. Having left home with the Junior Reserves, he died near Wilmington, and was buried there. His remains were brought to Salem, and re-interred in our Graveyard on Dec. 12, 1864.

Rogge, a daughter, born Nov. 23, 1864, in Liberty, to Augustus Rogge and Christine m.n. Parnell. Died Dec. 11, 1864.

James, Samuel Clement, born Apr. 14, 1828, in Surry County, to Benjamin James and Rebecca m.n. Hern. Died May 16, 1864. On June 17, 1861, he left for the army. He was present in many battles and skirmishes, but mercifully preserved until he received a mortal wound at Drury's Bluff, Va. He survived only one hour. His remains were buried near the battlefield, and re-interred in our Graveyard on Jan. 18, 1865.

Brooks, Charles Iverson, born Nov. 21, 1864, to Charles B. Brooks and Elizabeth C. m.n. Lemly. Died Jan. 19, 1865. Buried in Salem Cemetery.

Peck, Calvin, born Sept. 28, 1838, to William Peck and Elizabeth m.n. Kimmel. Married Feb. 15, 1859, to Amanda L. Ebert. Died Nov. 28, 1864. [Salem Diary: His remains were brought from Staunton, Va., where he died, and were re-interred in the Graveyard on Feb. 12, 1865.]

Pfohl, Frederick Siewers, born Apr. 27, 1862, to Augustus Pfohl and Elizabeth m.n. Siewers. Died Feb. 13, 1865.

Grunert, son of Maximilian Eugene Grunert and Maria Susanna m.n. Butner. Stillborn Feb. 24, 1865.

Grunert, Anna Josephine, born Feb. 14, 1857, in Bethania, to Maximilian Eugene Grunert and Emma Theresa m.n. Pfohl. Died Mar. 3, 1865. Poison was the cause of her death.

Blum, Anna Dorothea, born Sept. 22, 1784, at Bethlehem, Pa., to Massa Warner and Maria Dorothea m.n. Michel. Married Sept. 4, 1828, to John Jacob Blum. Died Apr. 30, 1865. [Salem Diary: She was weak in her mind for the last 28 years, and her departure for a better home was a great relief and blessing to herself and others. For 18 years she resided in the family of her stepson, Bro. Nath. Blum, where she was well taken care of.]

Friebele, (Henrietta) Sarah Elizabeth, born June 23, 1847, in New Hope, Jamaica, to John Adam Friebele and Henrietta Louisa m.n. Peterson. Died May 1, 1865.

Brösing, Christina Elizabeth, born Aug. 26, 1784, near Bethabara, to Andrew Brösing and Anna Joanna m.n. Steup. Died July 3, 1865.

Lick, Christina Elizabeth, born July 11, 1796, near Bethania, to Martin Lick and Christina Houser. Died July 8, 1865.

Lineback, Elizabeth, born Dec. 25, 1796, in Friedland, to Philip Snyder and Elizabeth m.n. Rominger. Married Nov. 17, 1822, to John Henry Lineback. Died July 7, 1865.

Rothaas, Caroline Charlotte, born Oct. 26, 1832, near Salem, to Jacob Rothaas and Maria Magdalena m.n. Vogler. Died Aug. 24, 1865.

Reich, Sarah Ann Imogen, born Aug. 20, 1859, near Salem, to Augustus Nathaniel Reich and Antoinette m.n. Nading. Died Aug. 27, 1865.

Reid, Martha Frazier, born June 14, 1861, at Mount Airy, to Dr. Wm. O. Reid and Jeanette Florentine m.n. Hagen. Died June 16, 1862. Buried at Mount Airy, but re-interred in our graveyard on Oct. 2, 1865.

Christman, Christina Elizabeth, born Feb. 3, 1785, to Daniel and Joanna Christman. Died Dec. 12, 1865.

Fisher, John Lewis Benzien, born Mar. 4, 1861, to James Fisher and Francisca L. m.n. Benzien. Died Oct. 20, 1865. [Recorded out of sequence.]

Miller, John William, born July 16, 1864, to Irwin Miller and Olive Victoria m.n. Boyer. Died Oct. 21, 1865. [Recorded out of sequence.]

Winkler, Henry Christian, born Sept. 10, 1851, to Christian Henry Winkler and Ruffina Amelia m.n. Reich. Died Jan. 1, 1866.

Fries, John Christian William, born Nov. 22, 1775, at Barby, Germany, to Peter Conrad Fries and Christine Elizabeth m.n. Jaeschke. Married Oct. 13, 1811, to Johanna Elizabeth Nissen. Died Jan. 26, 1866.

Cooper, Charles Alexander, born Mar. 22, 1810, at Germanton, to James Cooper and Joanna Maria m.n. Kushke. Married Oct. 29, 1835, to Paulina Rebecca Shulz. Died May 19, 1866.

Pfohl, John Jacob, born May 27, 1866, to Augustus Frederick Pfohl and Elizabeth m.n. Siewers. Died May 30, 1866.

Poole, Fannie, born Nov. 10, 1848, in Georgia. Died June 3, 1866. She was a pupil in Salem Female Academy.

Pfohl, Elizabeth, born Mar. 2, 1837, to Jacob Frederick Siewers and Matilda Amelia m.n. Winkler. Married Apr. 14, 1859, to Augustus Frederick Pfohl. Died June 18, 1866.

Swink, George Mumford, born Jan. 19, 1818, near Salisbury, to John Henry and Mary Swink. Married June 2, 1852, to Augusta Caroline Hall. Died Aug. 29, 1866.

Blum, John Henry, born Feb. 10, 1797, to John Henry Blum and Catherine m.n. Hauser. Married Oct. 21, 1841, to Anna Margaret Becker. Died Sept. 4, 1866.

Vogler, Mary Elizabeth, born Apr. 21, 1844, at Canaan, Cherokee Nation, to Miles Vogler and Sophia Dorothea m.n. Rüde. Died Oct. 3, 1866.

Reich, Sybilla Cecilia, born May 10, 1800, in Montgomery County, Pa., to John Dull and Elizabeth m.n. Cogan. Married June 17, 1824, to John Philip Reich. Died Oct. 19, 1866.

Schnall, Henrietta Dorothea, born Jan. 4, 1811, at Old Nazareth, Pa., to Jacob Schnall and Barbara m.n. Rank. Died Dec. 5, 1866.

Hendricks, Nathaniel, born Dec. 7, 1866, to Lee Hendricks and Martha Louisa m.n. Fisher. Died Dec. 13, 1866.

Winkler, William Parmenio, born June 1, 1812, to Christian Winkler and Elizabeth m.n. Danz. Married (1) Nov. 28, 1837, to Paulina M. Fisher (died 1858). Married (2) Mar. 1, 1859, to Sarah Ann Elizabeth Phillipps. Died Dec. 17, 1866.

Shaffner, Mary Lizette, born Feb. 13, 1866, to John Francis Shaffner and Caroline Louisa m.n. Fries. Died Dec. 24, 1866.

Salem Register: Non-Members, 1857-1866

Baptisms of Non-Members

Petri, Charles Alexander, born Oct. 7, 1856, to Wesley Petri and Amelia m.n. Stoehr. Baptized Feb. 18, 1857.

Hughes, William Henry, born Feb. 2, 1857, to Henry Hughes and Martha m.n. Collins. Baptized Mar. 23, 1857.

Reid, Alice, born May 11, 1857, to Christian Reid and Elizabeth m.n. Billeter. Baptized May 25, 1857.

Folz, George Micaiah, born June 14, 1856, to George Folz and Elizabeth m.n. Purnelle. Baptized July 3, 1857.

Banner, Julia Sophia, born Oct. 21, 1856, to Geo. Washington Banner and Clarinda m.n. Waterson. Baptized Oct. 21, 1857.

Fisher, Samuel Thomas, born May 16, 1857, to Jefferson Fisher and Laurette m.n. Blum. Baptized Oct. 29, 1857.

Mickey, Adelia Alice, born Dec. 7, 1856, to William Francis Mickey and Theresea m.n. Beckel. Baptized Jan. 6, 1857. [Recorded out of sequence.]

Spach, Maria Josephine, born Nov. 13, 1857, to David Spach and Maria m.n. Kimmel. Baptized Nov. 27, 1857.

Miller, Adolphus Rudelius, born Nov. 5, 1857, to Charles J. Miller and Mary m.n. White. Baptized Mar. 30, 1858.

Zink, John Henry, born Sept. 20, 1857, to Solomon Zink and Lucy Elisabeth m.n. Snyder. Baptized Mar. 31, 1858.

Holder, Edwin Sylverster, born May 24, 1858, to William Holder and Nancy m.n. Houser. Baptized Aug. 28, 1858.

Brewer, Mary Lydia Sophia, born Aug. 22, 1858, to Davidson Brewer and Louisa m.n. Fletcher. Baptized Oct. 22, 1858, in the Salem parsonage.

Brendle, John Henry, born Oct. 12, 1857, to [blank] Brendle and wife. Baptized Jan. 24, 1858. [Recorded out of sequence.]

Reich, Robert Alanson, born Aug. 8, 1857, to John Henry Reich and Maria Theresa m.n. Tesh. Baptized Mar. 21, 1858. [Recorded out of sequence.]

Faircloth, Francis Marsden, born Apr. 2, 1858, to Thomas and Louisa Faircloth. Baptized June 4, 1858. [Recorded out of sequence.]

Hughes, Laura Jane, born Dec. 12, 1858, to Henry Hughes and Martha m.n. Collins. Baptized Mar. 20, 1859, in the parents' house.

Weir, Paulina Eunice, born Feb. 16, 1859, to Robert Weir and Tempe m.n. Fisher. Mrs. Weir is a member at Friedberg, but living at Ashboro, Randolph Co., and being here on a visit to her relatives, requested her infant to be baptized. Baptized Apr. 25, 1859, in the Salem church.

Hicks, Alice Victoria, born May 16, 1859, to John Hicks and Mary Ann m.n. Boyles. Baptized July 24, 1859, in the Salem parsonage.

Reich, Sarah Ann Imogene, born Aug. 20, 1859, to Augustus Nathaniel Reich and Antoinette m.n. Nading. Baptized Dec. 1, 1859, in the Salem parsonage.

Petrie, James Edward, born Aug. 24, 1859, to Wm. Wesley Petrie and Antoinette Amelia m.n. Stare. Baptized Jan. 5, 1860, at the house of Charles Brietz.

Reich, Adelaide Augusta, born Sept. 16, 1859, to John H. Reich and Theresa m.n. Tesh. Baptized Jan. 26, 1860, at the parents' house.

Reed, Sarah Ellen, born Dec. 11, 1859, to Harrison Reed and Ernestina m.n. Blum. Baptized May 17, 1860, at the house of Br. David Blum at Waughtown.

Grubbs, John Samuel, born Mar. 12, 1859, to John Grubbs and Mary Ann m.n. Olridge. Baptized June 10, 1860, at Double Bridge schoolhouse.

Miller, Anna Elizabeth, born Oct. 24, 1859, to Charles Jeremiah Miller and Mary Elizabeth m.n. White. Baptized Aug. 6, 1860, at the parents' house in Liberty.

Blum, Mary Florence Sophia, born Aug. 7, 1860, to Rudolph Blum and Susan m.n. Snipe. Baptized Oct. 28, 1860, at the house of Br. Alex. Ackerman.

Crossland, Anna Louise, born Oct. 24, 1860, to Benjamin F. Crossland and Louisa M. m.n. Shober. Baptized Jan. 13, 1861, in the Salem church.

Parnell, Cicero Theodore, born Oct. 15, 1860, to Christina Parnell (now married to Aug. Regge). Baptized Mar. 23, 1861, at the mother's house.

Hege, Daniel Edwin, born May 9, 1860, to Daniel Hege and wife. Baptized May 12, 1861, at the Double Bridge schoolhouse.

Shouse, Alice Cordelia, born Jan. 13, 1861, to Wesley Shouse and wife. Baptized May 12, 1861, at the Double Bridge schoolhouse.

Merit, Edward Franklin, born May 22, 1861, to John Merit and Jane m.n. Standifer. Baptized Nov. 17, 1861, at the Double Bridge schoolhouse.

Reich, Anna Adela, born Oct. 2, 1861, to John H. Reich and Theresa m.n. Tesh. Baptized Dec. 31, 1861, at the house of the widowed Sr. Rudelphia Ackerman at Salem.

Faircloth, Sarah Elizabeth, born Oct. 4, 1861, to Thos. Faircloth and Louisa m.n. Rothaas. Baptized Jan. 11, 1862, at the house of the widowed Sr. Amelia Blum in Salem.

Brewer, Martha Isidore, born Nov. 13, 1861, to Davidsen Brewer and Louisa m.n. Fletcher. Baptized Jan. 29, 1862, in the Salem parsonage.

Blum, Olivia Leonora, born Feb. 1, 1862, to Rudolph Blum and Susan m.n. Leinbach. Baptized Apr. 11, 1862, at the parents' house.

Marshall, Benjamin Franklin, born Jan. 8, 1861, to William and Millie Marshall. Baptized July 20, 1862, at the Double Bridge schoolhouse. [Repeated below.]

Grubbs, Cornelia Elizabeth, born June 10, 1862, to Daniel Grubbs and Mary Jane m.n. Hendricks. Baptized Mar. 2, 1863, at the house of D. Grubbs, sen., the grandfather of the child.

Brewer, Francis Marion Lee, born Sept. 8, 1862, to John Brewer and Sophia m.n. Fletcher. Baptized Apr. 9, 1863, in the Salem parsonage.

Reed, Martha Ann Elizabeth, born Aug. 2, 1862, to Harrison Reed and Ernestina m.n. Blum. Baptized May 14, 1863, at the house of the widowed Sr. Amelia Blum at Salem.

Renigar, Theodore Keehln, born Jan. 30, 1863, to George H. Renigar and Margaret m.n. Warner. Baptized June 20, 1863, in the parents' house in Winston.

Fisher, George Oscar Lee, born Aug. 24, 1863, to Emanuel Fisher and Maria m.n. Kline. Baptized Jan. 16, 1864, at the parents' house in Winston.

Hughes, Samuel Hudson, born Aug. 16, 1861, to Henry Hughes and Martha m.n. Collins. Baptized Apr. 3, 1864, at the parents' house.

Hughes, Jefferson Cornelius, born Dec. 31, 1863, to Henry Hughes and Martha m.n. Collins. Baptized Apr. 3, 1864, at the parents' house.

Reich, Louisa Virginia, born Feb. 4, 1858, to Naaman Reich and Martha m.n. Harris. Baptized May 10, 1858, at the house of Br. Meller. [Recorded out of sequence.]

Grabb, Obey Eugene, born Dec. 10, 1860, to John Grabb and Mary m.n. Aldridge. Baptized June 5, 1862. [Recorded out of sequence.]

Marshall, Benjamin Franklin, born Jan. 8, 1861, to William Marshall and Millie m.n. Snow. Baptized July 20, 1862, at Double Bridge schoolhouse. [Repeated above.] [Recorded out of sequence.]

Holder, John Martin, born June 26, 1862, to Carlos Holder and Nancy m.n. Shelton. Baptized Sept. 14, 1862, at Pfafftown. [Recorded out of sequence.]

Flynt, Minerva Catherine Elizabeth, born June 2, 1862, to John Flynt and Lucy m.n. Petri. Baptized Sept. 14, 1862, at Pfafftown. [Recorded out of sequence.]

Transou, Mary Magdalene, born Apr. 17, 1862, to Julius Transou and Julia m.n. Conrad. Baptized Sept. 14, 1862, at Pfafftown. [Recorded out of sequence.]

Steward, Ellen Pamelia, born May 15, 1862, to William Steward and Nancy m.n. Pfaff. Baptized Sept. 14, 1862, at Pfafftown. [Recorded out of sequence.]

Kline, Isaac Rufus, born May 8, 1862, to Solomon Kline and Martha m.n. Pfaff. Baptized Sept. 14, 1862, at Pfafftown. [Recorded out of sequence.]

Petri, Alice Margaret, born Oct. 21, 1861, to Wesley Petri and Amelia m.n. Starr. Baptized Dec. 14, 1861, in Br. Ebert's house. [Recorded out of sequence.]

Shamel, Anna Martha Jane, born Feb. 14, 1862, to Eli Edward Shamel and Temperance m.n. Stolz. Baptized July 13, 1862, at Maple Springs. [Recorded out of sequence.]

Shamel, Sarah Elizabeth, born June 29, 1862, to Francis E. Shamel and Charity m.n. Livengood. Baptized Sept. 28, 1862, at Maple Springs. [Recorded out of sequence.]

Transou, Mary Beck, born Aug. 12, 1862, to Jacob Transou and Emmeline m.n. Steward. Baptized Jan. 9, 1863, at Pfafftown. [Recorded out of sequence.]

Saylor, Lewis Alexander, born Oct. 7, 1862, to William Saylor and Pauline m.n. Pfaff. Baptized Jan. 9, 1863, at Pfafftown. [Recorded out of sequence.]

Church, John Luther, born Nov. 12, 1862, to Charles Wesley Church and Lucinda m.n. Flynt. Baptized Jan. 9, 1863, at Pfafftown. [Recorded out of sequence.]

Krause, George Andrew Jackson, born Sept. 26, 1862, to Andrew Krause and Susan Elizabeth m.n. Krauss (Crews). Baptized July 19, 1863, at Pfafftown. [Recorded out of sequence.]

Transou, Caroline Viola, born June 4, 1863, to Julius Transou and Julia m.n. Conrad. Baptized July 19, 1863, at Pfafftown. [Recorded out of sequence.]

Petri, Robert Parmenio, born May 11, 1864, to John Joshua Petri and Angelica Justina m.n. Shulz. Baptized July 23, 1864, at the parents' house.

Blum, Rowan Keehln, born July 12, 1864, to Rudolph Blum and Susan m.n. Leinbach. Baptized Nov. 6, 1864, at the parents' house.

Brewer, Aemelius Roswell, born Oct. 1, 1865, to Wesley Brewer and Camilla m.n. Berryman. Baptized Jan. 31, 1866, at the parents' house.

Renigar, George Clement, born July 1, 1865, to Henry G. Renigar and Margaret m.n. Werner. Baptized Mar. 31, 1866.

Grubbs, Joseph Lee, born June 21, 1865, to Daniel Grubbs and Mary Jane m.n. Hendricks. Baptized June 9, 1866.

Waggoman, Eva Leonora, born June 26, 1866, to John Henry Waggoman and Martha Jane m.n. Hardgrave. Baptized Sept. 29, 1866, in the house of the child's grandmother.

Marriages of Non-Members

McCallum, Archibald, a widower from Twiggs County, Georgia, married May 7, 1857, to Emily Banner, daughter of Constantin Ladd Banner and Mary m.n. Bowman.

Rayle, Bartlet Y., of Guilford Co. married Oct. 14, 1861, to Ellen L. Lehman, daughter of Henry Lehman of Brookstown.

Henderson, John, married May 29, 1862, to Elizabeth Casey.

Joyner, John A., married July 3, 1862, to Salome Baumgardner.

Mosser, William, married Feb. 8, 1866, to Emma Snipe.

Reich, Columbus, married Lutitia Jones.

Deaths and Burials of Non-Members

[All burials are in the Salem God's Acre (the graveyard) unless otherwise stated.]

Kern, Julius Levering, born Dec. 24, 1819. Married in 1851 to Selma C. Spach. Died July 9, 1860. [Salem Diary: For several years past he has been residing at Louisburg, Franklin Co., N.C. He returned with his family last week to his father-in-law, David Spach, in the last stage of consumption. Owing to his having had his name taken off our list of members, and in accordance with the rule made by the Trustees that none but members should be interred in our graveyard, his remains were buried in Salem Cemetery.] [Board of Trustees on Feb. 19, 1861, permitted the remains to be reinterred in God's Acre.]

Chaffin, Nathan, born to Nathan and Julia Chaffin. Died Aug. 11, 1860. Buried in Salem Cemetery.

Hughes, Mary Elizabeth, born to Henry Hughes and Martha m.n. Collins. Died Sept. 4, 1860. Buried in Salem Cemetery.

Grubbs, Rosina, born Dec. 25, 1803, to Peter and Eve Michael. Married to George Grubbs. Died Feb. 2, 1861. Buried at Maple Springs.

Blum, Mary Florence Sophia, born to Rudolph Blum and Susan m.n. Snipe. Died Feb. 2, 1861. Buried at Liberty.

Smith, Elisha, born Sept. 10, 1814, in Montgomery County. Married in August 1854 to Annette L. Clewell, daughter of David Clewell. Died Feb. 24, 1861.

Tucker, John William, born July 3, 1860, to Amanda M. Tucker. Died Mar. 4, 1861. Buried at Liberty.

Byerly, Lucy Ellen, born Feb. 20, 1860, to Sandford Byerly and Eliza m.n. Masten. Died June 5, 1861. Buried in Salem Cemetery.

Casey, Thomas. Died June 9, 1861. Buried in Jerusalem Cemetery about one mile north of Salem.

Crossland, Anna Louise, born Oct. 24, 1860, at Portsmouth, Va., to B. F. Crossland and Louisa M. m.n. Shober. Died June 17, 1861.

Sink, Redellua Lee, born July 24, 1860, to W. L. Sink and wife. Died June 22, 1861. Buried at Waughtown.

Light (Leicht), John Simon, born Apr. 19, 1780, in Germany. Married (1) Aug. 9, 1812, to Sarah Rippel (died 1832). Married (2) Sept. 2, 1834, to Grace Shields. Died Nov. 5, 1861. Buried at Waughtown.

Cristman, Eliza Jane, born Feb. 1, 1858, at Waughtown, to Alvin and Charity Cristman. Died Nov. 29, 1861. Buried at Waughtown.

Banner, Sarah Ann, born May 4, 1837, in Germanton, to Const. L. Banner and Mary m.n. Bowman. Died Feb. 26, 1862. Buried in Salem Cemetery.

Wagaman, William Edward, born Aug. 20, 1840, near Salem, to John Wagaman and Lisette m.n. Shouse. Died Mar. 21, 1862.

Collins, David. Died Apr. 22, 1862. Buried at Liberty. [Salem Diary: He was a bricklayer who accidentally came to his death by a fall from a scaffold. He was not a member of any church. He leaves a widow and six children, the youngest an infant, and but little provision for their support.]

Patterson, Maria Louisa, born to John M. and Ann Eliza Morehead of Greensboro. Married to Rufus L. Patterson. Died May 3, 1862. Buried in Salem Cemetery.

Munsch, Catharine m.n. Lumly. Married to George Munsch. Died May 7, 1862. Buried in Salem Cemetery.

Faircloth, Mary Eleanora, born to Thomas Faircloth and Louisa m.n. Rothhaas. Died May 26, 1862.

Kingsbury, Lucy Ann m.n. Walls. Died July 18, 1862. Buried in Salem Cemetery.

Martin, Eva Catherine, born to Dr. Samuel Martin and Virlinda m.n. Miller. Died Sept. 5, 1862. Buried in Salem Cemetery.

Martin, Mollie, born to Dr. Samuel Martin and Virlinda m.n. Miller. Died Sept. 19, 1862. Buried in Salem Cemetery.

Shepperd, Jacob, born to A. H. Shepperd. Died Dec. 13, 1862. He fell in the battle of Fredericksburg. Buried in Salem Cemetery.

Banner, Henry C., born to Constantine L. Banner and Mary m.n. Bowman. Died Dec. 21, 1862, in Petersburg, Va., of a wound received in the battle of Fredericksburg. Buried in Salem Cemetery.

Remson, Eunice, born Aug. 17, 1846, to Ezra Remson and Mary m.n Marshall. Died Dec. 23, 1862. Buried in Salem Cemetery.

Lott, Eugene Smiley, born Dec. 16, 1862, to H. D. Lott and E. J. m.n. Lott. Died Jan. 16, 1863.

Stafford, John C. Died Jan. 24, 1863. Buried in Salem Cemetery.

Lott, Arthur Patterson, born Jan. 9, 1859, at Salem, to H. D. and E. J. Lott. Died Feb. 10, 1863.

Calhoun, James Y., born Aug. 11, 1836, in Guilford County, to Alfred Calhoun. Married May 3, 1859, to Mary Jenkins. Died Jan. 23, 1863, in the military hospital in Lynchburg, Va. Buried in Salem Cemetery.

Everhart, George Marlow, born July 21, 1859, at Huntsville, Ala., to Rev. Geo. M. Everhart and Cornelia A. m.n. Banner. Died Apr. 4, 1863, at Charlotte. Buried in Salem Cemetery.

Byerly, Lelia Ann, born Mar. 26, 1862, at Liberty, to Sanford and Eliza Byerly. Died May 23, 1863. Buried in Salem Cemetery.

Waugh, James R. Died May 1863. He was wounded at Chancellorsville, Va., and died in the hospital at Richmond. Buried in Salem Cemetery.

Horton, W. T., of the 19th Regiment, Georgia Troops. Died June 10, 1863. He arrived here sick on the 6th inst. Buried in Salem Cemetery.

Kingsbury, Selma Catharine, born Jan. 8, 1833, near Salem, to David Spach and Fredericka Charlotte m.n. Ebbeke. Married (1) Aug. 20, 1851, to Julius L. Kern (died 1861). Married (2) October 1862 to Henry Kingsbury. Died July 18, 1863.

Stafford, Betty Jackson, born July 13, 1862, at Winston, to A. J. and Cornelia Stafford. Died July 31, 1863. Buried in Salem Cemetery.

Martin, Jessie, born to Dr. Samuel Martin and Virlinda m.n. Miller. Died Sept. 6, 1863. Buried in Salem Cemetery.

Cook, Mary Jane, born Dec. 4, 1855, at Winston, to Nelson Cook and [blank] m.n. Stolz. Died Sept. 23, 1863. Buried at Liberty.

Lewis, Noah, born to Hasten Lewis and his first wife Tabitha m.n. Marshall. Died Sept. 25, 1863. He was a paroled prisoner of war. Buried in Salem Cemetery.

Shulz, Junius Edwin, born Sept. 3, 1836, to Thomas Shulz and Christina m.n. Mickey. Died Aug. 29, 1863. He was killed in battle and buried on the battlefield. Br. Bahnson preached the funeral Oct. 18, 1863, at Mt. Tabor.

Miller, Henry. Died Oct. 23, 1863. Buried at Bethabara.

Hensdale, David, born Dec. 11, 1841, in Forsyth County. Died Feb. 12, 1864. He was a volunteer in the army and had been absent from home for more than two years. On his way home to visit his widowed mother, he lost his life by being crushed at the railroad platform at Greensboro. Buried at Waughtown.

Reich, John William Thomas, born at Bethabara to Isaac and Sarah Reich. Died Sept. 11, 1863, age 5 years, 9 months, and 27 days. Buried at Bethabara. Funeral preached Feb. 28, 1864, at Bethabara.

Webb, Susan L., born Aug. 17, 1807, in Wilkesboro. Married in 1824 to Horatio M. Webb. Died Apr. 23, 1864. Buried in Salem Cemetery.

Shepperd, Augustine H., born Feb. 24, 1792, in Surry County. Married to Martha P. T. Turner. Died July 11, 1864. Early in life he was chosen a member of our legislature, and soon after elected to the U.S. Congress. He remained a member for many years. Buried in Salem Cemetery.

Reid, Phebe Elizabeth, born Dec. 25, 1851, in Forsyth County, to William Reid and wife. Died Dec. 7, 1864. Buried at Waughtown.

Faircloth, Sarah Elizabeth, born Oct. 4, 1861, in Davie County, to Thomas Faircloth and Louisa m.n. Rothaas. Died Dec. 13, 1864.

Smith, Thomas Plummer, born May 22, 1865, at Salem, to Jane Smith. Died June 25, 1865. Buried in Salem Cemetery.

Booze, J. W., of Surry County. Died July 7, 1865. Formerly of the 53d North Carolina Regiment. He arrived here sick on July 6. Buried in Salem Cemetery.

Veach, Rebecca, born May 26, 1795, in Rowan County. Married May 1, 1815. Died Feb. 11, 1866.

Salem Diary Entries, 1857-1866

[Church Register material that was recorded only in the Salem Diary. The following is the entirety of the material.]

Marriages

Harry and Betty, both members of our colored church, married June 20, 1858. Having joined the church lately they very properly thought it their duty to ask the blessing of the church on that connection in which they had lived for years without any church solemnity.

Deaths and Burials

Joyner, V. L., a boarding student at the Salem Female Academy. Died May 13, 1857. Her body was taken to Tarborough by her friends.

Waugh, Mrs. Funeral held July 26, 1857. Hers was the first burial in the new cemetery, which in its present condition still looks pretty wild.

Byerle, Mary Jane, an infant. Buried Jan. 10, 1858, in Salem Cemetery.

Atwood, Wm. F., an old neighbor of Salem. Died Jan. 23, 1858. Buried Jan. 24, 1858, in his family graveyard.

Macy, an old married woman who was baptized May 31, 1858. Funeral preached June 6, 1858, at the poorhouse.

Shepperd, Martha, wife of Hon. Augustine H. Shepperd, one of our near neighbors. Funeral preached June 19, 1858, followed by burial in Salem Cemetery.

Shulz, wife of Parmenio Shulz. Funeral preached by Christian Lewis Rights on Oct. 10, 1858, in Winston.

Frank, a negro convicted of murder. Executed Dec. 17, 1858, in Winston. Br. Holland had baptized him in the jail at Winston.

Senseman, Louisa, daughter of John Vogler and wife of Edw. T. Senseman. She died Aug. 15, 1854, at West Salem, Illinois, where her husband was pastor of the Moravian Congregation. Strong apprehensions having been expressed that the graveyard at West Salem, owing to the division between the English and German portions of that congregation, might not be kept up as a "Moravian" burying ground, the relatives of Sr. Senseman had her remains together with those of her deceased child removed to Salem, North Carolina, where they were re-interred Jan. 30, 1859, in God's Acre.

Tesh, George, an aged man who lived near the Clemmonsville road about 3 miles from Salem. Funeral preached Mar. 30, 1859, at Bethel Meeting House.

Hauser, Mary Ann Elizabeth, a daughter of Isaac Hauser, aged 21 years. Funeral preached July 30, 1859, at Waughtown.

Casey, James, a young man who died of consumption Nov. 20, 1859, at the paper mill. Funeral preached Nov. 21, 1859, in the Methodist Church at Winston. Burial in the "Jerusalem" graveyard.

White, Andrew, died Dec. 15, 1859, age 73 years, 5 months, and 10 days. Funeral preached Dec. 16, 1859, in the Methodist Church at Winston, where he was a member.

White, Thaddeus, 11-year-old son of Widow White in Liberty. Funeral preached Jan. 14, 1860, in the Methodist Church at Winston.

Murchison, Roderick, formerly a man greatly respected but latterly a mere wreck through intemperance. Funeral preached May 2, 1860, at Waughtown.

Riggs, Mrs. Funeral preached June 11, 1860, in the Methodist Church at Winston. Burial in Liberty graveyard.

Beeson, Noah, a young man in the employ of Br. J. N. Blum as miller. He accidentally met with his death July 8, 1863, by drowning while bathing in the creek before the mill.

Brown, a child of David Brown. Buried Aug. 24, 1864, in the County graveyard.

Shouse, Chas. Augt., a young man who fell Feb. 6, 1865, in the battle at Hatcher's Run near Petersburg. Funeral preached Mar. 8, 1865. [Buried in Salem Cemetery.]

Shay, Dennis, a member of one of the regiments of Palmer's brigade. Buried Apr. 16, 1865, in Salem Cemetery.

Church Book for the People of Colour in and about Salem, N.C. (St. Philips Register, 1857-1866)

Infant Baptisms

Ida Hunter, born Sept. 30, 1856, to Matilda and Alex., the property of E. Belo. Baptized Apr. 5, 1857.

Giles Arthur, born Aug. 17, 1856, to Lucy, the property of C. Banner, and Allen, the property of Mr. Fries. Baptized Apr. 26, 1857.

Samuel Rufus, born Nov. 12, 1856, to Paulina, the property of C. Banner, and George, the property of Mr. Bowles. Baptized Apr. 26, 1857.

Frances Octavia Cornelia, born Feb. 28, 1856, to Elizabeth, the property of C. Banner. Baptized May 12, 1857.

Laura Rebecca Elizabeth, born Aug. 16, 1857, to Daniel and Patsy, both the property of F. Fries. Baptized July 25, 1858.

Martha Jane, born Feb. 17, 1858, to Alexander and Matilda, both the property of E. Belo. Baptized July 25, 1858.

William Harris, born May 24, 1858, to Lucinda, the property of A. Butner, (and George? the property of Geo. Folz). Baptized July 25, 1858.

Charles Edward, born May 23, 1858, to Charlotte, the property of F. Fries, and David, the property of Eliz. Conrad. Baptized July 25, 1858.

Edward Francis, born Feb. 25, 1857, to Aggie, property of Eliz. Conrad. Baptized July 25, 1858.

Edwin Lewis, born Oct. 9, 1858, to Martin, property of C. Banner, and Caroline, property of Wm. Holland. Baptized Dec. 12, 1858.

Susan Baker, born Feb. 3, 1859, to Augustus and Mourning, belonging to Aug. H. Shepperd. Baptized Apr. 24, 1859.

Rebecca Theodosia, born Jan. 3, 1856, to Hezekiah Pinkney (Fries) and Epsie Dulcinea (Hege). Baptized July 24, 1859.

Francis Walter, born 1859 to Paulina (Banner). Baptized Oct. 30, 1859.

Rufus Alexander, born June 1859 to Aggie (Lemly). Baptized Oct. 30, 1859.

Isabella, born 1859 to Lucy (Banner). Baptized Oct. 30, 1859.

James Edward Leo, born Aug. 1, 1859, to Washington (Fries) and Harriet (Fries). Baptized Oct. 30, 1859.

Francis Augustus, born July 13, 1859, to John (Fries) and Amelia (Blum). Baptized Oct. 30, 1859.

Mary Caroline, born Feb. 7, 1860, to Fanny, servant of Mr. Chaffin. Baptized May 23, 1860.

Jane Sarah Emma, born July 16, 1860, to Martin (Banner) and his wife Caroline (Holland), both communicant members. Baptized Nov. 4, 1860, in the church.

Rosalie, born Mar. 6, 1861, to Augustus and Edmonia (Shepperd). Baptized May 26, 1861, in the church.

Mary Bell, born Apr. 16, 1861, to Lucinda (Adam Butner). Baptized July 28, 1861, in the church.

Sarah Bell, born Sept. 16, 1861, to Aggy (H. A. Lemly). Baptized Mar. 23, 1862, at H. A. Lemly's.

Sylvia Esther, born Mar. 16, 1862, to Giles (Fries) and Esther (Lemly). Baptized Apr. 28, 1862, in the church.

William Francis, born July 6, 1861, to Alick and Matilda, servants of Br. E. Belo. Baptized May 11, 1862, at the [Salem] parsonage.

Alice Isabella, born Sept. 16, 1862, to Henderson (servant of Dr. Martin) and his wife Ann (servant of Br. J. L. Fulkerson). Baptized Nov. 2, 1862, in the church.

Arabella, born July 17, 1862, to Lewis (Hege) and Mary Magdalene (Starbuck). Baptized Nov. 30, 1862, in the church.

James Milton, born Dec. 26, 1861, to Calvin (Taylor) and his wife Sophy (Waugh). Baptized Mar. 15, 1863, in the church.

Maria Louisa, born Feb. 3, 1856, to the md. sister Jane (Edw. T. Clemmons). Baptized May 31, 1863, in the church.

Laura Virginia, born May 23, 1858, to the md. br. and sr. Isaac and Jane, the servants of Br. Edwin T. Clemmons. Baptized May 31, 1863, in the church.

Mary Alice, born Sept. 7. 1860, to the md. Br. and Sr. Isaac and Jane, servants of Br. Ed. T. Clemmons. Baptized May 31, 1863, in the church.

Georgiana, born Mar. 16, 1863, to the md. Br. and Sr. Isaac and Jane, servants of Br. Ed. T. Clemmons. Baptized May 31, 1863, in the church.

Mary Lavinia, born June 18, 1856, to Jesse and his wife Judy, servants of Br. C. L. [Constantine Lazarus, not Christian Lewis] Rights. Baptized May 31, 1863, in the church.

Susan Adelaide, born Mar. 20, 1862, to Jack (Masten) and his wife, the md. Sr. Mary, servant of Mr. Edwin Light. Baptized May 31, 1863, in the church.

Josephine, born Aug. 22, 1856, to Fanny, servant of Mr. N. Chaffin. Baptized May 31, 1863, in the church.

Robert Henry, born Mar. 1863 to Robert (Banner) and Betty (Shepperd). Baptized July 19, 1863, in the church.

Hannah Johnson, born May 21, 1863, to Augustus (Shepperd) and Edmonia (Shepperd). Baptized July 19, 1863, in the church.

George Theodore, born June 5, 1863, to Martin (Banner) and Caroline (Vogler). Baptized July 19, 1863, in the church.

Henry Francis, born May 22, 1863, to Sanford (Hanes) and Lucinda (Butner). Baptized July 26, 1863, in the church.

William Henry, born Jan. 1, 1863, to Washington (Fries) and Harriet (Fries). Baptized July 26, 1863, in the church.

James Andrew, born Aug. 3, 1863, to William (Siewers) and Aggie (Lemly). Baptized Oct. 4, 1863, in the church.

Lee Henry, born Nov. 29, 1863, to Henderson (Martin) and his wife Ann (Fulkerson). Baptized May 29, 1864, in the church.

Sarah Ann, born Oct. 16, 1863, to Peter (Fries) and Rhoda (Fries). Baptized June 19, 1864, in the church.

Joseph Israel, born Feb. 13, 1864, to Washington (Fries) and Harriet (Fries). Baptized June 19, 1864, in the church.

Ella May, born May 14, 1864, to Mary (Leinbach) and John (Fries). Baptized June 19, 1864, in the church.

Lucinda Judea, born Feb. 22, 1864, to Calvin Taylor (free) and Sophie (Waugh). Baptized July 17, 1864, in the church.

Mary Ann, born Mar. 3, 1864, to David (Boner) and his wife Susan (Waugh). Baptized Oct. 16, 1864, in the church.

Ida Lenora, born July 18, 1864, to John Richard Montgomery and his wife Nelly Ann Dew, both free. Baptized Oct. 16, 1864, in the church.

Alberta Victoria, born Jan. 1865 to Ben and Mary, both of them formerly servants of Mr. Goodloe of Alabama. Baptized Aug. 6, 1865, in the church.

Rufus Eugene, born Mar. 31, 1865, to br. Martin (Banner) and his wife Caroline Jeretina (Vogler). Baptized Aug. 6, 1865, in the church.

James Irwin, born Feb. 12, 1865, to Ida (Ebert). Baptized Sept. 17, 1865, in the church.

James Alexander Leon, born Mar. 27, 1865, to Charity (Wm. Fries). Baptized Nov. 5, 1865, in the church.

John Henry, born Aug. 31, 1865, to Washington (Fries) and his wife Harriet (Fries). Baptized Nov. 19, 1865, in the church.

Francis Walter, born Sept. 25, 1865, to Henderson (Martin) and his wife Ann (Fulkerson). Baptized Nov. 19, 1865, in the church.

Harriet Lou Anna, born Oct. 6, 1865, to John (Fries) and Mary (Fulkerson). Baptized Nov. 19, 1865, in the church.

Banner, William Albert, born Sept. 4, 1865, to Robert and Betty Banner. Baptized Apr. 15, 1866, in the church.

Shepperd, Anna Mary, born Dec. 28, 1865, to Augustus and Edmonia Shepperd. Baptized Apr. 15, 1866, in the church.

Zevely, William Benjamin, born July 15, 1865, to Ben Zevely and Lavina (Hunt). Baptized Apr. 20, 1866, in the study of M. E. Grunert. [African Church Diary: He was born last July in Mississippi.]

(Clemmons), Isaac Granville, born Aug. 19, 1866, to Isaac (Clemmons) and Jane. Baptized 1866, in the church.

(Vogler), Maryland Thomas, born Aug. 22, 1866, to Alexander (Vogler) and Priscilla. Baptized 1866, in the church.

Adult Baptisms

Nancy Adelia, a single woman, property of Darius Starbuck. Baptized Oct. 11, 1857.

Betty Martin, a married woman, property of F. Fries. Baptized Mar. 21, 1858.

Rhoda Lauretta, a girl belonging to F. Fries. Baptized Mar. 21, 1858.

Anna Roseta, a girl belonging to E. A. Vogler. Baptized Mar. 21, 1858.

Alexander, a single young man, servant of Br. Elias A. Vogler. Baptized Oct. 23, 1859.

Julia Catharine Jarvis, a free brown girl, aged 17 years, indentured to Br. W. Thornton. Baptized Oct. 23, 1859.

David, a widower, aged 40 years, servant of Sr. Anna Shober. Baptized Jan. 15, 1860.

Esther, wife of Daniel, both servants of Br. Francis Fries. Baptized Jan. 15, 1860.

Peter, servant of Br. F. Fries, a young unmarried man. Baptized June 24, 1860.

Benjamin, servant of Dr. Zevely, aged 30 or thereabouts. Baptized June 24, 1860.

Isaac (servant of Edwin T. Clemmons). Baptized Dec. 9, 1860.

Jane (servant of Edwin T. Clemmons) and wife of Isaac. Baptized Dec. 9, 1860.

Lewis, a young man, servant of Br. George Hege. Baptized Apr. 14, 1861.

William Anderson, a young man, servant of Br. John D. Siewers. Baptized Apr. 14, 1861.

Thomas Jefferson, a young man, servant of Br. John D. Siewers. Baptized Apr. 14, 1861.

John Richard, a free boy, apprenticed to Br. Joshua Boner. Baptized Apr. 14, 1861.

Mary Magdalene, an unmarried young woman (hired at Br. Tr. F. Crist's). Baptized Apr. 14, 1861.

Rachel, a middle-aged woman, servant of Br. George Hege. Baptized Apr. 14, 1861.

Michael, aged about 36, servant of Mr. Samuel Lagenour. Baptized Sept. 28, 1862.

Jacob, aged about 16, servant of Dr. T. F. Keehln. Baptized Sept. 28, 1862.

Margaret, born Jan. 23, 1847, daughter of Lucy, servant of Br. C. L. Banner. Being confined to a sick bed, and her end evidently approaching, baptism was administered at her urgent request on May 13, 1863.

Rhoda, an elderly woman, servant of Mr. Reed. Baptized Mar. 13, 1864.

Charles, a young man, servant of Edwin T. Clemmons. Baptized Dec. 18, 1864.

Nathan, a boy in care of D. H. Starbuck. Baptized Dec. 18, 1864.

John Henry Jones, a free boy, indentured to Henry Hughes. Baptized Dec. 18, 1864.

Lucinda, a girl, servant of Julius Mickey. Baptized Dec. 18, 1864.

Julia, a girl, servant of O. A. Keehln. Baptized Dec. 18, 1864.

Pender, Laura Margaret, a girl living with the Sheppard family. Baptized July 22, 1866.

Foltz, Amanda Elisabeth (Betty). Baptized July 22, 1866.

Linda Cornelius or Sides, formerly servant of Christian Sides. Baptized July 22, 1866.

Marriages

Henry (Webb) married Dec. 25, 1859, to Nikotie (Waugh). [African Church Diary: He is a member of the Methodist church at Winston. The wedding took place at Mr. Waugh's in Waughtown.]

Alexander (Vogler) married Dec. 26, 1859, to Ann Lisette (Vogler).

Daniel, the servant of Fr. Fries, married Mar. 24, 1860, to Esther, the servant of Fr. Fries.

Isaac, servant of Br. Edwin Clemmons, married May 19, 1860, to Jane, the servant of Edwin Clemmons.

Haywood, servant of Addy Shober (he is hired to Edw. Clemmons), married 1860 to Paulina, servant of C. L. Banner.

Harris, servant of F. Fries, married Nov. 24, 1860, to Paulina, servant of Wm. Fries.

Henderson, servant of Dr. Martin, married Dec. 25, 1861, to Angeline (Ann), servant of Br. Fulkerson.

Boles, George, (hired to N. Chaffin) married Jan. 10, 1862, to Dorcas, servant of N. Chaffin.

Giles (servant of F. Fries) married Feb. 1, 1862, to Esther, (servant of A. H. Lemly).

William (servant of Jno. D. Siewers) married Nov. 15, 1862, to Aggie (servant of A. H. Lemly).

Peter (servant of F. Fries) married Dec. 25, 1862, to Rhoda (servant of F. Fries).

Richard (Dick), servant of Thos. J. Boner, married Aug. 25, 1863, to Susan, servant of Albert Waugh.

Montgomery, John Richard, married Nov. 26, 1863, to Nelly Ann Dew, both free persons of color, the former indentured to J. Boner.

David, servant of Mrs. Anna Shober, married Dec. 24, 1863, to Ellen, servant of Simon Light.

John, servant of H. W. Fries, married Oct. 1, 1864, to Lucinda, servant of the same.

(King), John, now of Jamestown, N.C., married Oct. 29, 1865, to Amelia (Lash).

Hege, Tom, married Jan. 2, 1866, to Amy Rights.

(Vogler), Alexander, a widower, married Feb. 3, 1866, to Scylla (Matthews).

(Hege), Lewis, a widower, married Mar. 20, 1866, to Dinah (Malone).

(Zevely), Ben, married Apr. 12, 1866, to Lavina (Hunt).

Fries, Carr, married May 10, 1866, to Miranda Butner.

Siewers, Richard, married June 2, 1866, to Anna Foltz. [African Church Diary: daughter of Lewis Foltz.]

Deaths and Burials

Lucy Ann Rosaline, the property of Mrs. Rights. Died Feb. 26, 1857. Her age was 1 year and 4 months.

P. Maria, the property of George Spach. Died Mar. 8, 1857. Her age was 35 years and 2 months.

Emma, the property of William Fries. Died May 30, 1857. Aged 6 years. [African Church Diary: She was the daughter of Lewis (Geo. Folz) and Mary (Wm. Fries).]

An unbaptized infant, the property of Wm. Fries. Died June 7, 1857. Aged about 1 year. [African Church Diary: The infant of Lewis (Geo. Folz) and Mary (Wm. Fries).]

David, the property of the Salem mill company. Died Oct. 8, 1857.

Betty, the property of Theod. Kelhln. Died Nov. 4, 1857.

Delilah, the property of Augustus Zevely. Died Nov. 10, 1857. Aged about 50 years.

Delilah, the property of Christian Hege. Died Mar. 20, 1858.

An unbaptized infant, the property of N. Chafin. Died June 10, 1858. Aged a few months.

Wellington, the property of Louisa Shober. Died Mar. 22, 1859. Aged about 50 years.

Joseph, the property of William Fries. Died Apr. 1, 1859. Aged about 20 years.

Betsy Ann, the property of Albert Waugh, Esq., wife of David (Shober). Died Oct. 1, 1859. Aged 24 years. She was buried at Waughtown.

An unbaptized infant of a servant of Wm. Fries and Daniel, servant of F. Fries.

George, servant of F. Fries. Died Nov. 26, 1859. Aged about 12 years. He came to his death accidentally. He was the first interment on the new cemetery for colored people.

Hamilton, servant of Mr. Waugh. Died Jan. 16, 1860. Interred at Waughtown.

Jenny, a communicant sr., aged about 70 years. Lived at the Widow Atwood's. Died Jan. 21, 1860.

Harry, a communicant Brother, servant of Br. Nathaniel Vogler. Husband of Betty (Fries). Died Feb. 22, 1860. His age was about 60 years.

Alvis, servant of Br. Francis Fries. Died Apr. 2, 1860. He died of lung disease. Aged about 36 years.

Susan, daughter of Augustus and [blank], servants of A. H. Shepperd. Died May 6, 1860. Age about 14 months. Interred at A. H. Shepperd's.

Betty, a communicant Sister, widow of Harry, servant of Br. Fr. Fries. Died May 21, 1860. She died suddenly of disease of the heart, aged about (50?). [African Church Diary: She has the testimony of having been a most faithful servant, as she was also a most steady and exemplary member of the church. A numerous company of blacks and whites was present at the funeral.]

Betty, a communicant member of the Methodist Church, servant of Dietrich Tewes. Died July 7, 1860. She died suddenly, probably of disease of the heart. Her age was 50 years (or upwards).

Lydia, daughter of Matilda, servant of E. Belo. Died July 20, 1860. Aged 15 months. Unbaptized. [African Church Diary: The first infant buried in the new cemetery for colored folks.]

Prid, a man (aged from 50 to 60), servant of E. Belo. He belonged to Wm. Hill of Surry till recently. Within 12 months past he came to Salem. Died of consumption July 25, 1860.

Phebe, daughter of Lewis (Folz) and Mary (Fries), servant of E. Belo. Died Aug. 4, 1860. Aged 17 years.

Ann, a communicant member, wife of Alick (both servants of Br. E. A. Vogler). Died Jan. 19, 1861. Her age was nearly 20 years. [African Church Diary: The funeral sermon was preached in the large church. A large procession of whites as well as colored people followed her remains to the grave.]

William, a lad, aged about 17 years, servant of Dr. T. F. Kuehln. Died Feb. 23, 1861.

Mary Caroline, child of Fanny, servant of Mr. N. Chaffin. Died Mar. 24, 1861. Age 1 year, 1 month, and 17 days.

Paulina, servant of C. L. Banner and wife of Haywood. Died June 8, 1861. Her age was about 26 years. Her remains were interred on Br. C. L. Banner's plantation.

Phebe, an aged communicant member, formerly the servant of the Unity Administration in Wachovia, for many years residing with her daughter Betsy at Br. John Beyerle's, where she was supported by a pension from the Unity Administration. Her age was about 90 years. Died Aug. 6, 1861.

Caroline, servant of Christian Hege. Died Aug. 13, 1861. Aged about 16 years.

Isaac, servant of Henry A. Lemly. Died Oct. 7, 1861. Aged about 22 years.

Epsey, wife of Pinkney (Fries) and servant of Christian Hege. Died Oct. 14, 1861. Aged about 33 years.

Mary, servant of Albert Waugh, Esq. Died Nov. 21, 1861. She was a candidate for confirmation. Her remains were interred at Waughtown. Aged 19 years, 10 months, and 1 day.

Rebecca, daughter of Pinkney (Fries) and Epsey (Hege), deceased. Died Mar. 6, 1862. Age about 6 years. [African Church Diary: She died Mar. 5, 1862; buried Mar. 6, 1862.]

Sarah Bell, daughter of Aggy (Lemly). Died Mar. 23, 1862. Aged 6 months and 7 days.

George Washington, son of Alex and Matilda (E. Belo). Died Apr. 13, 1862, in the 8th year of his age.

Esther, married woman, servant of H. A. Lemly. Died Apr. 6, 1862. Aged 20-odd years. [Recorded out of sequence.]

Unbaptized infant, daughter of Fanny, servant of N. Chaffin. Died Apr. 27, 1862. Aged 5 weeks.

Sylvia Esther, daughter of Esther, deceased. Died Apr. 30, 1862. Aged 1 1/2 months.

Daniel, a married man, servant of F. Fries. Died May 9, 1862. Aged about 65. [African Church Diary: He was the husband of Esther. He was a candidate for baptism, and but for providential hindrances would have been baptized on Easter Sunday. His end was said to have been very happy.]

Robert, a married man, servant of C. Hege. Died May 18, 1862. Aged about 50.

Mary, a married woman, servant of W. Barrow, Esq., of Winston. Died June 23, 1862. Aged about 35 years.

Mary, servant of Mrs. Phillips. Died Aug. 9, 1862. Aged about 16 years.

Adelaide Louisa Victoria, born Mar. 26, 1858, to David (Shober) and Betsy Ann (Waugh). Died Aug. 20, 1862. Interred at Waughtown.

John, son of Linda, servant of C. L. Banner. Died Dec. 21, 1862. Aged about 10 years. Interred at Mr. Banner's.

Arthur, son of Dorcas and George, servants of Mr. N. Chaffin. Died Jan. 30, 1863. Aged 4 months.

A girl, belonging to the estate of John Saunders. Died Feb. 5, 1863. Aged about 4 years.

Unbaptized infant, born Dec. 15, 1862, to Alick and Matilda (E. Belo). Died Mar. 16, 1863.

Nikotie, born June 23, 1839, a communicant Sister, wife of Henry (Webb) and servant of J. A. Waugh, Esq. Died Apr. 29, 1863.

Alice Isabella, born Sept. 16, 1862, to Henderson (Martin) and Ann (Fulkerson). Died June 9, 1863.

Humphrey, born May 12, 1831, servant of H. A. Lemly. Died June 10, 1863.

Henry Francis, born May 22, 1863, to Lucinda (Adam Butner) and Sanford (Hanes). Died Oct. 21, 1863.

Ben, servant of Dr. W. H. Wheeler. Died Jan. 15, 1864. A young man. Was found dead, sitting in his room; disease of the heart was the probable cause.

Catharine, a middle-aged woman, servant of Mr. N. Chaffin. Died Feb. 7, 1864. She was not connected with the church. The cause of her death was said to be rheumatism.

Mary Magdalene, born May 8, 1837, to Jerry and Letty, a quasi free woman of color. On April 14, 1861, she became a member of the church by baptism. The negro br. Lewis (Geo. Hege) was her husband. Died Feb. 14, 1864.

William Henry, born Jan. 1, 1863, to Washington and Harriet, both belonging to Henry Fries. Died May 12, 1864.

Jane, servant of Mrs. Louisa Crossland m.n. Shober. Died June 26, 1864. Her age was about 19 years.

Troy, son of Caroline, servant of Mr. Sam. Lagenour. Died July 28, 1864, of typhoid fever. Age about 7 years.

Wesley, servant of br. Jac. Fulkerson. Died Aug. 2, 1864, very unexpectedly of apoplexy, age about 21 years.

Mary, a communicant Sister, wife of Cyrus. Died Dec. 25, 1864. Her age is unknown. The corpse was buried without minister or company.

Lawson, Sophia, a communicant sister, free. Died Feb. 11, 1865. She died of typhoid fever, and was according to her request buried at her brother's house near Bethabara. [African Church Diary: where her mother was interred about a year ago.]

Phillis, a young married woman, living in the family of Mr. Henry Hughes. Died June 5, 1865. Her age was about 24.

Jemima, a communicant single sister, living in family of H. A. Lemly. Died June 15, 1865. Her age was about 32. [African Church Diary: Mrs. Lemly says she was more like a sister to her than a servant.]

Judy, a communicant sister, wife of Jesse, living with family of C. L. [Constantine Lazarus] Rights. Died July 15, 1865. Her age was 33 years and 13 days.

Josephine, born Mar. 13, 1861, unbaptized child of Daniel and Patsey, living on Fries' Quarter. Died July 18, 1865, of typhoid fever after a 16-day illness.

John Henry, born June 21, 1851, to David (Shober) and Betsy Ann (Waugh). Died July 27, 1865, of consumption.

Margaret Jane, born Dec. 10, 1851, to William (Spach) and wife Polly (Spach). Died July 27, 1865, of typhoid fever.

Mary, wife of Lewis (Foltz), who until a very short time since had lived in the family of br. William Fries. Died Aug. 31, 1865, of fever, aged 41 years. [African Church Diary: She had been servant of br. Wm. Fries, and only a few weeks ago she and her husband had moved on Zach. Rights' place, the old "Brüderplantage" (Single Brothers farm), to live together there. The grave was made on Fries' square.]

Amy, a widow, until lately living in the family of Const. L. Rights. She was a member of the Methodist Church. Died Sept. 19, 1865. Her age was upwards of 70.

John, living with Mr. David Blum in Waughtown. Married to Viney (Lavinia). Died Sept. 22, 1865. His age was about 57. [African Church Diary: His disease was contracted by drinking cold water while very warm. His age was 57 years, 4 months, 16 days.]

Ellen Susanna, born Nov. 12, 1849, to William (Spach) and wife Polly (Spach). Died Oct. 1, 1865, of typhoid fever. [African Church Diary: She was their youngest surviving daughter.]

Mary Bell, born Jan. 21, 1865, unbaptized daughter of John Mac, and Cynthia or Lucinda, both living with H. Fries. Died Oct. 15, 1865, of typhoid fever.

Jennie, an aged woman, member of Meth. E. church, who lived at Winston in the family of Mr. Crawley. Died Oct. 30, 1865. [African Church Diary: She had nursed Mr. Crawley in infancy, and remained with him all the time since then, bearing a good character for faithfulness and skill.]

Dora Elisabeth, born Oct. 3, 1864, to David Shober and wife Ellen (Light). Died Nov. 2, 1865.

Ben, formerly servant of David Blum of Waughtown, more lately of Dr. A. T. Zevely. Died Nov. 23, 1865. He had been for years a doorkeeper at the church, although not a member. His age was 60.

Henry, known as Henry Webb, formerly belonging to that family. A widowed brother who joined the church several years ago from the Methodists. Died Dec. 3, 1865, of consumption. [African Church Diary: He was a valuable member of the church and generally respected by white and colored.]

Amanda Pamelia, daughter of Jack(son) (Masten) and Mary (Light). Died Dec. 5, 1865, after a protracted illness. Her age was 14 years and about 9 months.

Rhoda, an elderly woman, and since her baptism a few years ago a faithful member of the church. She belonged until the emancipation to Mr. Reid. Died Apr. 11, 1866, rather suddenly of rheumatism.

Francis Walter, born Sept. 25, 1865, to Henderson Martin and Ann Fulkerson. Died Apr. 23, 1866.

Mourning Agnes, a communicant sister since 1843 who had lived for many years in the (Christian) Blum family. Died Apr. 28, 1866. She was probably nearly 80 years of age.

John Henry, born Aug. 31, 1865, to Washington and Harriet Fries. Died May 7, 1866.

Cyrus, an aged man, formerly the slave of the late br. Emanuel Shober. [African Church Diary: and afterwards of his son Charles, who gave him his freedom. Since then he lived where he could, mostly near the paper mill, the scene of his former labors. Finally

Martin (Banner) received him.] Died June 19, 1866. He fell down dead while walking in the yard of C. L. Banner. [African Church Diary: Sr. Herman paid for his grave.]

(Rottehaas), unbaptized infant of Willis (Rottehaas) and Amanda. Buried Sept. 27, 1866.

African American Church Diary Entries, 1857-1866

[Church Register material that was recorded only in the Diary of the African Congregation in Salem. *The following is the entirety of the material.]*

Infant Baptism

Casay, a child of Mr. Thos. Casay. Baptized Mar. 19, 1857.

Deaths and Burials

Henry Nelson, aged 2 years. Died in consequence of burns (scaldings). Buried Oct. 9, 1858, at Mr. Shepperd's.

Unbaptized infant [of?] Lewis Scott (Rights). Funeral preached Mar. 20, 1859, at the Salem colored church.

Charity (Nath'l. Blum). She died several months before her funeral was preached July 17, 1859, at the Salem colored church.

John, servant of the late Wm. F. Holland. Died autumn 1858. Funeral preached Aug. 28, 1859, at the Salem colored church.

Campbell, Lewis, an aged man who died about Christmas, 1859, in Iredell County. Funeral preached Mar. 25, 1860, at the Salem colored church. He had formerly resided in this vicinity, was well known and has relatives in the congregation. He was a zealous member of the Methodist church, and for many years past exhorted or preached as opportunity was given him. He bore the reputation of being a good man.

(Waugh), Dallas, born Dec. 14, 1855, to Br. David (Shober) and Betsy Ann (the mother departed this life several years ago). Died Jan. 17, 1862. Buried Jan. 19, 1862, at Waughtown. Funeral preached Feb. 2, 1862, at the Salem colored church.

(Siewers), Jefferson, an aged negro man, a very faithful member, who left the past weeks for his old home near Lynchburg, Va. Buried May 22, 1865, at Br. Const. Banner's.

Lawson, Anna. A member of Bethabara from infancy. Died June 1864. Funeral preached Aug. 20, 1865, at the Salem colored church.

Lawson, Jake, son of Anna Lawson. Shot during the war near his home near Bethabara by order, I [Br. Grunert] believe, of Capt. Wilson, C.S.A. Funeral preached Aug. 20, 1865, at the Salem colored church.

(Keehln), Jacob. He had left his home a few weeks since, contrary to his father's wishes, to get work on the railroad, and had died of typhoid fever. Heard Sept. 3, 1865, that he was buried yesterday at Midway.

Rights, Amie. Funeral held June 3, 1866, in Winston.

Bethania Register, 1857-1866

Infant Baptisms

Grunert, Anna Josephine, born Feb. 14, 1857, to Maximilian Eugene Grunert and Emma Theresa m.n. Pfohl. Baptized Mar. 22, 1857, in the Bethania church.

Leinbach, Reuben Claudius, born Jan. 9, 1857, to Joshua Leinbach and Elizabeth Lavinia m.n. Cooper. Baptized Mar. 28, 1857, at Pleasant Valley.

Marshall, Jacob Lewis, born Feb. 19, 1857, to Peter Marshall and Julia Antoinette m.n. Schultz. Baptized Mar. 28, 1857, at Pleasant Valley.

Conrad, John Henry, born Feb. 25, 1857, to Thomas Conrad and Louisa m.n. Schulz. Baptized Apr. 4, 1857, at Spanish Grove.

Matthews, Sarah Eliza, born Mar. 2, 1856, to William A. Matthews and Antoinette Melvina m.n. Transou. Baptized Apr. 26, 1857, in the Bethania church.

Matthews, Francis Leon, born Mar. 29, 1857, to William A. Matthews and Antoinette Melvina, m.n. Transou. Baptized Apr. 26, 1857, in the Bethania church.

Krause, Ellen Hortensia, born Dec. 20, 1856, to Andrew Krause and Susan m.n. Krause. Baptized May 12, 1857, at the house of Emmanuel Beck.

Butner, Eugene Edward, born Apr. 22, 1857, to Edward S. Butner and Mary Ann m.n. Wolffe. Baptized May 24, 1857, in the Bethania church.

Stoltz, Dora Camilla, born Mar. 27, 1857, to Parmenio Stoltz and Sarah m.n. Rothrock. Baptized May 24, 1857, in the Bethania church.

Kapp, Columbus Henry, born May 11, 1857, to William Kapp and Pamelia m.n. Shore. Baptized June 21, 1857, in the Bethania church.

Jones, Virginia Eliza, born Dec. 12, 1856, to Dr. Bev. Jones and Julia A. m.n. Conrad. Baptized July 15, 1857, at the house of Abraham Conrad.

Butner, Robert Oliver, born Apr. 19, 1858, to Alvin Emile Butner and Clarinda Caroline m.n. Oehman. Baptized June 6, 1858, in the Bethania church.

Hauser, Benjamin, born Aug. 6, 1858, to Joel P. Hauser and Licetta Margaret m.n. Pfaff. Baptized Dec. 4, 1858, at the house of William Leinbach near Bethania.

Pfaff, John Henry, born [Bethania Diary: Sept. 22, 1858] to Edwin P. Pfaff and Sarah M. m.n. Flint. Baptized Dec. 12, 1858, at Mickey's schoolhouse.

Theiss, Eugene Charles, born Nov. 10, 1858, to Solomon Theiss and Lauretta Sibilla m.n. Stockburger. Baptized Dec. 22, 1858, at the parents' house in Shoretown.

Kearney, William Henry Tobias, born Oct. 31, 1858, to William Alexander Kearney and Ann Caroline m.n. Rothrock. Baptized Dec. 26, 1858, at the parents' house near the Dutch meeting house.

Oehman, Luella Margaret, born Dec. 8, 1858, to Reinhold Ferdinand Oehman and Luisa Sophia m.n. Werner. Baptized Jan. 9, 1859, at the parents' house.

Shultz, Mary Selesta, born Nov. 20, 1858, to Edwin T. Shultz and Catherine A. m.n. Conrad. Baptized Feb. 27, 1859, at Spanish Grove.

Spoenhauer, Edwin Isaac, born Sept. 26, 1858, to William W. Spoenhauer and Pamelia L. m.n. Grabs. Baptized Apr. 30, 1859, at Crooked Run schoolhouse.

Butner, Virginia Elisabeth, born June 21, 1860, to Alvin Emile Butner and Clarinda Louisa m.n. Oehman. Baptized July 22, 1860, in the Bethania church.

Beck, George Frederick, born June 9, 1860, to Emanuel Beck and Mary Eliza m.n. Krause. Baptized July 22, 1860, at Spanish Grove.

Kapp, John William, born July 21, 1860, to William W. Kapp and Pamilia Catherine m.n. Shore. Baptized Oct. 7, 1860, in the Bethania church.

Stoltz, Henry Jacob, born Sept. 22, 1860, to William A. Stoltz and Martha C. E. m.n. Pursail. Baptized Nov. 4, 1860, at the parents' house in Bethania.

Conrad, Julius Ferdinand, born Nov. 5, 1860, to Thomas Conrad and Louisa Elisabeth m.n. Schultz. Baptized Nov. 13, 1860, at the parents' house near Pfafftown.

Butner, Charles Arthur, born Dec. 22, 1860, to Edward S. Butner and Mary Ann m.n. Wolf. Baptized Mar. 29, 1861, at the house of Henry Harman Butner in Bethania.

John Calvin, born Feb. 7, 1861, to Clemmentina, servant of br. H. H. Butner. Baptized Apr. 21, 1861, at the house of H. H. Butner. [This is the first slave baptism Br. Jacob Siewers recorded in the Bethania Register; it took place nine days after the shelling of Fort Sumter.]

Lash, Lillian May, born Nov. 5, 1861, to Thomas B. Lash and Wilhelmine Florina m.n. Stoltz. Baptized Nov. 24, 1861, at the parents' house near Bethania.

Marshall, Reuben Edwin, born Oct. 31, 1861, to Peter Marshall and Julia Antoinetta m.n. Schultz. Baptized Dec. 28, 1861, at Pfafftown.

Matilda Angelina, born Feb. 16, 1862, to Frank (Thomas Conrad) and Sarah Ann (Solomon Pfaff). Baptized Apr. 20, 1862, at Israel Lash's quarter.

Mary Eliza, born Mar. 3, 1862, to Levi (Israel Lash) and Maria (Israel Lash). Baptized Apr. 20, 1862, at Israel Lash's quarter.

Caroline Lucinda, born Feb. 11, 1862, to Stephen (Saml. Stauber) and Harriett (Israel Lash). Baptized Apr. 20, 1862, at Israel Lash's quarter.

Judith Lucretia, born Dec. 25, 1861, to Lucy (H. H. Butner) and John (Abraham Conrad). Baptized May 4, 1862, at the house of H. H. Butner.

Butner, Leon William, born Sept. 18, 1862, to Alvin Butner and Clarinda m.n. Oehman. Baptized Nov. 29, 1862, at the parents' house in Bethania.

Grabs, Emily Odelia, born Mar. 18, 1863, to Alexander Grabs and Jane m.n. Werner. Baptized Apr. 5, 1863, at the parents' house in Bethania.

Pfaff, Adana Salome Magdalene, born June 9, 1863, to Edwin P. Pfaff and Sarah M. m.n. Flint. Baptized July 12, 1863, at Mickey's schoolhouse.

Elisabeth, born Jan. 26, 1863, to Lydia, servant of Th. Lash, and George, servant of Sol. Transou. Baptized Sept. 13, 1863, in the Bethania parsonage.

Mock, Arthur Ulysses, born May 11, 1864, to Dr. Andrew Mock and Paulina m.n. Lehman. Baptized June 26, 1864, at the house of Br. and Sr. William Lehman.

Oehman, Edwin Grant, born Aug. 2, 1864, to Reinhold Oehman and Louisa m.n. Werner. Baptized Sept. 4, 1864, at the parents' house [Bethania Diary: br. Oehman having left the county].

Grabs, Minnie Olive, born Sept. 30, 1864, to William Grabs and Amelia m.n. Stoltz. Baptized Nov. 27, 1864, at the house of the grandmother, Sr. Sarah Stoltz.

William Henry and James Alpheus, twin boys born Sept. 25, 1864, to Tom (Conrad) and Clemmentine (Butner). Baptized Nov. 27, 1864, at the house of Br. H. H. Butner, their master.

Stoltz, James Alexander, born Nov. 21, 1865, to William A. Stoltz and Martha E. m.n. Pursail. Baptized Nov. 25, 1865, at the parents' house.

Dull, Ellis, born Feb. 19, 1866, to Edwin C. Dull and Florina N. m.n. Coltrain. Baptized Mar. 25, 1866, at Spanish Grove.

Shultz, Sarah Ann Elizabeth, born Jan. 27, 1866, to Edwin T. and Juliann Shultz. Baptized July, 23, 1866, at Spanish Grove.

Marshall, Mary Eliza, born May 24, 1866, to Peter Marshall and Julia m.n. Shultz. Baptized July 23, 1866, at Spanish Grove.

Adult Baptisms

Butner, William Nathan. Baptized June 2, 1866.

Glascock, William Samuel. Baptized July 16, 1866.

Faircloth, Catharine Louisa. Baptized July 16, 1866.

Marriages

Seitz, Henry Winston, born Oct. 5, 1833, to Franz Seitz and Christina m.n. Kapp, married Sept. 2, 1858, to Emily Krieger, born to Isaac Nathaniel Krieger and Louisa m.n. West.

Sink, N.L., born to Solomon Sink and Lucy m.n. Sneider, married June 15, 1859, to Susan Glasscoc, born to Julius Ceaser Glasscoc and Rachael m.n. Collet.

Shouse, John H., born Sept. 29, 1822, to Clarissa m.n. White, married Jan. 10, 1860, to Phebe L. Stewart, born May 1, 1837, to John Stewart and Susan m.n Wallace. [Bethania Diary: Shouse is a cripple and had to be carried into the house.]

Mock, Dr. Andrew L., born Nov. 15, 1835, to Peter Mock and Phebe m.n. Jones, married Nov. 13, 1862, to Paulina P. Lehman, born Apr. 4, 1843, to William E. Lehman and Anna Catherine m.n. Miller.

Ransom, Thomas, born Feb. 22, 1806, to Thomas Ransom and Elisabeth m.n. Tate, married Feb. 28, 1865, to Mary J. Stewart, born June 5, 1839, to John Stewart and Susan m.n. Wallace.

Porter, George W., married Dec. 27, 1865, to Florina Shore m.n. Strupe.

Buttner, William Nathan, married Aug. 26, 1866, to Mary C. Kearney.

Kearney, Edwin Wesley, married Aug. 28, 1866, to Mary M. Strupe m.n. Holder.

Stauber, Tobias M., married June 14, 1866, to Cornelia M. Lash. [Recorded out of sequence.]

Foltz, Edward, married Aug. 30, 1866, to Sarah Hunter m.n. Hauser.

Spach, Christian, married Oct. 9, 1866, to Lauretta Butner, born to Daniel Butner and Elizabeth m.n. Hage.

Shouse, E. A., married Dec. 12, 1866, to Susan P. Kiger.

Deaths and Burials

Leinbach, Susanna m.n. Lang, born June 4, 1778, in Surry (now Yadkin) County. Married Jan. 14, [year omitted], to Joseph Leinbach. [Bethania Diary: They had been married 57 years.] Died Feb. 3, 1857.

Butner, a stillborn daughter of Alvin Emil Butner and Clarinda Caroline Louisa m.n. Oehman. Buried Feb. 8, 1857.

Lehman, Christian Eugene, born Apr. 10, 1809, in Bethabara, to Joh. Christian Lehman and Elisabeth m.n. Schor widow Hauser. Married Apr. 30, 1837, to Sophia Amanda Butner. Died Mar. 16, 1857, in Baltimore, Md.

Stauber, Elisabeth m.n. Hauser, born Oct. 22, 1768, in Bethania. Married Apr. 24, 1792, to Francis Stauber. Died May 28, 1857. [Bethania Diary: By request Br. Jacob Siewers helped make the coffin.]

Moser, Sarah Elisabeth, born Aug. 24, 1855, to Thomas Moser and Frances m.n. Stauber. Died Aug. 7, 1857.

Hauser, Benjamin, born Jan. 24, 1783, in Bethania. Married (1) in his 22d year to Sarah Boner (died 1822). Married (2) Oct. 31, 1823, to Mary Christina Lash. Died Oct. 3, 1857.

Grabs, Christian Henry, born June 15, 1792, in Bethania. Married Aug. 13, 1815, to Susanna Transou. Died Dec. 18, 1857.

Shaub, Maria Salome m.n. Nisson, born Aug. 21, 1777, in Friedland. Married Aug. 8, 1797, to Jacob Shaub. Died Feb. 24, 1858.

Stoltz, Christina Gertrude m.n. Leinbach, born Nov. 5, 1787, near Bethabara. Married Oct. 18, 1810, to John Stoltz. Died Mar. 8, 1858.

Conrad, Elvira Lavenia, born Aug. 10, 1837, near Pfafftown, to Jesse Conrad and Nancy m.n. Leinback. Died Apr. 12, 1858.

Stauber, Calvin Edger, born Mar. 29, 1836, near Bethania, to Samuel B. Stauber and Sarah m.n. Shore. Died Aug. 2, 1858.

Marshall, Henry Theodore, born Jan. 3, 1855, to Peter Marshall and Julia Antoinette m.n. Shultz. Died Dec. 13, 1858.

Dull, Cornelia Catherine Elisabeth, born Dec. 28, 1858, to Edwin Dull and Sarah Ann Lisetta m.n. Shultz. Died Jan. 9, 1859.

Stauber, Sophia Elisabeth, born Apr. 18, 1838, to Samuel Benjn. Stauber and Sarah m.n. Shore. Departed Jan. 24, 1859.

Kearney, William Henry Tobias, born Oct. 31, 1857, to Alexander Kearney and Ann Caroline m.n. Rothrock. Died Mar. 3, 1859.

Kearney, Johanna Gertrude m.n. Hauser, born Apr. 2, 1792, in Bethania. Married Jan. 20, 1817, to John Kearney. Died Apr. 29, 1859.

Spach, Anna Catherine, born Aug. 4, 1805, near Friedberg, to John and Salome Holder. Married to Henry Spach. Died Sept. 19, 1859.

Schultz, Catherine Amanda m.n. Conrad, born Jan. 21, 1836, near Pfafftown, to William Conrad and his wife. Married Feb. 10, 1853, to Edwin Theodore Schultz. Died Nov. 18, 1859.

Leinbach, Joseph, born Sept. 13, 1774, about 3.5 miles north of Bethania on Muddy Creek. Married to Susanna m.n. Lang. Died Jan. 22, 1860.

Richmond, an infant of John M. Richmond and Elisabeth m.n. Crawley. Born and died May 25, 1860.

Dull, Eugene Luther, born July 11, 1856, to Edwin C. Dull and [Sarah] Anna Lisetta m.n. Schultz. Died June 7, 1860.

Schaub, John Christopher, born Dec. 14, 1781, in or near Bethabara, to John Shaub and Johanna m.n. Leinbach. Married May 29, 1810, to Anna Justina Sides. Died Aug. 21, 1860.

Pfaff, Emily Elisabeth, born Feb. 10, 1853, to Philip Henry Pfaff and Malinda m.n Stockburger. Died Nov. 17, 1860.

Dull, Rufus Seaton, born Mar. 28, 1860, to Edwin C. Dull and Sarah L. m.n. Schultz. Died Dec. 16, 1860.

Dull, Sarah Ann Lisetta, born Aug. 2, 1839. Married Sept. 6, 1855, to Edwin C. Dull. Died Dec. 27, 1860.

Thiss, a son of Solomon Thiss and Lauretta m.n. Stockburger. Born and died Jan. 18, 1861.

Stockburger, Anna Elisabeth m.n. Schultz, born Dec. 2, 1783, 3 miles west of Bethania on Muddy Creek. Married Apr. 12, 1810, to Joseph Stockburger. Died Apr. 11, 1861.

Conrad, Christian Thomas, born to Peter Conrad and Mary Magdalene m.n. Shoemaker. Married Feb. 8, 1848, to Louisa Elisabeth Schultz. Died Oct. 14, 1861.

Spach, Henry. Died Dec. 10, 1861. [Bethania Diary: His age was 59 y., 8 m., 17 days.]

Pfaff, John Peter, born Dec. 22, 1838, to Nathaniel Pfaff and Lavenia m.n. Kreager. Died Jan. 10, 1862. He was a volunteer in Captain Miller's Company at Manassas, Virginia, where he departed. Buried Jan. 14, 1862.

Conrad, William Augustus, born Apr. 1, 1842, near the Shallow Ford in Surry (now Yadkin) County, to Isaac Conrad and Antoinette m.n. Transou. Died Jan. 12, 1862. He was a volunteer in Captain Conolly's Company at Manassas, and died in one of the hospitals in Richmond. Buried Feb. 2, 1862.

Conrad, Catharina m.n. Spoenhauer, born July 28, 1775, near Bethania. Married Feb. 20, 1798, to John Conrad. Died Apr. 18, 1862.

Farcloth, John Augustus, born Feb. 16, 1855, in Forsyth County, to Abraham J. Farcloth and Mary Ann m.n. Holder. Died June 9, 1862.

Jordan, Sarah Ellen, born Apr. 29, 1860, to Abner Fields Jordan and Almede Elisabeth m.n. Hauser. Died Sept. 29, 1862.

Shore, Samuel Edgar, born Aug. 19, 1839, to Jacob Shore and Susan, m.n. Stoltz. Married Dec. 11, 1861, to Elisabeth Wier. Died Dec. 8, 1862.

Stauber, Julius Francis, born Sept. 3, 1842, near Bethania, to Samuel Benjamin Stauber and Sarah m.n. Shore. Died Aug. 14, 1862. He volunteered under Capt. Stow, was taken prisoner at Newbern, taken to Governors Island, and whilst at Fort Delaware was exchanged and returned to Richmond, and being sick went to the hospital, where after 10 days he departed this life. His remains were bro't here by his father and now rest in our church yard. Buried Dec. 14, 1862.

Schultz, John Parmenio, born Aug. 31, 1837, near Pfafftown, to John Henry Schultz and Anna Catherina m.n. Schaub. He volunteered June 8, 1861, in the 3d Company under Captain Miller, and was wounded in the engagements about Richmond, July 1st, in his thigh, the bone being broken several inches below the hip, and remained some time in the hospital in Richmond, from whence he was brought home. Died Dec. 19, 1862, after suffering upwards of 5 months.

Grabs, Edward Emil, born Jan. 9, 1841, in Bethania, to Christian Grabs and Susanna m.n. Transou. Died Dec. 23, 1862.

Transou, Sarah m.n. Loesch, born May 16, 1795, in Bethania, to John Christian Loesch and Johanna m.n. Hauser. Married Aug. 17, 1820, to Solomon Transou. Died Jan. 29, 1863.

Butner, Leon William, born Sept. 18, 1862, to Alvin Emil Butner and Clarinda Caroline m.n. Oehman. Died June 10, 1863. His father being absent in the Army of Virginia.

Grabs, Susanna m.n. Transou, born Oct. 11, 1798, in Bethania. Married July 11, 1820, to Christian H. Grabs. Died Apr. 1, 1863. [Recorded out of sequence.]

Moser, Mary Sophia, born Jan. 25, 1862, to Henry Thomas Moser and Lucia Francesea m.n. Stauber. Died July 20, 1863.

Chitty, John Benjamin, born June 30, 1834, in Salem, to John Jacob Chitty and Anna Dorothea m.n. Leinbach. Died Aug. 30, 1863.

Butner, Elisabeth m.n. Fry, born Oct. 29, 1770, at Townfork, to Michael and Dorothea Fry. Married (1) in 1793 to Abraham Lidy (died 1799). Married (2) June 5, 1814, to Adam Butner. Died Sept. 8, 1863.

Pfaff, Anna Magdalene m.n. Conrad, born Nov. 20, 1782, to Christian and Mary Conrad. Married Mar. 23, 1802, to Peter Pfaff. Died Sept. 25, 1863.

Strupe, Eugene Saml., born Oct. 23, 1834, to Ephraim Strupe and Salome m.n. Transou. His remains were brot here from the neighbourhood of Gordonsville, Virginia, where he died and was buried in the camp of instruction. Buried Dec. 23, 1863.

Devin, James Transou, born Feb. 13, 1862, to Rev. Mr. Robert J. Devin and wife. Died Apr. 15, 1864.

Stauber, Sarah m.n. Shore, born Sept. 15, 1804, to John Shore and Elisabeth m.n. Beckel. Married Nov. 30, 1828, to Samuel Benjamin Stauber. Died Apr. 17, 1864.

Spoenhauer, Levi Benjamin, born June 26, 1860, to Israel Spoenhauer and Elisabeth m.n. Folk. Died Nov. 8, 1864.

Shore, Israel Alexander, born Aug. 12, 1831, near Bethania, to Solomon Shore and Rebecca m.n. Werner. Married Mar. 31, 1853, to Florina Rebecca Strupe, daughter of Ephraim Strupe and Salome m.n. Transou. Died July 7, 1864, at the general hospital at Stanton, Virginia, from whence he was disinterred and bro't here for burial. Buried Feb. 14, 1865.

Shore, William Turner, born June 14, 1839, near Bethania, to Solomon Shore and Rebecca m.n. Werner. Married Feb. 28, 1860, to M. J. Dull, daughter of John Dull. Died July 22, 1864, in Virginia. His remains were transferred from thence to our graveyard. Buried Feb. 14, 1865.

Shore, Isaac, born Aug. 6, 1820, near Bethania, to John Shore and Elisabeth m.n. Beckel. Married Ernestina Werner, daughter of Jacob Werner and Gertrude m.n. Hege. Died Nov. 1, 1864, of camp diarrhea and erysipelas. Buried Feb. 14, 1865.

Hauser, Nerva Van Niman, born Feb. 1, 1828, to Benjamin Houser and Maria Christina m.n. Loesh. Married in 1862 to Biddie Nading, daughter of Christian Nading. Died Aug. 6, 1864, at the Winder Hospital, Virginia, from whence he was removed and brought here for interment. Buried Feb. 14, 1865.

Shore, John Henry, near Bethania, born Aug. 12, 1835, to Solomon Shore and Rebecca m.n. Werner. Married Dec. 8, 1864, to Martha A. Dull, daughter of John Dull. Died Feb. 19, 1865, in Virginia, from whence his remains were transferred for interment in the graveyard in Bethania. Buried Feb. 21, 1865.

Petree, an infant son of Joshua Petree and Angelica Justina m.n. Schultz. Died June 11, 1865. [Bethania Diary: Henry Schultz applied for permission to bury a grandchild (son) of his son-in-law Joshua Petree and wife Angelica Justina.]

Oehman, Edwin Grant, born Aug. 2, 1864, to Reinhold Oehman and Louisa m.n. Werner. Died June 16, 1865.

Oehman, Charles Florentine, born Aug. 11, 1855, to Reinhold Oehman and Louisa m.n. Werner. Died June 18, 1865.

Pfaff, Peter, born Jan. 28, 1773, in Friedberg. Married Mar. 23, 1802, to Anna Magdalene Conrad. Died June 22, 1865.

Strupe, James Erwin, born Sept. 1, 1829, near Bethania, to Samuel Strupe and Elisabeth m.n. Transou. Married in 1856 to Mary Elisabeth m.n. Anderson. Died July 5, 1865. [Bethania Report: He had recently returned from the West, and died of typhoid fever.]

Strupe, Edwin, born Aug. 17, 1831, near Bethania, to Samuel Strupe and Elisabeth m.n. Transou. Died Aug. 28, 1864. [Bethania Diary and Bethania Report: Died of typhoid feaver while in the Southern Army near Atlanta, Georgia, where his remains are. Funeral preached July 5, 1865.] [This register entry is crossed out.]

Miller, Jane, born Sept. 5, 1833, to John Michael Miller and Elisabeth m.n. Styers. Died Aug. 20, 1865.

Stoltz, James Alexander, born Nov. 21, 1865, to William Stoltz and Martha m.n. Pursail. Died Nov. 25, 1865.

Jordan, Loretta Elizabeth, born Oct. 8, 1863, to Abner Fields Jordan and Almeda Elizabeth m.n. Hauser. Died Dec. 12, 1865.

Mock, Beatus, born May 9, 1866, to Dr. Andrew L. Mock and Paulina P. m.n. Lehman. Died May 9, 1866.

Transou, Elizabeth m.n. Mickey, born Nov. 8, 1808, in Stokes (now Forsyth) County. Married in Nov. 1836 to Joseph Transou. Died Aug. 6, 1866.

Conrad, Catharine m.n. Spainhour, born May 28, 1787, in Stokes County. Married to Peter Conrad. Died Sept. 11, 1866.

Baptisms of Non-Members

Conrad, Betty Ann Caroline, born Nov. 30, 1856, to Emory Salathiel Conrad and Julia Ann m.n. Sailor. Baptized Feb. 26, 1857, at William Conrad's residence.

Snipes, James Edwin, born Oct. 26, 1856, to Andrew C. Snipes and Lydia Lavinia m.n. Pfaff. Baptized Mar. 8, 1857, at Pleasant Valley schoolhouse.

Pfaff, Isaac Rufus, born Nov. 3, 1856, to Calvin Christian Pfaff and Mary m.n. Ball. Baptized Mar. 8, 1857, at Pleasant Valley schoolhouse.

Werner, John Henry Theodor, born Jan. 15, 1857, to Tryphonius Elikthia Werner and Paulina Catharine m.n. George. Baptized Mar. 26, 1857, at Lewis Werner's residence.

Coller, Virgil Isaiah, born Jan. 8, 1857, to James Allen Coller and Charity m.n. Boose. Baptized April 25, 1857, at Pleasant Valley schoolhouse.

Spiess, Permilia Emeline, born Feb. 1, 1855, to Edwin Nathaniel Spiess and Antoinetta Elvira m.n. Steirs, daughter of Jesse Steirs, Sr. Baptized July 23, 1857, at the house of Edwin N. Spiess. Died July 26, 1857.

Spiess, John Leandor, born Apr. 12, 1857, to Edwin N. Spiess and A. Elvira m.n. Steirs. Baptized July 23, 1857, at the house of Edwin N. Spiess.

Petree, Lafayette Montgomery, born Aug. 6, 1857, to Francis William and Clementina Rebecca Petree. Baptized Aug. 13, 1857, at the parents' house.

Rothrock, Edwin Peter, born June 19, 1856, to William Emanuel Rothrock and Susan m.n. Koley. Baptized Aug. 16, 1857, at the house of Parmenio Stoltz.

Pfaff, Mary Jane, born May 27, 1857, to Emanuel Pfaff and Susan m.n. Ledford. Baptized Nov. 1, 1857, at Mickey's schoolhouse.

Waldraven, Edney Elendor Jane, born Nov. 16, 1856, to George Waldraven and Sarah Ann m.n. East. Baptized, Nov. 1, 1857, at Mickey's schoolhouse.

Buse, James Alexander, born Sept. 2, 1857, to Timothy and Rebecca Buse. Baptized Nov. 1, 1857, at Mickey's schoolhouse.

Shelton, Martha Louisa, born July 29, 1857, to Wiley Shelton and Matilda m.n. Myers. Baptized Jan. 24, 1858, at Spanish Grove.

Transou, Aurilious La Fayetta, born Oct. 10, 1857, to Jacob Transou and Emmaline m.n. Steward. Baptized Mar. 14, 1858, at Mickey's schoolhouse.

Steward, John Leon, born Feb. 5, 1858, to William Steward and Nancy m.n. Pfaff. Baptized Apr. 11, 1858, at Mickey's schoolhouse.

Sailor, Eugene Sandford, born Sept. 20, 1857, to William and Paulina Sailor. Baptized Apr. 11, 1858, at Mickey's schoolhouse.

Pfaff, Betty Ann, born Feb. 8, 1858, to Calvin and Mary Pfaff. Baptized Apr. 11, 1858, at Mickey's schoolhouse.

Shore, Louisa Jane, born Dec. 28, 1857, to Augustin E. Shore and Anne E. m.n. Geiger. Baptized Apr. 21, 1858, at the house of widowed Sr. Mary Shore.

Styers, Regina Elisabeth, born Oct. 15, 1857, to Abraham P. Styers and Paulina m.n. Geiger. Baptized Apr. 21, 1858, at the house of widowed Sr. Mary Shore.

Shouse, Edwin Leander, born Feb. 8, 1858, to James Leander Shouse and Mary Magdalene m.n. Spach. Baptized Apr. 25, 1858, at the house of Br. William E. Lehman.

Spoenhauer, Charles Rufus, born Oct. 22, 1857, to Ezra Spoenhauer and Elisabeth m.n. Folk. Baptized May 21, 1858, at the Bethania parsonage.

Sneider, Amanda Artancy, born Mar. 12. 1858, to Joel E. Sneider and Susan P. m.n. Spoenhauer. Baptized May 30, 1858, at Crooked Run schoolhouse.

Conrad, Emily Sybilla, born Mar. 4, 1858, to Emory Salathiel Conrad and Julia Ann m.n. Sailor. Baptized June 13, 1858, at the house of William Conrad [Bethania Diary: the grandfather] near Pfafftown.

Church, Sarah Ellen, born June 6, 1858, to Charles Church and Lucinda m.n. Flint. Baptized July 11, 1858, at Mickey's schoolhouse.

Johnson, Albert Benjamin, born June 21, 1857, to Thomas C. Johnson and Susan Jane m.n. Holder. Baptized July 18, 1858, at the parents' house in Bethania.

Flint, Aurelius Alexander, born Mar. 23, 1858, to John Procter Flint and Lucy Elisabeth m.n. Petree. Baptized Aug. 8, 1858, at Mickey's schoolhouse.

Transou, Issabella, born Oct. 11, 1858, to Evan Transou and Elisabeth m.n. Church. Baptized Oct. 13, 1858, at the parents' house. Infant died next day and was buried near Pfafftown.

Buse, Edwin Timothy, born Sept. 15, 1858, to Timothy Buse and Rebecca m.n. Henning. Baptized Dec. 12, 1858, at Mickey's schoolhouse.

Kline, Leon Thomas, born May 31, 1858, to Solomon Kline and Martha m.n. Pfaff. Baptized Dec. 12, 1858, at Mickey's schoolhouse.

Transou, Clara Ann, born Sept. 19, 1858, to Augustin Crawford Transou and Mary Elisabeth m.n. Alspaugh. Baptized Dec. 12, 1858, at the parents' house at Pfafftown.

Hauser, Silvanus David Davis, born Oct. 20, 1857, to Ezra Hauser and Mary Emmily m.n. McCullen. Baptized May 9, 1858, in the Bethania church. [Recorded out of sequence.]

Fulk, Rufus Sylvanus Levi, born Mar. 30, 1858, to Augustin Fulk and Ligustus Symphroni m.n. Hauser. Baptized May 9, 1858, in the Bethania church. [Recorded out of sequence.]

Conrad, Elliott Monroe, born Apr. 7, 1858, to John Conrad and Caroline Lisetta m.n. Conrad [Bethania Diary: daughter of Jesse Conrad]. Baptized June 27, 1858, at Spanish Grove. [Recorded out of sequence.]

Wood, Nancy Louisa, born Nov. 17, 1858, to James Wood and Margaret m.n. Leinbach. Baptized Feb. 27, 1859, at Spanish Grove.

Reginer, William Henry, born Dec. 10, 1858, to George H. Reniger and Margaret m.n. Werner. Baptized Mar. 27, 1859, at the house of Br. William E. Lehman.

Grabs, Ellen Dundena, born Nov. 24, 1858, to James Israel Grabs and Gazelle m.n. Glasscock. Baptized Apr. 22, 1859, at the parents' house.

Holder, Flora Angelica, born May 5, 1859, to William Carlos Holder and Nancy m.n. Stype. Baptized May 12, 1859, at the house of J. Martin Holder.

Wright, Mary Elisabeth, born Dec. 11, 1858, to William and Charlotte Wright. Baptized July 10, 1859, at Mickey's schoolhouse.

Shore, Flora Rebecca, born July 2, 1859, to Isaac Shore and Ernestina m.n. Werner. Baptized Sept. 11, 1859, in the Bethania church.

Culler, Sarah Lisetta, born June 15, 1859, to James Allen Culler and Charity m.n. Buse. Baptized Nov. 13, 1859, at Mickey's schoolhouse.

Schrivor, Mary Jane, born Jan. 15, 1859, to John Henry Schrivor and Elisabeth m.n. Fansler. Baptized Nov. 20, 1859, at the parents' house near Shoretown.

Church, George Henry, born Jan. 28, 1859, to Richard Church and Selena Catherine m.n. Flint. Baptized May 22, 1859, at Spanish Grove. [Recorded out of sequence.]

Sailor, Calvin Ellis, born Mar. 21, 1859, to William Sailor and Paulina m.n. Pfaff. Baptized Dec. 11, 1859, at Mickey's schoolhouse.

Conrad, Rufus Virgil, born Oct. 23, 1859, to John Leonard Conrad and Caroline m.n. Conrad. Baptized Dec. 18, 1859, at Spanish Grove.

Pfaff, Albert Hilliary, born Apr. 12, 1859, to Emanuel Pfaff and Susan m.n. Ledford. Baptized Jan. 8, 1860, at Mickey's schoolhouse.

Leinbach, Owen Lafayette, born Oct. 30, 1859, to Joshua Leinbach and [blank] m.n. Cooper. Baptized Feb. 26, 1860, at Spanish Grove.

Church, Flora Elisabeth, born Dec. 10, 1859, to Charles W. Church and Lucinda N. K. m.n. Flint. Baptized Mar. 11, 1860, at Mickey's schoolhouse.

Snipe, Mary Elisabeth, born Dec. 7, 1859, to Andrew and Lydia Snipe. Baptized Mar. 11, 1860, at Mickey's schoolhouse.

Dull, Rufus Seaton, born Mar. 28, 1860, to Edwin C. Dull and Sarah L. m.n. Schultz. Baptized Apr. 22, 1860, at Spanish Grove.

Krause, Margaret Celestia, born Feb. 10, 1860, to Andrew Krause and Susanna Elisabeth m.n. Krause. Baptized June 24, 1860, at Spanish Grove.

Spoenhauer, Levi Benjamin, born June 26, 1860, to Israel Spoenhauer and Elisabeth m.n. Folk. Baptized Aug. 5, 1860, in the Bethania church.

Steyers, Edwin Decator, born Sept. 27, 1859, to Abraham P. Styers and Paulina Jane m.n. Geiger. Baptized Aug. 5, 1860, at the Dutch meeting house.

Geiger, Oliver Abraham, born Oct. 29, 1859, to Henry W. Geiger and Mahala Jane m.n. Steyers. Baptized Aug. 5, 1860, at the Dutch meeting house.

Spiess, Leanna Francisca, born Oct. 7, 1859, to Edwin N. Spiess and Antoinetta Elvira m.n. Steyers. Baptized Aug. 5, 1860, at the Dutch meeting house.

Cramer, Christina Catherina, born Dec. 2, 1857, to William Cramer and Mariann m.n. Ingram. Baptized Aug. 5, 1860, at the Dutch meeting house.

Cramer, Charlotte Pamelia, born May 17, 1860, to William Cramer and Mariann m.n. Ingram. Baptized Aug. 5, 1860, at the Dutch meeting house.

Flint, Napolion Palmerston, born May 19, 1860, to John Procter Flint and Lucy Elisabeth m.n. Petrie. Baptized Sept. 23, 1860, at Mickey's schoolhouse.

Kline, Julia Bettyann, born June 26, 1860, to Solomon Kline and Martha m.n. Pfaff. Baptized Oct. 14, 1860, at Mickey's schoolhouse.

Grabs, Flora Evelyn, born Mar. 13, 1860, to James J. Grabs and Gazella m.n. Glasscock. Baptized Nov. 4, 1860, at the house of the widowed Sr. Christian Grabs.

Transou, Ann Isabella, born July 17, 1860, to Julius A. Transou and Julia m.n. Conrad. Baptized Nov. 25, 1860, at the parents' house in Pfafftown.

Moser, James Calvin, born Sept. 1, 1860, to Henry Thomas Moser and Lucia Francesca m.n. Stauber. Baptized Dec. 2, 1860, at the house of Wesley Kearney in Bethania.

Beck, James Douglas, born Dec. 7, 1859, to John Beck and Amy m.n. Hendrick. Baptized Dec. 5, 1860, at the parents' house near Pfafftown.

Fulk, Cornelia Margaret, born Jan. 4, 1861, to Augustus Fulk and Ligustus Symphroni m.n. Hauser. Baptized Apr. 30, 1861, in the Bethania church.

Boose, Lauretta Catherine, born Feb. 19, 1861, to Timothy Boose and Catherine m.n. Henning. Baptized May 12, 1861, at Mickey's schoolhouse.

Shore, Mary Elizabeth, born Oct. 13, 1860, to Augustin E. Shore and Anna E. m.n. Kieger. Baptized May 16, 1861, at the parents' house near the Dutch meeting house.

Reniger, Alice May, born Apr. 7, 1861, to George H. Reniger and Margaret m.n. Werner. Baptized July 8, 1861, at the house of William Lehman in Bethania.

Pfaff, Parmenio Sandford, born June 1, 1861, to Christian Benj. Pfaff and Minerva Magdalena m.n. Flint. Baptized July 28, 1861, at Spanish Grove.

Sailer, Julia Antoinette, born Jan. 24, 1861, to William Sailer and Paulina m.n. Pfaff. Baptized Aug. 18, 1861, at Mickey's schoolhouse.

Holder, Ellen Jeanetta, born July 1, 1861, to William Carlos Holder and Nancy m.n. Stype. Baptized Oct. 27, 1861, at the Bethabara church. [Duplicated in the Bethabara Register.]

Church, Mary Eliza, born Dec. 8, 1861, to Richard Church and Selena Catherine m.n. Flint. Baptized Dec. 28, 1861, in Pfafftown.

Strup, Charles Henry, born Mar. 22, 1862, to James Erwin Strup and Mary Elisabeth m.n. Anderson. Baptized May 11, 1862, at the house of Samuel Strup in Bethania.

Moser, Mary Sophia, born Jan. 25, 1862, to Henry Thomas Moser and Lucia Francesca m.n. Stauber. Baptized June 8, 1862, in the Bethania church.

Louisa Latetia, born [date blank] to Henry Zechariah (Thom. Lash's servant) and wife Malinda (Henry Shouse's servant). Baptized June 8, 1862, at Thomas Lash's quarter in Bethania.

Coller, Junius Lafayette, born Nov. 17, 1861, to James Allen Coller and Charity m.n. Boose. Baptized June 11, 1862, in the Bethania church.

Shore, Gideon Tobias, born July 12, 1862, to Isaac Shore and Ernestina Maria m.n. Werner. Baptized Oct. 19, 1862, in the Bethania church.

Spoenhauer, Aaron Lafayetta, born Sept. 26, 1862, to Louisa Ann Spoenhauer. Baptized Dec. 10, 1862, at the house of Augustus Folk about 2 1/2 miles west of Bethania.

Shore, John Augustine, born Sept. 22, 1862, to Augustine and Ann Elisabeth Shore. Baptized Apr. 11, 1863, at the house of widowed Sr. Mary Shore. (The father absent in the Southern army.)

Shore, Julina Susan, born Sept. 19, 1862, to Edward Henry Shore and Christina m.n. Geiger. Baptized Apr. 11, 1863, at the house of widowed Sr. Mary Shore. (The father absent in the Southern army.)

Shauss, Laura James, born June 12, 1863, to the late James Leander Shauss and Mary Magdalene m.n. Spach. Baptized Oct. 4, 1863, in the Bethania church.

Moser, Martha Cornelia, born Nov. 25, 1863, to Thomas Moser and Lucia Francesca m.n. Stauber. Baptized May 8, 1864, in the Bethania church.

Spoenhauer, James Goodman, born Mar. 8, 1864, to John Spoenhauer and Sarah Ann m.n. Anderson. Baptized Sept. 3, 1864, in the house of the widow of John Spoenhauer.

Kline, Laura Alice, born Oct. 20, 1861, to Edwin Kline (absent in the Army) and Felicia m.n. Massacup. Baptized Sept. 3, 1864, in the house of the widow of John Spoenhauer.

Holder, Leanna Delilah, born Nov. 19, 1864, to Carlos Holder and Nancy m.n. Stype. Baptized Mar. 7, 1865, at the house of Br. and Sr. Martin Holder.

Folk, Laura Gertrude, born July 1, 1864, to Augustus Folk and Ligustus Symphroni m.n. Hauser. Baptized Aug. 1 [July 31], 1864, in the graveyard near Pfafftown. [Recorded out of sequence.]

Flint, Sandford Isaac, born May 22, 1865, to John Proctor Flint and Lucy Elisabeth m.n. Petree. Baptized Oct. 9, 1865, at the house of Br. and Sr. S. Levin Grabs in Bethania.

Moser, Samuel Thomas, born Sept. 5, 1865, to Thomas H. Moser and Francisca m.n. Stauber. Baptized Dec. 3, 1865.

Conrad, William Edward, born June 1864, to Caroline Conrad. Baptized Apr. 28, 1866, [Bethania Diary: at the Negro church in Bethania].

Conrad, Ellen Abary Jane, born Aug. 1, 1865, to Caroline Conrad. Baptized Apr. 29 [28], 1866, [Bethania Diary: at the Negro church in Bethania].

Stauber, George Franklin, born Mar. 12, 1865, to Amanda Stauber. Baptized Apr. 29 [28], 1866, [Bethania Diary: at the Negro church in Bethania].

Spainhour, Laura Felicia, born Apr. 10, 1866, to William W. Spainhour and Pamelia m.n. Grabs. Baptized July 8, 1866, at Crooked Run.

Lash, Laura Elizabeth, born Aug. 5, 1865, to Henry and Malinda Lash. Baptized July 8, 1866. [Bethania Diary: formerly belonged to Thomas Lash.]

Stewart, James Alexander, born May 25, 1864, to William and Nancy Stewart. Baptized July 23, 1866, at Brookstown.

Beroth, Lizette Maria, born Apr. 28, 1866, to Jonathan Beroth and Rebecca m.n. Conrad. Baptized Sept. 23, 1866, at Spanish Grove.

Bethania Diary Entries, 1857-1866

[Church Register material that was recorded only in the Bethania Diary. The following is the entirety of the material.]

Baptisms

Strup, Samuel William, born Dec. 13, 1857, to James Ervin Strup and Mary Ann Elisabeth m.n. Anderson. Baptized Feb. 7, 1858.

Infant son of George (Sol. Transou's) and Lydia (Thom. Lash's). Baptized Sept. 5, 1858, at the negro church in Bethania.

Infant of John (Abraham Conrad's) and Lucy (Herman H. Butner's). Baptized Oct. 3, 1858, at the negro church in Bethania.

Infant daughter of Wesley (T. Lash's) and Viney (H. Kapp's). Baptized at the parsonage Apr. 24, 1859.

Grabs, infant son of Edwin Grabs. Baptized at the home of the grandparents, J. Grabs, May 29, 1859.

William Henry, infant of I. G. Lash's Henry and his wife Malinda, servant of Henry Shauss. Baptized Nov. 8, 1863, at the Negro houses.

Henly, infant daughter of Paulina Henly, a free colored woman. Baptized Mar. 6, 1864, at the house of Paulina Henly.

Stoltz, two infant daughters of Miranda Stoltz, a free colored woman, a daughter of the wife of Col. Henry Shouse. [The Bethania Report states that Miranda Stoltz was "a colored free woman, the reputed daughter of the wife of Col. Henry Shouse."] Baptized Mar. 6, 1864, at the house of Paulina Henly.

Fanny Elisabeth, born Feb. 3, 1864, to Frank, belonging to the estate of Thomas Conrad deceased, and wife Sarah, servant of br. Soln. Pfaff's. Baptized about 8 A.M. May 8, 1864, in the Bethania Church.

Mary Magdalene, born Jan. 2, 1864, to John, Kiser's servant, and Amanda, Lash's servant, his wife. Baptized May 15, 1864, at the former house of Abraham Conrad.

Julius Wesley, born Oct. 6, 1863, to Wesley, Lash's servant, and Wina, servant of William Kapp. Baptized May 15, 1864, in the Bethania Church.

William Isaiah, infant son of William, formerly Lash's servant, and Matilda, formerly belonging to Edwin Speace. Baptized June 4, 1865, in the Bethania Church.

Shore, William Aleader, born July 5, 1864, to Edward Henry and Christina Shore, m.n. Kiger. Baptized Sept. 30, 1865, at the parents' home.

Shore, grandson of Mary Shore. Baptized Nov. 14, 1866, at Sr. Shore's home.

Marriages

Devin, the Rev. Mr., of Oxford, married Aug. 22, 1860, to Mary Ann Transou, daughter of Solomon Transou.

Lash, Flavious, married Aug. 26, 1862, to the daughter of the widow Moore.

A colored couple, married Feb. 10, 1866, in the Bethania parsonage.

Deaths and Burials
[Note: The Dutch meeting house is Nazareth Lutheran Church.]

Spoenhauer, Jacob. Died unexpectedly and was buried Apr. 13, 1857.

Sides, Nathaniel C. Age 19. Funeral preached May 7, 1857, at Antioch Methodist Church.

Steirs, Jesse. Funeral preached July 7, 1857, at Nazareth Lutheran Church.

Sides, Christine. Died July 19, 1857. Buried at Antioch Methodist Church.

Petree, Lafayette Montgomery, born Aug. 6, 1857, to Francis William and Clementina Rebecca Petree. Funeral preached Aug. 20, 1857, in Pfafftown.

Harris, Johanna Ellen, born Apr. 5, 1856. Died Sept. 25, 1857. Buried at the Dutch meeting house.

Rothrock, William Eml. Died Oct. 23, 1857. Funeral preached Oct. 24, 1857, at Hickory Ridge.

Wolf, William A., 66 years old. Died Nov. 12, 1857. Buried at the Dutch meeting house.

Elijah. Buried Dec. 24, 1857, in the negro graveyard.

Eli (Thomas Lash's), found Mar. 29, 1858, in Abr. Conrad's pond. Funeral preached Mar. 30, 1858, text the 6th Commandment, "Thou shalt not kill."

Emanuel (Christian Grabs'), died Mar. 30, 1858.

Flint, William [Sr.]. Buried at his home Apr. 2, 1858.

Kline, a little son of Solm. Kline. Died June 2, 1858. Buried at Pfafftown.

Shouse, Henry. Died Aug. 23, 1857, aged 57 years, 9 months. Funeral preached Aug. 7, 1858, at the Dutch meeting house.

Shelton, Abner, died Sept. 14, 1857, age 15, and Robert Shelton, died Sept. 17, 1857, age 10. Funeral preached Sept. 11, 1858, at the home of their father.

Flint, John. Buried Sept. 23, 1858, at the home of the late William Flint.

Hauser, infant son of Lawrence and Sybilla Hauser m.n. Hauser. Funeral preached Dec. 1, 1858, at Crooked Run Schoolhouse. The infant was the first to occupy the new graveyard at Crooked Run.

Annie, an aged negress, mother of Dan Butner's Lucy. Funeral preached Dec. 3, 1858, at the negro church at Bethania.

Kraamer, Mathew. Funeral preached Jan. 12, 1859, at the Dutch meeting house.

Melvin, Mr. Funeral preached Apr. 30, 1859, at Mount Pleasant.

Corie, Rebecca, a maiden lady who lived on Isaac Spoenhouer's land, said to be 88 years old. Buried Oct. 31, 1859.

Daughter of Jacob and Viney, servants of Jonathan Spiese. Funeral preached Dec. 26, 1859.

Richmond, Elisabeth, m.n. Crawley. Married to John M. Richmond. Died June 3, 1860, shortly after the death of her newborn infant. Taken to Liberty for burial.

Flint, girl, age about 17 years, daughter of Allen Flint. Funeral preached Oct. 15, 1860, at the father's house.

Sides, infant son of Winston Sides. Funeral preached Oct. 17, 1860, at Antioch Methodist Church.

Transou, Owen, son of Ephraim Transou. On Sept 28, 1861, heard of his death in the army of Virginia.

Transou, Rubin, son of Ephraim Transou. On Oct. 23, 1861, heard of his death.

Barbour, child. Death noted Sept. 23, 1862.

Walls, John, husband of Gazeil Grabs's sister. He was bro't from the Camp on the Rappahannock, and was to be buried Apr. 8, 1863.

Virgil, [Bethania Report: son of Sandy and Betzy]. Died June 28, 1863, of typhoid fever, age about 13 years. Funeral preached June 30, 1863, at Thomas Lash's Quarter in Town.

Frances, daughter of Sandy and Betzy. Died July 22, 1863, age about 14 years. Funeral preached July 24, 1863, at Lash's quarter in Town.

Letitia, daughter of Alick. Died Sept. 11, 1863. Buried Sept. 12, 1863 at the negro graveyard.

Leinbach, Philemon Joseph, age 23 years, 9 months, son of William Leinbach. He fell near the Potomack on the retreat from Pennsylvania while defending the army trains. Funeral preached Sept. 13, 1863, at Mickey's Schoolhouse.

Wife of Alick. Died Oct. 6, 1863.

Infant son of Jacob Werner's Prince and his wife who lives with John Dull. Burial service held Jan. 1, 1864.

Kreager, Abraham. Died at Richmond. Funeral preached Feb. 23, 1864, at Antioch Methodist Church.

Infant daughter of Miranda Stoltz, a colored free woman. Burial service held Apr. 28, 1864, at a negro burial ground between Samuel Stauber's plantation and Thomas Kapp's.

Gerner, Eliza m.n. Chamerling, born Oct. 27, 1826. Widowed. Died May 19, 1864. Buried May 21, 1864, in Pfafftown graveyard.

Harriet, servant of I. G. Lash. Burial service held June 4, 1864, at the negro graveyard.

Infant daughter of Harriet. Died June 24, 1864. Buried June 26, 1864, in the negro graveyard.

Chamberlain, Rebecca. Funeral preached July 31, 1864, at Pfafftown burial place.

Spoenhauer, Elisabeth m.n. Helsabeck. Widowed. Funeral preached Sept. 3, 1864, at Antioch Methodist Church.

Spoenhauer, John, son of Elisabeth Spoenhauer m.n. Helsabeck. Shot, supposed accidentally, on Mar. 24, 1864, near Kingston. Funeral preached Sept. 3, 1864, at Antioch Methodist Church.

Spoenhauer, Evan Abraham, infant son of John Spoenhauer and Sarah m.n. Anderson. Died Sept. 18, 1863. Funeral preached Sept. 3, 1864, at Antioch Methodist Church.

Lizzie, about 10 years of age, daughter of Sandy and Betzy. Died Aug. 19, 1865. Buried Aug. 20, 1865, at the negro graveyard.

Ellick, about 13 years of age, son of Ellick and Johanna. Died of typhoid fever. Buried Aug. 22, 1865, at the negro graveyard.

John, a son of Sandy and Betzy. Died Aug. 29, 1865, of typhoid fever.

Dorcas, formerly the servant of Margaret Miller. Died Sept. 2, 1865. She leaves 5 little children to the care of her husband. Buried Sept. 3, 1865, at the negro graveyard.

Pratt, twin sons of William Pratt, both died during the war. The Rev. Solomon Helsabeck preached the funeral Sept. 17, 1865, at Bethabara.

Schause, James Washington, son of Miranda Schause (colored), aged 1 m., 19 days. Buried Sept. 20, 1865, between Saml. Stauber's and Thos. Kapp's.

Kiger, Armstead. He fell at the fight in the Wilderness May 5, 1864, age 30 years, 10 months, 12 days. Funeral preached Sept. 30, 1865, at the Dutch meeting house.

Shore, John A., infant son of Augustin and Anna Shore, m.n. Kiger. Died Sept. 25, 1864. Funeral preached Sept. 30, 1865, at the Dutch meeting house.

Kiger, Henry E., son of E. D. and Catherine Kiger. Died June 14, 1864. Funeral preached Sept. 30, 1865, at the Dutch meeting house.

Negro man, formerly belonging to Thos. Lash. Burial service held Nov. 5, 1865, at the negro graveyard.

Transou, widow of Phillip Transou. Buried Dec. 5, 1865, at Pfafftown.

Snider, John Henry, son of Alexander Snider and Christina m.n. Clotfelter. Buried Apr. 11, 1866, at Hopewell.

Hine, Lewis F., son of Matilda Hine. She died when he was 9, and he was bound to br. Solomon Tice near Bethania, and lived with him till he was grown. He was shot in Feb. 1864 in Caldwell County by one of the Home Guard from Watauga County in endeavoring to make his way through the lines and go North. Funeral preached June 24, 1866, in the Bethania Church.

Negro child of Henry and Malinda, formerly belonging to Thos. Lash. Funeral preached Aug. 12, 1866, in the Bethania Church.

Grubs, Eve. Buried Aug. 15, 1866, at Bethabara.

Kiger, Lewis. Buried Aug. 22, 1866, at the Dutch meeting house.

Swaim, infant daughter of William Swaim. Funeral preached Oct. 28, 1866, at the brick church in Winston.

Beards, infant child. Buried Nov. 10, 1866, at Winston.

Bethabara Register, 1857-1866

Infant Baptisms

Ledford, Martha Elisabeth, born Sept. 19, 1856, to Andrew Ledford and Eliza m.n. Pratt. Baptized Feb. 22, 1857, in the Bethabara church.

Spach, John Thomas, born July 31, 1857, to Thomas L. Spach and Maria L. m.n. Butner. Baptized Sept. 20, 1857, in the Bethabara church.

Hine, Adelia Catherine Elisabeth, born Jan. 15, 1858, to Edward Hine and Susan m.n Krause. Baptized Apr. 4, 1858, in the Bethabara church.

Flint, Henry Sandford, born Jan. 21, 1858, to William Flint and Antoinetta m.n. Butner. Baptized May 16, 1858, in the Bethabara church.

Shore, Emma Eliza, born Apr. 11, 1858, to John Henry Shore and Anna Catherine m.n. Hauser. Baptized May 16, 1858, in the Bethabara church.

Hege, Charles Eugene, born Oct. 13, 1857, to John Hege and Mary Magdalene m.n. Grubs. Baptized June 16, 1858, at the parents' house.

Hege, Louisa Jane, born Oct. 24, 1859, to John Hege and Mary Magdalene m.n. Grubs. Baptized Mar. 4, 1860, in the Bethabara church.

Spach, Elenor Victoria, born Apr. 9, 1860, to Thomas L. Spach and Maria Louisa m.n. Butner. Baptized May 20, 1860, in the Bethabara church.

Shore, Anna Christina, born Oct. 1, 1860, to John H. Shore and Anna Catherine m.n. Hauser. Baptized Dec. 2, 1860, in the Bethabara church.

Hine, John Joseph, born Dec. 18, 1860, to John Joseph Hine and Henrietta Dorothy m.n. Spach. Baptized Mar. 3, 1861, in the Bethabara church.

Hauser, Albert James, born Jan. 21, 1861, to Calvin Henry Hauser and Susan C. m.n. Foltz. Baptized Mar. 3, 1861, in the Bethabara church.

Hege, Ellen Susannah, born Sept. 15, 1861, to John Hege and Mary Magdalene m.n. Grubs. Baptized Nov. 3, 1861, at the Double Bridge schoolhouse.

Hine, Edward Alexander, born Nov. 13, 1862, to Edward Alexander Hine and Susan Christina m.n. Krause. Baptized Apr. 19, 1863, in the Bethabara church.

Hege, Daniel Mathias, born Sept. 1, 1863, to John Hege and Mary Magdalene m.n. Grubs. Baptized Nov. 29, 1863, at the Double Bridge schoolhouse.

Flint, Minerva Antoinetta, born Dec. 31, 1863, to William and Antoinetta Flint [Bethania Diary: m.n. Butner]. Baptized June 19, 1864, in the Bethabara church.

Hine, Charles Washington, born Feb. 22, 1866, to John Joseph Hine and Henrietta Catherine m.n. Spach. Baptized Apr. 15, 1866.

Butner, Allen Sylvester, born May 17, 1866, to Joseph Butner and Malvina m.n. Leinbach. Baptized June 17, 1866, in the Bethabara church.

Baptisms of Non-Members

Butner, Lewis Alston, born Dec. 5, 1856, to Samuel Butner and Martha m.n. Hauser. Baptized 1857.

Butner, Maria Lusena, born Mar. 13, 1857, to Augustus Zedekiah Butner and Serena m.n. Waldraven. Baptized Apr. 26, 1857, in the Bethabara church.

Shemel, James Francis, born Sept. 11, 1857, to Eli Shemel and Temperance m.n. Stoltz. Baptized Jan. 17, 1858, at the house of Eli Shemel.

Reich, John William Thomas, born Nov. 11, 1857, to Isaac and Sarah A. Reich. Baptized Jan. 17, 1858, at the house of Eli Shemel.

Schause, Silas Eugene, born May 7, 1857, to Wiley and Louisa Matilda Shause. Baptized Jan. 17, 1858, at the house of Eli Shemel.

Banner, Mary Adelaide Celestea, born Jan. 22, 1858, to John William Banner and Jane Adelaide m.n. Flint. Baptized May 16, 1858, in the Bethabara church.

Reich, William Leroy, born to Timothy Reich and Ann m.n. Taylor. Baptized Sept. 5, 1858, in the Bethabara church.

Davis, Laura Jane, born Jan. 19, 1859, to Hamilton Davis and Florina Elizabeth m.n. Butner. Baptized Apr. 24, 1859, in the Bethabara church.

Schemel, John Henry Abraham, born June 22, 1859, to Eli Edward Schemel and Temperance m.n. Stoltz. Baptized Nov. 6, 1859, in the Bethabara church.

Bowser, Lucinda Catherine, born Aug. 2, 1859, to Andrew Bowser and Fanny Edeline m.n. Miller. Baptized Jan. 15, 1860, in the Bethabara church.

Petri, William Robert, born Oct. 13, 1859, to Jacob Petri and Henrietta m.n. Krause. Baptized May 6, 1860, in the Bethabara church.

Butner, Thaddeus Marion, born Jan. 24, 1860, to Elias Josiah Butner and Susanne A. m.n. Stoltz. Baptized May 6, 1860, in the Bethabara church.

Hine, Aurlena Jeanetta, born May 3, 1860, to Edward A. Hine and Susan C. m.n. Krause. Baptized July 1, 1860, in the Bethabara church.

Dawson, Robert Armenius, born July 27, 1860, to William P. Dawson and Clemmentina L. m.n. Hine. Baptized Nov. 4, 1860, in the Bethabara church.

Davis, Sarah Ellen, born Oct. 24, 1860, to Hamilton Davis and Florina Elisabeth m.n. Butner. Baptized Mar. 3, 1861, in the Bethabara church.

Reich, Susan Catherine Martha, born July 12, 1860, to Timothy Reich and Anne m.n. Taylor. Baptized Mar. 19, 1861, at the house of Mary Reich 3 miles east of Bethabara.

Reich, William Wesley, born Aug. 19, 1860, to Ephraim W. Reich and Abigail m.n. Leibengood. Baptized Mar. 19, 1861, at the house of Mary Reich 3 miles east of Bethabara.

Shouse, Charles Alexander, born Nov. 4, 1858, to Christian Shouse and Sophia Elisabeth m.n. Wolf. Baptized Apr. 5, 1861, at the house of Henry Fogle.

Holder, Ellen Jeanetta, born July 1, 1861, to William Carlos Holder and Nancy m.n. Stype. Baptized Oct. 27, 1861, in the Bethabara church. [Duplicated in the Bethania Register.]

Hine, Charles Henry, born Aug. 10, 1861, to Theodore Hine and Mary Magdalene m.n. Shouse. Oct. 27, 1861, in the Bethabara church.

Bowser, Delsena Adeline, born July 12, 1862, to Andrew Bowser and Fanney Adeline m.n. Miller. Baptized Oct. 19, 1862, in the Bethabara church.

Butner, Mary Elias, born Mar. 17, 1863, to Elias Butner and Susanna A. m.n. Stoltz. Baptized May 17, 1863, in the Bethabara church.

Hine, John Madison, born May 3, 1858, to Charles William Hine and Phebe L. m.n. Ingram. Baptized Nov. 1, 1863, at the parents' house. [Bethania Diary: The father was about to return to the Army and desired to have his children baptized before leaving.]

Hine, Solomon Joseph, born Nov. 24, 1860, to Charles William Hine and Phebe L. m.n. Ingram. Baptized Nov. 1, 1863, at the parents' house.

Hine, Charles Edmond, born Aug. 25, 1863, to Charles William Hine and Phebe L. m.n. Ingram. Baptized Nov. 1, 1863, at the parents' house.

Hine, David Theodore, born Dec. 15, 1863, to Theodore Theophilus Hine and Mary Magdalene m.n. Shouse. Baptized Jan. 2, 1864, at the house of David Shouse.

Reich, Rebecca Jane Clementine, born Sept. 15, 1863, to Timothy Reich and Anna m.n. Taylor. Baptized Oct. 16, 1864, in the Bethabara church.

Grubs, Mary Lehama, born Aug. 2, 1863, to John Grubs and Mary Ann m.n. Aldridge. Baptized Dec. 11, 1864, at the house of Sr. Mary Magdalene Haga. The father is working at the saltworks in Virginia.

Marriages

Nicholas, S.L., married Nov. 17, 1859, to Emily C. Pratt, born to William Golson Pratt and Johanna Elizabeth m.n. Butner.

Beasley, John Quincy Adams, born to Edward Beasley and Martha m.n. Webb, married Jan. 22, 1860, to Maria E. Hauser, born Feb. 27, 1836, to Christian Hauser and Anna Johanna m.n. Spach.

Hauser, Calvin H., born Oct. 5, 1826, to Christian Hauser and Anna Johanna m.n. Spach, married Jan. 22, 1860, to Susan C. Foltz, born Feb. 16, 1839, to Theophilus Foltz and Elinora Elizabeth m.n. Walk.

Henning, Edward T., married Oct. 18, 1866, to widowed Delilah Styers m.n. Henning.

Deaths and Burials

Butner, John, born Nov. 26, 1778, in Rowan (now Davidson) County, to Thomas and Sarah Butner. Married (1) to Anna Maria Knauss (died Feb. 1839). Married (2) Aug. 20, 1839, to Elisabeth Spach. Died Jan. 2, 1857.

Reich, Henry Thomas, born Feb. 9, 1855, near Bethabara, to Ephraim W. Reich and Abigail m.n. Leibengut. Died Mar. 21, 1857.

Hine, John, born May 24, 1799, near Bethabara. Married Apr. 26, 1821, to Catherine m.n. Fiser. Died Jan. 1, 1858.

Reich, Thomas, born June 15, 1798, at Shober's paper mill near Salem. Married Jan. 29, 1822, to Mary Elisabeth Hauser. Died Mar. 9, 1858.

Hine, Catherine m.n. Fiser, born Dec. 28, 1798, in Davidson County, Tennessee, to John Fiser and Elisabeth m.n. Rank. Married Apr. 26, 1821, to John Hine. Died June 23, 1858.

Hine, William Perlemon, born Apr. 6, 1858, to Israel Levin Hine and Regina Catherine m.n. Beck. Died Aug. 23, 1858.

Reich, Mary Elisabeth, born Mar. 26, 1858, to Ephraim Reich and Abegail m.n. Livengood. Died June 3, 1859.

Shemel, Edwin Silvester, born Feb. 26, 1859, to Joseph Shemel and Sarah m.n. Hege. Died June 29, 1859.

Davis, Laura Jane, born Jan. 19, 1859, to Hamilton Davis and Florina Elisabeth m.n. Butner. Died Oct. 10, 1859.

Shouse, William H., born June 3, 1843, in Forsyth County, to Wiley Shouse and Matilda m.n. Stoehr. Died Dec. 11, 1859.

Eccles, Catherine, born Dec. 3, 1807, to John Rank and Catherine m.n. Vogler. Married to Jeremiah Eccles. Died May 19, 1860.

Butner, Junius Isaiah, born Sept. 30, 1838, in Bethabara, to Joseph Butner and Catherina m.n. Leinbach. Died July 28, 1860.

Butner, Harriet Lucinda, born June 13, 1854, to Elias J. Butner and Susanna A. m.n. Stoltz. Died Nov. 27, 1860.

Bowser, Lucinda Catherine, born Aug. 2, 1859, to Andrew Bowser and Fanny Adaline m.n. Miller. Died Mar. 11, 1861. [Bethania Diary: She was burned to death.]

Dawson, Clemmentina Louisa m.n. Hine, born Dec. 12, 1839. Married to William P. Dawson. Died Apr. 12, 1861.

Styers, a son, born Aug. 1, 1860, to John A. and Eliza Styers. Died June 22, 1861.

Spach, John, born Apr. 16, 1782, in Friedberg. Married (1) Apr. 5, 1804, to Catherine Knaus (died 1847). Married (2) Feb. 2, 1848, to Elisabeth Butner. Died June 23, 1861.

Spach, Elisabeth, born July 21, 1798, in Friedberg, to Herman Butner and Elisabeth m.n. Walk. Married Feb. 2, 1848, to John Spach. Died Aug. 11, 1861.

Hege, Amanda Augusta, born Oct. 10, 1855, to John Hege and Mary Magdalene m.n. Grubs. Died Nov. 27, 1861.

Hege, Alzena Paulina, born Dec. 21, 1846, to John Hege and Mary M. m.n. Grubs. Died Dec. 7, 1861.

Denny, Louisa Hortensia, born Apr. 20, 1833, at Bethabara, to Benjamin Krause and Susanna Rebecca m.n. Butner. Married. Died Feb. 25, 1862.

Butner, Permelia Catherine, born July 25, 1855, to Augustus Z. Butner and Serena m.n. Waldriven. Died Sept. 22, 1862. [Bethania Report: Her father was lately killed near Manasses in one of those engagements.]

Bowser, Andrew Augustus, born Mar. 13, 1853, to Andrew Bowser and Adaline m.n. Miller. Died Sept. 25, 1862.

Butner, Josiah Elias, born May 10, 1830, in Bethabara, to Thomas Butner and Mary Elizabeth m.n. Fockel. Married to Susanna A. Stoltz. Died Dec. 13, 1862. He fell in an action at Fredericksburg on the 13th of December whilst commanding his company.

Hine, Charles Henry, born Aug. 10, 1861, to Theodore T. Hine and Mary M. m.n. Shouse. Died Jan. 9, 1863.

Hine, Leonora Paulina, born Aug. 24, 1861, to Parmenio Hine and Clemmentine m.n. Beck. Died June 5, 1863.

Shemel, Amanda Elisabeth, born Apr. 6, 1855, to Eli Edward Shemel and Temperance m.n. Stoltz. Died July 22, 1863.

Shemel, John Henry Abraham, born June 22, 1859, to Eli Edward Shemel and Temperance m.n. Stoltz. Died July 23, 1863. The above [two] children were buried without asking the minister or Committee.

Miller, Henry. Died Oct. 23, 1863.

Shemel, Charles Daniel Abraham, born Apr. 3, 1864, to Joseph Shemel and Sarah m.n. Hege. Died June 25, 1864. [Bethania Diary: The Father is absent in the Army and has never seen his son.]

Krause, Anna Maria, born Dec. 9, 1793, near Bethabara, to Lewis Leinbach and Barbara m.n. Lauer. Married Nov. 26, 1816, to Samuel Krause. Died Feb. 10, 1865.

Krause, Susan Elisabeth, born Nov. 15, 1796, to Jacob Loesh and Susan m.n. Leinbach. Married June 14, 1821, to Thomas Krause. Died Feb. 12, 1865.

Spach, Thomas Lewis, born Oct. 9, 1819, near Bethabara, to John Spach and Anna Catherine m.n. Knaus. Married to Louisa Butner. Died Feb. 13, 1865.

Shemel, Eli Edward, born Aug. 28, 1828. Married Apr. 23, 1854, to Temperance Stoltz. Died July 3, 1865.

Haga, John, born Oct. 1, 1822, in Davidson County, to Mathais and Lydia Haga. Married to Mary Magdalene Grubs. Died Aug. 25, 1864. He was killed at Reem Station in a charge by the first shot fired on the 25th of August 1864. Not buried on our graveyard. [Bethania Diary: Funeral preached July 9, 1865, at Double-branch Schoolhouse.]

Grubs, John, born Oct. 4, 1823. Died Oct. 30, 1865. He was killed by his horse running away with the wagon.

Stiars, Eliza m.n. Riech, born May 4, 1820, near Bethabara. Married May 28, 1840, to John Stiars. Died Jan. 19, 1866.

Stiars, Hilary Edward, born Aug. 1, 1864, to John and Eliza Styers. Died Feb. 9, 1866.

Reich, Catharine m.n. Linebach, born Mar. 8, 1778, near Bethabara. Married John Reich. Died Aug. 30, 1866.

Rank, Mary Catharine, born Apr. 29, 1852, near Bethabara, to Permanio Rank and Margaret m.n. Miller. Died Nov. 7, 1866.

Friedberg Register, 1857-1866

Infant Baptisms

Shore, Alson Martin, born Oct. 29, 1856, to Thomas Shore and Mary m.n. Shutt. Baptized Jan. 29, 1857, at the parents' house.

Nading, Eliza Annestina Lizetta, born Feb. 2, 1857, to Matthias Nading and Mary Anna m.n. Snyder. Baptized July 12, 1857.

Johnston, Mary, born May 23, 1857, to William Costin Johnston and Saloma m.n. Seides. Baptized July 12, 1857.

Spach, Sarah Catharina, born July 4, 1857, to Trougott Spach and Nancy m.n. Haines. Baptized Aug. 30, 1857.

Fishel, Lewis Edwin, born July 15, 1857, to Gottfried Fishel and Regina m.n. Hardman. Baptized Aug. 30, 1857, at Friedberg.

Fishel, Jonas Sylvester, born Sept. 15, 1857, to Daniel Fishel and Eliza m.n. Mock. Baptized Oct. 25, 1857.

Swaim, Sarah Louisa, born Jan. 27, 1857, to Harrison Swaim and Anna Catharine m.n. Earnest. Baptized Dec. 19, 1857.

Rominger, John Benjamine, born Sept. 22, 1857, to Reubin Rominger and Mary m.n. Weasner. Baptized Jan. 10, 1858.

Tesh, Emmaly Regina, born Sept. 3, 1857, to Emmanuel Tesh and Charity m.n. Rothrock. Baptized Jan. 23, 1858.

Shore, Lucy Elizabeth, born Sept. 17, 1857, to Thomas Shore amd Mary m.n. Shutt. Baptized Jan. 27, 1858, at the parents' house.

Reich, Ellen Jane, born Nov. 5, 1857, to John Reich and Anna Minerva m.n. Tesh. Baptized Feb. 21, 1858, at Friedberg.

Rothrock, Julius Augustus, born Dec. 20, 1857, to Charles Rothrock and Lydia m.n. Fry. Baptized Feb. 21, 1858, at Friedberg.

Kanauss, Amanda Mary Ann, born Jan. 8, 1858, to Jesse Anderson Kanauss and Susan Anna m.n. Tesh. Baptized Feb. 28, 1858.

Shore, Nathan William, born Feb. 16, 1858, to William Shore and Lizetta Heneretta m.n. Walk. Baptized Apr. 4, 1858.

Rothrock, Charles Noah Winborn, born July 19, 1857, to Jacob Rothrock and Mary Ann m.n. Pope. Baptized Apr. 14, 1858, at the parents' house.

Burke, Emma Elizabeth, born Apr. 14, 1858, to John Burke and Elizabeth Caroline m.n. Spach. Baptized May 9, 1858, at Friedberg.

Rights, Florence Ellenor, born May 3, 1858, to Christian Lewis Rights and Elizabeth Balfour m.n. Hughes. Baptized May 30, 1858, at Friedberg.

Fishel, Sarah Catharine, born Mar. 19, 1858, to Timothy Fishel and Ann Margaret m.n. Rothrock. Baptized June 5, 1858, at Friedberg.

Mock, Jacob Alexander, born Apr. 22, 1858, to Nathaniel Mock and Maria Catharine m.n. Tesh. Baptized June 5, 1858, at Friedberg.

Mock, Sarah Elizabeth, born Apr. 22, 1858, to Nathaniel Mock and Maria Catharine m.n. Tesh. Baptized June 5, 1858, at Friedberg.

Sides, Alfred, born Mar. 10, 1858, to Elias Sides and Jane m.n. Longworth. Baptized Aug. 22, 1858, at Pleasant Fork.

Fishel, Lucinda Magdalena, born July 12, 1858, to Jonathan Fishel and Lucy m.n. Spach. Baptized Oct. 9, 1858, at Friedberg.

Kimmel, Emma Cornelia, born Aug. 22, 1848, to Sandford Kimmel and Eliza m.n. Brewer. Baptized Nov. 23, 1858, at the house of Archabald Sink.

Kimmel, Norman Sylvester, born Nov. 20, 1854, to Sandford Kimmel and Eliza m.n. Brewer. Baptized Nov. 23, 1858, at the house of Archabald Sink.

Crouse, Lewis Calvin, born Oct. 9, 1855, to William Harrison Crouse and Caroline Esther m.n. Faw. Baptized Nov. 25, 1858, at Friedberg.

Crouse, Mary Elvina, born June 23, 1857, to William Harrison Crouse and Caroline Esther m.n. Faw. Baptized Nov. 25, 1858, at Friedberg.

Foltz, Charles Lewis, born May 30, 1857, to John Foltz and Susan m.n. Crouch. Baptized Dec. 23, 1858.

Weasner, Mary Elizabeth, born Mar. 31, 1858, to Jacob Weasner and Sarah m.n. Rothrock. Baptized Dec. 26, 1858.

Tesh, Sarah Paulina, born Nov. 28, 1858, to Samuel Tesh and Elizabeth m.n. Evans. Baptized Jan. 30, 1859.

Spach, Leah Henrietta, born Dec. 18, 1858, to Trougott Henry and Nancy Spach. Baptized Feb. 13, 1859.

Armsey [Friedberg Diary: Armsworthy], Mary Catharine, born Nov. 18, 1858, to James Armsey and Caroline m.n. Kimmel. Baptized Feb. 27, 1859, at Friedberg. [Friedberg Diary: adopted by Archibald Sink.]

Rominger, Leminda Elizabeth, born Dec. 27, 1858, to Anderson Rominger and Antionet m.n. Shutt. Baptized Mar. 4, 1859.

Reich, Mary Elizabeth, born Jan. 12, 1859, to John Reich and Ann Minerva m.n. Tesh. Baptized Apr. 11, 1859.

Fishel, Jourdan David, born Dec. 11, 1858, to Michael Fishel and Mary Catharine m.n. Rothrock. Baptized Apr. 22, 1859.

Fishel, Laura Catharine, born Dec. 11, 1858, to Michael Fishel and Mary Catharine m.n. Rothrock. Baptized Apr. 22, 1859.

Tesh, Benjamine Francis, born May 15, 1859, to Solomon Tesh and Phoebe M. m.n. Perriman. Baptized June 19, 1859.

Spach, Mary Jane, born May 1, 1859, to Gottlieb Spach and Susanna m.n. Krautzfüsser. Baptized June 19, 1859.

Smith, Benjamine Alfred, born May 22, 1859, to John Benjamine Smith and Charlotta Christina m.n. Walk. Baptized July 24, 1859.

Earnest, Theodore Mannassah Rights, born June 23, 1859, to Sanford Daniel Earnest and Mary m.n. Swaim. Baptized July 24, 1859.

Fishel, Julius Franklin, born May 22, 1859 to Jesse Fishel and Caroline Elizabeth m.n. Tesh. Baptized July 30, 1859.

Mendenhall, John Henry, June 2, 1859, to Lemuel Mendenhall and Lucinda m.n. Rothrock. Baptized July 31, 1859.

Fishel, Amanda Leonora, born Oct. 9, 1855, to Sandford Fishel and Louisa m.n. Hoffman. Baptized Sept. 23, 1859, at the parents' house.

Fishel, Emma Elizabeth, born Apr. 4, 1857, to Sandford Fishel and Louisa m.n. Hoffman. Baptized Sept. 23, 1859, at the parents' house.

Fishel, Evander Samuel, born Mar. 3, 1859, to Sandford Fishel and Louisa m.n. Hoffman. Baptized Sept. 23, 1859, at the parents' house.

Johnston, Elizabeth, born Sept. 7, 1859, to William C. Johnston and Saloma m.n. Seides. Baptized Oct. 23, 1859.

Shore, Adelia Lucetta, born Oct. 6, 1859, to William Shore and Lucetta Henrietta m.n. Walk. Baptized Nov. 20, 1859.

James, David Theodore, born Sept. 6, 1859, to Franklin James and Jane m.n. Spach. Baptized Jan. 15, 1860.

Reich, Jacob Franklin, born Nov. 20, 1859, to James William Reich and Ellen m.n. Sink. Baptized Jan. 22, 1860.

Fishel, Francis Orestes, born Nov. 30, 1859, to Jacob Timothy Fishel and Anna Margaret m.n. Rothrock. Baptized Jan. 22, 1860, at Friedberg.

Crouse, Augusta Rosina, born Dec. 26, 1859, to Harrison Crouse and Esther Caroline m.n. Faw. Baptized Feb. 12, 1860.

Scott, George Washington, born Jan. 31, 1860, to Alexander Scott and Anna Maria m.n. Weaver. Baptized Mar. 11, 1860.

Tesh, Sarah Ann, born Sept. 6, 1859, to Emmanuel Tesh and Charity m.n. Rothrock. Baptized July 15, 1860.

Miller, Joseph Felix, born March, 1860, to Joseph Miller, Jr., and Rosina m.n. Delap. Baptized July 15, 1860.

Rothrock, Edwin Alexander, born June 28, 1860, to Charles Rothrock and Lydia Caroline m.n. Fry. Baptized Aug. 19, 1860.

Sides, Samuel, born Aug. 22, 1860, to Eli Sides and Jane m.n. Longworth. Baptized Oct. 28, 1860.

Reich, Samuel Augustus, born Sept. 24, 1860, to John Reich and Ann Minerva m.n. Tesh. Baptized Nov. 25, 1860.

Foltz, Matilda Lucy Ann, born Sept. 9, 1860, to John Foltz and Susan m.n. Crouch. Baptized Dec. 9, 1860.

Fishel, Benjamine Franklin, born June 21, 1860, to Jacob Fishel and Susanna m.n. Woosely. Baptized Dec. 26, 1860, at the parents' house.

Miller, Anna Sophia, born Sept. 7, 1860, to David Miller and Sarah Ann Elizabeth m.n. Fishel. Baptized Dec. 26, 1860, at the house of Jacob Fishel.

Earnest, Susan Jane, born Dec. 8, 1860, to Christian Earnest and Jane m.n. Jones. Baptized Jan. 13, 1861.

Spaugh, Orestis George, born Jan. 4, 1861, to Trougott Henry Spaugh and Nancy m.n. Hanes. Baptized Feb. 9, 1861, at the parents' house.

Smith, Louisa Victoria, born Nov. 22, 1860, to John Benjamine Smith and Christina Catharine m.n. Walk. Baptized Feb. 17, 1861.

Fishel, Paulina Sophia, born Oct. 6, 1860, to Jonathan Fishel and Louisa m.n. Spaugh. Baptized Feb. 24, 1861.

Shore, Amanda Catharine, born Jan. 22, 1860, to Thomas Shore and Mary m.n. Shutt. Baptized Mar. 15, 1861, at the house of Barney Kimmel.

Kanauss, Eliza Corneliann, born July 22, 1859, to Joseph Kanauss and Mary m.n. Fry. Baptized Sept. 25, 1859 ["registered for 1860"].

Johnston, Martha, born Jan. 22, 1861, to William Caustin Johnston and Saloma m.n. Sides. Baptized Mar. 29, 1861, at Friedberg.

Fishel, Juliann Hermina, born Jan. 9, 1861, to Sandford Jacob Fishel and Louisa m.n. Hoffman. Baptized Apr. 21, 1861, at Friedberg.

Fishel, Jacob Andrew, born May 4, 1861, to Jacob Timothy Fishel and Ann Margaret m.n. Rothrock. Baptized June 16, 1861.

Earnest, John Rufus, born Feb. 2, 1861, to Sandford Daniel Earnest and Mary m.n. Swaim. Baptized June 16, 1861, at Pleasant Fork.

Rominger, Eliza Jane, born May 4, 1861, to Anderson Rominger and Antionet m.n. Shutt. Baptized July 21, 1861.

Spaugh, Maria Anna, born Apr. 9, 1861, to Solomon Spaugh and Anna m.n. Green. Baptized Aug. 13, 1861.

Spaugh, Bertha Rebecca, born Sept. 1, 1861, to Lewis Nathaniel Spaugh and Emmaline m.n. Kimmel. Baptized Oct. 13, 1861.

Crouse, Sarah Madora, born Sept. 7, 1861, to Harrison Crouse and Esther Caroline m.n. Faw. Baptized Oct. 27, 1861.

Reich, Daniel Augustus, born Oct. 23, 1861, to William Reich and Ellen m.n. Sink. Baptized Nov. 24, 1861.

Tesh, Lucy Catharine, born Nov. 28, 1861, to Solomon Tesh and Phoebe m.n. Perriman. Baptized Jan. 12, 1862.

Mock, Alson Pinckston, born Oct. 23, 1861, to Alexander Benjamine Mock and Louisa m.n. Rominger. Baptized Jan. 14, 1862, at the parents' house.

Rothrock, Lewis Francis, born Jan. 4, 1862, to Charles Rothrock and Lydia m.n. Fry. Baptized Feb. 9, 1862, at Friedberg.

Fishel, Samuel Alexander, born Aug. 27, 1861, to Jesse Fishel and Caroline Elizabeth m.n. Tesh. Baptized October, 1861, at the parents' house. [Recorded out of sequence.]

Scott, Alexander, born Nov. 1, 1861, to Alexander Scott and Anna Maria m.n. Weaver. Baptized Mar. 9, 1862.

Spach, George Solomon, born Jan. 12, 1862, to Gottlieb Spach and Susanna m.n. Kreützfüsser. Baptized Mar. 9, 1862.

Burke, Amanda Clementine, born Jan. 14, 1862, to John Burke and Caroline m.n. Spach. Baptized Mar. 9, 1862.

James, Samuel Augustus, born July 26, 1861, to Franklin James and Jane m.n. Spach. Baptized Apr. 6, 1862, at Hope.

Long, Mary Elizabeth, born Feb. 5, 1862, to Lewis Long and Sarah m.n. Reich. Baptized Apr. 13, 1862.

Mendenhall, Joseph Emmanuel, born Mar. 26, 1862, to Lemuel Mendenhall and Lucinda m.n. Rothrock. Baptized June 29, 1862.

Shore, Eugene Benjamine, born Apr. 11, 1862, to William Shore and Lizetta m.n. Walk. Baptized June 29, 1862.

Knauss, John Wesley, born Mar. 22, 1862, to Joshua Joseph Knauss and Mary m.n. Fry. Baptized July 13, 1862.

Sides, Edward, born July 27, 1862, to Eli Sides and Jane m.n. Longworth. Baptized Sept. 14, 1862.

Reich, Rosa Isabel, born Aug. 12, 1862, to John Reich and Minerva m.n. Tesh. Baptized Oct. 19, 1862.

Hage, Cornelia Augusta, born Aug. 25, 1862, to Jacob Hage and Anna m.n. Spach. Baptized Nov. 16, 1862.

Miller, David Franklin, born Oct. 10, 1862, to David Miller and Elizabeth m.n. Fishel. Baptized Dec. 13, 1862.

Hardman, Phebe Rebecca, born Nov. 22, 1862, to Jesse Hardman and Anna Elizabeth m.n. Spach. Baptized Dec. 25, 1862.

Rominger, Samuel Augustus, born July 21, 1861, to Reubin Rominger and Mary m.n. Weasner. Baptized Oct. 20, 1861, at Pleasant Fork. [Recorded out of sequence.]

Tesh, Leonora Clementina, born Dec. 12, 1862, to Samuel Tesh and Elizabeth m.n. Evans. Baptized Mar. 8, 1863.

Spach, John Edwin, born Jan. 13, 1863, to Trougott Henry Spach and Nancy m.n. Hanes. Baptized Mar. 8, 1863.

Fishel, Clara Isabella, born Nov. 3, 1862, to Sandford Fishel and Louisa m.n. Hoffman. Baptized Apr. 3, 1863.

Lashmith, John Emmory, born Mar. 20, 1863, to John Lashmith and Malvina m.n. Transou. Baptized May 24, 1863.

Weasner, Joseph Floridore, born Apr. 13, 1863, to Ephraim Marcus Weasner and Catharine Matilda m.n. Mock. Baptized May 31, 1863.

Smith, Frederick Theodore, born Apr. 15, 1863, to John B. Smith and Christina m.n. Walk. Baptized June 13, 1863.

Johnston, Caustin, born May 1, 1863, to William Caustin Johnston and Saloma m.n. Sides. Baptized June 14, 1863.

Crouse, Jacob Franklin, born May 18, 1863, to Harrison Crouse and Esther Caroline m.n. Faw. Baptized June 28, 1863.

Hill, Clara Jane, born May 21, 1863, to Valentine Hill and Delilah m.n. Weaver. Baptized July 12, 1863.

Spach, Ida Elizabeth, born May 25, 1863, to Gottlieb Spach and Susanna m.n. Kreutzfüsser. Baptized Aug. 9, 1863.

Fishel, Delilah Rebecca, born June 6, 1863, to Jonathan Fishel and Lucy m.n. Spach. Baptized Aug. 15, 1863.

Fishel, Noah Benjamine, born July 4, 1863, to Jesse Fishel and Caroline m.n. Tesh. Baptized Aug. 15, 1863.

Earnest, William Sandford Harrison, born Aug. 20, 1863 to Daniel Sandford Earnest and Mary m.n. Swaim. Baptized Sept. 22, 1863.

Fishel, John Wesley, born July 2, 1863, to Jacob Timothy Fishel and Anna Margaret m.n. Rothrock. Baptized Oct. 25, 1863.

Fishel, Alice Victoria, born Nov. 4, 1860, to David Fishel and Nancy m.n. Steward. Baptized Nov. 29, 1863.

Shutt, Alice Ellenora, born July 13, 1860, to Louisa Shutt and Josiah Miller and adopted by Sr. Nancy Weasner. Baptized Nov. 29, 1863.

Miller, Sarah Margaret, born Sept. 30, 1863, to Joseph Miller and Rosa m.n. Delap. Baptized Jan. 17, 1864.

Floyd, Anna Paulina Catharine, born Dec. 3, 1863, to John Floyd and Susan m.n. Fishel. Baptized Jan. 31, 1864.

Tesh, Emanuel Valentine, born May 22, 1863, to Emanuel Tesh and Charity m.n. Rothrock. Baptized Feb. 22, 1864.

Reich, Louisa Sarah Ann, born Jan. 1, 1864, to John Reich and Minerva m.n. Tesh. Baptized Mar. 13, 1864.

Earnest, Levy Allen, born Apr. 1, 1864, to Christian Earnest and Jane m.n. Jones. Baptized May 12, 1864.

Sink, Mary Jane Elizabeth, born Feb. 27, 1864, to Noah Sink and Louisa Catharine m.n. Mock. Baptized May 29, 1864.

Knouse, Samuel Augustus, born Apr. 6, 1864, to Joseph Knouse and Mary m.n. Frye. Baptized June 19, 1864.

Rominger, Rosina Matilda, born Apr. 4, 1864, to Anderson Rominger and Antionet m.n. Shutt. Baptized June 19, 1864.

Hardman, John Wesley, born Aug. 3, 1864, to Jesse Hardman and Anna m.n. Spaugh. Baptized Sept. 10, 1864.

Reich, John Henry, born July 1, 1864, to William Reich and Ellen m.n. Sink. Baptized Oct. 15, 1864.

Theodesia Harriet Celeste, born Aug. 10, 1864, to the negro woman Martha belonging to brother Christian Spaugh. Baptized Mar. 14, 1865, at the house of Christian Spaugh.

Kern Monroe Sylvester, born Sept. 14, 1864, to the negro woman Calphene belonging to brother Christian Spaugh. Baptized Mar. 14, 1865, at the house of Christian Spaugh.

Sides, Saloma, born Nov. 9, 1864, to Eli Sides and Jane m.n. Longworth. Baptized Mar. 19, 1865. [Friedberg Report: The father is a prisoner at Camp Chase.]

Mendenhall, Clara Sarah Ann, born Jan. 1, 1865, to Lemuel Mendenhall and Lucinda m.n. Rothrock. Baptized May 23, 1865.

Crouse, Laura Maria, born Apr. 27, 1865, to Harrison Crouse and Esther Caroline m.n. Faw. Baptized July 9, 1865.

Miller, Amos Augustine, born Feb. 26, 1865, to Constantine Miller and Barbara m.n. Kreutzfüsser. Baptized July 23, 1865.

Shore, Ada Miranda, born May 27, 1865, to William Shore and Lizetta m.n. Walk. Baptized July 30, 1865.

Spaugh, Angeline Clara Isabella, born June 16, 1865, to Belinda Spaugh and James Shutt. Baptized Aug. 10, 1865.

Spaugh, William Eugene, born Apr. 25, 1865, to Trougott Henry Spaugh and Nancy m.n. Hanes. Baptized Aug. 20, 1865.

Fishel, Mary Elizabeth, born July 16, 1865, to Jacob Timothy Fishel and Anna Margaret m.n. Rothrock. Baptized Oct. 8, 1865.

Fishel, Theresa Sophia, born Sept. 26, 1865, to Jesse Fishel and Caroline m.n. Tesh. Baptized Dec. 7, 1865.

Johnson, Jane, born June 16, 1865, to William Johnson and Salome m.n. Seides. Baptized Dec. 16, 1865.

Spach, Amanda Rosina, born Nov. 12, 1865, to Gottlieb Spach and Susannah m.n. Kreutzfueser. Baptized Jan. 14, 1866.

Sink, Sarah Belinda, born Dec. 10, 1865, to David Sink and Paulina m.n. Mock. Baptized Mar. 11, 1866.

Tesh, Allen Lorenzo Lee, born Oct. 18, 1865, to Samuel Tesh and Elizabeth m.n. Evans. Baptized Feb. 11, 1866. [Recorded out of sequence.]

Reich, Rufus Franklin, born Feb. 14, 1866, to John Reich and Anna Maria m.n. Tesh. Baptized Apr. 22, 1866.

Floyd, Mary Louisa, born Feb. 12, 1866, to John Floyd and Susan m.n. Fishel. Baptized May 13, 1866.

Fishel, Selina Christina, born June 22, 1866, to Jonathan Fishel and Lucy m.n. Spach. Baptized Oct. 24, 1866.

Stoner, Charlotte Cornelia Ann, born Aug. 16, 1866, to Amos Stoner and Harriet Augusta m.n. Chitty. Baptized Nov. 11, 1866.

Adult Baptisms

Foltz, Susan m.n. Crouch. Baptized Oct. 24, 1858, at Friedberg.

Crouse, Esther Caroline m.n. Faw. Baptized Oct. 24, 1858, at Friedberg.

Miller, Derilda. Baptized Oct. 24, 1858, at Friedberg.

Delap, Felix. Baptized Oct. 24, 1858, at Friedberg.

Floyd, John. Baptized Oct. 24, 1858, at Friedberg.

Mendenhall, Lemuel. Baptized Oct. 24, 1858, at Friedberg.

Earnest, Jane Pyat m.n. Jones, born Jan. 2, 1821. Wife of Christian Earnest. Baptized Feb. 18, 1860.

Weaver, Henry. Baptized May 19, 1861.

Weaver, Angeline. Baptized May 19, 1861.

Sides, Jane m.n. Longworth. Baptized May 19, 1861.

Weaver, Alexander. Baptized Aug. 13, 1861.

Shoaf, William Naman. Baptized Dec. 8, 1861.

Tesh, Charity Maria. Baptized Dec. 8, 1861.

Cook, Maranda Catharine. Baptized Dec. 8, 1861.

Welfare, Daniel Thomas. Baptized Oct. 22, 1865.

Welfare, Anna Elizabeth. Baptized Oct. 22, 1865.

Armsworthy, Laura Elizabeth. Baptized Oct. 22, 1865.

Harmon, John. Baptized Aug. 13 [Friedberg Diary: Aug. 11], 1866.

Harmon, Charity m.n. Stewart. Baptized Aug. 13 [Friedberg Diary: Aug. 11], 1866.

Craver, Henry Harrison. Baptized Oct. 27, 1866.

Foltz, Sarah. Baptized Oct. 27, 1866.

Hyer, Enoch, born Jan. 15, 1838. Baptized Nov. 24, 1866.

Spach, Mary Elvina Rosina. Baptized Nov. 24, 1866.

Marriages

Spach, David F., born Feb. 5, 1831, to Daniel Spach, Sr., and Rebecca m.n. Weasner, married Feb. 15, 1857, to Maria Kimmel, born to Jacob Kimmel and Nancy m.n. Beockle.

Spach, Samuel Benton, married Dec. 13, 1857, to Sarah Green.

Fishel, Jesse, married June 8, 1858, to Caroline E. Tesh.

Reich, William, married Jan. 2, 1859, to Ellen Sink.

Spach, Lewis Nathaniel, born Dec. 8, 1833, to Daniel Spach, Sr., and Rebecca m.n. Weasner, married Feb. 9, 1859, to Emmaline Kimmel.

Sink, David, married Mar. 20, 1859, to Paulina Louisa Mock, born Oct. 23, 1839, to John Jesse Mock and Sarah Rebecca m.n. Kimmel.

Scott, Alexander, married Apr. 20, 1859, to Anna Maria (Nancy) Weaver, born July 23, 1834, to William Weaver and Christina m.n. Boeckle.

Floyd, John, married May 2, 1859, to Susan Rebecca Fishel, born July 29, 1836, to George and Catharine Fishel.

Fishel, Daniel, Jr., married Aug. 9, 1859, to Nancy Gorden.

Long, Lewis W., married Oct. 9, 1859, to Sarah Reich, born Oct. 28, 1838, to Phillip and Rosina Reich.

Mock, Alexander Benjamine, born May 20, 1838, to John Jesse Mock and Sarah m.n. Kimmel, married Feb. 7, 1860, to Louisa J. Rominger, born to Jordan Rominger and Catharine m.n. Hanes.

Reich, Benjamine Franklin, married Dec. 20, 1860, to Maria Catharine Sides, born July 10, 1843, to Christian David and Alpha M. Sides.

Lee, Henry T., married June 6, 1861, to Elizabeth J. Fry, born to Thomas Fry and Elizabeth m.n. Binkley.

Weasner, Ephraim Marcus, born to David Weasner and Anna Maria m.n. Hanes, married Dec. 19, 1861, to Matilda Catharine Mock, born to John Jesse and Sarah Mock.

Hardman, Jesse, married Feb. 16, 1862, to Anna Elizabeth Spach, born to Daniel Spach, Sr., and Rebecca m.n. Weasner.

Hill, Valentine, married Aug. 19, 1862, to Delila Rebecca Weaver, born to William Weaver and Christina m.n. Beockle.

Hanes, David, married Nov. 22, 1864, to Nancy Ripple.

Hill, Leander, married Aug. 10, 1865, to Maria Spaugh [Friedberg Diary: daughter of Daniel Spaugh, jun.]

Stoner, Amos, a soldier of the 9th Pennsylvania Cavalry (Gen. Sherman's army), married Nov. 16, 1865, to Harriet Chitty.

Pugh, Samuel Franklin, married Apr. 1, 1866, to Martha Elizabeth Smith.

Cooper, William Jacob, married July 3, 1866, to Jane Catharine Blum.

Wesner, William J., married Sept. 18, 1866, to Susannah R. Fishel.

Weaver, Henry F., married Sept. 19, 1866, to Theresa M. Wesner.

Hampton, Benjamin, married Nov. 22, 1866, to Eliza Reich.

Craver, Harrison, married Dec. 13, 1866, to Sarah Maria Foltz.

Stoltz, T. S., married Oct. 25, 1866, to Elizabeth Spach, born to Chr. Spach. [Recorded out of sequence.]

Deaths and Burials

Rights, Mabel Josephine, born Nov. 9, 1856, to Christian Lewis Rights and Elizabeth Balfour m.n. Hughes. Died Jan. 5, 1857.

Miller, Daniel, born Aug. 24, 1800. Died Jan. 15, 1857.

Swaim, Christina Salome m.n. Spach, born Oct. 30, 1807. Married July 19, 1829, to John Ledford Swaim. Died May 22, 1857.

Shore, Ellen Elizabeth, born Aug. 10, 1856, to William Shore and Lizetta Heneretta m.n. Walk. Died Aug. 30, 1857.

Foltz, Charles Martin, born Dec. 10, 1847. Died Sept. 5, 1857.

Hage, Susan Celeste, born Aug. 28, 1850, to Solomon Hage and Catharine m.n. Günther. Died Nov. 28, 1857.

Walk, John Henry, born Dec. 21, 1855, to John Joseph Wall and Mary Ann m.n. Berrier. Died Jan. 6, 1858.

Craver, Elizabeth m.n. Rothrock, born Nov. 13, 1778. Died Feb. 12, 1858.

Fishel, Gottfried, born Feb. 2, 1812, in Friedberg. Married Oct. 1, 1840, to Regina Hartman. Died Mar. 12, 1858.

Rominger, Eve Rosina m.n. Clause, born Jan. 16, 1778, in Shoeneck, Pa. Married Dec. 15, 1796, to Cornelius Rominger. Died Apr. 28, 1858.

Miller, Traugott, born July 25, 1840, to Jesse Miller and Maria Louisa m.n. Fishel. Died May 3, 1858.

James (Covis), Edmund George, born July 27, 1841, to John James (Covis) and Elizabeth m.n. Berril. Died May 7, 1858.

Spach, Christina m.n. Kimmel, born Apr. 24, 1795, near Friedberg. Married May 29, 1845, to John George Spach. Died June 13, 1858.

Mock, Maria Catharine m.n. Tesh, born Sept. 14, 1819. Married Oct. 18, 1838, to Nathaniel Mock. Died Oct. 12, 1858.

Mock, Jacob Alexander, born Apr. 22, 1858, to Nathaniel Mock and Maria Catharine m.n. Tesh. Died Oct. 15, 1858.

Earnest, Anna Louisa m.n. Herrman, born Jan. 20, 1796. Married in 1824 to Christian Phillip Earnest. Died Dec. 11, 1858.

Fishel, Catharine Eliza m.n. Mock, born Jan. 18, 1820, near Friedberg. Married Nov. 23, 1837, to Daniel Fishel. Died Apr. 25, 1859.

Crouch, Charles, born Nov. 22, 1796, in Davidson County. Married in 1820 to Catharine Glascock. Died Aug. 26, 1859.

Fishel, Daniel Sr., born Apr. 10, 1780, in Rowan County. Married (1) Apr. 12, 1803, to Sarah Elizabeth Ziglar (died 1806). Married (2) in 1807 to Maria Magdalina m.n. Schneider. Died Dec. 8, 1859.

Spach, Beatus and Beatus, stillborn twin sons of Lewis Nathaniel Spach and Emmaline m.n. Kimmel. Feb. 6, 1860.

Reich, Mary Elizabeth, born Jan. 12, 1859, to John Reich and Minerva Ann m.n. Tesh. Died May 30, 1860.

Spaugh, Orestes George, born Jan. 4, 1861, to Trougott Henry Spaugh and Nancy m.n. Hanes. Died Feb. 10, 1861.

Weasner, Emeline Rebecca, born Aug. 12, 1836. Died May 5, 1861.

Rothrock, Anna Margaretha m.n. Beockle, born Nov. 28, 1802, at Friedberg. Married July 4, 1820, to Daniel Rothrock. Died July 6, 1861.

Fishel, Ida Virginia, born Sept. 22, 1858, to David Fishel and Nancy m.n. Steward. Died July 27, 1861.

Phillips, William Jackson, born Oct. 26, 1860, to John Phillips and Ida Krutzfüsser. Died Sept. 24, 1861.

Earnest, John Rufus, born Feb. 2, 1861, to Daniel Sandford Earnest and Mary m.n. Swaim. Died Dec. 24, 1861.

Tesh, Beatus, born Feb. 10, 1862, to Emmanuel Tesh and Charity m.n. Rothrock. Died Feb. 14, 1862.

Spach, Martin, born Oct. 26, 1840. Died May 13, 1862. He was a volunteer in Captain Atwood's Company and died from the effects of measles at Goldsboro, N.C.

Padgett, Eliza Lauretta, born May 1, 1833. Died May 28, 1862.

Weasner, Beatus, born May 26, 1862, to Jacob Weasner and Sarah m.n. Rothrock. Died June 5, 1862.

Fishel, Rebecca, born Oct. 21, 1808. Died Oct. 22, 1862.

Shore, Verona m.n. Rominger, born Dec. 17, 1788, near Friedland. Died Oct. 31, 1862.

Mock, Alson Pinckston, born Oct. 23, 1861, to Alexander Benjamine Mock and Louisa m.n. Rominger. Died Nov. 24, 1862.

Miller, Thomas, born Aug. 28, 1839. Died Nov. 30, 1862.

Spach, Catharine, born Aug. 18, 1811, in Davidson County. Married Oct. 31, 1833, to Christian Spach. Died Nov. 25, 1862. [Recorded out of sequence.]

Spach, George Solomon, born Jan. 12, 1862, to Gottlieb Spach and Susanna m.n. Krützfüsser. Died Mar. 26, 1863.

Spach, Benjamine Alexander (non-member), born Mar. 3, 1834, in Davidson County. Married Sept. 15, 1859, to Elizabeth Hill. Died Feb. 14, 1863. A conscript in the [blank] North Carolina Regiment. He died at Burton's Hospital of typhoid pneumonia, and his remains were disinterred at Lynchburg, Va., and brought home.

Rothrock, Maria Catharine m.n. Beockle, born Feb. 28, 1794, in Rowan County. Married Feb. 27, 1817, to Christian Rothrock. Died May 27, 1863.

Rominger, Beatus (non-member), born May 22, 1863, to Eli Rominger and Lizana m.n. Hauser. Died June 12, 1863.

Peeler, Rosa Ann Christina (non-member), born May 20, 1844, in Davidson County, to Caleb Peeler and Saloma m.n. Rothrock. Died July 21, 1863.

Fishel, Sarah Maria, born June 27, 1854, in Davidson County, to Jonathan Fishel and Lucy m.n. Spach. Died July 29, 1863.

Hardman, Martha m.n. Vogler (non-member), born Aug. 1, 1820, in Forsyth County. Married to John Hardman. Died Oct. 11, 1863.

Knauss, John Wesley, born Mar. 22, 1862, to Joseph Knauss and Mary m.n. Frey. Died Oct. 24, 1863.

Spaugh, James Adam (non-member), born Aug. 2, 1838. Died May 10, 1863. He was a conscript and died at Richmond, Va., of typhoid fever. Buried Nov. 21, 1863.

Crouch, Augustine (non-member), born Jan. 11, 1839, in Forsyth County. Died Jan. 24, 1864. Buried Feb. 12, 1864. [Friedberg Diary: He was shot Jan. 25, 1864, at Orange Court House, Va., for desertion.]

Disher, Franklin Madison, born Mar. 10, 1860, to Christian Disher and Mary m.n. Evans. Died Feb. 25, 1864.

Hoffman, Mary Catharine, born June 18, 1860, to Phillip Hoffman and Susan m.n. Yonce. Died Apr. 3, 1864.

Ripple, John Wesley, born Sept. 23, 1843, in Davidson County [Friedberg Diary: to Phillip Ripple and Belinda m.n. Frye]. Died Apr. 10, 1864.

Earnest, William Sandford Harrison, born Aug. 20, 1863, to Sandford Daniel Earnest and Mary m.n. Swaim. Died May 31, 1864.

Foltz, Lucinda m.n. Sides, born Feb. 17, 1820, in Stokes (now Forsyth) County. Married Oct. 6, 1840, to Edward Foltz. Died May 31, 1864.

Spach, Jonathan, born Mar. 30, 1821, in Forsyth County. Died July 9, 1864. Died at Raleigh, where he was stationed as one of Provost Guard.

Long, Lewis W. (non-member), born Dec. 30, 1830, in Forsyth County. Died Sept. 17, 1864.

Spaugh, David Franklin (member of Salem), born Feb. 5, 1831, at Friedberg. Married Feb. 15, 1857, to Maria Kimmel. Died Feb. 14, 1865.

Hage, Anna Lucinda m.n. Spach, born Feb. 15, 1831. Married Jacob Hage, Jr., who was a volunteer in the Confederate Army and died near Petersburg, Va., in August 1862. She died Mar. 31, 1865.

Buttner, Louisa Catharine m.n. Walk (member of Bethabara), born Dec. 8, 1809, in Davidson County. Married Aug. 17, 1843, to Joseph Buttner. Died Apr. 4, 1865.

Floyd, Anna Paulina Catharina, born Dec. 3, 1863, to John Floyd and Susan m.n. Fishel. Died Nov. 7, 1865.

Rothrock, Sarah m.n. Spach, born Oct. 25, 1795. Married Jan. 1827 to Joseph Rothrock. Died Feb. 24, 1866.

Spach, Solomon Augustus, born Feb. 7, 1835. Died Sept. 9, 1862. In 1862 he was conscripted and entered the service. He was unwell when he left home, and exposure to camp life increased his indisposition, until on his way to Richmond he was compelled to stop at Jefferson, about 15 miles from Culpepper, being too sick to proceed any further. A stranger among strangers, he lay sick a few days, and died. Buried May 7, 1866.

Hampton, Malvina m.n. Shore, born Oct. 14, 1829, to Jacob Shore and Verona m.n. Rominger. Married Oct. 20, 1852, to Benjamin Hampton. Died June 14, 1866.

Spach, John George, born Sept. 3, 1786, near Friedberg, to Adam and Catharine Spach. Married (1) Mar. 11, 1811, to Mary Shore (died 1843). Married (2) May 29, 1845, to Christina Kimmel. Died June 24, 1866.

Fishel, Benjamin Franklin, born June 21, 1860, to Jacob and Susan Fishel. Died Aug. 22, 1866.

Mock, Christian Silvanus, born Apr. 12, 1841. Died Sept. 29, 1866. Fatally injured by a stone carelessly thrown.

Daniels, Columbus Franklin, born June 2, 1844. Died Oct. 24, 1866.

Spach, George, born Mar. 23, 1789, to John and Catharine Spach. Married (1) Apr. 23, 1815, to Catharine Sides (died 1827). Married (2) Apr. 23, 1829, to Elizabeth Shutt. Died Dec. 17, 1866.

Baptisms of Non-Members

Spach, William, born to William Spach and Lizetta m.n. Strupe. Baptized Aug. 23, 1857, at Pleasant Fork.

Earnest, Darius Scales, born Oct. 12, 1857, to Sandford Daniel Earnest and Julia Mary m.n. Swaim. Baptized Nov. 8, 1857, at Friedberg.

Rominger, Lewis Columbus, born July 24, 1857, to Solomon and Jane Rominger. Baptized Nov. 22, 1857, at Friedberg.

Chitty, Ellen Laura Ann, born Aug. 11, 1857, to Lafayette Chitty and Andeline m.n. Kimmel. Baptized May 16, 1858, at Hopewell.

Hage, Calvin Alexander, born Aug. 25, 1857, to Jacob Hage and Anna m.n. Spach. Baptized May 23, 1858.

Miller, Franklin Alexander, born Mar. 25, 1858, to Joseph Henry Miller and Rosina m.n. Delap. Baptized May 23, 1858, at Friedberg.

Chitty, Emma Jane, born Mar. 20, 1859, to Solomon Chitty and Sarah Ann m.n. Kimmel. Baptized July 10, 1859, at the house of Barnabas Kimmel.

Calvin James Obadiah (colored), born July 4, 1855, to Christian Spaugh's Martha and Delap's Alexander. Baptized Jan. 4, 1860, at the house of Christian Spaugh.

Ciscero Theodore Charles, born Oct. 5, 1859, to Spaugh's Martha and Delap's Alexander. Baptized Jan. 4, 1860, at the house of Christian Spaugh.

Pack, Paulina Elizabeth, born Sept. 21, 1859, to Reason Pack and Amanda m.n. Buttner. Baptized Mar. 25, 1860.

Spach, Hermina Clemmentina, born Apr. 10, 1860, to John Spach (son of John) and Christina m.n. Everhard. Baptized June 10, 1860.

Floyd, Emmanuel Madison, born Jan. 1, 1860, to John Floyd and Susan m.n. Fishel. Baptized Sept. 1, 1860.

Hage, Phoebe Jane, born Sept. 25, 1860, to Jacob Hage and Anna m.n. Spach. Baptized Nov. 25, 1860, at Pleasant Fork.

Swaim, Bridgett Lucina Elisabeth, born to Alfred Swaim and Gertrude Lisetta m.n. Nading. Baptized Nov. 25, 1860, at the house of Elisabeth Swaim.

Chitty, Victoria Elizabeth, born Jan. 22, 1861, to Solomon Chitty and Sarah Ann m.n. Kimmel. Baptized Mar. 15, 1861, at the house of Barney Kimmel.

Nading, Sarahann Christina, born Jan. 13, 1861, to Matthew Nading and Mary Ann m.n. Fishel. Baptized Apr. 21, 1861.

Foltz, Emmanuel Augustus, born Apr. 17, 1861, to Theophilis Foltz and Ann Malvina m.n. Heartel. Baptized June 12, 1861.

Hoffman, Mary Cath., born June 18, 1861, to Phillip Hoffman and Susan m.n. Yonce. Baptized Oct. 24, 1861.

Rominger, son of Reubin and Mary Rominger. Baptized Oct. 20, 1861, at Pleasant Fork. [Recorded out of sequence.]

Floyd, Maria Elizabeth, born Aug. 7, 1861, to John Floyd and Susan m.n. Fishel. Baptized Nov. 10, 1861, at Friedberg.

Mary Margaret (negro), born Jan. 7, 1861, to Christian Ripple's Hannah. Baptized Mar. 8, 1862, at the house of Br. Ripple.

Spach, John Franklin, born Feb. 8, 1862, to John Spach and Christina m.n. Everhard. Baptized May 11, 1862.

Miller, Maria Louisa, born Apr. 27, 1862, to Constantine Miller and Barbara m.n. Kreutzfüsser. Baptized Sept. 14, 1862.

Hage, Augusta Rebecca, born Aug. 19, 1862, to Samuel Hage and Elizabeth m.n. Beockle. Baptized Mar. 15, 1863, at Pleasant Fork.

Spach, James Franklin, born Oct. 14, 1865, to George S. and Elizabeth Spach. Baptized Mar. 11, 1866.

Miller, Solomon Augustus, born May 19, 1866, to Joseph H. Miller and Rosina m.n. Delap. Baptized July 8, 1866.

Shutt, David Franklin, born Mar. 16, 1866, to James Shutt and Mary m.n. Rothrock. Baptized July 8, 1866.

Hege, Samuel Augustus, born Apr. 19, 1866, to Samuel Hege and Elizabeth m.n. Boeckel. Baptized Aug. 12, 1866.

Deaths and Burials of Non-Members

Good, Sarah, born in Stokes County. Died May 6, 1857.

Hege, Catharine m.n. Weasner, born May 10, 1791, in Rowan County. Married June 21, 1820, to Jacob Hege. Died Aug. 14, 1857.

Rominger, Solomon, born Dec. 5, 1814. Died Dec. 4, 1857.

Reich, Nancy, died May 22, 1858.

Crouse, Beata. Stillborn daughter of Harrison and Esther Caroline Crouse. Aug. 31, 1858.

Armesworthy, Caroline, born Dec. 11, 1829. Married Sept. 13, 1849, to James Armesworthy. Died Dec. 9, 1858.

Hill, Sarah Lizetta m.n. Mock, born June 3, 1828, in Davidson County. Married (1) Mar. 7, 1851, to David Eader (died). Married (2) Aug. 26, 1858, to Leander N. Hill. Died

Jan. 19, 1860. A daughter was buried in the same coffin with the mother; it was born on Jan. 18 and lived two hours.

Hage, David, born in Davidson County. Married Dec. 18, 1832, to Elizabeth Sink. Died Jan. 22, 1860.

Foltz, Malchus Primins, born to Eli Foltz and wife. Died June 6, 1860.

Weaver, Elizabeth m.n. Tesh, born July 15, 1796, in Rowan County. Died Jan. 19, 1861.

Günther, Juliana m.n. Fiedler, born Feb. 2, 1785, at Friedland. Married Apr. 1819 to John Günther. Died May 25, 1861.

Floyd, Emmanuel Madison, born Jan. 1, 1860, to John Floyd and Susan m.n. Fishel. Died June 3, 1861.

Perril, Joseph, born Dec. 9, 1810, in Rowan County. Died Oct. 24, 1861.

Hanes, Phillip, born Dec. 30, 1824. Died Nov. 15, 1861. [Friedberg Report: He took an overdose of laudanum.]

Spach, Ellen Frances Josephine, born Dec. 10, 1860, to Adam Spach and Mary m.n. Berrier. Died Jan. 16, 1862.

Swaim, Benigna Louisa, born July 6, 1861, to Hamilton Swaim and Charity m.n. Crouch. Died Mar. 24, 1862.

Heartel, Edward, born Mar. 21, 1844, to Malvina Foltz, late Heartel. Died Apr. 18, 1862. [Friedberg Diary: He was a volunteer in Captain Atwood's Company, and died of brain fever at Raleigh. Buried Apr. 21, 1862, at Friedberg.]

Perril, Elizabeth m.n. Ader. Married (1) to a Mr. Hanes (died). Married (2) to Joseph Perril. Died May 29, 1862.

Craver, Joseph, born Nov. 16, 1807. Died June 2, 1862.

Miller, David, born May 3, 1838. Died July 26, 1862.

Floyd, Maria Elizabeth, born Aug. 7, 1861, to John Floyd and Susan m.n. Fishel. Died Aug. 11, 1862.

Spach, Beatus, born Sept. 18, 1862, to Adam Spach and Mary m.n. Berrier. Died Oct. 23, 1862.

Disher, Christian, born Dec. 23, 1837, in Davidson County. Died Nov. 15, 1862. He was taken sick in the army and came home on furlough.

Hage, Sarah Ellen, born Jan. 6, 1857, to Samuel Hage and Elizabeth m.n. Beockle. Died Dec. 7, 1862.

White, John, Sr. Died Mar. 20, 1863.

Earnest, Sandford Daniel, born Feb. 15, 1827. Died May 2, 1863.

Miller, Costantine. Buried June 17, 1865.

Rothrock, son of Tobias Rothrock and Edith m.n. Hoffman. Died 1865.

Foltz, Eliza, born Feb. 18, 1830. Married to Eli Foltz. Died Aug. 2, 1866. With her was buried in the same coffin her daughter Jane Missouri Foltz, born March 15, 1866, died July 27, 1866.

Painter, Philip Daniel, born Jan. 17, 1827, in Davidson County, to John Painter and Catherine m.n. Kreutzfueser. Died Nov. 19, 1866.

Painter, John, born Apr. 18, 1800. Died Nov. 23, 1866.

Friedberg Diary Entries, 1857-1866

[Church Register material that was recorded only in the Friedberg Diary. The following is the entirety of the material.]

Baptisms

Runniger, Mary Elisabeth, an infant. Baptized Apr. 2, 1857, in Liberty.

Cope, Elizabeth. Baptized June 12, 1857, at Macedonia.

Kerner, two children of Joseph Kerner. Baptized Aug. 20, 1857.

Hodges, Joseph. Baptized Dec. 11, 1857, at Macedonia.

Clark, Robert. Baptized Dec. 11, 1857, at Macedonia.

King, Minerva. Baptized Dec. 11, 1857, at Macedonia.

King, Mary Jane. Baptized Dec. 11, 1857, at Macedonia.
Hood, William. Baptized Dec. 11, 1857, at Macedonia.
Hodges, David. Baptized Dec. 11, 1857, at Macedonia.
Hodges, Elisabeth. Baptized Dec. 11, 1857, at Macedonia.
Clounch, Sarah. Baptized Dec. 11, 1857, at Macedonia.
Cope, Andrew. Baptized Dec. 11, 1857, at Macedonia.
Hodges, Martha. Baptized Dec. 11, 1857, at Macedonia.
Shaddock, David. Baptized Jan. 8, 1858, at Macedonia.
Miller, Henry F. Baptized Jan. 8, 1858, at Macedonia.
Shaddock, Sidney. Baptized Jan. 8, 1858, at Macedonia.
Jeffries, Temperance. Baptized Jan. 8, 1858, at Macedonia.
Hood, Mary. Baptized Jan. 8, 1858, at Macedonia.
Cope, Mary Jane. Baptized Jan. 8, 1858, at Macedonia.
Danner, Eli. Baptized Mar. 12, 1858, at Macedonia.
Allen, Rebecca Jane. Baptized Mar. 12, 1858, at Macedonia.
Wheeler, Martha. Baptized Mar. 12, 1858, at Macedonia.
Lee, Martha. Baptized Mar. 12, 1858, at Macedonia.
Wheeler, Margaret. Baptized Oct. 8, 1858, at Macedonia.
Lee, Henry. Baptized Oct. 8, 1858, at Macedonia.
King, Anderson. Baptized Oct. 8, 1858, at Macedonia.
Fry, Jane. Baptized Oct. 8, 1858, at Macedonia.
Austin, Amelia. Baptized Oct. 8, 1858, at Macedonia.
Etchison, Rebecca. Baptized Oct. 8, 1858, at Macedonia.
Longworth, Samuel. Baptized Oct. 8, 1858, at Macedonia.
Sheeks, Rachel (colored). Baptized Oct. 8, 1858, at Macedonia.
Clounch, Mrs. Baptized Apr. 14, 1860, at Macedonia.
Foltz, a child of Eli Foltz. Baptized June 6, 1860.
McBride, Wm. Greenland Bahnson, born Dec. 27, 1859, to John and Martha McBride.
    Baptized Aug. 17, 1860, at Macedonia.
Miller, infant daughter of Joseph Miller. Baptized July 30, 1862.
Nifong, youngest child of Adam Nifong. Baptized Aug. 3, 1862.
Nading, infant child of Matthew and Maria Nading. Baptized Oct. 18, 1863, at Pleasant
    Fork.

Marriage

Stoltz, Wm., married Oct. 25, 1866, to Elizabeth Spach.

Deaths and Burials

Vogler, Naoma, m.n. Eder. Funeral preached Mar. 25, 1857, at [Mt.] Olivet.
Mock, Adam, his daughter Belinda, and an infant son born since the death of the father.
    Funerals preached Mar. 29, 1857, at Midway.
Miller, Mary, a widow, age 87 years. Buried July 2, 1857, on old Mr. Woosely's place.
Miller, Mary, a widow, age 76 years. Buried July 9, 1857.
Hire, Rudolph. Died July 27, 1857.
Mock, Andrew. Funeral preached Oct. 18, 1857, at Midway.
Kimmel, widow of Sandford Kimmel. Funeral preached Nov. 14, 1857, at [Mt.] Olivet.
Essick, Alexander. Drowned Feb. 22, 1858, in Muddy Creek at his father's mill. [Friedberg
    Report: Alexander Essick, a young man 18 years old, in attempting to cross Muddy
    Creek in a boat at his father's mill, went over the dam and was drowned. His parents
    are worthy members of our Church at Muddy Creek. This young man was engaged in
    the mill, and some idlers lounging about there sent and procured some whisky, and
    persuaded him and his brother to drink with them. Some meal had to be taken across
    the creek in the boat, and he carried it over safe, but when attempting to return he
    pulled the wrong oar all the time and ran the boat over the dam, and even then he
    might have been saved had there been any one sober enough to render him assistance,
    for the boat at one time was within ten feet of the bank, where the water was but 3 feet
    deep. His brother was so drunk that he never found out what had happened till next

morning, and the others stood on the bank and hallo-ed, and never even tried to reach the poor fellow a pole. At last the boat drifted under the shoot, and he was knocked out and sunk to rise no more. A woman on the opposite bank witnessed the whole affair, and gave information of his death, or no one would have known what became of him. This was in the evening. His body was found on next day, and buried on Wednesday at Muddy Creek.]

Porter, a child of Ira Porter. Buried Mar. 26, 1858, at [Mt.] Olivet.

Daniels, Leminda, wife of Alexander Daniels and daughter of Robert Hampton, deceased. Buried June 7, 1858, on Ephraim Hampton's place, the family burying ground.

Lashmit, child of Franklin Lashmit. Buried July 7, 1858, at Bethel.

Ketner, a widow, m.n. Haines. Buried July 11, 1858, at Mt. Vernon.

Wood, Mrs., a aged lady who died the previous winter. Funeral preached Aug. 15, 1858, at Macedonia.

Disher child. Funeral preached Sept. 26, 1858, at Mt. Olivet.

Smith, Mrs. Elizabeth, mother of Br. John B. Smith. Funeral preached Nov. 14, 1858, at Gray's Chapel in Randolph County.

Hoffman, child of Phillip Hoffman. Buried Nov. 29, 1858, at Good Hope.

Shutt, a child of Solomon and Nancy Shutt. It died on Mar. 23, 1859, having lived nine hours. Buried Mar. 24, 1859.

Cecil, Elmina Lucretia, wife of Samuel Cecil. Died June 26, 1859. Buried June 28, 1859, at [Mt.] Olivet.

Kerner, two children of Joseph and Elmina [Malessa] Kerner. Funeral preached July 13, 1859, at Kernersville.

Evans, Julia, aged 8 years, daughter of Hendrick and Mary Evans. Buried Oct. 18, 1859, at Bethel meeting house.

Hodge, Albert Rights, infant son of Joseph Hodge and Jane m.n. Jefferies. Buried Nov. 22, 1859, at Macedonia.

Barnacastle, Francis. Buried Feb. 28, 1860, at Waughtown.

Yonce, John. Buried Mar. 12, 1860, at Good Hope.

Kerner, Elmina, wife of Israel Kerner of Kerner's Ville. Death reported Apr. 15, 1860.

Spach, Mary. Funeral preached June 10, 1860.

Harriet, servant of Christian Spach. Died June 14, 1860. Funeral preached June 24, 1860, at [Mt.] Olivet.

Hage, Mrs. Died June 27, 1860.

Hughes, Mary Elisabeth. Died Sept. 4, 1860.

Weasner, infant son of Jacob Weasner. Funeral preached Oct. 21, 1860, at Pleasant Fork.

White, William. Died suddenly Jan. 11, 1861, in Phillip Ripple's new ground where he had been at work. Age 23 years. Buried at Mt. Olivet.

Steward, Joseph, a Davidson Volunteer. Buried June 14, 1861, at Good Hope.

Hoffman, Susan m.n. Yonce, wife of Phillip Hoffman. Buried June 21, 1861, at Good Hope.

Hanes, Phillip. A volunteer, he died at Danville. Funeral preached Aug. 11, 1861, at Good Hope, where he was buried.

Hanes, Sarah, wife of David Hanes of Reedy Creek, sister of Francis Fishel. Died Jan. 4, 1862. Buried Jan. 6, 1862, at Good Hope.

Fishel, Andrew. Died Mar. 1, 1862, at Elizabeth City in Pasquotank County, where his remains were interred. Age 23 years, 8 months, and 5 days. Funeral preached Mar. 16, 1862, at Friedberg.

Zimmerman, Martin, a volunteer in Capt. Wheeler's company. Died Mar. 1, 1862, at Elizabeth City. Funeral preached May 11, 1862, at Friedberg.

Miller, infant daughter of Joseph Miller. Buried Aug. 4, 1862, at Midway.

Hage, George, and his infant son. Funeral preached Aug. 10, 1862, at Good Hope.

Byerly, Mrs. Funeral postponed from Aug. 24, 1862, at Sower's Church.

Brown, John. Wounded May 25, 1862, at the battle of Winchester, and died May 29. Funeral preached Oct. 5, 1862, beyond Clemmonsville.

Hage, Jacob. Funeral preached Nov. 9, 1862, at Friedberg.

Moss, Wesley, a deceased volunteer belonging to Capt. Atwood's Company. Funeral preached Nov. 23, 1862, at Bethel.

Scott, Alexander, husband of Nancy Scott. Died in the army. News received Jan. 5, 1863.

James, Amos Joseph and Allen Jacob, twin brothers. Amos died June 26, 1862, at Richmond from a wound, and Allen died Jan. 15, 1863, at Lynchburg from pneumonia. Funeral preached May 31, 1863, at Friedberg.

Null, Christopher Van. Died Aug. 20, 1862, near Orange Court House. Funeral preached June 7, 1863, at Hope.

Miller, Edwin, brother of Thomas Miller. Died Oct. 23, 1862, at Crenshaw Hospital, Liberty, Bedford County, Virginia. Funeral preached June 14, 1863, at Friedberg.

Snider, John Wesley. Died at Gettesburg from a shell wound. Funeral preached Oct. 18, 1863, at Pleasant Fork.

Fishel, David, Jr. Died Feb. 7, 1863, at Richmond. Funeral preached Nov. 29, 1863, at Friedberg.

Mock, Lewis. Wounded at the battle of Gettesburg and died July 10, 1863, in Pennsylvania. Funeral preached Dec. 13, 1863, at Friedberg.

Fishel, Charles. Wounded at the battle of Gettesburg and died Aug. 2, 1863, in Pennsylvania. Funeral preached Dec. 13, 1863, at Friedberg.

Frye, John Franklin. Funeral preached Dec. 19, 1863, at New Philadelphia.

Disher, Julia, wife of Henry Disher, jun. Funeral preached May 8, 1864, at [Mt.] Olivet.

Miller, Amos, son of Jesse Miller. Died spring 1864. He had been a prisoner of war at Point Lookout. Death reported May 23, 1864.

Stafford, Oscar, infant son of John Stafford. Died May 22, 1864, age 9 months. Buried May 23, 1864, at the old Stafford place.

Weaver, Alexander. Wounded Oct. 14, 1863, at Bristow Station and died the next day. Funeral preached July 10, 1864.

Snyder, John Wesley, born May 1, 1864, to Madison Snyder and Mary m.n. Disher. Died Aug. 9, 1864. Funeral preached Aug. 10, 1864, at Friedland.

Weasner, Samuel. Killed May 21, 1864, near Hanover Junction. Funeral preached Sept. 18, 1864.

Tesh, Solomon. Funeral preached May 14, 1865.

Fishel, Ephraim. Killed June 3, 1864, near Richmond. Funeral preached May 21, 1865.

Rominger, Reuben. Died Aug. 13, 1863, at Davids Island, N.Y. Funeral preached June 18, 1865, at Pleasant Fork.

Rominger, Priscilla. Buried July 21, 1865, at Friedland.

Zimmerman, a daughter of George Zimmerman. Funeral preached July 25, 1865, at Mt. Olivet. Age 10 years.

Pettacord, George. Funeral preached Sept. 3, 1865, at Hope.

Holder, Jacob. Funeral preached Sept. 3, 1865, beyond Clemmonsville.

Snyder, Daniel. Funeral preached Sept. 17, 1865, at Alexander Snyder's house.

Saunders, Miss Emma Delphine. Funeral preached Oct. 6, 1865, in the Methodist Church in Winston.

Spach, Lewis N. Funeral preached Oct. 8, 1865.

Beochle (Pickle), Samuel R. Funeral preached Oct. 8, 1865.

Bruer, Reuben. Funeral preached May 20, 1866, at Muddy Creek.

Veitch, Mrs. Rebecca. Funeral preached June 17, 1866, at Muddy Creek.

Ellis, Ezekiel. Funeral preached June 17, 1866, at Muddy Creek.

Swink, G. Died Aug. 29, 1866.

Hope Register, 1857-1866

Infant Baptisms

Seides, James Emmory, born Jan. 18, 1857, to George M. Seides and Abagail Frances m.n. Lashmet. Baptized Apr. 5, 1857.

Hauser, John Thomas, born Jan. 24, 1857, to Permanio Hauser and Maria m.n. Styars. Baptized Apr. 5, 1857.

Bevil, Eliza Rebecca, born Jan. 27, 1857, to Allen Wm. Bevil and Julia m.n. Rians. Baptized Apr. 5, 1857.

Seides, Elizabeth Jane, born June 4, 1857, to Christian David Seides and Alpha m.n. Vawter. Baptized July 5, 1857.

Jones, Sarah Corianna, born May 12, 1857, to Solomon Jones and Pamelia m.n. Styers. Baptized June 19, 1858.

Sides, Phebe Jane, born Apr. 26,1859, to George M. Sides and Abagail F. m.n. Lashmit. Baptized Aug. 7, 1859.

Libengood, Mary Elizabeth, born June 19, 1859, to John and Sophia Libengood. Baptized Sept. 4, 1859.

Ball, Martha Rebecca, born July 21, 1859, to William Ball and Rebecca m.n. Essick. Baptized Sept. 4, 1859.

Jones, Joseph Emmory, born May 24, 1860, to Solomon Jones and Pamelia m.n. Stiars. Baptized Aug. 25, 1860.

Sides, David Franklin, born Jan. 11, 1861, to George Michael Sides and Abagail Frances m.n. Lashmith. Baptized May 5, 1861.

Ball, John Emmory, born Mar. 7, 1861, to William Ball and Rebecca m.n. Essick. Baptized May 5, 1861.

Jones, Albert Lafayette, born Apr. 19, 1861, to Thomas Jones and Margaret Saloma m.n. Miller. Baptized Sept. 1, 1861.

Reich, Ambrose Jesse, born Jan. 22, 1862, to Benjamin Franklin Reich and Mary Catharine m.n. Sides. Baptized Apr. 6, 1862.

Jones, Viva Jane Rebecca, born Aug. 25, 1862, to Solomon Jones and Pamelia m.n. Stiars. Baptized Oct. 5, 1862.

Holder, John Francis, born Mar. 30, 1860, to Jacob and Elizabeth Holder. Baptized Oct. 5, 1862.

Hicks, Jane Isabella, born Aug. 23, 1862, to Daniel and Louisa Hicks. Baptized Oct. 5, 1862.

Thompson Roxana, born Sept. 13, 1861, to Giles and Mary Ann Thompson. Baptized Oct. 5, 1862.

Vogler, Minerva Ellen, born June 24, 1862, to Matthew and Nancy Vogler. Baptized Oct. 5, 1862.

Miller, William Francis, born Sept. 29, 1862, to William Miller and Jane m.n. Strupe. Baptized May 7, 1863, at Hope.

Seides, Rosina Isabella, born Mar. 12, 1863, to Christian David Seides and Alpha Monroe m.n. Vawter. Baptized May 7, 1863, at Hope.

Ball, Rhoda Caroline, born Feb. 4, 1863 [Friedberg Diary: 1862], to William Ball and Rebecca m.n. Essick. Baptized July 5, 1863, at Hope.

James, Emmory Franklin, born June 25, 1863, to Franklin James and Jane m.n. Spach. Baptized Dec. 6, 1863, at Hope.

Jones, Augusta Elizabeth, born Dec. 17, 1863, to Thomas Jones and Margaret m.n. Miller. Baptized July 3, 1864, at Hope.

Brown, Ida Bell, born Sept. 25, 1864, to John and Belinda Brown. Baptized Sept. 3, 1865.

Whit, Henderson, born Feb. 18, 1864, to Watson and Sarah Whit. Baptized Sept. 3, 1865.

Non-Member Baptism

James, Edward Luther, born Mar. 5, 1866, to Franklin and Jane James. Baptized June 3, 1866, at Hope.

Adult Baptisms

Ball, William, born Aug. 25, 1815. Baptized Feb. 6, 1859.

Peddycord, Amos, born Apr. 11, 1842, to DeOrsay Peddacord and Lucy m.n. Beeson. Baptized Feb. 6, 1859.

Holt, Washington, born to Ephraim Holt and Sarah m.n. Peddacord. Baptized Apr. 1, 1860.

Holt, Rebecca, born to Washington Holt and Nancy m.n. Painter. Baptized Apr. 1, 1860.

Marriages

Faw, Amos, married Dec. 16, 1858, to Rebecca Sides, born Sept. 22, 1840, to Christian David Sides and Alpha Monroe m.n. Vauter.

Michael, John, a widower, married June 14, 1859, to Rebecca Wommack m.n. Rominger.

Deaths and Burials

Styars, Maria Saloma m.n. Seides, born Nov. 26, 1798, in Friedland. Married July 1, 1819, to John Stiars. Died Sept. 30, 1857.

Seides, Rebecca, born Jan. 17, 1811, in Friedland. Died Jan. 14, 1858, at the house of her nephew Alexander Bevil in Liberty.

Eccles, Sarah Jane, born to Harrison M. Eccles and Christina m.n. Mock. Died Feb. 15, 1858.

Libengood, Jacob, born Dec. 23, 1795, in Rowan County. Married Mar. 20, 1823, to Elizabeth Seides. Died Mar. 23, 1858.

Holland, Frederick William, born Feb. 1, 1817, in Salem. Married Feb. 17, 1842, to Susan Hampton. Died Sept. 12, 1858.

Holland, Benjamin Franklin, born June 28, 1850, in Forsyth County, to Frederick William Holland and Susan m.n. Hampton. Died Oct. 14, 1858.

Holland, Cynthia Cornelia, born Dec. 27, 1843, to Frederick William Holland and Susan m.n. Hampton. Died Dec. 17, 1858.

Libengood, Phillippina Elizabeth m.n. Sides, born Oct. 10, 1796, near Friedland. Married Mar. 20, 1823, to Jacob Libengood. Died Apr. 13, 1859.

Fisher, Sarah m.n. Hamilton, born Feb. 20, 1784, in Stokes County. Married May 19, 1822, to George Fisher. Died June 25, 1859.

Cook, Jacob, born Jan. 12, 1814, in Davidson County. Died Oct. 13, 1859. He has left a wife and 8 children, and one died before him. On Wednesday morning, 12th, he fell from the hay mow in his barn (he had been packing fodder away). The fall injured his head, and although he was able to go into the house without assistance and gave directions to send for a physician, in an hour after he fell he became insensible, and remained so till he died on Thursday night about 10 minutes before 12 o'clock. He was a man greatly esteemed by his neighbors, and a worthy church member.

Jones, Joseph Emmory, born May 24, 1860, to Solomon Jones and Pamelia m.n. Stiars. Died Jan. 6, 1861.

Pettacord, De Orsay, born Sept. 12, 1809. Died Jan. 16, 1862.

Eccles [Friedberg Diary: Susan Pauline, daughter of Harrison Eccles. Died Oct. 11, 1862, age 8 years, 29 days. Buried Oct. 12, 1862, at Hope. Funeral preached July 5, 1863, at Hope.]

Lowder, Phebe Ann, born Apr. 17, 1846, near Friedland, to Samuel Lowder and Catharine m.n. Snyder. Died Feb. 10, 1863.

Reich, Benjamine Franklin, born May 17, 1833, in Stokes County. Died Sept. 3, 1863. [Salem Diary: He had returned from the army in May last, with symptoms of dropsy, of which disease he died. In 1859 or 1860 he attended lectures (at Salem) preparatory to confirmation and applied for admission as a communicant, but was advised to wait for a time till some business settlement which he had in obligation at the time should be disposed of. The present miserable war had a very disheartening effect on him. He entered the army very unwillingly as a conscript. His naturally strong constitution was soon broken down, and he died in the prime of life leaving a widow and one child. His remains were interred at Hope, of which congregation his wife (a daughter of Br. Christian Sides) is a member.]

Boner, Anna Margaret m.n. Gerber, born June 1, 1793, in Stokes County. Died Oct. 11, 1863.

Null, Catharine m.n. Buttner, born Dec. 29, 1798. Married Jan. 26, 1823, to Frederick Null. Died Feb. 12, 1864.

Holt, Nancy m.n. Painter, born Jan. 7, 1817. Married to Washington Holt. Died Dec. 3, 1864.

Null, Frederick. Married to Catharine m.n. Buttner. Died Dec. 25, 1864. [Friedberg Diary: Age 87 years, 8 mos., and 16 days.] For 36 years Brother and Sister Null were Stewards of the Hope Congregation and served with fidelity and faithfulness.

Eccles, Christina m.n. Mock, born Jan. 11, 1816, in Davidson County. Married to Harrison Eccles. Died Apr. 26, 1866.

Friedland Register, 1857-1866

[The original Friedland Register No. 2 was lost many years ago. The following records were compiled from several original sources: register extracts for 1859 and 1860, the Friedland Register begun by C. L. Rights in 1889 (with earlier material added), the Friedland Diary and Reports to Ministers Conference, the (New) Philadelphia Diary and Reports, the Kernersville Diary and Reports, and the Private Diary of R. P. Leinbach. The death register made use also of a listing of gravestone inscriptions copied in 1936 by William J. Hall.]

Infant Baptisms

Schneider, Ann Elvira Louisa, born to Alexr. and Ann Mary Schneider. Baptized May 10, 1857.

Kerner, Marilla Eliza, born Mar. 3, 1857, to Israel and Elmina Kerner. Baptized June 21, 1857.

Kinneman, Philip Louis Emmanuel, born to Andrew and Elizabeth Kinneman. Baptized Nov. 29, 1857.

Kerner, Nancy Ella, born to Elias Kerner and Partha m.n. Dicks. Baptized July 13, 1859.

Kerner, Robah Bascombe, born to Elias Kerner and Partha m.n. Dicks. Baptized July 13, 1859.

Weavil, Medora Paulina, born to Walter Weavil and Sarah m.n. Phillips. Baptized July 17, 1859.

Ried, Christian Frederic, born Feb. 1, 1859, to Christian Reid and Elizabeth m.n. Billeter. Baptized Jan. 15, 1860.

Gibbins, William Leander, born Apr. 20, 1860, to William Gibbins and Partha [Martha] m.n. Williard. Baptized June 10, 1860.

Fetter, Elizabeth Adelia, born Oct. 7, 1859, to William Fetter and Paulina m.n. Shore (nonmembers). Baptized Feb. 19, 1860.

Kinneman, a daughter of Andrew and Elizabeth Kinneman. Baptized Mar. 3, 1861.

Steward, two children of John Steward and Sarah m.n. Sapp. Baptized May 12, 1861.

Steward, infant son of John Steward and Sarah m.n. Sapp. Baptized Aug. 31, 1862.

Reed, infant daughter of C. Emanuel Reed and Nancy m.n. Louder. Baptized Jan. 4, 1863.

Steward, infant daughter of Jacob Wesley and Phebe Malinda Steward. Baptized June 7, 1863.

Kerner, infant daughter of Nathaniel M. Kerner and Martha E. m.n. Stockton. Baptized July 19, 1863.

Steward, a child of J. Steward. Baptized Apr. 9, 1865.

Reed, infant child of Em. Reed. Baptized May 28, 1865.

Gibbins, infant child of W. Gibbins. Baptized May 28, 1865.

Steward, a child of John Steward. Baptized May 13, 1866.

Steward, a child of Jacob Steward. Baptized May 13, 1866.

Kerner, a child of Phillip Kerner. Baptized June 10, 1866.

Weavil, a child of Walter Weavil. Baptized Sept 9, 1866.

Adult Baptisms

Sill, Moses, age 46. Baptized Jan. 9, 1859.

Stewart, Phebe Malinda m.n. Sell. Baptized Jan. 19, 1862.

Johnson, Henry Wesley. Baptized Feb. 2, 1862.

Weavel, Malinda Susanna. Baptized Feb. 2, 1862.

Weavel, Emily Adaline. Baptized Feb. 2, 1862.

Smith, Maria Leucretia. Baptized Sept. 16, 1866, at Friedland.

Hepler, Lousena Ellen. Baptized Sept. 16, 1866, at Friedland.

Motsinger, Louisa. Baptized Sept. 16, 1866, at Friedland.

Piccard, Martha Jane. Baptized Sept. 16, 1866, at Friedland.

Pitts, Martha Jane. Baptized Sept. 16, 1866, at Friedland.

Weavil, William Andrew. Baptized Sept. 16, 1866, at Friedland.

Smith, Eli. Baptized Sept. 16, 1866, at Friedland.

Porter, Thomas Alexander. Baptized Sept. 16, 1866, at Friedland.

Weavil, William Albert. Baptized Sept. 16, 1866, at Friedland.

Weavil, Walter. Baptized Sept. 16, 1866, at Friedland.

Marriages

Schneider, Charles F., married May 24, 1857, to Phoebe Schneider.

Reid, Samuel, married Jan. 18, 1866, to Elizabeth Crouch.

Hine, J. Nelson, married Apr. 12, 1866, to M. Elizabeth Ried, at the Friedland parsonage.

Steward, Moses G., married Aug. 12, 1866, to Emily Mathews.

Deaths and Burials

Swaim, Polly, born June 4, 1784. Died Apr. 23, 1857.

Sides, Elisabeth. One of our old members. Buried May 7, 1857.

Reed, Alice, born May 11, 1857. Died May 26, 1857.

Reed, Lydia Caroline, born Mar. 8, 1854. Died June 6, 1867.

Weavil, Phebe, born June 14, 1850. Died Aug. 8, 1857.

Nissen, Lewis Henry, born Apr. 5, 1851. Died Aug. 24, 1857.

Weavil, infant daughter of Eli and Katharine Weavel. (No dates on stone.)

Hine, infant daughter of Joseph and Elizabeth Hine. (No dates on stone.)

Teague, W. F., born and died Oct. 5, 1857.

Crumpler, Erastus A., born Sept. 30, 1857, to James Crumpler and wife. Died Oct. 20, 1857.

Girl, 1850-1857.

Smith, Beatus. Died 1858.

Hine, Joseph L., born Nov. 5, 1824, at Friedland. Died July 25, 1858. He was thrown from a buggy and so badly injured that he died in a few hours. Formerly connected with Friedland congregation, later with Oldside Baptists.

Girl, 1852-1859.

Huff, Beatus, born and died Jan. 22, 1859.

Hine, Margaret Louisa, born Apr. 30, 1859. Died June 18, 1859.

Ried, Elisabeth m.n. Vogler, born Apr. 8, 1791. Married to Charles Ried. Died Oct. 22, 1859.

Reid, Mary Octavia, born June 6, 1856, to Harrison Reed. Died Dec. 20, 1859.

Hiatt, Anne, born Nov. 1859, to Charles Hiatt and wife (non-members). Died Jan. 2, 1860.

Smith, Hannah Loretta, born Mar. 12, 1853, to John Smith and wife. Died Feb. 11, 1860.

Smith, Martha Elizabeth, born 1858. Died 1860.

Swim, Parmenio, born Jan. 19, 1840, to John Swim and Salome m.n. Lagenauer. Died Feb. 27, 1860.

Crumpler, Leander Lewis, born Nov. 25, 1859, to James Crumpler and Louisa m.n. Steward (non-members). Died June 16, 1860.

Voss, James (non-member). Died Sept. 1, 1860, of a wound inflicted by Moses Smith.

Weavil, Eli Madison (non-member), born Dec. 12, 1853, to Eli Weavil and Catharine m.n. Smith. Died Oct. 12, 1860.

Schneider, Philip, born June 17, 1786, to Cornelius Schneider and wife. Married Aug. 26, 1809, to Catharine Hummel. Died Oct. 31, 1860.

Weavil, Phalba, an unmarried woman, her infant having been born the preceding day. Died Apr. 11, 1861.

Chamelin, Eli E., born Sept. 12, 1859, to J. H. and P. J. Chamelin. Died June 1, 1861.

McCuiston, Charles Terry, born to R. D. and L. McCuiston. Died July 3, 1861.

Reid, infant daughter of Harrison and Ernestina Reid. Funeral sermon preached July 21, 1861.

Hine, Mary D., born Apr. 4, 1859. Died Dec. 5, 1861.

Crumpler, Charles L., born Mar. 2, 1861. Died Sept. 18, 1861.

Weavil, Fabe Elizabeth, daughter of Phalba Weavel. Funeral preached Nov. 10, 1861.

Reed, Elizabeth m.n. Lagenauer, born Jan. 22, 1782, at Friedland. Married (1) in 1806 to Jacob Rothrock (died 1807). Married (2) Dec. 23, 1813, to Joh. Samuel Ried. Died Nov. 22, 1861.

Stafford, Martha Jane, born May 9, 1860. Died Jan. 16, 1862.

Chamelin, Phebe E., born Sept. 8, 1860, to J.H. and P.J. Chamelin. Died June 16, 1862.

Teague, R. C., born May 30, 1862. Died July 23, 1862.

Teague, R. E., born May 30, 1862. Died Aug. 4, 1862.

Smith, Eli, born Nov. 7, 1855. Died Sept. 1, 1862.

Gibbins, John Christian, born Jan. 18, 1845, to Wm. Gibbins and Martha E. m.n. Williard. Died Sept. 24, 1862.

Kinnamon, Andrew, born July 8, 1805. Died Nov. 17, 1862.

Phillips, Catharine m.n. Sides, born May 27, 1782. Died Nov. 28, 1862.

Steward, Laura. Died Aug. 19, 1863.

Swaim, Rachel, born July 19, 1845. Died Oct. 3, 1863.

Swaim, John. Married to Sally Swim. Died Dec. 1863. [Friedland Report: He died unexpectedly, supposedly from the effects of a snake bite last summer. Buried without any service.]

Gibbins, Eli M., born Jan. 24, 1864, to William Gibbins and wife. Died Mar. 6, 1864.

Williard, Laura C., born Dec. 12, 1856, to Alvereus Williard and wife. Died May 18, 1864.

Melton, Mrs., buried May 29, 1864.

Petticoard, Mrs. Grazella. Buried June 7, 1864.

Ried, Penelope, born 1862 to Emmanuel Ried and wife. Buried June 7, 1864.

Chamelin, Anderson L., born Oct. 23, 1862, to John H. Chamblin and wife (nonmembers). Died June 14, 1864.

Reed, Mary Lauretta, born Mar. 10, 1848, to Christian Ried and Elisabeth m.n. Billeter. Died July 19, 1864.

Williard, William P. Born and died in 1864.

Ried, Penelope, born 1862, to Emmanuel Ried and wife. Died 1864.

Kinnamon, Mary E., born Apr. 5, 1846. Died Jan. 22, 1865.

Kinnemon, Elisabeth Barbara m.n. Reed, born Sept. 25, 1823. Married to Andrew Kinnemon. Died Feb. 25, 1865.

Huff, David, born Apr. 5, 1833. Died Mar. 16, 1865. [Friedland Report: He was shot by members of the 1st N.C. Battalion. On July 9, 1865, a funeral sermon was preached by Rev. Mr. Clark, Chaplain of the 10th Ohio Cavalry.]

Kinnamon, Phebe M., born Aug. 30, 1849, to Andrew and Elizabeth Kinnamon. Died Mar. 17, 1865.

Swim, John L. Funeral preached May 28, 1865.

Crumpler, Maggie L., born Sept. 19, 1864. Died July 3, 1865.

Rominger, Priscilla, wife of Amos Rominger. Buried July 21, 1865.

Weavil, Miss Mary. Funeral preached Aug. 13, 1865.

Weavil, John. Died Sept. 9, 1865.

Cook, Philip. Killed at the battle of Spottsylvania Courthouse. Funeral preached Sept. 10, 1865.

Smith, David, born July 28, 1820. Married to Caroline Swaim. Died Nov. 14, 1865.

Rothrock, Frank, 1862-1865.

Nicholson, two children. Funeral preached May 6, 1866.

Girl, July 1865-June 1866.
Ried, Phebe R., born Oct. 27, 1864, to E. Reed and wife. Died June 31, 1866.
Swaim, Andrew J., born Sept. 21, 1848. Died Sept. 2, 1866.

Friedland Reports Entries, 1857-1866

[Church Register material that was recorded only in the Friedland Reports. The following is the entirety of the material.]

Baptisms

Louder, Jonathan. Baptized Oct. 7, 1866, at Hope.
Boner, Sarah Jane. Baptized Oct. 7, 1866, at Hope.
Boner, Wesley. Baptized Oct. 7, 1866, at Hope.

Deaths and Burials

Brendle, a child of James Brendle. Funeral preached Sept. 22, 1866, at the Waughtown church.

R. P. Leinbach Diary Entries, 1857-1866

[Church Register material that was recorded only in the Private Diary of R. P. Leinbach. The following is the entirety of the Diary material.]

Baptisms

Shore, a child of Paulina Shore. Baptized Feb. 19, 1860, at the Factory in Salem.
Brown, Wm. Francis Cecil, born to Mrs. Malinda Brown. Baptized Oct. 4, 1863, at Macedonia.

Deaths and Burials

Hart, Wm. Funeral preached Oct. 16, 1861, at Union Hill Baptist Church. His body had been brot from Manassas.
Parish, Wm. Funeral preached Dec. 15, 1861, at Muddy Creek. He was the husband of Br. Reuben Bruer's daughter. He enlisted as a soldier, and went to Manassas, where he subsequently died.
Weaver, wife of Wm. Weaver. Buried May 22, 1862.
Hall, two colored children of Jane and Augustus Hall. [Macedonia Report: Funeral preached Aug. 10, 1862.]
Cooper, an elderly woman between 85 and 90 years of age. Buried Oct. 30, 1862, at Muddy Creek.
Williams, Alex. Killed near Richmond. Funeral preached Nov. 2, 1862.
Douthit, Ava. Died Mar. 20, 1863. Funeral preached Mar. 22, 1863, at Mr. Douthit's.
Daniels, daughter of Alex Daniels, age 7 years. Buried Apr. 17, 1863.
Thompson, Gills. Funeral preached July 19, 1863, [Macedonia Report: at Muddy Creek].
Yancey [Yonce?], W. L. Learned Aug. 2, 1863, of his death.
Peck, Charles. Died in 1861 at Manasses. Funeral preached Aug. 16, 1863, at Muddy Creek.
Eccles, Henry. Funeral preached Sept. 20, 1863, at Clemmonsville.
Davis, a child of Evan Davis. Died June 1862. Funeral preached Oct. 18, 1863, at Macedonia.
Leinbach, Emanuel. Funeral preached Dec. 6, 1863, at Bethlehem Methodist Church in Davie County.

Doty, Isaac. Slain in the battle of Sharpsburg Sept. 17, 1862. [Friedland Report: he joined the church at Muddy Creek in Br. Hagen's time in 1853.] Funeral preached Feb. 21, 1864, at Muddy Creek.

Sheek, a child of Richmond Sheek. Buried Apr. 13, 1864, at Macedonia.

Parish, a child of Angelina Parish. Funeral preached May 15, 1864, at Muddy Creek.

Covis [James], Harrison. Buried June 18, 1864.

Perry, Wm. Slain in battle. Funeral preached Oct. 2, 1864, at Macedonia.

Two children of Rachel, servant of D. Sheek. Funeral preached Nov. 6, 1864, at Macedonia.

Stevens, an elderly man. Funeral preached Jan. 1, 1865, at Macedonia.

Riddle, Emily Ellen, born June 18, 1860, to Emerson and Jane Riddle. Died Nov. 12, 1864. Funeral preached Feb. 5, 1865, at Macedonia.

Miller, Calvin, infant son of Wiley Miller, about 4 years old. Funeral preached Aug. 20, 1865, at Muddy Creek.

Eccles, James. Funeral preached Oct. 15, 1865.

Macedonia Register, 1857-1866

Baptisms

Sheek, Sarah Elizabeth, born Dec. 29, 1853, to Daniel Sheek and Anfield m.n. Berryman. Baptized June 12, 1857.

Sheek, Mary Francis, born to Richmond Sheek and Emeline m.n. Riddle. Baptized June 12, 1857.

Boner, Lisetta Elizabeth, born to William Boner and Ginsey m.n. Longworth. Baptized June 12, 1857.

Boner, Edwin, born to William Boner and Ginsey m.n. Longworth. Baptized June 12, 1857.

McBride, Amanda Ardelia, born to Leonard McBride and Nancy m.n. Armsworthy. Baptized June 12, 1857.

Smith, Jonathan Wesley, born to John W. Smith and Sarah m.n. Bachiem. Baptized June 12, 1857.

Sheek, Rachel Amanda Jane, born to Ransom Douthit and Rachel Sheek, col. Baptized June 12, 1857.

McBride, Louisa Florida, born to John McBride and Margaret m.n. Kinneman. Baptized Aug. 6, 1858.

Sheek, Albert Rights, born May 6, 1858, to Richmond and Emeline Sheek. Baptized Aug. 6, 1858.

Sheek, Eliza Jane, born Aug. 1857 to Daniel Sheek and Anfield m.n. Berryman. Baptized Aug. 6, 1858.

Jeffries, Emily Jeffries, born to Jacob Jeffries and Sarah m.n. Danner. Baptized Aug. 6, 1858.

Shadrick, Theodore Rights, born to David and Minerva Shadrick. Baptized June 7, 1859.

Sheek, Martha Jane, born May 28, 1861, to Richmond Sheek and Emeline m.n. Riddle. Baptized Feb. 9, 1862

Lee, Eleanora Mabel, born July 5, 1862, to Henry Lee and Elizabeth m.n. Fry. Baptized [blank].

Lee, Addie Louisa, born Dec. 17, 1863, to Henry Lee and Elizabeth m.n. Fry. Baptized July 3, 1864.

Lee, William Henry Caswel, born Feb. 10, 1866, to Henry Lee and Elizabeth m.n. Fry. Baptized July 1, 1866, at Macedonia.

Adult Baptisms

Faircloth, Elizabeth. Baptized Oct. 7, 1866.

Fry, Mary. Baptized Oct. 7, 1866.
Dunn, Dorcas. Baptized Oct. 7, 1866.
Wood, Emily Jane. Baptized Oct. 7, 1866.
Baton, Sarah Elizabeth. Baptized Oct. 7, 1866.
Bullard, Eliza. Baptized Oct. 7, 1866.

Marriage

Boner, Joseph Wesley, born to Joseph and Anne Boner, married Sept. 12, 1861, to Sarah Jane Louder, born to Samuel Louder and Jane m.n. Snyder.

Deaths and Burials

Shiek, Eliza Jane, born Aug. 3, 1857, to Daniel Shiek and Anfield m.n. Berryman. Died Sept. 3, 1861.

Hall, Henry Francis, born Apr. 7, 1842, to John Hall and Mary m.n. Stockberger. Died Sept. 6, 1861. He had enlisted and joined the army, and whilst encamped at Manassas was seized with the typhoid fever, which carried him off in twelve days. His body was subsequently bro't home, and interred at Macedonia Oct. 29, 1861.

Miller, Lucinda Bell, born Mar. 18, 1858, to Jonathan Miller and Mary m.n. Wood. Died Feb. 4, 1863. She is believed to have died from effects of poison.

Miller, Edward Wiseman, born Aug. 12, 1855, to Jonathan Miller and Mary m.n. Wood. Died Feb. 6, 1863. Also supposed to have been poisoned.

Miller, Mary m.n. Wood, born Feb. 20, 1829. Married Aug. 8, 1849, to Jonathan Miller. Died Feb. 11, 1863. She as well as her children are believed to have died from the effects of poison, administered, as was supposed, by the black woman.

McBride, Nancy Margaret m.n. Kinnick, born Dec. 27, 1829. Married to John McBride. Died Feb. 13, 1863. She is said to have died of the same disease as Sr. Miller and her children.

Miller, Nancy Amanda, born May 10, 1850, to Jonathan Miller and Mary m.n. Wood. Died Feb. 27, 1863. She was the last victim of that terrible disease which carried off the above named persons. From the fact that the disease corresponded perfectly with the symptoms laid down in medical works under the head of Belladonna, it is supposed that they were poisoned by a preparation of its roots, etc.

Hall, Ferdinand Eugene, born July 16, 1840, to John and Mary Hall. Died May 3, 1863. Slain in the battle at Chancellorsville. Whilst charging a battery, he received a death shot from a ball, which instantly terminated his earthly career. His body was subsequently bro't home and interred at Macedonia.

Hall, Mary m.n. Stockburger, born May 7, 1818. Married Oct. 8, 1839, to John Hall. Died Sept. 28, 1863.

Jones, Henry. [Friedland Report: He was slain at Upperville in the Pennsylvania campaign. Funeral preached Jan. 3, 1864.]

Cope, Andrew Jackson, born July 18, 1825. Died Dec. 4, 1863. Died in the hospital at Wilmington. He left home Sept. 28th to join the army. Having always enjoyed the full protection of the old government, he saw no necessity of a new one, and was unwilling to fight for the establishment. He was, however, "coerced" into measures, but was called to a better land where "the wicked cease from troubling, and the weary are at rest."

Claunch, Sarah, born Jan. 10, 1823. [Friedberg Diary: Buried Apr. 10, 1866.]

Smith, Sarah P., born Mar. 19, 1821. Married to John W. Smith. Died Sept. 25, 1865.

Coly, Sarah m.n. Smith, born July 25, 1846. Married to James Coly. Died Oct. 17, 1866. Like her mother, she died of consumption after about 6 months illness.

New Philadelphia Register, 1857-1866

Infant and Adult Baptisms

Transou, Rebecca Laura Ann, born Feb. 25, 1857, to Carlos Transou and Amanda m.n. Kettner. Baptized Aug. 13, 1857.

Creter, Miranda Victoria, born May 13, 1857, to Levi Jacob Creter and Sarah Susannah m.n. Ketner. Baptized Aug. 13, 1857.

Transou, Isabel Dundena, born Dec. 27, 1857, to Timothy Transou and Sarah m.n. Miller. Baptized Feb. 28, 1858.

Burkard, Henry Samuel, born Mar. 18, 1858, to Frederick Burkard and Alina m.n. Oehman. Baptized May 30, 1858.

Fletcher, John Henry, born Feb. 27, 1858, to Andrew Fletcher and Charlotte m.n. Rhines. Baptized July 25, 1858.

Fletcher, James Calvin, born Feb. 27, 1858, to Andrew Fletcher and Charlotte m.n. Rhines. Baptized July 25, 1858.

Norman, Adelaide Antoinette, born Feb. 4, 1858, to Meredith Norman and Belinda m.n. Miller. Baptized July 25, 1858.

Transou, William Joseph, born Aug. 9, 1858, to Carlos Transou and Emanda m.n. Ketner. Baptized June 19, 1859.

Crater, Amos Martin, born May 6, 1859, to Levi Crater and Sarah m.n. Ketner. Baptized June 19, 1859.

Ciger [Kiger], EUJane [Eugene] Francis, born May 30, 1859, to Armsted Ciger and Sarah m.n. Norman. Baptized July 10, 1859.

Rominger, Flora Anna Rebecca, born June 15, 1859, to James and Lydia Paulina Rominger. Baptized Aug. 13, 1859.

Transou, Emma Virginia, born Dec. 25, 1859, to Timothy Transou and Sarah m.n. Miller. Baptized Mar. 11, 1860.

Norman, Alace Ellen, born June 27, 1859, to Meradith Norman and Belinda m.n. Miller. Baptized Mar. 11, 1860.

Fletcher, Nancy Sofia, born May 4, 1861, to Andrew Fletcher and Charlotta m.n. Rhines. Baptized July 28, 1861.

Crater, Elen Sophia, born July 5, 1861, to Levi Crater and Sarah m.n. Ketner. Baptized Aug. 11, 1861.

Spach, Franklin Alexander, born Mar. 25, 1861, to Alexander Spach and Charlotte m.n. Moss. Baptized Aug. 25, 1861.

Kiger, John Cicero, born Aug. 5, 1861, to Armsted Kiger and Sarah m.n. Norman. Baptized Dec. 1, 1861.

Crater, Delia Catharine, born Dec. 27, 1861, to Allen Crater and Anna m.n. Ketner. Baptized Feb. 9, 1862.

Bevil, William Alen, born to Wm. Alen Bevil and Julia Elizabeth m.n. Rhins. Baptized May 18, 1862.

Jones, Marthaann Elizabeth, born Mar. 22, 1862, to Calvin Theodore Jones and Maryann m.n. Frye. Baptized July 13, 1862.

Transou, John Rufus, born July 14, 1862, to Timothy Transou and Sarah m.n. Miller. Baptized Oct. 19, 1862.

Crater, Francis Levi, born Oct. 3, 1862, to Levi Crater and Sarah m.n. Ketner. Baptized Nov. 16, 1862.

Lee, Eleanor Mabel, born July 5, 1862, to Henry Jackson Lee and Elizabeth June m.n. Frye. Baptized Dec. 28, 1862.

Fletcher, Phebe Jane, born Aug. 6, 1862, to Andrew Fletcher and Charlotta m.n. Rhines. Baptized Aug. 9, 1863.

Jane Eliza, born 1864 to a negro woman belonging to Br. Martin Rominger. Baptized Aug. 28, 1864.

Crater, Lisetta Maria, born Nov. 26, 1864, to Allan Crater and Anna m.n. Ketner. Baptized Jan. 8, 1865. [Philadelphia Diary: The father was not present, having been ordered back to the army some weeks since, altho quite disabled from his wounds.]

Transou, Henry Calvin, born Jan. 3, 1862, to Carlos Transou and Amanda m.n. Ketner. Baptized Sept. 17, 1865.

Transou, Maria Catharine, born Mar. 5, 1860, to Carlos Transou and Amanda m.n. Ketner. Baptized Sept. 17, 1865.

Spach, Rufus Arminius, born Nov. 5, 1865, to Thomas Spach and Melvina m.n. Lash. Baptized Mar. 4, 1866.

Spach, Walter Thomas, born Nov. 5, 1865, to Thomas Spach and Melvina m.n. Lash. Baptized Mar. 4, 1866.

Rominger, Harriet Elmira, born Feb. 10, 1866, to Martin Rominger and Emma [Emily] m.n. Davis. Baptized Apr. 15, 1866.

Crater, Mary Cornelia, born Mar. 9, 1866, to Allan Crater and Anna m.n. Ketner. Baptized Apr. 29, 1866.

Crater, Lewis Luther, born July 27, 1866, to Reuben Crater and m.n. Alpha Jane m.n. Reich. Baptized Sept. 2, 1866.

Lashmet, Mary Maria, born May 31, 1866, to John Lashmet and Paulina Henrietta m.n. Transou. Baptized Sept. 2, 1866.

Ketner, Joseph Francis, born May 31, 1844, to Sandford Ketner and wife. Baptized Oct. 14, 1866.

Rominger, Chloe Elizabeth, born Feb. 14, 1850, to David Rominger and wife. Baptized Oct. 14, 1866.

Rominger, Lucy Emeline, born Nov. 23, 1851, to David Rominger and wife. Baptized Oct. 14, 1866.

Chitty, Helen Cornelia, born July 26, 1866, to Henry Chitty and Laura m.n. Transou. Baptized Nov. 10, 1866.

Marriages

Rominger, Martin, married Jan. 31, 1865, to Emily J. Davis.

Crater, Reuben J., born to Br. and Sr. John Crater, married June 29, 1865, to Alpha J. Reich, born to Daniel Reich.

Chitty, Henry N., born to Br. and Sr. Traugott Chitty, married Nov. 30, 1865, to Laura Elisabeth Transou, born to Br. and Sr. Timothy Transou.

Deaths and Burials

Transou, Cornelia, born Feb. 16, 1854, to Carlos Transou and Amanda m.n. Kettner. Died July 5, 1857.

Bevel, Ellen Magdalen, born July 21, 1856, at Winston, to Christian Alexander Bevel and Sarah Catherine m.n. Miller. Died Dec. 9, 1857.

Waterson, John, born Jan. 13, 1780, Londonderry, Ireland. Died Dec. 5, 1858.

Rominger, Rebecca m.n. Crater, born Apr. 6, 1789. Married to John Martin Rominger. Died June 19, 1862.

Rominger, James Mansom, born Feb. 7, 1829, to John Martin Rominger and Rebecca m.n. Crater. Died Feb. 12, 1863. [Philadelphia Report: He was a conscript, and was brought home from a hospital in Virginia in a distressed condition.]

Crater, Levi, born to John Crater and Catharine m.n. Essig. Died Jan. 29, 1864.

Frye, Thomas, born June 23, 1802, in Rowan County, to George and Elizabeth Frye. Married Oct. 1, 1833, to Louisa Elizabeth Brinkley. Died Mar. 31, 1864.

Crater, Uriah, born Jan. 7, 1865.

Jones, a son born to Thomas Jones and Margaret m.n. Miller.

Miller, Beatus, born to Br. Webster and Jane Miller. Lived a few days.

[The above three entries constitute a single penciled burial entry dated Jan. 31, 1865.]

Crater, John Leonard, born Oct. 11, 1855, in Forsyth County, to Levi Crater and Sarah m.n. Ketner. Died Mar. 16, 1865.

Philadelphia Diary Entries, 1857-1866

[Church Register material that was recorded only in the (New) Philadelphia Diary and Reports. The following is the entirety of the material.]

Baptisms

Kiger, Armsted, a married man. Baptized Nov. 28, 1858, at Philadelphia.

Marshall, John. Baptized Nov. 28, 1858, at Philadelphia.

Kiger, Sarah, a married woman. Baptized Nov. 28, 1858, at Philadelphia.

Jones, Temperance. Baptized Nov. 28, 1858, at Philadelphia.

Jones, Jane. Baptized Nov. 28, 1858, at Philadelphia.

Jones, Calvin T. Baptized Mar. 27, 1859, at Philadelphia.

Willyard, John A. Baptized May 22, 1859, at Philadelphia.

Willyard, Mahala C. Baptized May 22, 1859, at Philadelphia.

Star, Jonas Lafayette. Baptized Dec. 14, 1862, at Philadelphia.

Morgan, Goerge Washing. Baptized Dec. 14, 1862, at Philadelphia.

Rominger, Sarahann. Baptized Dec. 14, 1862, at Philadelphia.

Jones, Lutecia. Baptized Dec. 14, 1862, at Philadelphia.

Jones, Mary Elizabeth. Baptized Dec. 14, 1862, at Philadelphia.

Marriage

Riddle, Thos. C., married Dec. 12, 1861, to Sophia Regina Butner.

Deaths and Burials

Riddle, Mrs. Funeral preached Mar. 8[?], 1860, at Macedonia.

Norman. A young man. Died Apr. 20, 1860. Funeral preached Apr. 21, 1860, at Sharon.

Miller. An old man. Died Apr. 26, 1860. Buried Apr. 27, 1860, at Shiloh.

Olaver, three youths, children of Israel Olaver. Funeral preached Sept. 16, 1860, at Muddy Creek.

Woosley, infant son of William Woosley. Buried Oct. 15, 1860.

Slater, Mr. Buried May 15, 1861.

Alspaugh, a female member of the Methodist Episcopal Church, aged 92 years. Buried July 10, 1862.

Reich, John, son of Daniel Reich and a volunteer. Buried Jan. 28, 1863.

Vogler, two young men who died in the army. Funeral preached May 31, 1863.

Slater, two men, one of which was killed at Fredericksburg and the other died in the hospital. Funeral preached June 14, 1863.

Transou, Carlos. He died of disease in Virginia February 1863 whilst with the army, age 30. Funeral preached May 14, 1865, at Philadelphia.

Bevil, a man who died during the war [Bethania Diary: of a wound received at or near Winchester, Virginia]. Funeral preached Oct. 8, 1865, at Philadelphia.

INDEX

Pratt, Johanna Elisabeth, m.n. Butner, 6382
Pratt, William Golson, 6248, 6249, 6287, 6337, 6376, 6377, 6459
Pratt, Sr. William Golson. *See* Pratt, Johanna Elisabeth, m.n. Butner
Prayer meetings: at African Church in Salem, 6523, 6524, 6527, 6575, 6633, 6634, 6635; at Bethabara, 6336-37; at Bethania, 6292; for females, 6448; at Friedberg, 6254, 6296; at Friedland, 6346, 6608, 6663; at Macedonia, 6344; at Salem Congregation, 6262, 6268, 6269, 6274, 6302, 6304, 6305, 6306, 6308, 6309, 6310, 6337, 6351, 6360, 6394, 6399, 6401, 6444, 6567, 6570, 6630, 6631; week of, 6359, 6376, 6396, 6421, 6626, 6638
Prayer, fasting, humiliation, days of, 6394, 6396, 6397, 6400, 6409, 6411, 6421, 6423, 6424, 6428, 6429, 6430, 6432, 6438, 6439, 6443, 6458, 6459, 6473, 6474, 6493, 6495, 6498, 6514, 6519, 6537, 6541, 6558, 6561, 6570, 6588, 6591, 6605. *See also* Thanksgiving, days of
Presbyterian church in Winston, 6373, 6412, 6515, 6524
Presbyterians, 6230, 6376, 6511
Presbyters, consecration of, 6381, 6386, 6389, 6391
Prisoners of war, 6495, 6511, 6518-19, 6541, 6555, 6566, 6597, 6600-1
Prohibition, 6625, 6628
Property. *See* Salem Congregation: land and lots owned by
Proprietor (Emil Adolphus de Schweinitz), 6212, 6213, 6237, 6490, 6528. *See also* Administrator
Protracted meetings (revivals), 6255, 6291, 6300, 6309, 6380, 6381, 6426, 6430, 6476, 6594, 6599, 6608, 6621, 6656-57, 6660, 6661, 6666. *See also* Camp meetings
Provincial (Wachovia) Administration (Sustentation), 6284, 6479; annual accounts: *1857-58*, 6286; *1857-59*, 6332; *1859-60*, 6375; *1860-61*, 6420; *1861-62*, 6456; *1862-63*, 6492; *1863-64*, 6535; *1864-65*, 6586; *1865-66*, 6653; constitution of, 6238, 6273, 6569-70; financial condition of, 6594, 6663; horse, 6286; library, 6375. *See also* Sustentation House
Provincial (Wachovia) Synods, Southern Province, 6316; *1858*, 6262, 6264, 6266, 6282, 6285, 6351; *1864*, 6510, 6520, 6559, 6540, 6549; *1865*, 6559, 6569-70, 6577, 6586, 6594, 6598, 6615, 6616
Provincial Elders Conference, 6262, 6264, 6282, 6301, 6308, 6316, 6331, 6333, 6339, 6368, 6369, 6375, 6377, 6405, 6409, 6435, 6490, 6497, 6515, 6532, 6534, 6549, 6559, 6577, 6583, 6586, 6594, 6615, 6620, 6621, 6636, 6637, 6643, 6649; president of, 6273, 6276, 6283, 6577; president's office abolished, 6570; report to, 6615-21
Provincial Financial Board, 6264, 6276, 6278-79, 6455, 6534, 6549; investment policies of, 6285; minutes: *1858*: 6282-86; *1859*, 6331-34; *1860*, 6374-76; *1861*, 6419-20; *1862*, 6455-57; *1863*, 6491-92; *1864*, 6534-36; *1865*, 6586; *1866*, 6652-53
Prussians, 6630
Puryear, 6602

R

Railroads and rail travel, 6224, 6330, 6361, 6364, 6448, 6464, 6496, 6506, 6546, 6555, 6557, 6559, 6562, 6563, 6596, 6599, 6600
Rains, 6269, 6290, 6291, 6305, 6339, 6346, 6379, 6459, 6464, 6473, 6501, 6502, 6568, 6569, 6587, 6596, 6599, 6624, 6633, 6660, 6665
Raleigh, North Carolina, 6400, 6461, 6463, 6464, 6498, 6525, 6545, 6572, 6589
Rank, Catharina. *See* Schaffner, Catharina, m.n. Rank, widow Hauser
Rank, Charles, 6251
Readmittances, 6337, 6654
Reed. *See also* Ried
Reed, Christian Emanuel, 6345, 6346, 6544, 6545, 6547, 6610
Reed (Reid), Jeannette, m.n. Hagen, 6242
(Reed), Rhoda, 6476, 6477
Reed, William O., Rev., 6250
Reed, Sr. William O. *See* Reed (Reid), Jeannette, m.n. Hagen
Reed, family of, 6431
Reedy Creek, Davidson County, 6430
Reeves, Capt., 6397
Regimental bands: 21st North Carolina, 6474; 26th North Carolina, 6511, 6543; 33d North Carolina, 6492
Reich, Augustus Nathanael, 6525, 6596
Reich, Catharine, m.n. Linebach, 6657
Reich, Emanuel, 6602
Reich, Frank, 6489, 6490, 6528, 6529
Reich, Jacob, 6628
Reich, James A., 6398
Reich, Johanna Paulina. *See* Vierling, Johanna Paulina, m.n. Reich
Reich, Sr. Johannes. *See* Reich, Catharine, m.n. Linebach
Reich, John, 6525
Reich, Joseph H., 6398, 6473
(Reich), Margaret, 6446
Reich, Naaman, 6539
Reich, Philip, 6223, 6304